The New Presidential Elite

The New Presidential Elite

Men and Women in National Politics

JEANE KIRKPATRICK

with the assistance of

Warren E. Miller
Elizabeth Douvan
William Crotty
Teresa Levitin
Maureen Fiedler

New York
Russell Sage Foundation and The Twentieth Century Fund

Library of Congress Catalog Card Number: 76–1816
Standard Book Number: 87154–475–X

For Kirk

Contents

Tables and Figures

Tables

Appendix B

Figures

Foreword

It is with a great deal of professional pride and pleasure that we mark the completion and publication of this landmark report on the 1972 national political conventions. In this jointly supported project, the Twentieth Century Fund's continuing interest in political and social institutions and Russell Sage Foundation's commitment to the study of social change have been fused. Private foundations seldom undertake cooperative efforts of this type; we hope that the results of our joint effort will encourage others in the foundation world to undertake similar collaborations.

The Twentieth Century Fund and Russell Sage Foundation share a commitment to social science research as a means of promoting better understanding of contemporary social problems and changing institutions in our society. Both foundations have traditionally endeavored to provide scientific analyses of problems and to draw out their implications for the future before such problems emerged as priority items on the agendas of other organizations. When Jeane Kirkpatrick and her colleagues sought support for this project, both the Fund and the Foundation welcomed the opportunity to produce a detailed analysis of the changing political conditions embodied in the 1972 national political conventions. This collaboration has gone beyond funding, for the staffs of the Fund and the Foundation have remained intimately involved in the project throughout both research and writing. The result is a unique document that sheds light on current and future changes in political participation in the nation.

Professor Kirkpatrick and her colleagues studied the delegates to the 1972 political conventions and found that the McGovern rules for the national Democratic Convention were an early manifestation of and response to a growing trend on the American political scene, precipitating significant changes in political participation. The study examines the "new breed" of participants in presidential selection, giving special attention to the increased activity on the part of women. The book is significant not only as a systematic and detailed survey of the 1972 convention delegates and as an insightful analysis of the 1972 presidential selection process, but also as a solid framework within which to examine presidential selection in the election years to come.

Both the Twentieth Century Fund and Russell Sage Foundation consider this study a notable contribution to the understanding of the American political process. We are grateful to Professor Kirkpatrick and her colleagues for the meticulous research and analytical flair that underlie this important and standard-setting work.

M.J. Rossant
Director, Twentieth Century Fund
Hugh F. Cline
President, Russell Sage Foundation

Preface

This study has a long and rather complex history which began in August 1970 when a group interested in research on women met in Chicago. Various approaches to the study of women in politics were considered before a decision was made to utilize women delegates to the two national conventions as a cross section of women who were active in American politics. Various criticisms can be made of this decision, but it is not easy to identify a level of American politics at which women are sufficiently numerous that they can be studied not as idiosyncratic individuals, but as examples of a class. The conventions provided women from various levels of the two parties, from all states, and of diverse ideological persuasions. The conventions also provided a "matched" sample of male activists, required in order to determine what constituted "distinctively feminine" characteristics and experiences. For these reasons the conventions seemed a strategic point at which to cut into national politics to study the experience of women in the national political process.

A team consisting of Warren Miller, director, Center for Political Studies, University of Michigan; Elizabeth Douvan, professor of psychology, University of Michigan; William Crotty, professor of political science, Northwestern University; and myself developed a proposal for such research. The Twentieth Century Fund and Russell Sage Foundation provided the funds necessary to finance the project. Naturally I am very grateful to them.

The early statement of the project's goals stated the purposes of the study as follows:

> To gain new understanding of the political characteristics and experience of women in American politics. To identify the social, cultural, psychological, and political characteristics of those who became active. To illuminate the reasons many women do not seek public office. To identify new trends affecting the participation of women in political power. To explore some potential consequences of women's greater participation in power.

The four of us met repeatedly to devise research instruments appropriate to the task. It was decided that a mail questionnaire would be sent to all delegates and that face-to-face interviews would be conducted with a carefully structured sample of delegates to both the Democratic and Republican conventions. All four team members participated actively in development of the questionnaire and interview schedule and in development of codes. The sample was drawn, the interviewing conducted, the data coded by the Center for Political Studies under the direction of Warren Miller. Teresa Levitin also participated actively in the development of the questionnaire and the plans for coding.

Once the tapes were available, the principle site of activity on the project was changed from the Center for Political Studies in Ann Arbor to Washington, D.C., and Georgetown University. Elizabeth Douvan provided some measures concerning women. Teresa Levitin provided some measures of activism and attitudes toward women and made suggestions for analysis. William Crotty provided an index on professionalism, and Warren Miller made a detailed comparison of the mail questionnaire and interview samples concluding that in almost all respects important for our purposes the two were identical. (See Appendix B.) Maureen Fiedler, R.S.M., joined the project as my research assistant and through two years has provided valuable help. All of the computer analysis for the book was carried out by her. The initial draft of the chapter on convention participation was written by her. Except for that chapter, I wrote the book.

It is not the book that was originally planned. Reality has a way of undoing even very carefully laid plans. Foremost among the realities that altered the structure and focus of this book were the unexpected similarity of women's and men's attitudes and behavior and the extraordinarily interesting implications of the data for aspects of politics unrelated to sex.

The result is a book that treats women as one part of what I have come to call "the presidential elite." I believe that the chapters on women accomplish most of the original goals. And I hope that the remaining chapters illuminate some aspects of the mid-elite that are so influential in presidential politics.

Survey research is expensive, especially when it involves hundreds of face-to-face interviews. In assessing the value of such undertakings, it is important to bear in mind the intrinsic value of the data collected. Thanks to the generosity of Russell Sage Foundation and the Twentieth Century Fund and the meticulous work of the Center for Political Studies, a large body of data of lasting value on this level of political activists is now available to other researchers, supplementing Herbert McClosky's pioneering study of delegates to the 1956 conventions. Such collections of data through time are indispensable to the development of an accurate map of political and social change.

Thanks are due to others who assisted in various phases of the project. Wendy Hoag and Barbara Farah attended most sessions on questionnaire construction and coding and saw to it that decisions made in those meetings were implemented. Joyce Horn and Charlotte Fisher have struggled valiantly with my crabbed penmanship and poor spelling. Jan Larsen of the Georgetown University Computer Center helped out on problems of machine analysis. All data analysis was carried out at that Computer Center. Various persons on both the Twentieth Century Fund and Russell Sage Foundation staffs have offered comfort and assistance throughout the project, but Selma Campbell and Herbert McClosky deserve special thanks.

I am especially indebted to my husband and to Austin Ranney for having painstakingly read and commented on the entire draft. Their criticism, help, and encouragement were sorely needed and greatly appreciated. I desire also to acknowledge my cumulative debt to Harold Laswell who not only read this manuscript but who, through long evenings of conversation stretching over two decades, has contributed greatly to my understanding of social process. I am also grateful to Howard Penniman, Thomas Mann, and Anthony King, each of whom read portions of the manuscript, and to Nancy Edgerton who helped surmount the last obstacles.

Finally, a word about pronouns. After pages of saying "he or she," "him or her," I determined to sacrifice ideology to style. Following standard English usage, I have consistently used "he," "him," and "man" as impersonal pronouns. I trust the reader will understand them as such.

Jeane Kirkpatrick

Georgetown University
March 1976

The New Presidential Elite

PART I

The Presidential Elite and the Presidential Parties

CHAPTER 1

A New Breed? A New Politics?

In virtue of class circulation, the governing elite is always in a state of slow and continuous transformation. It flows on like a river, never being today what it was yesterday. From time to time sudden and violent disturbances occur. There is a flood—the river overflows its banks. Afterwards, the new governing elite again resumes its slow transformation, the flood has subsided, the river is again flowing normally in its wonted bed.[1]

This book is inspired by the belief that American politics is being transformed in some important, fairly fundamental ways by the ascendancy to power in the majority party of large numbers of new men and women whose motives, goals, ideals, ideas, and patterns of organizational behavior are different from those of the people who have dominated American politics in the past. I call this belief the "new breed" hypothesis. Its investigation is the central purpose of this book. Whether new people have made their way into the national political elite in significant numbers, how they differ from traditional American political participants, and what kinds of institutional changes are suggested by their characteristics: these are the questions with which this book is concerned.

Until relatively recently the standard interpretation of American politics has described politics and politicians as pragmatic rather than ideological, as more firmly attached to parties than to particular programs, as moderate rather than extreme. Because politicians and politics are pragmatic—the familiar interpretation asserts—they value victory above all, adopt policies favored by the electorate, abandon positions unpalatable to voters, and choose candidates on the basis of voter appeal rather than because of their relation to a body of doctrine. Because they lack firm doctrinal commitments—the theory continues—American parties and political leaders can easily accommodate diverse interests, compromise diverse points of view, and orient their campaigns toward that happy hunting ground of pragmatic vote seekers—the moving center. Obviously, the presidential politics of 1972 did not fit this description.

Was 1972 an atypical year—an aberration without progeny, a fluke resulting from a particular set of historical circumstances created by the Vietnam war and not likely to be repeated in our lifetimes?

If one considers the candidacy of George McGovern in a historical vacuum looking neither at its antecedents nor its contemporaries, it may seem reasonable to regard it as an isolated event caused by a particular conjunction of events: the war in Southeast Asia, a division among his Democratic rivals, and the special sophistication of McGovern and his strategists in taking advantage of the reformed rules. All these were important aspects of the situation: necessary but not sufficient causes of George McGovern's successful quest for the Democratic nomination. The "McGovern phenomenon," I will argue, was less a unique occurrence than a rather dramatic episode in a process that includes at least the "Goldwater phenomenon," the "McCarthy phenomenon," the "Wallace phenomenon," and perhaps the "Cambodian spring," "Kent State," and "Watergate" phenomena. The politics of 1972 were a part of the process of the continuing transformation of American parties and political life. That process has accelerated so rapidly that the reality of change has outstripped our descriptions of past and present, confusing our base lines and confounding both our comparisons and predictions. We often speak as though Plunkitt of Tammany Hall were the norm in contemporary American politics,[2] and George McGovern the aberration. Surely the reverse is more nearly true. The policy-oriented liberal who makes his own party and country the object of his reformist zeal is as familiar as the policy-oriented conservative whose goals are first to capture his party and then to restore his nation to traditional virtues.

Robert MacIver once noted that ". . . a process is continuous. Since, therefore, it cannot be explained by the conjuncture of forces at any one moment we must look for determinants that are themselves persistent, that work more deeply in the soil of society, that are congenial and understandably related to the direction of the process."[3] I do not seek, in this inquiry, to locate and identify the origins of this process, in part because I have neither the skills nor the appetite for the historian's task, in part because I have been convinced by R.G. Collingwood that ". . . processes are things which do not begin and end but turn into one another. . . ."[4] This book deals with symptoms and diagnosis rather than causes. It joins the work of others who have been impressed by the accumulating body of evidence that suggests important, probably basic, alteration in American political characteristics.

It is not only the nominations of Barry Goldwater[5] and George McGovern that call into question the conventional characterization of the national political elite, though these, occurring within a decade, constitute rather dramatic evidence to the contrary. The decline of party identification and the growth of split ticket voting; the appearance of a third party; the increased reliance on public relations techniques rather than organization; the decreased confidence in government and in other public institutions; the appearance of direct action—assassinations, sit-ins, demonstrations, draft evasion; the progressive breakdown of consensus on such basic values as patriotism, obedience to law, and compromise; the rise of new kinds of pressure groups and new kinds of issues; the perfection of direct mail campaigns which, like electronic media, bypass parties; the proliferation of primaries that weaken the role of party organizations in the nominating process; the Democrats' reformed rules that reduce the role of the party's leaders in candidate selection; the persistence of "cross cutting" issues that cut across traditional party alignments; the landslide defeat of the majority party's presidential candidate; "Watergate" and all that it implies about the decline of restraint in the use of power—these and many other phenomena of the recent past argue that the American political system is undergoing quite fundamental changes.

Popular descriptions of 1972 Democratic politics painted the conflict within the Democratic party in large part as a contest between oldtimers and newcomers. The former were presumably found among the supporters of traditional "establishment" candidates, Edmund Muskie, Hubert Humphrey, Henry Jackson, and, to a lesser extent, George Wallace. They were said to be the people who had dominated American politics for decades, had made a mess of things at home and abroad, had developed moral calluses from having labored so long in the political vineyards. Juxtaposed to them were the newcomers, who, legend had it, had been stimulated by passionate concern with the issues of the late 1960s—civil rights, war, ecology—to enter the political arena. Many of these newcomers, it was widely believed, were women—a new breed of women whose greater interest in issues and power brought them into politics in search simultaneously of public goals and personal fulfillment. And youth—in the early 1970s the rhetoric of revolution was commonplace, and it was frequently asserted that a youth revolution was under way, politicizing new voters as the women's revolution politicized women, luring large numbers of the young into politics to canvass, to organize, and to transform the system. The McGovern movement was frequently described as a product of this surge into politics of thousands of Americans who had a rising sense of social justice and social outrage. Similar characteristics were sometimes attributed to Wallace's supporters. On the Republican side, President Nixon's talk of a new majority was laced with references to the new roles of youth and newcomers in Republican politics of that year.

The fact that many organization leaders were not delegates to the Democratic Convention and that many of those who became delegates were relatively unknown and inexperienced enhanced the impression that a revolution had taken place in the Democratic party. Nearly one-third of Democratic delegates had had less than five years experience in politics. Fewer than one-half had had experience that stretched back further than the election of John Kennedy, and only 17 percent had ever attended a previous convention. Furthermore, the inexperienced were especially numerous in the most influential candidate group—notably, that supporting George McGovern. Nearly one-half of this group had become active after domestic passions concerning the Vietnam war had been aroused. (See Tables 1-1 and 1-2.) The experience of McGovern delegates was qualitatively as well as quantitatively low. About one-fifth had held party office beyond the district level, and persons with experience in public office were still more scarce. Wallace delegates had similarly brief, low-level political experience, and although seasoned regulars with longer experience in party organization were relatively numerous in the Humphrey and Muskie camps, the convention took its tone from the numerically dominant McGovern group. The scarcity of established party leaders and the presence of the large numbers of relative newcomers became the principal theme of journalists covering the Democratic Convention. *Time*'s comment is typical of popular accounts.

> Actually, there are two Democratic parties now. One was in the convention hall, relishing its ascension to power. The other, beaten and bitter, was on the sidelines. It was not just Richard Daley, but included scores of Democratic Governors, Senators, Congressmen, state party chairmen, local officeholders—all the regulars unhorsed by the McGovern reforms and outorganized by what is now the McGovern machine. Only 19 of the nation's 30 Democratic Governors came to Miami Beach, and none played a significant role.[6]

The Republican Convention, in which most delegates had longer experience and at higher levels, provided a sharp contrast. Only 7 percent had been active less than five years, and 17 percent had become active before 1945. Even at the Republican Convention, only 30 percent of delegates to that convention had previously served as delegates.[7] However, it is meaningful to speak of the Republican Convention as a meeting of party officials: 92 percent held party office and 57 percent held offices at the state or national level, as compared to 74 percent of Democrats, a large majority of whom had experience only at the local level. (See Table 1-3.)

The expectation of change is a salient aspect of the national culture. It conditions us to expect continuing revisions of our political practices, although as compared with those of most other modern nations, our political institutions have been unusually stable. The expectation of change is also closely, if not necessarily, related to the demand for change, and from the late 1960s to the 1972 presidential election the claim was frequently

Table 1-1. Political Generations[a] by Party and Candidate Preference (%)

	Democrats	Republicans	McGovern	Humphrey	Wallace	Muskie	Nixon
Pre–1945	11	17	6	20	20	23	17
1946–1959	29	39	23	41	17	38	39
1960–1967	30	38	31	24	29	29	38
1968–1972	30	7	40	15	35	10	7
$N =$	1565	819	875	199	66	138	787

[a]"Political Generation" is a measure of the time a delegate first became active in politics. There are four generations defined here. Those who became active: (1) before the end of World War II (1945); (2) in post-war years (1946–1959); (3) in the Kennedy/Johnson years (1960–1967); (4) in the Nixon first term (1968–1972)–newcomers.

NOTE: These data are from the mail questionnaire sample. Percents do not necessarily add to 100 percent due to rounding.

Table 1-2. Median Age and Years of Political Experience by
Party and Candidate Preference

	Median Age	Median Years Political Experience
Party		
Democrats	41.0 (n=1572)	11.5 (n=1565)
Republicans	46.9 (n=817)	14.7 (n=819)
Candidate Preference		
McGovern	36.9 (n=880)	7.6 (n=875)
Humphrey	47.6 (n=196)	16.2 (n=199)
Wallace	42.0 (n=67)	10.5 (n=66)
Muskie	47.5 (n=136)	15.7 (n=138)
Nixon	47.1 (n=785)	14.7 (n=787)

NOTE: These data are from the mail questionnaires.

heard—especially from those dissatisfied with politics as usual—that people entering politics had changed and that the political system *must* change to accommodate the new habits and demands of the new people!

Less has been heard about the "forces for change" in the period since the landslide defeat of Democratic candidate George McGovern, but the evidence of significant political transformation accumulates. The changes that have so far occurred have not necessarily fit the predictions, nor fulfilled the hopes of those who advocated and facilitated reform. But they provided good grounds for believing that by 1972 the character of many activists influential in presidential politics—I will call them the "presidential elite"—had undergone a more than routine alteration.

A great deal was heard in the years preceding the last presidential election of the new men and women with new motives, goals, ideals, ideas, values, and patterns of behavior. The principal political characteristics of the new type were said to be greater idealism, more interest in nonmaterial values and in issues and ideology, more concern about policy than party and a parallel tendency to give ideology priority over electoral victory, unusual reluctance to compromise principles, and unprecedented willingness to invest large amounts of time in support of a candidate or a cause without material or self-interested rewards.

Persons sympathetic to the changing style of American politics welcomed the arrival to national prominence of a hypothetical new breed as evidence that people of principle were replacing the opportunistic bosses and machine politicians of yesterday. Other observers were less sanguine, believing that they perceived in the new political type a tendency to intransigence as well as principle. Those enthusiastic about the new political types saw promise of a new maturity in American politics, of responsible parties and rational choices. Those less sure that the new breed embodied political progress worried about the progressive polarization of the electorate and about the compatibility of ideological movements with two-party politics and representative government. Both the optimists and the pessimists agreed that change had occurred and that new people had risen to positions of influence in the presidential parties.

Many of the characteristics attributed to the new people were those of the reform politics style that had been noted and described by political scientists during the previous decade or so. Observed especially in the political clubs of the Northeast and Far West, in the state Democratic parties of Minnesota and Wisconsin, and in certain affluent suburbs and practiced especially by the college educated, this style of volunteer politics had been described and labelled by James Q. Wilson, who called its practitioners "amateur democrats," Aaron Wildavsky, who termed them "purists," and Leon Epstein, who called the syndrome the "middle-class" political style.[8] The people whom they described were urban and suburban, college educated, geographically and socially mobile, had relatively high incomes, young, heavily Jewish, largely liberal types who brought to politics distrust for party organization, disdain for the organization regulars and the paid professionals who staffed the organizations, distaste for a politics based on party loyalty, and a high regard for verbal skills and the articulation of issues and for politics based on ideology rather than on economic interests.

An aspect of reform politics noted by Epstein and of special interest here was the prominence of women.[9] The new political breed of the 1970s was said to contain large numbers of new women who differed from traditional women even more sharply than the new men differed from their traditional male counterparts.[10] The new woman was said to be distinguished especially by her demand for a more equal share of power and her willingness to compete with men for it. The new politics practiced by the new breed, it was asserted, would differ from the old in its willingness to honor the claims for power of women and other "hitherto disadvantaged" groups who had been, it was said, frozen out of the power structure.

Not all the relevant symptoms of change fit the "reform" politics model. Similar political characteristics were noted elsewhere—among the southern whites, the industrial workers, and the young and old who swelled George Wallace's audiences and filled his coffers. This new breed was less likely to be college educated and affluent, less likely to be urban or Jewish, and certainly less likely to be liberal. But, like the Goldwater volunteers of the

Table 1-3. Party and Public Office Experience by Party and Candidate Preference (%)

	Democrats	Republicans	McGovern	Humphrey	Wallace	Muskie	Nixon
Highest Level Party Office Presently Held							
National level	9	16	7	14	10	17	17
State level	15	40	10	22	12	27	40
District level	5	5	5	3	0	3	4
County level	17	22	17	15	14	15	22
City-local level	18	9	21	16	22	14	9
None held now	36	8	40	30	43	24	8
N =	1252	683	716	153	51	107	655
Highest Level Party Office Ever Held							
National level	12	20	10	17	12	16	21
State level	18	41	12	25	16	34	41
District level	9	7	10	6	6	6	7
County level	16	20	17	15	18	14	20
City-local level	17	7	20	14	16	11	6
None ever held	28	6	32	23	32	19	6
N =	1601	848	890	202	68	140	814

Highest Level Public Office Ever Held

National level	2	4	1	4	3	5	4
State level	11	17	7	15	7	26	17
Local level	15	19	11	20	13	19	19
None ever held	71	60	31	61	77	49	60
N =	1601	848	890	202	68	140	814

Relationships: Highest party office presently held by party, V = 0.39.
Highest party office ever held by party, V = 0.36.
Highest public office ever held by party, V = 0.12.

NOTE: These data are from the mail questionnaires.

previous decade, they shared with the reform types a high level of ideological interest, a distaste for the regular party organization, and an indifference to parties and candidates between whom there was not a "dime's worth of difference."

The new breed hypothesis has broad implications; it involves assertions and predictions of change in the modal political personality, in the dominant political culture, and in political institutions. If it is true that large numbers of new men and women with new identifications, expectations, and demands have entered the political system and achieved influence within it, this obviously foreshadows enormous change in the American political system and 1972, like 1964, will prove to have been a predictor of the shape of the politics of the future. If the new breed hypothesis is not true, then many of the expectations concerning the shape of the future will be confounded, and the decisions intended to be farsighted will prove merely mistaken.

Because politics is people interacting to specified ends in specified arenas, the influence of actor and interaction is reciprocal. The goals, resources, and style of actors influence the character of interaction in a political arena, and the character of the interactions influences who is (and who is not) attracted into the arena. The new breed hypothesis, like all other assertions that American politics is changing in fundamental respects, assumes change in the goals, resources, and styles of those active in politics. This book is devoted to an inquiry into the goals, resources, and styles of the 1972 presidential elite and their implications for the future of American politics.

CONSTITUTIONS AND THE CHARACTER
OF ELITES

This study was inspired by a tradition of political investigation that stretches at least from Plato through Harold Lasswell, Herbert McClosky, and Robert Dahl.[11] The conviction that the quality of government depends on the character of the political elite is an ancient one that was enunciated and illustrated by Plato: "Constitutions cannot come out of sticks and stones; they must result from the preponderance of certain characters which draw the rest of the community in their wake."[12]

In Book Eight of *The Republic*, Plato described the manner in which the socialization of the ruling class produced new character types who in turn transformed the political system. Underlying each type of constitution were the distinctive interests and passions of the ruling elite. Two thousand years later, Gaetano Mosca articulated a new theory of the ruling class that shared these assumptions. Mosca, too, was convinced that political change originated in conflict *within* the elite and not between elite and mass (as Marx had supposed). With Plato, Mosca saw that the character of the government and the society is dependent on that of the ruling class. Mosca drew a distinction—important to us—between the top governmental leaders, "the highest stratum of the ruling class" and the second stratum that is "much more numerous and comprises all the capacities for leadership in the country." This second stratum is very important.

> Without such a class any sort of social organization would be impossible. . . . In the last analysis, therefore, the stability of any political organism depends on the level of morality, intelligence and activity that this second stratum has attained. . . . Any intellectual or moral deficiencies in this second stratum, accordingly, represent a graver danger to the political structure, and the one harder to repair, than the presence of similar deficiences in the few dozen persons who control the workings of the state machine.[13]

This second, more numerous, stratum of the elite that has a collective rather than an individual impact on the policy includes bureaucrats who interpret and implement the decisions of the top leaders and also incumbents of other influential positions. It is such a second stratum elite with which we are concerned in this study. Mosca perceived a plurality of elites, outside the governing class, each representing an important social force and each a potential contender for top power in the legal government. He shared with Plato, Vilfredo Pareto, and others the conviction that political change derived from competition among these elites.

The composition and circulation of political elites has also been a focus of continuing attention and controversy among modern social scientists: whether societies and institutions are necessarily, inevitably governed by ruling elites, as Robert Michels argued; whether a capitalist elite might finally be replaced by the equal distribution of power and other values as Karl Marx predicted; whether revolutions result only in the replacement of one narrow elite by another as Pareto argued; or whether the major transformation of our time is the decline of economic elites (especially business) and the rise to power of intellectuals and semi-intellectuals, as Waclaw Machajski and Lasswell have argued. What *is* has attracted as much attention as what will be. The debate on whether the United States is governed by a unified corporate elite, a military-industrial complex, or by plural, competing elites has given rise to a large literature in which the names of Robert Dahl and C. Wright Mills loom large. Some of this literature has emphasized intra-elite relations, some mass-elite relations; some has argued that those relations are necessary, inevitable; others that they are indeterminate.[14]

Intra-elite competition is the principle but not the exclusive focus of this study. In this study I assume only that elite characteristics are important and that intra-elite differences may be a significant source of political change, not that they are the only source. Potentially significant intra-elite differences include social, economic, psychological, and ideological characteristics.

No society has a static ruling elite. The human life cycle alone guarantees continuing circulation of those in power roles. The interplay of ambition, generation, and skill insures circulation of elites; social and cultural change accelerate the rate of circulation. A change of rulers does not necessarily entail significant change in the character or composition of the elite or in the political system. But as Plato pointed out, and as Ortega y Gasset has argued, new political generations may differ in fundamental respects from their predecessors and the ascension to power of a generation with new psychological and social characteristics may mark the beginning of a new political epoch.

In principle, changes in the personal predispositions (character), resources, and styles of political actors may occur independently of one another: a ruling elite's personal concerns may change without occasioning parallel changes in its social or personal resources or its style of behavior; an elite may be replenished with persons who, though recruited from different social strata, share the goals and styles of the higher status actors; the style of elite political behavior may change while goals and resources remain the same. However, history indicates that major changes are usually characterized by a change in both the psychological and social characteristics of the ruling elite.

Despite the popular notion that fundamental changes in the composition and vocabulary of the ruling elite are precipitated by revolution and war, close investigation confirms Plato's insight that the evolutionary change within the ruling class is a major source—probably the major source—of fundamental alteration of political regimes. The belief that just such a change is under way is the point of departure for this inquiry.

The absence of trend data makes impossible a straightforward comparison of past and present presidential elites and forces reliance on incomplete accounts of past conventions and on intra-elite comparison. Fortunately, the organization of the two conventions facilitates comparison. The Republican Convention was organized on the basis of traditional notions about what a national convention should be; its delegates were recruited from among party leaders and regulars in conventional ways. Presumably a significant portion of those delegates possessed the personal and social traits characteristic of American politics as it had been in recent decades. That convention also contained substantial numbers of persons recruited to politics in the half-decade preceding the convention and so provides an opportunity to determine whether a Republican variant of the new breed had made its way into the national arena by 1972. On the Democratic side, generational diversity was supplemented by the presence of some candidates—notably Wallace and McGovern—who symbolized a departure from Democratic politics as usual and other candidates—Humphrey, Muskie, and Jackson—who represented the traditional liberal Democratic politics that had dominated the party since the New Deal. These latter may have rallied traditional liberal Democrats around them, while candidates who purported to stand for something new (McGovern and Wallace) may have attracted significant numbers of carriers of a new politics—if such new people were indeed present on the scene. Both Republican and Democratic conventions contained unprecedented numbers of women delegates. If women have distinctive political characteristics and a special proclivity for the new politics, their enlarged presence enhanced the likelihood that a new political type was present in significant numbers among the decision makers in national politics in 1972.

THE PSYCHOLOGICAL BASES OF INSTITUTIONAL STABILITY AND CHANGE

A political party, like any other institution, is an enduring pattern of interactions based on stable expectations and reciprocal behaviors. The stability of the expectations guarantees the character of the interaction; the reciprocity of the behavior confirms for participants and witnesses the correctness of the expectations at the same time that it achieves the institutional goal.

An institution lasts just as long as the shared understandings and reciprocal behaviors last. When a generally accepted understanding concerning the purposes or modes of an institution changes, behavior changes, the pattern of interaction changes, and the institution changes. The stability of institutions depends on the stability of culture, that is, on the stability of understandings about the goals, purposes, and modes of appropriate behavior. What we call "forces for change" are people who propose new patterns of interaction because they have a new conception of what a given activity is, or ought to be. What we call "the demand for change" is the demand that people interacting in a given arena scrap old understandings and agree on new ones—that they behave differently.

A demand for reform develops when some persons develop new expectations about the nature of an institution and the behavior appropriate to it. When new expectations become widespread or when they spread to many participants in an interaction, the consensus required to maintain the patterned interaction is already gone.

The structure, rigidity, and flexibility of groups, the skill of leaders, and other environmental demands affect the speed and the ease with which changing expectations restructure institutions. Neither the government nor political parties are at every moment a reflection of the individuals who comprise them. But, in the absence of coercion, institutions eventually change with the changing expectations of those who comprise them. The pattern of reciprocity evaporates as the behavior of some participants changes to conform to new understandings about the nature of the interaction. And institutional practices disappear in the debris of confounded expectations.

THE PRINCIPAL HYPOTHESIS

The principal hypothesis of this study is that there were among the delegates to the two conventions of 1972 political types whose personal and political goals, resources, and styles differed in identifiable ways from those of the political actors who have dominated presidential politics in the past decades; that these distinctive traits were associated with sex, political generation, candidate preference, and social structure; and that they have important political implications for the future of the presidential parties.

Personal goals should be reflected in personal predispositions, incentives, role conceptions, modes of participation; political goals should be reflected in incentives, role conceptions, and especially in the content and style of political ideology. Resources include past political and other organizational experience, income, education, occupation, and ethnic identification. Style integrates psychological, ideological, and behavioral traits.

The null hypothesis is not that there were no differences in the goals, resources, or styles of delegates (previous research suggests variety in all these), but that there were no differences distributed so as to indicate that one modal type is being replaced by another modal type, specifically that they were not significantly related to sex, to political generation, to social structure, or to candidate preference group, and finally, that the projection of such differences as exist does not suggest significant change in the presidential parties.

It is important to distinguish between the circulation of elites and their transformation. The former concerns turnover; the latter involves significant change, not merely in the incumbents but in their characteristics. Rapid turnover may be evidence of circulation of elites, not of their transformation; it may mean that there are important social changes under way that have been registered in the political system; it may indicate intra-elite factionalism and dispute as in France of the Fourth Republic; it may reflect the relative unattractiveness of political office. The fact of rapid turn-over of elected officeholders in the United States has been repeatedly documented: Charles Hyneman's research established the rapid turnover of state legislators;[15] Heinz Eulau and others have demonstrated that this is a widespread and continuing pattern.[16] A profile of the 1974 Congress pointed out that 38 percent of all congressmen had been first elected since 1970. The data on attendance at national conventions documents rapid circulation in the presidential parties' elites: only one-third of delegates to the 1968 Democratic Convention had attended a previous convention.

Diversity within the elite is also not necessarily an indicator that a process of elite transformation is under way, because successive studies have established that diversity of motives, goals, and styles is a normal characteristic of American politics. Virtually every study of American officeholders has confirmed that different kinds of people seek office for different reasons. James David Barber, Samuel Eldersveld, Edward Banfield, James Q. Wilson, Frank Sorauf, Leon Epstein, Jeane Kirkpat-rick, Heinz Eulau, Dwaine Marvick,[17] and others have documented the existence of substantial diversity in the motives of political activists.

Social mobility in and of itself also does not constitute evidence of system change because a high level of social mobility is a well-established characteristic of officeholders. More than most, persons elected to public office are likely to have better educations, higher incomes, and higher social status than their parents.[18] The continuation of established patterns of mobility is evidence of continuity not of transformation. Divergence from the established pattern of mobility would signal new paths for arriving at elite status.

THE SCOPE OF THE INQUIRY

The new breed hypothesis postulates change in political actors and processes. The hypothesis itself calls attention to the existential continuity of individual, group, and political system; its investigation requires investigating all relevant levels of action and interaction. The problems posed by multilevel inquiry are not problems of "linkage," in the sense that one subject unit, an individual, is "linked" to another subject unit or group. The problem is rather one of viewing the same subject unit from the appropriate observational standpoints—as individual actors, as factions, and as an elite of the presidential parties. If there is under way a process of political change based on the changing character of individuals who com-prise the elite of the presidential parties, then it should be reflected in the persons, factions, and presidential elites of the two parties.

The scope of this study is broad in that it deals with individual political actors, political parties, and the party system, narrow in that it is based largely on one category of political actors, the delegates to the 1972 Republican and Democratic conventions. Much of its value depends on the author's assumption that the delegates to the two conventions constituted a cross section of the effective elite of the presidential parties and that for this reason they constituted a promising perspective from which to observe the American political scene.

Disclaimers, as Lionel Trilling once noted, are part of the ritualized decorum of modern social science.[19] These disclaimers are not merely tactics of self-defense; they also reflect researchers' sensitivity to the differences among what it is possible to prove, what it is possible to make informed guesses about, and what is simply not known. I think I am aware of the limitations of this sample, but also of its strength. I want to focus first on the strengths and reserve the disclaimers for later in this chapter.

STUDYING ELITES

In recent years elites have been studied less frequently and less systematically than masses. Perhaps the reason is that masses were so long neglected. Perhaps the reason is that masses are easier to sample, to interview, and to aggregate. It is certainly true that traditionally historians have written history as the history of kings, princes, despots, presidents, and their advisors and their enemies and that until recently political scientists, too, have focused their attention on rulers and on their ideas. The lives and views of ordinary citizens have been largely ignored by both, perhaps because they had little influence on large events or perhaps because the methodological problems of studying masses, and especially the values and purposes of masses, were overwhelming until the development of probability statistics, standardized interviewing, and the sample survey. In the approximately three decades since these techniques have made subjectivities of masses available for study, political scientists of behavioral persuasion have lavished effort on the systematic study of large populations, while elites have been relatively neglected. In consequence, our understanding of mass electorates and mass culture has grown enormously, but our understanding of elites has remained largely impressionistic. The late V. O. Key noted this discrepancy between our knowledge of the electorate and what he called "the leadership corps" in 1956.[20]

Not only is the number of studies of political activists and professionals small, but with the notable exception of Herbert McClosky's pioneering work, most of these studies are based on small samples of small universes. The lack of major national elite studies and the availability of mass data have distorted the picture of political reality, encouraging (though not causing) us to treat all opinions as though they were equal (the democratic fallacy) and to treat collectivities as mere aggregates of individual characteristics (the individualistic fallacy), when, as group theorists long ago pointed out, politics proceeds through organized groups hierarchically structured so that the preferred outcomes of participants have unequal weight. Even in democracies mass preferences have only a cumulative, indirect effect on the decisions of parties and governments. Elites have a much greater, much more direct impact on who governs and to what ends.

Political elites are, by definition, persons with more influence than most others on outcomes with significance for the entire community. We are partial in our times to explaining political events by reference to "forces," but "forces," if such exist, are manifested only through people and especially through people who make decisions with important consequences. Many public events and almost all public policies can be understood only by reference to elite perspectives, and these perspectives must be studied directly. The behavior of elites cannot be inferred from that of masses, anymore than mass perspectives and behavior can be inferred from elites.

Political elites differ from masses in some crucial respects. They are more politicized, more interested in public affairs, more informed about them, and more emotionally involved in public decisions.[21] Elites compromise people who see their personal fate as linked in a significant way to public events and desire to influence public decisions affecting themselves and others. Because politics is important to them, they are much more likely to have developed a comprehensive map of the political world and a closely related ideology that positions the self and others in relation to political events. But because the members of a political elite share some characteristics, it does not follow that all persons who are influential in relation to some set of political outcomes share all characteristics. It does follow, for example, that an entire elite shares class origins or ideologies. In referring to the elite nothing is implied about the unity, cohesion, or durability of the political influentials with whom I am concerned. In speaking of "an" elite or "the" elite, I intend only to conform to standard English usage, not to suggest the existence of a single unified ruling class. The term is intended here to refer to a *political class*, a category of persons who were influential in some decisions that had important consequences for the society.[22] This conception states only that particular persons exercised more influence than most people in specified decisional processes. It identifies and inquires. It prejudges nothing concerning the scope of the bases of the influence, nor concerning the position of this elite in any broader decisional system.

THE ELITE OF THE PRESIDENTIAL PARTIES

No claim is made that the 1972 convention delegates constitute a representative sample of the entire American political elite. Such a sample would include more governors, congressmen, mayors, campaign managers, state legislative leaders, political bosses, and influential advisors. But such a sample would be much more likely than this to capture the characteristics of today's leadership corps and to understate or miss entirely the symptoms of change.

I do not even claim that the convention delegates constitute a sample of the dominant elites of the Republican and Democratic parties. Republican delegates probably were representative of the influential Republicans in 1972, but for obvious and insurmountable technical reasons I cannot be sure because we do not in fact know the characteristics of the whole group of Republican influentials. There are good grounds for supposing that the delegates to the Democratic Convention were less representative of the leadership of the Democratic party throughout the nation. One of the newsworthy characteristics of the convention was the exclusion of so many prominent Democrats. It seems likely that the most important organizational impact of the Democrats' pre-convention reforms was to separate delegate selection from the regular party structures. When delegates to a national convention were chosen from among and/or by leaders of the state and local parties, the continuity of influence from state parties to presidential politics was assured. But when, as in 1972, convention delegates are selected independently of the regular party structure, then continuity between the presidential party elite and the state and local parties cannot be assumed but becomes instead a matter for investigation. However, there are persuasive grounds for believing that convention delegates constituted a significant political elite whether or not they were representative of either the ongoing party organizations or the rank and file of their own parties.

Although most of the major functions of American political parties are still controlled by state and local parties, the importance of the national parties has increased dramatically in recent years and is still increasing. Conventions are the principal institution of the national parties. National conventions have always been multifunctional institutions. Their most famous function is, of course, the choice of a presidential nominee, a task whose importance can hardly be overestimated. While voters normally must choose between only two persons, each of the parties chooses one person from among many, and the one chosen has one chance in two of becoming president. But national conventions not only choose governors, they govern. As the highest decision-making body they can bind a party, speak in its name, adopt a platform, and overhaul the rules and structures of the party. Delegates to the national conventions not only make decisions affecting an upcoming election, they also make decisions about what parties and politics will become. In the present period when progressively more power is being claimed and exercised by the national parties,[23] the role and influence of delegates is important even though the actual choice of a nominee may be largely or even wholly decided by the outcome of primaries, conventions, and other processes that preceded the convention.[24]

Whether or not the delegates to the two conventions were personally influential in local political contexts, each may be reasonably considered a political influential in the context of the 1972 presidential politics. Power, as Lasswell has reminded us, is not an object that can be lugged about, carried from one place to another.[25] It exists only in specific contexts and specific relations. In Chicago's Democratic party, in Illinois, with voters in the city of Chicago, in the state legislature, among other mayors, vis-à-vis the federal government, Mayor Richard Daley doubtless had and has far more influence than Reginald Williams, a reform slate member who replaced Daley as a delegate. But in the context of the 1972 Democratic Convention, Reginald Williams was probably more directly influential than Daley; he had a vote on issues before the convention and a voice in the proceedings of the Illinois delegation and was part of a network of like-minded persons who, collectively, constituted a majority of the convention's delegates.

Furthermore, the presence of delegates at the conventions indicates that they were sufficiently skillful and/or influential in local communities to be chosen as delegates. In many instances delegates who did not occupy influential positions in local decision structures were leaders and activists in a counter-elite, some faction that had sufficient skill and/or support to win out over regulars in contests conducted under the new rules.

Delegates are influential participants in the presidential parties. Presidential parties are collectivities that make decisions about which persons and issues will be presented to the national electorate under the party's label in a given presidential year. The elite of the presidential parties includes all persons with influence on the selection and presentation of candidates and issues in a presidential election. The mass of presidential parties are party identifiers and other voters whose ballots decide among candidates and issues in primaries and general elections. National conventions are arenas in which important decisions are made affecting presidential parties. Primary elections, state caucuses, state conventions, and smoke-filled leadership conferences are other such arenas.

Delegates to national conventions are interesting to students of politics because, for the period that they serve as delegates, they are members of *the elite political class*, persons whose decisions are felt throughout the political system. "A class," Lasswell has asserted, "is a major aggregate of persons engaging in practices giving them a similar relation to the shaping and distribution (and enjoyment) of one or more specified values."[26] The political elite is that political class that has more influence than others in the shaping of specified values through political processes. Collectively, they embody the human, social, and political characteristics of a national party. Collectively, the delegates constitute a slice of American political life broad enough to include persons from every state and thick enough to include representatives of all political levels. No political leader is too important to attend his party's national convention, but in 1972 many a precinct leader or insurgent was important enough.

THE DATA

This study is based on 2,449 questionnaires returned by delegates to the two conventions and on face-to-face interviews with 1,336 delegates to the two conventions. Mail questionnaires were sent to all delegates in advance of the convention. In the case of disputed delegations, chosen only at the convention, questionnaires were hand delivered to the delegates in Miami. Repeated follow-up efforts yielded a response rate of 51 percent of the Democratic delegates and 63 percent of the Republican. These questionnaires constitute an important body of data, especially because detailed comparisons between questionnaire responses and face-to-face interview data established that the mail questionnaire sample, although self-selected, was very similar to the carefully structured sample with which face-to-face interviews were conducted.

The most important data base of this study, however, is the personal interviews conducted by the University of Michigan's Center for Political Studies with a representative sample of delegates to the two conventions. This sample was structured to take account of geographical distribution, sex, and candidate preference. More Democrats than Republicans were interviewed, because the Democratic delegates constituted a much more heterogeneous group and also because they were believed more likely to include the new men and women, if such existed, and to reflect new political styles.

Altogether these constitute one of the largest bodies of data ever collected on delegates to the national conventions. It is important that the number of persons interviewed (and queried by mail) was large enough to permit the identification and analysis of subgroups. It thus becomes possible to investigate hypotheses relevant to different political generations, age groups, personality types, ideological groups, and many other political subgroups.

Questionnaires and interviews were carefully designed to include data on the various aspects of delegates' identity, experience, and perspectives. More specifically, the following types of data were collected.

Basic Demographic and Political Biographic Data

If new kinds of people have achieved elite status in American politics, some of their social characteristics may differ from those of traditional elites. Information on age, income, occupation, social participation, family status, and education was gathered, because such traits may constitute personal resources useful in politics, because these and other traits deriving from social location may influence political perspectives and behavior, and because whatever their impact on individual political behavior they provide information concerning the characteristics most useful in gaining influence at a particular time and place.

Data on the past political experience of delegates were collected in detail, and these data, too, constitute valuable information on individuals, factions, and party elites. Length of political activity, continuity, party and public officeholding, and recruitment experiences are among the types of political information that should illuminate the political characteristics of delegates and their integration into the party elites.

Data on Perspectives

The perspectives of the political elite are critical to the new breed hypothesis, which postulates the arrival to political influence of persons with distinctive goals, motives, role conceptions, and belief systems. Distinctive perspectives lead political actors to act in distinctive ways. "A perspective," Lasswell has noted, "is a pattern of identifications, demands, and expectations."[27] Perspectives define the boundaries of the self, establish purposes and priorities, and state relations. Understanding political behavior depends on knowledge of those elements of the actors' perspectives that are relevant to politics.

History and social science alike demonstrate that the relations between social position and perspectives are indeterminate; perspectives cannot be inferred from social position, nor social position from perspectives. Even a casual student of the twentieth century must be aware, for example, that the leadership of all major revolutions of the century—communist, nazi, fascist, Peronist, democratic—has come from middle income skill groups.[28] Repeated studies have demonstrated that neither parental social class, nor income, nor nationality are universally or necessarily reliable predictors of a person's ideology.[29] The point is not that there is no relation between social position and perspectives but that the relationship must be established empirically for every time and place.

Therefore, a systematic effort was made to collect data on the identifications, expectations, and demands of delegates.[30]

Identifications

Identification creates the political "we." Identifications locate an individual in a tradition, in an ethnic, religious, regional, or racial group, in a party, in a cause. Identification both extends and limits empathy. Normal people acquire multiple identifications in the process of growing up. Parents are the first "others" incorporated into the self via identification. Later come place, school, church, team, party, and all the social groups through which one defines oneself. Identifications cannot be inferred because the process of acquiring a social identity varies idiosyncratically. One person identifies with income group or geographical region or sex, another does not. The intensity and durability of identifications vary, as do their priority. A person's identifications are not necessarily compatible; on the contrary, the pull of mutually incompatible identifications is an important source of internal conflict.

The identifications of delegates are extremely important to our inquiry. The new breed hypothesis postulates some basic changes in the identifications and priorities of political activists: away from parties and traditional interest groups toward moral issues and new groups based on physical characteristics, such as sex, race, and age. Hypotheses that predict the breakup of the parties and/or realignment postulate that party identification will become less important than identifications based on other factors, such as issue consistency, political style, sex, age, color, or ethnic background.

Expectations

Expectations, as employed here, include all matter-of-fact assumptions and beliefs about the nature of things, including one's own position in the world. Expectations comprise the individual's cognitive map of the universe. They constitute the "reality principle" that states causes and consequences and promises rewards and punishments. Expectations are, in sum, what a person believes to be true about the world and his position in it. Obviously they have an important impact on political beliefs, policy preferences, and behavior. The extent to which expectations condition the effects of identification and demands is often underestimated. They may harmonize apparent conflicts among identifications. Differences in expectations also exacerbate conflicts. For example, a person who believes that economic deprivation is the principal cause of crime will, if he desires to reduce crime, staunchly advocate the adoption of programs aimed at eradicating poverty. The same person may oppose beefing up law enforcement as basically irrelevant to the problem. But one who believes that crime is rooted in human orneriness and is best discouraged by firm and certain punishment will support tightening law enforcement and regard poverty programs as basically irrelevant to the problem of controlling crime. Each of these hypothetical persons finds the proposed solution of the other silly, not because of a disagreement about values (assuming both truly desire to reduce crime), but because of disagreement about causes and effects. Many quite intense political conflicts are rooted in just such disagreements about facts. Since "the facts" about many complex social issues are exceedingly difficult to establish, conflicts based on differing belief systems are often as enduring as those grounded on conflicting values.

Data on expectations are, of course, crucial to the exploration of our subject for inquiry. If there are new kinds of women and men in the presidential elite, they will have new views about what conventions can and should do, about what political parties are and can be, about what people like themselves can do, about what groups with which they are associated, such as women, are and can become. If the parties are to persist in roughly their present forms, then there must be a general consensus about what the political world is like, about the proper functions of parties in that world, and about the nature of the various groups that comprise them.

Demands

Demands concern the "delusively simple question": "What do elites want?" What values do they seek to maximize as individuals and members of a collectivity through particular institutions? As political party activists and leaders, are they more interested in feeling virtuous? Feeling victorious? Feeling loved? In winning or in educating?

Demands refer to outcomes that the individual seeks to obtain. They may refer either to the value position of the self or to that of the collectivity. The same delegate may, for example, desire to be elected chairman of his state delegation, to get his candidate elected, and to get the party to adopt his issue priorities as its priorities.

An individual's demand system is the totality of his demands and their respective priorities. A person's demand system is closely related to his identifications and perspectives, but it cannot be inferred from them because identifications and expectations may be combined in various and sometimes unexpected ways, and any number of demands may be associated with each permutation. Neither can a demand system be inferred from the arena of his activity because most institutions provide the opportunity for maximizing various values. There is substantial evidence that people become active in politics, for example, for quite different reasons and will bring to that arena quite different demands and priorities.

Note also that individuals' demands may be made in the name of collectivities. The character of demands made in the name of groups—such as a political party or a candidate support group—is determined by the interactions of the most influential participants (and not necessarily by the majority). The multifunctional character of major political institutions, such as parties, and the multiple interests of participants make it impossible to infer the value priorities and demands of collectivities from their formal functions. Political parties, for example, do not necessarily give top priority to winning elections.[31]

Mutually compatible demands are a condition of a unified, harmonious elite. Conflict within an elite may arise because members of the elite desire the same scarce values or because different portions of the elite seek goals that are incompatible with one another. Conflict over the same values, e.g., power, status, wealth, most frequently leads to changes in political personnel but not in the basic characteristics of the political system; conflict arising from the pursuit of different values and goals frequently presages major, fundamental change in a political system. The new breed hypothesis postulates the existence of this second type of conflicting demands within the presidential elite.

THE ENVIRONMENT

The boundaries between the environment and the subject of research are, of course, always determined by the observer's standpoint. What is subject and what is environment change as the observational viewpoint changes. A given set of actors and acts may constitute the focus of attention at one level of inquiry and environment at another. When one speaks of data on the environment, therefore, reference is always made, at least implicitly, to an analytic viewpoint.

In principle an environment is almost infinitely expansible and can include party rules, formal and informal; local party practices, including the personalities of local leaders, the level of competition, and the character and resources of other contenders; the weather; the economy; the state party, its leadership, rules, and practices; the contest for the presidential nomination, including staffs, tactics, and outcomes—locally and national-ly; media treatment of the nomination contest; the social, political, educa-tional background of the delegates and other contenders for the nomination, their past participation in politics; and so forth. Every political act takes place in a broad social and cultural context and the interdependence of social events means that in fact any given interaction takes place in an endlessly expansible environment. However, the researcher's task is eased by the facts, first, that not all aspects of environment are equally relevant to his concerns and second, that the relevant aspects of the more remote environment are frequently present in the proximate context.

Every researcher makes decisions about which aspects of environment are most relevant to the inquiry and about how much of the environment must be considered. A great deal depends on the quality of these decisions since overlooking significant aspects of context may doom the analysis. Placing events in the appropriate social and temporal context is not merely desirable, it is essential, because "empirical significance requires that the propositions of social science, rather than affirming unqualifiedly universal invariances, state relations between variables assuming different mag-nitudes in different social contexts."[32]

Presidential parties exist in a national political system in which they perform certain functions—notably the nomination of candidates for the presidency, the stating of general positions, the contesting of elections; they function within a national political culture and subcultures that include norms, beliefs about the interrelation of elements including causation, views about what is and is not fitting, expectations concerning what categories of people should make rules for the society, and so forth; they exist, too, in the context of a social structure—class hierarchies, an economic organization, family and community organizations, and a myriad of patterned expectations and practices concerning rights, obligations, opportunities, indulgences, and deprivations.

The aspects of environment that have special relevance for this study are three: first, the general characteristics of the political system that affect the kinds of persons attracted to and successful in politics; second, the rules and laws that governed access to delegate status in 1972; and third, the political contests of 1972 that also affected the kinds of people attracted into the arena of presidential politics.

Some other aspects of environment—such as class, region, occupation, religion—enter the analysis as attributes of individuals, factions, and par-ties. Other contextual characteristics are constructed in the course of the analysis. A more inclusive unit constructed from less inclusive units may be treated as the context for interactions of lower level units.

STRATEGY OF ANALYSIS

It is clear by now that this study is based on individual data, but that it concerns factions, parties, and the party system as well as individuals. Interviews with individuals and questionnaires completed by them constitute the data base of this study. The subject is always the individual political actor; the object is alternatively individual political actors, factions, the Republican and Democratic parties, and the party system.

Each delegate was an individual with distinctive perspectives and experiences who occupied a role in one or more decisional structures. It is the role (or roles) that defined the individual as a political influential, however role selection and definition are influenced by personal factors and by the structures of which the role is a part. The individual traits with which I am here concerned are social attributes, personal predispositions, political hstories, political perspectives, and political style. The delegate attributes of interest are role definition and convention participation.

Presidential parties are not mere aggregates of individuals, and their characteristics are not only the sum of the characteristics of the individuals who comprise them. Not only do they have integral qualities, such as unity, homogeneity, continuity and congruence, but these integral qualities are not necessarily accessible through the simple aggregation of individual traits. The characteristics of a convention or party may not reflect the "average" of the characteristics of all delegates, but only the characteristics of the numerically dominant faction. The large variations in individual attributes and the structure of decision making mean that an adequate analysis will include consideration of factions—groups comprising likeminded individuals—as intervening units between delegates and presidential parties, for, as Eulau commented ". . . if there is a great deal of variation among subject unit properties, either of sub-unit or super-unit, one must ask whether their properties can be used to describe unit properties and whether the transformed properties can be used in analysis of between-unit variations."[33] Like parties, factions have integral qualities, such as unity, cohesion, and homogeneity. Finally, the individual delegates, factions, and parties constitute a promising perspective from which to view the presidential party system, especially the extent to which it provides choice and representation.

If multilevel inquiry is complex, it is because the reality in question is complex: that reality consists of individuals filling roles in institutions which in combination comprise a party system. The social scientist who wishes to explore complex social realities—such as the impact on politics of the accession to elite status of new types of persons—has little choice but to adopt a multilevel strategy of analysis, recalling that, as Eulau pointed out, "Mobilizing all levels of analysis in behalf of understanding or explaining the manifold of events that constitute one particular phenomenon . . . is a strategy of research, not a confusion of levels of analysis."[34]

SEX AND POLITICS

At each level of analysis special attention is given to sex. The characteristics of participants are examined in order to determine distinctive and common characteristics of male and female participants: the analysis of the delegate's role includes a search for sex specific patterns of role perception, role definition, and role behavior; the analysis of parties will explicitly investigate the role and possibilities of women within each of the parties. Finally, some questions concerning the representation of women in the policy process are examined.

In the pursuit of explanations of political behavior, social scientists have explored social class, economic class, occupation, race, anti-Semitism, group affiliations, and a variety of other aspects of human identity less definitive than sex. Meanwhile, differences between the sexes have been extolled in song and verse, celebrated in marriage rituals, and nurtured and protected by distinctive socialization practices, but rarely scrutinized to determine their consequences for such major areas of human life as politics. It is past time that political scientists fill this particular gap.

Subsequent political traumas have invited us to forget that 1972 was an extraordinary political year not only because the presidential candidate of the majority party suffered a landslide defeat for the first time in American history, but especially because that year saw the arrival and the ascent to power of new doctrines about what democratic politics is and should be, new practices that reflected these new expectations and demands, new faces said to represent a new political type, and new forces said to provide alternative power bases. Because an unusually large number of these new faces were female, the 1972 conventions provide an especially good opportunity to study the experience and prospects of women in American politics.

NOTES

1. Vilfredo Pareto, *The Mind and Society: A Treatise on General Sociology*, trans. Andrew Bongiorno and Arthur Livingston (New York: Dover Publications, Inc., 1935), vol. 3, p. 1431.
2. William L. Riordan, *Plunkitt of Tammany Hall* (New York: E. P. Dutton and Co., 1963).
3. R. M. MacIver, *Social Causation* (New York: Harper and Row, 1964), p. 133.
4. R. G. Collingwood, *An Autobiography* (New York: Penguin Books, 1944), p. 67.
5. See especially Aaron Wildavsky, "The Goldwater Phenomenon: Purists, Politicians and the Two-Party System," *Review of Politics* 27 (1965): 413.
6. *Time*, July 17, 1972. One list entitled "Who Is Not Voting in Miami Beach?" named the following as "casualties of the party's new reform rules": "Boston's Mayor Kevin White; Harvard political scientist Sam Beer, who helped the McGovern Commission write the new rules; Massachusetts Congressman Thomas O'Neill; New Jersey Senator Harrison Williams; former New Jersey Governors Richard Hughes and Robert Meyner; former New York Governor Averell Harriman; former New York City Mayor Robert F. Wagner; former Pennsylvania State Chairman John Rice; Seattle Mayor Wes Uhlman; Florida State Treasurer Thomas O'Malley, and Secretary of State Richard Stone."
7. This figure is not abnormally low. In the 1968 Democratic Convention, which was widely believed to be a classic example of a "controlled" convention of "hand picked" delegates, only 30 percent had prior experience as delegate to a national convention. William Baum found that only 27 percent of those who attended the 1960 Republican convention were present in San Francisco in 1964 and only 31 percent of the 1968 delegates had attended the 1964 convention. "Between 1956 and 1964 almost half the Republican state delegations had a turnover which was total or within one of being so. This high level of turnover," he added, "takes place at all levels and affects both leadership and the rank-and-file levels to a substantial degree." Donald Bruce Johnson, "Delegate Selection for National Conventions," in *Practical Politics in the United States*, ed. Cornelius Cotter (Boston: Allyn & Bacon, 1969), p. 224.
8. The literature of political science on this subject proves that the reform politics style is not so new as the new breed hypothesis indicates. Variants of the type have been described for nearly two decades: Frank J. Sorauf, "Extra-Legal Political Parties in Wisconsin," *American Political Science Review* 48 (1954): 692–704; see, inter alia, James Q. Wilson, *The Amateur Democrat: Club Politics in Three Cities* (Chicago: University of Chicago Press, 1962); Francis Carney, *The Rise of Democratic Clubs in California* (New York: Holt, Rinehart and Winston, 1958); Stephen A. Mitchell, *Elm Street Politics* (New York: Oceana Publications, 1959); Robert S. Hirshfield, Bert E. Swanson, and Blanche D. Blank, "A Profile of Political Activists in Manhattan," *Western Political Quarterly* 15 (1962): 489–507; Robert H. Salisbury, "The Urban Party Organization Member," *Public Opinion Quarterly* 29 (1965–1966): 550–564; Dennis S. Ippolito, "Motivational Reorientation and Change among Party Activists," *Journal of Politics* 31 (1969): 1098–1101; Leon D. Epstein, *Political Parties in Western Democracies* (New York: Frederick A. Praeger, 1967), pp. 122–126; Donald C. Blaisdell, *The Riverside Democrats*, Cases in Practical Politics, No. 18 (New Brunswick, N.J.: Eagleton Institute, 1960); C. Richard Hofstetter, "Organizational Activists: The Bases of Participation in Amateur and Professional Groups," *American Politics Quarterly* 1 (1973): 244-276.

9. Epstein, *Political Parties*, p. 126.
10. McGovern strategist Frederick G. Dutton emphasized the new characteristics of women and youth in *Changing Sources of Power: American Politics in the 1970s* (New York: McGraw-Hill, 1971).
11. Well-known treatments of this subject are Gaetano Mosca, *The Ruling Class* (New York: McGraw-Hill, 1939); Pareto, *Mind and Society*; Plato, *The Republic*; Harold D. Lasswell, *Politics: Who Gets What, When, How* (New York: McGraw-Hill, 1936); Robert Michels, *Political Parties* (Hearst's International Library, 1915); Robert A. Dahl, *Who Governs? Democracy and Power in an American City* (New Haven: Yale University Press, 1961); Herbert McClosky, et al., "Issue Conflict and Consensus Among Party Leaders and Followers," *American Political Science Review* 54 (1960): 406–427; Edward A. Banfield, *Political Influence* (Glencoe, Ill.: The Free Press, 1961).
12. *The Republic of Plato*, trans. Francis Macdonald Cornford (London: Oxford University Press, 1941), p. 261. An interesting analysis of this theme is Harold D. Lasswell, "Political Constitution and Character," *Psychoanalysis and the Psychoanalytic Review* 46 (1969): 1–18.
13. Mosca, *Ruling Class*, pp. 404–405.
14. Michels, *Political Parties*; Karl Marx, *Communist Manifesto, Das Kapital*; Pareto, *Mind and Society*; Wactaw Machejski, discussed in Max Nomad, *Rebels and Renegades* (New York: Macmillan, 1932), pp. 206 ff.; Dahl, *Who Governs*; C. Wright Mills, *The Power Elite* (New York: Oxford University Press, 1956). Also important in this controversy are Nelson W. Polsby, *Community Power and Political Theory* (New Haven: Yale University Press, 1963); Raymond E. Wolfinger, "Reputation and Reality in the Study of 'Community Power'," *American Sociological Review* 25 (1960): 636–644; Robert Presthus, *Men at the Top: A Study in Community Power* (New York: Oxford University Press, 1964). For a reasonably good bibliography on the study of political power, see Roderick Bell, David V. Edwards, and R. Harrison Wagner, *Political Power: A Reader in Theory and Research* (New York: The Free Press, 1969).
15. Charles S. Hyneman, "Tenure and Turnover of Legislative Personnel," *Annals of American Academy of Political Science* 195 (1938): 21–31.
16. Heinz Eulau, William Buchanan, LeRoy Ferguson, John C. Wahlke, "Career Perspectives of American Legislators," in *Political Decision-Makers: Recruitment and Performance*, ed. Dwaine Marvick (Glencoe, Ill.: The Free Press, 1961), pp. 218–263.
17. James David Barber, *The Lawmakers: Recruitment and Adaptation to Legislative Life* (New Haven: Yale University Press, 1965); Jeane J. Kirkpatrick, *Political Woman* (New York: Basic Books, 1974); John Wahlke, Heinz Eulau, William Buchanan, and LeRoy C. Ferguson, *The Legislative System: Explorations in Legislative Behavior* (New York: John Wiley & Sons, 1962), pp. 95–120; Samuel J. Eldersveld, *Political Parties: A Behavioral Analysis* (Chicago: Rand McNally & Co., 1964), pp. 272–303; Wilson, *Amateur Democrat*; Dwaine Marvick and Charles Nixon, "Recruitment Contrasts in Rival Campaign Groups," in *Political Decision-Makers*, ed. Marvick, pp. 193–217; Banfield, *Political Influence*; Frank J. Sorauf, *Party and Representation* (New York: Atherton, 1963); Leon D. Epstein, *Politics in Wisconsin* (Madison: University of Wisconsin Press, 1958).
18. Some studies which identify social mobility as a characteristic of elected officeholders are Edward A. Shils, "The Legislator and His Environment," *University of Chicago Law Review* 18 (1951): 1581 and Epstein, *Politics in Wisconsin*, pp. 112–113. See also Wahlke, et al., *The Legislative System*, p. 489; Sorauf, *Party and Representation*, pp. 75–81; Kirkpatrick, *Political Woman*, pp. 32–33; Seymour Martin Lipset and Reinhard Bendix, *Social Mobility in Industrial Society* (Berkeley: University of California Press, 1959), pp. 33–42.

19. Lionel Trilling, *The Liberal Imagination* (New York: Doubleday & Co.), p. 184.
20. V. O. Key, Jr., *American State Politics: An Introduction* (New York: Alfred A. Knopf, 1956), p. 255.
21. Differences between masses and elite that are relevant to politics have been explored in McClosky, et al., "Issue Conflict"; also McClosky, "Consensus and Ideology in American Politics," *American Political Science Review* 58 (1964): 361–382; J. W. Prothro and C. M. Grigg, "Fundamental Principles of Democracy: Bases of Agreement and Disagreement," *Journal of Politics* 22 (1960): 276–294; S. A. Stouffer, *Communism, Conformity and Civil Liberties* (Garden City: Doubleday & Co., 1955); Dahl, *Who Governs?;* Charles F. Cnudde, "Elite Mass Relationships and Democratic Rules of the Game," *American Behavioral Scientist* 13 (1969): 189-200.
22. I define class here and throughout the book in relation to specific values; the political class is thus defined in relation to the possession of influence. Harold D. Lasswell and Abraham Kaplan, *Power and Society: A Framework for Political Inquiry* (New Haven: Yale University Press, 1950), p. 62.
23. Saloma and Sontag emphasize that "conventions have steadily become more national and centralized political institutions . . ." as part of a nationalizing trend affecting American politics. John S. Saloma, III, and Frederick H. Sontag, *Parties: The Real Opportunity for Effective Citizen Politics* (New York: Alfred A. Knopf, 1972), p. 55. An especially interesting question that has been given little attention is *why* the state parties acquiesced in the McGovern guidelines. William Cavala, "Changing the Rules Changes the Game: Party Reform and the 1972 California Delegation to the Democratic National Convention," *American Political Science Review* 68 (1974): 27–42, presents some interesting conjectures. So does Austin Ranney in his *Curing the Mischiefs of Faction: Party Reform in America* (Berkeley: University of California Press, 1975).
24. The diminishing freedom of delegates to choose anyone other than the popular front-runner is emphasized by William G. Carleton. "How Free Are the Nominating Conventions," *Virginia Quarterly Review* 40 (1964):205–223. But we see also Eugene B. McGregor, Jr., "Rationality and Uncertainty at National Nominating Conventions," *Journal of Politics* 35 (1973): 459–478; and William H. Luch, "Polls, Primaries and Presidential Nominations," *Journal of Politics* 35 (1973); 830–848.
25. Lasswell and Kaplan, *Power and Society* pp. xiv–xix.
26. Ibid., p. 62.
27. Ibid., p. 25.
28. Harold D. Lasswell and Daniel Lerner, eds. *World Revolutionary Elites: Studies in Coercive Ideological Movements* (Cambridge, Mass.: MIT Press, 1965). James Q. Wilson emphasizes the same point in *Political Organizations* (New York: Basic Books, 1974), pp. 56–75.
29. This fact should be readily grasped by Americans since our recent history is filled with upper-class revolutionaries and conservative workers, as well as upper-class conservatives and liberal laborers.
30. I prefer the Lasswell categories for analyzing subjectivity (identifications, expectations, and demands) to the Parsonian categories popularized in political science by Gabriel Almond, Sidney Verba, and others, because the Lasswell categories seem to focus more directly on aspects of subjectivity of special relevance to politics and because they bypass sticky, probably insoluble, questions concerning distinctions between facts, values, and desires. The following discussion of perspectives rather closely follows his framework. The most comprehensive statement on these concepts is Lasswell and Kaplan, *Power and Society*, Chapter 2.

31. European socialist parties, for example, came into being before the working classes were enfranchised. See Epstein, *Political Parties*, ch. VI.
32. Lasswell and Kaplan, *Power and Society*, p. xxi.
33. Heinz Eulau, "Some Aspects of Analysis, Measurement and Sampling in the Transformation of Micro and Macro-Level Unit Properties" (Paper prepared for presentation at the Conference on Design and Measurement Standards for Research in Political Science, Lake Lawn Lodge, Delevan, Wisc., May 13–15, 1974). I wish to thank Professor Eulau for making this paper available to me and for permitting its citation.
34. Heinz Eulau, *Micro-Macro Political Analysis: Accents of Inquiry* (Chicago: Aldine Publishing Co., 1969), p. 134. For further discussion of this strategy, see Harold D. Lasswell, "Person, Personality, Group, Culture," *Psychiatry 2 (1939):* 553–561. Also, Heinz Eulau and Kenneth Prewitt, *Labyrinths of Democracy: Adaptation, Linkages, Representation, and Policies in Urban Politics* (Indianapolis: Bobbs-Merrill, 1973), pp. 30–60.

CHAPTER 2

Contexts

The character of presidential parties as of other institutions is importantly influenced by the character of the people who fill their roles, but the identity of those incumbents is importantly influenced by the institutional practices that regulate access to those roles and define their functions. Delegates both are and are not self-selected. The desire to be a delegate is an important qualification, but no one becomes a delegate merely by willing it. Becoming active in politics grows out of a "fit" among an *internal personal predisposition* to seek a value that might be available through politics, *role perceptions* that confirm the relevance of the institution to the desired values, *skills* and other resources needed in the relevant processes, and the *opportunity* provided in the environment for achieving the desired role.

Existing political practices constitute the environment to which individuals react, assessing whether they do or do not desire to participate, and in which they must act if they decide to invest time, energy, and effort in politics. These practices vary greatly through time and space. Politics dominated by a landed gentry is very different from politics dominated by corporate economic power. "Marketplace" politics dominated by economic interests is very different from the politics of intellectuals, each acting in the name of the public interest. Each type of politics has distinctive styles and distinctive requirements. These change, but for any individual the existing institutions are given. They prescribe rules and define appropriate behaviors; they exert a major influence over who will be attracted to politics and who repelled; who will become influential and who remain on lower rungs. The impact of the situation on leadership recruitment is clearest in times of crises—when a man who might not otherwise win power—a Churchill, a de Gaulle, a Hitler—arrives at the top. But the environment of participation has a continuing, less dramatic influence on who seeks and wins influence: particular issues or candidates may mobilize persons never before active in politics; rules may encourage or discourage various kinds of people from seeking office by the obstacles they impose or the assistance they offer.

Only a few aspects of the demographic, social, and political context of 1972 presidential politics will be mentioned: first, some ubiquitous characteristics of American political life with special relevance to the delegate recruitment process; second, the party rules and state laws that governed the recruitment of delegates; and third, the political contests around which delegate selection was organized on the Democratic side.

THE NATIONAL CONTEXT OF PRESIDENTIAL POLITICS

Presidential politics differs from local and state activity in focus and style. Local party activity is concerned with local problems and more concrete issues and is probably most attractive to persons with local perspectives—to those who participate in politics because they see it as a form of civic activity. Local politics also more frequently holds the promise of material rewards. Its effects on participants are relatively direct, concrete, personal. But presidential politics deals or purports to deal with the big issues and offers an opportunity to debate broad questions. Its consequences for those who participate tend to be remote, impersonal, uncertain.

Even in "normal" political years the ideological content of presidential politics is higher than that of local and state politics, and studies of the 1972 presidential election agree that the ideological content was much higher than in elections of the recent past. Unusually large numbers of voters had opinions on various national problems and related those opinions to the contest among candidates.[1] It seems likely that decreased national consensus and increased salience of divisive issues may have attracted to the political arena persons with more general ideological concerns than characterize the persons active in politics at local and state levels.

SOME WIDELY SHARED CHARACTERISTICS OF POLITICAL LIFE

Delegates are chosen as members of particular parties and as inhabitants of particular states. Although the political culture and practices of the states differ in important respects from one another, state parties resemble one another in some important ways. Indeed there are fundamental similarities in American politics at all levels. Here I consider briefly the voluntary character of American politics, the diversity of activity carried on in American parties, and the highly social character of political relations. Each of these characteristics influences who becomes active.

The Voluntary Character of Political Activity

An essential feature of American politics that affects virtually all aspects of its organization and activities is that it is *voluntary*—normally undertaken in response to internal purposes rather than external constraints, such as the need to earn a living or to avoid going to jail. All but a few political actors are volunteers in another sense as well—that they engage in politics as a leisure time activity—one distinct from (though not necessarily unrelated to) their principal economic role.

The fact that American political organizations are dependent on volunteers to accomplish almost all their objectives and the parallel fact that more volunteers are needed than are available profoundly affect the composition and interactions of the organizations, rendering them more permeable and less bureaucratic than most organizations. Perhaps a local party exists here or there that is ruled by a tight self-perpetuating oligarchy, but virtually all serious students of American politics are impressed with the ease with which newcomers move into positions of leadership in party organizations. The victories of the Goldwater and McGovern movements are two recent illustrations of the permeability of American parties and the ease with which one dominant elite is replaced by another. There are local counterparts to these events in many cities, counties, and states. Samuel Eldersveld, describing the parties in Detroit, Michigan, commented on the relation between scarce volunteers and the circulation of elites: "The scarcity of talent and lack of intensive and sanctioned control make it unlikely that those 'in power' can or will deny entrance to those with ability, drive and/or local support."[2]

Candidates for the presidential nomination are also dependent on volunteers for achieving their goals. Because they are ad hoc special purpose organizations, candidates' campaign groups often reflect the characteristics of volunteer politics with special intensity.[3]

The loose, relatively unstructured, permeable, volunteer character of political organizations means that political activity normally provides a large leeway for individuals to find and to devise their own roles. In loosely organized groups, roles are not defined with specificity and authority; therefore, individuals may find their way into activities and roles suited to their interests, adapt existing roles to those interests, or restructure the organization to provide scope and support for their concerns and predispositions. Far more quickly than tighter, more highly structured institutions, loosely structured, permeable parties reflect the changing dispositions and interests of the people who comprise them. Richard Stearns, who became Senator McGovern's manager for the nonprimary states understood well the high permeability of the parties: "Even the most diabolical party machinations have never long resisted determined citizens. The theme of political history in America, at least from the organizational standpoint, is the (often temporary) victory of reform over party."[4]

It is this permeability of American politics that gives plausibility to the new breed hypothesis. Permeability permits new political generations to move rapidly into leadership positions, permits outsiders to move in, and generally accelerates the circulation of those in power. Permeability permits incongruent modal personality types to enter the organization and makes it possible for incongruent members to gain sufficient power to change the organizational structure. When the society produces significant numbers of new people interested in achieving political influence, the permeability of the parties provides them an opportunity to achieve it.

The loose organization of American parties is also closely related to the voluntary character of American political activity; it is probably impossible to build a permanent hierarchical bureaucratic nationwide organization of volunteers. Volunteers come and go; they cooperate but they do not take orders.

Eldersveld has pointed out that interpersonal relations in party organizations are characterized not by the giving and taking of orders, but by what he termed "reciprocal deference."[5] Leaders need activists, both know it, and the knowledge gives an egalitarian cast to interpersonal relations. This limits the potential for hierarchical relations. It is easy to exaggerate the rationality and hierarchical character of bureaucracies and to underestimate the importance of informal interactions, but the interactions in bureaucratic organizations are nonetheless characterized by a degree of structure, permanence, and rational purposiveness that distinguish them sharply from American political organizations.

It is believed that the big city machine had a fairly high degree of structure, permanence, and professionalism, and it is significant that many of its lieutenants were paid professionals linked therefore to their roles by the same kinds of material incentives that link civil servants to a government bureaucracy.[6] Informed observers of the American political scene agree that such few bosses and urban machines as remain appear to be living on borrowed time. Most of the county courthouse gangs that practiced patronage politics in a rural setting have already lost their grip on power. I do not suggest that patronage has disappeared from presidential politics, but as compared to politics in those countries where political campaigns are run by professional election agents, and as compared to the politics of our past, volunteers play an unusually large role. The volunteer character of politics presumably has important effects on the class characteristics and the psychological characteristics of participants. The relative scarcity of financial rewards through politics (insightfully explored by James Q. Wilson in *The Amateur Democrat* and *Political Organizations*)[7] renders political participation less attractive to persons who need or want to spend their leisure supplementing their incomes. The absence of concrete material rewards almost certainly decreases the participation of lower-class and working-class persons and increases the attractions of politics to middle and upper middle-class persons.[8] The egalitarian relations within the party permit the integration of large numbers of persons of essentially identical status and background. Although delegates are recruited from all levels of politics, as well as from every state, great diversity in their social characteristics was not expected.

The Diversity of Political Activity

Varied and diverse activities are carried out in and by political organizations, and for this reason political organizations need not only people, but different kinds of people—people who will pour coffee, stuff envelopes, make phone calls, collect dollars, host teas and coffees and lunches and dinners, run meetings, raise money, map strategy, organize a precinct, manage a campaign, write speeches, and run for office. No party could survive, even in one town or state, if all its members wanted to run for office, manage campaigns, or map strategy. Despite the fact that political activity at its most visible and dramatic level involves the quest for power, no party is made up only of power seekers. Even such small power-oriented groups as the early Nazis and Bolsheviks required, and contained, persons with a fairly wide variety of predispositions: theoreticians, managers, agitators, errand boys, technicians, and a leader. Research on state and county organizations indicates that even among those who become party officials a large portion, perhaps a majority, have no desire to run for public office and never do so.[9] As Dwaine Marvick has noted, "The development of a modern democratic theory must proceed by exploring the ways in which a great multiplicity of personalities, skills, attitudes, predispositions, and general characteristics are employed in the intricate web of relationships that constitutes the working political order."[10]

Although diverse temperaments and skills are needed and accommodated by modern party organizations, it seems unlikely that all the types of persons found in political activity at the lowest levels would have been present in the two conventions.

The Social Character of Political Activities

As conducted in the United States in 1972, politics involved an almost endless round of diverse activities, most of which had only a remote relationship to winning and exercising power, many of which were tedious and tiring, and all of which involved numbers of people engaged in joint efforts to accomplish some common goal. Politics is never a solitary pursuit, and though its interactions are purposive in the sense that they are more or less explicitly oriented toward a group goal, they have more in common with a social club than with an army or a civil service. In political organizations people are moved by persuasion, agreement, and enthusiasm. This fact alone "socializes" political relations; it means that they must be reasonably "pleasant" to participants if they are to endure. Because politics involves endless socializing, those who engage in it are most likely to be gregarious people who have a habit of joining with others to achieve goals.

Political activity in the United States is characterized by a ubiquitous purposive friendliness that involves warm affect and low commitment. Robert Dahl commented on this requirement for political participation.

> Perhaps the most obvious requirement that one must have is an unusual tolerance for creating and maintaining a great number and variety of personal relationships. This does not mean that the professional (politician) actually likes other people to any unusual degree or even that he has an unusual need to be liked by others. Indeed a study by Rufus Browning indicates that among businessmen the need for affiliation—the desire to have the liking and approval of others—is lower among those who are active in politics than those who are inactive, and it is lower among leaders than among subleaders. Browning's findings suggest the tantalizing hypothesis that the distinguishing characteristic of the professional is an inordinate capacity for multiplying human relationships without ever becoming deeply involved emotionally.[11]

The characteristics described earlier—volunteerism, permeability, diversity, sociability, national focus—are enduring, but not necessarily permanent, attributes of American presidential politics. Studies of many localities document that in Detroit, Elm City, Chicago, New York, and New Haven[12] parties need workers, that there is a high turnover of leaders, a low control over recruitment, and short periods of apprenticeship, and that they are filled with large numbers of public spirited volunteers more attracted by doing good and associating with like-minded others than by enriching themselves at the public till. Collectively, these attributes constituted the social and human context of presidential politics of 1972.

THE RULES

In the century and a half since the emergence of national conventions, both Republicans and Democrats held conventions that were basically conferences of party leaders and regulars—conferences of people who had devoted and would continue to devote large amounts of time, energy, and sometimes money to the party. Obviously, the rise and spread of presidential primaries affected the character of conventions since the selection of delegates by primary provided a vehicle for the representation of voters' views in conventions—and not merely those of state party leaders.[13] But (even in states with primaries), slating, endorsements, and apathy have generally resulted in delegations filled by persons who "tended to be representatives of the regular party organizations in their state."[14]

The test of a convention was generally believed to be its ability to pick a winner. Its responsiveness to the rank and file was secured—or believed to be secured—by the party's need to attract and mobilize local party activists, to attract voters, and to win elections.[15]

In 1972 the Republican Convention was organized on the basis of these traditional notions about what a national convention should be.[16] But the ties of the Democratic Convention to the regular organization were fewer and more tenuous.[17]

The McGovern-Fraser Commission guidelines constituted a self-conscious effort to bring participatory democracy to the national convention: an effort based on a new conception of participation, a new conception of representation, and a new conception of what a national convention should be.

These new conceptions were embodied in the guidelines authored by the Democratic party's Commission on Party Structures and Delegate Selection (popularly known as the McGovern Commission or the McGovern-Fraser Commission). That commission, established by the 1968 Democratic Convention[18] for the purpose of assuring that all Democrats had "full and timely opportunity to participate" in the delegate selection process, revolutionized delegate selection in the Democratic party. It is still controversial. Some Democrats see the commission's report as a landmark in the struggle for party democracy, an emancipation proclamation that frees the party from control by bosses and entrenched interests. Others view it as a mistaken though well-intentioned effort—one that cripples party organization, exacerbates party divisions, and makes electoral victory much more difficult to achieve. For still others, the guidelines constituted a naked power grab by one faction that used its control of the reform commission to write rules that assured it an advantage in the contest for the nomination.[19] Then and now controversy over the rules included their substance and the procedures by which they were adopted. A majority of the commission took the position that the guidelines were binding once adopted by the commission, that they did not fall within the jurisdiction of the National Committee, and that the commission was an instrument of the 1968 convention and was only responsible to the next convention whose members would be chosen under its rules.

The notion that many Democrats (especially anti-war, anti-Humphrey, anti-Johnson Democrats) had been frozen out of participation in the nominating process in 1968 was premise to the deliberations of the McGovern-Fraser Commission. The determination to wrest control of the party from the entrenched leadership and to "open" the party to the participation of all—especially those formerly frozen out—was the overriding goal of the commission. Primaries are the historic device for democratizing the nominating process. But the McGovern Commission eschewed the "national primary" route to reform and explicitly endorsed diversity in nominating procedures.

Fear that one or both political parties have fallen victim to oligarchical control is a recurring theme in American political history, most recently and most incisively described by Austin Ranney.[20] American suspicion of organization as somehow not democratic feeds this fear, and the political culture reinforces it. The charge that bosses have prevented the "people" from having their way is always available to explain a political defeat and to justify reforms that hobble those who have power and abet those who seek it.[21]

According to the commission, the guidelines were designed "to stimulate the participation of all Democrats in the nominating process and to reestablish public confidence in the National Convention."[22] Commission member Austin Ranney confirms that "Most of the guidelines were consciously designed to maximize participation by persons who are enthusiasts for a particular aspirant or policy in the year of the convention."[23] Many commission members agreed with reform commission member and McGovern strategist Fred Dutton that "This society is already taking off on still another great surge matched only a few times in the past, and possibly never before. To attempt to hold back politically can only intensify the potential strains and dangers. . . . The need now is for a public transition such as that from Hoover to Roosevelt—in short, the crossing of a great historical threshold."[24] To accomplish this the commission proposed to eliminate or amend rules and practices that tended to "inhibit access to the delegate selection process . . .," to "dilute the influence of a Democrat in the delegate selection process . . . ,"[25] and to adopt new rules that would guarantee full participation of all interested Democrats.

We are concerned here not with the rules as such but with those aspects of the rules that affected who sought and won delegate contests. The provisions most important for these purposes are 1) those that aimed at "opening" the processes to participation by all interested Democrats and 2) those that aimed at limiting the control of party officials over delegate selection.

The commission sought to achieve the goal of "opening" the nominating process by removing barriers to full participation and by requiring "open" procedures at each stage. Most of these regulations were non-controversial: most important of these were Guideline C-1, which called for "adequate public notice" concerning times and places of meetings, including a specific explanation of the relation between the meeting and the delegate selection process; Guideline C-3, which required that "an opportunity to participate in the delegate selection process must be open to all persons who wish to be Democrats and who are not already members of another party . . ."; and Guideline C-6, which required that meetings at which slates were formed be publicized and open to all Democrats.

As a part of its effort to open the party, the guidelines took special note of the plight of persons who had in the past found the gateways to participation barred to them—notably women, blacks, and youth. It was noted that "representation of blacks, women, and youth at the 1968 convention was substantially below the proportion of each group in the population," and Guidelines A-1 and A-2 were drafted requiring all states to "overcome the effects of past discrimination by affirmative steps to encourage representation on the national convention delegation of young people—defined as people of not more than 30 nor less than 18 years of age—and women in reasonable relationship to their presence in the population." An identical requirement applied to blacks and other minorities. These controversial requirements expressed in Guidelines A-1 and A-2 resulted in the presence at the Democratic Convention of larger numbers of women, blacks, persons under 30, American Indians, and Chicanos than at any previous convention.

A second major concern of the reform commission was to eliminate the practices that would "dilute" the influence of Democrats who participated in the delegate selection process. The exercise of "disproportionate" influence by party notables was perceived as one important means through which the influence of rank and file Democrats was diluted. John Stewart, an astute and expert observer of the Democratic scene, believes these rule changes had the greatest effect on outcomes: "Whatever benefit McGovern acquired from the new rules resulted from the less publicized changes that greatly reduced the control of established party leaders in selecting delegates or in influencing their selection."[26]

A number of the provisions that "opened" the party and guaranteed that the influence of participants was not diluted also had the effect of reducing the influence of party leaders. In this category fall the prohibition of ex officio delegates, the requirement of a quorum of 40 percent for all party committee meetings concerning delegate selection, the requirement of "timelines," i.e., all delegates to be chosen in the calendar year of the convention, the prohibition of the unit rule at all stages of the delegate selection process, and the prohibition of proxy voting. Naming the party's leading officers and officeholders to the state's delegation was a standard practice in both parties prior to 1972. The prohibition of ex officio delegates meant that party leaders would have to compete "on an equal basis" for positions in the delegation. This, in turn, often required a party leader to make an early commitment to a candidate for the nomination and forfeit advantages that might accrue from maintaining neutrality and a good bargaining position among the contenders. It also required party leaders who might have preferred to remain neutral to risk their prestige by joining a slate whose fortunes would be determined by political factors with little relevance to state politics. The prohibition of ex officio delegates operated to reduce substantially the number of leading Democrats present at the convention.

With its prohibition of "any practices by which officials elected or appointed before the calendar year . . . propose or endorse a slate of delegates,"[27] the commission expressed in clearest form the majority view that a convention should be a meeting of persons interested in the nomination contest. How, argued the commission, could the rank and file participate in the nominating process if delegates were chosen before "the issues and candidates that characterized the politics . . ." of the year "had clearly emerged"? The commission not only required that delegates be selected during the calendar year of the convention, but it stipulated that "timeliness" prohibited participation in the delegate selection process of ". . . governors, state chairmen, state, district and county committees who are chosen before the calendar year of the convention. . . ."[28]

The effect of this requirement was clearest in the Illinois challenge where it was argued that one of the reasons the Daley slate should be ousted was the participation of Daley and other regulars not chosen in the calendar year 1972. A related guideline (C-5) stated the reform commission's view that committee systems were an undesirable method of delegate selection because they "offer fewer guarantees for a full and meaningful opportunity to participate than other systems" and limited the proportion of a state's delegation that could be chosen by committee, thereby further reducing the possibility that other party, community, and interest group leaders could be appointed to the state's delegation without competing for a seat. In fact, fewer than 20 percent of delegates were selected by party committees.

The Democratic reforms also affected the composition of the Republican Convention. Favorable discussion of the Democratic reforms created pressure on the Republicans to increase the representation of women, blacks, and youth in party proceedings. Though no formal requirements were adopted, Republican national chairman Robert Dole said in April 1972 that the party was trying to "make certain that half the delegates are male, half are female, that we have young and minority representation in every delegation. . ."[29] and, in fact, more women, youth, and minorities were present at the 1972 Republican Convention than at previous conventions.

Rules have both intended and unintended effects, both direct and indirect consequences. One of the most important consequences of the new rules was to further accelerate the nationalization of American politics. The development and enforcement of national guidelines governing delegate recruitment weakened the role of state parties in the recruitment process and also in convention proceedings; it strengthened the role of candidate campaign staffs and heightened the importance of the new constituencies as compared to traditional areal constituencies.

A convention brings together for a brief period persons who may not otherwise be associated with one another; its role structure derives in part from rules of procedure and in part from the structure of subgroups, such as state parties and candidate groups that antedate the convention. Traditionally, state parties have been the principal subunits of a national convention, and their structures have had great relevance for its structure and operations. Emphasizing the importance to delegates' behavior of membership in state parties, Nelson Polsby and Aaron Wildavsky counsel, "it must never be forgotten that delegates come from state parties with internal lives of their own. The delegates spend over 1,400 days every four years as members of their state parties and less than a week at the national convention."[30] But the impact of state parties on convention structures varies with rules and practices. When the rules prescribe that the preexisting structures, such as state parties, shall control recruitment and prescribe that state delegations shall be the action units of the convention, the structure and composition of state parties will have a large impact on conventions. The same understandings that structure their ongoing relations in the state party will structure the interactions of a delegation comprising state party regulars. Delegates chosen as representatives of state parties may have different political experience, interests, and role expectations than delegates chosen as supporters of a particular candidate. Democratic rules that restricted direct participation of state party organizations in the delegate selection process and that prohibited the imposition of the unit rule had an indirect effect on the internal organization of delegations. John Saloma and Frederick Sontag noted that various factors "have served to erode the control of state political bosses, further increasing the national authority of the convention—the decline of patronage as the basis for state and urban party machines, the rise of nationwide interest groups like organized labor, and, more recently, national Democratic party guidelines for state delegate selection procedures and apportionment of representatives on convention committees on the basis of population."[31]

A concomitant of the declining influence of state and local organizations on convention composition and proceedings is the greatly enhanced importance of candidate groups. Candidate groups are ad hoc collectivities that coalesce around the presidential aspirations of particular men. Usually they come into existence only in the year preceding the convention and function as loose, temporary coalitions whose actors know one another only slightly and interact rarely. Their greater size and unstructured membership facilitate highly centralized decision making. Rules prohibiting unit voting by state delegations also paved the way for increased influence of candidate organizations.

When the impact of state organization on convention proceedings is diminished, the relevance of areal constituencies to convention proceedings is also greatly decreased even though the formal structure of the national convention is still based on areal units. The relation of a convention delegate to an areal constituency is in any case substantially different from the relation of a legislator to his geographical constituency. The congressional electoral system anchors each legislator in a district and accountability guarantees that the legislator who desires to be reelected must demonstrate concern for the district from which he is elected. No such guarantee is built into the process of selecting delegates to national conventions. Most of the structural elements that link a legislator to an area are missing in the relationship between a delegate and a geographical district. In some states, delegates are selected indirectly through votes cast for a presidential contender; in others, slating, statewide contests, two and three step convention processes alter and perhaps eliminate entirely a relation between an area and a delegation. It seems clear that an indirect but perhaps inevitable effect of rules that attenuate the role of the state party organization is to further diminish the extent to which delegates are oriented to area constituencies.

STATE PRACTICES

New York *Times* analyst R. W. Apple called the 1972 revisions in state rules for choosing delegates "one of the most important modifications in the recondite but often decisive mechanics of American politics since the progressive era produced the initiative, referendum, and recall; the direct election of Senators; and the Presidential primary in the nineteen-twenties."[32]

One unanticipated consequence of the reforms was the increase in the number of primaries from seventeen in 1968 to twenty-two (plus the District of Columbia) in 1972. Changed rules were not the only reason for the proliferation of primaries; the desire to attract publicity to the state and widen participation in presidential nominating politics played a role in some states. But it was clear that some states changed to delegate selection by primary, because it seemed the simplest way to conform to the new Democratic rules. By 1972 nine of the ten largest states had adopted primaries as the means for choosing delegates (Texas was the exception). Furthermore, as James Lengle and Byron Shafer point out, "The increase in the number of 'effective' primaries was even greater, however, because (required) reforms upgraded previously less significant arenas into serious campaign sites. In fact, the biggest rise in the number of delegates along the primary route came not from new entries but from changes in old ones."[33] In consequence of these changes, some 1,900 votes, 63 percent of the total to the 1972 convention, were chosen by primary as compared to 41 percent in 1968. In 1972, 1,509 votes were needed to be nominated. Because only four states were winner-take-all states able to bring blocs of delegates to the convention, winning primaries did not necessarily guarantee the nomination. As *Congressional Quarterly* noted, "a candidate could win a majority of votes in all twenty-three primaries in 1972 and still fall as many as 250 votes short of the number needed to nominate."[34] It became clear very early that no candidate would take a commanding lead through the primaries and, therefore, that candidates must pursue the contest for delegates in nonprimary states.

There was procedural diversity in both primary and nonprimary states. Primaries were open and closed, binding and nonbinding. Most were closed and binding but many of these differed in their specific requirements concerning how long delegates were bound and who could release them. The basis for distributing seats also varied in the primary states: four states—California, Oregon, Rhode Island, South Dakota—and the District of Columbia retained winner-take-all primaries in which the winner of the statewide primary won all seats. A second type of primary—found in Florida, Indiana, Massachusetts, Tennessee, and Wisconsin—adopted the winner-take-all principle at the level of the congressional district. A third type of primary, utilized in nine states, provided for the selection of individual delegates to the national convention without committing the individual elected to support any particular candidate. A fourth type of primary provided that delegates be chosen on the basis of the statewide popularity of the presidential candidates.[35]

Practices also varied in the nonprimary states, but they varied within limits set by the new rules. The reform rules required that at least 75 percent of the delegates be chosen at the congressional district level; most states chose about that portion of their delegates through conventions at the congressional district level and at-large delegates at a state convention. The McGovern-Fraser guidelines also required that the delegate selection process be open to all enrolled party members and that the times, places, and rules for public meetings be publicized well in advance of the meeting.

EFFECTS OF RULES

In both parties rules of the national parties influenced (and sometimes determined) the process and terms of delegate selection everywhere. No rules are entirely neutral. Each favors some type of power base over another, some skills, associations, personal qualities over others. The 1972 Democratic rules had some indisputable effects: notably producing increased numbers of women, persons under 30, blacks, and other minorities and heightening the importance in American politics of these "new constituencies" as compared with areal constituencies;[36] decreasing the influence on delegate selection of state party organizations; increasing the power of candidate organizations; and reducing the numbers of elected officials and party leaders present in Miami.

Debate continues over other effects of the reform rules: whether they purified the party or only transferred power from an organizational elite to an ideological counter-elite; whether they were or were not responsible for the party's landslide defeat; whether they made the party more or less democratic.[37] But there is no debate over whether the new rules accelerated the circulation of the Democratic presidential elite and facilitated the accession to influence of new people who without the rules would surely have found it more difficult to win influence in presidential politics.[38] Concerning the extent of change, *Congressional Quarterly* commented on convention eve:

> The closer the Democrats come to the opening gavel of their national convention, the greater the uncertainty grows over the convention's procedures and outcome. The only certainty is that the 5,000 delegates and alternates to the four-day assembly in Miami Beach July 10-13 will participate in a gathering unlike any other ever held by a political party in the United States.[39]

Both Democratic and Republican delegates were generally satisfied with the process by which they were selected. Eighty percent of Democrats felt that the delegate selection process was fairer than before; 87

percent said it was more open than in the past; and 82 percent said it produced a more representative slate. Over 90 percent of McGovern's delegates felt that the process was fairer than before; and a bare majority of all Democratic delegates (52 percent) thought the 1972 procedures were likely to produce a winner. Wallace delegates felt differently on both questions.

The new rules were not the sole determinants of the composition of the Democratic Convention. Indeed, in retrospect it seems likely that most contemporaneous accounts exaggerated the impact of the reform rules on the composition of the Democratic Convention. The collapse of the Muskie campaign which had attracted the support of so many Democratic notables, the success of George McGovern in rallying round him the party's left, the existence of multiple candidates competing for the support of moderate and conservative Democrats, the failure of the Wallace organization to adapt fully to the new rules, and the unanticipated proliferation of primaries—each played a role in determining the convention's composition. But outcomes are always a consequence of the interaction of rules, events, and actors, and no serious observer doubts that the rules had an impact on who ran and who was selected as a delegate. Lengle and Shafer demonstrate authoritatively that "In the last presidential nomination race, the beneficiary of the power hidden in the order of the games was Senator George McGovern."[40]

POLITICAL CONTEXT

The events of 1972 are too recent to require detailed reconstruction, but succeeding political events have been so traumatic that they may have blurred the outlines of the contest. It is especially important to recall that by 1972 a decade of war, civil disobedience, and violence had exacerbated passions as well as divisions, producing what Alexander Bickel termed a "moral firestorm"[41] which threatened to engulf traditional political identifications and voting patterns as it had already engulfed the traditional limits of political behavior and mutual tolerance. Only the major features of the contests are mentioned.

REPUBLICANS

On the Republican side, the most important political fact was the existence of an incumbent, Richard Nixon, who was popular in his own party and generally regarded as having a very good chance to win reelection. In the months preceding the Republican Convention when delegates were chosen, polls showed Nixon running strongly against all potential Democratic candidates. The existence of a popular incumbent and the absence of a significant opponent—neither Congressman McCloskey on the left nor Congressman Ashbrook on the right were able to mobilize a significant challenge to Nixon's dominance of his own party—meant there was no contest over candidates or issues to stimulate "outsiders" to try to win seats at the Republican Convention. Party rules and procedures normally are changed as the result of intraparty strife, and no intense factional rivalries or insurgencies had racked the Republican party since 1964. Rules governing recruitment to the Republican Convention had been repeatedly updated and were revised again prior to the 1972 convention. But these revisions neither reflected nor caused important changes in the composition or procedures of the convention. In the absence of any internal contests over candidates or issues, the Republicans were free to concentrate during the pre-convention period on developing issues and positions that would be useful in the general election and to watch the Democrats defeat one another.

DEMOCRATIC CONTEST

Although the number of voters who identified with the Democratic party continued to be very large, new issues and new passions threatened to fracture the loose New Deal coalition that had dominated American politics for most of four decades.

Badly split since 1967, that party entered 1972 presidential politics divided on issues, candidates, and party organization. Among Democrats the wounds of 1968 had by no means healed. An important faction of the party still felt that it had been cheated of a fair voice and an appropriate role in the 1968 nomination process; others did not doubt that "spoilers" inside and outside the 1968 convention were responsible for Hubert Humphrey's narrow loss and Nixon's election. On the party's right and left there were Democrats who despaired of getting a hearing in the party. Some of these were Southerners, white workingmen, and the elderly who threatened defection to Wallace or to the Republicans. Others were found at the opposite end of the conventional political spectrum swelling the ranks of McGovern supporters. The "peace movement" had apparently become a permanent faction in the party, one united by perspectives that stretched beyond Vietnam to the most basic questions of national identity and purpose. Many of the regulars remained in the party's "center," squeezed between increasingly hostile factions.[42]

A dozen candidates sought the Democratic nomination in New Hampshire. Half a dozen of these were at one time or another believed to have a real chance to win the nomination: front-runner Edmund Muskie was the clear favorite of the party's top leadership and led the public opinion polls in mid-winter. He was crowded by Hubert Humphrey who longed for a rematch with Nixon and by Henry Jackson who argued he best represented the New Deal tradition—both contested Muskie for the right to be the mainstream candidate. On the left, anti-war crusader George McGovern was "faced with several liberal campaigns, each of which seemed to have some initial advantage: McCarthy began with greater strength in the polls; Lindsay had glamor, money, and a good press . . . ; and Chisholm appeared to be attracting support among both black and active women's groups."[43] And there was Alabama Governor George Wallace who insisted that *he* most closely represented Democratic rank and file and mounted a determined challenge from the right. The appeal of George Wallace to a substantial Democratic constituency had been demonstrated by the 13 million votes he obtained in 1968; but long before the primaries Wallace had announced his determination to compete in 1972 for the *Democratic* nomination, and while no one was certain of his potential strength among Democratic primary voters, informed observers did not discount it.

The ideological spectrum represented by these candidates was broad, but no broader than that found in 1972 among Democratic voters. The issues salient in 1972 were not the bread and butter and welfare state issues on which Democrats were (and are) relatively united; they were instead the new social and cultural issues on which there were strongly held opinions and clashing views within the party.

Large-scale American participation in the Vietnam war had ended, but disagreement on foreign policy continued—between those who desired to end all American support for South Vietnam and those who did not; between those who desired large cuts in the national defense budget and those who did not; and between those who favored a diminished American military role in Europe and Asia and those who did not. George McGovern made these issues the centerpiece of his successful campaign for the Democratic nomination and his unsuccessful campaign for the presidency. McGovern called on Americans to "reorder" their priorities: to clean up their cities and water, to cut defense expenditures, and to expand domestic ones. Hubert Humphrey and Henry Jackson emphasized economic issues and counseled caution on defense cuts warning that the world was still a dangerous place, that the Soviet military might continue to grow at an accelerating pace, and that negotiating mutual arms limitations depended on not disarming unilaterally.

Rioting in cities and on campuses had ended but Democratic disagreement on how to deal with urban and campus "unrest" (as it was then called) merged with disagreement on broader law and order issues. Did the imperfections of the society cause and justify dissidence, civil disobedience, and violent assaults on the social order? If so, then crime, disobedience, and "unrest" could and should be dealt with by abolishing poverty and eliminating social injustice. If not, then repression and punishment were required and justified to defend social peace. Disagreement on the causes and cure of crime was mixed with disagreement about the general worthiness and virtue of the society: two bumper stickers of the period reflected Democratic divisions on this issue: "America: Love it or leave it," on the one hand; "America: Change it or forget it" on the other. Wallace hammered the law and order theme from the outset of his campaign (until a would-be assassin's bullet cut him down in a Maryland shopping center) denouncing permissive judges and politicians who pampered criminals but did not protect law-abiding taxpayers against crime and attacking civil disobedience and amnesty and those who advocated it.

These were not the only disagreements that divided Democrats. The desirability and constitutionality of "forced" busing to achieve "racial balance" aroused intense conflict in some areas, and always, the most intense disagreement was among Democrats. The capacity of busing to move primary voters was demonstrated in Florida's early primary and again in Michigan.

Because the issues of 1972 expressed and involved basic identifications and values, they stimulated unusually intense interest and mobilized some who had not previously participated in presidential politics to seek delegates' positions. The divisions among Democrats—symbolized by the mutual antagonism of the three Georges (Wallace, Meany, and McGovern)—pitted the traditional political culture against the values of the new politics.[44] Ideology played an unusually important part in this contest for the nomination, as in the succeeding election, and brought into the Democratic arena persons not moved by organizational politics as usual. At least this was widely believed to be the case. It was said again and again that many of the people who took part in the contest within the Democratic party for the nomination were different from the regulars who had dominated it in the preceding decade. Probably the claim is accurate. Just how different is the heart of this inquiry.

The months between New Hampshire's March 7 primary and California's June 6 winner-take-all contest saw the progressive narrowing of the Democratic field. The pre-convention proceedings gave good grounds for concluding that a major change had overtaken American politics: that the old leaders would be replaced by a new elite. The candidates supported by the party's top leaders were unable to translate their support in the organization and in the public opinion polls into delegate victories. It had already been established in 1968 that for a front-runner to win a media victory as well as a victory at the polls it was not enough to win in New Hampshire; it was necessary to win big, and Muskie's showing (like that of Johnson before him) had not satisfied media expectations. Muskie's poor showing in Florida, where he ran fourth, was a nearly mortal blow to his presidential hopes, and it was the burying ground of Lindsay's well-financed campaign. George Wallace's victory in that state dramatized the opportunity primaries offered to an insurgent. His success in Michigan, over the urgent efforts of the UAW leadership, dramatized the national character of his appeal.

All the long shots save one dropped out early and were soon followed by Lindsay, Jackson, and Muskie; a bullet put an end to George Wallace's campaign at a time when he led all contenders in popular votes. The loss in California diminished Humphrey's fading hopes. By July, George McGovern, the remaining long shot, an ex-Methodist minister, who preached peace and moral awakening, had nearly captured his party's nomination. The McGovern "movement"—as it was always called—was a clear descendant of the "movement" that rallied round Eugene McCarthy four years earlier and which in the intervening years had conducted an unceasing agitation against the war in Vietnam. By 1972, however, the movement had acquired some new characteristics: the most important of these were organizational skill and sophistication. McGovern's army of largely young, white, college-educated, upper income, ideologically motivated volunteers[45] came prepared in 1972 with a direct mail solicitation campaign that startled seasoned political observers with its effectiveness (despite the fact that Barry Goldwater's campaign for small contributions had enjoyed great success among Republicans eight years earlier), highly motivated cadres, an organization in every state, and an understanding of the new rules that surpassed that of all other candidates. It was largely these McGovern volunteers who gave rise to the new breed hypothesis: the belief that American politics was being transformed because large numbers of new, more idealistic, more sophisticated, more educated, more independent people were entering presidential politics and winning influence. In caucuses, state conventions, and primaries, the supporters of George McGovern demonstrated that their presumed inexperience was no handicap.

McGovern ran first in primaries in Massachusetts, Wisconsin, California, and New York; Muskie led the field in New Hampshire and Illinois; Humphrey, in Ohio and Pennsylvania; and George Wallace finished first in Florida, Michigan, and Maryland. McGovern fared still better in states where delegates were chosen by caucus and convention. From the beginning McGovern's organization in the nonprimary states astonished rivals and observers with its audacity and effectiveness.

The McGovern campaign in the nonprimary states was headed by Richard Stearns who, as an intern on Kenneth Bode's staff, had prepared state-by-state analyses of the delegate selection processes. Stearns' detailed knowledge of the procedures was an undoubted asset to the McGovern campaign, as was his hard-headed understanding of the dynamics of elite mobilization. Still, he himself commented "My ideas couldn't have worked for McGovern if not for the reform commission." Washington *Post* reporter, William Chapman, described the contest for delegates in these nonprimary states as "a quiet patient struggle to pack caucuses at the local level and then win the congressional district and state conventions which select national convention delegates."[46] McGovern supporters carried the contest even into the home states of his opponents and into areas not generally hospitable to proponents of the new liberalism, winning, for example, nineteen delegates in Minnesota, thirty-four delegates in Texas, six in Georgia, and ten in Oklahoma.

Commenting on the South Dakota senator's nonprimary victories, the New York *Times* noted, "First in Iowa, later in states, such as Vermont and Idaho, McGovern cadres in precinct caucuses confronted unsuspecting and ill-prepared party leaders, committed in each case to the nomination of Senator Edmund S. Muskie."[47]

John Stewart explained the success of McGovern's forces similarly. "The impact of these changes was especially evident in nonprimary states. Precinct leaders who would routinely meet with a known group of friends and neighbors to choose delegates for county or state conventions suddenly encountered a mass outpouring of new people who arrived early, stayed late, and, more often than not, supported George McGovern."[48]

By the eve of the convention, George McGovern had won 27 percent of the popular vote cast in the primaries, was the first choice of 31 percent of Democratic voters, and had accumulated over 1,350 delegates. Only the "California challenge" stood between him and the nomination, and that outcome was clear enough once acting Chairman Larry O'Brien ruled that the majority of that state's delegates could vote on the challenge and that the issue could be resolved by a simple majority of those eligible to vote (not an absolute majority of convention delegates).[49]

McGovern's feat was the more impressive because it was accomplished in spite of the fact that Muskie had early established his position as the favorite of many party leaders; that George Wallace had cornered the loyalties of a large share of dissatisfied, anti-organization Democrats; and that Humphrey enjoyed the active support of COPE, the AFL-CIO, and a large share of the civil rights leadership, and, once the Muskie campaign faltered, most of the party leadership.[50] In retrospect it seems clear that McGovern's success rested on the existence of highly motivated, readily mobilized supporters who were easily transformed into a core of volunteers in every state, on an efficient organization, on the mistakes and division of his opponents, and on the new rules that he had helped to write as chairman of the McGovern Commission.

Observers agreed that the McGovern leaders understood far better than their rivals the political implications of the new rules and the requirements of the new style of participatory politics.[51] Richard Stearns, McGovern's coordinator for nonprimary states, foresaw that "the 1972 campaign would require wide organization but relatively small numbers of people"; and McGovern upsets would be easiest, he decided, "in states where relatively closed party structures had discouraged mass support and were all the more vulnerable to sudden bursts of outside interest."[52]

Going into the convention, McGovern had a commanding but not a conclusive lead: *Congressional Quarterly* gave McGovern 1,383 delegates to 367 for Humphrey, 370 for Wallace, 171 for Muskie, 162 for assorted other candidates, and 562 uncommitted.[53]

The new rules and the intensity of the Democratic contest had combined to reduce the number of uncommitted delegates. Most delegates were selected as supporters of particular presidential candidates. Candidate preference not only structured the convention, it dominated the recruitment process: the overwhelming majority of delegates ran as partisans of a particular presidential hopeful and were elected as such. The rules and the politics of 1972 so discouraged the selection of uncommitted delegates that only 562 of 3,016 delegates were uncommitted at the time of their selection, and the preferences of a good many of these were known by the time of the convention.

Altogether it was a very unusual political contest. The front-runners had faltered. Both Wallace and McGovern were the enemies of politics as usual. Both had bypassed and challenged regular Democratic organizations. Both had registered major victories. These victories did not *prove* that one American elite had been replaced by another, but they provided reasonable grounds for thinking so.

NOTES

1. Arthur H. Miller, Warren E. Miller, Alden S. Raine, and Thad A. Brown, "A Majority Party in Disarray: Policy Polarization in the 1972 Election" (Paper presented at the annual meeting of the American Political Science Association, New Orleans, La., September 4-8, 1973).
2. Samuel Eldersveld, *Political Parties: A Behavioral Analysis* (Chicago: Rand McNally & Co., 1964), p. 120.
3. The Goldwater and the McGovern campaigns demonstrated that campaigns with a high ideological content may have a special capacity to motivate and mobilize volunteers. See Aaron Wildavsky, "The Goldwater Phenomenon: Purists, Politicians and the Two-Party System," *Review of Politics* 27 (1965): 386–413. Also, Theodore H. White, *The Making of the President 1964* (New York: Atheneum, 1965) and *The Making of the President 1972* (New York: Atheneum, 1973).
4. Richard G. Stearns, "The Presidential Nominating Process in the United States: The Constitution of the Democratic National Convention" (Thesis submitted to Balliol College, Oxford University, June, 1971), p. 149. I wish to thank Mr. Stearns for making this thesis available to me.
5. Eldersveld, *Political Parties*, p. 9.
6. Edward C. Banfield and James Q. Wilson, *City Politics* (Cambridge, Mass.: Harvard University Press, 1963).
7. James Q. Wilson, *The Amateur Democrat* (Chicago: University of Chicago Press, 1962). This point is emphasized and explored by James Q. Wilson in *Political Organizations* (New York: Basic Books, 1973). Also see Leon D. Epstein, *Political Parties in Western Democracies* (New York: Frederick A. Praeger, 1967). But note that some state studies have found that national incentives continue to be important to some, e.g., James David Barber, *The Lawmakers: Recruitment and Adaptation to Legislative Life* (New Haven: Yale University Press, 1965).
8. Wilson, *Political Organizations*, ch. 3; also Edward C. Banfield, *The Unheavenly City: The Nature and Future of Our Urban Crisis* (Boston: Little, Brown Co., 1970), especially ch. 3.
9. Samuel C. Patterson, "Characteristics of Party Leaders," *Western Political Quarterly* 16, no. 2 (1963): 332-352. Also Leon D. Epstein, *Politics in Wisconsin* (Madison: University of Wisconsin Press, 1958), p. 91. Samuel Eldersveld spoke of the "unique careerist dilemma" confronting parties: ". . . the party," he said, "needs power-aspiring careerists because it is a power-seeking and power-converting group; but it cannot afford too many aspirants because of the resulting threat to structural viability." *Political Parties*, p. 122.
10. Dwaine Marvick and Charles R. Nixon, "Recruitment Contrasts in Rival Campaign Groups," in *Political Decision-Makers: Recruitment and Performance*, ed. Dwaine Marvick (Glencoe, Ill.: The Free Press, 1961), p. 215.
11. Robert Dahl, *Who Governs? Democracy and Power in an American City* (New Haven: Yale University Press, 1961), p. 298. This study cites Rufus Browning, "Businessmen in Politics" (Ph.D. diss., Yale University, 1960). On the same theme, Lester Milbrath commented, "Sociable personalities are more likely to enter politics than nonsociable personalities; this is especially true of political activities that require social interaction." *Political Participation: How and Why Do People Get Involved in Politics?* (Chicago: Rand McNally & Co., 1965), p. 75.

12. Eldersveld, *Political Parties;* Stephen A. Mitchell, *Elm Street Politics* (New York: Oceana Publications, 1959); Edward C. Banfield, *Political Influence* (Glencoe, Ill.: The Free Press, 1961); Wilson, *Amateur Democrat;* Dahl, *Who Governs?*

13. William H. Lucy, "Polls, Primaries and Presidential Nominations," *Journal of Politics* 35 (1973): 830–848, provides an account of the relations of these three.

14. David W. Abbott and Edward T. Rogowsky, "The Linkage Process: An Essay on Parties and Opinion," *Political Parties: Leadership, Organization, Linkage,* eds. Abbott and Rogowsky (Chicago: Rand McNally & Co., 1971), p. 518. Until 1972 the characterization of David, Goldman, and Bain remained essentially accurate: "The party conventions bring together a cross section of officialdom from the executive and legislative branches of all levels of government and also from all parts of the party hierarchy." Paul T. David, Ralph M. Goldman, and Richard C. Bain, *The Politics of National Party Conventions* (Washington, D.C.: Brookings Institution, 1960), p. 342.

15. A persuasive defense of traditional nominating conventions is Herbert McClosky, "Are Political Conventions Undemocratic?" *New York Times Magazine,* August 4, 1968, pp. 15-21. A good description of the traditional convention is Nelson W. Polsby, "Decision-Making at the National Convention," *Western Political Quarterly* 13 (1960): 609-619. A good description of the entire presidential nominating process is Nelson W. Polsby and Aaron B. Wildavsky, *Presidential Elections: Strategies of American Electoral Politics,* 4th ed. (New York: Charles Scribner's Sons, 1976). Also useful is Gerald Pomper, *Nominating the President: The Politics of Convention Choice* (New York: W.W. Norton and Company, Inc., 1966). Also, Aaron B. Wildavsky, "On the Superiority of National Conventions," *Review of Politics* 24 (1962): 307-319. Note that Senator George McGovern, writing on the 1968 Democratic Convention, not only criticized it, but noted that it "was governed by essentially the same rules as those which nominated Woodrow Wilson, Franklin Roosevelt, and John F. Kennedy." George McGovern, "The Lessons of 1968," *Harpers Magazine,* January 1970, p. 43.

16. Though note that the Republican party adopted new rules that aimed at providing "timely" selection and wider representation of rank and file.

17. The absence of a contest in the Republican party doubtless enhanced the identification of the party organization and the convention.

18. The mandate is contained in the "Minority Report of the Rules Committee," adopted by the convention on August 27, 1968, and reprinted in *Mandate for Reform.,* Report of the Commission on Party Structure and Delegate Selection (Washington, D.C.: Democratic National Committee, 1970), p. 53.

19. Richard Stearns, for one, had no illusions about the proper aim of reform. "As this thesis demonstrates, proponents of reform fail, again and again, to grasp the essential weakness of 'pure' democracy—the apathy of most citizens, whose interest and involvement in politics extends little beyond the formal act of voting. Consequently, the real task of reform has been misunderstood—it is not to dismantle leadership, but to make it fluid and competitive—not to eliminate elites, but to make their displacement easier." "Presidential Nominating Process," p. vii.

20. Austin Ranney, *Curing the Mischiefs of Faction: Party Reform in America* (Berkeley: University of California Press, 1975).

21. See the discussion of the "conspiracy theory" in Sir Karl R. Popper's *The Open Society and Its Enemies* (New York: Harper and Row, 1963), vol. 2, pp. 94-96; also his *Conjectures and Refutations: The Growth of Scientific Knowledge* (New York: Harper and Row, 1963).

22. The guidelines are published as *Mandate for Reform*, Report of the Commission on Party Structure and Delegate Selection to the Democratic National Committee.

23. Ranney, *Curing the Mischiefs*, p. 153.
24. Fredrick G. Dutton, *Changing Sources of Power: American Politics in the 1970s* (New York: McGraw-Hill, 1971).
25. Ibid.
26. John G. Stewart, *One Last Chance: The Democratic Party 1974–76* (New York: Frederick A. Praeger, 1974), p. 56.
27. *Mandate for Reform* (Guideline C-4); see also the discussion on p. 12, which expressed in clearest form the majority view that a convention should be a meeting of persons interested in the presidential nomination contest.
28. *Mandate for Reform* (Guideline C-4), p. 47. Richard Stearns noted that the commission "gave the most liberal reading possible to the Convention's resolution," "Presidential Nominating Process," pp. 113-114. That 1968 enabling resolution stated only that "The Convention shall require . . . that all feasible efforts have been made to assure that delegates are selected through . . . procedures open to public participation within the calendar year of the National Convention." *Minority Report of the Rules Committee, 1968 Democratic National Convention*, August 27, 1968, p. 247.
29. Quoted in *Congressional Quarterly*, April 29, 1972, p. 946. Note that the 1968 Republican Convention had directed its national committee to propose methods for eliminating discrimination in party affairs (Rule 32) and that most of the recommendations of the Committee on Delegates and Organization (known as the DO committee) appointed in pursuance of this directive were adopted by the 1972 convention and will be binding on the 1976 convention.
30. Polsby and Wildavsky, *Presidential Elections*, p. 119.
31. John S. Saloma, III, and Frederick H. Sontag, *Parties: The Real Opportunity for Effective Citizen Politics* (New York: Alfred A. Knopf, 1972), p. 56.
32. R. W. Apple, New York *Times*, February 10, 1972, p. 24.
33. James I. Lengle and Byron Shafer, "Primary Rules, Political Power, and Social Change," unpublished manuscript which I wish to thank Byron Shafer for having made available to me.
34. *Congressional Quarterly*, April 29, 1972, p. 942.
35. Primaries also differed in the role they assigned to party organizations. Statutes in California, Oregon, South Dakota, and Nebraska ignore the party altogether. Wisconsin, New Mexico, New Hampshire, and Delaware parties have limited apportionment or appointment powers. In some states—Illinois, Maryland, New York, and Pennsylvania—state party committees could directly appoint delegates; in two others (Rhode Island and New Jersey) they could endorse candidates on the ballot; in two others (Massachusetts and Indiana) they nominated a majority of the delegates; in eight primary states committees have full powers of apportionment. Stearns, "Presidential Nominating Process," pp. 108-109.
36. There is no agreement on the number of each of these present at the Democratic Convention. Neither, however, is there much disagreement. The Democratic National Committee puts the figures at 39.9 percent women, 21.4 percent youth (under 30); and 15.2 percent blacks. Reported in *Congressional Quarterly*, July 8, 1972, p. 1642.
37. Note that Richard Stearns had said that "the real task of reform . . . is not to eliminate elites, but to make their displacement easier." Stearns, "Presidential Nominating Process," p. vii. A critical analysis of the reform guidelines was prepared by a task force of the Coalition for a Democratic Majority, *Toward Fairness and Unity for '76*, co-chairmen Congressman Richard G. O'Hara and Richard Schifter.
38. Theodore White asserts that ". . . the mechanisms of the quotas . . . had little effect on the primary campaigns and the triumph of George McGovern at the Democratic conven-

tion. . . ." *Making of the President 1972*, p. 33. It was the nonprimary states where these and other provisions of the reformed rules had their greatest impact.

39. *Congressional Quarterly*, July 8, 1972, p. 1635.

40. Lengle and Shafer, "Primary Rules," p. 2. Their extremely interesting paper demonstrates the consequences in members of delegates of various rule changes. A good description of the use of reform to gain partisan advantage is Richard Stearns' of how the MaCarthy forces conceived, organized, financed, and orchestrated the (Howard) Hughes "Commission on the Democratic Selection of Presidential Nominees." "Presidential Nominating Process," pp. 25-29.

41. Alexander M. Bickel, "Watergate and the Legal Order," *Commentary*, January 1974, p. 20.

42. For example, a Gallup poll in the first week of February reported that Muskie was the first choice of 29 percent of Democratic voters; Kennedy and Humphrey followed with 24 percent and 23 percent respectively; George McGovern was the first choice of 5 percent. A January Gallup poll had reported Muskie running neck and neck in a three-man race with Nixon and Wallace.

43. William Cavala, "Changing the Rules Changes the Game: Party Reform and the 1972 California Delegation to the Democratic National Convention," *American Political Science Review* 68 (1974): p. 34. Cavala is describing McGovern's situation in California, but it applies equally well elsewhere.

44. Jeane J. Kirkpatrick, "The Revolt of the Masses," *Commentary* 2 (1973): 58–62.

45. This characterization of the McGovern volunteers is based on the agreement of most journalists who covered the politics of 1972.

46. Washington *Post*, April 9, 1972, p. A3.

47. Christopher Lydon, New York *Times*, May 9, 1972, p. 24.

48. Stewart, *One Last Chance*, p. 57.

49. O'Brien's ruling remains controversial. In fact, however, an absolute majority voted for the McGovern position to overturn the Credentials Committee ruling on seating the California delegation.

50. A poll of county chairmen conducted in early May revealed that these party officials preferred Humphrey to McGovern by a margin of more than two to one; among the "pros who had favored Muskie the preference for Humphrey over McGovern was three to one; and officials supporting Jackson preferred Humphrey to McGovern by a ratio of more than ten to one." The Gallup Poll, reported in the Washington *Post*, May 8, 1972, p. A2

51. Cavala, "Changing the Rules," p. 36.

52. Lydon, New York *Times*, p. 24.

53. *Congressional Quarterly*, July 8, 1972, p. 1641.

CHAPTER 3

Some Social and Personal Characteristics

The ruling class is the class from which rulers are recruited and in whose interest they exercise power. . . .[1]

"Not all elements of this conclusion are capable of proof with the evidence currently available, but of the broad outlines of the change there is no doubt. The delegates of recent years were better educated, less boss-ridden, better adjusted to the requirements of an open political system, and generally more trustworthy in all respects than those of half a century earlier."[2]

Thus the Brookings Institution authors described the convention delegates of 1952–56 in their massive study of the Republican and Democratic conventions of that time. The comment not only serves to remind us that there has been, at least since the 1950s, a persistent concern with the "quality" of delegates, but that some of the criteria for judging quality have been remarkably stable: the desire to eliminate the influence of "bosses," the desire to have an "open" system, the desire for well-educated, "trustworthy" decision makers.

The Brookings description also illustrates how in the recent past as well as the present persons writing about politics have postulated links between socioeconomic traits and political attitudes. The "better education" of delegates, it is implied, is related to the fact that they are more trustworthy, more independent, more attuned to "open politics." Karl Marx's political philosophy provides the modern prototype of an explanation of political behavior by way of class position. But Marx's argument stood in a long tradition. The notion that social and economic characteristics "determined" political behavior was already familiar in fifth century B.C. Athens. Plato postulated causal links between class, predispositions, and regime; Aristotle explained why a commonwealth of independent

61

farmers was more hospitable than an urban society to democratic political institutions, a view echoed by Thomas Jefferson more than two thousand years later, but only after Montesquieu, Adam Smith, and others had argued or assumed that social function was closely related to political type.

Recently, various critics have suggested that the changing social characteristics of the American political elite have been accompanied by important changes in the political system. Kevin Phillips has argued that "an increasingly large, affluent slice of America earns its bread from handling and applying knowledge, and that this new segment of the economy is already a powerful vested interest for social change and liberal politics."[3] Lionel Trilling, Daniel Bell, Seymour M. Lipset, Herman Kahn, and others have postulated some version of a new class based in the knowledge and communications industries whose distinctive social base is accompanied by unique political values and styles.[4] Since the characteristics attributed to this new class often resemble those attributed to our hypothetical new breed, these hypotheses have special interest for this study. The social and economic characteristics of elites are, in any case, necessarily a concern of this study: first, because the socioeconomic characteristics of the elite provide an important part of the answer to questions about who has influence in the society and what resources are most useful in gaining access to influence; and second, because social location may affect individuals' perspectives and characteristic strategies. Childhood poverty or opulence is generally believed to have permanent effects; ethnic and religious groups constitute distinctive subcultures from which expectations and goals are imbibed and habits acquired. For these reasons elite studies generally include information on social and economic characteristics. In fact, a large part of what we know about political leaders concerns gross physical, social, and economic traits that are judged relevant to political roles. Such information on the leadership corps of a society is especially illuminating when collected over a long enough time period to permit the detection of changes in the social composition of political elites.

In this chapter those questions relevant to social and economic characteristics of the delegates to the two conventions are examined. What social characteristics were most useful in gaining access to decisional processes of the national parties in 1972? How homogeneous or divisive were the members of the presidential elite? Were the two conventions of 1972 dominated by the new class? Answering these questions requires first reviewing the social characteristics of the delegates to the two conventions.

INCOME, OCCUPATION, STATUS

In their seminal study, Paul David, Ralph Goldman, and Richard Bain commented concerning delegates to the 1948 conventions: "The most noteworthy features . . . are the concentrations of lawyers and businessmen, the large number in other middle class occupations, and the generally close similarity of the occupational distributions in the two parties. . . ."[5] By 1972 the similarity in occupational backgrounds of the elites of the two parties was still striking; lawyers were still numerous, but the proportion of businessmen had declined in both parties.

These data confirm what journalists reported at the time: namely, that the reforms and upheavals of 1972 did not fundamentally alter the relationship between socioeconomic status and political participation. As compared to most other people, delegates went to school longer, made more money, and had better jobs. They were, in brief, an overwhelmingly middle-class group, and they knew it. Both conventions were filled with highly educated persons engaged in occupations for which they were prepared by higher education. Virtually all the delegates easily qualified for membership in what David Apter termed the "national elite."[6] Apter termed this skill-based professional elite "the establishment" and noted that their growing domination of American society has occurred alongside the progressive decline of business.[7]

It is no surprise that delegates should have been a middle to upper middle-class group. Successive studies of political elites have confirmed that relatively high income, high educational achievement, and high status occupations are characteristic of political influentials at all levels of the political process: in local communities, at the state level, and in Congress.[8] Comparative research has established that these socioeconomic advantages are shared by political elites in the systems as diverse as those found in China, Cuba, the U.S.S.R., the Middle East, the U.A.R., France, Britain, and Argentina.[9]

Delegates' income reflects this middle-class status. Although a majority of American families had incomes of under $10,000 per year in 1972, fewer than one-tenth of the delegates had such low incomes, and students comprised a large portion of that few. Republicans were somewhat more well off financially than Democrats: 23 percent of Republicans made over $50,000 a year. Table 3–1 shows that, like political activists generally, most convention delegates were neither rich nor poor but solidly middle to upper middle class. Their incomes were consistent with their occupations: they were the incomes of professionals, technical experts, and managers.

Table 3-1. Delegate Income by Party and Candidate Preference (%)

	Democrats	Republicans	McGovern	Humphrey	Wallace	Muskie	Nixon
Less than $10,000	13	6	16	14	15	3	5
$10,000–20,000	35	18	37	32	33	37	17
$20,000–30,000	26	31	26	31	28	23	32
$30,000–50,000	14	23	12	13	9	23	23
Over $50,000	12	23	9	10	15	14	23
Weighted N =	2579	1062	1317	420	123	286	1038

Income question: "Please look at this card and tell me the letter of the income group that includes the income of all members of your family in 1971 before taxes. This figure should include dividends, interest, salaries, wages, pensions and other income."

Relationships: Income by party, V = 0.25.

NOTE: These data are from the interviews.

A SKILL-BASED ELITE

Domination of the presidential elite by a skill-based middle class was even more complete in 1972 than in 1948–1952. (See Table 3–2.) Among delegates who were employed, approximately 35 percent of Democratic delegates and 32 percent of Republicans were professionals; another 22 percent of Democratic and 26 percent of Republican delegates had managerial positions; only 7 percent of Democrats and 13 percent of Republicans were self-employed. Lawyers were the most numerous category of professionals if we consider the presidential elite as a whole. But representatives of other professional callings—notably teaching—were also present in large numbers. In the McGovern ranks, teachers outnumbered lawyers. The occupations of Republican delegates were very similar to those of the 1948–1952 delegates (except for the presence of more housewives), but two striking changes had occurred in the composition of the majority party's elite in the two decades since the Brookings study: the number of businessmen had declined to less than one-half of their previous proportion of delegates, and the proportion of teachers present had risen dramatically. Because many of the current diagnoses and prognoses concerning American politics focus on the "knowledge elite," a more detailed analysis was undertaken to determine the various types of professions present in the elite. Such an inquiry is desirable in any case, because the various professions attract persons of differing predispositions, and the initial differences are further enhanced by the education and training specific to each profession. Education for some of the professions—notably law and the humanities—emphasizes the development of persuasive skills and critical abilities. Some 10 percent of all delegates were clergy and teachers, and approximately 12 percent were lawyers. These were not evenly distributed between the parties or among candidate preference groups. Lawyers comprised 16 percent of Republicans and only 11 percent of Democrats; clergy and teachers comprised 15 percent of Democrats and 4 percent of Republicans. Among McGovern supporters, teachers and clergy outnumbered lawyers by three to one. In all other candidate preference groups lawyers were more numerous than teachers and clergy, and among Nixon supporters, they outnumbered teachers and clergy by more than four to one. The role of the professional class in presidential politics was enlarged further by the number of university students (4 percent of all delegates), most of whom were doubtless headed for the professions, and by the number of women who, though themselves housewives, were married to professionals. (See Table 3–2.)

Lawyers, teachers, and clergy were not the only delegates with higher education. Approximately 60 percent of delegates in both parties had finished college and 38 percent of Democratic males and 43 percent of

Table 3-2. Delegate Occupation and Spouse's Occupation by Party (%)

	Own Occupation			Spouse's Occupation		
	All	Democrats	Republicans	All	Democrats	Republicans
Professional–Technical	34	35	32	29	32	22
Managers–Salaried	23	22	26	7	8	5
Manager–Self-employed	9	7	13	5	5	6
Clerical Workers	7	8	5	7	8	4
Sales Workers	3	3	4	2	2	4
Craftsmen	1	2	0	2	2	3
Operatives	1	2	0	2	2	0
Service Workers	1	1	0	2	2	0
Farmers and Farm Managers	1	1	1	2	0	2
Laborers	0	0	0	0	0	0
Housewives	14	13	17	41	36	53
Students	4	5	1	1	1	0
Unemployed	2	2	1	0	0	0
Weighted N =	3731	2623	1108	2887	1995	892

Questions: "What is your main occupation? What sort of work do you do?" "What is your spouse's main occupation? What sort of work does he/she do?"

NOTE: These data are from the interviews.

Republican males held some postgraduate degree. The rise of the educated classes to political power is dramatized by contrast with 1948, when only 12 percent of Democratic and 9 percent of Republican delegates held graduate or professional degrees. (See Table 3.3.)

BASE VALUES

If we ask "What skills and resources were most useful in gaining admission to the presidential elite in 1972?", the answer appears to be higher education, especially higher education in management or in the persuasive skills. At least two prior resources are required to achieve such expertise: a relatively high level of intelligence and an achievement orientation strong enough to cause persons to submit themselves to the disciplines of higher education and to make the necessary effort. But beyond these personality attributes are some more tangible skills.

Education provides professional qualifications that are then used to accumulate economic advantages. But that is not all. Education of certain kinds also provides verbal skills, an ability to manipulate abstract concepts and to make and state a case. Rational argument is the stock in trade of lawyers, teachers, college students, ministers, and related professionals. And in an age when marketing, advertising, and interpersonal relations have assumed large importance, verbal skills are important to managers. Specialists in persuasion have a distinctive advantage in arenas where decisions are made on the basis of developing and stating cases. Furthermore, persons trained in the liberal arts, the social sciences, law, and the ministry develop a special skill in dealing with normative categories.

Since influence is a property of interpersonal relations, verbal persuasiveness (and other interpersonal skills) has always been useful to rulers and indispensable to their advisors. But it is not equally useful to heads of government in all types of regimes. The right heredity is the crucial attribute in monarchies and some types of aristocracy. The ability to control the instruments of violence is the chief power base in some other types of regime, notably military dictatorships. Managerial skills have also proved crucial to the consolidation of power, as in Stalin's case. Wealth is a base value of famous potential in politics, particularly in regimes of the feudal type in which economic and political power are united. But in a democracy with loosely organized political parties, the ability to speak persuasively is important to winning leadership roles in either parties or governments.

In considering verbal skills as a base value, differences among types of verbal skills and training should be noted. These distinctions become

Table 3-3. Delegate Education by Party and Candidate Preference (%)

	Democrats	Republicans	McGovern	Humphrey	Wallace	Muskie	Nixon
Less than high school	4	2	2	8	17	3	2
High school graduate	13	11	8	25	23	11	11
Some college	27	28	26	27	27	27	29
College graduate	27	27	32	21	20	26	27
M.A.	12	8	17	7	0	8	8
Ph.D. or equivalent	4	3	6	1	0	3	3
Ll.B.	12	18	9	10	12	20	18
M.D.	1	3	1	1	1	2	3
Weighted N =	2641	1104	1334	435	148	288	1080

Education question: "What was the highest grade of school or year of college you completed?"

Relationships: Education by party, V = 0.12.

NOTE: These data are from the interviews.

more interesting because of the distribution of different types of symbol specialists in candidate support groups. (See Table 3–4.) Teachers, lawyers, ministers, and politicians are all skilled in articulating conceptions of the public good. All are trained in "culture-oriented studies which are typically concerned with the symbolic environment of a society—both with the prevailing system of values and goals that constitute the 'myth' and, particularly in times of troubles, with the literature of protest that accompanies the formation of contending values and goals into rival ideology."[10] But in recent decades liberal arts education has emphasized the communication of liberal and critical perspectives, and there is a growing body of data indicating that in our times higher education in the humanities and social sciences strongly predisposes the recipients toward liberal perspectives. As we shall see in a later chapter on delegates' ideological perspectives, the amount and kind of a delegate's education is related to his views on issues and ideologies. Persons with graduate degrees in the arts and social sciences tend to be more liberal on a variety of issues than persons with less education or than lawyers or physicians, and teachers in these fields are especially liberal.[11]

Moral criticism, which was a cardinal feature of the McGovern movement, involves some specialized skills including the ability to judge existing arrangements and institutions against some standard that is not given in the situation and to articulate criticisms. In our times, universities are the institutions that specialize in articulating the moral critiques of the society that play an ever more important role in our politics. Once comprehensive moral criticism becomes a feature of the politics of a period, one can expect to find increasing numbers of intellectuals in political roles, and vice versa. Once intellectuals become numerous in a political process, one can expect more attention to moral dimensions. Edward Shils noted that ". . . in modern times, first in the West and then, in the nineteenth and twentieth centuries, at the peripheries of Western civilization and the Orient, the major political vocation of the intellectuals has lain in the enunciation and pursuit of the ideal."[12] Once the vision of the ideal enters politics, both critics and defenders of social institutions must be articulate, persuasive, and skilled in moral and social criticism.

The relatively small numbers of self-employed businessmen, farmers, and workers at the two conventions are the other side of the coin of their domination by professionals. Self-employed businessmen constituted only 5 percent of McGovern delegates, and, as already indicated, fewer than 1 percent of McGovern delegates were craftsmen or industrial workers of any kind. Among Humphrey and Muskie delegates businessmen comprised approximately 12 percent of the total candidate support group.[13] Craftsmen and industrial workers were absent from the Muskie

Table 3-4. Occupational Type by Party and Candidate Preference (%)

	Democrats	Republicans	McGovern	Humphrey	Wallace	Muskie
Symbol specialists	15	6	21	9	2	9
Lawyers	11	16	7	10	10	19
Material specialists	13	14	10	16	27	15
Housewives	13	17	16	7	10	14
Students	5	1	7	2	1	3
Clerical and sales workers	11	9	12	9	20	9
Public employees	8	13	5	10	8	6
Salaried managers	6	10	5	6	9	6
Health personnel	2	3	1	1	6	4
Other professionals	8	7	9	9	5	6
Others	10	4	8	22	2	8
Weighted *N* =	2653	1110	1343	435	154	286

NOTE: These data are from the interviews. See Appendix C for a full description of the occupations included in each category.

candidate support group and constituted only about 6 percent of Humphrey delegates. Businessmen were somewhat more numerous among Nixon supporters (14 percent), and workers were absent. Only among Wallace delegates did persons self-employed in business or industry constitute as much as one-fourth of the group. Once again, however, industrial workers, craftsmen, and farmers were virtually absent.

It may be that the small numbers of businessmen, farmers, and workers present at the two conventions did not imply that either were unrepresented or that their interests were not taken account of. Lawyers are trained to represent the interests of others, and lawyers in the various delegations may have spoken for the interests and points of view of different economic constituencies. In any case, we are concerned here not with representation but with what the composition of the conventions can tell us about the skills and resources most useful in gaining access to political arenas. We do not know how many owners of retail stores, real estate and insurance agencies, contractors, and manufacturers sought to become delegates. Neither do we know how many carpenters, plumbers, and steel and automobile workers ran for delegates' positions. The relative absence of these occupations may reflect only the relative lack of interest in volunteer politics of persons in these positions. But we can at least conclude that the composition of the two conventions indicates either that businessmen, workers, and farmers (like physicists, chemists, and engineers) had little desire to participate in the political arena or that their skills were not those required to gain access to political influence in the presidential parties. Whatever the reason for the relatively small direct participation of these two occupational categories in presidential politics in 1972, it is important to note that both these two groups—independent businessmen and workers—are famous (or in some circles, infamous) for their concern with material rewards and incentives. Self-employed businessmen seek profits; workers are aggressively concerned with wages, hours, and working conditions. Both groups are frankly self-interested. Professionals, by contrast, are more likely to see themselves as participating in politics for reasons unrelated to material rewards. The business and trade union ethos alike stresses economic self-interest as a legitimate incentive. The professional ethos stresses service. This does not mean that the professional is necessarily more altruistic than the businessman or worker; it does mean that a politics dominated by professionals will differ in style and probably also in substance from a political process in which businessmen and workers are more numerous.

Politics conducted by professionals will probably feature more emphasis on the symbolic aspects of politics and less on the output of goods and services. In processes in which enlightenment and rectitude are dominant concerns, the importance of material factors is likely to be downgraded. James Q. Wilson has emphasized the declining prestige and importance of material incentives in American politics and the concomitant rising importance of "purposive" incentives. He notes further that: "If purposive organizations become important . . . then leaders capable of producing concerted action on the basis of ideas become more influential."[14] Politics dominated by professionals is likely to have a higher ideological content and the political process is more likely to be conceived as an arena for setting public agendas and resolving moral problems than as an arena for winning and compromising material interests. Conversely, politics with a high issue content is doubtless more attractive to professionals than to persons principally concerned with "broker" functions. In any case, the small number of industrial entrepreneurs and workers, merchants and clerks, carpenters and homebuilders in both conventions both documents and illustrates the decline of business and business values in politics.[15]

MOBILITY

In considering the socioeconomic status of the presidential elite, it is important to note that these upper income, upper education, middle and upper middle-class delegates were not necessarily born into their current class status. That upward social mobility is a characteristic of American (and other) political activists and politicians has been frequently noted in previous studies.[16] It also characterized the delegates of the two conventions. The extent of professional and educational mobility of both Republican and Democratic delegates is striking.

Occupational changes from fathers to delegates indicate rapidly rising social status. At least twice as many McGovern, Humphrey, and Nixon delegates were professionals as were their fathers, and the contrast is sharper still among Wallace supporters. While the percentage of professionals was lower among Wallace delegates than the supporters of any other candidates, their upward mobility was the most dramatic: roughly 31 percent of them were professionals as compared to only 5 percent of their fathers. Conversely, while approximately one-fourth of all Democratic and one-seventh of Republican delegates had fathers with working-class occupations, among the delegates themselves these occupations were almost entirely absent.

The upward mobility of the delegates is also indicated in the contrast between the education of delegates and their fathers. The difference is even greater than that between their occupations. Two-thirds of McGovern delegates had at least a college education as compared to one-third of their fathers; 57 percent of McGovern delegates' fathers had not gone beyond high school as compared to only 7 percent of McGovern delegates. The contrasts are similar among Republicans. Sixty percent of Nixon delegates had finished college as compared to 26 percent of their fathers; 58 percent of Nixon delegates' fathers had a high school education or less as compared to 13 percent of the delegates. Among Humphrey supporters the intergenerational contrast is still greater, and while educational levels of delegates and fathers alike are lowest among Wallace supporters, the contrast between generations holds.

Especially notable is the disappearance from one generation to the next of the "uneducated" class, that is, of delegates with no more than eight years of schooling. While very few delegates had less than a high school education, over 40 percent of Humphrey, Muskie, and Wallace delegates had fathers who had not gone beyond the eighth grade.

The extent and scope of intergenerational upward mobility is also reflected in the dramatic changes in education between women delegates and their mothers. The educations of women delegates' mothers and fathers are very similar—more similar in fact than that of male and female delegates themselves. Many of the women had mothers as well as fathers who had not gone past eighth grade, and many more who had ended their educations with high school. The daughters, like the sons, proved ready to take advantage of improved opportunities for education. Virtually all of them finished high school and well over one-half finished college as well. Education is the first arena available to a child for demonstrating an achievement drive; it is also a tool for winning other values later in life. The dramatic educational advance from one generation of females to the next not only demonstrates the increased availability of education to both sexes, it also is evidence that in this important respect political women are similar to political men.

Providing that one counts leaving the status of housewife for a remunerative employment as progress, then women delegates also showed upward occupational mobility. In fact, the occupation of housewife is a classless status that does not exist on the occupational status ladder. It is a classification broad enough to include the wives of both the rich and poor, although one might have three servants and grown children and the other be the overburdened mother of nine in a small apartment. Employment outside the home increased greatly from mother to daughter. While over one-half of the mothers of all delegates were housewives, fewer than one-half the women delegates so classified themselves. The distribution of housewives varied by support group, ranging from 26 percent of the McGovern delegates to 50 percent of the Wallace women. Also indicative of upward mobility was the greatly increased number of women who had become professionals: approximately three times as many of the women delegates had achieved this status as did their mothers.

In part, these intergenerational contrasts reflect the national trend toward higher levels of education. But the gap between generations is much greater than the national average. And it is this that proves that delegates constitute an unusually mobile group and one whose rise has been closely associated with the acquisition of specialized skills through formal education. Political influence was only one of the values that they had maximized.

The social mobility of the delegates has implications for the political system and for the status and perspectives of participants. It demonstrates that the national presidential elite does not comprise a hereditary ruling class in which membership is passed from generation to generation. The presence of persons with diverse class backgrounds reflects a continuing circulation of elites and testifies to the absence of a static, socially homogeneous ruling class. The point deserves some emphasis because of the continuing popularity of the notion that there exists a basically hereditary, closed ruling class that dominates political, economic, and social institutions in the United States.[17]

Second, as David Apter and others have argued, the *durability* of class status may have a powerful effect on how the individual views his relations to society.[18] For those who move up or down the social ladder, perspectives acquired in childhood influence those of the adult. The stings of relative deprivation are frequently enduring, and those who have felt them may harbor permanent resentments against those more favored by heredity or fortune. The individual who uses education as a lever to raise himself submits to further deprivation and discipline in the form of long years of study. Not infrequently those deprivations become the subjective basis of a claim on society: for deference, status, power, wealth. While there is a rather large lore concerning the habits and outlook of the nouveau riche, there has been little scrutiny of the opinions, values, and behavior of the newly educated classes or the first generation professional. The fact that income and status are dependent on skills gives them a contingency and impermanence as compared to income and status based on the ownership of property. A land-based ascriptive upper class and a mobile skill-based upper class resemble one another in that members have at their disposal more money, more prestige, and more control of their time than most other people. But the "vested" interests of the upward (and potentially downward) mobile professional do not necessarily coincide with the interests of persons whose upper economic status derives from the ownership of capital assets. A principal "vested interest" of the professional class, for example, is having intellectual (and closely allied moral) values serve as a basis for participation in power processes and in *not* having power awarded on the basis of such other values as wealth, heredity, physical strength or beauty, or organizational skill.

Research findings on the impact of mobility on political perspectives are mixed, probably because the consequences of mobility vary in different contexts. V. O. Key points out that "white collar men who have been upward mobile (in comparison with their fathers) tend toward the Republican party, while blue collar upward mobile men tend toward the Democratic party."[19] Exhaustive analysis of the relations between social mobility on the one hand, and perspectives on the other, revealed no significant association between the two, but the presence of so many upwardly mobile persons among those active in presidential politics remains significant, whether or not it has observable effects on political attitudes.

In sum, it is clear that the delegates to the two conventions enjoyed a middle to upper middle-class status, including relatively high incomes, high education, and high status occupations, and that many had the kinds of jobs that provide the free time and/or flexibility conducive to political activity. Many were also the kinds of jobs that require verbal skills for success and provide their practitioners with continuous practice in the persuasive arts. Self-employed businessmen were scarce as compared to two decades earlier, and the proportion of farmers had also declined. Workers and their representatives continued to be scarce in the Democratic Convention and virtually absent from the Republican. Managers who are also the product of prolonged, specialized education and whose position rests on these skills were also numerous, but rather less so than suggested by standard accounts of the role of managers in a post-business civilization.[20] Finally, the occupational and professional characteristics of delegates indicate that recruitment practices by which delegates to the two conventions were chosen were especially suited to the skills and resources of the professional and managerial classes. Perhaps all of politics as it is practiced today (in America and elsewhere) has characteristics that invite domination by middle and upper income skill groups. These are possibilities whose probabilities and implications will be considered later in this study.

SOME SIMILARITIES IN THE PERSONAL AND SOCIAL STYLES OF DELEGATES

On the assumption that major changes in the characteristics of activists in presidential politics might be reflected in delegates' personalities and styles of citizenship, questions were included that probed delegate self-conceptions and patterns of participation. In the attempt to maximize the strengths of the data to limit its negative consequences, we focused on traits rather than whole personalities.[21] Various questions were posed that were designed to investigate the presence or absence of some characteristics that previous research had identified as having special relevance for politics: among these were self-esteem, efficacy, ego strength, ability to compete, and related traits. Confidence in the findings is enhanced by the high consistency of the responses. Some characteristics of delegates are revealed not by responses to specific questions but by responses to all questions on personal motives and characteristics. For example, delegates of both parties and all ideological persuasions seemed to have clearly formulated self-conceptions that they were not reluctant to share with interviewers. Very few questions on personality elicited refusals or "don't know" responses from anyone.

It is significant, too, that delegates were not inhibited in expressing good opinions of themselves. The fact that they were willing to ascribe many laudatory traits to themselves in itself indicates the kind of high self-esteem and self-confidence that equips political actors to "blow their own horns" in the effort to achieve desired political goals.

High self-esteem, which is a significant characteristic of these delegates, has been repeatedly found to correlate positively with both social and political participation.[22] Its principal components are a good opinion of the self, low anxiety and internal conflict, and a sense of integrated autonomy, of personal competence, and of self-control. The internal conviction that one is worthy and deserving of respect is generally associated with basic self-acceptance and reasonably stable psychological integration and with both social and political participation. People with reasonably high self-esteem are more comfortable than others in interpersonal relations oriented to impersonal goals in which the participants do not receive constant assurances that they are appreciated, admired, loved, and respected. They are better able to take risks. Participation in public processes entails a level of psychological risk (of failing, of being rebuffed or ignored) that can be borne comfortably only by those with quite good opinions of themselves.

These activities—risking, involving oneself without fear of being overwhelmed, asserting oneself, achieving goals, functioning in relatively impersonal contests—also require a strong ego or a functional facsimile. Stable integration renders the self unthreatening and permits assertion without fear of aggression and violence, compromise without abandonment, and commitment without the threat of destruction. The person with a strong ego can mobilize his resources in the service of conscious purposes and can adapt his purposes to reality. He is therefore able to engage in competition, to set goals and achieve them, and to risk and lose without jeopardizing the self.

Effective political participation in democratic contexts does not necessitate virtue or outstanding personal strength, but it does seem to require not being very insecure about one's basic worth or skills, not having a strong need for a continuous flow of affection in all interactions, and not fearing conflict and competition. Large majorities of convention delegates attributed just such capacities and skills to themselves and, in so doing, demonstrated how comfortable they were with a good opinion of themselves. Over 80 percent of all candidate groups described themselves as confident, rational, sympathetic, decisive, and independent.

They did not see themselves as shrinking violets; large majorities said that they are ambitious and competitive and have no trouble asserting their views in arguments, competing with others, or losing. The ability to "lose," to contemplate rejection by fellow party members and/or voters, is a psychological requirement for running for any public office or party office that is also sought by someone else. Most public offices and many party offices fall in this category. One might, therefore, expect that persons who had sought and held such offices would have less fear of losing than those who had not. Such is not the case. In this elite group of participants, fear of losing was no more common among those who had not held public office as those who had.

There is no recognizably desirable trait that a majority of delegates in all candidate groups did not attribute to themselves. In addition to describing themselves as rational, confident, decisive and independent, more than 50 percent of the supporters of all candidates also claimed to be flexible, straightforward, and tranquil.

This good opinion of themselves did not, however, lead delegates to claim that they have transcended all human problems. Over one-half said that they have trouble dividing their time among their various activities, nearly one-half said they find loss of privacy a problem, and about an equal number confessed that they do not find it easy to take criticism. But the major personal problems admitted by delegates are difficulties that in fact constitute virtues. About three-quarters said that they find it difficult to compromise their convictions and to work with incompetent people, but presumably all moral people find it difficult to compromise their convictions, just as intelligent, efficient people find it exasperating to work with incompetents.

Another set of questions aimed at probing personalities inquired of delegates about the traits that, in their opinion, suited them for politics. The tendency to attribute good qualities to the self again asserts itself.

Both successes and failures seemed to the delegates to be due to their abundance of virtues. The qualities judged most useful to political success are social: "liking" people and being good at communicating with others. The personal traits judged liabilities in politics are also virtues: being too honest and the closely related lack of tact and diplomacy.

Delegates conceived themselves as high-minded, effective people who have special skills in interpersonal relations.[23]

Like McClosky's study of delegates in the 1950s, this one finds no psychological correlates of party identification.[24] Analysis of composite measures developed on the basis of factor analyses to tap competitiveness, orderliness, subjectivity, defensiveness, and self-confidence reveals no significant difference between the parties. (See Table 3–5.)

This analysis of gross personal orientation indicates that there are no hard and fast psychological requirements for participation in American politics. People with quite different traits can and do become active and achieve influence. But if a range of personality traits is compatible with participation, not all traits would appear to be equally so. *The modal effective volunteer personality in presidential politics is ambitious and competitive and knows it, is open rather than defensive, leads a busy, structured life and likes it that way, feels he knows himself but not too well, and is not greatly concerned about his subjective life. The modal political participant thinks well of himself, believes himself effective, realistic, and capable of influencing events.*

Unfortunately, comparable data are not available for the general population; in consequence we cannot know with certainty whether these traits are possessed by most people or are distinguishing characteristics of participants generally, or of effective participants more specifically. It is not, in any case, general relationships but the distribution of these traits among parties, generations, and candidate support groups that is most relevant to this inquiry. But the data indicate that there were no significant differences in the global psychological characteristics of the different portions of the elite. The same general personality traits characterized McGovern, Nixon, Wallace, Humphrey, and Muskie delegates. Though some popular stereotypes associate Wallace supporters with extreme right authoritarianism and the McGovern movement with radical confrontation politics, these groups attracted much the same kinds of activists as found elsewhere in American politics, probably because although some persons in both movements engaged in direct action in support of their policy views—especially concerning race and war—both McGovern and Wallace campaigned for the presidency in conventional ways: through primaries, caucuses, and direct mail campaigns. Both operated within the system in which both had successful careers. The rhetoric of recent politics has invited exaggeration and misconception concerning the political

Table 3-5. Personality Traits by Party and Candidate Preference (%)

	Democrats	Republicans	McGovern	Humphrey	Wallace	Muskie	Nixon
Competitiveness–Aggression							
Low	5	4	8	1	0	2	4
	32	32	37	29	32	24	32
High	63	64	55	70	69	74	64
Weighted N =	2599	1082	1329	423	146	281	1058
Subjectivity							
Low	9	17	5	15	13	12	17
	72	68	69	73	67	78	69
High	20	15	26	12	21	11	15
Weighted N =	2607	1080	1331	426	144	286	1056
Defensiveness							
Low	37	36	33	47	33	37	36
	56	55	58	48	63	52	56
High	8	9	9	5	4	11	9
Weighted N =	2628	1078	1332	432	149	290	1054
Rationality–Confidence–Decisiveness							
Low	5	3	5	4	8	2	3
High	96	97	95	96	92	98	97
Weighted N =	2596	1076	1323	426	146	278	1050

Relationships: Competitiveness–Aggression by party, V = 0.01.
Subjectivity by party, V = 0.13.
Defensiveness by party, V = 0.02.
Rationality–Confidence–Decisiveness by party, ϕ = 0.03.

NOTE: Data are from the interview sample. For method of index construction and the specific constituent variables that comprise these indexes, see Appendix C.

spectrum and the kinds of people found in it. Although the McGovern and Wallace campaigns each had a marginal relation to the extreme anti-system politics of the years just prior to 1972, neither campaign had anything in common with conspiratorial or authoritarian politics. There were no American Nazis or Weathermen at the national nominating conventions—at least not as delegates.

This finding that the personalities of delegates of both parties are generally similar does not imply absence of significant differences in their personal and political goals or their perceptions or styles. It indicates only that the basic personality structure of delegates was similar, and it suggests that any new type of political actor is not very different in basic character from the political types with which we are familiar.

In various other ways delegate characteristics were consistent with those attributed to political activists by previous research.[25] As compared to most adults, they were more likely to have lived for a long time in one place (see Table 3–6), more likely to have had parents who were active in politics (about one-third had at least one politically active parent),[26] and more likely to have a spouse and friends who were interested in politics. They were also more likely to be joiners active in one or more civic, religious, or social associations.[27] (See Table 3–7.)

There were some suggestive differences among candidate groups with regard to some demographic characteristics. McGovern delegates were more geographically mobile than supporters of other candidates (only 26 percent had lived in their communities for twenty years or more as compared to 60 percent of Humphrey delegates, 62 percent of Muskie delegates, and about 51 percent of Nixon and Wallace delegates), and they were also the most urban of the candidate support groups. (See Table 3–6.)

SOME ASCRIPTIVE CHARACTERISTICS

The literature on political development agrees that a defining characteristic of modern societies is that roles are distributed on the basis of personal achievement rather than on the basis of ascription. The belief that rewards should go to persons qualified by skill and achievement rather than by hereditary status has been a crucial—perhaps *the* crucial—moral claim of the middle classes who have invoked it to batter down special privileges based on noble blood, race, or religion.

In fact, physical characteristics have had a continuing relevance to the distribution of most values—and perhaps especially to power—throughout the modern period. Race is the most obvious example of an ascriptive trait which until the 1965 Voting Rights Act served as an effective obstacle to blacks' access to political power. But the increasing numbers of blacks elected as congressmen, mayors, and other public officers

Table 3-6. Years in Local Community, Size of Local Community by Party and Candidate Preference (%)

	Democrats	Republicans	McGovern	Humphrey	Wallace	Muskie	Nixon
Years in Local Community							
One year or less	3	1	5	1	0	1	1
2–5	16	7	22	8	15	5	7
6–10	16	12	18	10	9	13	11
10–20	26	29	29	22	25	19	29
Over 20	39	52	26	60	51	62	52
N =	1575	813	877	200	67	139	782
Size of Local Community							
Over 350,000	24	20	28	21	8	14	20
100,000–350,000	15	15	12	22	25	17	15
30,000–100,000	23	21	25	17	27	27	21
2,500–30,000	30	34	28	30	34	28	33
2,500 or less	9	10	7	10	6	15	11
Weighted N =	2669	1116	1346	441	154	290	1090

Question: "How many years have you lived in your present community?"

Relationships: Years in local community by party, $V = 0.17$.
Size of local community by party, $V = 0.06$.

NOTE: Data on number of years in local community are from the mail questionnaires. Size of community data are from the interviews. Size of local community was based on census size of delegate's present locality.

Table 3-7. Civic Participation by Party and Candidate Preference (%)
(Number and Type of Memberships in Voluntary Associations)

	Democrats	Republicans	McGovern	Humphrey	Wallace	Muskie	Nixon
Total Number of Memberships							
None	18	18	19	10	28	17	18
1–2	37	26	44	35	28	22	26
3–4	32	38	29	38	37	41	38
5 or more	12	18	9	18	7	19	19
N =	1601	848	890	202	68	140	814
Professional, Service, Social Club Memberships							
None	54	36	66	35	49	31	35
Some activity	39	52	32	54	43	52	52
A great deal of activity	7	13	2	11	9	16	13
N =	1601	848	890	202	68	140	814
Female–Civic Group Memberships (Feminist Groups, League of Women Voters, Civic Groups)							
None	56	69	49	63	72	63	69
Some activity	41	30	46	37	28	33	30
A great deal of activity	3	1	4	0	0	4	1
N =	1601	848	890	202	68	140	814
Church–School Group Memberships							
Neither	55	43	60	42	49	42	42
One	28	30	28	27	31	31	31
Both	18	27	12	31	21	27	27
N =	1601	848	890	202	68	140	814

Relationships: Number of memberships by party, V = 0.13.
Professional, etc. memberships by party, V = 0.18.
Female–civic memberships by party, V = 0.15.
Church–school memberships by party, V = 0.13.

NOTE: These data are from the mail questionnaire sample. For the method of index construction and the specific constituent variables comprising these indexes, see Appendix C.

testify to the declining importance of race as a barrier to political power. Sex has, if anything, been a greater obstacle to participation in power processes. Although women constitute something over 50 percent of the population, they are scarce in all of the society's decision-making structures. Despite a great deal of rhetoric about the women's revolution, there is still no woman in the Senate, no woman mayor of a major city, one woman governor, and only nineteen women in the House of Representatives. Obviously, sexual characteristics are related to the distribution of power.

Age is another biological characteristic whose association with power has been demonstrated by repeated elite studies that show that in the United States as in other societies major positions in power processes are filled largely by males of middle age or more. Age differs from other ascriptive qualities in some important respects: first, because it is not a permanent characteristic (everyone who lives long enough is every age) and second, because of its special relationship to biological and social maturation. No one seriously argues that ten-year-olds should vote, much less occupy roles in decisional structures. Views about the appropriate period of apprenticeship vary by field of endeavor, but in most political systems (except a monarchy) long periods of preparation precede access to power. Age is, therefore, an innate if not permanent biological attribute with undeniable relevance to power distribution.

Until recently, liberals and liberal doctrines emphasized providing equal access to power (as to other values). It was believed that abolition of legal discrimination and of discriminatory practices satisfied the requirement of equal access; from that point, ability, ambition, hard work, and luck were expected to serve as the basis of selection. But in the late 1960s notions about what was and was not "liberal" and "just" underwent some important changes. Not the least of these was the appearance of the belief that justice required more than equal access to values and that equal access required more than legal access. With the growing egalitarianism of modern American society, and especially of modern liberalism, came the conviction that a just distribution of values required special assistance for hitherto disadvantaged or underprivileged groups.

It would be necessary to write a cultural history of the period to account for the fact that attention was progressively focused on three of the many groups of "hitherto disadvantaged" persons: blacks, women, and youth. Suffice it to say here that blacks, whose predicament had been dramatized by the civil rights movement, were a blatant example of a group who because of race had been heavily restricted in its pursuit of values. The Vietnam war and the obligations of military service had focused attention on youth who during the war seemed to many to incur more responsibilities than rights from the political system. The rise of the women's movement dramatized the very low participation of women in power processes. The attention of the cultural elite had shifted, at least for a period, away from economic problems and groups to preoccupations with the political advantages of middle-aged white males.

Since the categories of blacks, women, and youth had in common the fact that each was based on a physical characteristic that presumably had an important influence on their social and political experience, 1972 saw new attention paid to these ascriptive properties, particularly by the Democratic party.

The McGovern Commission announced that after examination, it "found that each of the groups (blacks, women, and youth) was significantly lacking in representation"[28] and proposed a plan for remedying the problem.[29] These decisions of the Democrats received a great deal of largely laudatory comment and constituted pressure on the Republicans to demonstrate that women and youth and blacks were also to be found wielding power in the Republican party. One result was the presence of large and unprecedented numbers of women, youth, and blacks at the Democratic and to a lesser extent at the Republican conventions. Another result was to give the affected traits—femaleness, negritude, youth—a significant institutional advantage. The specific institutional support enjoyed by these traits under the "McGovern" guidelines means that they must be interpreted somewhat differently than traits that lacked such specific support, such as socioeconomic status, education, or ethnic group membership.

On the Democratic side the percent of women was up from 13 percent of all delegates in 1968 to an unprecedented 39 percent in 1972.[30] Between 1892 when three women were seated as alternates at the Republican Convention and the ratification of the women's suffrage amendment, few women had attended either convention. After 1920 intermittent increases brought the total number of women to 252, or 14 percent of the Democratic Convention of 1936. But by 1952 the proportion of women at the Democratic and Republican conventions had declined to 13 percent and 11 percent respectively.[31]

The participation of significant numbers of blacks in national politics did not begin until after southern blacks were effectively enfranchised by the Voting Rights Act of 1965. Most estimates suggest that blacks constituted approximately 5 percent of Democratic delegates in 1968 and about 15 percent in 1972. The increase of participation of persons under 30 was still more dramatic. In 1968 they comprised 2.6 percent of Democratic delegates and in 1972, 22 percent. Democratic delegates under 30 outnumbered their Republican counterparts by about three to one, but there were twice as many Republicans as Democrats 65 years and older.

Neither blacks nor youth were distributed evenly between the parties or among candidate groups. Blacks were most numerous among Humphrey delegates, of whom they comprised nearly one-fourth. As Table 3–8 shows, persons under 30 were most numerous among McGovern's supporters and comprised about 30 percent of that candidate's support group. McGovern's supporters were easily the youngest delegate group: over half were under 40; fewer than one-fifth were over 50. Even with the special support of quotas for women, blacks, and youth, it remained true that a majority of both conventions were male, white, and middle-aged (See Table 3–8.)

Quotas constituted an important asset of blacks, women, and youth— one that enabled them to attain elite status although they had somewhat fewer other assets. The income of black delegates was lower than that of non-blacks (although, of course, still much higher than the national average). Thirty-five percent of black delegates had incomes over $20,000, as compared to 57 percent of white delegates. Forty-one percent of blacks and 33 percent of whites made between $10,000 and $20,000. Nearly one-quarter of black delegates made under $10,000, as compared to 11 percent of non-blacks; of these 10 percent were students. Delegates drawn from these three groups resembled white males over 30 in socioeconomic characteristics; however, while their educations, incomes, and occupational status were high as compared to the whole population, they were less advantageous than the middle-aged white male.[32] Still, women and blacks were clearly members of the middle income skill-based elite. The quotas did not result in the recruitment of persons very different socially from those who did not benefit from quotas; they merely reduced the advantage of being white, male, and over 30.

ETHNIC COMPOSITION

Certain other traditional ascriptive advantages had shrunk by 1972, and some traditional disadvantages had all but disappeared. The percent of WASPs declined concomitantly with the rise of other ethnic groups; the numbers of Jews increased sharply. In part, the ethnic composition of the two parties and candidate support groups reflects the realities of ethnic politics in America. Blacks and Jews vote overwhelmingly Democratic and were more numerous in the Democratic Convention. WASPs and Germanic ethnic stock are more frequently found voting Republican and constituted a larger portion of Republican delegates.[33]

Neither party was ethnically homogeneous, but the Democrats were more ethnically heterogeneous than the Republicans. Persons of Anglo-Saxon descent comprised less than one-fourth of Democratic delegates; blacks were nearly as numerous as the Irish (16 percent and 18 percent

Table 3-8. Delegate Age and Religion by Party and Candidate Preference (%)

	Democrats	Republicans	McGovern	Humphrey	Wallace	Muskie	Nixon
Age							
Less than 30	22	8	29	9	28	12	7
30–39	22	16	27	14	16	18	16
40–49	29	35	26	33	20	40	36
50–65	24	32	16	37	34	26	33
Over 65	4	9	2	8	2	4	9
Weighted N =	2652	1100	1335	439	154	290	1074
Religion							
Protestant	52	79	41	67	81	49	79
Catholic	25	17	24	28	17	35	17
Jewish	11	2	18	3	0	12	2
Other religions	1	1	1	1	0	0	2
Atheists, agnostics, no religion	11	2	16	2	2	5	2
Weighted N =	2601	1106	1298	429	154	290	1080

Question: "Is your religious preference Protestant, Catholic, Jewish, or something else?"

Relationships: Age by party, V = 0.22.
Religion by party, V = 0.28.

NOTE: These data are from the interviews.

respectively); and the portion of Jews was equal to those of Germanic descent (10 percent each). The value position of Jews was distinctive. Their incomes were much higher than those of delegates generally, with nearly one-third in the over $50,000 bracket and 71 percent over $20,000 (as compared to 14 percent of other delegates who had incomes of $50,000 or more and 40 percent who made more than $20,000 annually). There were more blacks, Jews, Irish, Italians, and Chicanos at the Democratic Convention; more Anglo-Saxons, persons of Germanic stock, and Scandinavians at the Republican Convention. As expected, the religious composition of the conventions followed their ethnic characteristics except for the large numbers of Democrats who described themselves as having no religious affiliation. (See Table 3–8.)

There were suggestive differences among the candidate support groups. Wallace delegates were heavily (81 percent) Protestant; the McGovern group contained the fewest Protestants (41 percent), the most Jews (18 percent), and the most persons without a religious affiliation (16 percent). (See Table 3–8.)

SUMMARY AND CONCLUSIONS

So far, we have identified several distinctive characteristics of the McGovern group: of all candidate support groups they had the smallest percentage of lawyers, and the largest proportion of teachers and clergy; they also had the highest portion of delegates with advanced degrees, the largest shares of women, Jews, and persons without religious affiliation, and the smallest portion of Anglo-Saxons.

The Republicans more closely resembled the traditional political elite: Anglo-Saxons, lawyers, and Protestants predominated and income levels were still higher than those of the Democrats. Altogether, the 1972 Democratic delegates constituted a very economically, occupationally, and educationally homogeneous group and a sexually, racially, ethically heterogeneous group.

Comparison of the 1972 and 1948 presidential elites makes clear that there had been no revolution in their social composition. However, the changes were significant. The declining number of delegates drawn from business, the rising numbers of teachers and clergy, the higher education levels, the presence of a significant number of secularists, and the progressive displacement of the white Anglo-Saxon Protestants—these trends present in the majority party suggest a circulation of elites that involves change in more than the identity of the rulers. In combination, these changes could support a new political type. Culture and politics can change without corresponding changes in the socioeconomic characteristics, but the presence of significant changes in the composition (or vocabulary) of an elite is an indicator of the probability that significant political change has occurred.

We can also say with some confidence that *no new patterns of ego organization nor of citizenship are revealed by this analysis*. The small but statistically significant tendency for some supporters of McGovern and Wallace to be somewhat more "subjective" and less fond of schedules and order may constitute an early symptom of the arrival of a new type of activist. But at this stage, these differences constitute no more than a possible clue. Just as the socioeconomic characteristics of the presidential elite are similar, *so are the global personality characteristics and patterns of social participation of most. There is little evidence here of a new modal personality, nor of a new modal pattern of citizenship*. Compared to most people, delegates exemplified a participant style of citizenship.

NOTES

1. Harold D. Lasswell and Abraham Kaplan, *Power and Society: A Framework for Political Inquiry* (New Haven: Yale University Press, 1950), p. 206.
2. Paul T. David, Ralph M. Goldman, and Richard C. Bain, *The Politics of National Party Conventions* (Washington, D.C.: The Brookings Institution, 1960), p. 353.
3. Kevin P. Phillips, *Media-cracy: American Parties and Politics in the Communications Age* (Garden City, N.Y.: Doubleday & Co., 1975).
4. Lionel Trilling, *Beyond Culture: Essays on Literature and Learning* (London: Seeker and Warburg, 1966); Daniel Bell, *The Coming of Post Industrial Society: A Venture in Social Forecasting* (New York: Basic Books, 1973); Seymour Martin Lipset and Herman Kahn, contributions to a symposium "America Now: A Failure of Nerve" 60 *Commentary* (1975).
5. David, et al., *Politics*, p. 337.
6. David Apter, "Ideology and Discontent," *Ideology and Discontent,* ed. Apter (Glencoe, Ill.: The Free Press, 1964), pp. 33–34.
7. Ibid.
8. On political participation and socioeconomic resources, see, inter alia, Sidney Verba and Norman Nie, *Participation in America: Political Democracy and Social Equality* (New York: Harper and Row, 1972), especially pp. 125–137. Also, Philips Cutright, "National Political Development: Its Measurement and Economic Correlates," in *Politics and Social Life,* eds. Nelson W. Polsby, Robert A. Dentler, and Paul A. Smith (Boston: Houghton Mifflin, 1963), pp. 569–582. Also Norman H. Nie, Bingham Powell, Jr. and Kenneth Prewitt, "Social Structure and Political Participation," *American Political Science Review* 63 (1969): 361–378. For a summary and further bibliography, see Lester Milbrath, *Political Participation* (Chicago: Rand McNally & Co., 1965), pp. 114–128, and James Q. Wilson, *Political Organizations* (New York: Basic Books, 1973), especially pp. 56–77. Also Murray Hausknecht, *The Joiners* (New York: Bedminster Press, 1962), and Kenneth Prewitt and Heinz Eualu, "Social Bias in Leadership Selection, Political Recruitment and Electoral Context," *Journal of Politics* 33 (1971): 293–315. D. R. Matthews, *The Social Background of Political Decision Makers* (Garden City, N.Y.: Doubleday & Co., 1954); Robert A. Dahl, *Who Governs? Democracy and Power in an American City* (New Haven: Yale University Press, 1961); Harold D. Lasswell and Daniel Lerner, eds. *World Revolutionary Elites: Studies in Coercive Ideological Movements* (Cambridge, Mass.: MIT Press, 1965); Frederick Frey, *The Turkish Political Elite* (Cambridge, Mass.: MIT Press, 1965); Jose Luis de Imaz, *Los Que Mandan* (Buenos Aires: Editorial Universitario de Buenos Aires, 1966); Dario Canton, *El Parlemento Argentino en Epocas de Cambio: 1890, 1916 y 1946* (Buenos Aires: Editorial del Instituto, 1966), are good examples of the effective use of basic socioeconomic data in elite analysis.
9. Lasswell and Lerner, eds. *World Revolutionary Elites*; W. L. Guttsman, ed. *The British Political Elite* (New York: Basic Books, 1964); Frey, *Turkish Elite*; De Imaz, *Los Que Mandan.*
10. Daniel Lerner, Ithiel de Sola Pool, and George K. Schueller, "The Nazi Elite," in *World Revolutionary Elites*, eds. Lasswell and Lerner, p. 223.
11. Everett Carll Ladd, Jr., and Seymour Martin Lipset, *The Divided Academy: Professors and Politics* (New York: McGraw-Hill, 1975); and a series of Gallup polls showing the highly liberal cast of college liberal arts and social science faculties, and the tendency of students to become more liberal during the years of their college educations and of graduate students to be the most liberal of all.

12. Edward Shils, *The Intellectuals and the Powers and Other Essays* (Chicago: University of Chicago Press, 1972), p. 9.
13. Note that CBS asserts that 29 percent of Democratic delegates were businessmen, 17 percent were union members, and 5 percent labor representatives. Obviously, different criteria were used.
14. Wilson, *Political Organizations*, p. 344.
15. See Apter, "Ideology and Discontent," p. 34, for perceptive comments on this decline. Talcott Parsons also notes that the professions think of themselves as "disinterested" and of business as "self-seeking" in *Essays in Sociological Theory: Pure and Applied* (Glencoe, Ill.: The Free Press, 1949), p. 186. Also Harold D. Lasswell, *Power and Personality* (New York: W. W. Norton, 1948) and F. A. Hayek, "The Intellectuals and Socialism," *University of Chicago Law Review*, Spring 1949, p. 417. James Q. Wilson notes that the disaffection "of one segment of the urban middle class from conventional business mores and political practices" was "endemic" and "these persons regarded big business and machine politics as two manifestations of gross incivility based on materialistic self-seeking," *The Amateur Democrat: Club Politics in Three Cities* (Chicago: University of Chicago Press, 1962), p. 27.
16. Milbrath, *Political Participation*, ch. 5. Also Malcolm E. Jewell and Samuel C. Patterson, *The Legislative Process in the United States*, 2nd ed. (New York: Random House, 1973), p. 73, and William J. Keefe and Morris Ogul, *The American Legislative Process: Congress and the United States* (Englewood Cliffs, N.J.: Prentice-Hall, 1968), pp. 121–132, for a discussion of the upward mobility of American state legislators. Also, Jeane Kirkpatrick, *Political Woman* (New York: Basic Books, 1974).
17. The most famous version of this doctrine is C. Wright Mills, *The Power Elite* (New York: Oxford University Press, 1956).
18. David Apter suggests of persons with temporary status: "Knowing their tenure status is temporary, they do not have the same sense of obligation or duty to the community that a more permanent high-status group might develop." *Ideology and Discontent*, p. 31.
19. V. O. Key, Jr., *Public Opinion and American Democracy* (New York: Alfred A. Knopf, 1961), p. 146. For a further discussion of the effects of mobility on perspectives, see Richard Centers, *The Psychology of Social Classes: A Study of Class Consciousness* (Princeton: Princeton University Press, 1949); Heinz Eulau, "Identification with Class and Political Perspective," *Journal of Politics* 18 (1956): 232–253; Bruno Bettelheim and Morris Janowitz, "Ethnic Tolerance: A Function of Social and Personal Control," *American Journal of Sociology* 55 (1949–50): 137–145; Philip E. Converse, "The Shifting Role of Class in Political Attitudes and Behavior," in *Readings in Social Psychology*, 3rd ed., eds. Eleanor Maccoby, T. Newcomb, and E. Hartley (New York: Holt, Rinehart, and Winston, 1958), pp. 388–399; Angus Campbell, Philip E. Converse, Warren E. Miller, Donald E. Stokes, *The American Voter* (New York: John Wiley & Sons, 1960), ch. 13.
20. The most famous version of the rise of managers is, perhaps, James Burnham, *The Managerial Revolution: What is Happening in the World* (New York: John Day Co., 1945).
21. Survey research is, of course, the ideal tool for the study of the subjectivities of aggregates. However, it imposes certain limits. The data collected in this fashion consists of reports on the self: activities recolleted, priorities stated, and personal characteristics of the self described by the self. Furthermore, while collecting comparable data requires asking comparable questions, the question and answer procedure may interfere with the expression of subjective connections that can illuminate psychic functioning, as, for example, through free association. But delegates were too numerous to permit

depth interviews of a representative sample. Standardized interviews risk imposing the researcher's presuppositions and cognitive structures, but the only practical alternative to them is to forego investigation entirely and simply make guesses about the personal character of elites and masses. Herbert McClosky's work has demonstrated the utility of survey research for the investigation of the subjectivity of large numbers. Herbert McClosky, *Political Inquiry* (New York: Macmillan, 1969). See also Harry C. Triandis, et al., *The Analysis of Subjective Culture* (New York: John Wiley & Sons, Interscience, 1972); Alex Inkeles and David H. Smith, *Becoming Modern: Individual Change in Six Developing Countries* (Cambridge, Mass.: Harvard University Press, 1974); and Daniel Lerner, *The Passing of Traditional Society: Modernizing the Middle East* (Glencoe, Ill.: The Free Press, 1958).

22. Milbrath, *Political Participation*; James David Barber, *The Lawmakers: Recruitment and Adaptation to Legislative Life* (New Haven: Yale University Press, 1965); Paul Sniderman, *Personality and Democratic Politics: Correlates of Self-Esteem* (Berkeley: University of California Press, 1975); Robert E. Lane, *Political Life: Why People Get Involved in Politics* (Glencoe, Ill.: The Free Press, 1959); Edmond Costantini and Kenneth Craik, "Women as Politicians: The Social Background, Personality and Political Careers of Female Party Leaders," *Journal of Social Issues* 28, no. 2 (1972), 217–236. Also relevant are Guiseppe Di Palma and Herbert McClosky, "Personality and Conformity: The Learning of Political Attitudes," *American Political Science Review* 64 (1970): 1054–1073; Kirkpatrick, *Political Woman* and Campbell, Converse, Miller, and Stokes, *The American Voter*.

23. This finding of the similarity of persons active in democratic politics is consistent with other studies. Edmund Costantini and Kenneth Craik, "Competing Elites Within a Political Party: A Study of Republican Leadership," *Western Political Quarterly* 22 (1969): 901. Also, Milbrath, *Political Participation* and Wilson, *Political Organizations*.

24. Herbert McClosky, "Conservatism and Personality," *American Political Science Review* 52 (1958): 27–45.

25. Wilson, *Amateur Democrat*, p. 10. Jewell and Patterson, *The Legislative Process in the United States*, p. 71; Leon D. Epstein, *Politics in Wisconsin* (Madison: University of Wisconsin Press, 1958); Frank Sorauf, *Party and Representation: Legislative Politics in Pennsylvania* (New York: Atherton, 1963), p. 71; Donald R. Matthews, *U.S. Senators and Their World* (Chapel Hill: University of North Carolina Press, 1960).

26. Milbrath, *Political Participation*, pp. 113–114. See also M. Kent Jennings and Richard G. Niemi, *The Political Character of Adolescence: The Influence of Families and Schools* (Princeton: The Princeton University Press, 1974).

27. Donald Matthews documents the multiple membership of senators in *U.S. Senators*. Frank Sorauf describes the gregarious habits of Pennsylvania legislators in *Party and Representation*, p. 79. Milbrath makes the same point in *Political Participation*. Verba and Nie document this relationship in *Participation in America*. Also, Ingunn Nordesval Means, "Women In Politics: The Norwegian Experience," *Canadian Journal of Political Science*, September 1972, p. 379, and Kirkpatrick, *Political Woman*, pp. 42–45. All these findings confirm Tocqueville's insight. Alexis de Tocqueville, *Democracy in America*, eds. J. P. Mayer and Max Lerner (New York: Harper and Row, 1966), pt. 2, chs. 5, 6, 7.

28. *Mandate for Reform*, Report of the Commission on Party Structure and Delegate Selection (Washington, D.C.: Democratic National Committee, 1970), p. 26.

29. This is not the time or place to pursue the very interesting question of how these groups came to be the beneficiaries of "quotas" within the state delegations, when the McGovern Commission report explicitly wrote that "It is the understanding of the

Commission that this is not to be accomplished by the mandatory imposition of quotas," *Mandate for Reform*, p. 40, but to note that some interesting permutations of the doctrine of equal access were advanced, and quotas were imposed guaranteeing large, unprecedented representation for all three groups in the Democratic Convention.

30. Democratic National Committee figures put it at 36 percent.

31. For further information on women in national conventions, see Marguerite J. Fisher and Betty Whitehead, "Women and National Party Organization," *American Political Science Review* 38 (1944): 895–903; and David, et al., *Politics*, pp. 327–329.

32. These findings concerning women and blacks are consistent with that of Wolfinger concerning ethnics—namely, that achievement of political influence occurs after the achievement of middle-class status. See Raymond E. Wolfinger, "The Development and Persistence of Ethnic Voting," *American Political Science Review* 59 (1965): 905.

33. The greater ethnic and religious heterogeneity of Democratic leadership is noted in Charles W. Wiggins and William L. Turk, "State Party Chairmen: A Profile," *Western Political Quarterly* 23 (1970): 332. The heterogeneity of the party rank and file has been emphasized and documented by Lloyd A. Free and Hadley Cantril, *The Political Beliefs of Americans: A Study of Public Opinion* (New Brunswick, N.J.: Rutgers University Press, 1967), pp. 152–156.

CHAPTER 4

Incentives to Participation in Presidential Politics

The motives of leaders probably more than any other perspective determine the character of the individual's relationship to the party, as well as the drive potential of the group collectively.[1]

The motives of political actors figure importantly in many classic and contemporary explanations of political change. Plato, Mosca, and Pareto[2] shared the conviction that the dominant passions (values) of its elite shaped a society's political institutions and that changes in these passions precede and cause changes in the constitution. They agreed, too, that the elite whose intense predispositions had such influence was not limited to the topmost rulers but extended to that more numerous class—which Mosca termed the "second stratum" on whom all regimes are dependent for the implementation of their designs.[3] In our own times, the work of such diverse scholars as Harold Lasswell, Edward Banfield, James Q. Wilson, Anthony Downs, William Riker, and Samuel Eldersveld reflects the conviction that the motives of political activists have determinative influence on the character of political institutions.[4] Many contemporary students agree with Wilson that the effects of participants' motives (and other aspects of their personalities) are greatest—and clearest—in voluntary institutions.

> The kinds and value of incentives supplied to the members of an association, the conflicts between those who compete for a particular inducement, and the differences in behavior among those who seek dissimilar incentives within an organization will importantly affect the character of any organization but will be a principal influence on the character of a voluntary association.[5]

Obviously political parties with their frequently shadowy intermittent structure, low role articulation, and high turnover are examples of such institutions. The manifest difficulties of studying motives (variously termed "purposes," "goals," "values," "intense predispositions," "dominant passions") and their consequences have seemed less forbidding to many students of political parties than trying to explain parties' composition and functions without recourse to these subjective phenomena.

Not all those who have emphasized motives in the study of political parties have approached the problem in the same way: some, among whom Downs and Riker are notable, have *postulated* actors' single goals and assumed maximizing behavior.[6] They are frequently reproached for oversimplification. Others, among whom Eldersveld and Wilson[7] are notable, have eschewed such stipulation in favor of descriptive analysis of the stated purposes of political activists and have been reproached for failure "to predict the direction of party activity."[8]

The assumption that parties can be explained as a team of single-minded men "seeking to control the governing apparatus by gaining office in a duly constituted election"[9] simplifies the task of predicting their behavior.[10] But, empirical studies have repeatedly found that party activists and leaders seek multiple values through political activity and that political parties are characterized by a "motivationally complex and pluralistic structure."[11] The *fact* of diverse motivations constitutes a persuasive argument against any approach that attempts to explain the behavior of political parties with reference to a single motive. It is probably true that the clarity of the rational office seeker model (or any other single causation model) cannot be equaled by any explanation that takes into account the multiplicity of motives of party leaders and activists, but the predictive power of the model lies less in the attribution to all actors of a single goal than in the maximization postulate. Lasswell's value institutional approach provides an alternative that combines motivational complexity with a maximization postulate that permits the projection of the probable consequences of various motivational syndromes.[12] Wilson's *Political Organizations* also features the combination of a relatively complex motivational model and an assumption of value maximization, but Lasswell's value categories are more comprehensive and differentiated than Wilson's and his framework more highly elaborated. Because it permits both complexity and prediction, the value institutional approach will be utilized in this discussion of the motives of delegates.[13] In this chapter I propose first to describe the motives of delegates to the two conventions noting evidences of changes in the values and, second, to discuss some possible institutional consequences of the motivational composition of the two parties.

Because the discussion of the motives of political actors, itself complex, has been further complicated by the proliferation of terms, a brief note on the terms, concepts, and assumptions to be employed should clarify this discussion. Purposes, goals, motives, incentives, and goal events are all terms that refer to the preferred outcomes that stimulate a person to take a particular action. Such decisions, to take one course of action rathe⁻ than another, do not occur in a vacuum. They are guided by personal predispositions to prefer one value (one kind of preferred outcome) over another. Value predispositions antedate particular acts of valuation and are more enduring components of the self-system. Value predispositions and acts of valuation shape responses to incentives. The *desire* to maximize that value is the motive, or purpose, or goal. Perceiving an opportunity to maximize a desired value is an *incentive* to participation. Value predispositions influence preception, because they sensitize an actor to particular aspects of the environment. That sensitivity may lead one person to see opportunity where another sees only discouragement. The perception of politics as an arena for the maximization of desired values is a function of the environment, the value predispositions, the imagination, and the intelligence of the individual.[13]

The value institutional approach postulates that in analyzing human interactions, it is useful to assume that "man seeks to maximize valued outcomes; he does something in the expectation of being better off than if he did something else."[14] This approach does not assume that political behavior is self-interested in any banal material sense, only that it is purposive in the sense that people have personal reasons for becoming and remaining active.[15] The value institutional approach is distinguished from "positive theory" or the "rational office seeker" model, because it postulates an indeterminant relation between motives and institutions and assumes that the motives of actors in any arena must be established empirically rather than assumed. The value focus of an institution serves to attract to that arena persons with a special interest in the pursuit of the relevant value. However, since major institutions are multifunctional, diverse types of people fill roles in the institution simultaneously.[16] Changing balances among the various types of persons in an institution may "tilt" it, causing a reorientation of its value specialization.

Not only do the reasons for which people spend time and energy on politics differ, but the dominant value orientation of political institutions themselves change with changes in their environment and/or composition, and these changes in turn affect the kinds of people who choose to become active.

The more porous and permeable an institution, the more readily such reorientation can take place. Many observers believe that such a change in the orientation of American political parties is in process and was accelerated by the entrance into political activity in 1972 of people whose motives differed substantially from those who have dominated American politics in the recent past. While research on the motives and goals of American political leaders and activists in the last half-century indicates that fame, fortune, romance, reputation, power, moral passion, and social position have all served as motives for becoming and remaining active in politics, the values that participants have most often sought to maximize through political participation are:

1) Material values (wealth): Getting or keeping a job through patronage, attracting new clients or customers, securing a government contract, eliciting a bribe are examples of ways in which wealth can be maximized through politics.
2) Solidary values: Solidary values concern the sense of well-being that derives from comradeship, friendship, a sense of belonging, of solidarity with like-minded others. Solidary values have either an interpersonal or an organizational focus. Solidary values are frequently focused on groups with which an individual has identified. Where identification with a collectivity exists, an individual may seek and enjoy maximization of collective rather than personal goods. This process of identification creates the "we" that lies at the center of political phenomena,[17] and creates a social self who can seek and enjoy collective as well as purely personal benefits. This capacity for identification conforms to psychological reality and distinguishes Lasswell's value maximizing man from the extreme individualist of most economic models[18] and makes it possible to take account of some aspects of political reality (e.g., party loyalty) with which the individualistic models cannot deal.
3) Moral or rectitude values: Moral values include all views concerning what is right, good or moral, or wrong, bad, or immoral for the polity. Rectitude values are pursued in politics through support for policies or candidates one has invested with moral status.
    Note that the pursuit of rectitude in politics is focused on altering the behavior and the value position of others as contrasted with the rectitude goals that aim at perfection of the self. The latter pursuit emphasizes self-mastery, the former requires power over others.
4) Status values: Honor, fame, prestige, preferments of various kinds are sought and won in political arenas.
5) Power: The capacity to participate in decisions that affect the policies of others is the historic prize available to political leaders.

Recent research on the American mid-elite indicates the declining importance of material incentives and the increasing importance of rectitude concerns as incentives to political activity,[19] as well as the continuing significance of solidary incentives (including both socializing and party loyalty).[20] It has also identified links between the motives of participants and attitudes toward organization and, in some circumstances, to ideology as well.[21]

The fact that not all reasons for political participation enjoy equally good reputations creates problems for the researcher and probably means that a person's description of his motives tells us something about group norms as well as about his own reasons for becoming active in politics.

MOTIVES OF DELEGATES: THE MULTIPLE
GOALS OF POLITICAL ACTIVITY

The study included both open-ended and closed questions concerning reasons that the respondents originally became active in politics, satisfactions they derive from political activity, and reasons for desiring to become a delegate. In most cases these turn out to be the same.

Like many other human activities, political participation provides an opportunity to maximize multiple values. Table 4-1 shows that most delegates in fact sought multiple goals through political participation.

Almost all sought to maximize moral values through their political activity; many sought solidary values; a minority sought status values and/or power; and a few attempted to maximize material values in political processes. Only 5 percent said they sought only one or two rewards through political participation. About one-fifth described fewer than five incentives as important to their political participation; over one-half described five to eight reasons as important; while the remainder reported nine or more important incentives to participation.

The pattern of delegate incentives suggests that party-oriented participants were most likely to be motivated by multiple values. Republicans, delegates supporting Humphrey and Muskie, and those with long experience were more likely than newcomers or supporters of McGovern and Wallace to have multiple reasons for participation. (See Table 4-1.) Political generation was also related to the number of incentives regarded as important.

In both parties, those who became active before the end of World War II were twice as likely as those who became active after 1968 to describe more than nine incentives as important stimuli to political activity, but this association between generation and multiplicity of motives does not establish whether participation itself breeds increased interests in politics or whether the newcomers were distinctively single-minded. There are grounds for believing both that contemporary politics may be more attractive to single value types and also that most persons attracted to politics because of a single issue or candidate either develop broader interests or drop out.[22]

Table 4-1. Number of Important Incentives to Politics by Party, Candidate Preference, Political Generations (%)

Number of Important Incentives	Party ID		Candidate Preference					Political Generations			
	Dems.	Reps.	McGovern	Humphrey	Wallace	Muskie	Nixon	Pre-1945	1946–1959	1960–1967	1968–1972
Only 1 or 2	7	2	9	1	18	2	2	4	3	5	11
3–4	25	13	32	8	34	16	12	15	17	17	36
5–8	52	57	53	50	43	52	57	47	55	57	48
9–12	24	30	16	42	23	32	30	38	28	26	16
N =	1446	742	824	178	56	126	720	252	688	710	486

Question: "We are interested in peoples' reasons for being involved in politics. How important are each of the following reasons to your own participation in politics?" Possible answers: extremely important, quite important, not very important, not at all important. The *specific reasons* to which delegates were asked to give one of the above answers were:

1. Personal friends or members of my family are active in the party.
2. I want to see particular candidates elected.
3. Party work helps me make business or professional contacts.
4. Politics is a part of my way of life.
5. I am strongly attached to the party and want to give it my support.
6. I enjoy the friendships and social contacts I have with other people in politics.
7. I like the fun and excitement of elections and campaigns.
8. I want to have a personal career in politics.
9. Party work gives me a sense of fulfilling civic responsibility.
10. I want to get the party and its candidates to support the policies I believe in.
11. I like the feeling of being close to people who are doing important work.
12. Party work gives one visibility and recognition.

This table gives the percentages of those in each category who regarded a certain number of incentives as "quite important" or "extremely important." Percents do not necessarily add to 100 due to rounding.

Relationships: Number of important incentives by party, V = 0.15; by political generations, gamma = −0.23.

NOTE: These data are from the mail questionnaires. For an explanation of this index, see Appendix C.

Among Democrats the number of goals sought through political activity was also associated with experience in party office and with ideology. Those who had held state or national office were more likely to seek multiple goals through politics than those who had not (gamma .38), and the more offices a person held, the more likely he was to have multiple goals. Persons who explain their participation by reference to few incentives were more numerous among Democrats than Republicans and were more likely to be drawn to politics by issues (gamma .40) than by attachment to party, local or state interests, or personal associations. They were also less likely to have held party office (gamma .51). Among both Republicans and Democrats the more single-minded political actor is not in politics because he enjoys it (gamma .50 for Democrats and .51 for Republicans), nor for recognition, nor from an interest in party reform; he is in politics because of an overriding concern with a candidate and/or an issue. Among Democrats (but not Republicans) the fewer the incentives to political participation, the greater the intensity with which policy views were held and the more consistent and comprehensive the ideological orientation.[23] Conversely, persons seeking many different satisfactions from politics tended to have less intense and less holistic ideological orientations.

Multi value types are the norm at the level of the mid-elite. It is not clear whether multi-value perspectives are also most numerous at the highest levels of politics or only at the middle and lower levels of democratic politics where rewards must be found in the process itself or whether they are characteristic of political actors in all kinds of systems.

The multiplicity of incentives characteristic of most of the delegates does not imply that all—or nearly all—members of this strategic mid-elite were alike. Tables 4-2 and 4-3 make clear that the two parties and the candidate preference groups featured varying motivational mixes.

MORAL INCENTIVES: CIVIC DUTY AND ISSUES

Moral incentives to political participation may take the form of a general commitment to good citizenship and desire to help the community solve its problems, support for particular programs, or commitment to a comprehensive ideology or plan for redemption. The civic action or public service orientation to politics that conceives politics as civic activity is not necessarily tied to any ideology, program, or policy and is often associated with a pragmatic, non-ideological approach to politics. The type of moral concern that links concern for the public good with programmatic and/or ideological goals is associated with "issue politics." Obviously these two orientations are not mutually exclusive. In fact most

Table 4-2. Important Incentives to Politics by Party, Candidate Preference, Political Generations (%)

Incentives	Party ID		Candidate Preference					Political Generations			
	Dems.	Reps.	McGovern	Humphrey	Wallace	Muskie	Nixon	Pre-1945	1946–1959	1960–1967	1968–1972
Support particular candidate	97	95	99	96	96	96	95	96	97	97	96
Influence party on policy	90	81	93	83	95	86	80	85	87	87	88
Sense of civic responsibility	74	89	68	87	72	81	89	87	84	80	66
Politics is my way of life	71	79	67	83	50	82	80	82	81	75	56
Support the party	58	89	44	89	46	83	90	84	81	69	42
Friendships and social contacts	57	68	48	73	55	65	69	71	62	62	49
Fun and excitement	54	63	47	67	54	62	64	63	56	60	48
Near people doing important work	44	49	36	57	55	48	49	56	45	45	40
Want career in politics	35	34	34	41	24	37	34	30	33	37	37
Visibility and recognition	31	36	23	43	39	39	37	43	32	33	24
Family, friends active in party	28	35	20	42	29	33	35	44	32	29	23
Business-professional contacts	11	12	6	18	15	14	12	14	12	11	9
N =	1572	825	881	195	67	138	794	300	752	766	521

Question: "We are interested in peoples' reasons for being involved in politics. How important are each of the following reasons to your own participation in politics?" Possible answers for each incentive listed: extremely important, quite important, not very important, not at all important.

This table describes those for whom each incentive was "extremely important" or "quite important."

NOTE: These data are from the mail questionnaires. *N*'s reflect responses to the "support a candidate" item. Other *N*'s are comparable in size.

Table 4-3. Important Incentives: Rank-Ordered by Party and
Candidate Preference (%)

Democrats (N = 1564)		*Republicans (N = 820)*	
Influence policy	90%	Support party	89%
Civic duty	74%	Civic duty	89%
Support party	58%	Influence policy	81%
Enjoy social contacts	57%	Enjoy social contacts	68%
McGovern Supporters (N = 878)		*Humphrey Supporters (N = 194)*	
Influence policy	93%	Support party	89%
Civic duty	68%	Civic duty	87%
Enjoy social contacts	48%	Influence policy	83%
Support party	44%	Enjoy social contacts	73%
Wallace Supporters (N = 65)		*Muskie Supporters (N = 137)*	
Influence policy	95%	Influence policy	86%
Civic duty	72%	Support party	83%
Enjoy social contacts	55%	Civic duty	81%
Support party	46%	Enjoy social contacts	65%

Question: "We are interested in people's reasons for being involved in politics. How important are each of the following reasons to your own participation in politics?" Possible answers: extremely important, quite important, not very important, and not at all important.

This table describes those in each party and candidate support group for whom a given incentive was "extremely important" or "quite important."

NOTE: Data are from the mail questionnaires. *N*'s reflect responses to "influence policy." Other *N*'s are comparable in size.

delegates described both as important incentives to political activity. One important difference between these two types of motivation is probably that "civic duty" more often focuses on *common* problems and ideological or policy concerns on *divisive* ones. There was a slight but consistent tendency for supporters of the traditional candidates to emphasize civic duty as an incentive to political activity and for the McGovern and Wallace supporters to emphasize the desire to influence party policy as an incentive to activity. But the identification of political activity with civic obligation was shared by most, and for most politics seemed the most important of their civic activities. Roughly two-thirds of Nixon, Muskie, and McGovern delegates but only 37 percent of Wallace delegates said political activities were more important to them than other community memberships. Policy concerns were also an important incentive to participation for almost all delegates and important to their decisions to seek a delegate position.

The fact of nearly universal mid-elite concern with rectitude incentives is not consistent with many descriptions of American politics in this century. The ubiquity of policy concerns of 1972 delegates cannot be explained merely as a function of the unusually intense ideological divisions within the Democratic party because among Republicans, where there was a very high degree of consensus on issues, four-fifths of all delegates described concern with party policy as an important incentive to political participation (as compared to 90 percent of Democrats). The relatively even distribution of policy interests across age cohorts proves, too, that policy incentives have not become important only recently. The 1972 delegates did not reflect a sudden upsurge of issue concern; there was no Old Guard unconcerned with the content of politics, no Young Turks separated from their elders by the former's concern with issues and the latter's indifference to policy. It has been nearly two decades since Sorauf, Wilson, Epstein, and others first observed, analyzed, and labelled the middle-class amateurs for whom policy has distinctive importance.[24] There has been time for these to grow in numbers and influence, time for the decline of urban organizations staffed by paid lower-class precinct captains, for the explosion of higher education, for the rise of the electronic media, and for the rise to influence of yesterday's policy-oriented insurgents.[25]

While policy was important to all, it was not equally important. In response to open-ended questions on the reasons for their original involvement in politics and their reasons for becoming delegates, McGovern and Wallace supporters were more likely than others to cite concern with the issues involved in a particular campaign as the original reason for becoming active in politics. Among Humphrey, Muskie, and Nixon delegates party ties and social incentives prompted the entrance of more delegates into politics than did policy concern. (See Table 4-2.)

Rectitude specialists—here defined as persons for whom policy was an important incentive to political activity, but support for party was not—comprise 27 percent of this mid-elite. Table 4-5 shows that they were by no means evenly distributed, but comprised 39 percent of Democrats and 8 percent of Republicans. Among Democrats they were concentrated in the McGovern and Wallace ranks—comprising over one-half (about 54 percent) of each group, while among Humphrey supporters they were barely more numerous than among Republicans. In both parties rectitude specialists were relatively more numerous among persons who became active during or after 1968; however, fewer than one-half the rectitude specialists in each party were of this generation. Approximately 25 percent of Democratic rectitude specialists became active before 1960, one-third in the Kennedy-Johnson years, and somewhat over two-fifths during or after 1968. The largest portion first became active during the period that their party featured candidates and platforms with heavy moral emphasis: the Goldwater years on the Republican side and the McCarthy/McGovern years on the Democratic. The presence of substantial numbers of rectitude specialists among persons with fairly long experience indicates that *persons recruited to politics do not necessarily develop attachment to the party or drop out*. Some stay in their parties, acquiring know-how without developing a sense of institutional identification.

SOLIDARY INCENTIVES: ORGANIZATIONAL

All—or almost all—the presidential elite was motivated by concern with candidate selection and issue positions but there was less unanimity concerning the importance of party solidarity. In their reactions to candidates and issues, there were large statistically significant differences between supporters of Humphrey, Muskie, Nixon[26] on the one hand and Wallace and McGovern on the other. For over four-fifths of the supporters of traditional candidates attachment to party was an important incentive to political participation; for over one-half of the followers of McGovern and Wallace it had little or no importance. The sharp dichotomy between traditional and nontraditional candidate support groups suggests that we are here dealing with an important distinction between old and new political types.

A large body of research demonstrates that attachment to party is a major source of the stability and continuity in democratic political systems[27] and an important incentive to activists.[28] Elite attachment to party has special importance for parties' strength and durability. Masses change election outcomes by the strength or weakness of their attachment to party, but leaders can split parties. Party solidarity not only affects election outcomes, it also affects the character of interactions within a party. Identification with a party and its prospects softens debate and limits conflict within a party.

Responses to both open-ended and fixed alternative questions revealed that among Republicans and Humphrey supporters support for party was the most widely shared incentive for political participation. It was far less important in the McGovern and Wallace ranks. For example, 19 percent of Humphrey delegates, 26 percent of Nixon delegates, 7 percent of McGovern delegates, and 5 percent of Wallace delegates mentioned party solidarity in their initial answer to an open-ended question about why they happened to run for delegate.

The importance of party solidarity as an incentive to activity was related to age, political generation, and party role. In general, the longer a person had been active in politics, the more likely he was to describe party as an incentive to activity—a finding consistent both with studies demonstrating that the intensity of party identification increases with age and with Eldersveld's finding that persons who became active through party solidarity are very likely to remain active.[29] Almost four-fifths of those who became active before 1960 say that supporting the party was an important incentive to political activity; somewhat fewer of those who became active between 1960–1967 considered it an important incentive, but the precipitous decline in party solidarity as a motive to political action occurred among people who became active during or after 1968. A high level of organizational solidarity was the norm for Wallace delegates through 1945, for Muskie delegates through 1967, and for Humphrey and Nixon delegates through 1971; and there was a substantial minority of McGovern delegates for whom party solidarity had never been important—regardless of their length of activity. For example, only 57 percent of McGovern delegates who entered politics in the postwar years 1946–1960 described party as a significant incentive, as compared to 90 percent of Humphrey delegates, 84 percent of Muskie delegates, and 94 percent of Nixon supporters.

The relation between age and party solidarity is consistent with the preceding findings concerning political generation. Among McGovern, Wallace, Muskie, and Nixon delegates there is a discernible tendency for older delegates to be more motivated by party ties than younger delegates. In these candidate support groups attachment to party was a less important incentive to delegates under 40 than to those over 40. But the strong attachment to party of young Humphrey delegates demonstrates that youth is not necessarily associated with weak party ties. The data suggest that length of activity may reinforce ties to party and enhance its motivating power, but they are also compatible with the hypothesis that strength of party loyalty is diminishing.

The importance of party solidarity was also positively related to the quality of political experience. Among delegates of all ages, generations, and persuasions, party loyalty was associated with having held party office. (See Table 4-4.) Holding public office had the same effect, but the relation of public office and party solidarity was less strong than that be-

Table 4-4. Important Incentives by Party Officeholding
Experience (%)

Incentives	Ever Held Party Office? Yes	No
Participation of friends and family	32	24
Support of particular candidate	97	95
Business/professional advantage	12	9
Politics part of way of life	78	57
Desire to support party	75	45
Enjoy social contacts	65	44
Enjoy fun and excitement	60	44
Want career in politics	36	30
Civic duty	83	63
Desire to influence party policy	86	91
Be near people doing important work	46	41
Enjoy recognition	35	25
$N =$	1912	485

Question: "We are interested in people's reasons for being involved in politics. How important are each of the following reasons to your own participation in politics?" Possible answers: extremely important, quite important, not very important, and not at all important.

This table describes those for whom each incentive was "extremely important" or "quite important" in each office-experience category.

NOTE: Data are from the mail questionnaires. *N*'s reflect responses to "support a particular candidate." Other *N*'s are comparable in size.

tween party office and solidarity (the gamma is .57 for party office and .40 for public office).

The disappearance of the policy neutral regulars is reflected in the very small numbers of solidary specialists in this presidential elite. Solidary specialists (here defined as persons for whom party was an important incentive to activity while policy was not) comprise 10 percent of the total sample—fewer than one-half the number of rectitude specialists. Solidary specialists were most numerous among Republicans and the Humphrey and Muskie supporters, but while rectitude specialists comprised one-half of the McGovern and Wallace delegates, solidary specialists constituted less than one-fifth of any candidate group. In the Democratic (but not the Republican) party solidary specialists were found mainly among persons recruited to political activity before 1968. (See Table 4-5.)

Table 4-5. Motivational Types (%)

	Solidary Specialists	Rectitude Specialists	Synthesizers	Neither	*N*
Party					
Democrats	7	39	51	3	1547
Republicans	17	8	72	3	813
Candidate Preference					
McGovern	4	54	39	3	866
Humphrey	15	9	74	3	193
Wallace	2	53	42	3	64
Jackson	13	13	69	5	77
Muskie	13	16	70	2	136
Ideological Self- Classification					
Radical	0	67	28	5	116
Very liberal	5	52	42	2	634
Somewhat liberal	10	23	62	4	530
Moderate	17	12	68	4	475
Somewhat con- servative	16	10	73	1	436
Very conservative	9	18	71	2	126
Generations (Democrats)					
Pre-1945	10	19	69	2	165
1946–59	9	26	64	2	436
1960–67	7	43	49	2	458
1968–72	5	55	34	6	460
Generations (Republicans)					
Pre-1945	15	7	74	3	125
1946–59	17	6	77	1	306
1960–67	17	9	71	3	301
1968–72	22	22	50	6	54

NOTE: Solidary specialists are delegates who said that party was an important incentive to participation but policy was not. Rectitude specialists are delegates who said that policy was an important incentive to participation but party was not. Synthesizers are delegates who said that party and policy were important incentives to participation. Others said neither party nor policy were important incentives to participation.

SOLIDARY INCENTIVES: PERSONAL

Party loyalty is a complex phenomenon in which are linked personal and political values, hereditary identifications, social characteristics (such as class, race, and ethnic and sectional identification), and expectations. The party with which any individual identifies is in part a moral posture, in part an abstraction independent of particular people and policies, and in part the flesh and blood persons who "are" the party at a particular time and place.[30] Like other types of voluntary organizational activity, politics entails a particular type of socializing in which people meet regularly and establish limited "friendly" relationships within the context of cooperative endeavor toward an impersonal goal. Although pleasant, social contacts remain functional, but although functional, pleasant.

Studies of traditional politics suggest that strong ties of personal loyalty may develop among political co-workers and that these reinforce bonds of shared purpose. When *amicitia* exists among those allied in the pursuit of power, personal political goals become more inclusive, less egocentric. As Henry Fairlie emphasized in a discussion of the contribution of *amicitia* to political morality,[31] personal bonds temper and limit the pursuit of power and deference.

Patterns of value preference confirm that solidary incentives were highly compatible with one another: friendship, socializing, family participation, and attachment to party are positively associated with one another and with status drives and material incentives.[32] But social incentives were almost never a *sufficient* cause of participation among these elite actors. Those who valued socializing had multiple motives, of which sociality was one.

Like party solidarity, sociality is related to age, candidate preference, party role, and political experience. Socializing is somewhat more important to older than to younger delegates, to supporters of the traditional candidates (Nixon, Humphrey, and Muskie) than to McGovern's and Wallace's boosters, and to persons who have held party office.

Sociality should not be confounded with affiliation needs. Table 4-6 shows that few of the presidential elite scored high on the Affiliation Index, although most said that enjoyment of social contacts is an important incentive to participation. Another indication of the non-intimate nature of political socializing was the fact that only one-half as many delegates reported that the participation of friends and family was important to their participation as so rated enjoyment of social contact.[33]

A factor analysis of incentives suggests that among this mid-elite party solidarity, civic duty, and the habit of political participation comprise a single dimension of political motivation. Presumably this dimension that

Table 4-6. Personality Traits by Party and Candidate Preference (%)

	Democrats	Republicans	McGovern	Humphrey	Wallace	Muskie	Nixon
Affiliation Index							
Low 1	21	18	24	22	14	18	18
2	35	36	36	37	41	31	36
3	30	26	28	29	37	26	26
4	10	16	9	10	5	19	16
High 5	4	4	4	3	3	6	4
Weighted *N* =	2544	1040	1287	410	148	284	1020
Achievement Index							
Low 1	1	2	1	0	2	3	2
2	10	6	10	8	6	9	6
3	26	17	28	19	31	21	17
4	35	36	33	39	30	42	36
High 5	29	40	28	34	31	25	40
Weighted *N* =	2544	1040	1287	410	148	284	1020
Power Index							
Low 1	14	28	10	19	11	22	28
2	28	28	28	27	29	24	28
3	30	26	31	28	39	35	25
4	21	14	23	22	18	14	14
High 5	7	5	7	5	3	6	5
Weighted *N* =	2544	1040	1287	410	148	284	1020

Relationships: Affiliation Index by party, V = 0.08. Achievement Index by party, V = 0.15. Power Index by party, V = 0.17.

NOTE: Data are from the interview sample. For method of index construction and the specific constituent variables that comprise these indexes, see Appendix C.

links habit, group solidarity, and civic obligation taps the traditional "public service" conception of political participation and stands in contrast to both ideology and the hope of personal gain. When the items in this factor were combined to form a Solidarity Incentives Index, Republicans and Humphrey delegates proved most likely and McGovern supporters least likely to score high on this index. Scores on the Solidarity Incentives Index were positively correlated with enjoyment of politics (r .31) and status needs (r .50); they were negatively correlated with political generation (r -.33), party reform interests (r -.23), and policy-maker role orientation (r -.23).

STATUS INCENTIVES

Two items tapped status needs as motives for political activity: the desire for visibility and recognition and the satisfaction derived from feeling close to people engaged in important activities. Slightly over one-third of all the delegates described the former as an important reason for political activity, and nearly one-half so described the latter. Status values were positively associated with material, solidary, and power values. The association of status and solidary values is further underscored by a factor analysis in which the two status incentives occur in the same motivational dimension as enjoyment of social contacts. A Status Incentive Index constructed from this factor also proved to be positively associated with the Solidary Incentives Index. (The association is r .48 among Democrats and r .42 among Republicans.)[34]

Apparently, the attraction to status incentives may be part of a relatively traditional political style. Status values are less attractive to persons recruited after 1968 than to those who have been active longer and less important to the political activity of McGovern delegates than supporters of other candidates, and there was a negative relation between status index scores and interest in policy and party reform.

The desire for deference, for feeling that one "counts" in the affairs of the community is self-regarding in the sense that it involves a change only in the value position of the self and has no direct relation to any collective good. But the positive association of status and solidary incentives suggests that status seeking through politics is compatible with strong collective identifications, and the equally strong association of status incentives and enjoyment of politics (r .48) indicates that a feeling of enhanced importance may be one of the emotional by-products of purposive socializing. Lasswell has emphasized that status values belong to the same general family as power: both involve desire to feel, in relation with others, that one is the object of respect and esteem.[35]

The relations between solidarity and status found here are very similar to those reported by Lester Milbrath and Walter Klein. Their Esteem Scale "seems to measure self-esteem as well as a desire for receiving esteem from others." They report that this scale, which was highly correlated with their Sociality Scale, "performed much better than Dominance and slightly better than Sociality in separating participants from nonparticipants."[36]

POWER VALUES

The study of motives and goals is complicated at best, but the identification of persons interested in maximizing power poses special problems. Pursuing power has little prestige and activists are frequently reluctant to reveal power goals. But there is another more basic problem in identifying power-oriented personality types. As Lasswell pointed out long ago in his famous formula, $p \{d\} r = P$, political man displaces private motives onto public objects and rationalizes them in terms of the public interest.[37] All power seeking is motivated by "purposive" goals; all those who seek political power are characterized by an identification of the self with some larger group (a family, clique, nation, race, or sex) and a purpose that links personal goals to this larger group. Neither the identification nor the rationalization is a stratagem undertaken to fool an unwary public. Both are fully incorporated into the self. Since the motive for maximizing personal power is always presented to the ego as well as to others as a means of achieving a public goal, questions inquiring directly about motives are unlikely ever to result in responses that affirm the desire to maximize power as a principal purpose. The "power" incentive exists in contexts that tend to obscure its presence.

Although all political power seekers have public concerns, the reverse is not necessarily true. A predisposition to value power cannot be assumed from the mere fact of participation in politics, any more than preoccupation with rectitude can be inferred from participation in ecclesiastical institutions or a special concern with enlightenment can be inferred from presence in an educational institution. Enormous amounts of power are associated with high political positions, but participation in politics at lower levels is not necessarily a route to participation in power. In his essay, "The Selective Effect of Personality on Political Participation," Lasswell pointed out that persons for whom power is a dominant concern may find democratic politics an inhospitable arena,[38] and Robert Lane concluded that "the search for power is just as likely to be expressed in non-political areas as in political areas."[39] Studies of the motivations of political activists at lower levels have repeatedly found that power is not a significant incentive for most. It is hardly surprising that this should be the case since the volunteer character of American politics gives intraparty relations an egalitarian flavor that must be unattractive to many power seekers.[40]

In considering power seeking in politics it is crucial to distinguish between lower level offices and activities to which little influence attaches, and high politics which offers the opportunity for making decisions that affect the lives of many. Most political participants are, of course, found at the lower levels and most of the empirical investigations of the motives of politicians have low level political actors as subjects. Rufus Browning and Herbert Jacob's findings caution against generalizing findings from one level of actor and type of politics to other levels and types: "Opportunities for exercising power and for achieving . . . vary not only among offices within local political systems but also from one system to another." They found that "the distribution of opportunities among political offices are related to the motivational make-up of officeholders."[41] The greater the power opportunity, the more persons with high achievement and power needs. Presidential politics holds the promise of large influence over large questions and, in principle, should attract some persons with a driving need to shape the choices of others. Some of these persons would not have been present in a sample of delegates but were candidates, candidate staff, and convention officials.

Two measures were utilized to identify delegates with intense power predispositions: one tapped a generalized orientation to influence in interpersonal relations; another measured political ambition and achievement needs in politics specifically. The former measure was part of a broad effort to identify the relative strength of power, affiliation, and achievement values in interpersonal relations. Both power and achievement orientations might be related to a predisposition to value and seek influence. A three-item Achievement Index, a three-item Power Index and a three-item Affiliation Index were constructed, and the distributions (shown in Table 4-6) are consistent with the findings of previous inquiries: relatively few delegates scored high on the Power Index; many scored low. Still fewer delegates scored high on the Affiliation Index than on the Power Index, and low scorers were far more numerous. But most delegates scored high and few scored low on the Achievement Index. These findings are consistent with those of other investigations of the personalities of political participants.[42]

A second set of measures was designed to tap political ambition specifically. In these measures desire for high level and/or party office was interpreted as an indicator of power predispositions; level of effort which a respondent was prepared to invest in achieving that office was interpreted as an indicator of the intensity of the predispositions. The need for power, Alexander George has argued, is expressed in activities whose overt goal is to dominate or deprive others, in efforts to secure oneself against domination or influence by others, and/or in the drive for political achievement.[43] In political circles the desire to influence public events is generally considered laudable, while a generalized desire to dominate situations and people is often unacceptable. Therefore, questions concerning political ambition provide the respondent with an opportunity to express a desire for power in a nonpejorative context. To measure political ambition respondents were asked "Thinking of all the possible offices and positions in politics, from local to national and from public office to position in the party organization, which of the following would you most like to be if you could have your personal choice? First, consider public office." Public offices from president to municipal council were listed, and in another question party offices from national party chairman to local organization were listed. For both public and party offices major positions were included at the national, state, and municipal levels (and for party, county, and district as well). To provide an indication of the seriousness of the goal, of its centrality for the person, a second question inquired how hard the respondent would work to achieve the desired position. Would the respondent "work harder and make more sacrifices than for any other goal in life," "work harder than before," or "make some additional effort"? Indexes were constructed on the basis of responses to these two questions. The most interesting findings are summarized below.

First, the 1972 Republican and Democratic conventions contained a large number of persons of high political ambition. Over one-half of all delegates (54 percent) expressed a desire to hold public office at the national level, and only one-fourth of the presidential elite had no desire for public office. There was also wide interest in holding party office. About two-fifths of the delegates said they would like to hold party office at the national level and another 19 percent at the state level where power has been traditionally vested. The overall relation between ambition for party and public office was gamma .40.

Second, 29 percent of delegates said that they were prepared to give top priority to political ambition—to work harder and sacrifice more than for any other goal. Presumably, this group had intense power predispositions. Another 22 percent of the delegates expressed high political ambition and were willing to work hard to achieve it but not to give these efforts top priority in their lives.

Third, evidence that many desired influence over public events, and not only status or fame, is implied in the fact that only one-third as many would work as hard for high party office as for high public office. It is public office that gives direct access to the major power processes of the society; party office provides less influence on authoritative decisions.

The percent of high ambition/high achievement delegates was about the same in both parties and was very similar in all candidate groups, but there were significant differences between the sexes. In both parties and all candidate groups substantially fewer women than men expressed high ambition and achievement values. There were also expected, but not large, differences among generations, with high ambition most common among the youngest delegates. The relation between political ambition and attachment to party was less expected. Although fewer Democrats than Republicans were strongly attached to party, about the same proportion of each desired high party office and gave top priority to achieving it, making clear that the desire for power in party processes was not necessarily associated with attachment to party.[44] Ambition is apparently rooted in personal characteristics unrelated to institutional identification.

As compared to persons with less ambition, the most ambitious were slightly *less* likely to be motivated by solidary values (whether of party or sociality); they were slightly less likely to be moved by civic responsibility or stimulated by status concerns. On the other hand, delegates with high ambition and high achievement drive were somewhat more likely than others to value politics as an opportunity for business or professional advancement, and they were definitely more likely than the unambitious to be interested in influencing party policy.[45]

The fact that persons with high ambition were numerous and that most of them sought to maximize *other* values than power through their political activities casts doubt on the validity of a sharp distinction between the motives of "office seekers" and their supporters. Only the candidate will occupy the office, but his supporters may enjoy enhanced power and status just as he derives important solidary and rectitude satisfactions.

PATTERNS OF MOTIVATION:
A SUMMARY DESCRIPTION

The preceding description of delegate motivation indicates that there were no sharp discontinuities in the personal and political goals of old and new political generations, women and men, or candidate support groups. Each party, political generation, age, sex, and candidate group was characterized by motivational diversity. Like the parties of Detroit studied by Eldersveld, the mid-elites of presidential parties are "motivationally complex and pluralistic structure(s)."[46] But while there are no sharp discontinuities or subgroups with monolithic motivations, there were nonetheless significant differences among age groups, political generations, and candidate support groups. Younger delegates, less experienced delegates, and McGovern and Wallace supporters were more likely to be motivated by overriding issue commitments and power values, and to be unconcerned with solidary and status values.

The elites of the two parties differed less in the level of their concern with issues than in their attitudes to party. When Eldersveld studied Detroit, he found material and solidary incentives more important to Democrats than moral or "purposive" incentives.[47] And David Nexon reached the same conclusion from his examination of "occasional activists" from 1956–1964.[48] *By 1972, both presidential parties were saturated with policy concerns*. The presence of rectitude concerns among supporters of all candidates, age groups, and political generations means that they are an attribute of presidential politics, not merely of a single faction or subgroup. Obviously, stereotypes of the policy neutral regulars and the ideological activists are outdated if indeed they ever described the modern political world.[49] Furthermore, in 1972 the trend was toward the declining importance of party and the increased importance of policy as a motive. (See Tables 4-2 and 4-4.)

The most important intra-elite differences concerned attitudes toward party. All available data confirm that attachment to party is part of a broader solidary incentive that links party to other goals: enjoyment of social contacts (r .43); civic duty (r .40); enjoyment of the fun and excitement of politics (r .37); feeling a part of important activities (r .46); gaining recognition (r .42). Orientation to party is linked to many other dimensions of social and political life: to political generation; to length of residence in one's community; to number of memberships in voluntary associations; to ideology and ideological style; to role perception. No other incentive was strongly related to so many other aspects of political life: presumably, therefore, attitudes to party were a central factor in the politics of 1972. Table 4-7 shows some linkages between incentives and role perceptions.

Available evidence suggests that by 1972 the attenuation of attachment to party had affected the elites of both parties and all elite factions but was especially strong among newcomers to politics and the elite supporters of Wallace and McGovern. Because attachment to party is related to many aspects of political behavior, *a continued trend away from solidary incentives will probably mean a major and fundamental change in the American political system.*

Table 4-7. Incentives and Organizational Perception:
Most Inclusive Factor

Desire to support party	.69	Incentive
Delegate should be one who		
will work for party	.69	
will represent party interests	.61	Role requirement
will represent state interests	.39	
Delegate should		
reward party service	.68	
work for harmony	.41	Role definition
stress party organizational role	.60	
take a firm position	-.38	
Convention should		
reform party	-.42	Institutional function
unify party	.38	

NOTE: Data are from the mail questionnaires. Factor loadings above from Varimax rotation. Problem included all responses to all questions concerning motives, role qualifications and definition, and convention function included in the mail questionnaires.

One consequence of increased numbers of activists seeking to maximize other than solidary values should be decreasing willingness to tolerate frustration of either policy preferences or ambitions. In Albert Hirschman's terms, fewer activists and leaders will be moved by "loyalty" to prefer "voice" over "exit."[50] *Identification* with a party gives activists a stake in its well-being even when they disagree with particular decisions on candidate or platform. An instrumental attachment to party provides much less basis for enduring the frustrations typically associated with the broad-scale aggregation of diverse perspectives and interests characteristic of two-party systems.

A second probable consequence of increased numbers and/or importance of mid-elite activists not motivated by party attachment is the declining emphasis on winning as the party's principal (and legitimate) goal. Respondents who believed that picking a winner was an important task for a convention were most frequently those for whom party loyalty was a motive to participation. (See Table 4-8.) A deemphasis on winning would profoundly alter the fundamental characteristics of American political parties by neutralizing the "discipline of the market." It would lessen a party's interest in tolerating and compromising conflict, render it less sensitive to voter opinion, and less likely, therefore, to move to the center in search of voters.

A third important consequence grows out of the distinctive ideological characteristics of some of those whose activity was not motivated by

Table 4-8. The Job of the Convention by Motivational Type (%)

	Solidary Specialists	Rectitude Specialists	Synthesizers	Neither
Pick a Team That Can Win				
	($N = 171$)	($N = 347$)	($N = 936$)	($N = 44$)
High priority	85	57	81	75
	($N = 12$)	($N = 156$)	($N = 99$)	($N = 4$)
Low priority	6	26	9	7
Unify the Party				
	($N = 89$)	($N = 81$)	($N = 419$)	($N = 17$)
High priority	43	13	36	29
	($N = 53$)	($N = 409$)	($N = 439$)	($N = 27$)
Low priority	26	66	38	47
Adopt Correct Issue Positions				
	($N = 89$)	($N = 372$)	($N = 547$)	($N = 29$)
High priority	42	61	47	48
	($N = 48$)	($N = 85$)	($N = 230$)	($N = 8$)
Low priority	23	14	20	13

Question: "What do you think are the most important things a convention can do?" Respondents were asked to rank order five roles of a convention: the three listed plus "reform the party" and "nominate a deserving candidate." "High priority" means that the respondent ranked that function of first or second importance; "low priority" includes those who ranked it fourth or fifth.

NOTE: Data are from the mail questionnaires.

support for party. Rectitude specialists tended to the ideological extremes: a substantial majority classified themselves as either "radical," "very liberal," or "very conservative," while delegates for whom the party solidarity inspired activity were much more likely to be moderates—"somewhat liberal," "moderate," or "somewhat conservative." (See Table 4-5.) A high degree of intensity and of internal consistency was also characteristic of the ideological style of many rectitude specialists; in contrast, persons for whom solidary values were important were more eclectic in their views. More important is the fact that among Democrats the increasing importance of issues was accompanied by the decreasing pull of party.

NOTES

1. Samuel J. Eldersveld, *Political Parties: A Behavioral Analysis* (Chicago: Rand McNally & Co., 1964), p. 272.
2. *The Republic of Plato*, trans. with Introduction and Notes, Francis MacDonald Cornford (London: Oxford University Press, 1941); Gaetano Mosca, *The Ruling Class* (New York: McGraw-Hill, 1939); Vilfredo Pareto, *The Mind and Society: A Treatise on General Sociology*, trans. Andrew Bongiorno and Arthur Livingston (New York: Dover Publications, Inc., 1935).
3. Mosca, *Ruling Class*, pp. 404–405.
4. An earlier argument for making power maximization the central concept of the discipline was George E. G. Catlin, *The Science and Method of Politics* (Hamden, Conn.: Archon Books, 1964; originally published in 1927); Anthony Downs, *An Economic Theory of Democracy* (New York: Harper and Brothers, 1957); Mancur Olson, *The Logic of Collective Action: Public Goods and the Theory of Groups* (New York: Schocken Books, 1968); Albert O. Hirschman, *Exit, Voice and Loyalty: Responses to Decline in Firms, Organizations and States* (Cambridge, Mass.: Harvard University Press, 1970); James Q. Wilson, *Political Organizations* (New York: Basic Books, 1973) and Wilson, *The Amateur Democrat: Club Politics in Three Cities* (Chicago: University of Chicago Press, 1962); Eldersveld, *Political Parties*; Dwaine Marvick and Charles R. Nixon, "Recruitment Contrasts in Rival Campaign Groups" in *Political Decision-Makers: Recruitment and Performance*, ed. Dwaine Marvick, (Glencoe, Ill.: The Free Press, 1961); Lewis Bowman, Dennis Ippolito, and William Donaldson, "Incentives for the Maintenance of Grassroots Political Activism," *Midwest Journal of Political Science* 13, no. 1 (1969): 126–139; M. Margaret Conway and Frank B. Feigert, "Motivation, Incentive Systems, and the Political Party Organization," *American Political Science Review* 62, no. 4 (1968): 1159–1173; Robert S. Hirshfield, Bert E. Swanson, and Blanche D. Blank, "A Profile of Political Activists in Manhattan," *Western Political Quarterly* 15, no. 3 (1962): 489–506; David Nexon, "Asymmetry in the Political System: Occasional Activists in the Republican and Democratic Parties, 1956–1964," *American Political Science Review* 65 (1971): 716–730; John W. Soule and James W. Clarke, "Issue Conflict and Consensus: A Comparative Study of Democratic and Republican Delegates to the 1968 National Conventions," *Journal of Politics* 33 (1971): 72–91; Lewis Bowman and G. R. Boynton, "Recruitment Patterns Among Local Party Officials: A Model and Some Preliminary Findings in Selected Locales," *American Political Science Review* 60 (1966): 667–676; Robert H. Salisbury, "The Urban Party Organization Member," *Public Opinion Quarterly* 29 (1965–1966): 550–564; Harold F. Gosnell, *Machine Politics: Chicago Model* (Chicago: University of Chicago Press, 1937); Sonya Forthal, *Cogwheels of Democracy: A Study of the Precinct Captain* (New York: William-Frederick Press, 1946); J. T. Salter, *Boss Rule: Portraits in City Politics* (New York: McGraw-Hill, 1935). Edward Banfield, *Political Influence* (Glencoe, Ill.: Free Press, 1961) describes the importance of material incentives to political party organizations of the recent past. On the study of incentives in other nations, see James Payne's *Labor and Politics in Peru* (New Haven: Yale University Press, 1965), and Nathan Leites, *On the Game of Politics in France* (Stanford, Calif.: Stanford University Press, 1959).
5. Wilson, *Political Organizations*, p. 32.
6. Downs, *Economic Theory*; William H. Riker, *The Theory of Political Coalitions* (New Haven: Yale University Press, 1962).
7. Eldersveld, *Political Parties*; Wilson, *Amateur Democrat*.
8. Joseph A. Schlesinger comments that "Traditional descriptive analysis arrives at an impasse, however, in trying to predict the direction of party activity." "The Primary Goals

of Political Parties: A Classification of Positive Theory," *American Political Science Review* 69 (1975): 840–849.

9. Downs, *Economic Theory*, p. 25.

10. Brian Barry recently noted that the Downs model "does not *predict*, . . . except in the sense of predicting that when the axioms are satisfied the outcomes deduced from them will occur." "Review Article: 'Exit, Voice and Loyalty'," *British Journal of Political Science* 4 (1974): 103.

11. Eldersveld, *Political Parties*, p. 302.

12. The value institutional approach is presented in various of Lasswell's works. A comprehensive statement is Harold D. Lasswell and Abraham Kaplan, *Power and Society: A Framework for Political Inquiry* (New Haven: Yale University Press, 1950), and a good summary is found in Harold D. Lasswell, "Introduction: The Study of Political Elites," in *World Revolutionary Elites: Studies in Coersive Ideological Movements*, eds. Harold D. Lasswell and Daniel Lerner (Cambridge, Mass.: MIT Press, 1965).

13. The terms and the theory are those of Lasswell.

14. Lasswell and Lerner, eds. *World Revolutionary Elites*, p. 8. Lasswell adds that the maximization postulate is not only useful, but "intuitively plausible, especially since the postulate holds even when human beings make erroneous calculations and in retrospect wish they had acted differently."

15. This assumption is not inconsistent with Robert Salisbury's warning against overestimating the purposive character of political activity and underestimating the possibility and/or the extent to which political activity is habitual. Research on political activists establishes that political activity—like most human activities—most often develops in supportive environments that shape and reinforce personal inclination. Presumably, people who become active as an aspect of early socialization internalize the motives for activity as well as the habit. "The Urban Party Organization Member," *Social Science Quarterly* 49 (1969): 800–815.

16. Eldersveld, *Political Parties*, p. 302. Also. Marvick and Nixon, "Recruitment Contrasts," pp. 207–208.

17. Lasswell and Kaplan, *Power and Society*, pp. 11–12.

18. Olsen, *Logic of Collective Action*, is an exception. Also, Hirschman, *Exit, Voice and Loyalty*. His concept of loyalty assumed identification but does not develop it.

19. Wilson, *Political Organizations*, ch. 6; Wilson, *Amateur Democrat*; Bowman and Boynton, "Recruitment Patterns"; Marvick and Nixon, "Recruitment Contrasts," p. 208; Heinz Eulau, William Buchanan, Leroy C. Ferguson, and John C. Wahlke, "Career Perspectives of American State Legislators," in *Political Decision-Makers*, pp. 241–247.

20. Eldersveld, *Political Parties*, p. 303; Wilson, *Political Organizations*, pp. 110–115.

21. Wilson, *Amateur Democrat*; also John W. Soule and James W. Clarke, "Amateurs and Professionals: A Study of Delegates to the 1968 Democratic National Convention," *American Political Science Review* 64 (1970): 888–898; C. Richard Hofstetter, "The Amateur Politician: A Problem in Construct Validation," *Midwest Journal of Political Science* 15 (1971): 31–56. Dan Nimmo and Robert L. Savage, "The Amateur Democrat Revisited," *Polity* 5, no. 2 (1972): 268–276; Vicki G. Semel, "Ideology and Incentives Among Democratic Amateurs and Professionals" (Paper prepared for delivery at the annual meeting of the American Political Science Association, New Orleans, La., September 4–8, 1973), p. 408. An excellent discussion of many of the relations is Nelson W. Polsby and Aaron B. Wildavsky, *Presidential Elections: Strategies of American Electoral Politics*, 3rd ed. (New York: Charles Scribner's Sons, 1971), pp. 35–59.

22. Bowman, Ippolito, and Donaldson noted that though "the local party . . . can attract activists through purposive incentives . . . the maintenance of activism requires, to some extent, the eventual positive orientation of the activist toward the party as a group and

toward his position in the party." "Incentives," p. 138. Also, Eldersveld, *Political Parties*, p. 293.

23. The study included numerous questions on ideology; measures of intensity and of ideological consistency across issue areas were developed, and their relation to incentives analyzed. These measures are discussed in Chapter 6.

24. Frank J. Sorauf, "Extra-Legal Parties in Wisconsin," *American Political Science Review* 48 (1954): 692–704; Wilson, *Amateur Democrat*; Francis M. Carney, *The Rise of the Democratic Clubs in California* (New York: Holt, Rinehart, and Winston, 1958); Joseph P. Harris, *California Politics* (San Francisco: Chandler, 1967), ch. 2; Leon D. Epstein, *Politics in Wisconsin* (Madison: University of Wisconsin Press, 1958), ch. 5.

25. In his study of political activists from 1956 to 1964 David Nexon found that "The Republicans are a high participation party with an amateur base composed of right wing ideologues, while the Democrats are a low participation party with a professional base not dependent on ideological incentives to activism." "Asymmetry," p. 717. Of course, Nexon's generalization was based on lower level activists. However, there are other grounds for believing his characterization of the two parties applied at other levels. It is consistent with Eldersveld's findings for Detroit, *Political Parties*, and with a widespread impression created, for example, by the sharp contrast between the Goldwater and Johnson conventions.

26. Kennedy and Jackson supporters resemble those of other traditional candidates.

27. The outstanding essay on this subject is Philip E. Converse and Georges Dupeux, "Politicization of the Electorate in France and the United States," *Public Opinion Quarterly* 26, no. 1 (1962): 1–23. See also the interesting discussion of party identification in Donald Stokes and David Butler, *Political Change in Great Britain: Forces Shaping Electoral Choice* (New York: St. Martin's Press, 1969).

28. Because it has such importance for the political system, all evidence concerning change in patterns of organizational solidarity is important. Evidence of such change is accumulating rapidly. The rise of split-ticket voting and the increasing numbers of independents who identify with neither party have been widely noted as have the development and persistence of ideological schisms in the majority party. Since 1948 we have watched "presidential Republicans" in the South demonstrate with their votes that some issues were more important to them than their traditional Democratic party identification, and since 1968 defections and threats of defection on the left have signaled the rise of new issues for which some liberals were prepared to desert their party. On the importance of party as an incentive for activists, see, for example, Marvick and Nixon, "Recruitment Contrasts," p. 208, and Eldersveld, *Political Parties*, ch. 11.

29. Eldersveld, *Political Parties*, p. 140.

30. Austin Ranney, "The Concept of 'Party'," in *Political Research and Political Theory*, ed. Oliver Garceau (Cambridge, Mass.: Harvard University Press, 1968), pp. 143–162.

31. Henry Fairlie, "Lessons of Watergate," *Encounter* 43, no. 4 (1974): 8–27.

32. Lester W. Milbrath and Walter W. Klein emphasize the centrality of sociality to political participation in "Personality Correlates of Political Participation," *Acta Sociologica* 6 (1962): 53–66; also Milbrath, *Political Participation: How and Why Do People Get Involved in Politics* (Chicago: Rand McNally & Co., 1965), pp. 74–76. Gabriel Almond and Sidney Verba, *The Civic Culture: Political Attitudes and Democracy in Five Nations* (Princeton: Princeton University Press, 1963), ch. 10, report that nations high on social activity were high in levels of political participation. The relationship between organizational and personal loyalties is also stressed in Peter B. Clark and James Q. Wilson, "Incentive Systems: A Theory of Organizations," *Administrative Science Quarterly* 6, no. 2 (1961): 129–166.

33. Robert A. Dahl noted the unusual sociability of the politician and commented "This does not mean that the professional actually likes other people to any unusual degree or even

that he has an unusual need to be liked by others.'' *Who Governs? Democracy and Power in an American City* (New Haven: Yale University Press, 1961), p. 298. Dahl cites, in support of this point, Rufus Browning, *Businessmen in Politics* (Ph.D. diss., Yale University, 1960).

34. Clark and Wilson, "Incentive Systems," pp. 141–146, also emphasize the affinity of solidary and status rewards.
35. Lasswell and Kaplan, *Power and Society*, pp. 55–56.
36. Milbrath and Klein, "Personality Correlates," p. 119.
37. This formulation is presented in various of Lasswell's works; it is stated with great clarity in *Power and Personality* (New York: W. W. Norton, Compass Books, 1948), pp. 20–58.
38. Harold D. Lasswell, "The Selective Effect of Personality on Political Participation," in *Studies in the Scope and Method of "the Authoritarian Personality,"* Richard Christie and Marie Jahoda, eds. (New York: The Free Press. (1954)), pp. 197–225.
39. Robert E. Lane, *Political Life: Why People Get Involved in Politics* (Glencoe, Ill.: The Free Press, 1959), p. 127. See also Milbrath and Klein, "Personality Correlates," pp. 53–66.
40. Milbrath, *Political Participation*, p. 82.
41. Rufus P. Browning and Herbert Jacob, "Power Motivation and the Political Personality," *Public Opinion Quarterly* 28 (1964): 87, 89. Also Milbrath, *Political Participation*, pp. 48–89.
42. E.g., Browning and Jacob, "Power Motivation," pp. 75–90.
43. Alexander George, "Power as a Compensatory Value for Political Leaders," *Journal of Social Issues* 24, no. 3 (1968): 35.
44. Detailed analysis of the role orientations and incentives establishes that in each party persons with low attachment to party are as likely as those with strong attachment to have high ambition for public office and high achievement needs. Those with strong organizational concerns are only slightly more likely than persons with weak organizational concerns to have high ambition/high achievement needs for party office.
45. Joseph A. Schlesinger, *Ambition and Politics: Political Careers in the United States* (Chicago: Rand McNally & Co., 1966), emphasizes that political ambition has both attitudinal and behavioral consequences. On ambition and politics, see also Gordon S. Black, "A Theory of Political Ambition: Career Choices and the Role of Structural Incentives," *American Political Science Review* 66 (1972): 144–159, and Black, "A Theory of Professionalization in Politics," *American Political Science Review* 64 (1970): 865–878; John W. Soule, "Future Political Ambitions and the Behavior of Incumbent State Legislators," *Midwest Journal of Political Science* 13 (1969): 439–454; Kenneth Prewitt, "Political Ambitions, Volunteerism and Electoral Accountability," *American Political Science Review* 64 (1970): 5–17; Michael L. Mezey, "Ambition Theory and the Office of Congressman," *Journal of Politics* 32 (1970): 563–579. Note, however, that Schlesinger emphasizes the impact of the desire for reelection as affecting politicians' behavior in conjunction with ambition p. 2.
46. Eldersveld, *Political Parties*, p. 302.
47. Ibid., p. 287.
48. Nexon, "Asymmetry," p. 724.
49. By 1972 virtually all delegates to the national conventions belonged to Pareto's Type A category: people moved by ideas about the public good. *Mind and Society*, pp. 1609–1610. Also Bowman, Ippolito, and Donaldson, "Incentives," pp. 137–138; and Conway and Feigert, "Motivation," p. 1172.
50. Hirschman, *Exit, Voice and Loyalty*.

CHAPTER 5

Role Expectations and Institutional Stability

Even though "Parties are more important as labels than as organizations,"[1] they are nonetheless confronted with such standard problems of organizational maintenance as recruiting members, training and testing leaders, formulating purposes, securing needed contributions, establishing communications, and coordinating activities. Like other organizations, a political party is threatened by internal conflict over purposes and strengthened by consensus; like any other organization, its persistence requires some sense of corporate identity that distinguishes it from other organizations that compete for loyalty, time, energy, skills, and other scarce resources; and finally, like any other organization, it needs decision makers who are committed to preservation of the organization. The requisites for organizational maintenance include an incentive system that will reward devotion, effort, and success; a decision-making system that ensures that decisions will be made by persons with some concern for organizational maintenance; and a process for recruiting new members and leaders, communicating group norms and practices, and training and testing replacements for the leadership corps.[2]

The widespread tendency of leaders to develop an intense interest in the welfare and persistence of the organization for which they make decisions was noted by Wilson who asserted that

> Those responsible for maintaining the organization will be powerfully constrained in their actions by the need to conserve and enhance the supply of incentives by which membership is held in place. This constraint, which we shall argue is the chief constraint on organizational leaders, sets the boundaries around what is permissible and impermissible political activity.[3]

Most of the literature on political parties assumes that presidential parties will be headed by persons with a strong commitment to the party's organizational interests: to winning, to forging and preserving party unity, and to strengthening and preserving the party's resources and good reputation. But this assumption does not take account of the anti-organizational trends in American reform politics. The inclination to equate organization with oligarchy and to associate democratization with anti-organizational strategies has led to a variety of efforts to "democratize" politics by way of reforms that weaken party organization. Initiative, referendum, recall, and the direct primary are clear examples. The McGovern–Fraser reforms are the most recent example of reform that coupled an effort to "open" the parties with sharp limitations on the influence of organizational leaders. Characteristically, reforms look toward the correction of past abuses but often have consequences unrelated either to their goals or expectations. One unintended effect of the McGovern–Fraser reforms may have been to elevate into positions of influence within the Democratic party persons with little concern for organizational preservation.

This chapter examines the attitudes of delegates toward the institution in which they served. These attitudes, which are embodied in role expectations, can have a major impact on the level of intraparty harmony and conflict and on other aspects of organizational maintenance.

Role expectations concern what actors in a given interaction must do, should do, may do, and may not do; shared, these expectations structure interactions among people; stabilized, these shared expectations comprise the structured behavior we call institutions. Institutions function because shared expectations lead to reciprocal behavior. They remain stable as long as there is broad consensus on goals and appropriate behaviors.

The looser the organization, the less continuous the interactions, the faster the turnover, the more diverse the recruitment practices, the greater the opportunity for development of divergent role perceptions and for institutional change. Structures reinforce and perpetuate themselves by communicating role requirements clearly and by structuring incentives to reward appropriate behavior and punish inappropriate behavior. Less structured institutions often cannot preserve themselves, because they lack the mechanisms for communicating, socializing, rewarding, and depriving. A national convention lacks most of the institutional requisites for stability: it meets briefly and rarely, lacks continuity in membership, and has no distinctive rewards and deprivations that can be manipulated to encourage delegates to behave in desired ways.[4] The relative stability of convention behavior in past years presumably derived from the fact that a large portion of its membership, especially those in leadership roles, were also members of other, ongoing organizations.[5] Rules may have important effects on the character and stability of role expectations. Rules that permit the selection of individuals who are not part of state organizations, who have not shared socializing experiences (such as those provided by joint activity in previous enterprises), who are part of diverse role structures (e.g., party organization, candidate groups, or issue groups), and who are not responsible or committed to an ongoing organization increase the likelihood that delegates will have diverse and possibly incompatible understandings of what a convention is and what a delegate does. The rules under which the Democrats operated in 1972 enhanced the already high potential for role conflict in that party. In the case of the Republicans, the absence of conflict and the pattern of organizational recruitment enhanced the harmony of role expectations.

ROLE CONFLICT AND POLITICAL CONFLICT

Because there is a strong tendency for stabilized roles to be assigned the character of legitimate expectations, deviation from expected behaviors is frequently perceived as a violation of rules, trust, and acceptable behavior.[6] Conflicting role expectations and role behavior lead quickly to mutual charges of bad faith and of perversion of the political process. There is a parallel tendency for demands to be presented as descriptions of appropriate or legitimate functions rather than as advocacy; for example, the view that the "nature" of a political party requires that a party articulate and adopt clear issue positions and programs is, in fact, a demand that parties do this. Because the range of goals that may be sought and achieved through politics and political parties is large, the potential for disagreement on role expectations is also large. Since a role expectation is a segment of culture embedded in a total culture, times of rapid cultural change are especially likely to produce conflicting role conceptions. The existence of diverse regional and political subcultures further enhances the likelihood that there will be present in any national convention persons with quite different understandings of what should be and could be undertaken there.

Much of the debate and most of the acrimony surrounding the Republican Convention of 1964 and the Democratic Conventions of 1968 and 1972 arose from clashing conceptions of what a convention should do and the closely related question, what a party should be. In general, liberal Democratic reformers and Republican conservatives have desired to build national programmatic parties and have perceived national conventions as arenas for the affirmation of clearly formulated conceptions of the public good, while Democratic regulars and less conservative Republicans have attempted to preserve the national parties as loose electoral alliances of persons who feel some common interest or identity—however vague—as "Democrats" or "Republicans" and conventions as arenas of aggregation and compromise. Echoes of role conflict were present in 1964, 1968, and 1972 as advocates of programmatic parties called the regulars "power brokers" and reproached them for unconcern with principle; and supporters of aggregative parties reproached the reformers as "purists" who desired to rule or ruin. In general, regulars are believed to have an abiding and, it is sometimes charged, overriding concern for organizational maintenance, while reformers are more concerned with ideological correctness of decisions than with their impact on party organization.

Because roles are complementary and reciprocal, widely shared role expectations facilitate easy communication and cooperation. Disparate role expectations breed misunderstanding as well as change. In addition to structing behavior, role expectations serve as the criteria for evaluating the performances of both individuals and institutions. A "good" procedure for choosing delegates is one that conforms to prevailing standards of fairness and results in the selection of delegates with the expected characteristics. If the job of a convention is to produce a winner, a convention that does not do so is a failure; if the job of a convention is to reform the party, a convention that preserves the status quo is a failure. If a delegate should be one with an abiding concern for party, then recruitment processes that produce delegates with concern for party are good processes. But if a delegate should be a young person who cares deeply about a particular issue—e.g., war—then recruitment processes that select party regulars are bad processes. Disagreement on role requirements signals the absence of agreed upon criteria for evaluating performance. Was the 1968 Democratic Convention a failure because it consisted mainly of party regulars chosen through traditional procedures, or was it, as compared to 1972, a success because it nominated a team that nearly won? Was the 1972 convention a success because it embodied party reforms and contained many delegates who gave priority to matters of principle? Or was it a failure because it nominated a candidate who was massively rejected by voters? In the absence of shared criteria, it is impossible to settle such questions.

Role conflict may occur within a single individual or between individuals. However uncomfortable internal role conflict is for the afflicted individual, it is role conflicts *among* people (commonly termed "role strains") that have the most serious consequences for institutions.

This chapter explores the diverse and conflicting views among delegates to the two conventions concerning what a convention should be and what a delegate should do, inquires into some reasons for these differing orientations, and considers some likely consequences for presidential parties of the persistence of existing trends. It argues that the diversity of delegates' role conceptions was not merely that characteristic of loose, decentralized parties but was patterned so as to suggest growing disagreement about what a presidential party is and what its principal institution, the national convention, can and should do, and disagreement about whether delegates have responsibility for organizational maintenance. These disagreements, I suggest, constitute important evidence of the presence among persons influential in national politics of new people with conceptions of politics substantially different from those of the people who have dominated American politics in the past.

THE JOB OF A CONVENTION

Most descriptions of national conventions emphasize the functions of picking a winner and aggregating interests. Polsby and Wildavsky note that "the great search at most conventions is for 'The Man Who Can Win'."[7] Delegates, say Polsby and Wildavsky, "want to gain power, to nominate a man who can win the election, to unify the party and to obtain some claim on the nominee, to protect their central core of policy preferences, and to strengthen their state party organization."[8] But they also point out that these goals are not distributed equally among all delegates. V. O. Key had no doubt about the most important job of a convention. "The function of the convention," he asserted, "is to settle the conflict among factions of the party for the presidential nomination."[9] More recently, Judson James emphasized the aggregative functions of national conventions, the need to "make this voluntary assembly of the elements of the party into a unit with common goals and cooperative attitudes."[10]

The kind of candidate nominated, platform adopted, and rules agreed upon have profound consequences for a presidential party's electoral fortunes and subsequent strength. These decisions depend in significant measure on delegates' conceptions of the job of a convention. To determine these conceptions, a question asked delegates to rank order five possible functions of national conventions. The five functions named were the aggregative function, "unifying the party"; the electoral function, "picking nominees who could win the election"; the articulation function, "adopting correct positions on important national issues"; the self-perfection function, "reforming the party"; and the reward function, "nominating the most deserving candidate." (See Table 5-1.) Four of these functions concern intraparty matters; one—putting together a winning team—concerns interparty competition.

Table 5-1. Delegate Role Perceptions: The Job of the Convention by Party, Candidate Preference, and Political Generations (%)

Role Perception	Party ID		Candidate Preference					Political Generations			
	Dems.	Reps.	McGovern	Humphrey	Wallace	Muskie	Nixon	Pre-1945	1946–1959	1960–1967	1968–1972
Choose a winning team	69	85	61	87	47	86	85	77	81	77	58
Adopt correct issue positions	49	52	56	27	74	42	52	45	46	52	56
Nominate deserving candidates	37	28	45	32	37	25	28	36	31	30	42
Unify the party	30	32	16	56	25	44	32	39	36	28	21
Reform the party	18	6	25	5	18	7	6	10	9	14	24
N =	1435	785	819	179	61	127	756	255	692	722	501

Question: "What do you think are the most important things the convention can do?" Respondents were asked to rank-order the five roles of a convention. This table describes those who ranked each role first or second in importance.

NOTE: *N*'s reflect responses to "reform the party" item. Other *N*'s are comparable in size.

The Electoral Function: Putting Together a Winning Team

It is generally agreed that major parties in democratic systems normally give very high priority to winning elections. The desire to win is thought to be the motivating force that makes parties sensitive to voter opinions and prompts them to seek party unity.

Tables 5–1 and 5–2 show that in 1972 delegates to the two conventions were far from unanimous about the priority of winning. Republicans and

Table 5-2. The Priorities of a Convention by Candidate Preference Group (%)

	McGovern	Humphrey	Wallace	Muskie	Nixon	Democrats
Nominating a Team Who Can Win the Election						
Most important	37⎫ 61	63⎫ 87	20⎫ 47	66⎫ 86	63⎫ 85	45⎫ 69
Second most important	24⎭	24⎭	27⎭	20⎭	22⎭	24⎭
Third most important	17	10	35	8	9	15
Fourth most important	17⎫ 23	3⎫ 4	12⎫ 18	6⎫ 6	4⎫ 6	13⎫ 17
Least important	6⎭	1⎭	6⎭	0⎭	2⎭	4⎭
Unifying the Party						
Most important	3⎫ 16	19⎫ 56	10⎫ 25	9⎫ 44	8⎫ 32	8⎫ 30
Second most important	13⎭	37⎭	15⎭	35⎭	24⎭	22⎭
Third most important	19	19	27	29	34	21
Fourth most important	25⎫ 65	18⎫ 25	27⎫ 48	14⎫ 27	26⎫ 35	23⎫ 51
Least important	40⎭	7⎭	21⎭	13⎭	9⎭	28⎭
Adopting Correct Positions on National Issues						
Most important	22⎫ 56	7⎫ 27	30⎫ 74	11⎫ 42	15⎫ 52	18⎫ 49
Second most important	34⎭	20⎭	44⎭	31⎭	37⎭	31⎭
Third most important	28	47	12	30	32	31
Fourth most important	10⎫ 17	21⎫ 26	10⎫ 14	22⎫ 28	13⎫ 16	14⎫ 20
Least important	7⎭	5⎭	4⎭	6⎭	3⎭	6⎭
Reform Party						
Most important	6⎫ 25	1⎫ 5	3⎫ 18	3⎫ 7	1⎫ 6	5⎫ 18
Second most important	19⎭	4⎭	15⎭	4⎭	5⎭	13⎭
Third most important	27	12	15	21	12	22
Fourth most important	35⎫ 49	35⎫ 83	23⎫ 67	38⎫ 73	28⎫ 82	35⎫ 60
Least important	14⎭	48⎭	44⎭	35⎭	54⎭	25⎭
Nominating Deserving Candidate						
Most important	33⎫ 45	11⎫ 32	31⎫ 37	11⎫ 25	13⎫ 28	24⎫ 37
Second most important	12⎭	21⎭	6⎭	14⎭	15⎭	13⎭
Third most important	10	16	19	13	15	13
Fourth most important	12⎫ 45	17⎫ 53	21⎫ 44	17⎫ 62	27⎫ 57	15⎫ 50
Least important	33⎭	36⎭	23⎭	45⎭	30⎭	35⎭
N =	819	179	61	127	756	1435

Note: Data are from the mail questionnaires. For the question, see Table 5-1. *N*'s reflect responses to "reform the party." Other N's are comparable.

supporters of traditional Democratic liberals gave greater priority to winning than did the followers of new politics candidates, McGovern and Wallace. Slightly more than three-fifths of the Republican presidential elite and 45 percent of Democrats agreed that putting together a winning team is a convention's *most* important task, and 85 percent of Republicans and 69 percent of Democrats agreed that it had either first or second priority. Intraparty differences among Democrats were large enough to indicate clashing views of institutional function in that party. Supporters of traditional liberal Democrats, Muskie and Humphrey, put high priority on winning: 66 percent and 63 percent respectively described this as the *most* important task of a convention as compared to only 37 percent of McGovern and 20 percent of Wallace supporters. Among Democrats (but not Republicans) persons who became active in or after 1968 were substantially less concerned with winning than those who had been active longer.

The Aggregative Function: Unifying the Party

For those who want to win, achieving party unity is believed to take on special urgency. An occasional aberration, such as Truman's 1948 victory in the face of the Dixiecrat and Wallace revolts, does not alter the fact that victory in a national election normally requires the support of a unified party. This is a reason that students of politics have attached great importance to the capacity of a convention to "bind its participants into a 'we' feeling that will support joint efforts beyond the convention into the campaign."[11] There is also reason to believe that for many long-time participants party unity and consensus have value independent of their utility in winning elections.

Democratic delegates were sharply and significantly split on the importance of the aggregative function, and the divisions coincided roughly with the split between exponents of traditional politics and new politics. Few delegates saw achieving unity as the *chief* function of the conventions, but it was much more important for Humphrey delegates, over one-half of whom described this as one of the two most important functions of a convention, than for McGovern delegates, 40 percent of whom considered it the *least* important of the five functions, and two-thirds of whom considered it relatively unimportant (Table 5–2), perhaps because 85 percent already expected that their candidate would defeat Nixon (as compared to 19 percent of the supporters of Humphrey, 26 percent of Muskie delegates, and 3 percent of the Wallace delegates).[12] This finding is consistent with the impressions of many observers that McGovern delegates were unusually unconcerned with compromising differences, and with the findings of Sullivan, et al., that even after winning the nomination, many McGovern delegates seemed uninterested in rallying support-ers of defeated candidates to support the nominee.[13] Supporters of George Wallace were similarly unconcerned with forging party unity. Muskie supporters more nearly resembled Humphrey delegates in their attitudes on this subject. Republicans, for whom unity was no problem in 1972, were less concerned about party unity than the Humphrey–Muskie candidate support groups and more so than the McGovern–Wallace groups.

Democratic political generations differed in their attitudes toward the aggregative function: the post-1968 generation was more than twice as likely as those recruited earlier to be unconcerned with party unity, but the fact that this generational relationship did not hold for Republicans nor for Humphrey supporters indicates that there is no necessary ten-dency for newcomers to devalue party unity, just as the presence of some delegates with long experience who remained indifferent to achieving party unity means that experience does not *necessarily* breed apprecia-tion of the utilitarian or moral value of consensus.

The Articulation of Issues: Taking Correct Positions

Conventional lore concerning relations between winning, achieving unity, and adopting platforms suggests that controversial and divisive issues should be compromised if possible or fuzzed and swept under the rug if no compromise can be found. Both Democrat and Republican groups concerned with winning and unity gave least priority to the articu-lation of correct issue positions. The candidate support group least con-cerned with winning (Wallace) was most united in the conviction that conventions should take correct positions on issues; in this group 74 percent saw issue articulation as important, as compared with 47 percent who were similarly concerned with winning. The same relationship was reflected among Humphrey delegates, only one-fourth of whom rated the articulation of correct issue positions as one of the two most important convention functions as compared to 87 percent who gave such priority to winning. McGovern delegates were more split on the relative importance of these functions: 61 percent saw the electoral functions as important; 56 percent so ranked the articulation of correct positions on issues. Republi-cans, were also more likely to give priority to both electoral and issue articulation functions.

There were also differences between the generation that became active in 1968 and its predecessors. In both parties those who became active only during or after 1968 were more likely than others to give priority to articulating correct issue positions.

The Reward Function: Nominating a Deserving Candidate

Who is a deserving candidate? And what are the obligations of a national convention to such a man? From the perspective of an organization man, a deserving candidate would be one who had faithfully served the party and met all its requirements for apprenticeship. For an issue or style enthusiast, a deserving candidate is one whose capacity for personal or moral leadership qualifies him as party leader. In 1972 the supporters of regular candidates were less concerned than McGovern and Wallace supporters with nominating a deserving candidate and more concerned with nominating a winning candidate. There were no generational differences concerning this function; neither did party experience matter. Democrats most interested in picking a winning team and unifing the party were least concerned with selecting a deserving candidate. This pattern indicates that—for most delegates—the deserving candidate was one with outstanding personal and moral qualities, not an organizational leader.

The Self-Perfection Function: Reforming the Party

For most delegates reforming the party was the least important function of the convention. Interest was greatest among McGovern and Wallace supporters, but was low even in these groups (perhaps because of a feeling that their party had already been reformed). In both parties political experience was negatively associated with interest in party reform and youth was more likely to see it as important than were older delegates.

ROLE QUALIFICATIONS AND DEFINITIONS

Who is equipped by training, temperament, point of view, reputation, and experience to be a delegate? Views on this subject tell us a great deal about what delegates think a convention, a national party, and a presidential nominee should be. Should a national convention be a conference of state party representatives—as most of the literature of political science suggests? In this case, delegates should be persons who can represent state party organizations, party leaders who hold or have held responsible positions in state and local parties. Is a convention an assemblage of the party faithful who gather to recommit themselves to the party, to iron out differences, and to choose a candidate and plan strategy for the upcoming national election? In this case, delegates should be persons of proven devotion to the party who will represent party interests and take care to nourish party unity. Should it be a national meeting of like-minded people who gather to express their point of view and choose a standard-bearer who shares their views and will carry them to the people? If a convention is above all an arena for advocating and contesting issue positions, then delegates should above all be the persons who share the appropriate beliefs and will stand firm for them.

Most discussions of delegates to national conventions have focused on the organizational characteristics of delegates, perhaps because until recently "delegates to national conventions [have been] chosen, after all, as representatives of the several state organizations. . . ."[14] But institutional changes—notably the proliferation of primaries, the rise of nationwide preconvention campaigns that aim at voters and potential activists as well as party leaders, the prohibition of the unit rule, and Democratic reforms restricting the role of state party organizations and leaders in the nomination contests—have increased the likelihood that persons chosen as delegates may not be party leaders or "representatives" of their state parties. Corresponding changes in the political culture and in the character of presidential contests—including the declining prestige of party regulars among portions of the "political class" and the appearance of the crusading candidate (Goldwater, McCarthy, McGovern)—have further affected views about the appropriate qualifications of delegates to national conventions and the character of persons actually selected as delegates.

Delegates' views concerning delegate qualifications confirm the disagreement concerning the appropriate relation of decision makers in presidential politics to party organizations.

The norms of apprenticeship require that delegates be chosen from among persons who have been in the party long enough to have understood its institutional identity and structure, to have internalized its norms, and to have demonstrated reliable identification with these norms. The belief that conventions are (should be) national conferences of party leaders who have served such apprenticeships leads naturally to the expectation that delegates will be persons who have experience in elected public office and/or in some of the thousands of party offices from precinct leader through national committeeman. This view of national conventions is so widespread among persons who write about political conventions that it comes as something of a surprise that a minority of Republican and Democratic delegates believed it important that delegates should have held party office, and almost none thought they should necessarily have experience in public office.

Three general views of delegate qualifications were present in the Democratic Convention. There were some who thought delegates should be devoted to the party and have held party office. These comprised well under one-half of Democrats; they were most numerous in the ranks of

Humphrey supporters. A second group emphasized devotion to the party's interest but were relatively unconcerned with delegates' organizational experience. This orientation was relatively widespread among Humphrey and Muskie delegates and was present in McGovern and Wallace ranks. A third type—most numerous in Wallace and McGovern ranks—viewed past relation to party as without importance and saw support for preferred issue positions as the qualification for delegate status. From this last perspective a presidential nomination was a matter to be settled among those who cared about the policies and personalities of the presidential nominating contest. For these, commitment and activism were the qualifications for delegate status; organizational experience was irrelevant.

The third (non-organizational) view was found chiefly among Democrats and was most numerous among Wallace supporters.[15] Republican perspectives on delegate qualifications emphasized either objective or subjective attachment to party. Relatively more Republicans than Democrats thought delegates should be recruited from among party officers; virtually all Republicans believed delegates should be devoted to the party's interests.

The influence of the non-organizational orientation has increased in the last decade. Polsby and Wildavsky described the demand "for immediate access to positions of party power" as characteristic of the supporters of Eugene McCarthy in 1968.[16] McGovern–Fraser Commission member Austin Ranney said, "Most of the guidelines were consciously designed to maximize participation by persons who are enthusiasts for a particular presidential aspirant or policy *in the year of the convention*."[17] Certainly, the McGovern–Fraser reforms made it easier to translate issue and candidate enthusiasm into delegate status.

Other views of delegate qualifications were consistent with these organizational orientations. Those who emphasized party office as a qualification also generally emphasized the representation of state and local interests, and vice versa. Among McGovern supporters only 36 percent described concern for state interests as a very important qualification, as compared to 72 percent of Nixon delegates, 61 percent of Humphrey delegates, and 56 percent of Muskie supporters. Wallace delegates were more favorable to state interests and more likely than McGovern delegates to emphasize the importance of local reputation and personal attractiveness as delegate qualifications.

ROLE CONCEPTIONS

Role conceptions were tapped more directly in a question which asked, "In thinking about the decisions that will be made at the convention, which of the following factors will you favor and which will you oppose? Counting service to the party heavily in nominating candidates? . . . ," etc. through seven possible criteria for decision. For each factor, respondents were asked whether they would "strongly favor," "favor," "oppose," or "strongly oppose," or had "no opinion."

The pattern of responses can be predicted from the previous analysis. Two broad orientations were evident: one emphasized taking account of party interests in decision making; the other emphasized issue concerns and participation. The former orientations were strongest among Republicans and supporters of Humphrey and Muskie, and though concern for organization was present among McGovern and Wallace delegates, in both those candidate support groups there were substantial minorities who attached little importance to party: 41 percent of Democrats opposed attaching any importance to past party service; 48 percent opposed giving any weight to party organizational role; 43 percent favored standing firm even if it meant resigning from the party; and 36 percent opposed any compromise on the issues. Most of each type were found in the McGovern and Wallace ranks.

ROLE EXPECTATIONS AND ORGANIZATIONAL MAINTENANCE: DEMANDS AND SUPPORTS

Although widely employed for the analysis of whole systems, the systems perspective is rarely brought to bear on political parties themselves which, after all, confront fundamentally the same problems of system maintenance as any other large complex institutions. Although "the political party, at least in the United States, is a conspicuous exception to the general tendency for society to become increasingly organized, rationalized, and bureaucratized,"[18] it is nonetheless confronted with standard problems of organizational maintenance. Even though a presidential party is little more than a quadrennial meeting of persons who "coordinate their activities so as to influence the choice of candidates,"[19] it must secure the needed contributions from members, formulate purposes, and recruit and retain members and leaders.

Convention delegates are persons who speak for the national party organization. The demands they make on the party and the support they offer it are crucial to organizational maintenance. To what extent can we assume that they are committed to the preservation of the organizations in whose name they speak?

From the perspective of systems maintenance some role conceptions emphasize system *support;* others state *demands.* The requirement that delegates have worked hard for the party, made financial contributions, held party or public office, and been devoted to its organizational interests involves system support. So do the requirements that, in making decisions, delegates count service to the party and seek consensus. Those role requirements provide for the selection of delegates who have been thoroughly socialized, who have demonstrated the strength of their identification and devotion to the party, and who, in making decisions, will bear in mind their impact on party organization.

But respondents could also define the role of delegate in terms of demands on the party: notably the demand that delegates share views on policy and press these regardless of their impact on party unity. The closely related view that commitment is the only serious delegate qualification constitutes a demand that norms of apprenticeship be rejected. These expectations reflect negative or indifferent attitudes toward organizational maintenance: first, because persons with records of party service are most likely to know and care about the organization and, second, because the refusal to reward service removes a major incentive to service.

Table 5-3 reflects the distribution of demands and supports by candidate support group. It demonstrates the strong orientation to organizational support of the regulars who comprised the Republican party's presidential elite and the higher level of demands than supports characteristic of the McGovern and Wallace groups. These differences between McGovern and Wallace delegates on the one hand and supporters of "mainstream" candidates, Humphrey, Muskie and Nixon, on the other, are important indicators that organizational attitudes may be as important as ideology in distinguishing between traditional and new types of political actors. Sharp generational differences are also revealed.

A factor analysis of role expectations of Democrats confirms the presence of two major dimensions: one dimension, which I term the "Organizational Support Index," measures orientations to organizational maintenance and takes no account of ideology or policy. The second dimension relates to the adoption of policies and takes no account of organizational maintenance. Two measures are required, because in this delegate population (as in the case of Hofstetter's activists in Columbus, Ohio)[20] individual role sets cannot necessarily be organized along a single dimension. Some delegates whose incentives and role conceptions emphasize organizational supports also emphasize the policy-maker role. Others who are greatly concerned with policy have anti-organizational attitudes. Still others are chiefly oriented to organizational maintenance and are less concerned with policy concern. Democrats were more likely than Republicans to react to issue and organizational concerns as a single dimension; Republicans were much more likely than Democrats to react to policy and party as unrelated dimensions.

Table 5-3. Demands and Supports by Party, Candidate Preference, and Political Generations

	Party		Candidate Preference					Political Generations			
	Dems.	Reps.	McGovern	Humphrey	Wallace	Muskie	Nixon	Pre-1945	1946–1959	1960–1967	1968–1972
Supports											
Select a winning team[a]	69	85	61	87	47	86	85	77	81	77	58
Unify the party[a]	30	31	16	56	25	44	32	39	36	28	21
Works hard for party[b]	81	97	75	93	73	93	97	91	92	89	72
Contributes financially to party[b]	27	42	16	49	37	36	42	46	38	31	16
Held or ran for public office[b]	19	28	17	22	27	27	28	35	28	18	15
Held party office[b]	19	45	14	28	18	29	45	39	34	29	13
Well-known in local community[b]	70	71	65	78	72	74	71	87	73	67	62
Will represent best interests of party[b]	86	98	81	98	81	94	98	96	93	92	80
Counting service to party heavily in decision[c]	59	90	45	86	54	82	90	84	79	72	47
Working to minimize disagreement[c]	93	97	91	98	95	98	97	96	96	95	90
Playing down issues to win[c]	64	70	64	75	32	68	70	67	69	68	59
Demands											
Articulate issues[a]	49	53	56	27	74	42	52	45	46	52	56
Reform the party[a]	18	7	25	5	18	7	6	10	9	14	24
Nominate deserving candidate[d]	37	28	45	32	37	25	28	36	31	30	42
Strong policy views[b]	82	70	89	68	91	66	69	76	73	79	85
Standing firm even if it means resigning[c]	43	29	54	16	71	17	28	38	30	36	52
Minimizing role of party organization in nomination[c]	52	19	66	29	64	27	19	35	30	39	63
Selecting a nominee strongly committed on issues[c]	95	95	99	88	97	93	95	94	94	96	97
N[d] =	1382	705	808	166	49	125	678	212	637	701	490
Overall support score[e]	56	69	50	70	51	67	69	69	65	61	48
Overall demand score[f]	54	43	62	38	65	40	42	48	45	49	60
Demand-support average[g]	+2	+26	–12	+32	–14	+27	+27	+21	+20	+12	–12

[a] The percentages for these variables represent those in each category who regarded this institutional role perception as first or second in importance.

[b] The percentages for these variables represent those in each category who regarded each delegate-role-qualification as "very important" or "somewhat important."

[c] The percentages for these variables represent those in each category who regarded each role definition in convention decision making.

[d] The N's presented here are those for the "selection of a winning team." Other N's are comparable in size. These data are from the mail questionnaires.

[e] The Overall support score is simply the average percentage of delegates in support positions.

[f] The Overall demand score is simply the average percentage of delegates in demand positions.

[g] The Demand-support average is the overall demand score subtracted from the overall support score. A positive number here means supports exceed demands; a negative number, demands exceed supports.

THE ORGANIZATIONAL SUPPORT INDEX

The Organizational Support Index combines an incentive (desire to support party) as a motive for political participation with views on delegate qualification (service to party and dedication to party interests) and role defi1 ition (taking account of service to party in making convention decisions, working to minimize disagreement, and taking account of party organizational roles). In combination these items comprise a measure of broad orientation to party organization that is suitable for either Republicans or Democrats.[21] This index is unidimensional, internally homogeneous, and discriminates among known groups. It can be used to continue the exploration of generalized orientations to party organization that was pioneered by Wilson, and Polsby and Wildavsky, and continued by Soule and Clarke, Semel, Roback, and others.[22] Note, however, that the Organizational Support Index is not identical with Wilson's Amateur/ Professional types nor with the measures utilized by Hofstetter, Soule and Clarke, and others.[23] As compared to most of these, the Organizational Support Index focuses more explicitly on organizational demands and supports; it is less concerned with internal democracy and more concerned with organizational supports, such as rewarding the faithful, emphasizing party service, and seeking party unity. I have declined to term this an index of "professionalism" because so few of the high scorers are "professionals" within the ordinary meaning of the term: they are not attracted to politics by the hope of material gain, nor are they remunerated for their work, and they do not work at politics "full-time" in the manner of paid precinct captains in urban machines or of British election agents. They are volunteers for whom politics is an avocation. However many attitudes a person who works full-time at politics may share with a volunteer, there remain some important differences between their situations, differences of a type likely to influence their perspectives. The authentic professional who pursues politics for a living and is tied to the organization by material as well as other interests has a more tangible personal stake in political outcomes than anyone except the public officeholder; furthermore, he is likely to have longer and more intensive experience and, in consequence, to be more knowledgeable and more skilled. Full-time, paid professionals feel the impact of organizational gains and losses more personally, more directly, more tangibly, and more certainly than do volunteers whose ties are subjective and for whom the personal impact of organizational misfortunes can be obviated by changing the focus of attention and withdrawing affect. Differences between an activist attached to party for material reasons and a genuine professional for whom politics is a vocation rather than avocation are closely related to the differences between organizations that rely on material incentives and those that rely on solidary incentives to attract and hold members.

Because solidary organizations have characteristics quite different from those maintained by material rewards, it seems desirable to adopt a terminology that clearly distinguishes between paid political professionals or persons attracted to politics by material incentives, on the one hand, and volunteers attached to organizations by identification and personal ties, on the other. Both *may* share similar role expectations and offer equally high levels of organizational support. But this is an appropriate subject for investigation, not assumption.

In "Incentive Systems: A Theory of Organizations,"[24] Clarke and Wilson discuss some differences between solidary organizations and "utilitarian organizations," which rely largely on material incentives. Utilitarian organizations (which are peopled with *real* professionals) are characterized by clarity concerning benefits, low attention to substantive goals, high flexibility concerning activities, and conflict resolution through bargaining. Solidary organizations (which are peopled with volunteers) offer diffuse general benefits, pay more attention to substantive purposes (which must be nondivisive), usually cultivate opportunities for enhancing members' prestige, have less flexibility in changing organizational goals and tactics, have a high turnover of leadership, low continuity, and less experienced elites, and are more subject to conflicts concerning status.[25]

Solidary organizations not only feature but *require* a high level of group agreement. Clarke and Wilson note "First and foremost, they must be noncontroversial, since solidary benefits are weakened by any risk that the goal of the association might divide the membership or impair its prestige."[26] Divisions, for example on issues, are especially dangerous to solidary organizations. Such divisions are not only hostile to the maintenance of organizational identifications, but they are *especially repellent* to persons for whom solidary values are important. Persons to whom the satisfactions of group solidarity, fellowship, and good feeling are incentives to political action will find rifts and schisms particularly distasteful, just as participants preoccupied with issues and ideologies will be sensitive to diversion of collective attention and energy from rectitude goals to any others including organizational maintenance and fun and games.

INSTITUTIONAL PRESERVERS AND INSTITUTIONAL TRANSFORMERS

In *Political Organizations,* Wilson argued ". . . that many persons active in politics and policy-making, in and out of government, are persons speaking for, or acting as part of, formal organizations and that the constraints and requirements imposed by their organizational roles are of great significance in explaining their behavior."[27] High scorers on the Organizational Support Index (Table 5-4) are such people. They not only identify with their party, they also define their role as guardian of the institution. For this reason it is reasonable to term these high scorers "institutional preservers" understanding that we mean by that concern with preservation of the parties as *organizations*. Low scorers (Table 5-4) can be reasonably termed "institutional transformers" with the understanding that we intend by this nomenclature indifference or hostility to the preservation of the parties as they have in fact existed. Institutional preservers defined their roles as offering *support* to the organized party; institutional transformers were, at best, indifferent to organizational support and held goals that frequently threatened party organizations. Some institutional preservers (especially Republicans) were also policy makers, that is, they also defined their role of delegate in terms of advocacy and promotion of particular policies. (See Table 5-5.) Many policy makers were institutional transformers rather than preservers. These were most numerous in McGovern and Wallace ranks. (See Figure 5-1.)

The presence of non-organization men and women at the 1972 Democratic Convention was emphasized by most observers of that convention. Theodore White, for one, contrasted the "McGovern Army" with the regulars in his discussion of "the discontinuity, the rupture of past from present."[28] George McGovern himself emphasized his separation from the party's leadership with references to "old established politicians" and "the establishment." The reformed Democratic rules embodied a reform conception of party organization; the delegate envisioned by these rules was not necessarily distinguished by service to the local party. When it "opened" the party to people whose only necessary qualification was activity in the year of the convention, the reformed rules paved the way for the admission into the convention of large numbers of persons unconcerned with organizational maintenance, and, in fact, Table 5-4 shows that *more than two-fifths of Democratic delegates were unconcerned with or opposed to giving weight to organizational maintenance.* Most but not all of these were found among McGovern's supporters (63 percent of whom were low scorers on the Organizational Support Index) or Wallace supporters (50 percent of whom were low scorers). They were present in much smaller numbers among Republicans and the supporters of traditional Democratic candidates Humphrey and Muskie, of whom they comprised 9 percent, 13 percent, and 18 percent respectively. The fact that substantial percentages of McGovern and Wallace delegates scored high on this institutional support measure demonstrates that these groups were not simply charismatic communities organized around a leader with an issue but

Table 5-4. Organizational Support by Party, Candidate Preference, Political Generations (%)

| | Party | | Candidate Preference | | | | | Political Generation | | | |
	Dems.	Reps.	McGovern	Humphrey	Wallace	Muskie	Nixon	Pre-1945	1946–1959	1960–1967	1968–1972
Very low	20	1	31	1	26	2	1	5	6	11	32
Low	24	8	32	12	24	16	7	10	13	18	30
High	31	34	27	31	29	36	33	32	35	32	27
Very high	26	58	10	56	21	46	59	53	46	39	12
N =	1113	670	617	159	38	105	648	236	580	567	362

Relationships: Party, V = 0.41; political generation, gamma = –0.41.

NOTE: These data are from the mail questionnaire sample. For a complete explanation of this index, see Appendix C.

Table 5-5. Policy Orientations by Party, Candidate Preference, and Political Generations (%)

	All Delegates	Party		Candidate Preference					Political Generation			
		Dems.	Reps.	McGovern	Humphrey	Wallace	Muskie	Nixon	Pre-1945	1946–1959	1960–1967	1968–1972
Very low	3	3	5	1	5	0	6	5	4	4	3	3
Low	26	21	38	10	41	17	43	39	24	32	26	17
High	44	43	47	44	48	35	44	47	48	44	45	42
Very high	26	34	11	46	5	48	8	10	24	20	25	38
N =	1865	1271	594	755	150	48	101	573	217	569	603	439

Measures of association for this table are: party, V = 0.26; political generations, gamma = 0.17.

NOTE: Data are from the mail questionnaire sample.

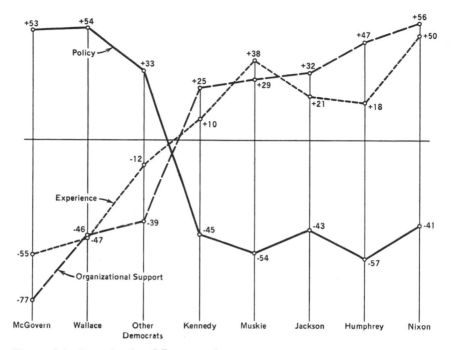

Figure 5-1. Organizational Support, Political Experience, and Policy Orientation by Candidate Preference: Z-scores

included significant numbers of men and women with a concern for the party. However, when we differentiate among *levels* of concern, the relative unconcern of McGovern and Wallace delegates is still more sharply revealed. Ten percent of McGovernites, 21 percent of Wallacites, 56 percent of Humphrey delegates, 46 percent of Muskie supporters, and 59 percent of Nixon delegates scored very high on the Organizational Support Index.

EXPERIENCE AND ORGANIZATIONAL MAINTENANCE

The pattern of candidate support scores on the Organizational Support Index establishes that substantial numbers of persons without a strong commitment to the Democratic party had found their way into decision-making roles by way of the McGovern and Wallace movements and that such attitudes were virtually absent at the Republican Convention. Since these are also the groups with least political experience, it is reasonable to ask whether concern with organizational maintenance is a function of experience, and a still more interesting question: is *un*concern with organizational maintenance compatible with extended experience? Wilson notes the high turnover of amateur activists[29] and discusses the special problems of "institutionalizing" the amateur's spirit so that amateurs will continue to be active "beyond the initial assault on the system."[30] He notes that "Many, but not all, of the amateurs with long experience and personal stakes in politics acquire the habits and motives of the professional." History, he says, suggests that "Eventually, the amateur either loses interest or becomes a professional and plays the game by professional rules."[31] He notes the existence of pseudo-amateurs whose rhetoric is that of the amateur, but whose practice marks him as a professional and whose organizational concerns and skills hold the group together.

Bowman, Ippolito, and Donaldson also found that the level of party loyalty was an important determinant of continued political activity. Persons without a strong attachment to party were more likely to drop out than those strongly oriented to party.[32] And Eldersveld commented, "Especially noticeable is the large number of idealistic recent joiners who became disillusioned."[33] But Semel reported that "purposive sustaining motivations remained predominant" in the New Democratic Coalition members she studied.[34] Note, however, that the activists she studied were relative newcomers to politcs.

In considering this problem a distinction should probably be made between organizational skills and organizational commitments. It may be that the pseudo-amateurs observed by Wilson had the skills but not the commitment associated with the professional, just as some may have a material interest in a party without feeling either identification or commitment. But although prolonged association with an institution is theoretically compatible with continuing indifference to its well-being, most previous investigation indicates that persons who have remained politically active for a long time usually have developed an identification with their party and a concern with its well-being.[35] Such a relationship between experience and solidarity holds among Democratic delegates (r .42) but is much weaker among Republicans (r .22).[36] However, while the quantity and quality of political experience are associated with attitudes to organizational maintenance, the relationship is neither necessary nor uniform. One-fourth of the Democrats who became active before 1960 score low on the Organizational Support Index, as do 13 percent of those who became active before the end of World War II, and 40 percent of Democrats who became active during or after 1968 scored in the high half of this index.[37] Although the general relationship between political experience and organizational support is weaker among Republicans than Democrats, Republicans who became active after 1967 were also least likely to score very high on organizational support and most likely to score low.

SOCIALIZATION AND ORGANIZATIONAL SUPPORT

Political experience is the previous experience that is most directly relevant to organizational orientations, but there are other antecedent life experiences that can have an impact on the kind of attachment a person develops to the political organizations with which he is associated. Age, place of origin, education, income, ethnic characteristics, length of time in his community, and parents' political activity have been found by one or more previous investigations to be related to attitudes to party. Wilson and Epstein noted that reformers tended to be young, college educated, and residents of large cities or suburbs and have relatively high incomes. They also reported that reformers were more likely than professionals to be newcomers to their place of residence.[38] Hofstetter also found fairly strong correlations between age, education, and organizational orientations.[39] Soule and Clarke also found correlations between age and "amateurism" but little relation between organizational orientations and education or income.[40] They also reported that professionals were more likely than amateurs to have developed political interests early in life and to come from families who were also interested in politics.[41]

Some of these associations between antecedent influences and organizational orientations were found among delegates to the Democratic Convention, but no such relations were found among Republicans. Democrats who scored high on the Organizational Support Index were more likely than others to have been born in small towns or rural areas, to have longer periods of residence in their local community, and to belong to multiple local organizations. Even among Democrats, however, there was almost no association between education, income, and parental activities, on the one hand, and organizational support scores, on the other. And among Republicans there was no relation between these social factors and organizational orientations. The fact that place of origin, geographical mobility, age, income, and integration into local community were unrelated to Republican attitudes toward party underscores the fact that weak party attachment is not a necessary psychological attribute of geographical mobility, or age, or education, or place of origin, or community integration. Once it is clear that weak party attachment is not a necessary concomitant of living in a city or suburb, or moving about, or having gone to college, it becomes clear that the Democrats among whom these characteristics coexist are not a necessary product of history but a particular political type or types who no more reflect "contemporary reality" or the wave of the future than do others who share social attributes characteristic of the contemporary scene (e.g., social and geographical mobility) but have quite different attitudes toward political parties. Finally, the absence of expected relations between social and political characteristics among Republicans is a reminder of the extent to which conceptions of the contemporary political scene are based on the study of Democrats—and especially of the liberal wing of that party.[42] Polsby and Wildavsky and Epstein have pointed to differences as well as similarities between the Goldwater phenomenon and the McCarthy and McGovern movements—the most important of these differences being that Goldwater enjoyed the support of Republican regulars while McCarthy and McGovern drew an important part of their strength from outside the ranks of the regular party.[43] Apparently, Goldwater "purism" was not accompanied by anti-organizational attitudes. Failure of political scientists to study Republicans and Democrats in more detail may have resulted in an inadequately differentiated map of the contemporary political world.

IDEOLOGY AND ORGANIZATIONAL SUPPORT

The fact that reform politics has frequently featured liberal ideology and anti-organization emphasis has suggested to some observers that there may be an intrinsic and predictable connection between ideology and organizational maintenance. The additional fact that some contemporary liberals reject other traditional group loyalties—school, locality, state, nation—strengthens the impression that some process of de-identification with traditional groups and organizations is an aspect of one strain of contemporary liberalism.[44] However, similar indifference to party loyalty is displayed by some conservative groups and leaders. In 1968 and 1972 threats of walking out were frequently heard among leaders and followers of the McCarthy and McGovern movements, but in 1968 it was George Wallace and his followers who actually established a third presidential party, and in 1974–1975, third and fourth party talk was most frequently heard on the right—among conservative Republicans dissatisfied with Ford's leadership and among Wallace and his lieutenants, who do not preclude the possibility that if Wallace is denied a place on the Democratic ticket he will again run as a third party candidate.

Wilson argued that there was no substantive relation between amateur and professional orientations and either liberalism or conservatism but that there might be such a relationship between these and ideological extremism,[45] and an analysis of the relation between motives of delegates and their ideological positions reveals that extreme ideological views were most common among persons who had little concern for party. The relation between ideological and organizational style is more definitively established by analysis of the ideologies of delegates with differing role conceptions. Democrats who classified themselves as either very liberal or very conservative were more likely than moderates to score low on the Organizational Support Index (r .38); 73 percent of the self-described "radicals" scored low on organizational support as compared to 51 percent of the "somewhat liberal," 11 percent of the "moderates," 16 percent of the "somewhat conservative," and 43 percent of the "very conservative." Relations between ideological and organizational orientations are weaker among Republicans (r .21), almost all of whom were committed to organizational support.

A second dimension of ideological style was also related to organizational maintenance: Democrats with comprehensive, internally consistent ideologies were less likely than those with more eclectic issue orientations to score high on the Organizational Support Index (r .33);[46] delegates with more extreme issue positions were also less inclined toward organizational support.

Substantive political attitudes were still more strongly related to organizational maintenance. Among Democrats the correlation between cultural conservatism and attitudes toward organizational maintenance is r .51 and attitudes toward "sanctions" and organizational support is r .46. As always, relations were weaker among Republicans (r .30 and r .23 respectively). In both parties cultural liberals were less concerned than cultural conservatives with organizational maintenance, and persons hostile to the use of force as an instrument of social policy were less likely than others to define the delegate's role in terms of institutional maintenance. These relations between ideology and party conform to the popular impression that persons of intense, relatively extreme ideological persuasion were less likely than moderates to take personal responsibility for the well-being of their party. Apparently those who entered politics to express fairly specific, fairly extreme issue orientations did not see their goals as linked in an enduring way to the strength of a party, or else they did not perceive a party as an organization that requires a continuing flow of supports.

ORGANIZATIONAL SUPPORT AND OTHER ATTITUDES

The significance of attitudes toward organizational maintenance is enhanced by its relation to other aspects of role conception, style, and behavior. High scorers on the Organizational Support Index were more likely to believe a convention should give priority to picking a winner and achieving party unity (relations are r .39 and r .36 respectively) and less likely to give priority to party reform and issue articulation (r −.36 and r −.28 respectively). Among Republicans who were much more united in their concern for party preservation, the relations between organizational support scores and convention functions were weaker but all in the same direction.

Some other motives of participants (besides the desire to support the party) were also associated with attitudes to organizational maintenance. In both parties status incentives were positively related to organizational support scores (r .38 for Democrats and r .28 for Republicans); so were "social" incentives (r .23 for Democrats and r .24 for Republicans). These findings are consistent with those of Eldersveld who emphasized the importance of social and status satisfactions to the "regulars" in both parties;[47] Conway and Feigert reported that in both suburban counties studied by them social contacts were apparently the most important single incentive to continued (as contrasted with initial) involvement;[48] and Semel found that among the New Jersey Democrats she studied "the regular is sustained by sociable rewards to a much greater extent than is the reformer."[49] They are also consistent with Wilson's views concerning the relationship between organizational and personal loyalties.[50] The pattern seems to be reasonably clear: in contemporary American politics organizational identification and concern for organizational maintenance are linked to particular people, to sociality, and to enjoyment of esteem and recognition.[51] For persons most attached to party, it remains true that "A party is a social group, and the personal motivational relationship in the party is basically the same, apparently, as in other social groups."[52]

Most interesting theoretically were the negative relations among Democrats of role conceptions that emphasized organizational maintenance and role definitions that emphasized policy making (r −.42). While most delegates had some interest in both party and policy, no candidate support group was equally concerned with both these dimensions. Those who saw the delegate as policy maker and the party as a policy vehicle were most numerous in those candidate support groups with least concern for organizational support.

Almost one-half of McGovern and Wallace supporters scored very high on the Policy-Maker Index, but fewer than one-half as many scored as high on the Organizational Support Index. Conversely, while over one-half of Humphrey and Nixon delegates scored very high on the Organizational Support Index, no more than 10 percent of these groups scored as high on the Policy-Maker Index. Even among Republicans, relatively few delegates gave equal importance to both functions. Figures 5–1 and 5–3 graphically depict these negative associations. And Figure 5–2 shows that opposition between policy concerns and organizational support was strongest among persons with least political experience, especially among those who became active after 1967. The negative relation between these two types of role conception indicates that for many Democrats commitment to building an ideological party was not accompanied by an equally strong commitment to strengthening the party organization.

CO-RELATIONAL TYPES[53]

Role conceptions do not exist in the abstract; they are held by people who have many other attributes. As part of the effort to identify the personal and social characteristics of the institutional preserver and the institutional transformer, profiles were constructed that depicted the personal and social characteristics that might have played a role in shaping and/or preserving orientations to political organization. To achieve

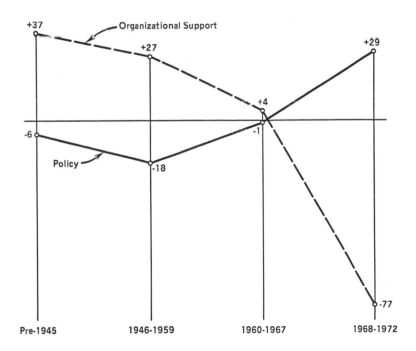

Figure 5-2. Organizational Support and Policy Orientation by Political Generation: Z-scores

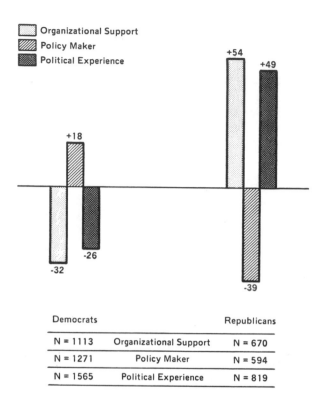

Figure 5-3. Organizational Support, Political Experience and Policy Maker by
Party: Z-scores

maximum clarity concerning these relations, only "pure" types were considered: the institutional preservers whose characteristics are described are those who scored in the highest quartile of the Organizational Support Index; the institutional transformers are those who scored in the lowest quartile. Institutional preservers comprise 38 percent of the total sample ($n = 672$); institutional transformers comprise 13 percent ($n = 229$).

As already indicated, institutional preservers were very likely to be Republicans or supporters of the traditional Democratic candidates (Humphrey, Muskie, or Jackson).[54] Almost all the institutional transformers were McGovern supporters. (While Wallacites were likely to score low on the Organizational Support Index, few scored in the lowest quartile.)

The institutional preserver was more likely to have been born in a small town or rural area, to be at least 40, and to be a Protestant or Catholic and had probably lived for at least ten years in his present community and belonged to at least three local organizations. Politically, the institutional preserver was a regular who became active before 1968 and had held at least two, and probably more than three, party offices. Most of the time he voted a straight ticket. Though he was not unconcerned with issues, he saw the principal jobs of the convention as picking a winner and achieving party unity, and particularly if he was a Democrat, he was unlikely to define the delegate's role principally in terms of issues. Delegates, he believed, should be people who had held party office and who enjoyed a good local reputation. For the institutional preserver, reforming the party had lower priority than electoral and organizational functions. Ideologically, he was very likely to be a moderate, liberal, or conservative, whose political opinions were relatively eclectic and did not comprise a comprehensive, internally consistent ideology. On cultural matters the institutional preserver was likely to be relatively conservative: to believe that the use of force is sometimes necessary to protect society and to take a dim view of those who deny the legitimacy of the society's basic institutions; to prefer the policeman to the militant, the military to the demonstrator. The institutional preserver was also relatively (but not very) conservative on relations between the sexes: he (or she) probably believed that there are innate sex differences that are relevant to politics, denied that women have suffered much discrimination in politics, and emphasized the political clout women have through auxiliary roles. In sum, though the institutional preserver might have been a liberal Democrat dedicated to welfare state economics and social policies, he or she was relatively conservative on basic cultural and social questions.

The institutional transformer was more likely to be under 40, to have grown up in an urban or suburban setting, and to be Jewish, atheist, or agnostic. He was probably a relative newcomer to his community and belonged to few local groups; his parents were probably not active in politics. Most institutional transformers had relatively little experience in politics: most became active after 1967, many had held no party offices, and few had held more than one office—and that at the local level. And they were unlikely to vote a straight ticket. For them, the essence of politics was policy: the primary requirement of a delegate was that he have strong policy views; the primary job of the convention was to articulate clear, correct issue positions. Doing this had higher priority for the institutional transformer than the electoral functions, and he was less concerned than the institutional preserver with socializing and the excitement of politics.

In 1972, most institutional transformers were "very liberal" or "radical" in political views. For the institutional transformer both the legitimacy and the virtue of society's social and cultural organization were in doubt; he probably had more sympathy for the demonstrator who challenged existing patterns than for the cop who defended them. In international affairs he was pro-United Nations, pro-philanthropy, and anti-military. Sex roles as well as party institutions seemed to him (or her) in clear need of reform to end discrimination against women, and he (or she) was convinced that women's inferior roles reflect the prejudices of society not the laws of nature.

Attitudes toward parties then were part of larger attitude syndromes. One syndrome was basically supportive of existing social and political institutions; the other was oriented to basic changes. The institutional preserver accepts organizational maintenance as his task; the institutional transformer is less concerned with protecting either the party or the other institutions of the society than with perfecting them. On issues as superficially diverse as crime, welfare, police, the military, the institutional preserver favored preservation of existing arrangements, and the transformer opposed policies oriented to preservation.

The differences between these two types were above all differences in beliefs and values. In many other ways they resemble one another closely. There are roughly equal numbers of women and men in each group. Social class composition was very similar; both groups were middle class, though the institutional preservers had somewhat higher incomes. Compared to most people, both types were well-educated, though the institutional transformer may have had a bit more schooling. In personality, both were confident, decisive, but the institutional transformer was probably somewhat less competitive, less orderly, and more given to subjective explorations.[55]

CONCLUSIONS

A good deal has been written about divisive issues in the politics of 1972. The issues that are normally described as distinguishing different political groups are public policy questions—busing, war, crime, inflation, unemployment. This analysis demonstrates that activists in the politics of 1972 were also divided in their attitudes to political organization.[56] The extent to which a delegate did or did not see himself as having responsibility for the preservation of his party was perhaps the most important factor that distinguished supporters of traditional candidates and politics as usual from the delegates representing the new candidates—McGovern and Wallace. To the extent that these attitudes toward the parties persist, it seems clear that the fissiparous tendencies already apparent in the Democratic party will be accelerated.

Democratic disagreements on public issues will be exacerbated both by disagreement about what a party should be, by what its decision makers should do, and by the lack of organizational loyalties of some parties to the debate.

Despite a popular impression to the contrary, it seems clear that strong party identification is not simply a function of agreement with a party's platform. If this were the case, then party identifications would not survive for decades, often for generations, through changing problems and changing party platforms. Research on socialization indicates that party identification antedates any clear notion of where a party stands on particular issues and often persists in spite of disagreement with a party's position and candidates. Identification serves as the basis of diffuse, as compared to specific, support. Agreement with a party's platform serves as ground for specific support. But specific support provides no basis for concern for the long-term well-being of the organization. Loyalty to party modifies the impact of disagreements on specific issues. It provides a context of shared identification and common interest (in the welfare of the party) within which conflicting interests and perspectives can be reconciled or compromised. If a party's decision makers and activists do not feel an attachment to that party that transcends a particular election or issue, an important incentive to compromise will be removed.

A second powerful incentive to compromise is the desire to win elections. Most observers agree that the desire to win stimulates parties' efforts to broaden their coalitions (by accommodating as many interests and perspectives as possible), to harmonize their differences, and to seek candidates and platforms acceptable to voters. This process of aggregation, accommodation, and conflict resolution is carried out by party elites of whom delegates to national conventions are an important component. The presence of substantial numbers of delegates who do and do not give winning elections high priority will surely precipitate bitter controversy concerning priorities and increase the likelihood that decisions will be made that make winning harder rather than easier.

But the most direct impact of decision makers with a negative attitude toward organizational support will be on the organization itself. An organization based largely on non-material, intangible collective benefits is difficult to maintain at best. One held together by a shared "cause" has a still more tenuous existence. The dramatic decline in the importance and prestige of material benefits has already left American parties heavily dependent on solidary and ideological incentives. If solidary incentives also decline in importance and prestige, only ideology and personality are left as bases of organization. "Movements" based on principle and personality, such as the McCarthy, McGovern, or Wallace movements have the flavor of redemptive organizations, value spontaneity, and resist institutionalization. They may be early examples of a politics in which high issue concern is linked with low organizational support. The similarities in the attitudes toward organization of McGovern and Wallace supporters are the more striking given their intense disagreement on all substantive issues. The facts that younger delegates, less experienced delegates, and those associated with the McGovern and Wallace movements scored lowest on organizational support and that older, more experienced delegates who supported conventional candidates (Nixon appeared to be a conventional candidate) scored highest on these qualities suggest a trend away from domination of the presidential parties by activists who provide the parties with strong, diffuse support.

The fact that Democrats most likely to define their roles in terms of policy were also most negative in their attitudes to organizational support strongly argues that these issue enthusiasts are not the harbingers of responsible parties of the British types. Although they are "not the centralized, highly integrated, tightly disciplined, and hierarchically organized structures described in the standard political science textbooks,"[57] British parties are characterized not only by policy concern but also by relatively strong, relatively bureaucratic party organizations and by a type of party governance that vests control in the party's leaders, officeholders, and organization men. There are no primaries that deprive the party organization of control of the nominating process, no "timeliness" rules that prevent the participation of persons elected before a given calendar year in a national convention, no barring of ex-officio leaders, and no doctrine of "openness" that juxtaposes leadership and organization on the one hand and democracy on the other. And there are paid professional election agents in most constituencies who "view organization building and maintenance as the most important function they perform. . . ."[58]

It is possible, of course, that absence of concern for organizational maintenance among Wallace and McGovern Democrats says little about attitudes toward organization per se and is merely a reflection of the estrangement of these delegates from the existing Democratic organization. But such an interpretation rests on a purely instrumental conception of party identifications, and, as indicated, a purely instrumental view does not square with what we know about the acquisition and durability of party identification. It also could not explain why defeat of their preferred candidates did not result in a comparable withdrawal of organizational support among the supporters of Humphrey, Muskie, and Jackson.

The alternative explanation, that presidential parties are in transition, is more consistent with what we think we know about parties. The supporters of traditional candidates displayed the attitudes that the textbooks describe as characteristic of American political activists—intense concern for winning, achieving unity, party loyalty, and rewarding the faithful. These attitudes were significantly less common among the young, the inexperienced, and the supporters of the movement style of personalist/ ideological candidates. The most straightforward interpretation of this configuration would seem to be that in 1972 we were moving away from a traditional organizational style toward one featuring parties that are less permanent, less broadly based, and less oriented to winning.

NOTES

1. James Q. Wilson, *Political Organizations* (New York: Basic Books, 1973), p. 95.
2. Chester I. Barnard, *The Functions of the Executive* (Cambridge, Mass.: Harvard University Press, 1938).
3. Wilson, *Political Organizations,* p. 27.
4. Note that delegates do not personally suffer or profit from their decisions, nor are they held accountable for them. For further discussion of this unusual relationship among delegates, those who choose them, and voters in their districts, see Chapter 9.
5. Nelson W. Polsby and Aaron Wildavsky, *Presidential Elections, Strategies of American Electoral Politics,* 3rd ed. (New York: Charles Scribner's Sons, 1971), p. 124, emphasizes this point.
6. The tendency of expectations to acquire intrinsic value for those who hold them is an interesting example of the relations between "is" and "ought."
7. Polsby and Wildavsky, *Presidential Elections,* p. 116.
8. Ibid., p. 122.
9. V. O. Key, *Politics, Parties and Pressure Groups,* 5th ed. (New York: Thomas Y. Crowell, 1964), p. 425.
10. Judson L. James, *American Political Parties in Transition* (New York: Harper and Row, 1974), p. 111. James's account of the conventions emphasizes coalition building.
11. Ibid., p. 112.
12. McGovern strategists' belief that he could win by uniting an "army of the alienated" was a counterpart to the Goldwater team's belief that a "hidden conservative majority" would give them victory.
13. Denis G. Sullivan, Jeffrey L. Pressman, Benjamin I. Page, and John J. Lyons, *The Politics of Representation: The Democratic Convention of 1972* (New York: St. Martin's Press, 1974); James, *American Political Parties,* exaggerates the McGovern team's interest in coalition building in his description of the Illinois challenge and the Democratic platform, pp. 120-122. Note that the data of Sullivan, et al., indicate relatively little interest in achieving party unity among McGovern ranks.
14. Polsby and Wildansky, *Presidential Elections,* p. 124.
15. It is generally agreed that the Goldwater movement constituted a triumph of grass roots Republican organization leaders. Leon D. Epstein demonstrates the greater affinity of organizational Republicans for Goldwater in Wisconsin than of Democrats for McGovern. "Who Voted for McGovern: The Wisconsin Case," *American Political Quarterly* 1 (1973): 465-478.
16. Polsby and Wildavsky, *Presidential Elections,* pp. 43-45.
17. Austin Ranney, *Curing the Mischiefs of Faction: Party Reform in America* (Berkeley: University of California Press, 1975), p. 153 (his emphasis). The "timeliness" requirement, the diminution of leaders' roles in slate making and elsewhere all had the effect of enhancing the opportunities of persons outside the leadership corps of local parties.
18. Wilson, *Political Organizations,* p. 95.
19. Ibid., pp. 95-96.
20. These dimensions are similar to those identified by Hofstetter in his interesting study of political activists in Columbus, Ohio. C. Richard Hofstetter, "The Amateur Politician: A Problem in Construct Validation," *Midwest Journal of Political Science* 15 (1971): 31-56. I might add that this study is not intended as an exercise in construct validation. The possibilities that a changing political elite will have subsections with different characteristics seems too great to suggest that a construct, developed to describe a

segment of the mid-elite more than a decade ago, can be invalidated because it fails to describe a national elite in 1972.

21. Certain items were omitted which were part of this dimension when the factor analysis was limited to Democrats or expanded to include the entire delegate population, but which were not suitable for use with Republicans, nor with certain Democratic subgroups. Attitude toward party reform is an example: while it was positively and fairly strongly associated with attitudes to organization by most Democratic delegates, notably McGovern delegates, it had a different meaning in the Republican context and was differently related to other organizational attitudes.

22. James Q. Wilson, *The Amateur Democrat: Club Politics in Three Cities* (Chicago: University of Chicago Press, 1962); also John W. Soule and James W. Clarke, "Amateurs and Professionals: A Study of Delegates to the 1968 Democratic National Convention," *American Political Science Review* 64 (1970): 888-898. Hofstetter, "Amateur Politician"; Dan Nimmo and Robert L. Savage, "The Amateur Democrat Revisited," *Polity* 5 (1972): 268-276. Vicki G. Semel, "Ideology and Incentives among Democratic Amateurs and Professionals" (Paper prepared for delivery at the annual meeting of the American Political Science Association, New Orleans, La., September 4-8, 1973); also Polsby and Wildavsky, *Presidential Elections*, esp. pp. 35-59. Also E. Gene De Felice, "Pre-Convention Politics: The Surge of Amateur Delegates from Illinois, 1972" (Paper delivered at the annual meeting of the American Political Science Association, Washington, D.C., September 5-9, 1972); Thomas Roback, "Amateurs and Professionals Among 1972 Republican National Convention Delegates" (Paper delivered at the annual meeting of the American Political Science Association, New Orleans, La., September 4-8, 1973).

23. It should be noted that these are also not identical with one another. Hofstetter's scale, "Amateur Politician," p. 36, for example, emphasizes internal party procedures more heavily than Soule and Clarke, "Amateurs and Professionals," p. 890.

24. Peter B. Clarke and James Q. Wilson, "Incentive Systems: A Theory of Organizations," *Administrative Science Quarterly* 6 (1961): 138-146.

25. Ibid. Also Wilson, *Political Organizations*, esp. pp. 30-55. Also Wilson, *Amateur Democrat*, pp. 315-316; Barnard, *Functions of the Executive;* Mancur Olson, *The Logic of Collective Action: Public Goods and the Theory of Groups* (New York: Schocken Books, 1968).

26. Clarke and Wilson, "Incentive Systems," p. 142.

27. Wilson, *Political Organizations*, p. 9.

28. Theodore H. White, *The Making of the President 1972* (New York: Atheneum, 1973).

29. Wilson, *Amateur Democrat*, p. 15.

30. Wilson suggests that the "clubs" are a response to this problem. Ibid., p. 29.

31. Ibid., p. 5.

32. Lewis Bowman, Dennis Ippolito, and William Donaldson, "Incentives for the Maintenance of Grassroots Political Activism," *Midwest Journal of Political Science* 13 (1969): 126-139, especially pp. 135-136.

33. Samuel J. Eldersveld, *Political Parties: A Behavioral Analysis* (Chicago: Rand McNally & Co., 1964), p. 288.

34. Semel, "Ideology and Incentives," p. 14.

35. Soule and Clarke suggest that ". . . the professional learned that the party was not only a means to certain substantive ends, but that it assumed some intrinsic value." "Amateurs and Professionals," p. 892.

36. A composite measure is utilized to measure total experience. It includes length of activity plus officeholding. When length of activity alone is considered the correlation is .34

among Democrats and −.07 among Republicans, while the correlations between solidarity and officeholding experience is *r* .32 for Democrats and −.27 for Republicans.

37. The conditional gamma for the relation of political generation and solidarity for Democrats is −.43 and for Republicans is −.13.
38. Leon D. Epstein, *Political Parties in Western Democracies* (New York: Frederick A. Praeger, 1967), pp. 122-126; Wilson, *Amateur Democrat*, p. 11.
39. Hofstetter, "Amateur Politician," pp. 31-56.
40. Soule and Clarke, "Amateurs and Professionals," p. 891.
41. Ibid., p. 892.
42. I do not intend to suggest that the Republicans have not been studied. See, inter alia, Aaron Wildavsky, "The Goldwater Phenomenon: Purists, Politicians and the Two Party System," *Review of Politics* 27 (1965): 386-413; and Roback, "Amateurs and Professionals."
43. Epstein, "Who Voted for McGovern."
44. This process of de-identification is noted and discussed by Harold R. Isaacs, *Idols of the Tribe: Group Identity and Political Change* (New York: Harper and Row, 1975).
45. Wilson, *Amateur Democrat*, p. 2.
46. Measures were constructed which tested consistency within and between various issue dimensions. Those measures established the comprehensiveness and consistency of an ideological orientation.
47. Eldersveld, *Political Parties*, p. 303.
48. M. Margaret Conway and Frank B. Feigert, "Motivation, Incentive Systems, and The Political Party Organization," *American Political Science Review* 62 (1968): 1172.
49. Semel, "Ideology and Incentives," p. 11. Note that Semel also reports that both sociability and status are more important motivations for initial political activity for "regulars" than "reformers," p. 8.
50. Wilson, *Political Organizations*, p. 44.
51. Note that when incentives alone are considered, the relationship of status and sociality incentives is *r* .48 and note also that the Sociality Scale developed by Milbrath and Klein measures both solidarity and status. Lester W. Milbrath and Walter W. Klein, "Personality Correlates of Political Participation," *Acta Sociologica* 6 (1962): 53-66.
52. Eldersveld, *Political Parties*, p. 303.
53. Following Laswell, a "nuclear" type connects a political role with intense predispositions of the total personality. Co-relational types identify other traits associated with the nuclear traits, and developmental types "describe a set of terminal, adult reactions and relate them to those critical experiences in the antecedent life of the individual which dispose him to set up such a mode of dealing with the world." Harold D. Lasswell, "A Note on 'Types' of Political Personality: Nuclear, Co-Relational, Developmental," *Journal of Social Issues* 24 (1968): 81-91.
54. Nine percent were McGovern supporters.
55. The gammas relating scores on the Organizational Support Index to various other personal characteristics are as follows: age .33; income .17; education .14; political generations .41; experience .54; political offices .49; party offices .47; public offices .21; community membership .20; years in local community .28; parental activity .20; social incentives .37; status incentives .42; reform incentives −.19; policy maker .43; party leaders .33; local leaders .20; job of the convention: unify the party .45; pick a winning team .43; articulate issues −.25; reform party .45; choose a deserving candidate −.16. Concerning ideology the gammas are: self-classification .55; sanctions .64; international idealism .59; military policy .48; cultural conservatism .65. Concerning women the gammas are: innate sex differences .39; perception of discrimination −.43; role conflict .22; power behind the throne .44. Concerning personality they are: confident .26; competitive-ambitious .17;

order and schedules .23; defensiveness −.02; subjectivity .38. Cramer's V's: for region of origin .16; sex .08; religion .22; race .03; place of birth .13; occupation .17; ethnicity .25; candidate preference .35. Gammas reflecting the relations between organizational support scores and straight ticket voting were .55 for Democrats and .50 for Republicans.

56. If, to facilitate comparability, we combine the two dimensions here treated separately into a single Amateur/Professional Index which more closely resembles those used in most of the studies patterned on Wilson's study, the differences between the parties and among candidate preference groups are confirmed, indeed magnified.

Amateur/Professional Index

Desire to influence party policy
Delegate should have strong views on party
Favor/oppose counting service to party heavily in nominating candidates
Favor/oppose minimizing role of party organizations in nominating candidates
Favor/oppose playing down some issues if it will improve chances of winning
Favor/oppose encouraging widespread participation in making party decisions
Favor/oppose selecting a nominee strongly committed on the issues.

"Amateurs" are much more numerous among Democrats than Republicans and are concentrated in McGovern and Wallace ranks. Conversely, "professionals" are concentrated in Humphrey, Muskie, and Nixon ranks. Among Democrats "amateurism" is strongly related to both experience and ideology, among Republicans these relations are much weaker. (The gamma for relation between amateur/professional scores and political generation is Democrats .38; Republicans .03. For political experience, it is Democrats −.48; Republicans .25. For ideology (self-classification), it is Democrats .53; Republicans .02.)

Amateurs and Professionals by Candidate Preference and Party (%)

		McGovern	Humphrey	Wallace	Muskie	Nixon	All Democrats
Professional	1	6	54	11	47	48	22
	2	40	41	29	44	45	40
Amateur	3	55	5	60	9	7	39
$N =$		578	133	35	86	499	995

NOTE: The columns do not total 100 percent because of rounding; only those candidate groups were included where the candidate maintained a concerted campaign and accumulated a significant number of delegates. Jackson and Kennedy delegates resembled the Humphrey/Muskie pattern. For a complete explanation of this index, see Appendix C.

57. Robert Frasure and Allan Kornberg, "Constituency Agents and British Party Politics," *British Journal of Political Science* 5 (1975): 474.
58. Ibid., p. 473.

CHAPTER 6

Political Perspectives

Political actors internalize identifications and adopt views of the public interest. Identifications define the collectivity in whose name goals are sought; they identify the "we" and the "they" through which politics proceeds. Conceptions of the public interest express the public goals of the "we" that guide, explain, and justify political behavior. Identifications may be inclusive or exclusive, open or closed; conceptions of the public interest may be broad or narrow, general or detailed, elaborated or vague, systematic or casually organized. In any given individual, identifications and conceptions of the public interest coexist with expectations that define possibilities and suggest strategies.[1]

Perspectives include beliefs and their associated effects. Perspectives comprise cognitive, affective, evaluative elements which, though they may be separated for analytic purposes, exist as integral, usually indistinguishable parts of an individual's perspective on the world.

This chapter deals with the classification, salience, direction, coherence, scope, and intensity of the political perspectives of the 1972 presidential elite. Classification concerns how the delegates described their own views; salience refers to the position of a public problem in an individual's focus of attention; direction refers to substantive position taken on political issues; coherence relates to the organization of attitudes, to what "hangs together"; scope refers to the range of issues that comprise a perspective on the politics of 1972; intensity refers to the tendency of persons to take extreme or moderate positions on issues. Coherence, scope, and intensity are dimensions of ideological style.

The central hypothesis of this study is that there were, among the delegates to the two conventions, new political types whose personal goals and political perspectives differed in identifiable ways from those of the people who had dominated presidential politics in the past. Marked differences in delegates' incentives and role perceptions have been established, and it has been noted that these differences were associated with candidate preference, age, and experience. The substantive ideological differences among the candidates and their supporters were public knowledge. This chapter inquires into whether these were accompanied by differences in ideological style and whether they were related to differences in organizational style and social structure. In this chapter it is argued that important differences in ideological style did exist among delegates, especially Democratic delegates, that the ideological styles of many McGovern and Wallace supporters were distinctive in their comprehensiveness and intensity, and that ideological styles were related to personal goals and organizational styles. It is widely recognized that ideological style is a very important aspect of a political system. Therefore, the appearance of new ideological styles among influential activists is interpreted as an important indicator of significant change.

Accounts of 1972 agree that questions of policy and morals played an unusually large role in the preconvention contests in the Democratic party and in the subsequent election. The tumultuous politics of the late 1960s featured new issues that challenged the wisdom, morality, and legitimacy of American government and politics. From the Great Depression to the mid-1960s American politics was dominated by welfare state issues: how to guard the society against drastic and catastrophic economic fluctuations, how to provide minimum economic well-being for all, how to use government's power to stimulate economic growth, how to pay for new services and public activities—all without destroying the fundamental elements of the free enterprise system. Questions concerning government's proper role in the economy and in the economic lives of citizens provoked ardent debate and "structured" the electorate into Republican and Democratic parties, but rarely challenged the legitimacy of the society's basic institutions. United States entry into World War II quieted the debate on intervention that preceded it and produced a spirit of bipartisan cooperation in foreign affairs that lasted through the Korean war and into the period when large numbers of American troops were committed to Vietnam. But the consensus of the World War II and postwar decades was eroded by the rise of new issues to which old agreements seemed less and less relevant. Civil rights issues were associated with civil disobedience by both sides; "massive resistance" in the South challenged the authority of federal courts; urban rioting challenged the legitimacy of property rights and public authority; the antiwar movement pressed further these challenges to the legitimacy of decision processes in political parties and government.

The politics of the last tumultuous decade brought into the political arena varied and divisive questions of domestic and foreign policy, of national purpose and morality. They were characterized by recurring challenges to the authority and legitimacy of political institutions and decisions, by declining levels of consensus and by the progressive abandonment of restraint by partisans inside and outside of government. The deepening schisms within American society dominated the 1972 presidential contests.

The design of this study took account of the content and structure of the political debates that were important to the politics of the period: issues and policies emphasized by candidates for the presidency in the course of the long preconvention period, discussed in the media, and revealed by the public opinion polls to be important to substantial numbers of voters. These included questions of the authority and legitimacy of government, questions of foreign policy, economic policy, welfare policy, race relations, and the "women's revolution." For each of these areas two or more measures were included that were designed to supplement, reinforce, and cross-check one another. Direct questions concerning policy were posed; thermometers were utilized to elicit attitudes to groups. In addition, delegates were asked to describe their political orientations and place themselves on a liberal/conservative spectrum.

SALIENCE

Not all social problems become political issues; not all political issues reflect social problems. The indeterminate relation between public problems and public issues is basic to understanding the relations between public opinion and political outcomes. A social problem may be defined as a situation that affects a fairly large number of people and diverges in significant respects from the desired state. A political issue is the subject of debate between parties or individuals who advocate or are perceived to advocate different courses of action by government.

There are various reasons for which problems do not become political issues. There may be consensus with the political elite about both goals and strategies, as there was broad consensus about United States goals in World War II. There may be little interest in a problem among the political elite—as before Arab oil boycotts suddenly called attention to the world's dwindling oil resources. Sometimes problems debated at the elite level fail to become political issues, because the public pays little or no attention. Sometimes such problems fail to become political issues, because the public is not convinced that the problem would be or could be resolved no matter who is elected.

For a public problem to become a political issue it must attract widespread attention and be perceived as an issue on which the parties to a political conflict have different views which they seek to translate into public policy. When respondents in this study were asked what they considered the principal problems facing the government or themselves, the responses told us whether or not a particular problem had attracted widespread elite attention; they did not tell us whether respondents regarded the problem as relevant to a particular political contest. Therefore, salient problems are not necessarily identical with salient political issues. In societies where there is widespread political cynicism, for example, the feeling that corruption is a major problem may be accompanied by the conviction that nothing will be done about it. In societies at war, ending it may be regarded as the principal problem facing government, as it surely was in World War II, but there may be no conviction that one party could be or would be more effective than another in bringing about this desired state. Attitude measures that investigate salience rarely measure other qualities, such as the relevance of a particular issue to a particular political contest. But whether or not they are relevant to the structure of partisanship in an election, salient problems are always at least latent issues. All parties to a political contest must pay attention to salient problems if only to neutralize them, that is, to prevent the opposition from turning the problem into a useful issue.

Obviously, it is impossible to infer a respondent's *position* on an issue from the *salience* that issue has for him. In 1972, for example, both McGovern and Nixon supporters regarded foreign policy questions as the most important, but they had different views about how these issues should be resolved and who could best resolve them.

To explore the salience of public problems, delegates were asked two questions. One inquired, "What do you personally feel are the most important problems facing our government?" The second asked, "What do you feel are the most important problems facing people like you these days?" First responses to such questions provide insight into the problems in the *forefront* of attention. We therefore look separately at the first problem mentioned by a respondent and next at the total of delegates' replies. Responses (shown in Table 6–1) confirm the impressions of contemporary observers: there were significant differences in the focus of attention of various people of the political elite. The hierarchy of concern of McGovern and Wallace delegates differed sharply. Their first responses to the question establish that McGovern delegates were most concerned about foreign affairs (41 percent), the integrity of government (23 percent), and economic issues (10 percent); Wallace delegates' priorities were economic issues (36 percent), race and law and order (22 percent), and integrity of government (20 percent).

When the first three issues mentioned by respondents were compared, the resulting priorities confirm the distinctiveness of the McGovern and Wallace groups. While economic problems, social welfare, and foreign affairs ranked in the top three for Humphrey, Muskie, and Nixon delegates (though not necessarily in that order), economic issues did not occur in McGovern delegates' top three, nor social welfare in Wallace delegates' top three.

The relatively low importance of economic issues for McGovern delegates is especially interesting when it is recalled that 57 percent of Democrats in the electorate identified economic problems as the most important problem facing government (as compared to 42 percent of Democrats who rated foreign affairs most important), and that the Democratic party is popularly believed to be the most competent to deal with economic questions. Since the depression economic questions have had a unique relationship to the structure of partisanship in the United States; they have also had special salience for Democrats. Their relatively low importance for the dominant Democratic faction may signal a major alteration in ideological perspectives. Focus of attention may turn out to be a distinguishing characteristic of the new breed.

Many of the issues that figured importantly in campaign rhetoric of primaries and the analyses of pundits were not mentioned frequently by respondents: welfare policy, for example, was emphasized at one time or another by all candidates; so was busing to achieve racial balance in public schools.

POLITICAL VIEWS: IDEOLOGICAL SELF-CLASSIFICATION

One simple, direct, uncomplicated way to measure a person's orientation in the political world is to ask him to place himself on a liberal/conservative spectrum. The problem with this approach derives from the ambiguity of these terms. "Liberal" and "conservative," "radical" and "reactionary" are not terms with definite referents agreed upon by all English speakers or all Americans, or even all educated politically active men and women. Because liberal and conservative are comparative terms one answer to the question, "Are you a liberal?" must be, "Compared to whom?" and another, "In relation to what?" Regulation of the economy? Capital punishment? Abortion? Women's liberation? Epistemology? Construction of the Constitution? Drug legislation?[2] What is generally understood by this question is, "Are you liberal or conservative on the dominant political issues of the times?" Knowing this does not solve the problem. The knowledgeable person is bothered by the shifting views about what is liberal and what conservative. The original liberals on the

Table 6-1. Public Issue Salience by Party and Candidate Preference (%)

Most Important Issue	Democrats	Republicans	McGovern	Humphrey	Wallace	Muskie	Nixon
Unemployment	3	1	2	7	0	3	1
Aid to education	1	1	1	1	0	1	1
Health–Medical care problems	2	1	1	0	0	0	1
Housing and urban problems	3	3	3	2	1	2	3
Poverty, welfare, hunger	2	3	3	4	2	2	3
Other social welfare problems[a]	2	1	1	1	0	4	1
Agriculture–Natural resources[b]	0	0	1	3	0	3	0
Labor–Management problems	0	2	0	1	0	0	2
Race–Civil rights	5	0	6	2	8	5	0
Other minority–Civil rights[c]	0	0	0	0	0	1	0
Protect whites	0	0	0	0	2	0	0
Civil liberties	1	0	1	2	0	1	0
Law and order[d]	2	5	0	0	12	1	5
Drug problems	1	0	0	1	0	0	0
Moral decay[e]	1	1	1	4	1	1	2
Inflation	3	7	1	4	10	5	7
Taxation	2	1	1	1	1	3	1
Redistribution of wealth	2	0	2	1	0	0	0
Other Economic–Business–Consumer problems[f]	10	22	6	17	25	11	22
Vietnam	25	15	30	23	13	30	15
Other foreign affairs problems[g]	10	14	11	6	1	10	14
National defense[h]	2	3	2	4	0	3	3
Ethics in government	4	1	6	1	4	2	3
Trust in government	5	3	5	4	0	4	3

Other government functioning problems[i]	10	11	12	7	16	5	11
Miscellaneous[j]	5	5	6	6	2	4	5
Weighted N =	2667	1116	1349	436	154	290	1090

[a]"Other social welfare problems" includes population, day care, reference to women, assistance to the aged, assistance to minorities, and references to class structure and polarization.

[b]"Agriculture–Natural resources" includes farm economics, farm labor, pollution, conservation of resources, and development of natural resources.

[c]"Other minority–Civil rights" includes any mention of minority rights without specification of race or sex.

[d]"Law and order" includes campus disorders, general public disorder, black riots, war protests, street violence, gun control, crime, control of extremists, revolutionary ideas, and hijacking.

[e]"Moral decay" includes religious decay, school prayer, and youth problems, such as drinking, sex, etc.

[f]"Other Economic–Business–Consumer problems" includes economic growth, government spending, foreign investment, profit control, interstate commerce control, highway expansion, consumer protection, and tariffs.

[g]"Other foreign affairs" includes the Middle East, war prevention, foreign involvement in general, United Nations, communism, foreign affairs in relation to domestic priorities, and relations with the U.S.S.R. and People's Republic of China or parts of the world other than Vietnam.

[h]"National defense" includes: disarmament, size of armed forces, selective service, influence of military, national morale or patriotism, and weapons development.

[i]"Other government functioning problems" includes rearrangement of government priorities, quality of public employees, size of government bureaucracy, pervasiveness of government controls over citizens, government secrecy, representativeness of political leaders, lobbyists, government catering to minorities, fair election procedures, federal-state relations, power of president, Congress, or Supreme Court, ineffectiveness of government, and preservation of ideas of Founding Fathers.

[j]"Miscellaneous" includes general references to quality of life, apathy, motivation, lack of concern for people, technological complexity, political ideology, erosion of "Protestant ethic," socialization of minorities, keeping informed, discontent, fear, materialism, and bringing about change.

Relationships: Public issue salience by party, V = 0.28.

NOTE: This table gives the percentages of delegates who mentioned each problem as the *"most important"* problem. These data are from the interviews.

political scene opposed government intervention in economic affairs and ardently supported laissez-faire economic policies on grounds that government regulation constituted an unwarranted and undesirable interference with individual freedom and that leaving each individual free to pursue his own economic interest would result in the greatest production of wealth for the whole society.[3] However, by the second decade of the present century, the liberal position came to be associated with advocacy of welfare state policies that entailed the progressive involvement of government in the economy. In the United States, between the New Deal and the late 1960s, liberals were generally understood to be persons who championed labor as against business, social security as against economic insecurity, economic planning as against reliance on the free market. There is also a traditional association between liberalism and civil liberties—free speech, free press, free assembly. During the last two to three decades, attitudes toward racial questions have served as still another basis for classification as "liberal" and "conservative." Relations between domestic liberalism/conservatism and attitudes to foreign policy have also varied. Alfred Hero points out that during the Roosevelt period differences were slight in the foreign policy views of those calling themselves "liberal" and those calling themselves "conservative." During the Truman period there continued to be little difference on such major policies as the Marshall Plan, NATO, military aid, and the defense establishment, but differences existed on such issues as optimism about avoiding war, technical and economic aid to underdeveloped nations, support for national independence aspirations, and trade with Yugoslavia. After a period of feeble linkage during the Eisenhower period, foreign policy differences between self-perceived liberals and conservatives increased slightly. Meanwhile, policies dealing with race had gained salience, and weak positive correlations developed in attitudes toward race and international affairs.[4] Vietnam introduced a new dimension into relations between foreign and domestic policy.

Each time new issues enter the political arena the spectrum must be stretched, bent, or twisted to accommodate new dimensions. Since many new issues have no direct or obvious relationship to those already on the spectrum, this process can become very complicated. Frequently "liberal" is used to describe persons who desire change of any kind whatsoever, and "conservative," those who resist change of any kind whatsoever.[5] Self-placement is always complicated by the different amounts of prestige that these symbols enjoy in different milieus. Changing referents, changing contexts, and changing opinions lead to a continuing alteration of position on a reified spectrum. Yesterday's liberal may be tomorrow's radical or conservative. A further complication arises from the fact that people may take a liberal position on one issue or type of issue and a conservative position on others.

In spite of all these complications, at any given time many people have some notion about what a conservative is and what a liberal is, many have views about who are the liberals and who the conservatives. In his famous discussion of mass belief systems in the 1950s, Philip Converse estimated that 2.5 percent of the total population make active use of some "relatively abstract and far-reaching conceptual dimension as a yardstick against which political objects and their shifting policy significance over time were evaluated,"[6] and that an additional 9 percent were familiar with such abstractions. But the recent polarization of American politics has been accompanied by increased salience of ideology, and it seems clear that ever larger numbers of people have a conception of a liberal/conservative spectrum on which they can and do place parties, candidates, and themselves.[7] Virtually all observers agree that the content and utility of such abstractions as liberal and conservative increase sharply as one moves from the electorate, much of which has little information or interest concerning politics, to an informed, involved, active elite.

The fact that the self-classification of the presidential elite is remarkably consistent with its views on multiple issues indicates that however confusing or inconsistent the liberal/conservative categories may seem to the student of intellectual history and political philosophy, most delegates had sorted themselves and the issues on this spectrum. Self-classification also confirms that the ideological spectrum of the 1972 activists was broad. Seventy-two percent of McGovern delegates classified themselves as either radical or very liberal as compared to 20 percent of Muskie delegates, 15 percent of Humphrey delegates, and no Wallace or Nixon delegates. It is not a balanced spectrum; while 12 percent of McGovern delegates are self-described radicals, no one called himself a reactionary. Thirty-seven percent of Wallace delegates and 11 percent of Nixon delegates described themselves as very conservative. If this spectrum of delegates were mounted as a seesaw, radical and very liberal delegates would never get the others off the ground. McGovern and Wallace delegates constituted the two extremes of this spectrum. Nixon delegates were the moderately conservative counterparts of moderately liberal Humphrey and Muskie supporters. (See Table 6–2.) But while Wallace and McGovern delegates were polar opposites, Wallace delegates did not constitute an ideological counterweight to McGovern delegates, not only because the latter were much more numerous, but because McGovern delegates were more ideologically homogeneous. This homogeneity is reflected in the self-classification. Only 4 percent of McGovern delegates described themselves as moderates, and 1 percent as conservative. The remaining 95 percent described themselves as either somewhat liberal (24 percent), very liberal (60 percent), or radical (12 percent), while among Wallace delegates 17 percent described themselves as moderate, 8 percent as somewhat liberal, and 76 percent either as somewhat conservative (39 percent) or very conservative (37 percent). (See Table 6–2.) Nixon and Humphrey delegates were less ideologically homogeneous than Wallace and McGovern delegates and, when juxtaposed, fit the familiar American pattern of interparty conflict in which moderate liberals oppose moderate conservatives with each group containing some representatives of all ideological orientations.

Judged by ideological self-placement of delegates, the two parties provided the electorate a clear-cut choice between moderate conservatives and persons of very liberal persuasion. Self-perception does not necessarily predict either the position on particular issues nor the perception of masses. However, among this ideologically sophisticated and committed elite, positions on specific attitudes on cultural, social, and foreign policy are highly correlated with self-classification on the liberal/conservative spectrum.

AUTHORITY AND AUTHORITY FIGURES

"Ideologies," Edward Shils tells us, "are always concerned with authority."[8] In Shils' view, ideologies, which are "a product of man's need for imposing intellectual order on the world,"[9] arise in times of crisis and challenge the most fundamental claims of the existing order: the claims to legitimacy. Because of the intimate relationships among legitimacy, authority, and force, the involvement of agents or instruments of legitimate coercion (police, military) in political conflict almost always signals the presence of fairly basic ideological conflict.

Governments are institutions that claim the right to make certain decisions for the whole society and to enforce those decisions by the use of force if necessary. The possession of instruments of force with which to coerce compliance with its decisions is a defining characteristic of government. Legitimacy has a special and intimate relation to coercion. Exercised on behalf of a legitimate government by officers of that government, force is said to be legitimate. Its legitimacy differentiates it from force exercised by others—by private rather than public agents. Legitimacy gives *authority* to government actions and differentiates them from other policies that are enforced by severe sanctions or the threat of severe sanctions. Agents of the government who make decisions and exercise force in behalf of governments are called "authorities," because they partake of the legitimacy of government.

Table 6-2. Delegates' Ideological Self-Classification by Party and Candidate Preference (%)

	McGovern	Humphrey	Wallace	Muskie	All Democrats	All Republicans
Radical	12 ⎫	1 ⎫	0 ⎫	1 ⎫	8 ⎫	0 ⎫
Very liberal	60 ⎬ 96	14 ⎬ 64	0 ⎬ 8	19 ⎬ 69	41 ⎬ 79	1 ⎬ 10
Somewhat liberal	24 ⎭	49 ⎭	8 ⎭	49 ⎭	30 ⎭	9 ⎭
Moderate	4	26	17	29	13	35
Somewhat conservative	1 ⎫	11 ⎫	39 ⎫	3 ⎫	6 ⎫	44 ⎫
Very conservative	0 ⎬ 1	0 ⎬ 12	37 ⎬ 76	0 ⎬ 3	2 ⎬ 8	13 ⎬ 57
Reactionary	0 ⎭	1 ⎭	0 ⎭	0 ⎭	0 ⎭	0 ⎭
$N =$	874	200	65	138	1568	834

Question: "How would you describe your political views?"

NOTE: These data are from the mail questionnaires.

But as Lasswell has reminded us, it is the attitudes of the governed that confer legitimacy, and, as the governed can bestow legitimacy on the decisions of government, they can also deny legitimacy.[10] The politics of the late 1960s and early 1970s featured repeated challenges to the legitimacy of particular policies and to the processes through which those policies were made. Racial and war policies were the focus of these challenges.[11]

Both sides in the various civil rights struggles over desegregation in the South denied the legitimacy of existing laws and of the processes by which they were made. On the one side it was asserted that state laws were invalid because blacks had been excluded from the decision process, or because the laws violated the constitutional rights of black citizens, or because they violated natural rights of men. On the other side, it was claimed that federal laws were invalid because they represented an unconstitutional usurpation of legislative power by the Supreme Court, or because they represented an unconstitutional usurpation of power by the federal government from the states, or because they violated the constitutional rights of white citizens. Civil disobedience undertaken by the civil rights movement may have received more publicity but in fact posed a less serious challenge to the legitimacy and authority of government than did the southern policy of "massive resistance" to decisions of the Supreme Court. The Wallace movement is a direct descendant of massive resistance. And the 1972 charges that courts and pointy-headed bureaucrats had usurped the powers of the people continued a challenge to the legitimacy of authoritative decisions.

The antiwar movement echoed and broadcast the charge. United States involvement in Vietnam was criticized not only as mistaken, but as illegitimate either on grounds that the government lacked the legal right to commit troops to Southeast Asia, or that it lacked the moral right to do so, or both. Sometimes it was argued that the decisions of government relating to the war were illegitimate, because segments of the population had been frozen out of decision-making processes.[12] The McGovern movement was a direct descendant of this challenge. The politics of 1972 were therefore distinctive in their inclusion of questions of legitimacy not normally found in election contests in the United States.[13]

The law and order position rests ultimately on the beliefs that authority is legitimate, that citizens are obliged to obey, and that strong measures are justified to ensure obedience and counter disobedience. The anti-law and order position justifies urban riots, student disorders, massive resistance, or antiwar violence with a denial of legitimacy to government and the invocation of some "higher" principle—such as social justice, states' rights, self-determination. Attitudes toward authorities and those who challenge authority are therefore useful indicators of views concerning the legitimacy of government.

Foreign policy, especially military policy, may also be associated with legitimacy, and attitudes toward the military establishment are indicators of views about some important agents of official purposes.

The questionnaire and interview on which this study is based contained several items designed to communicate orientations to authority and its agents. Among these were three thermometer items, two of which emphasized attitudes to authority figures who use force, namely, policemen and the military; a third is a group that is frequently associated with civil disobedience, namely, political demonstrators. The rating of these items by delegates revealed sharp and expected differences in orientations toward authority and legitimacy.

McGovern delegates displayed a distinctive orientation toward authority. They were least likely to have a good opinion of the military and most likely to have a good opinion of political demonstrators. They were also somewhat less favorable to the police than were other candidate support groups. Wallace delegates were also distinctive. They were most favorable to the guardians of authority and least favorable to political demonstrators. Nixon delegates most closely resembled Wallace delegates in the intensity of their hostility to demonstrators and their support for the military. Humphrey and Muskie delegates closely resembled the Nixon and Wallace groups in their support for police but fell between the others on the other measures. This distribution of attitudes toward the police and demonstrators indicates that one group whose antecedents are rooted in civil disobedience (Wallace delegates) strenuously supported the symbols of authority and opposed the challengers to authority. The appearance in American politics of a group which both supports law enforcement officers and denies the legitimacy of some government actions may signal something new in contemporary American politics: namely, *a significant movement which opposes the existing government in the name of older conceptions of legitimacy.*[14] McGovern supporters demonstrated antiauthority trends more by their support for those who challenged authority than by their opposition to those symbols of authority, the police.

Responses to these three symbols of authority and challenge are significantly intercorrelated, and a factor analysis of responses to groups reveals that in the attitudes of this highly educated and informed population, attitudes to police, military and political demonstrators also were linked to attitudes to civil rights leaders, rock festivals, welfare recipients, and black militants.[15]

The rotated factor analysis confirms the connections among force-wielding authority figures, namely the police and the military, and some groups which are commonly perceived as challenging or threatening the legitimacy of traditional social and legal arrangements: civil rights leaders challenged the laws and practices associated with traditional (discriminating) race relations; black militants and political demonstrators posed more forceful challenges to the social and legal order; rock festivals were for a period the capitals of the counter culture, and were characterized by anti-war, anti-establishment, anti-authority attitudes. However, while there were fairly strong negative correlations among military, police, demonstrators, and black militants and civil rights leaders, there was a much weaker association between police and military on the one hand and welfare recipients or rock festivals on the other. (See Table 6–3.)

A four-point index based on responses to questions eliciting views on military strength and crime, and feelings about the military establishment and the police provides a composite measure of attitudes toward the use of force in both domestic and foreign policy. Distributions of delegates on this measure are shown in Table 6–4.

Policemen keep the peace, military establishments protect the nation: this at least is the *raison d'être* of these institutions in the United States and elsewhere. The theoretical relationship between support for government and support for these authority figures is therefore persuasive. Was it reflected in the attitudes of delegates toward government? Did those with a more positive attitude toward authorities who apply sanctions also have a more positive evaluation of government generally? Questions used to measure the electorate's confidence in government were also submitted to these delegates. Delegate responses (shown in Table 6–5) to these widely used questions on "trust in government" confirmed the general impression that McGovern and Wallace supporters had an especially low opinion of those who controlled the government. However, analysis of these responses also indicates the absence of any association between attitudes toward authorities and sanctions and confidence in government. McGovern delegates had a low regard for government *and* for force-wielding authorities; Wallace delegates had a low regard for government and a high regard for sanctions. Confidence in government was low in all candidate groups, but lowest of all among delegates supporting McGovern and Wallace.

Part of what appears to be cynicism may in fact only be a result of intense partisanship. Nearly 80 percent of the Republican delegates believed government was run for the interests of all, suggesting that the apparent cynicism of the Democrats was only the complaint of the "outs" against the "ins." (See Table 6–5.) The same partisanship probably influenced responses to the question of whether the government could be trusted to do the right thing. A majority of Republicans answered affirmatively. But if only partisanship were involved in responses to these questions, then all

Table 6-3. Orientations Toward Authority Figures and Challengers to Authority (Pearson's *R* Correlations)

	Civil Rights Leaders	Police	Rock Festival People	Military	Welfare Recipients	Political Demonstrators	Black Militants
Civil Rights leaders		-.40	.50	-.48	.56	.67	.64
Police	-.40		-.22	.67	-.18	-.43	-.46
Rock festival people	.50	-.22		-.33	.47	.56	.51
Military	-.48	.67	-.33		.22	-.49	-.47
Welfare recipients	.56	-.18	.47	.22		.59	.52
Political demonstrators	.67	-.43	.56	-.49	.59		.74
Black militants	.64	-.46	.51	-.47	.52	.74	

Question: "This next card is called a 'feeling thermometer,' and we would like you to use it to measure your feelings toward various groups. If you don't feel particularly warm or cold toward a group, then you should place it at the 50° mark. If you have a warm feeling toward a group, you would give it a score somewhere between 50° and 100°. On the other hand, if you don't feel very favorably toward a group, then you would place it somewhere between 0° and 50°."

NOTE: These data are from the interviews.

Table 6-4. Sanctions: A Summary View (%)

Support for Sanctions	McGovern	Humphrey	Wallace	Muskie	Nixon
Low	49	13	0	15	1
Middle	49	56	27	65	29
High	2	31	73	20	70
Weighted N =	857	192	55	162	703

NOTE: These data are from the interviews. For method of index construction and a complete explanation of the Sanctions Index, see Appendix C.

Democrats would have held equally negative views of government. In fact among supporters of Humphrey and Muskie distrust and partisanship were tempered by a large admixture of confidence in government—even in a government run by the opposition.

This finding is consistent with the general view that McGovern supporters were more hostile to "the system" than was typical for the party out of power and, conversely, that Humphrey and Muskie delegates were associated with an older tradition of greater mutual tolerance. Drastic decline in confidence of the political elite is reflected in a comparison of the responses to a sample of delegates to the 1956 Republican and Democratic conventions with those of delegates in 1972. Although McClosky's questions were not identical, several were very similar. The responses of delegates studied by McClosky reflected high confidence in government and high diffuse system support in 1956, and responses of 1972 delegates reflected low levels of confidence. For example, only 8 percent of McClosky's informants agreed that "the laws of this country are supposed to benefit all of us equally, but the fact is that they're almost all 'rich man's laws'," while 91 percent of McGovern supporters, 63 percent of Humphrey delegates, 84 percent of Wallace delegates, and 61 percent of Muskie delegates agreed that government was run not for the benefit of all, but for a "few big interests." (Note, though, that only 21 percent of Nixon delegates agreed.) Among 1956 delegates, 82 percent agreed that "I usually have confidence that the government will do what is right."[16]

Obviously, these high levels of elite disaffection from government are incompatible with the widespread view based on mass studies that "persons who feel cynical about or alienated from politics are much less likely to participate in politics."[17] Comparative studies have already demonstrated the existence of widespread cynicism among the elites of some nations, and Robert Putnam's study established that a major difference between British and Italian political elites is precisely the lesser cynicism of the former and the greater cynicism of the latter.[18]

Delegates' low opinion of government and, inferentially, of those who govern may be something new on the American political scene. It almost surely has important implications since legitimacy, restraint, and obligation are all closely bound beliefs concerning the virtue of government. Cynicism about government and governors can justify diverse assaults on the public order. The demand for radical change is one well-known response. Corruption is another. Why *not* steal from the public treasury or bug one's opponents or help sympathetic interests if "everyone does it"? The belief that government is corrupt itself becomes a corrupting factor. When the political elite holds such beliefs, political dialogue is likely to be shrill or cynical or both. Redemptive zeal and cynical manipulation are the normal products of a loss of confidence in the political institutions of the society. The especially low confidence in government expressed by McGovern and Wallace delegates illustrates the relations between these attitudes and challengers to the legitimacy of government policy.

There is an interesting contrast between delegates' optimistic views of human nature and their low opinions of government. Responses to the widely used "faith in people" measures reveal a very good opinion of people shared by Republicans and Democrats alike and by supporters of all candidates. (See Table 6–6.) It is interesting, though, that on all three questions, Wallace delegates were less optimistic than others. More of them doubted that you can trust most people, more believed that people are basically out for themselves and that others are prepared to take advantage of you when it is in their interest to do so. While this difference is theoretically interesting, it should not be overemphasized, because even Wallace delegates were quite sanguine about human nature.[19]

It would be intellectually satisfying to be able to report that the often assumed relationship between views of human nature and national policies was reflected in candidate support patterns. But it was not. Apart from the greater pessimism of the Wallace delegates, there are no other significant differences among the candidate support groups. On each of three questions at least two-thirds of the delegates associated themselves with the optimistic position. The relatively equal distribution of optimists and pessimists among all candidate groups except Wallace suggests that the view on human nature had no relevance to a preference for Nixon, McGovern, Humphrey, or Muskie. Not only did abstract views of human nature have no relation to support for candidate preference (always excepting Wallace), they also had little relation to the delegates' views on specific policy questions to which their relevance would seem greatest.

Table 6-5. Confidence in Government (%)

	McGovern	Humphrey	Wallace	Muskie	Nixon
Government Wastes Money					
A lot	68	60	97	55	71
Some	30	37	3	42	27
Not much	2	3	0	4	2
N =	874	197	65	139	795
Government Will Do What Is Right					
Always	0	1	0	1	2
Most of the time	17	63	26	51	69
Some of the time	83	36	74	49	30
N =	872	198	66	136	793
Government Run for Whom					
Benefit of all	9	37	16	39	79
Few big interests	91	63	84	61	21
N =	851	188	64	132	744

What Government Knows

Knows what it's doing	43	64	31	55	61
Doesn't know what it's doing	57	36	69	46	39
N =	852	191	65	134	772

How Many Crooked People

Hardly any	8	22	5	26	29
Not many	54	64	46	57	65
Quite a lot	38	15	50	17	7
N =	871	197	66	136	789

Questions: "Do you think people in the government waste a lot of the money we pay in taxes, waste some of it, or don't waste 'very much of it?" "How much of the time do you think you can trust the government in Washington to do what is right—just about always, most of the time or only some of the time?" "Would you say the government is pretty much run by a few big interests looking out for themselves, or that it is run for the benefit of all the people?" "Do you feel that almost all of the people running the government are smart people who usually know what they are doing, or do you think that quite a few of them don't seem to know what they are doing?" "Do you think quite a few of the people running the government are a little crooked, not very many are, or do you think hardly any of them are crooked at all?"

NOTE: The data are from the mail questionnaires.

Table 6-6. Faith in People Index (%)

	McGovern	Humphrey	Wallace	Muskie	Nixon
Low	19	22	44	15	14
High	81	78	56	86	86
Weighted N =	1276	417	142	283	1032

Questions: "Here are a number of statements about other people. First, generally speaking, would you say that you can trust most people or that you can't be too careful in dealing with most people?"

"Would you say that most of the time people try to be helpful or that they mostly look out for themselves?"

"Do you think most people, if they are given a chance, try to take advantage of you or do you think most people try to treat you fairly?"

NOTE: These data are from the interviews.

Presumably the belief that people are or are not basically self-interested, prepared to take advantage of others, and be trusted would be related to views about defense and foreign policy. If others will *not* take advantage, presumably there would be little need to defend oneself against them. If they cannot be trusted, prudence would dictate an attitude of vigilance and a policy of preparedness. *But in fact there turns out to be almost no relationship between views on human nature and on foreign policy.* Optimism about human nature did not lead delegates to give military strength lower priority; pessimism did not increase the tendency to advocate preparedness. Optimists and pessimists were about equally likely to advocate withdrawing troops from Asia and keeping them there and to support or oppose the withdrawal of American troops from Europe. But there was a tendency for those with greater faith in people to support programs of international cooperation, aid, and organization.

Although political philosophy and psychological theory alike lead us to expect a relationship between faith in people and views about the use of force in society (it is not necessary to repress good, cooperative instincts); in fact, there is only a weak relationship between the two.

Apparently, optimism about others is part of the generalized optimism characteristic of the participant personality in democratic societies. As Walter Bagehot pointed out nearly a century ago, democratic government requires extraordinarily high levels of mutual trust among citizens.[20] How, Bagehot asked, could one conceivably agree to have important decisions made by a majority of one's fellow citizens unless one trusts their fundamental good sense, goodwill, and good judgment? If one's neighbors are fools or knaves, their mere numbers will not give their actions legitimacy. The importance of trust to democracy makes it important that a large majority of the presidential elite is basically sanguine about the decency and fairness of others.

This optimism has important implications for other attitudes as well. In principle, a good opinion of others will reinforce the mutual restraint and legitimacy that are crucial to stable democratic institutions. Knaves could not be trusted to observe lawful procedures in achieving their aims. They could not be expected to be restrained in their pursuit of preferred outcomes. Restraint is closely related to trust because the restraint of one party in a conflict requires trust that other parties will observe the same legal and moral restraints. Democratic competition is conflict limited by law and characterized by the mutual restraint of the contending parties. This restraint involves above all the renunciation of force and fraud: *not* breaking up opponents' meetings, *not* attempting to overthrow the government, and *not* bugging opponents' headquarters.

Trust is related to legitimacy in yet another way. It limits conflict, because it extends even to one's opponents. Opponents of whom one expects the worst can hardly be regarded as legitimate decision makers for the society. They themselves can hardly be expected to observe legal restraints to the use of power and to rule with a decent regard for the interests of all. For this reason we would expect a generally good opinion of others to be accompanied by a reasonably high level of confidence in government. The fact that it is not casts doubt either on our theory, our measures, or both. Or perhaps it merely warns against oversimplifying the relations between views of human nature and attitudes toward government. While a certain trust of others is required to support democratic practices, it is also true that low faith in people may coexist with high confidence in government. The Founding Fathers distrusted human nature and had a generalized distrust of governments. This led them to organize government to prevent and correct the expected abuses of power. Conversely utopianism combines a buoyant optimism about human nature with harsh condemnation of existing institutions, because real institutions are never worthy of imagined human perfections.

FOREIGN POLICY

As debates concerning United States policy in Vietnam made clear, the foreign policies of a nation involve an assessment of human nature, force, legitimacy, and authority. In 1972 Southeast Asia continued to be a matter of intense concern to many Americans. This issue, which created dissension among Democrats as early as 1966, played a major role in the decision of then President Lyndon Johnson to retire from politics without seeking another term as president, became a focus of violence outside the Democratic Convention in 1968, crippled the Democratic party which was already injured by the Wallacite defections, and played a small but important role in Richard Nixon's narrow victory over Hubert Humphrey in that year.[21] In the primaries and in the subsequent general election George McGovern, the candidate of the peace movement, presented himself as the man who gave ending the war supreme priority. By 1972 the antiwar position had become dominant within the Democratic party, and although most American troops had been withdrawn, the Nixon administration, supported by a majority of the Congress, continued a policy of massive aid to South Vietnam, Laos, Cambodia, and Thailand. This commitment remained a major target of the peace movement and of its candidate, George McGovern.

The survey included two questions on Vietnam policy: one inquired about views on withdrawing troops from Southeast Asia; another inquired about the desirable extent of continued support for South Vietnam. (See Tables 6–7 and 6–8.) These measures confirmed that only McGovern supporters were united on Southeast Asian policy. Other candidate support groups, including the Nixon delegates, reflected ambivalence and indecision. Even the Wallace delegates, who shared a single point of view on many questions, were of several minds on this one.

Southeast Asia was not the only foreign policy issue that divided the electorate and the elite. The Vietnam war served as a stimulus to a more general examination of United States military and foreign commitments. The bitterness and domestic turmoil that accompanied the war, the emphasis of the Nixon administration on détente, the winding down of the

Table 6-7. Withdrawing Troops from Asia by Candidate Preference (%)

	McGovern	Humphrey	Wallace	Muskie	Nixon
Strongly agree	77 ⎱ 91	33 ⎱ 60	19 ⎱ 42	44 ⎱ 76	9 ⎱ 30
Somewhat agree	14 ⎰	27 ⎰	23 ⎰	32 ⎰	21 ⎰
Uncertain	1	6	8	4	3
Somewhat disagree	7 ⎱ 8	23 ⎱ 33	26 ⎱ 50	16 ⎱ 20	38 ⎱ 67
Strongly disagree	1 ⎰	10 ⎰	24 ⎰	4 ⎰	29 ⎰
Weighted N =	1339	433	151	284	1058

Question: "Please tell me whether you strongly agree, somewhat agree, somewhat disagree, or strongly disagree. All United States troops should be withdrawn from Asia."

NOTE: These data are from the interviews.

Table 6-8. Aid to Southeast Asia by Candidate Preference (%)

		McGovern	Humphrey	Wallace	Muskie	Nixon
No aid to						
Southeast Asia	1	57	16	19	19	3
	2	28	15	2	17	4
	3	8	12	5	26	8
	4	4	23	14	18	16
	5	2	16	7	12	22
	6	1	7	9	2	17
Military and economic aid to Southeast Asia	7	1	11	44	6	30
$N =$		776	178	57	126	747

Question: "Even though most of the American troops have been withdrawn from South Vietnam, there is still a lot of discussion about the United States action in Indochina. Some people think we should end all American military assistance and economic aid to Southeast Asia. Others say we should give military assistance and economic aid to the governments of South Vietnam, Cambodia, and Laos. Where would you place yourself on the following scale, ranging from agreement with no United States military assistance or economic aid to agreement with United States military assistance and economic aid?"

NOTE: These data are from the mail questionnaires.

cold war, the prosperity of Europe, the rise of balance of payments problems in the United States, and the presence of a new generation with no personal memory of either the nazi holocaust or communist expansionism—these and related developments precipitated a broad reconsideration of both the assumptions and the policies associated with the cold war consensus.

A number of questions probed elite orientations to fundamental questions of foreign policy: the defense establishment, collective security commitments to Europe and Asia, economic aid policies, the United Nations, and the use of nuclear weapons were explored. (See Table 6–11.)

Two of these items (Tables 6–9 and 6–10) are so basic to all other views on foreign and military affairs that they deserve separate attention: Respondents were asked about their level of agreement or disagreement with the following statements:

American military superiority should have priority in American foreign policy.

The United States should give more support to the United Nations.

Table 6-9. American Military Superiority Should Have Priority
in American Foreign Policy (%)

	McGovern	Humphrey	Wallace	Muskie	Nixon
Strongly agree	2	22	70	14	44
Somewhat agree	15	33	21	33	38
Uncertain–don't know	2	6	2	2	2
Somewhat disagree	28	27	6	33	12
Strongly disagree	53	12	1	18	4
Weighted N =	1341	435	151	284	1070

Table 6-10. The United States Should Give More Support
to the United Nations (%)

	McGovern	Humphrey	Wallace	Muskie	Nixon
Strongly agree	52	17	4	28	8
Somewhat agree	26	36	4	24	21
Uncertain–don't know	6	2	1	7	5
Somewhat disagree	13	30	17	29	31
Strongly disagree	3	16	74	12	35
Weighted N =	1336	433	151	282	1068

If the world is a dangerous place, more specifically, if the aggressive designs of the great communist powers are kept in check only by fear of retaliation, then it is important for the United States, as the most powerful non-communist nation, to maintain military superiority. If communist intentions pose no threat to the vital interests of the United States and we should not attempt to safeguard other non-communist nations, then it does not make sense to spend our nation's wealth maintaining the world's most powerful military establishment. If the world is not a dangerous place, then a strategy of international cooperation is obviously more appropriate (and more enlightened and humane) than a strong defense posture. Divisions among delegates on these two questions reflect profoundly different views about the nature of the contemporary world. While the questions do not pose mutually exclusive alternatives (it is entirely possible to think *both* that the United States should give more support to the United Nations *and* that it should maintain military supremacy), many delegates responded as if they did. The question on military

Table 6-11. The Use of Nuclear Weapons by the United States
Would Never Be Justified (%)

		McGovern	Humphrey	Wallace	Muskie	Nixon
Strongly agree	1	55	24	3	32	12
Somewhat agree	2	21	18	8	11	16
Uncertain–don't know	3	3	5	4	9	6
Somewhat disagree	4	17	38	37	28	39
Strongly disagree	5	4	16	48	21	27
Weighted $N =$		1337	429	147	284	1060

Question: "I will now read you several statements on American foreign policy. For each, please tell me whether you strongly agree, somewhat agree, somewhat disagree, or strongly disagree."

NOTE: Data are from the interviews.

superiority also involves the use of force as an instrument of policy. There was a persistent and probably basic disagreement among delegates concerning the use of force that was reflected in responses to other questions about policy in other areas.

McGovern delegates were most opposed to giving priority in foreign affairs to maintaining military superiority; their attitudes were distinctive within their own party and stood in sharp contrast to the views of Wallace and Nixon delegates. They were also most widely and intensely in favor of greater United States support for the United Nations—a position that was opposed with special unanimity and intensity by Wallace delegates.

A factor analysis of the foreign affairs items establishes the presence of two dimensions. One concerns military policy (see Table 6–12). The second factor focuses on international cooperation as an alternative to a strong defense policy (see Table 6–13). The first factor includes attitudes toward keeping American troops in Asia and/or Europe, toward the circumstances under which the United States might resort to war, and toward the use of nuclear weapons. The second includes items on the United Nations, aid to needy nations, and relations with Cuba. The importance of maintaining American military superiority and the use of nuclear weapons occur in both factors. These two dimensions of orientation toward foreign affairs persisted on all factor problems in which these items were involved.

Table 6-12. Military Policy Index by Candidate Preference (%)

		McGovern	Humphrey	Wallace	Muskie	Nixon
Do not use						
military force	1	68	25	7	35	10
	2	30	57	53	55	48
Use military						
force	3	2	18	40	10	42
Weighted N =		1323	426	147	281	1038

NOTE: These data are from the interviews. For method of index construction and a list of the constituent variables in the Military Policy Index, see Appendix C.

Table 6-13. International Idealist Index by Candidate Preference (%)

		McGovern	Humphrey	Wallace	Muskie	Nixon
Idealist	1	71	26	0	40	5
	2	29	67	21	55	69
Non-idealist	3	1	8	79	5	26
Weighted N =		1323	428	146	280	1052

NOTE: These data are from the interviews. For method of index construction and a list of the constituent variables in the International Idealist Index, see Appendix C.

Indexes were constructed on the basis of these factors to provide a single measure of respondents' attitudes toward each of these dimensions. Significant differences emerged among delegates supporting the various candidates.

As Table 6–12 makes clear, McGovern delegates were distinctively opposed to the use of military force as an instrument of American foreign policy; Nixon delegates most supportive of it. Muskie and Humphrey delegates were divided. Wallace delegates were less unanimous on this index than on many other questions, although over one-half definitely supported the use of military force as an instrument of foreign policy. Since the collective security agreements signed by the United States since World War II are involved in this index, the McGovern delegates' position implies rejection of the alliances and commitments that have dominated American foreign policy in the postwar era. Their scores confirm that the McGovern delegates were not merely opposed to involvement in South Vietnam, Laos, and Cambodia, but to the web of collective security treaties and commitments negotiated in the postwar years.

Scores on the International Idealist Index provide evidence that *it was not isolationism but rejection of force* as an instrument of foreign policy that prompted McGovernite opposition to United States commitments in Asia and Europe. Support for the United Nations, aid to needy nations, and closer ties with Cuba were the attractive modes of international involvement. Perhaps McGovern delegates were also rejecting nationalism and patriotism as part of a process of extending the scope of their identifications from the national to the supranational. Perhaps they were identifying with the international underdogs. Note that only among Wallace delegates was there a majority who *opposed* a policy of aid and cooperation. Large majorities of delegates supporting other candidates had mixed views on these questions. Wallace delegates, among whom nationalism was much stronger, were explicitly opposed to policies that assumed higher degrees of commitment to international organizations. Here, as on many other issues, Wallace and McGovern delegates constituted opposing ends of an ideological spectrum that will become more familiar in the following pages.

ECONOMIC ISSUES

Among the whole electorate economic problems were regarded as the most pressing in 1972. More than war, public morality, crime, or environment the people were concerned about making ends meet, about the high cost of living, high taxes, actual and threatened unemployment, and a variety of associated "pocketbook" issues. The salience of these issues in 1972 should not surprise us. Most American troops had been brought back from Vietnam, and therefore few families were threatened by personal loss through foreign policy. Domestic disorders had diminished dramatically: the campuses and cities alike were quiet as compared with the years just past. Crime continued its steady rise, but the rate of increase was lower than in previous years. But the economy was already showing signs of acute strain in shifting from a wartime to a peacetime basis and from the impact of Republican economics. Since most people have a limited interest in abstract or remote or general political questions and a much greater concern about the concrete problems of daily life, it takes dramatic, unusually frightening events—wars, disasters, revolutions—to turn their attention away from wages, prices, and taxes to the big questions about how to order the society. The elites who made decisions for the two parties in 1972 were less concerned than voters about economic questions, but they could not be indifferent to the bread and butter issues on which elections so frequently turn.

Three measures tapped the economic orientations of respondents: a proximity measure inquired about the appropriate role for government in fighting inflation, and attitudes toward two historic contenders in the economic arena—business interests and labor unions—were elicited via a thermometer rating.

The results are interesting, if not surprising. They testify to the withering away of laissez-faire economics and demonstrate that at the elite level the economic "right" is no more. Almost no one among the presidential elite believed that government should take no action to combat inflation (see Table 6–14). McGovern and Wallace delegates who were polar opposites on many questions contained the highest number of governmental activists: 46 percent of both groups described their views as fully committed to all necessary government action against inflation. Wallace ranks also provided the largest number of hold-outs against government economic initiatives with 15 percent strongly opposed to government action. Controlling inflation proved one of the few issues on which Democrats were basically united: almost all thought government should do something. While fewer Nixon delegates were fully committed to full government action, on balance two-thirds favored government intervention to combat inflation and only 12 percent opposed it.

The relatively weak correlation (gamma .32) between respondents' views about government's appropriate role in fighting inflation and ideological self-placement (Table 6–15) also reflects the fact that this issue was peripheral to the issues that in 1972 stimulated members of the political elite to think of themselves as liberals, conservatives, radicals, or whatever. By contrast the relation of ideological self-placement to busing was gamma .76; for aid to Southeast Asia, it was gamma .67; for military policy, it was gamma .71; for welfare policy, it was gamma −.62. Even most "conservatives" supported government action to end inflation.

Orientations toward business interests and trade unions indicate the persistence of traditional differences. Table 6–16 shows that Democrats were more favorable to union leaders than Republicans and Table 6–17 shows that Republicans were more favorable to business interests than Democrats. There were nonetheless some significant differences among supporters of McGovern, Humphrey, Muskie, and Wallace.[22] The historic alliance between organized labor and the Democratic party had weakened seriously. The AFL-CIO declined to endorse Democratic candidate George McGovern on grounds that he was an unreliable supporter of labor. Differences in foreign policy and in cultural style also created tensions and animosities between the devotees of the new politics and the

Table 6-14. Government Action Against Inflation by Candidate Preference (%)

		McGovern	Humphrey	Wallace	Muskie	Nixon
All necessary government action vs. inflation	1	46	37	46	37	23
	2	34	22	7	21	18
	3	13	22	7	24	22
	4	6	12	20	15	25
	5	2	2	0	2	7
	6	1	2	6	1	4
No government action	7	0	3	15	1	1
$N =$		824	183	55	126	729

Question: "There is a great deal of talk these days about rising prices and the cost of living in general. Some feel that the problem of inflation is temporary and that no government action is necessary. Others say the government must do everything possible to combat the problem of inflation immediately or it will get worse. Where would you place yourself on the following scale, ranging from agreement with total government action against inflation to agreement with no government action against inflation?"

NOTE: These data are from the mail questionnaires.

Table 6-15. Opinions About Government Action Against Inflation by Ideological Self-Classification (%)

	Radical	Very Liberal	Somewhat Liberal	Moderate	Somewhat Conservative	Very Conservative
Maximum government action vs. inflation						
1	63	45	34	30	24	31
2	18	35	28	19	15	15
3	12	13	22	24	19	12
4	3	5	12	20	27	16
5	3	2	1	4	7	10
6	2	1	2	2	6	7
No government action vs. inflation 7	1	1	1	1	2	9
$N =$	112	608	493	439	403	122

Question on inflation: "There is a great deal of talk these days about rising prices and the cost of living in general. Some feel that the problem of inflation is temporary and that no government action is necessary. Others say the government must do everything possible to combat the problem of inflation immediately or it will get worse. Where would you place yourself on the following scale, ranging from agreement with total government action against inflation to agreement with no government action against inflation?"

Question on ideology: "How would you describe your political views?"

NOTE: These data are from the mail questionnaires.

Table 6-16. Union Leaders: Thermometer Rating (%)

		Democrats	Republicans	McGovern	Humphrey	Wallace	Muskie
Frigid	0	3	15	2	2	20	2
	10	3	11	3	2	11	3
	20	5	12	6	3	6	4
	30	6	12	7	2	11	6
	40	8	10	10	5	8	7
Neutral	50	25	23	24	22	32	27
	60	13	7	14	8	8	14
	70	14	5	14	16	3	12
	80	11	4	11	14	2	16
	90	6	1	5	10	0	4
Hot	100	5	0	3	18	0	6
N =		1542	809	862	194	65	137

The question asked respondents to rate union leaders on a feeling thermometer that ranged from 0 to 100.

NOTE: These data are from the mail questionnaires.

Table 6-17. Business Interests: Thermometer Rating (%)

		Democrats	Republicans	McGovern	Humphrey	Wallace	Muskie
Frigid	0	13	1	15	7	14	5
	10	9	2	12	4	3	8
	20	12	3	15	7	5	8
	30	11	2	13	8	8	13
	40	9	5	12	6	3	5
Neutral	50	25	29	20	32	33	36
	60	8	15	6	12	9	11
	70	6	18	4	12	5	5
	80	5	16	2	8	6	7
	90	2	6	1	4	5	2
Hot	100	1	6	0	1	9	2
$N =$		1533	804	863	192	64	133

The question asked respondents to rate business interests on a feeling thermometer that ranged from 0 to 100.

NOTE: These data are from the mail questionnaires.

labor leadership. These tensions were reflected in McGovern delegate rankings of labor union leaders.[23] One-fifth of these were unfavorable to union leaders, and few were very strong in their support. More McGovern delegates were, for example, warmer in their support for political demonstrators, women's liberation, welfare recipients, party reform leaders, liberals, and the National Women's Political Caucus than for labor union leaders. Humphrey delegates were much more favorable than McGovern delegates to labor leaders and Muskie delegates slightly more so. As compared to Nixon supporters, however, McGovern delegates were partisans of the unions' leadership. Over one-half of Nixon delegates expressed unfavorable views on union leaders. Fewer than one-fifth were at all supportive. Wallace delegates were still more hostile to the union leadership despite Wallace's success in winning blue collar support.

If McGovern delegates were lukewarm in their feelings toward labor union leaders, it was not from love of business. The extent of McGovern delegates' animosity to business was unique among Democrats (Table 6–17). Sixty-seven percent were unfavorable to business and only 13 percent at all favorable. The fact that McGovern delegates were very anti-business without being very pro-labor leaders is interesting, particularly when the relatively low salience of economic issues for this group is also considered. Apparently McGovern delegates viewed both the major proponents on the economic scene—big labor and big business—with a certain distaste, as an arena devoid of heros. The Humphrey delegates provide an interesting contrast between McGovern delegates' anti-business, lukewarm labor attitudes. Humphrey delegates were the most pro-labor leaders of all Democratic groups and also the most favorable to business of any Democratic candidate group. Wallace delegates, in contrast, were the most negative to labor and second only to McGovern delegates in their percentage of unfavorable ratings of business. Wallace delegates were sharply split in their attitudes toward business, because some, reflecting the populist trends of the movement, were very hostile, and others, presumably more traditional conservatives, were definitely pro-business.

Business found widest support among Nixon delegates. It is notable and potentially important that Nixon delegates' favorable attitude to business was not as intense as McGovern delegates' *un*favorable attitude. The widespread pro-business orientations of the Republicans proves that elite attitudes were consistent with the image of the Republican party as having a special relationship with business. To be sure, friendly feelings toward business do not support the view that the Republican party is dominated by big business, any more than friendly feelings toward labor indicate the reverse. But the strong pro-business orientations do indicate that the Republican leadership believes that business serves the public interest. It has not been long since almost all Americans believed that business was a principal foundation (if not *the* foundation) of the nation's prosperity. The decline of this view among Democrats, especially new politics supporters, is notable *and may be a preface to unprecedented future debates about the structure of ownership and control of the economy. It may be significant for the future that while one numerous portion of the political influentials was very antagonistic to business interests, this antagonism was not balanced by equally warm support from any quarter. The imbalance of intensity among detractors and supporters in the political elite provides a basis for expecting continuing erosion of business' political position and, when coupled with the virtual absence of elite support for laissez-faire economic policies and the low participation of businessmen in politics, probably presages continued movement away from an economy dominated by private business.*

The distinctively anti-business orientation of McGovern delegates received little attention in 1972, doubtless because economic issues were peripheral to the central political conflicts of the 1972 campaign. These distinctive economic attitudes have clear relevance to the appraisal of the new breed hypothesis. At a minimum they constitute one more distinctive characteristic of McGovern delegates. At a maximum they presage the emergence of new economic issues and new political conflicts.

WELFARE POLICY

Sometime in the late 1960s welfare policy collided with the achievement ethic and the resultant sparks became part of the political fireworks of the decade. The basic principle of the welfare state had been established and almost universally accepted long before.[24] By the 1960s there were few Americans who disagreed with the proposition that governments should provide public funds to help those unable to help themselves to achieve a minimum standard of physical well-being. But there was much less agreement on the definition of poverty, the definition of eligibility, and especially, the relationship of what came to be called "welfare" payments to work. Poverty is always relative to a time, a place, and a general standard of living. In the 1960s President Lyndon Johnson's "war on poverty" defined poverty to include larger numbers of people. About the same time eligibility requirements for public relief were relaxed. And requirements were progressively abandoned that able-bodied recipients of welfare payments work. By 1970 the "progressive" policies of the New Deal, which provided public works for able-bodied unemployed, seemed to many to be reactionary, if not inhumane.

Expanding welfare rolls and high taxes prepared the electorate for charges (launched principally by George Wallace and some leading Republicans) that "welfare cheaters" lived in comfort off the toil of honest workingmen and women. Debates on welfare created supporters for the more conservative candidates and problems for John Lindsay and especially George McGovern whose flawed welfare policy proposals became an albatross.

Once basic beliefs about the personal and social value of work became entangled with questions about how, when, and under what circumstances government should expend public funds to support the needy, the welfare policy debate took on a new intensity and importance.[25] In the minds of both elite and voters, welfare policy was linked to such apparently unrelated topics as busing, crime, and Vietnam.

The fact that the achievement ethic (sometimes called the "work ethic") was also a target of the counter culture which was in turn associated with the McGovern movement intensified the involvement of welfare policy in the politics of the period.

Two items were included in the interview that tapped attitudes toward work and welfare. The sharp differences among delegates and candidate support groups confirmed the involvement of these issues in partisan politics. The most interesting of these two measures did not test attitudes for or against public support of the needy but, like the actual political issue, tested priorities and attitudes toward work. (See Table 10–1.) This measure also involves views concerning deprivations and indulgences, because to provide public support for able-bodied persons who do not work is a kind of indulgence and to require that able-bodied persons work, regardless of their inclinations, constitutes an effort to enforce policy with deprivations. Attitudes toward indulgence and deprivation as social incentives have an obvious theoretical relationship to the use of other sanctions. It is therefore not surprising that delegate views were very similar on both. McGovern delegates were uniquely supportive of abolishing poverty without regard to work (75 percent supported this position); an even higher percentage of Wallace delegates (95 percent) took the opposite view. Though there was less agreement among delegates supporting other candidates, there were significant differences in emphasis. About three-fourths of Nixon delegates emphasized the obligation to work, as compared to 45 percent of Humphrey and 33 percent of Muskie delegates.

A second measure utilizing a thermometer to test feelings toward welfare recipients revealed somewhat different distributions (Table 10–6): large majorities of delegates supporting McGovern, Humphrey, and Muskie expressed warm feelings toward welfare recipients; a large majority of Wallace delegates, cool feelings. In combination the two measures confirm the especially strong opposition between the views of McGovern and Wallace delegates and the tendency of the others to be ranged on a spectrum that moved from McGovern to Muskie to Humphrey to Nixon to Wallace.

RACE RELATIONS

By 1972 controversy concerning government action in the field of race relations centered on the question of whether it was desirable or constitutional to require busing of school children across district lines in order to achieve racial balance within the schools in a district. Particularly intense conflict raged over the question of busing between inner cities (mainly lower class and black) and suburbs (mainly middle class and white) and across county lines. "Forced busing" had little salience nationally, but intense importance within some states, for example, Florida, Michigan, and Maryland, where court decisions requiring busing inflamed local opinion. All candidates were forced to take public positions on busing and these positions became ammunition in the hands of their opponents. And in the interesting ideological chemistry of 1972, busing was subjectively linked to other superficially unrelated issues that divided both elite and electorate. The correlation between busing and welfare policy was r .64; between busing and crime policy, r .68; and between busing and Southeast Asia policy, r .60.

On this policy, as on the issues to which it was linked, McGovern delegates had distinctive views: an overwhelming majority (87 percent) were favorable to busing to further integrate schools, while in no other candidate group did more than 41 percent support this policy. Humphrey and Muskie supporters were nearly evenly split on whether it was more desirable to bus to integrate or to maintain neighborhood schools; Nixon and Wallace delegates were overwhelmingly opposed to busing. (See Table 10–2.)

Busing was (and is) a complex issue that involves dimensions besides race. Busing children out of neighborhood schools involves mixing cultures and classes as well as races. It deprives parents who must use public schools of control over the environment in which their children are socialized. The busing controversy was but one example of how questions of race and civil rights had become intertwined with other questions of social policy. Civil disobedience is another. Thermometer ratings of civil rights leaders and black militants indicate that *most Humphrey and Muskie delegates distinguished the two—approving civil rights and disapproving busing and disobedience; however, persons in other candidate support groups tended to either approve or disapprove both.*

COHERENCE: STRUCTURE

Opinions may be analyzed one by one but they exist not in isolation but in structured constellations. The coherence of political beliefs—how they "hang together"—is an extremely important determinant of how a political system functions. As Converse noted, beliefs are "bound together by some form of constraint or functional interdependence."[26] How they are bound together has practical as well as theoretical consequences.

The coherence of political attitudes is affected by various factors including the character of the political culture, the character of conflictive issues, and the experience and temperament of the individual. What hangs together for one person is not necessarily perceived as related by another. For the student of politics, it is the individual's perception of interrelations that matters, since it is his perception that affects his political behavior.

Exploring the coherence of political beliefs poses serious problems to which there are a limited number of approaches. Depth interviews of each respondent provide the most reliable insight to how ideas and feelings hang together for a particular person, but the problems of generalizing such information are acute. Where large numbers are involved, as in the present study, two other strategies are available: factor analysis may be relied on to report which beliefs and attitudes hang together, or tests may be developed to determine respondents' consistency in answering questions that seem to the researcher to belong together. Both these approaches are utilized in this study.

Robert Lane has commented, "The mistake underlying reliance on the constraints implied by statistical clustering, scalar ordering, or acceptance of an idea cluster by an authoritative elite is based on the fallacious view that if some people see idea-elements properly clustering in a certain way, others should too," and he adds, "Such 'constraints' or clusterings refer to neither logic nor rationality."[27] But there is no compelling reason (no constraint?) why clusters and factors and scales must be associated with "the fallacious view that if some people see idea-elements properly clustering in a certain way, others should too." Statistical techniques can be used to map configurations and alternatives as well as to measure conformity to norms.

I assumed that the delegates were rational, involved, reasonably well-informed, and reasonably effective people and that their beliefs and the relations among them made sense to them and some of the people who chose them as delegates. I did not assume that an elaborate deductive political ideology in which multiple specific applications may be deduced from one or two architectonic principles is superior to perspectives in which views about specific policies derive from the examination of discrete problems and some perhaps inarticulate general views about the world. The techniques of statistical analysis utilized in this examination carry with them no constraints that violate these assumptions.

COHERENCE OF BELIEFS: A FACTOR ANALYSIS APPROACH

When all questions concerning policies, issues, and potentially related groups were combined in a single problem, the resulting most inclusive factor confirmed that broad and diverse issues became linked in the political divisions of 1972. That factor, which is termed the Political Culture Factor, is shown in Table 6–18.

What is the ideological dimension reflected in the Political Culture Factor? Perhaps we should begin by noting what is not included in this dimension. Vietnam policy, believed by many to have been the core of the McGovern movement, is not.[28] It occurred in a factor with other items relevant to United States military policy. Economic policy is not included. Although several items relevant to the traditional economic-based left-right dichotomy were included in the factor analysis, none was related to the constellation of cultural and political items included in the Political

Table 6-18. Political Culture: The Most Inclusive Factor in Varimax Rotated Solution

Busing	.47
Crime	.50
Liberals	−.41
Military priorities	−.47
United States give economic aid	.51
United States recognize Cuba	.51
No nuclear weapons	.42
United States support United Nations	.59
Welfare policy	−.58
Rock festivals	−.56
Military	.48
Welfare recipients	−.49
Political demonstrators	−.54
Black militants	−.52

NOTE: These data are from the intersect sample. Interview questions 82, 86, and 87 and mail questionnaire questions 39, 40, 41, 42, and 43. All delegates were included in this factor problem. The cut-off point for inclusion in the Political Culture Factor was .4.

Culture Factor. Since it is economic issues and attitudes toward economic groups that have "structured" the party alignment of the post-New Deal period, it is interesting that they were not related to the questions of value and policy that dominated the politics of 1972.

Inclusion or exclusion of subjects in the Political Culture Factor does not imply that those excluded were less important than those included, only that they did not figure in the most inclusive dimension of ideological conflict. But if these issues that have had such salience in American politics were not included in the Political Culture dimension, what is that dimension that played so important a role in structuring political conflict?

Perhaps the coherence of the disparate items on the Political Culture Factor can best be understood by reference to the maintenance of social order.[29] The relation between welfare, military preparedness, busing, and crime then would be understood not as logical but as existential. Traditional society included (and includes) a belief that work has intrinsic value for persons and societies; that those who can work should and only those who cannot should be supported by public funds; that conflict is a permanent feature of politics; that power is necessary to maintaining social peace; that to be safe, the nation must be strong, preferably stronger than any other nation; that authority rests on force as well as consent; that authority must be protected and preserved; that citizenship requires obedience to laws with which one disagrees; that breaking the law undermines authority and threatens social peace; that lawbreakers should be punished.[30] The inclusion in a single factor of crime, liberals, military policy, the United Nations, welfare, political demonstrators, and black militants makes sense because all involve attitudes to authority, power, and work. Busing is involved with preserving traditional society because it threatens the ability of parents to transmit traditional values and manners. Rock festivals, the United Nations, economic aid, recognizing Cuba have in common a rejection of some elements of the traditional culture: its inhibitions, nationalism, and anti-communism.

These issues cohered in the attitudes of some of the political influentials because they cohered in traditional American society. They hung together for large numbers of McGovern supporters because they were involved in a comprehensive rejection of traditional practices, and they hung together for Wallace and Nixon supporters because they were mobilized for a general defense of the traditional institutional practices.

Table 6–19 shows that Muskie and Humphrey supporters clustered in the middle of the political culture spectrum, because most were not engaged on this cultural battlefield. That some delegates (and non-delegates) saw busing, welfare, political demonstrations, and defense policies as related and others did not does not indicate a weak intellect or insensitivity on the part of either. It signifies that different mind sets organized the

Table 6-19. Political Culture Index by Candidate Preference (%)

		McGovern	Humphrey	Wallace	Muskie	Nixon
Cultural transformers	1	57 }98	4	0	21	1
	2	41	54 }91	0	40 }71	9
	3	2	37	30 }101	31	57 }90
Cultural preservers	4	0	4	71	8	33
Weighted N =		748	163	44	155	623

NOTE: These data are from the intersect sample. For method of index construction and a complete explanation of the Political Culture Index, see Appendix C.

issues of the year differently. But if, following Rokeach, "we define importance solely in terms of connectedness" so that "the more a given belief is functionally connected or in communication with other beliefs, the more implications and consequences it has for other beliefs and, therefore, the more central the belief,"[31] then the presence in this factor of such multiple and diverse subjects as rock festivals, busing, welfare, economic aid to developing nations, and political demonstrators provides further confirmation that such questions were centrally involved in the politics of that year.[32]

The links between culture, authority, and policy orientation reflected in this rotated factor analysis were believed by many to be the most significant feature of the politics of 1972. A counter culture had developed in the late 1960s alongside the growth of civil disobedience and protest. The counter culture and the politics of protest alike denied the authority and morality of traditional values and practices. The counter culture was broader than its political manifestations and included new attitudes toward work, sex, drugs, crime, language, dress, hair styles, childrearing, music, science, reason, discipline, spontaneity, and a variety of other topics some of which had little relevance for politics. The counter culture entered the national political arena by way of antiwar demonstrations and the new politics of the McCarthy and then the McGovern movements. Not all of the exponents of the new politics embraced the life styles and social doctrines associated with the counter culture. But the two were related by a shared antagonism to many traditional symbols and practices, by the conviction that many of the society's institutional practices lacked legitimacy, and by bonds of mutual tolerance.

Many of the major political issues of 1972 were perceived to be involved in the clash of cultures. The antiwar demonstrations, for example, not only attacked American policy in Southeast Asia, but celebrated new life styles. Welfare policy became involved in conflicting views of the work ethic. Government financed and administered child care programs were debated by persons with different views about the roles of wives, mothers, and women's liberation. Law enforcement policy became entangled with questions concerning the legitimacy of the social order and the morality of the outcast. Foreign policy became enmeshed in culture conflict not only because of the affinity between the counter culture and the antiwar movement, but because new conceptions of national purpose had become the subject of hot debate. Even pollution and "the environment" were involved in culture conflict as counter culture accused traditional culture of overvaluing technology and justifying rape of the environment. Disagreement on values and morals accompanied debate on candidates and social policy and added special intensity to the politics of 1972.[33]

The political culture factor and the coincidence of scores on that factor with candidate preference reflect the broad involvement of culture in the political conflicts of 1972.

Another indicator of the extent to which culture was involved in the politics of 1972 is the very high correlation between respondents' views of their position on the political spectrum and their scores on the Political Culture Index and various other measures involving authority.

The salience of political culture to presidential politics at the elite level is reflected in Table 6–20. The lesser centrality of economic issues to the politics of the year is reflected in its lesser relation with political self-classification.

The Political Culture Factor constitutes persuasive evidence that for the political elite, many discrete issues were perceived as parts of a broader whole relevant to that year's presidential politics. But ideological coherence among policies, issues, and groups was not limited to this one dimension. There was also coherence across dimensions and coherence among issues and groups not included in the Political Culture Factor. Although Vietnam policy did not appear in this factor, it was correlated with all the items in the factor—and with other issues and groups (Table 6–21).

For large portions of the elite existential political constraints linked domestic and foreign policy, culture, and politics. The high coherence of issues and symbols signified political conflict whose scope was unusually broad for people famous for eclectic perspectives.

CONSISTENCY

Delegates' opinions were also analyzed within and across six issue areas. To determine the ideological consistency of attitudes concerning race, authority, foreign policy, economic policy, women, and the counter culture, six indexes were developed, and for each it was determined how many delegates took a consistently liberal or conservative position *on all three items in the index*. Those who were consistently liberal or conservative across five or six of these subject areas are termed "holists." Those who were consistently liberal or conservative on two, three, or four issue areas are called "programmatic" delegates; persons consistent across one or two issue areas are called "eclectics," and those consistent on none are termed "very eclectic." Obviously the investigator's opinion is crucial in deciding which item related to which issue and what constituted the liberal and conservative ends of these scales. The measure is vulnerable to the criticisms Robert Lane levelled against using the interviewer's

Table 6-20. Ideological Self-Classification: Relation to Specific
Issues and Political Culture (Gammas)

Inflation[a]	.32
Busing[a]	.76
Vietnam[a]	.67
Crime[a]	.71
Welfare[a]	− .62
Political Culture Index	.88

[a]Proximity measures.

NOTE: The welfare and political culture measures are from the intersect sample; the remainder is based on data from the mail questionnaire. For a complete explanation of the Political Culture Index, see Appendix C.

conception of interrelations as a standard by which to measure others' consistency.[34] But the items in these scales are very simple, and all the items in each measure occurred in a single dimension in some factor problem. The decision as to what was liberal and what conservative was made not by the author's idiosyncratic understanding of these traditions, but on the basis of the delegates' perceptions of these issues in 1972. And, as Sartori has emphasized,[35] internal consistency is an important characteristic of political beliefs, it is one criterion for distinguishing what is often termed "ideological" politics in which political actors are guided by a comprehensive deductive belief system from political systems characterized by pragmatic orientations and lesser conflict.

The results of this analysis (Table 6–22) confirm the presence in an elite of persons who displayed extraordinary ideological consistency on a broad range of issues and subjects. Holists amounted to 18 percent of the supporters of McGovern, 21 percent of Wallace supporters, and no Humphrey delegates. Programmatics, who also displayed unusually high levels of ideological consistency, comprised 43 percent of McGovernites and 31 percent of Wallace supporters and 20 percent of Republicans.

The existence of a high degree of ideological consistency in political actors does not necessarily imply the presence of a "rationalistic" or "ideological" mentality—in the sense that these terms are employed by Sartori, Shils, and Oakshott.[36] As defined by Sartori, "The *rationalistic* processing-coding tends to approach problems as follows: i) deductive argumentation prevails over evidence and testing; ii) doctrine prevails over practice; iii) principle prevails over precedent; iv) ends prevail over means; and v) perceptions tend to be 'covered up,' doctrine-loaded, typically indirect."[37] Though the rationalistic approach to politics involves

Table 6-21. Vietnam Policy: Its Relation to Other Issues
(Pearson's R Correlations)

Busing[a]	.60
Crime[a]	.59
National Women's Political Caucus[b]	−.45
Conservatives[b]	.62
Party reform leaders[b]	−.49
Women's lib[b]	−.50
Blacks[b]	−.44
Liberals[b]	−.61
Business interests[b]	.46
Military superiority[c]	−.55
Withdraw troops from Southeast Asia[c]	.61
United States/Cuba relations[c]	.45
Withdraw troops from Europe[c]	.45
No nuclear warfare[c]	.40
United States support United Nations[c]	.44
Welfare policy[a]	−.52
Civil rights leaders[b]	.52
Policemen[b]	.43
Rock festivals[b]	−.35
Military[b]	.57
Political demonstrators[b]	−.53
Black militants[b]	−.49

Question on Vietnam: "Even though most of the American troops have been withdrawn from South Vietnam, there is still a lot of discussion about the United States' action in Indochina. Some people think we should end all American military assistance and economic aid to Southeast Asia. Others say we should give military assistance and economic aid to the governments of South Vietnam, Cambodia, and Laos. Where would you place yourself on the following scale, ranging from agreement with no United States military assistance or economic aid to agreement with United States military assistance and economic aid?"

[a]Proximity measures.
[b]Feeling thermometers.
[c]"Strongly agree" to "strongly disagree" statements.

NOTE: All data above the dashed line are from the mail questionnaires; the remainder is from the intersect sample. The cutoff point for inclusion in this table was .35.

Table 6-22. Ideological Holism by Party, by Candidate Preference, and by Ideological Self-Classification (%)

	Dem.	Rep.	McGovern	Humphrey	Wallace	Muskie	Nixon	Radical	Very Liberal	Somewhat Liberal	Moderate	Somewhat Conservative	Very Conservative
Very eclectic	7	12	4	10	0	24	13	3	5	12	17	7	0
Eclectic	46	66	35	76	49	52	66	15	36	65	66	66	44
Programmatic	34	20	43	14	31	17	20	51	42	18	16	23	46
Holist	13	2	18	0	21	6	2	31	17	5	1	4	10
Weighted N = 1178	501		692	139	39	140	481	109	539	387	277	278	78

NOTE: Data on parties and candidate support groups are from the interviews; data on ideological self-classification are from the intersect sample. Cramer's *V* for the parties is .25.

Gamma for ideological self-classification is –.36.

The holism index is based on six issue area indexes; holists are those who were consistently liberal or conservative in their responses to *each* item in five or six area indexes; programmatics were consistently liberal or conservative in responses to *each* item of three or four issue area indexes; eclectics were consistent in responses to each item of one or two issue area indexes, and very eclectics were not consistent in their responses to all items in any index. For a complete explanation of this holism measure, see Appendix C.

more than a high level of ideological consistency, a comprehensive, consistent perspective is an important element of ideological politics. And it stands in contrast to the pragmatic, incremental approach to politics that treats problems as discrete questions whose resolution derives from situational and technical factors rather than as "pieces" of ultimate questions.

The 1972 presidential elite probably contained few persons operating from a comprehensive, systematic, rational doctrine of which Marxism is, in our time, the prototype. But as the high correlations between ideological self-placement and issues make clear, many in this elite positioned themselves not only in relation to specific policies and issues, but with reference to much more general abstract principles. Consistently conservative and liberal responses to subject areas not only indicate "consistency," they indicate that the choice of positions on specific issues is being guided by more general principles. In 1972 these principles were the conflicting values and notions of causation embodied in the traditional culture and the subculture that challenged it. It is probably always the case that culture guides responses to diverse phenomena and gives those responses a unity and consistency that is apparent only when compared with reactions deriving from a different culture. If culture can function in the same fashion as a comprehensive ideology, so can a counter culture. As a comprehensive ideology may constitute the basis of a subculture within a society (the Marxism of the French Communist party has functioned as the basis of a counter culture within French society), so may a counter culture function as an ideology. Something of this sort seems to have happened in the United States in recent years. The political perspectives of many in the political class changed in response to changed values, goals, and tastes. Rokeach has noted that "A person's value system may . . . be said to represent a learned organization of rules for making choices and for resolving conflicts—between two or more modes of behavior or between two or more end-states of existence."[38] The effect was the same as if opinions had been derived from a comprehensive ideology—though no such ideology existed: within a few years, the opinions and loyalties of thousands of the enlightened classes changed in strikingly similar ways. Charles Reich described as the "greening of America" the process in which large portions of the elite abandoned traditional assumptions, values, and life styles in favor of new beliefs about authority, power, discipline, rewards and punishments, political obligation, and political morality.[39] The appearance of a challenge to traditional culture and practices called attention to relations among political issues and between them and basic values, which relations would probably have passed unnoticed had the culture itself not become an issue, and stimulated self-conscious defense of the culture. The values and beliefs of both culture and counter culture functioned as the tenets of a deductive ideology. The result was conflict whose scope, salience, and intensity is typical of "ideological politics" in a polity in which the actions of virtually no one were guided by an explicit political ideology. The direct, explicit involvement of basic values in political conflict increases the *scope* of conflict by emphasizing connections between specific objects of disagreement and many other issues, because values concern "a desirable mode of behavior that has a transcendental quality to it, guiding actions, attitudes, judgments and comparisons across specific objects and situations and beyond immediate goals to more ultimate goals. . . ."[40] The direct involvement of basic values in political conflict increases the *intensity* of that conflict because "values occupy a more central position than attitudes within one's personality makeup and cognitive system, and they are therefore determinants of attitudes, as well as of behavior."[41] Because they have an important motivational component and serve important adjustive and ego-defensive functions for the persons who hold them, the explicit involvement of basic values in a political arena enhances interest in the arena by leading more people to feel a *personal* stake in political outcomes.

The type of orientations of major actors within a political system determines the scope and intensity of conflict; It determines whether politics are "pragmatic" or "ideological." Where there is general consensus on identity and purpose, demands of competing groups will be limited to changes in specific policy or perhaps to the inauguration of new programs. Although anthropologists (and even political scientists) may perceive coherence between any set of political demands and basic cultural precepts, the objective existence of coherence among basic cultural assumptions, social structures, and policy preferences does not mean that all the elements of a culture are involved in political competition at all times. Indeed all possible questions are never debated in a political arena. That all possible modes of social organization are not debated by political actors in a democratic system does not indicate a conspiracy to prevent discussion of fundamental issues; it merely indicates the existence of broad consensus on these issues. The failure of the American parties to debate and decide whether or not the society should reestablish slavery as an alternative to existing unemployment, or practice infanticide as a form of population control, or nationalize all enterprises with a capital value of over $100,000 reflects the existence of widespread agreement in the society on these questions.[42]

In political systems where basic questions of identity, value, and belief are not at issue, they are not an issue. Where the goals of political parties are to achieve specific limited improvements or to end specific abuses as, for example, to eradicate black lung and indemnify its victims or to provide better medical care for the aged, then fundamental aspects of social and cultural systems are, in fact, not involved in the competition between the parties. Similarly, when the chief question to be resolved in an election is *who* among various contenders with similar perspectives will rule, the fundamental structure of the society or its basic beliefs is not involved. Fundamental questions about reorganizing society and reforming the culture become *political* questions, because some group of political actors challenges existing values in the political arena.

Orientations change, and yesterday's areas of consensus may be tomorrow's hotly contested issues. Political systems change, and into the system that yesterday considered only discrete policies there may come new generations with new comprehensive orientations.

The inclusion of basic questions of value and causation in the political sphere has a powerful effect on the quality of political interactions. Politics is only one of the social processes through which questions may be debated and decided. Churches, families, and the individual conscience are other arenas through which matters of faith, morals, and purpose may be resolved. By formal provisions and habits of forebearance, constitutional governments exclude some issues from resolution through politics. Matters of religion and life style, for example, have long been regarded as inappropriate matters for public decision.[43]

Questions of rectitude are not only less easily compromised than questions of economic interest, but they are associated with special intensity and intransigence, because they have special relation to a person's core values and commitments. Almost no students of political ideologies doubt that some elements of a belief system are more important than others. Converse, for example, asserts that ". . . idea elements within a belief system vary in a property we shall call *centrality,* according to the role they play in the belief system as a whole."[44]

When the question of centrality is approached in relation to the self-structure rather than in relation to some intellectual construct, such as a right/left spectrum, the special centrality of culture becomes clear. Central symbols and rudimentary beliefs ("I am French") are identifications incorporated into the self.[45] We know from Freud, Erikson, Sullivan, and other students of personality development that the process of incorporation begins in the very earliest stage of a child's development but that not all identifications are acquired at the earliest stage of life and that, whenever acquired, identifications are anchored in the self-system and integrated into it. Erikson has emphasized the role of ideology in the resolution of the "identity crisis" through which each of us passes on our way to maturity. Ideologies are incorporated into the self because they help to answer those more fundamental questions, "Who am I and what should I do?" Ideologies "create a world image convincing enough to support the collective and the individual sense of identity."[46] These questions are answered by an explicit ideology only when they have, for whatever reason, not been answered by the culture. But whenever acquired, and from wherever, symbols of identification define the "we" in whose name demands are made. They are to politics what money is to the economy. They are currency with which other values are sought and gained.[47] Basic symbols of identification are foundations on which may be built elaborate ideological edifices (such as Marxism) or simple demands (such as "Freedom for Catalonia!").[48] Ideologies whose symbols of identity are different from those of the dominant culture symbolize counter cultures.

Values are also basic elements of a culture, which internalized, become central elements of the self. As Lasswell, Rokeach, Sartori, and others have emphasized, values may be viewed either as elements of a culture or internalized as personal predispositions.[49] A politics in which basic identifications and values are at stake will be more intense and more bitter than a politics that involves interests, because while the former is felt to involve questions of *survival* (of the self and the culture that supports and reinforces it), the latter involves only *aggrandizement*. However desirable, aggrandizement is never as crucial as survival.

The preceding data on the perspectives of the presidential elite demonstrate the centrality of basic values and identifications to the presidential elite in 1972, as voting studies have demonstrated the parallel importance of these issues among voters. Not only did the University of Michigan's Center for Political Studies' authors find that ". . . as an explanation of the vote in 1972 issues were at least equally as important as party identification,"[50] they also found that "The war issue—including Vietnam policy, amnesty, and cutbacks in military spending—and social issues—incorporating policy alternatives for dealing with urban problems and unrest, government aid to minorities, protection of individual civil liberties in criminal cases, and alternative modes for dealing with student demonstrations—were the issue domains that attributed significantly, the explanation of the vote."[51] The low salience of economic issues for the elite and the high coherence of cultural and social issues establishes not only that economic issues no longer "structured" the electorate and elite in 1972, but that issues that did were issues with a great potential for intensely involving the individual by way of his crucial self-conceptions.

CULTURAL PRESERVERS AND CULTURAL TRANSFORMERS: CO-RELATIONAL TYPES

To determine the personal, political, and social characteristics of those members of the presidential elite who were most united in their alienation from the traditional political culture, those who scored highest and lowest on the Political Culture Index were isolated and analyzed. Persons scoring in the highest fourth comprise 14 percent of the total sample ($n=297$); they are termed "cultural liberals." Those scoring in the lowest fourth comprised 26 percent of the sample ($n=577$); they are termed "cultural conservatives." These two categories of persons differed from one another in many ways.

The cultural liberal was more likely to be under 40, highly educated, and urban in origin. Though also a joiner, the cultural liberal was probably not active in as many community organizations as the cultural conservative.

Politically, the cultural liberal was almost surely a Democrat and very probably a McGovern supporter. His political experience was likely to be relatively brief, and the little experience he had in party office was probably at very low levels. A strong liberal or radical, he came to politics out of intense interest in issues and remained relatively unconcerned with party organization. Party reform and increased participation were of greater concern to him than unifying the party or winning the election. Like amateurs the cultural liberal had intense views across a wide spectrum of issues, and tended to be holistic in perspective.

Personally, he differed from many other delegates in his greater subjectivity and lesser concern with order in his life.

Cultural liberals comprise a very homogeneous category whose members shared most social and political characteristics. In background and style, ideological and organizational perspectives they closely resembled Wilson's "amateur," Polsby and Wildavsky's "purist." Cultural conservatives were more diverse, and shared few of the amateur's characteristics. Less intense, less holistic ideologically, and deeply attached to party, the cultural conservative focused more on building party unity and winning elections than on articulating correct issue positions—not because he was uninterested in policy, but because he was also strongly attached to the party by fun, friends, and status satisfactions, and party loyalty as well as policy. These attitudes were seasoned by years of political activity and experience in party office. Representatives of these two cultural types often differed from one another in religion, education, and demographic background, and, quite possibly, in occupation. Both Protestants and Catholics were more numerous among the cultural conservatives; agnostics and Jews among the liberals. Rural and small town origins were more numerous among the cultural conservatives; urban backgrounds among the liberals. In occupation, the cultural conservative was less likely to be engaged in a profession that featured symbol manipulation (journalism, teaching, clergy), but symbol specialists were overrepresented among the cultural liberals.

CONCLUSION

Did the cultural liberals comprise the new breed? Not exactly, since persons with "new" organizational perspectives and incentives were also found at the other end of the political spectrum. Many of the pure cultural liberals shared motives and organizational attitudes that differentiated them from the supporters of traditional candidates. However, cultural conservatives also shared these new attitudes toward parties and politics. Among the 1972 presidential elite cultural liberals with high concern about politics and low organization support were more numerous—much more numerous—than cultural conservatives with these attitudes. However, the presence of some pure cultural conservatives with anti-organizational concerns demonstrates that the newer orientations to political life were not an attribute of a single ideological position.

In a later chapter relations among these dimensions are analyzed in an effort to determine the existence and characteristics of the new people whom so many believe embodied and represented new forces in American politics.

NOTES

1. This conception of perspectives is, of course, that of Harold D. Lasswell and Abraham Kaplan, *Power and Society: A Framework for Political Analysis* (New Haven: Yale University Press, 1950), pp. 16–28. There is no generally accepted terminology to discuss political beliefs and feelings associated with them. "Belief system," "political culture," "ideology," are all terms used to describe constellations of beliefs, feelings, and attitudes concerning politics. The word one uses to describe these elements and constellations does not seem to me important providing that it is defined so that it links the individual into the political system and includes beliefs and their associated effect. Useful discussions of the elements of ideology are Giovanni Sartori, "Politics, Ideology and Belief Systems," *American Political Science Review* 63 (1969): 398–411; Robert Dahl, "Ideology, Conflict and Consensus: Notes for a Theory" (Paper prepared for the International Political Science Association World Congress, Brussels, Belgium, 1967); Roger W. Cobb, "The Belief-Systems Perspective: An Assessment of a Framework," *Journal of Politics* 35 (1973): 121–153; Edward Shils, "The Concept and Function of Ideology" in *The International Encyclopedia of the Social Sciences* (New York: Macmillan, 1968), vol. 7, pp. 66–75; and Shils, "Ideology and Civility: On the Politics of the Intellectual," *Sewanee Review* 66 (1958): 450–480. Also Robert D. Putnam, *The Beliefs of Politicians: Ideology, Conflict, and Democracy in Britain and Italy* (New Haven: Yale University Press, 1973); Robert Lane, *Political Ideology: Why the American Common Man Believes What He Does* (New York: The Free Press, 1962).

2. A good discussion of these problems is Donald E. Stokes, "Spatial Models of Party Competition," in *Elections and Political Order,* eds. Angus Campbell, et al. (New York: John Wiley & Sons, 1966), pp. 161–179. See also Donald D. Searing, John J. Schwartz, and Alden E. Lind, "The Structuring Principle: Political Socialization and Belief Systems," *American Political Science Review* 67 (1973): 415–432. Also Eugene Litwak, Nancy Hooyman and Donald Warren, "Ideological Complexity and Middle American Rationality," *Public Opinion Quarterly* 37 (1973): 317–332.

3. This was, of course, the view of the "philosophical radicals": Jeremy Bentham, James and John Stuart Mill, David Ricardo, and Adam Smith. For a good account of the thought of the original liberals, see John Plamenatz, *The English Utilitarians* (Oxford: Blackwell, 1966); Ely Halevy, *The Growth of Philosophic Radicalism* (Boston: Beacon Press, 1955).

4. Alfred O. Hero, Jr., "Liberalism-Conservatism Revisited: Foreign vs. Domestic Federal Policies, 1937–1967," *Public Opinion Quarterly* 33 (1969): 399–408.

5. For arguments supporting this interpretation, see Samuel P. Huntington, "Conservatism as an Ideology," *American Political Science Review* 51 (1957): 454–473. Also, Robert Waelder, "Protest and Revolution Against Western Societies" in *The Revolution in World Politics,* ed. Morton A. Kaplan (New York: John Wiley & Sons, 1962), pp. 3–27.

6. Philip E. Converse, "The Nature of Belief Systems in Mass Publics" in *Ideology and Discontent,* ed. David E. Apter (New York: The Free Press, 1964), pp. 215–218.

7. A useful discussion of issues and voting is the series of articles in the *American Political Science Review* 66, No. 2 (1972). These include Gerald M. Pomper, "From Confusion to Clarity: Issues and American Voters, 1956–1968," 415–428; Richard W. Boyd, "Popular Control of Public Policy: A Normal Vote Analysis of the 1968 Election," 429–449; Richard A. Brody and Benjamin I. Page, "Comment: The Assessment of Policy Voting," 450–458; John H. Kessel, "Comment: The Issues in Issue Voting," 459–465.

Kessel's article also provides comprehensive references to the literature on this subject. There is broad consensus on the growing importance of ideology in American politics. The University of Michigan's Center for Political Studies' analysis of the 1972 election augments this growing consensus. Arthur H. Miller, Warren E. Miller, Alden S. Raine, and Thad A. Brown, "A Majority Party in Disarray: Policy Polarization in the 1972 Election" (Paper presented at the 1973 American Political Science Association in New Orleans, La., September 4–8, 1973).

8. Shils, "Concept and Function of Ideology," p. 68.
9. Ibid., p. 69.
10. There are, of course, well-known problems concerning the relations of consent and legitimacy. I do not intend to imply that all governments that *exist* are legitimate, nor that all obedience gives consent. Obedience can be coerced as well as given. Still, it is true that governments that most subjects actively oppose cannot be said to be legitimate. For a discussion of these and related problems, see, e.g., T. H. Green, *Lectures on the Principles of Political Obligation* (London: Longmans, Green and Co., 1895); R. M. MacIver, *The Modern State* (Oxford: Oxford University Press, 1926), and *The Web of Government* (New York: Free Press, 1965).
11. Civil disobedience is the denial that one is obligated to obey an *il*legitimate law.
12. The efforts of the McGovern Commission to secure "equal" participation of all potential Democratic voters are directly related to this charge. So was the enfranchisement of 18-year-olds.
13. The election of 1860 was the last that featured serious challenges to legitimacy. Of course, many conservatives denied the legitimacy of much of the New Deal. The courts' dramatic reversals contributed to questions of legitimacy concerning the New Deal and school segregation.
14. This combination of attitudes is more common elsewhere. France's O.A.S. is a clearcut example of insurgency in the name of an older conception of authority. So perhaps was the southern position in the Civil War. There are various events in recent American politics that pitted agents of authority (police) against other agents of authority (e.g., civilian review boards).
15. However, the key authority figures, police and military, were also related to another cluster of items in another factor.
16. Herbert McClosky, "Consensus and Ideology in American Politics," *American Political Science Review* 58 (1964), p. 370.
17. Lester W. Milbrath, *Political Participation: How and Why Do People Get Involved in Politics?* (Chicago: Rand McNally & Co.,1965), p. 79. Also Gabriel Almond and Sidney Verba, *The Civic Culture: Political Attitudes and Democracy in Five Nations* (Princeton, N.J.: Princeton University Press, 1963); Angus Campbell, "The Passive Citizen," *Acta Sociologica* 6 fasc. (1–2): 9–21; Donald Stokes, "Popular Evaluations of Government: An Empirical Assessment," in *Ethics and Bigness,* eds. Harlan Cleveland and Harold Lasswell (New York: Harper and Row, 1962). However, Leites, Putnam, and others have documented the political cynicism of some elites in France, Italy, and elsewhere: Nathan Leites, *The Game of Politics in France* (Stanford: Stanford University Press, 1959); Putnam, *Beliefs of Politicians;* James L. Payne, *Patterns of Conflict in Columbia* (New Haven: Yale University Press, 1968); and Payne, *Labor and Politics in Peru* (New Haven: Yale University Press, 1965).
18. Putnam, *Beliefs of Politicians*, and Leites, *Game of Politics*.
19. In considering these findings note that the three measures do not postulate perversity or enjoyment of wickedness but only emphasize self-interest and suggest that where possible people will prefer their own advantage. This was, of course, the assumption on

which the Founding Fathers acted, which led them to divide and limit power. *The Federalist Papers,* for example, affirm and reaffirm the view that people will prefer their own interests to those of their neighbors, that they will readily fall into mutual animosities and violent conflicts, that the control of these self-interested passions (and the factions to which they lead) is a principal function of government. Obviously, the presidential elite who wrote the Constitution had different, less rosy expectations than the present one about human nature and conduct. *The Federalist Papers,* especially Nos. 51 and 10.

20. Walter Bagehot, *The English Constitution* (London: Cox and Wyman, Ltd., Fontana Library ed., 1963). Also, Harold D. Lasswell, "Democratic Character," in *Political Writings* (Glencoe: The Free Press, 1951), pp. 495–503.

21. The precise role of Vietnam in the defeat of Hubert Humphrey in 1968 is disputed among experts. For a discussion of the impact on the election's outcome of the defection from Humphrey of doves, hawks, and others, see Philip E. Converse, Warren E. Miller, Jerrold G. Rusk, and Arthur C. Wolfe, "Continuity and Change in American Politics: Parties and Issues in the 1968 Election," *American Political Science Review* 63 (1969): 1083–1105; Robert B. Smith, "Disaffection, Delegitimation and Consequences: Aggregate Trends for World War II, Korea and Vietnam," in *Public Opinion and the Military Establishment,* ed. Charles C. Moskos (Beverly Hills, Calif.: Sage Publications, 1971); E. M. Schreiber, "Vietnam Policy Preferences and Withheld 1968 Presidential Votes," *Public Opinion Quarterly* 37 (1973): 91–98.

22. Outstanding among other studies confirming distinctive orientations of the parties on economic issues are V.O. Key, *Politics, Parties, and Pressure Groups,* 4th ed. (New York: Thomas Y. Crowell, 1958), p. 239; Herbert McClosky, Paul J. Hoffmann and Rosemary O'Hara, "Issue Conflict and Consensus Among Party Leaders and Followers," *American Political Science Review* 54 (1960): esp. p. 411.

23. Note though that McClosky, et al. noted the existence of a widespread support among the Democratic presidential elite for increased government regulation of trade unions and commented: ". . . it may signify that the party's perspective toward the trade unions is shifting somewhat." McClosky, et al., "Issue Conflict," pp. 415–416. Since his comment was based on the delegates to the 1956 convention, it suggests that tensions within the Democratic party concerning trade unions may be of relative long standing.

24. Richard M. Scammon and Ben J. Wattenberg emphasize the wide acceptance of the welfare state in *The Real Majority* (New York: Coward-McCann, 1970). Public opinion polls of the 1960s confirm this interpretation.

25. On the relations among work, religion, and the American tradition, see, e.g., Max Weber, *The Protestant Ethic and the Spirit of Capitalism* (London: G. Allen and Unwin, Ltd., 1930); Richard Henry Tawney, *Religion and the Rise of Capitalism: A Historical Study* (New York: Harcourt Brace and Co., 1926); Perry Miller, *The New England Mind: The Seventeenth Century* (New York: Macmillan, 1939); Max Lerner, *America as a Civilization: Life and Thought in the United States Today* (New York: Simon and Schuster, 1957).

26. Converse, "Nature of Belief Systems," p. 207.

27. Robert E. Lane, "Patterns of Political Belief," in *Handbook of Political Psychology,* ed. Jeanne N. Knutson (San Francisco: Jossey-Bass, 1973), p. 103.

28. But when Democrats only were included in the problem, Vietnam did enter as the most inclusive factor, as did a number of items relating to women and women's liberation.

29. Samuel P. Huntington described attitudes toward the social order as the basis of conservative and liberal orientations in his article, "Conservatism as an Ideology." Also, Waelder, "Protest and Revolution," and Robert Waelder, *Progress and Revolution* (New York: International University Press, 1967).

30. This description paraphrases a larger discussion of the contrast between the old and new politics. Jeane Kirkpatrick, "The Revolt of the Masses," *Commentary* 2, (1973): 58–62.

31. Milton Rokeach, *Beliefs, Attitudes, and Values: A Theory of Organization Change* (San Francisco: Jossey-Bass, 1968).

32. Note that McClosky, et al. found relatively low differences between parties on "style" issues—in which category he included the United Nations, international alliances, foreign aid, immigration, and segregation. Items relevant to all of these except immigration occur in the Political Culture Factor, on which we will see there are large differences among delegates. McClosky comments that one explanation of the low differences on his other categories of issues is that they are "not so likely to be part of the common core of values upon which the community structure rests." McClosky, et al., "Issue Conflict," p. 418. The presence of these items in the political arena signifies that a good many of the "core values" of the community were disputed in the political arena (or perceived as being) in 1972. Note also that McClosky's findings were consistent with those of the Elmira, New York, study. See Bernard R. Berelson, Paul F. Lazarsfeld, and William M. McPhee, *Voting* (Chicago: University of Chicago Press, 1954), ch. 9.

33. Analysis of the election outcome has established the importance of cultural conflict to the defecting Democrats. See especially, Miller, et al., "Majority Party," p. 61. These interrelations are reflected in the Political Culture Factor.

34. Lane's criticism occurs in his discussion of constraint in "Patterns of Political Belief," in *Handbook*, ed. Knutson, pp. 98–105.

35. Sartori, "Politics, Ideology," p. 401. Also, Shils, "Concept and Function of Ideology," emphasizes the comprehensive rationalistic quality of ideological politics. Indeed, both defined ideology as partaking of just such qualities.

36. Michael Oakshott's *Rationalism in Politics and Other Essays* (New York: Basic Books, 1962) is an important examination of the implications and consequences of rationalistic political mentality and habits. On the same subject, see John Arthur Passmore, *The Perfectability of Man* (London: Duckworth, 1970), which traces rationalistic and utopian political thought through the history of western political philosophy.

37. Sartori, "Politics, Ideology," p. 402.

38. Rokeach, *Beliefs, Attitudes*, p. 161.

39. Charles Reich, *The Greening of America: How the Youth Revolution is Trying to Make Life Livable* (New York: Random House, 1970). Also, Theodore Roszak, *The Making of a Counter Culture: Reflections on the Technocratic Society and Its Youthful Opposition* (Garden City, N.Y.: Doubleday, Anchor Books, 1969).

40. Milton Rokeach, *The Nature of Human Values* (New York: Free Press, 1973), p. 18.

41. Ibid.

42. The notion that questions that are *not* decided in the political realm—"nondecisions"—result from the machinations of the powerful is in essence an argument that culture is conspiracy. This position ignores the fact emphasized by such diverse scholars as Karl Marx, Max Weber, and Sigmund Freud that culture molds personality, including the personality of the "ruling elite," and not the reverse. The argument that questions not considered are excluded by the ruling class is, of course, made by Peter Bachrach and Morton S. Baratz, "Two Faces of Power," *American Political Science Review* 56 (1962): 947–952. But see also Nelson W. Polsby, *Community Power and Political Theory* (New Haven: Yale University Press, 1963); Robert A. Dahl, "A Critique of the Ruling Elite Model," *American Political Science Review* 52 (1958): 463–469.

43. The Bill of Rights is explicitly devoted to defining some spheres as off limits for governments. John Stuart Mill was not alone in his belief that limiting the power of government

to act on questions of life style and morality was the foundation of personal liberty. The distinction between state and society has long been regarded by exponents of personal freedom as crucial to its preservation. See, inter alia, Mill, *On Liberty;* Green, *Lectures;* MacIver, *Web of Government.*

44. Converse, however, is concerned with logical relations among ideas about the nature of the world. Converse, "Nature of Belief Systems," p. 208.

45. Note that Robert Lane has emphasized the centrality of identifications in political perspectives. Lane, *Political Ideology.* Also, *Political Thinking and Consciousness: The Private Life of the Political Mind* (Chicago: Markham, 1969) and "Patterns of Political Belief," in *Handbook*, ed. Knutson.

46. Erik H. Erikson, *Young Man Luther: A Study in Psychoanalysis and History* (New York: W. W. Norton and Co., 1958), p. 22.

47. History provides no examples of a ruler who ruled only in his own name without reference to collective symbols. The simplest program is that which merely affirms a collective identity—as "we Catalans"—and in the process distinguishes that collectivity from all others. The most familiar collective symbols of the period are those of nationality—language, culture, territory—which in the past two centuries have served both to unite smaller groups (in nation-states) and to divide them with separatist movements (e.g., Bangladesh, Basque, Ireland). As Merelman noted there is already evidence "indicating a link between positive identification and the development of moral and cognitive skills." Richard Merelman, "The Development of Political Ideology: A Framework for the Analysis of Political Socialization," *American Political Science Review* 63 (1969): 758.

48. Symbols of identification are not always clear. In Marxism, for example, it is not clear whether it is in fact an intellectual elite with the power to penetrate and manipulate the laws of history, or "the workers of the world." Frequently ideologies with the broadest, most inclusive symbols (e.g., mankind, workers of the world, international brotherhood) also offer the possibility of identification with a small, exclusive group, e.g., the priesthood, the vanguard, etc. or simple advocacy of discrete policies (as with "consumers deserve protection from . . ." or "women demand more representation . . .").

49. Harold D. Lasswell's value institutional approach is based on just this relation of personality, culture, and social institution; Milton Rokeach emphasizes the relationship in *The Nature of Human Values*; also, Sartori, "Politics, Ideology." Other observers have emphasized the centrality of values as a determinant of behavior. See, inter alia, Gordon W. Allport, *Pattern and Growth in Personality* (New York: Holt, Rinehart, and Winston, 1961), pp. 296–304.

50. Miller, et al., "Majority Party," p. 69.

51. Ibid., p. 73. Cultural issues, defined narrowly as abortion, equality for women, and the legalization of marihuana, "proved less potent." Note that I have defined culture more broadly—to include questions of authority, legitimacy, and force.

CHAPTER 7

Styles of Convention Participation

Little is known about patterns of participation at national party conventions prior to 1972. Images of delegate activity from earlier accounts range from the "oligarchy model" where party "bosses" sequestered themselves in back rooms to make decisions[1] to the "marketplace" model which featured hard bargaining and compromise among multiple participants to produce a winning consensus at the ideological center of presidential politics[2] to the "theater" model where uncertain, passive delegate-actors received their voting cues from announced trends in balloting.[3] It is widely believed that decision making has traditionally rested with persons of long party experience among whom state party leaders have been regarded as "kingmakers."[4]

Compared to legislatures or party committees, where patterns of influence, structures of participation, norms of deference, and the process of earned entry into decision-making circles can be analyzed in detail over years and decades, conventions are ephemeral institutions in which interactions are too brief and intermittent to permit the development of established expectations.

The fact that the political experience of so many 1972 delegates was brief and limited to the lower levels of the party also meant that they would be less bound by habitual patterns. The fact that many had won delegate status by taking part in a campaign unrelated to the state party organization suggested that the state party might have little importance for them, especially since state and locality had little interest for some.

Just because of their short life span and large turnover, conventions are less structured and more open to new forms of participation than are more highly institutionalized bodies. Therefore, they may be good arenas for discerning new trends in elite political activism. Various aspects of the presidential politics of 1972 appear to have illuminated and accelerated these trends away from traditional geographical constituencies and toward racial, age, youth, and other interest groups. The abolition of the unit rule in the Democratic Convention meant that states had been weakened as "action units" of the convention; the proliferation of primaries and the reform rules combined to lend new importance to the candidate group as a unit of convention organization and action. It was believed that delegates might reflect the declining importance of geographical political units and the rise of the so-called new constituencies.

Any exploration of delegate participation begins from the fact of indeterminate relations between activity and influence. Majorities of both Republican and Democratic delegates are expected to influence the activities of their state delegations and candidate preference groups.[5] But the activities of individual delegates may or may not have an impact on convention outcomes. A delegate (or an observer) may mistake four or five days of frenzied activity for influence on decision making. But activity is not influence.

Although patterns of participation can tell us little about the larger outcomes of a convention, they can provide information on the questions that are of concern here: whether presidential elites in 1972 exhibited new and distinctive patterns of political behavior, and whether newcomers were especially likely to seek new arenas.

Each convention constituted a distinct arena that provided its delegates with greater or lesser opportunities for participation. The Democrats arrived in Miami with multiple disputes, interests, and candidates, poised for the political confrontation of the decade. Every dispute—credentials contests, platform fights, rules decisions, the struggle for the nomination—offered opportunities for participation. Caucuses of women, blacks, youth, and reformers enhanced the potential for participation beyond the more traditional labor and state delegation caucuses.

The Republicans, by contrast, gathered in Miami to formalize and celebrate the nomination of Richard Nixon. With the single exception of the disagreement over Rule 30, there were neither credentials nor platform disputes. Nevertheless, state delegations and interest groups (including women, blacks, and youth) provided opportunities for Republican participation.

Because of their differences, the conventions are analyzed separately; levels and styles of delegate activity are defined and analyzed in the appropriate institutional context. Each provides an opportunity to investigate the extent to which participation was channeled through state delegations and candidate groups or the new special interest caucuses.

ARENAS FOR PARTICIPATION: THE
CONVENTIONS COMPARED

Because Democrats were engaged in a full-scale intraparty battle over reform, issues, and candidates while the Republicans produced a "neat, tidy and punctual . . ."[6] ceremony of renomination and reaffirmation of unity, the Democratic Convention had more arenas for participation.

To determine the arenas of activity, delegates were asked to name the "two main things they did in addition to voting" and were asked about the extent of their involvement in state delegation meetings, candidate activities, credentials, platform, and rules decisions, and "other groups" that met at each convention.

As Table 7-1 indicates, Democrats' activity focused on disputes while Republicans were involved first in organizational activity (over 40 percent mentioned it as a significant mode of participation, while Democrats mentioned it only one-half as often) and social functions (which Republicans mentioned seven times more frequently than Democrats).

Both conventions reported roughly equal percentages of persons engaged in either "issue-related" tasks relating to credentials, platform, or rules decisions, or such activities as "keeping informed," "listening to speeches," "general lobbying," and "consulting with others." The fact that Republicans reported as much issue-related activity as Democrats belies the notion that activity is mainly generated by disputes.[7] Faced with a rather peaceful convention, Republicans apparently spent their time reinforcing their agreements and dealing with the one dispute they confronted—Rule 30. Democrats, faced with multiple disputes, spread their energies around among candidate and interest groups, platform debates, and the crucial credentials challenges. Concern for policy, reflected in the relative weight given to platform, was equally strong at both conventions.

Table 7-2 illustrates other similarities in delegates' convention behavior. Despite the demise of the unit rule in Democratic procedures, state delegations remained the central units of participation at both conventions. At both conventions delegates were heavily involved in the disputes that had the greatest bearing on control of national parties: the nomination and credentials disputes on the Democratic side, and at the Republican Convention the Rule 30 debate that was widely believed to be important to control of the 1976 convention.

Democrats reported somewhat greater involvement than Republicans in unofficial groups that met during their conclave, doubtless because

Table 7-1. Types of Convention Participation by Party (%)

Convention Activities	Democrats			Republicans			Percentage Difference Between Combined Party Responses
	First Response	Second Response	Combined Responses	First Response	Second Response	Combined Responses	
Formal organization[a]	28	11	21 (N = 870)	49	28	42 (N = 659)	21
Interest groups[b]	14	15	14 (N = 568)	3	9	5 (N = 82)	9
Candidate groups[c]	22	18	21 (N = 838)	4	6	4 (N = 70)	17
Issues[d]	8	12	10 (N = 394)	9	12	10 (N = 157)	0
Other[e]	28	42	33 (N = 1347)	30	37	32 (N = 514)	1
Social functions[f]	0	2	1 (N = 45)	6	9	7 (N = 106)	6

[a]Includes membership in formal convention committees (rules, platform, credentials, etc.), state delegation positions, and podium speeches.

[b]Includes participation in "factional" groups, such as caucuses of women, blacks, youth, senior citizens, labor, Chicanos, etc.

[c]Includes work for any candidate for president, vice-president, Senate, or House of Representatives.

[d]Includes any reference to credentials challenges or platform or rules issues.

[e]Includes general lobbying, keeping informed, consultations with others, and listening to speeches.

[f]Includes any mention of social functions or receptions.

Question: "Once the convention was under way, what were the main things you did in addition to voting?"

NOTE: Percentages do not necessarily add to 100 due to rounding. All *N*'s in this table are weighted *N*'s. The question came from the interview sample.

Table 7-2. Participation Scores for Convention Activities by Party:
The Conventions Compared

Convention Activity	Democrats	Republicans	Participation Difference Between Parties
State delegation	+86	+88	2
	(N = 2645)	(N = 1114)	
Candidate meetings	+52	+10	42
	(N = 2597)	(N = 1016)	
Platform decisions	+8	+5	3
	(N = 2641)	(N = 1100)	
Credentials decisions	+12	-32	44
	(N = 2645)	(N = 1076)	
Rules decisions	-7	+41	48
	(N = 2645)	(N = 1104)	
Other groups	-4	-22	18
	(N = 2633)	(N = 1084)	

NOTE: Participation scores for each category were calculated by subtracting the percentage of those who reported "no participation" and "not very much participation" in a given activity from those who reported a "great deal of participation" or "some participation." A positive value indicates a preponderance of the group measured (parties, in this case) were relatively active in a given arena of participation; a negative score indicates lower activity. All N's in this table are weighted. The questions came from the interview sample.

minority, female, and youth caucuses proliferated as a part of the Democratic party's "reform" effort, because the reform rules required unprecedented numbers of women, youth, blacks, Chicanos, American Indians, and related groups, and because the most militant leaders of such groups were found within the Democratic party.[8]

LEVELS AND STYLES OF ELITE PARTICIPATION

In *Political Participation*, Lester Milbrath conceptualized political activity as unidimensional and cumulative and suggested that "gladiatorial" activities presupposed participation in less demanding activities.[9] Sidney Verba and Norman Nie challenged this theory, developing in its place a typology of citizen styles that was not dependent on the notion of progressively demanding political acts, but on identification of discrete "modes" of citizen participation.[10] Neither work analyzed elite participation per se, but both approaches offered possibilities for the exploration of elite behavior. Both are utilized here to determine whether levels or types of delegate activity were linked in discernible patterns to new breed political characteristics.

There was no reason to expect that delegates supporting traditional candidates should have been any more or less active than new breed delegates, but there was reason to believe that the new interest groups might have been distinctively important for new types of delegates. Therefore, it was thought that types of participation (the Verba and Nie approach) would be more useful than the Milbrath participation levels approach for discerning new participation patterns, if such existed.

In Milbrath's categories, all convention delegates would be gladiators. Therefore, a refined scale of involvement was needed to discriminate between those delegates who did little more than listen to speeches and those who spent great time and energy in struggles over platforms, candidate selection, and/or party rules.

In devising a scale, differences between the conventions were respected, levels of delegate activism were defined in general terms, and care was taken not to overemphasize official activities with limited access. The final measure of activism tapped the *quality, scope, and intensity* of reported activities in each convention. "High" activists were distinguished from others by the political significance, diversity, and intensity of their convention participation. Emphasis was on defining the extreme categories of this scale where one would expect to find the greatest differences. Table 7-3 presents the resulting distributions. The levels of participation were high at both conventions; only 16 percent of either body reported low levels of participation.

Were these levels of activism related to other political characteristics, to ideology, incentives to political activity, role conceptions, or orientation to party and policy? Briefly, the answer is no. No one *level* of participation characterized any particular style of actor at either convention. In

Table 7-3. Levels of Elite Activism by Party (%)

	Democrats	Republicans
"High" activity	22	23
"Moderate" activity	64	61
"Low" activity	14	16
Weighted N =	2631	1088

NOTE: The data are from the interviews. See Appendix C for a description of the measure.

both parties, the only characteristics to which levels of activism were significantly linked were perceptions of personal political information and personal political influence. Delegates who were most active also perceived themselves as influential; less active delegates were less sanguine about their influence.

The most active had few distinctive characteristics. He or she (sex made no difference) was most likely to be under 50, with a moderate amount of political experience and a college degree. Neither race, religion, nor income had any consistent, significant relation to elite activism,[11] and neither did the system through which a delegate was recruited to the convention. Primary victors were as likely to be active as were state convention winners and vice versa, and those who relied on friends to get them to Miami were no less active than those who campaigned hard for the delegate position.

Among Republicans, level of activity was associated with party officeholding experience, but among Democrats, level of activity tended to be higher among the less experienced McGovern supporters. Only Wallace's women supporters were distinctively inactive. (See Table 7-4.)

There was no important association between level of activity and other characteristics. It was type of activity rather than amount, intensity, or level that turned out to be associated with other aspects of political behavior.

STYLES OF PARTICIPATION: THE DEMOCRATS

Three arenas of the convention were foci of Democrats' participation; the traditional state delegation unit, special interest caucuses, and the disputes over platform, credentials, and rules.[12] As Table 7-5 indicates, delegates were classed according to their range and type of activities.

Table 7-4. Levels of Activism by Candidate Preference (%)

	McGovern	Humphrey	Wallace	Muskie	Nixon
Low	11	16	18	23	16
Moderate	61	72	67	56	61
High	28	12	15	21	23
Weighted N =	1338	428	152	290	1062

NOTE: These data are from the interview sample. Cramer's V for level of activism by candidate preference is 0.11.

Table 7-5. Operational Definitions of Styles of Elite Participation: Democrats

	State Delegation Participation[a]	Interest Group Activity[b]	Dispute Orientation[c]	Percentage of Delegates
General activists	+	+	+	26
Interest group specialists	0	+	0	7
Dispute specialists	0	0	+	6
State delegation specialists	+	0	0	12
Interest groups and disputes	0	+	+	7
Interest groups and state delegations	+	+	0	12
State delegations and disputes	+	0	+	19
Observers	0	0	0	10
Weighted N =				2378

[a]State delegation participation was measured by an index combining the following questions:

a. "Once you got to the convention, how much did you participate in the activities of your state delegation?"
   Possible answers: a great deal, somewhat, not very much, none.

b. "Compared to others in your state delegation, were you more active, as active, or less active in state delegation caucuses?"
   Possible answers: more active, as active, less active.

Since almost all delegates reported high state delegation participation, this index was used to ascertain the *most active* participants. On an index with possible scores ranging from 1 to 6, those who scored 5 or 6 were given a "+" in this column and considered significantly active state participants.

[b]A "+" in this column simply means that a delegate reported participating in *some* interest group activity at the convention, including: caucuses of women, blacks, Chicanos, youth, senior citizens, labor, gay liberation, the New Democratic Coalition, or other minority or interest groups. It also included any mention of sub-state delegation caucuses.

[c]Dispute orientation was measured by an index of participation in platform, rules, and credentials decisions—the "great disputes" at the Democratic Convention. The basic questions) on which the index was based were:
   "How much did you participate in: credentials decisions?
                                       decisions on platform issues?
                                       decisions on rules issues?"

Possible responses to each question included: a great deal, somewhat, not very much, none.
   Those who scored on the upper half of this index were given a "+" in this column. (A preliminary factor analysis indicated that these three dispute-related arenas of participation comprised a single dimension of participation.)

The eight resulting participation types are, of course, statistical aggregates not groups based on common identifications. They constitute qualitatively different styles of participation that might be expected to attract different types of delegates. Did politically experienced, party-oriented delegates concentrate on state delegation units? Did reform-minded delegates participate heavily in nongeographical interest caucuses? What were the relationships between political style, ideology, and participatory behavior?

General Activists

More than one-fourth of the Democratic delegates spread their energies to all three arenas of participation. This heterogeneous aggregate included experienced party officeholders and political newcomers, conservatives and radicals, but blacks, other racial minorities, and a significant proportion of women in every candidate preference group[13] were "overrepresented" in this group. So were advocates of party reform (26 percent considered reform the first or second priority among convention tasks). The most widely shared qualities among these high activists were a desire to influence party policy and confidence in the ability to do so. They were determined, confident persons with a high estimate of their competence in politics and a conviction that they were more influential and better informed than most delegates.

Interest Group Specialists

Interest group specialists were persons whose activities were focused exclusively on the new demographic constituencies. Seventy-three percent of this category were women. Indians, Chicanos, and other nonwhite, non-black delegates were also overrepresented, comprising 4 percent of the convention but 12 percent of the interest group specialists. Most of this small contingent (7 percent) within the convention were newcomers to politics, very few had significant party experience, and scarcely any had ever held public office. None had ever held national or state public office.

Interest group specialists were most notable for their political style which combined high policy concern with little or no interest in party preservation or solidarity. These were not the confident, self-assured policy advocates and reformers who dominated television screens in July 1972. Many had relatively low education and low self-estimates. They did not see themselves as influential or well-informed, nor as competitive and aggressive personalities. In the aggregate, they looked like a group of relatively low status amateurs clinging to demographic identifications as they ventured somewhat uncertainly into presidential politics.

Dispute Specialists

Only 6 percent of all Democratic delegates "specialized" in credentials, platform, or rules disputes to the virtual exclusion of other forms of participation. These dispute specialists were mostly white and male, except for the contingent of Wallace women virtually none of whom shared the interests or activities of the women's caucus. Few in this group had long political experience, but almost all had some party experience at the local level.

They tended to be ideological moderates, slightly more conservative than the convention on some issues and close to the norm on others. National issues were very important to this group: 78 percent (more than any other participant category) saw the "adoption of correct positions on national issues" as either the first or second convention priority. Some perhaps concentrated on disputes in the effort to modulate and compromise issue positions they perceived as extreme, others with the hope of securing the adoption of their preferred positions. Though they did not perceive themselves as very influential or very well-informed, they remained determined to try to influence outcomes.

Dispute specialists were comparatively uninterested in the activities of women, minorities, and youth; many were engaged in combating the reforms that had given new influence to these groups.

State Delegation Specialists

State delegations are the traditional action units of presidential conventions.[14] Delegates in 1972 who focused most of their energies here conformed to traditional descriptions of convention delegates. This was the preferred arena for experienced party and public officeholders. The pre-1945 generation was overrepresented, and newcomers to politics comprised only 16 percent of the group although they represented 33 percent of the convention as a whole. Only 10 percent of these delegates were under 30, and only 25 percent were McGovern supporters—a lower proportion than in any other participation category. Men (especially white men) were more likely than women to focus their efforts on state delegations.

The typical state delegation specialist was ideologically moderate to conservative and likely not to be a supporter of party reform; he was apt to have been helped in becoming a delegate by friends or associates. He saw the convention's first task as selecting a winning team for the November election and gave high priority to establishing party unity. The state delegation specialist acted through the traditional units of party organization to achieve his goals—many of which concerned the well-being and preservation of the party.

Other Participation Patterns

Numerous delegates were active in two types of arenas. Convention disputes and interest groups (but not state delegation activities) claimed the attention of approximately 7 percent of Democratic delegates. These delegates provided a suggestive contrast to both the inexperienced and inefficacious interest group specialists on the one hand, and, on the other, to delegates oriented to traditional patterns of participation through state delegations. Seventy-one percent of them were McGovern delegates; *no* Wallace supporters fit this pattern of activity. Newcomers predominated; persons with experience in public or party office were scarce. Lack of concern with organizational preservation was a hallmark of this group: they were least likely to see party support as a reason for seeking a delegate position and were least likely to ascribe importance to the selection of winning candidates. Radical and very liberal delegates, racial minorities, and women were overrepresented in this category and enthusiasm for reform was higher here than anywhere else. In spite of their low experience, these delegates were thoroughly convinced of their own efficacy in convention politics.

Another 12 percent of Democrats combined interest group and state delegation activity. In this heterogeneous group, blacks, racial minorities, and women were overrepresented, with Muskie women especially prominent and Wallace women totally absent. Few public officeholders but many party officers adopted this pattern of activity. Most delegates in this category had at least five years' experience in politics, and many had been active as long as ten to fifteen years. Though they tended to be liberal and favorable to reform, they also were strongly attached to party, concerned with winning, and with achieving party unity.

Another group, comprising about 19 percent of all delegates, were active in state delegations and in the convention's credentials and platform fights but not in interest groups. These delegates were predominantly white, male, and experienced in party and/or public office. Muskie supporters were overrepresented in this group; McGovern supporters underrepresented. These were "party people," who were prepared to do battle for traditional conceptions of party and politics. Most were ideological moderates whose opinions were somewhat more conservative than the norm of this very liberal convention. Though not entirely unfriendly to party reform, these delegates were nevertheless more skeptical about its benefits than were most other groups at the convention. For them, the traditional tasks of nominating a winning team and welding party unity had high priority. A high sense of efficacy, a generalized self-confidence, and a conviction that they were well-informed differentiated these delegates from those who were active only in state delegations and had no significant involvement in the convention's great disputes. But both groups consisted of seasoned regulars concerned with preservation of the institution in which they had invested time and energy through the years.

About 10 percent of Democratic delegates participated little in any convention activities. These tended to be fun-loving and politically inexperienced moderates and conservatives. Only about one-third of this group were McGovernites; all other candidate preference groups were overrepresented. Although they included older as well as younger delegates, very few had been party officials. Nonetheless, they valued institutional preservation and party victory, but they differed from the real professionals in their low policy orientation, lack of experience in office, and extremely low estimates of personal influence.

Conclusions: The Democrats

In 1972 state delegations remained a major arena of convention activity—neither the abolition of the unit rule, the rise of the new constituencies, nor the increased importance of the candidate organization led most delegates to ignore their delegations. Those who did were less experienced, less confident, and probably less effective than others. Their decisions to ignore the state delegation activity may have resulted more from inexperience than ideology. More significant were the much larger number who were active in both state delegations and the new demographic interest groups. These were drawn principally from McGovern ranks, and many (though not all) persons who eschewed the new interest groups were supporters of Humphrey, Muskie, and Jackson. Among Democrats, patterns of convention activity were related to attitudes toward both ideology and organization.

STYLES OF PARTICIPATION: THE REPUBLICANS

In 1972 the Republican Convention was untroubled by conflict over candidates or platforms, but state delegations and special interest groups remained significant in the convention. As Table 7-6 indicates, some delegates were active in both types of arenas, others in only one, and a few were simply observers. State delegations' activities were important for most Republican delegates. Only one-fourth did not report participation in delegation activities, and slightly over one-fourth were active in both state delegations and an interest group. Most of those active in both types of arenas were women, because the women's caucus was the largest interest group.

Table 7-6. Elite Styles of Participation: Republicans

	State Delegation Participation[a]	Interest Group Activity[b]	Percentage of Delegates
General activists	+	+	27
Interest group specialists	0	+	7
State delegation specialists	+	0	49
Observers	0	0	17
Weighted N =			1014

[a]State delegation participation for Republicans was measured in the same way as for Democrats. See footnote a, Table 7-5.

[b]A "+" in this column simply means that a delegate reported participating in *some* interest group at the Republican Convention. Caucuses of women, blacks, and youth were the principal interest groups active at this convention, although small groups of labor representatives, Chicanos, and a caucus interested in the distribution of 1976 delegates also reported meeting.

General Activists

Like the most active Democrats, the most active Republicans rated themselves high on influence, information, and self-confidence. They brought to the diverse political arenas strong, positive self-images and a conviction that their participation would make a difference.

State Delegation Specialists

The state delegation specialists who comprised almost one-half of the Republican Convention were in some respects very much like their Democratic counterparts. Delegates most likely to concentrate exclusively on state delegations were predominantly male (90 percent) with top political experience. In both parties, persons who held public office, especially at state or national levels, were likely to focus their activity in their delegations. Again like the Democrats, the Republican state delegation specialists were strongly oriented to party and to organizational maintenance. Republican state delegation specialists tended to be consistently conservative on national and international issues. Their experience doubtless contributed to their self-confidence, information, and the conviction that they could influence events. The combination of self-confidence, high efficacy, ambition, and experience were distinctive characteristics of this group.

Interest Group Specialists

In both parties the delegates whose activity was exclusively focused on interest groups were largely female (71 percent in the Republican case) and without experience in party or public office. They did not feel well-informed or influential, and they saw themselves as uncompetitive and introspective.

Among Republicans interest group activities were not associated with negative attitudes to party and to organizational maintenance. Unlike the Democrats, who were active in the new interest groups, Republican interest specialists were able to harmonize subjectively the interests of their sex or race group with their organizational identifications. They were also issue-oriented conservatives who conceived their role in terms of policy making as well as organizational maintenance. In other words, multiple incentives played a role in the political activity of Republican interest group activists. They found the friendships, excitement, and learning process of politics alluring and exhilarating; they exhibited a strong interest in enhancing personal status and strong concern for party and policy alongside their interest in women or youth or blacks.

These relatively young Republicans were issue-oriented beginners who no doubt looked to the day when they might play a more prestigious role in the party whose preservation they valued.

Observers

Approximately 17 percent of Republican delegates were inactive in the convention. Like most other Republicans these were attached to party and concerned with its victory and welfare. They were relatively inexperienced, and their relative inactivity was accompanied by a low estimate of personal style and personal characteristics.

Altogether the similarities between the parties were striking. Public officeholders stationed themselves in close proximity to their state delegations, operating within the human environment with which they were familiar and on which they were dependent. Women and minorities often opted for patterns relevant to their sex or race identifications. Weaker personalities often simply filled an "observer" role. Those who engaged in across-the-board activity were also those who saw themselves as influential people. Republican and Democratic elites at the national conventions of 1972 were different in ideological outlook, but their participation styles and the associated personal characteristics were quite similar.

Among Republicans, however, participation in new groups was integrated into preexistent patterns of commitment and participation. Only among Democrats was there a discernible tendency for new concerns and activities to replace traditional areal and institutional patterns of participation.

ACTION GROUPS: THE SPECIAL INTEREST CAUCUSES

At both 1972 conventions, some delegates participated in groups organized around identifications based on interests other than state or candidate group. The reform movement in the Democratic party invited the formation of caucuses around those identifications given special consideration in the McGovern-Fraser guidelines: women, racial minorities, and youth. Special interest caucuses were not new to that party; the labor caucus had been a factor in Democratic conventions for two decades. In 1972, however, new action groups proliferated: gay liberation, the New Democratic Coalition of former McCarthy supporters, senior citizens, and Chicanos organized to press demands. Over one-half of the Democratic Convention (52 percent) reported participation in some special interest activity.

By contrast, only one-third of Republicans reported participating in action caucuses. Women's groups proved most attractive to Republican delegates. Labor, black, and youth groups met, but their numbers were small and their activities minimal. Debate on Rule 30 stimulated some activity.

Among Democrats, interest group activity was most attractive to McGovern delegates, to women of all candidate preferences (except Wallace women), to newcomers to politics, and to members of minority races and youth. (See Table 7-7.) Among Republicans it was especially attractive to women. (See Table 7–8.)

Women's Activities

Women's activities at presidential nominating conventions are nothing new. Both conventions have provided women's programs focusing on issues believed to be of special interest to that sex (child care, education, health, etc.); both have held women's luncheons featuring the candidates' wives and have organized other ladylike activities. However, with women attempting to function as a pressure group in 1972, the character of organized "women's" activities underwent a significant change.

Sixty-four percent of Democratic women and 71 percent of Republican women reported participation in some women's activity. The Republican women who participated in women's activities were virtually identical to other Republican delegates in regard to age, education, ideology, and

Table 7-7. Political and Demographic Characteristics of Action Group Participants: Democrats (%)

	All Democrats	Women's Groups	Black Groups	Youth Groups	Labor Groups	All Groups
Sex						
Male	58	7	65	52	80	42
Female	42	93	35	48	20	58
Candidate Preference						
McGovern	52	68	56	75	26	64
Humphrey	17	11	18	7	57	13
Wallace	6	1	1	6	0	2
Muskie	11	8	3	5	9	7
Jackson	6	3	2	1	8	3
Political Generations						
Pre-1945	7	5	4	2	24	5
1946–1959	32	27	27	12	54	28
1960–1967	31	33	39	35	9	31
1968–1972	30	36	31	51	14	36
Age						
Under 30	22	25	22	72	3	28
30–39	22	23	25	17	19	24
40–49	29	29	30	6	33	28
50–65	24	20	21	6	37	18
Over 65	4	4	2	0	7	3
Race						
White	80	79	14	77	71	68
Black	16	16	82	16	23	25
Other races	4	5	4	7	6	7
Education						
Less than high school	4	2	3	0	30	4
High school graduate	14	12	12	10	23	13
Some college	25	30	32	35	18	28
College graduate	19	22	16	25	18	21
College plus	38	34	38	31	10	35
Ideology						
Radical	8	11	16	15	9	12
Very liberal	42	46	36	44	14	44
Somewhat liberal	30	32	31	24	46	29
Moderate	12	8	14	10	19	11
Somewhat conservative	6	2	3	3	14	3
Very conservative	1	1	0	4	0	1
Party Office						
None	56	55	70	54	50	57
One	16	14	15	23	23	17
Two	10	11	7	8	20	10
Three or more	18	20	8	15	7	17
Public Office						
None	83	87	86	90	87	88
One	13	10	10	6	13	9
More than one	4	3	4	3	0	3
Weighted *N* =	2630	750	378	292	99	1379

NOTE: This table describes each of the special interest caucuses of the 1972 Democratic Convention according to a number of political and demographic characteristics. Percentages do not necessarily add to 100 due to rounding. Data are from the interviews (candidate preference, sex, age, race, and education) or the intersect samples (generations, ideology, and officeholding).

Table 7-8. **Political and Demographic Characteristics of Interest Group Participants: Republicans (%)**

	All Republicans	Women's Groups	Black Groups	Youth Groups	All Groups
Sex					
Male	66	0	43	74	23
Female	34	100	57	26	77
Political Generations					
Pre-1945	14	16	20	0	15
1946–1959	41	43	40	0	39
1960–1967	36	33	20	75	37
1968–1972	9	8	20	25	10
Age					
Under 30	8	8	0	58	11
30–39	16	7	43	26	15
40–49	35	37	29	16	32
50–65	32	39	29	0	32
Over 65	9	9	0	0	9
Race					
White	94	93	21	95	90
Black	5	6	71	5	9
Other races	1	1	7	0	1
Education					
Less than high school	2	1	0	0	1
High school graduate	11	15	7	5	14
Some college	27	39	57	32	35
College graduate	19	24	14	32	23
College plus	41	21	21	32	28
Ideology					
Very liberal	1	2	30	0	3
Somewhat liberal	11	11	10	23	12
Moderate	35	39	50	39	38
Somewhat conservative	41	39	0	39	35
Very conservative	12	9	10	0	12
Party Office					
None	34	25	29	32	24
One	9	5	0	16	7
Two	13	15	29	26	16
Three or more	44	55	43	26	53
Public Office					
None	72	77	50	79	73
One	17	19	43	11	21
More than one	11	4	7	11	6
Weighted N =	1090	266	28	38	364

NOTE: This table describes each of the special interest caucuses at the 1972 Republican Convention according to a number of political and demographic characteristics. Percentages do not necessarily add to 100 due to rounding. Data are from the interviews (age, sex, race, and education) or intersect (generations, ideology, and officeholding) samples.

political experience. On the Democratic side, newcomers to politics were relatively more numerous than women with longer experience, and Wallace's women supporters were noticeably absent, perhaps because their culturally conservative views about female roles in society and politics afforded them little common ground with those engaged in organized women's activities. Newcomers to politics found women's activities more attractive than did those with long experience, but delegates of all ages participated in almost representative proportions. So did women with various levels of experience in politics.

The media publicized the women's activities as largely "feminist" in orientation. And at the Democratic Convention those active in women's affairs were in general agreement about women's roles in politics, and they were more united than the rest of the convention on the so-called "women's issues": they favored a nonrestrictive abortion policy, a national day care program, equal treatment of men and women with regard to employment, and were favorable to the women's liberation movement. They rejected almost unanimously the notion that men are the natural governors of society, and they saw few, if any, incompatibilities between political life and wife/mother roles. Generally speaking, they perceived their sex as suffering discrimination in politics and were rather skeptical about women having exercised power "behind the thrones" on which male politicians sit. Democratic women activists were issue-oriented "liberals" and "feminists" who combined a desire for cultural change regarding the role of women with broader social interests. They had limited common ground with women who were not active in convention women's groups. On all issues except military policy these two types of women were as distant from each other as from men.

Republican women active in women's groups were less united than their Democratic counterparts in their views on these subjects and less divergent from the non-active Republican women. Still, they were markedly more "feminist" than other Republicans in their denial that there are innate sex differences relevant to politics, their perception of sex discrimination in politics, and their belief that traditional nurturant roles and political careers are compatible. Compared to other Republican women, they were slightly less negative in their view of women's liberation. But they were much more ready than Democratic activist women to believe that women had exercised political power in auxiliary roles "behind the throne." Unlike their Democratic counterparts, 75 percent of Republican women were experienced party officeholders. Perhaps this experience convinced them that women had exercised more influence than was apparent.

Republican female activists' views on "women's issues" were not much different from those of the Republican Convention as a whole: they were a bit more inclined toward abortion on demand and a national day care program and somewhat less negative in their outlook on women's liberation. But on these, as on other questions, Republican women activists were considerably more conservative than the Democrats active in women's groups. Unlike the Democratic women activists, Republican feminist views were not part of a general perspective on domestic and international affairs. Only on questions of military policy did Republican women's views depart from the Republican norm.

In other regards as well, Democratic and Republican women activists differed from one another and resembled the dominant characteristics of their own parties. Democratic women activists were dedicated to party reform and more concerned with issues than with the party and were less willing than most of their colleagues to sacrifice issue commitments to achieve party unity or win elections. Altogether, their style tended to be that of the political amateur with strong convictions and a single-minded concern with issues—including the issue of women's political role. At least 55 percent scored low on party support, and 18 percent extremely low. Women's activities at the Democratic Convention were part of a movement away from traditional areal constituencies and organizational concerns and toward new patterns of political identification and interaction.

In contrast, although issues were important to most Republican women activists and even took priority over party unity for some, Republican women were basically party loyalists whose style blended party and policy commitments.

The self-images of women active in women's groups differed little from the rest of the convention's, although they saw themselves as slightly less competitive, and somewhat more subjective, defensive, and schedule-oriented than their colleagues. They believed themselves more influential and well-informed in convention decisions than did non-activist women.

Black Activists

Most black voters vote Democratic and most black leaders are Democrats. Blacks therefore constitute an interest group of considerable importance inside the Democratic party. The fact that they were also beneficiaries of "quotas" in the 1972 Democratic delegate selection process further enhanced their influence in that convention. They were much less numerous and less influential at the Republican Convention where they nonetheless functioned as a caucus.

Just as the women's group in the Democratic Convention was not entirely female, the black caucus was not entirely black. Three percent of whites and 14 percent of those who reported neither black nor white racial identifications joined 73 percent of the Democratic blacks in this action group. McGovern and Humphrey delegates were especially numerous in black activities, so were black public officials. Unlike many of the women activists, black caucus participants did not see racial identifications and activities as incompatible with attachment to party. Delegates active in black affairs gave high priority to winning and were less concerned with party reform. Nearly 50 percent (compared to only 29 percent of the rest of the convention) put achieving party unity as first or second among convention tasks. Since race-related interests have historically focused on domestic policy, it is not surprising that black affairs activists had especially intense feelings concerning domestic issues—nor that they emphasized the policy-making role of the delegate. But these commitments did not take precedence over party. In political style, they were party loyalists.

At the Democratic Convention, activists in black affairs had distinctive views only on busing, crime, and welfare. On all other issues, they closely resembled the rest of the Democratic Convention.

At the Republican Convention activists in black affairs were few, comprising only 3 percent of delegates, and they differed from the majority of Republicans in several important respects. They were more liberal—90 percent classified themselves as "moderate" to "very liberal" and this self-designation proved consistent with their views on all substantive issues. Their relatively liberal views diverged most sharply from those of most Republicans on welfare, busing, and crime—where they shunned tough-minded policy options. Most were committed to international aid and cooperation, and many were skeptical about pro-military policy options. As compared to Democrats, most were cultural conservatives and supported the use of force as an instrument of policy, but on both counts, this group was more liberal than Republicans in general. Like Democratic activists, these Republicans held more extreme views than fellow party members on matters of domestic policy.

In both parties, activist blacks were concerned about sexual as well as racial discrimination; they were less willing than most men to believe that innate sex differences disqualified women for politics and much more willing to recognize women as victims of political exclusion.

Some of the differences between Republican and Democratic activist blacks presumably derived from the difference in their situations within the two parties. As compared to other Republican delegates, that party's black activists did not believe themselves either influential or well-informed except in areas related to their special interest. This self-perception was perhaps due to their small numbers in the convention and/or the deviances of their policy views from other Republicans. They aspired to high public office, but no one in the caucus expressed a desire for high party office. By contrast, the aspirations of Democratic black activists for high party or public office equalled those of others, and they believed themselves more influential and better informed than the rest of the convention.

In both parties black activists combined an interest in party reform with a high concern for their party; and in both they combined high policy interests with commitment to organizational maintenance. Both, in sum, reflected a mixture of political styles.

Youth Activists

Eleven percent of Democrats and 3 percent of Republicans participated in youth activities at the convention. Definitions of youth are flexible, and in fact some 28 percent of Democrats and 42 percent of Republicans who took part in the youth activities were over 30.

In both parties those interested in youth affairs were a diverse group. Most of the Republicans were moderate, the Democrats liberal. In both parties the youth activists were more liberal than the average for their convention.

The most distinctive characteristic of youth activists in both parties was their political ambition. Almost all expressed an interest in running for public office, many aspired to high office, and expressed confidence in their ability to achieve these goals.[15] The level of aspirations suggests that "youth" activities constituted an arena in which very ambitious, power-oriented personalities can win influence at a time that they lack the experience and other resources needed to exercise power in the national party.

In both parties youth activists were attracted to politics for various reasons—including enjoyment of politics, sociability, and policy concerns. As usual, Republicans were more experienced and more strongly attached to party than Democrats. Republican concern with party and with organizational maintenance constitutes a reminder that weak attachment to party (such as characterized many Democrats) is not a necessary political attribute of youth.

Labor Groups

Since the Roosevelt coalition was forged in the 1930s, labor has been a traditional constituency of the Democratic party. In 1972, labor activists, who comprised about 4 percent of Democratic delegates, were supporters of mainstream candidates: Humphrey, Muskie, and Jackson. Most were political veterans at least 40 years old, and most (80 percent) were men.

As a group, they were less liberal in ideological identification than the median of this convention. In many ways labor was the most distinctive group at the Miami conclave. Staunch party loyalists, they gave top priority to winning candidates and achieving party unity. None rated party reform an important convention task. They came to preserve the party, not reform it. Commitment to party was the distinctive characteristic of this group. Ideologically, they were eclectic and in spite of intense views on domestic policy, they did not conceive the delegates' role in terms of policy. Instead, they saw themselves as agents of the party responsible for its well-being and preservation.

Labor activists, who were losers in many intraparty struggles in 1972, believed themselves to be most influential in state delegations and candidate groups and less so in the disputed areas of platform, credentials, and rules. These were men schooled in the American party tradition, which has historically valued winning, unity, and compromise over ideological purity. They were bearers of traditional politics at a Democratic Convention that featured change.

NOTES

1. See, for example, M. Ostrogorski, *Democracy and the Organization of Political Parties* (New York: Macmillan, 1902), vol. II, pp. 270–279; E. E. Schattschneider, *Party Government* (New York: Holt, Rinehart, and Winston, 1942), p. 179.
2. This is the model of Richard M. Scammon and Ben J. Wattenberg, *The Real Majority* (New York: Coward-McCann, 1970), ch. 11; and Judith Parris, *The Convention Problem* (Washington, D.C.: The Brookings Institution, 1972), pp. 82–83.
3. Eugene B. McGregor, Jr., "Rationality and Uncertainty in National Nominating Conventions," *Journal of Politics* 35 (1973): 459–478.
4. The importance of state delegations and leaders is implicit in the discussions of Ostrogorski, *Democracy*; V.O. Key, *Politics, Parties and Pressure Groups*, 5th ed. (New York: Thomas Y. Crowell Co., 1964), ch. 15; Nelson W. Polsby, "Decision-Making at the National Conventions," *Western Political Quarterly* 13 (1960): 609–619.
5. Although supporters of the most numerous candidate preference group might have been expected to feel especially influential, McGovern delegates were no more likely than others to expect that they would have influence in their state delegations and Wallace supporters were most likely to think they would be influential in their candidate group. The absence of major contests did not leave Republican delegates feeling inefficacious; 86 percent of Republicans expected to have some influence in their state delegations. Most delegates did not expect to wield a great deal of influence in either their state delegations or candidate groups but neither did they expect to function as rubber stamps. The fact that delegates did not feel influential in all arenas indicates that more than a generalized predisposition to feel efficacious is reflected in these expectations. Although their interest in credentials and platform decisions was high, few delegates expected to have much opportunity to influence decisions on these matters.
6. See, for example, Theodore White, *The Making of the President 1972* (New York: Bantam Books, 1973), p. 319.
7. Democrats did tend to give this type of activity a *first* mention more often than Republicans, but when first and second responses are combined, approximately 10 percent of the central activity of each convention involved either national policy issues or convention issues.
8. See, for example, White's description, *Making of the President*, pp. 320–321.
9. Lester Milbrath, *Political Participation: How and Why Do People Get Involved in Politics?* (Chicago: Rand McNally & Co., 1965), pp. 16ff.
10. Sidney Verba and Norman H. Nie, *Participation in America: Political Democracy and Social Equality* (New York: Harper and Row, 1972), ch. 4 esp.
11. One exception to this was the Republican Jews, considerably more active than most Republicans.
12. When six questions on various modes of participation were factored for Democrats, these three forms of participation factored together on a single "dispute" dimension.
13. Because of the importance of the women's caucus at both conventions, female delegates tended to be overrepresented in any category of activity that included special interests.
14. Ostrogorski, *Democracy*; Key, *Politics*, ch. 15; Polsby, "Decision-Making."
15. This is in line with the findings of Joseph A. Schlesinger in *Ambition and Politics: Political Careers in the United States* (Chicago: Rand McNally & Co., 1966).

CHAPTER 8

A New Class? A New Breed?

Were there then *new* types of political actors present in the presidential elite? How can we decide this question? It is abundantly clear that political activity is a complex phenomenon prompted by different motives and conducted in different ways and that there were various types of political actors present in the two conventions. Whether one or more of these types constituted a new political type in presidential politics is another question: there are no comparably clear and comprehensive base lines against which to measure the 1972 delegates. Certain changes in the delegate population can be established by comparing descriptions of the 1972 delegates with those of 1948. In addition to reporting information on the 1952 and 1956 conventions, the David, Goldman, and Bain study also reports data collected in 1948 by Charles Tuttle. David, Goldman, and Bain describe delegates that were overwhelmingly white, male, middle-aged in physical characteristics, middle class in status, and characterized by relatively high education and high income. David and his colleagues summed up the social characteristics of the 1948 delegates this way: "The most noteworthy features . . . are the concentrations of lawyers and businessmen, the large number in other middle-class occupations, and the generally close similarity of the occupational distribution in the two parties."[1] Although this resembles a description of the 1972 presidential elite, there are significant differences between the two delegate populations. Women, blacks, and other racial and ethnic minorities were much more numerous in 1972; both the average and median age of delegates had declined substantially; delegates were more highly educated in 1972 than two decades earlier; and some interesting changes in occupations had occurred. The proportion of businessmen had dropped sharply, as had the percentages of trade unionists and farmers. But the proportion of teachers, social scientists, college professors, social workers, writers, and related types of symbol specialists had increased in both parties. These changes were more marked among Democrats than Republicans and were especially characteristic of McGovern supporters.

Still more changes have taken place in the *political* characteristics of delegates in the past two decades. David, Goldman, and Bain reported:

> Four-fifths of the respondents to the Tuttle study of the 1948 delegates indicated that they regularly attended state and county party organization meetings. At least three-fifths either were or had been county organization officers; nearly one-half were or had been state party officers. Most delegates, in other words, are active party workers who frequently hold party office at about the rank of county chairmen or state committee members. Few of these party offices pay salaries. . . . In 1952, as in 1948, the typical delegate appeared to be the kind of individual who devotes much of his time and energy to politics as an engrossing side line, but looks to some other occupation for his principal sources of income.[2]

These state and party officers were supplemented by large numbers of elected officials—including two-thirds of the governors in each party, nearly two-thirds of the senators, and many of the congressmen.[3] These were conventions of party leaders. The age of volunteer politics had already arrived, but the volunteers who attended the conventions were organization regulars. In 1972 substantially fewer delegates, especially Democratic delegates, had experience in party office above the local level; they reflected a trend toward progressively weaker ties between state parties and national conventions—a trend that perhaps has its parallel in the trend toward distinctive presidential voting patterns.

David, Goldman, and Bain also noted that various legal and organizational changes—the Hatch act, women's suffrage, the advent of primaries, Republican reapportionment—had altered national conventions during the first half of this century. And they identified certain "intangible factors" as having a still more important impact on the composition of presidential conventions.

> These include the coming of age of the immigrant groups and the changing nature of the big city political machines; the virtual disappearance of the state-wide bosses of the Platt type; civil service reform and more frequent enforcement of standards of honesty in the awarding of government contracts; the growing importance of organized labor and its interest in direct political action; the increasingly active interest in the party organizations of both parties taken by middle- and upper-class people with a public service orientation; a noteworthy shift in political power from the party officials . . . to elected officials with a direct responsibility to the public, . . . and finally, the rising standards of education and social responsibility throughout the country.[4]

Obviously, some of the trends associated with the new politics were already present in the early 1950s: the rise of a well-educated middle class with a "public service" orientation, the decline of the bosses and their paid political aides, and the decreased power of the party leaders were clear. The Stevenson candidacy served as a catalyst, attracting unprecedented numbers of middle-class amateurs to campaign on behalf of the articulate, urbane Adlai Stevenson, a figure whose appeal to amateurs has hardly waned. And there is already present in David, Goldman, and Bain the fascinating distinction between "citizen" participation and "professional politicians"[5] (as though the professionals were not citizens).

The increased participation of the educated middle class and the decline of the immigrant based urban machine were also reported in investigations of urban politics during the 1950s and 1960s. Robert Dahl's classic study of political change in New Haven[6] described one such transition from a patrician elite to "new men." There was general agreement about the characteristics of the educated middle-class politicians and activists: their "public service" orientation, their greater independence, their lesser interest in patronage. Whether they were "amateurs" on the Wilson model or "professionals" of the Dahl variety, the educated middle-class political actors were said to be "better adjusted to the requirements of an open political system."[7] David, Goldman, and Bain, and most other contemporary observers thought as well of the public-spirited delegates of two decades ago as most commentators thought of the highly educated policy-oriented delegates who gathered in Miami in 1972.[8]

> The facts suggest that the great majority of the delegates were well qualified to deal with the problems of their political parties, that they were about as reputable a group of individuals as could reasonably be expected in any large political assembly in this imperfect world.[9]

By 1972, virtually all delegates to national conventions were members of the large category of middle to upper middle-class Americans who, as compared to most people, are more interested in issues, more well-informed, more active, and more "public spirited" in the sense that they feel some sort of personal stake in public decisions and so desire to influence them. The types of actor in the two conventions constitute subspecies of this more general category.

Four types[10] of political actor were discerned from an analysis of the conjunction of motives, role perceptions, ideological style, convention participation, and political experience.[11] I have called these the "traditional liberal," the "traditional conservative," the "new liberal," and the "new conservative." Traditional liberals and conservatives are characterized by strong commitment to party and a habit of seeing themselves as representatives of a party. As compared to the new conservatives and liberals, the traditionals had been active longer, held more political offices, and were more concerned about organizational support and maintenance. Their ideological commitments were eclectic, and their opinions were more moderate than extreme. At the convention they acted through delegations and candidate groups and remained relatively uninvolved with the various special interest groups. In combination, these traits constituted a political style shared by many liberals and conservatives at the two conventions. Only policy preferences separated the traditional liberals and conservatives, and because the liberals were mostly moderate liberals and conservatives moderate conservatives, because their perspectives were eclectic and none too intense, the limited policy differences that divided them would not prove too difficult to compromise, ignore, or obfuscate, especially since defense of preferred policies did not have top priority for them. Persons for whom party unity and preservation are more important than articulating policy positions would probably be prepared to compromise policy preferences for the sake of either party or national unity especially since consensus is also a value for this group.

Because most textbooks ascribe to American political parties characteristics consistent with the attitudes of traditional liberals and conservatives it seems justified to assume that these characteristics—strong party identification and solidarity, moderate, eclectic policy commitments, areal organizational ties, long political experience—were in fact attributes of the political activists who have dominated presidential politics in the recent past. And if this is so, then it is also reasonable to describe delegates who do not share these characteristics as nontraditional or as representing a new political type.

The nontraditional or new breed actors in the 1972 presidential elite had relatively weak ties to party and conceived politics as an arena of clashing policy conceptions and world views. Whether he was liberal or conservative, the new type of political actor was much more likely than the traditional to have a comprehensive ideological orientation and relatively extreme views. At the Democratic Convention, liberal, new breed types also displayed low areal orientations. The new conservative had a stronger areal focus, but he, too, probably had not been active long and had little experience in a responsible position in a local or state party organization.[12]

Traditional liberals and conservatives had most of the attributes of what have been called party "professionals." Their priorities included building party unity, winning electrons, and preserving the party. Their satisfactions were social as well as moral; their virtues were, in large measure, the virtues of a good team member: solidarity, perseverance, service, and determination to win. It is not hard to see why traditional liberals and conservatives were offended by the new liberal and conservative unconcern for party unity, and victory, nor why the new liberal or conservative had a low opinion of the traditionals who seemed to value organization

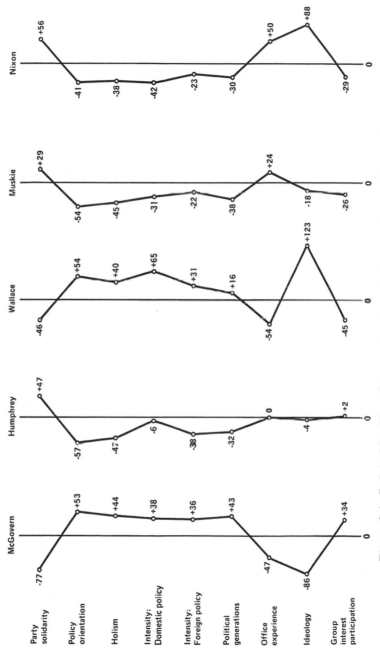

Figure 8-1. Political Profiles of Major Candidate Preference Groups (Z-score graphs)

above the substance of politics. The tendency of the new liberal or conservative to see particular issues and questions as parts of larger wholes meant that questions contested in the political arena were likely to be seen as "fundamental" matters of conscience. The intensity and the priority that policy had for these new liberals and conservatives meant both that it was harder for them to compromise positions and that there was little incentive for doing so. The ideological distance between the new liberal and conservative was very large, and their attachment to particular policies strong. The desire to win was real, but both the inclination and the potential for coalition building were low.

Neither the new liberal nor conservative was in fact new on the American political scene. The activists who peopled the reform clubs, the Goldwater, Wallace, McCarthy, and McGovern movements clearly shared many, if not all, the characteristics of the new liberals and conservatives. Why then call them "new"? Only because they stand in rather sharp contrast to the kinds of activists who are believed to have constituted the majority at most national conventions of both parties since World War II, because they do not resemble the picture of party activists still purveyed in most of the textbooks, and because their ascendancy in American politics is still sufficiently recent that the full effects on the party system and the political system have not yet been felt. There are good grounds for expecting that the influence of new conservatives and liberals will not soon wane.

The new breed hypothesis with which this study began not only postulated the presence of political types whose personal and political goals, resources, and styles differed in identifiable ways from those of persons who have dominated presidential politics in the recent decades, it also postulated that these distinctive traits were associated with sex, political generation, candidate preference, and social structure. This hypothesis was only partly confirmed: there were new political types, they were concentrated in the McGovern and Wallace ranks, and they were mainly newcomers to politics. But the relation of these new types to social structure is more complex.

Since most delegates to both conventions were part of a middle-class, skill elite, the intense disagreement within the presidential elite did not express a classical economic class struggle. Like most of the political conflicts of the modern period, the conflicts of 1972 were carried out between segments of the middle class. The interesting question is whether it is possible to identify any social correlates of this intraclass conflict.

One currently fashionable hypothesis postulates a politics dominated by a different kind of class struggle, one which has been variously described as pitting the "intelligentsia against the middle Americans," the knowledge elite against everyone else, or the "producers—businessmen, manufacturers, hard hats, blue-collar workers, and farmers—against a new and powerful class of nonproducers composed of a liberal verbalist elite (the dominant media, the major foundations and research institutions, the educational establishments, the federal and state bureaucracies) and a semi-permanent welfare constituency. . . ."[13] Kevin Phillips' latest book, *Mediacracy*, describes the privileged position of the knowledge elite; William Rusher makes the postulated opposition of the knowledge elite and others the basis for a hypothetical new party system. But it is not only conservatives who have noted the rise of an adversary intelligentsia of even greater numbers. A growing number of intellectuals with liberal Democratic affiliations—for example, Seymour Martin Lipset, David Bell, Lionel Trilling[14]—have also called attention to the rising political importance of a new adversary intelligentsia. Lipset's recent work is pervaded by preoccupation with this class of whom he recently wrote:

> The new intelligentsia is an outgrowth of conditions in post-industrial society which made a mass phenomenon of the educated class, the producers of knowledge and culture and their followers in the upper rungs of the tertiary sector of the economy, those involved in communications, in the application of scientific technology, in welfare related activities. . . . In many countries the educated young, inside and outside the university, together with many in intellectualized elites, reject traditional values. As David Bell has aptly put it, the "new class" which dominates the media and the culture [has developed] values centered on "personal freedom" [which] are profoundly anti-bourgeoisie.[15]

Herman Kahn has also made this class which he terms (for want of a better name) "upper-middle-class progressives" a focal concern of his diagnosis of the contemporary scene.

> This group includes an overwhelming portion of the high-culture and the educational and media establishments. . . . It is usually supremely self-confident in its basic attitude and opinions, especially those which are so basic they are unnoticed. . . . [It is] almost totally unaware of how blind and committed it was in following its class interests versus those of many other groups in our society.[16]

In another discussion of the 1972 election, I described the new class as consisting mainly of "intellectuals enamored with righteousness and possibility; college students, for whom perfectionism is an occupational hazard; portions of the upper classes freed from concern with economic self-interest; clergymen contemptuous of materialism; romantics derisive of Babbitt and Main Street," and noted that "The values of the counter

culture, spread throughout the population by expanding college enroll-
ments, were purveyed to the public at large by magazines oriented to
intellectual fashion and by the mass media."[17]

Many commentators on the contemporary scene agree that an intelligentsia, or knowledge elite has arisen in the United States, that it is
based on the elite universities, the media, and related knowledge industries, and that its members share an adversary orientation to traditional
American values and institutional practices. These formulations link a
functional class to a specific ideology and to class interests.[18] As described by most critics, the adversary intelligentsia is a close relative of
the amateur or purist, but its disenchantment with American politics is
more complete.

The convention provided an opportunity to investigate the postulated
linkages between political style and occupation and to determine whether
political activists associated with the knowledge producing and consum-
ing occupations have distinctive attitudes, including alienation from traditional political culture and institutions.

To test the hypothesis that persons involved in the creation, criticism,
and transmission of culture had distinctive attitudes and a distinctive role
in the politics of 1972, delegates were divided into functional categories
designed to illuminate the characteristics of various occupational types. A
category comprising clergy, teachers, college professors, social scientists,
social workers, authors, and publishers was developed. This category is
termed "symbol specialists" because of its members' professional involvement with formulating and transmitting opinions about the nature
and meaning of events. Although lawyers also have highly developed
verbal skills, they have long had a distinctive political role and were
treated as a separate category. Because self-employed businessmen, trade
unionists, and farmers are engaged in the production of material goods
and are frankly interested in the maximization of economic benefits and
because analysis demonstrated that they shared many attitudes toward
politics, they were treated as a single category and termed "material
specialists." The other categories are self-explanatory. Analysis of the
elite within these categories makes the paucity of self-employed businessmen, laborers, and their representatives even more striking. Symbol specialists were more numerous than self-employed businessmen, farmers,
laborers, and union officials combined. The composition of this mid-elite
does not reflect a politics dominated by rural-industrial cleavages of the
recent past, but neither does it suggest the trend toward greater representation of scientific competence that Brzezinski regards as appropriate to
a modern society.[19]

Some of each category of persons were found in each candidate preference group, but the proportions differ markedly. Symbol specialists con-

stituted approximately two and one-half times as large a portion of Democratic as of Republican delegates. And within the Democratic Convention they were most numerous in McGovern ranks where they comprised 21 percent of all McGovern supporters and least numerous in Wallace ranks where they constituted only 2 percent of the total. Lawyers were most numerous in Muskie and Nixon ranks and least so among McGovern supporters. Material specialists were most numerous in the Wallace group, where they constituted 27 percent of the whole, and least numerous among McGovern supporters.

Each group had distinctive ideological characteristics. Table 8-2 shows that symbol specialists and students were most likely to be radical or very liberal and least likely to be conservative. Material specialists, salaried managers, and health personnel were most likely to be conservative. Of all groups, public employees most often described themselves as moderates. Table 8-3 shows that symbol specialists and students were more prone to comprehensive, internally consistent intense ideologies; they were most likely to pursue politics from a near exclusive concern with policy and indifference to party. Of all groups except students, they were most alienated from the traditional political culture. Another evidence of their cultural distinctiveness was the large number of persons without religion who fell in this category. (See Tables 8-1 and 8-3.)

Table 8-1. Occupation by Religion (%)

	Protestant	Catholic	Jewish	Atheist—Agnostic
Symbol specialists	10	13	13	25
Lawyers	12	14	15	10
Material specialists	15	12	15	3
Housewives	15	10	18	15
Students	3	4	5	7
Clerical and sales	11	11	8	11
Public employees	9	13	6	7
Salaried managers	8	6	5	7
Health personnel	3	0	4	1
Other professionals	7	9	4	11
Others	9	8	8	3
Weighted *N* =	2213	832	305	299

NOTE: These data are from the interviews.

Table 8-2. Occupation by Ideology (%)

	Symbol Specialists	Lawyers	Material Specialists	Housewives	Students	Clerical and Sales	Public Employees	Salaried Managers	Health Personnel	Other Professionals	Others
Self-Classification											
Radical	11	2	2	4	23	5	3	6	6	6	3
Very liberal	48	19	16	28	40	25	17	16	27	43	37
Somewhat liberal	22	31	17	22	20	32	28	13	8	17	34
Moderate	9	25	21	20	8	22	42	24	6	17	14
Somewhat conservative	9	18	32	19	9	13	11	33	44	12	11
Very conservative	1	4	11	7	0	4	0	9	8	6	2
Weighted N =	305	273	271	391	90	282	180	174	48	164	197
Political Culture Index											
Very liberal 1	47	21	9	31	54	31	11	12	26	33	17
2	32	33	24	23	35	31	41	19	4	33	48
3	14	37	31	29	11	27	42	46	22	23	28
Very conservative 4	6	9	36	18	0	12	6	24	48	11	7
Weighted N =	259	217	193	337	74	249	136	140	46	141	146

NOTE: These data are from the intersect sample. For a complete explanation of the Political Culture Index, see Appendix C.

Table 8-3. Ideological Style and Convention Participation by Occupation (%)

	Symbol Specialists	Lawyers	Material Specialists	Housewives	Students	Clerical and Sales	Public Employees	Salaried Managers	Health Personnel	Other Professionals	Others
Holism											
Very eclectic	5	8	7	7	3	8	22	10	14	7	12
Eclectic	38	59	50	57	38	52	56	57	43	53	56
Programmatic	40	25	31	30	30	31	22	27	36	31	21
Holists	17	8	11	7	29	9	0	6	7	8	11
Weighted N =	242	193	151	291	69	210	108	111	42	122	130
Domestic Policy Intensity											
Low 1	9	13	7	12	0	14	19	13	0	3	16
2	32	55	27	38	47	38	53	41	57	59	35
High 3	59	32	66	50	53	48	28	46	44	38	49
Weighted N =	290	248	203	331	76	245	133	154	46	149	155
Foreign Policy Intensity											
Low 1	1	1	3	1	3	0	0	1	0	1	0
2	31	49	44	36	33	39	42	41	34	36	34
High 3	68	50	53	63	65	62	58	58	66	64	66
Weighted N =	458	441	471	506	144	390	330	262	83	277	294
Convention Participation											
Number of Subgroups											
None	52	87	68	35	32	53	68	74	75	48	65
One	38	10	27	60	42	33	24	20	25	39	27
Two	9	2	4	5	23	11	6	4	0	11	8
Three or more	2	0	1	0	3	3	3	1	0	2	0
Weighted N =	464	461	484	520	144	398	354	270	83	287	298

NOTE: Data on holism and domestic policy intensity are from intersect sample, and convention participation data are from the interviews. Foreign policy intensity is from the interviews. For a complete explanation of these indexes, see Appendix C.

Table 8-4. Organizational Style by Occupation (%)

	Symbol Specialists	Lawyers	Material Specialists	Housewives	Students	Clerical and Sales	Public Employees	Salaried Managers	Health Personnel	Other Professionals	Others
Solidarity											
Low 1	26	3	5	9	42	13	9	11	32	12	6
2	23	13	18	18	25	17	13	12	18	21	29
3	23	53	36	28	12	20	41	30	9	41	40
High 4	29	31	41	44	21	50	36	47	41	26	25
Weighted N =	212	224	190	285	57	179	119	130	34	108	137
Policy Orientation											
Low 1	2	5	1	2	0	1	2	2	0	2	8
2	18	45	27	27	15	17	34	32	39	21	24
3	43	33	48	50	52	50	46	39	17	42	47
High 4	36	18	24	22	33	32	19	27	44	36	21
Weighted N =	240	224	187	285	67	223	122	130	41	130	152
Specialties											
Solidary specialists	2	17	14	19	2	11	8	10	18	11	6
Rectitude specialists	49	18	22	29	47	30	22	21	56	42	30
Synthesizers	48	63	63	49	51	59	66	69	27	47	62
Neither important	1	3	0	3	0	1	3	0	0	0	2
Weighted N =	295	273	263	383	90	274	174	171	45	156	194

NOTE: These data are from the intersect sample. For a complete explanation of these indexes, see Appendix C.

In all their principal attitudes and attachments, students closely resembled symbol specialists, but Table 8–2 shows that greater numbers of students classified themselves as political radicals, still fewer were concerned with organizational maintenance, still more were alienated from the traditional political culture, still more viewed politics by way of comprehensive, consistent ideologies, and still larger numbers took part in the convention activities of the new interest groups. Since over two-thirds of the students present at the convention were McGovern supporters, it is hardly surprising that they would display the characteristics associated with that position. That students tended to the extremes of the McGovern position may reflect a temporary consequence of the Vietnam war or may be the harbinger of change.

Material specialists, persons whose occupations are explicitly concerned with the production of goods rather than services, also had distinctive ideological characteristics. Table 8–2 establishes that they were among the most conservative of the functional groups and felt more intensely about domestic than foreign policy. Most were motivated by an attachment to both party and policy (Table 8–4); many took responsibility for party preservation. Persons without religion were especially rare in this category. (See Table 8–1). The organizational and ideological characteristics of salaried managers closely resembled those of material specialists.

The analysis of perspectives of functional groups offers confirmation of the view that occupation was systematically but not necessarily related to political perspectives. Verbalists among the mid-elite did have unusually liberal perspectives on a wide range of issues and were least supportive of the traditional political culture and most alienated from government. They tended not to see themselves as protectors of party organization. Neither their motives nor role conceptions emphasized party support. The proclivity of symbol specialists for cultural revolution and institutional reform went beyond the conventional characterization of the amateur. Their uniquely low confidence in government reflects disenchantment with the institutions of the society, and their uniquely low support for the traditional culture reflects disenchantment with the values of society. Their distinctive alienation from traditional orientations to party was expressed in the low priority they gave to building party unity and to winning elections. The symbol specialists in this elite shared the defining characteristics of the adversary intelligentsia.

Although no class is monolithic in its ideological perspectives and style, these patterns provide some important evidence to support the contention that contemporary American political conflict does reflect a class struggle—but a struggle between functionally distinct sectors of the same economic class. The heavy concentration of symbol specialists and students in the dominant McGovern ranks magnified their influence beyond what numbers alone would suggest.

In 1951 Lasswell described the contours of the "post-bourgeois" revolution. While the bourgeois revolution marked the rise of the businessman and the decline of feudal aristocracy, the "major transformation" from the bourgeois to the post-bourgeois era "is the decline of business (and of earlier social formations) and the rise of intellectuals and semi-intellectuals to effective power." It was, Lasswell noted, the Polish Marxist Waclaw Machajski who first identified intellectuals as the ascendant social class.[20] Modern politics and technology, it was argued, make the "persuasive skills" of intellectuals indispensable to the capture of political power. Education has replaced blood and capital as the indispensable qualification for political power. Lasswell, Lerner, and associates documented the rise to power of members of middle income skill groups in the century's principal revolutionary movements: the Nazis, the Bolsheviks, the Italian Fascists, the Kuomingtang, and the Chinese Communists were examples. But examination of the ruling elite of democratic nations reveals the same trends in recruitment. It could as easily be said of Lyndon Johnson, Richard Nixon, Gerald Ford, Edward Heath, Margaret Thatcher, Harold Wilson, George Pompidou, or François Mitterand, as of Mao or Lenin, that "it was through their education that these individuals acquired the skills they used to articulate their political ideologies and organize their political movements.[21] Experts in the persuasive and organizational skills are as valuable in democratic as in revolutionary politics. In fact, the democratic leader's need to win approval and votes makes him peculiarly dependent on persuasive abilities— reinforced by organizational effort. Where in past times and other places organizations could be built with material rewards, today in the United States organization, too, often depends on the persuasive powers of the leader. The organizational expert builds after a leader mobilizes followers. Solidary organizations are less dependent than ideological groups on the verbal skills of leaders, but nevertheless require periodic articulation of purposes and verbalization of common commitments. The ideological—or rectitude based—organization is singularly dependent on the agitational skills of its leaders to state and reiterate the purposes that are its raison d'être. In their special dependence on the rhetorical output of leaders such organizations resemble charismatic communities. *The highly educated activists that people both parties constitute the special constituencies of the persuasive leader. The influence of symbol specialists rests not just on their numbers, but on the extent to which other portions of the highly educated elite value the skills of articulation and argument.*

Persons in the symbol specialist group—the teachers, journalists, clergy, social scientists—had no single point of view. Neither did their first cousins, the lawyers. The diversity of point of view within these functional groups is most dramatically illustrated by some leading political figures. Contending Democrats George McGovern and Hubert Humphrey were both university teachers whose persuasive skills and related political abilities enabled them to create organizational bases where none had previously existed. George Wallace, Henry Jackson, Richard Nixon, and Edmund Muskie are lawyers, but they did not acquire the same perspectives on politics from the study of law any more than William Buckley, Tom Wicker, George Will, and James Reston, all of whom are eastern establishment commentators on politics and society, reach the same conclusions about the meaning of events. The point is clear enough. The writers, teachers, and lawyers who parlay verbal skills into political influence do not necessarily share the same perspectives on political events, not even those who went to Ivy League Schools, or grew up in small midwestern towns, or share a southern accent. But though there is no necessary relation among education, function, and ideology, there is nonetheless a tendency for the symbol specialist to embrace liberal, adversary positions. If symbol specialists constitute the ascending portion of the middle-class political elite and material specialists are declining in influence, then the attractions of power will probably encourage ever larger numbers of lawyers, whose skills are in any case very similar to those of other verbal experts, to adapt their perspectives to fit ascendant styles of belief and behavior.

There are class interests and predilections that characterize all parts of the verbalist elite. One common interest is in having the parties adopt practices that favor the skills of this class as opposed to wealth, birth, or beauty. Symbol specialists share a concern with discussion and advocacy of the ideological aspects of politics. *A symbol specialist may be said to have a vested interest in the intellectual and moral aspects of politics because he is expert in articulating, analyzing, criticizing, and moralizing.* These skills are especially useful in ideological politics. The greater numbers of symbol specialists in the McGovern ranks almost surely affected the success of that movement in communicating with communicators, just as the presence in Wallace ranks of more persons without verbal sophistication stimulated negative comment among those who value verbal skills.

The rise of ideological politics in this country has accompanied the growing importance of symbol specialists in American politics and government. It appears that the broker conception of government is giving way to a public interest conception of government that involves much larger roles for planners and explainers. It appears, too, that political salience of bread and butter issues has been declining while style, image, and abstract issues of principle are of steadily increasing importance.

Ideas, values, and issues are the currency with which symbol specialists pursue politics. What money is to the businessman and manpower is to the trade unionist, *words* are to the symbol specialist: they are the base value utilized in the effort to win other values—power, status, moral approval, wealth. A special relation exists in politics between rectitude concerns and verbal skills. Obviously, verbal skills are needed to dramatize moral concerns, but moral concerns are also needed to make persuasion *persuasive*. Moral claims are readily available to the middle income symbol specialist. *Unlike wealth, status, knowledge, and health—rectitude can, for all practical political purposes, be had for the claiming.* Lasswell noted that "Social conflicts afford ready opportunity for advancement by the use of 'ought' words. Symbol specialists are demanded who can invent or elaborate the language of justification for the exercise, or the denial of authority."[22] Moral claims are the resource most readily available to persons lacking the wealth, numbers, social status, legitimacy, and other attributes with which political power is won. Moral claims and critiques are the principal resource available to the revolutionist or reformist group which is long on critical and verbal skills and short on other values. The greater the prominence of ideology in a political struggle or in a regime, the more elevated is the role of the symbol specialist. "The pattern for mythmaking by intellectuals," Lasswell noted, "was, set for our society by Plato, who dreamed poetically of the 'philosopher king' in whom omniscience was at one with omnipotence."[23] Ideology is the preferred political instrument of the intellectual classes. History—both recent and remote—establishes the ability of upwardly mobile, intellectually skilled persons to attach themselves to rulers who have won power by other means. But moral criticism, ideology, and value manipulation are the symbol specialists' preferred instrumentality in the political spheres—doubtless because this is his own terrain.

Lasswell and Lerner have documented the role of the symbol specialist in this century's principal revolutionary regimes, and Edward Shils has emphasized the intellectual's role in the politics of the new nations.[24] Meanwhile elite studies have documented the growing prominence of verbal skill groups in American, British, and French politics.

Because of their training and proclivities, symbol specialists have a special aptitude for the "demoralization" and "remoralization" of politics. The process of demoralization consists of criticizing and undermining the myths and legitimacy of established institutions. The process of remoralization consists of providing new myths and new authorities. Both processes offer the opportunity to define reality; both involve attractive opportunities to reinforce definitions and conceptions of morality with power.[25]

The processes of demoralization and remoralization of American politics are already far advanced.[26] *The effort to demoralize and to remoralize politics involves interpreting specific questions as parts of larger wholes and linking all questions to basic values. In brief, it involves reversing the processes and habits of incrementalism.* The end of ideology and convergence hypotheses argue that in technologically complex societies more and more problems will be perceived and treated as technical rather than political and that government will more and more become a series of technocratic solutions to technical problems. Such a development appeared particularly plausible in the early stages of the demoralization of politics. But just as problems formerly perceived as political may be treated as technical problems, so can problems previously perceived as technical be redefined as political problems. (Many of the central "ecological" issues consist of questions that have until recently been perceived and treated as technical questions.) The remoralization of politics proceeds by investing small questions with larger meaning and moral significance. One consequence of this process is intensification of political conflict. Verbal sophistication becomes an ever greater political asset; lack of verbal skills, an ever more crippling liability. An early consequence of this process is to increase greatly the need for symbol specialists. The resulting increase in numbers of symbol specialists leads to the further "moralization" of politics and policy making which further increases the need for symbol specialists, and so forth. The result is a continuing process, whose end is not yet in sight, in which the need for and number of symbol specialists engaged in political and quasi-political activities increases geometrically. Their increased numbers lead to even greater emphasis on ideology and style, and the more important ideology and style become in politics, the more likely politics is to attract persons who are sensitive to and affectively involved with ideologies. Personality and political systems interact reciprocally. The character of political actors affects the character of the political process, and the character of the process affects who is attracted into it. The dominance of presidential politics by a skill-based professional class of verbal specialists will have continuing consequences in American politics—whether or not that class remains divided among itself or achieves unexpected unity. Some of those consequences will be discussed in the following chapters.

NOTES

1. Paul T. David, Ralph M. Goldman, and Richard C. Bain, *The Politics of National Party Conventions* (Washington, D.C.: Brookings Institution, 1960), p. 337.
2. Ibid., p. 338.
3. Ibid., pp. 344–348.
4. Ibid., p. 352.
5. The distinction between "citizen" politics and "professional politicians" is interesting on two counts: first, because almost none of those called "professionals" are in fact that but are instead volunteers; and second, because the juxtaposition implies that "professionals" must not be engaging in "citizen" politics. For recent use of the concept of "citizen" politics as something different from participation through the parties, see John S. Saloma and Frederick H. Sontag, *Parties: The Real Opportunity for Effective Citizen Politics* (New York: Alfred A. Knopf, 1972).
6. Robert A. Dahl, *Who Governs? Democracy and Power in an American City* (New Haven: Yale University Press, 1961).
7. David, et al., *Politics*, p. 353.
8. James Q. Wilson was a notable but not unique exception to this generally favorable assessment. His *The Amateur Democrat: Club Politics in Three Cities* (Chicago: University of Chicago Press, 1962) provides a cogent critique of the negative potential of this style of politics.
9. David, et al., *Politics*, p. 353.
10. As in all taxonomic enterprises the strategy is to abstract common features and classify *types* of regularities. Greenstein noted that the process is "possibly as fundamental as any aspect of cognitive functioning." Fred I. Greenstein, *Personality and Politics: Problems of Evidence, Interference, and Conceptualization* (Chicago: Markham, 1969) provides an excellent discussion of strategies for studying personality and politics. On typologies, see also Paul F. Lazarsfeld and Allen Barton, "Qualitative Measurement in the Social Sciences: Classification, Typologies, and Indices" in *The Policy Sciences: Recent Developments in Scope and Method*, eds. Daniel Lerner and Harold D. Lasswell (Stanford, Calif.: Stanford University Press, 1951), pp. 155–192. Also Edward A. Tiryakian, "Typologies," *International Encyclopedia of the Social Sciences* (New York: Macmillan, 1968), vol. 16. Carl G. Hempel, "Typological Methods in the Social Sciences" in *Philosophy of the Social Sciences*, ed. Maurice A. Natanson (New York: Random House, 1963), pp. 210–230. Eduard Spranger, *Types of Men: The Psychology and Ethics of Personality*, 5th ed. (Halle, Germany: Niemeyer, 1928). Also, Harold D. Lasswell, "A Note on 'Types' of Political Personality: Nuclear, Correlational, Developmental," *Journal of Social Issues* 24 (1968): 81–91, emphasizes these attributes of the type of typologies.
11. R. M. MacIver, *Social Causation* (New York: Harper and Row, Torchbook, 1964), p. 377.
12. The fact that experience in the state and local organization is not necessarily related to concern for local or state party organizations increases the likelihood that areal focus is more a function of culture than of experience.
13. William A. Rusher, *The Making of the New Majority Party* (New York: Sheed and Ward, 1975), p. xxi.
14. Lionel Trilling, *Beyond Culture: Essays on Literature and Learning* (London: Secker and Warburg, 1966); Daniel Bell, *The Coming of Post-Industrial Society; A Venture in Social Forecasting* (New York: Basic Books, 1973); Seymour Martin Lipset and

Everett C. Ladd, Jr., *The Divided Academy: Professors and Politics* (New York: McGraw-Hill, 1975).

15. Seymour Martin Lipset, contribution to a symposium entitled "America Now: A Failure of Nerve," in *Commentary* 60, no. 1 (1975): 59.

16. Herman Kahn, in the symposium "America Now," p. 47.

17. Jeane Kirkpatrick, "The Revolt of the Masses," *Commentary* 55, no. 2 (1973): 58–62, p. 61.

18. Most observers do not include lawyers in this intelligentsia, although the two groups share many common characteristics. That lawyers as a class are not usually included in the adversary knowledge elite is probably explained by the fact that lawyers typically function inside the system as representatives and advocates rather than outside it as critics. Recent developments in legal education and practice suggest the rising importance of adversary orientations in legal education and the legal profession.

19. Zbigniew Brzezinski, *Between Two Ages: America's Role in the Technotronic Era* (New York: The Viking Press, 1970), pp. 216–217.

20. Cited in Harold D. Lasswell, "The World Revolution of Our Time," in *World Revolutionary Elites: Studies in Coersive Ideological Movements*, eds. Harold D. Lasswell and Daniel Lerner (Cambridge, Mass.: MIT Press, 1965), p. 86.

21. Daniel Lerner, "The Coercive Ideologists in Perspective," in *World Revolutionary Elites*, p. 460.

22. Harold D. Lasswell, *Politics: Who Gets What, When, How* (New York: Whittlesey House, 1936), p. 145.

23. Lasswell, *Politics*, p. 152.

24. Edward Shils, *The Intellectuals and the Powers, and Other Essays* (Chicago: University of Chicago Press, 1972).

25. An interesting discussion of intellectuals' role in the definition of reality is Peter L. Berger, *Pyramids of Sacrifice: Political Ethics and Social Change* (New York: Basic Books, 1974); also Peter L. Berger and Thomas Luckman, *The Social Construction of Reality: A Treatise in the Sociology of Knowledge* (Garden City, N.Y.: Doubleday, 1966).

26. "Remoralization" is Harold D. Lasswell's term. He applies it specifically to the "destiny" of middle income skill groups. *Politics*, pp. 177–178.

CHAPTER 9

Factions in the Presidential Parties

Political parties have sometimes been regarded as identical with factions, and sometimes sharply distinguished from them. George Washington, James Madison, and David Hume, for example, viewed parties as factions and took a dim view of both.[1] By contrast, Robert MacIver argued that "the difference between faction and party is as important as the difference between oligarchy and democracy," because while factions merely seek power, "parties contest for control of government by constitutional means."[2] F. E. Schattschneider also saw important differences between parties and factions, differences that extended to both goals and means. A party, Schattschneider insisted, was not merely a group of power seekers, it was "an organization which makes a bid for power" by constitutional majoritarian processes and methods.[3] Its most distinctive characteristics derived from the need to attract a majority. To win the support of a majority, a party "must subordinate many other things." "The symmetry of programs must be bent, amended, and amputated to fit the cruel necessities of compromise on a multitude of fronts. It is idle to talk as if parties would not find it necessary to compromise if politicians were sufficiently high minded. To refuse to make concessions and to refuse to develop a many-sided program is simply to refuse to make a bid for power."[4] In Schattschneider's view, to refuse to compromise and aggregate diverse interests and perspectives is to be a faction rather than a party.

Others have distinguished factions from parties on the basis of their arena of contention rather than their goals or methods. Leiserson, for example, observes that factions "exist within every party as rival leadership groups seeking to control the party structure just as the parties themselves are factional with respect to the total body of citizens who accept as legitimate the authority of government."[5] And Lasswell and Kaplan asserted, "A faction may be described then as a continuing alignment within a decision-making group: a subgroup concurring in all decisions relating to a specified interest."[6]

Ambiguity and disagreement concerning the characteristics of factions and their relation to parties is of a piece with continuing disagreement on the nature of political parties. Like factions, parties have been defined with regard to their object (to win power, to promote policies), with regard to their bases (interest, affection, ideology), and with regard to their methods (constitutional, non-constitutional, aggregative, non-aggregative). Most relatively contemporary commentators have defined parties either like Burke, as a group of like-minded persons, "united, for promoting by their joint endeavors the national interest, upon some particular principle in which they are all agreed"[7] or, like Herring, as "an association which is, above all, concerned with attaining to office, rewarding its followers, adding to its power, and continuing its life."[8] And, as in the past, discussion about what parties and factions should be frequently colors views about what they are. Many of those who define party in terms of issues also believe that citizens *should* be actively involved in policy decisions and that programmatic parties will stimulate greater voter interest and participation than will parties that lack clear ideological definition. Those writing in the tradition of Schattschneider and Herring are less concerned with having parties provide clear policy alternatives (the feasibility of which they question on other grounds) than with the preservation of parties as institutions capable of aggregating interests, "structuring" the vote, and recruiting and screening leaders.[9]

Whether the parties *should be* programmatic associations comprising persons with a common view on salient problems or whether they should be alliances of office seekers and potential governors who adopt programs in response to the views of voters is not at issue here. It is desirable to examine the characteristics of the factions present at the conventions because just as "Merely adding atoms of course does not make for molecules . . . ,"[10] merely adding delegates does not explain a presidential party. Not infrequently, the delegates who comprise conventions are organized into subunits that serve as foci of identification and as decision groups. Eulau observed that "A unit composed of individuals is an action unit—or 'collective actor' when it has, as an integral or global property, a decision rule or set of rules, formal or informal, that enables the individuals in the unit to act in common and commit the unit as a whole or other units to a course of action."[11] Factions, such as candidate groups and special action caucuses, have the capacity for collective actions. The data on 1972 convention delegates illuminate the extent to which presidential parties in 1972 actually were ideologically and/or socially homogeneous; they provide the information needed to identify the "factional leadership groups struggling for control of the formal structure of political authority."[12]

For the purposes of this discussion the presidential parties are viewed as including all those individuals and factions who met in the convention to attempt to influence the selection of the party's standard-bearer and/or the articulation of its program, and political factions are defined as coalitions of delegates who make demands in the name of some shared goal on a party. This image conforms to Leiserson's view that the essential difference between a faction and a party is that persons who comprise a faction choose to compete (at least initially) within a party rather than as a party.

The bases of the various factions who struggled for control of a party's label and resources are investigated rather than assumed. Geography, a state's economics, and culture have all served as bases of political faction in the United States. V.O. Key emphasized the importance of sectionalism in structuring American political competition: "For its two party form and for the persistence of that form," he observed, "American politics probably owes a considerable debt to an underlying dual sectionalism, which, for well over a century, contributed to a partisan dualism; and undoubtedly aided in molding enduring political habits."[13] But he also did not neglect the influence of demographic shifts on either the character or durability of political cleavages. "An urban electorate," he noted, "may be susceptible to wider shifts in partisan attachment than would have been expected of the rural electorate of an earlier day."[14] The names of Robert Alford and Seymour Martin Lipset[15] are prominently associated with the argument that American political cleavages have reflected economic classes. More recently cultural divisions have claimed increasing attention as a basis of political alignments.

The appeals of particular candidates also have a demonstrated capacity to affect political alignments. In his important article, "Some Dynamic Elements of Contests for the Presidency," Donald Stokes asserted that in a period (1952 to 1964) when there was little change in party identification, candidates had dramatic effects on electoral behavior.

> It is therefore evident that the dynamism of popular attitude is peculiarly tied to the emergence of new candidates for the Presidency. The attitudes toward the parties are not inert. The shift in the relative assessment of the parties over the period of this research has been enough to alter the parties' strength by something like six million votes on a turnout equal to that of 1964. But the change, impressive as it is, nevertheless is moderate by comparison with the change induced by succeeding pairs of candidates. The fluctuations of electoral attitudes over these elections have to a remarkable degree focused on the candidates themselves.[16]

While some theoretical frameworks—for example, Marxism—postulate some factors as basic and others as "superstructure," historical evidence suggests that the bases of political cleavage can and do change.

In presidential politics the nature of the contest and the rules under which it is conducted increase the likelihood that candidates will become the rallying points for political factions. Sectional, economic, or ideological groups need a leader who can win the nomination and election in their behalf. And ambitious leaders need supporters. The dynamics of pre-convention competition make it extremely likely that factions will coalesce around the candidacies of persons competing for the presidential nomination. While contemporary discussion often assumes that activists coalesce around issues, making their decision about whom to support less on the basis of a candidate's leadership skills, integrity, charm, or ability to win than on the basis of what he "stands for," not all candidate support groups were ideological factions—even in the polarized politics of 1972. The Democratic Convention provided clear-cut examples of candidate groups that were ideological factions and of candidate groups that were alliances of ideologically heterogeneous persons united in support of leaders who had inspired loyalty and confidence.

Table 9-1. Ideological Consensus in Candidate Groups: Rank-Ordered

Humphrey Candidate Group		*Muskie Candidate Group*	
Police	+81	Police	+81
Inflation	−74	Inflation	−78
Politicians	−74	Civil rights leaders	+73
Civil rights leaders	+63	Politicians	+64
Military	+56	Liberals	+54
Welfare recipients	+52	Lay off women first	+50
Union leaders	+52	Abortion	+48
Cultural conservatism	+51	Conservatives	−43
Black militants	−45	Military policy	−43
Lay off women first	+44	Vietnam	−42
Liberals	+41	Crime	−40
Conservatives	−37	Black militants	−39
Crime	−31	International idealism	−39
Women's Lib	−27	Welfare recipients	+33
Sanctions	+26	Union leaders	+30
Abortion	+24	Military	+21
International idealism	+22	Cultural conservatism	+19
Busing	+13	Women's lib	−16
Welfare	−12	Sanctions	+14
Vietnam	−9	Welfare	+13
Military policy	−9	Business interests	−12
Business interests	+5	Busing	0

The McGovern and Wallace groups were characterized by consensus on many issues and by relatively high ideological consistency and intensity. (See Table 9–1.) Neither was a single issue faction. Though agreement on Southeast Asian policy was high in the McGovern candidate support group, that was by no means the only issue that united this group. There was high consensus on other aspects of foreign and domestic policy including the use of force as an instrument of foreign policy, the importance of military strength, foreign aid, the United States relations with Cuba, busing, civil disobedience, and crime.

Wallace group consensus was highest on welfare, police, busing, and black militants—all issues that have at least a peripheral relation to race. But agreement extended beyond these to foreign policy—support for the military, desire to keep the nation strong, disdain for supranational

Table 9-1. Ideological Consensus in Candidate Groups: Rank-Ordered (Continued)

McGovern Candidate Group		Wallace Candidate Group	
Civil rights leaders	+98	Sanctions	+100
Crime	−93	Cultural conservatism	+96
Liberals	+92	Welfare	−93
Inflation	−90	Busing	+93
Vietnam	−89	International idealism	−92
International idealism	+85	Black militants	−86
Conservatives	−84	Police	+85
Busing	−80	Liberals	−82
Military policy	−80	Military	+81
Cultural conservatism	−73	Conservatives	+71
Sanctions	−73	Civil rights leaders	−70
Political demonstrators	+70	Crime	+68
Abortion	+70	Political demonstrators	−58
Women's lib	+66	Women's lib	−50
Lay off women first	+66	Welfare recipients	−49
Welfare	+63	Union leaders	−43
Welfare recipients	+59	Inflation	−39
Business interests	−54	Vietnam	+34
Military	−46	Military policy	+25
Police	+41	Abortion	−17
Black militants	+22	Lay off women first	+8
Union leaders	+19	Business interests	+1

NOTE: Consensus scores were calculated by subtracting the percent of a group favorable to a symbol or issue from the percent of a group unfavorable to the symbol or issue.

bodies, and détente with Cuba—and to non-racial domestic issues relevant to the traditional authority structure.

Both the McGovern and Wallace groups had some distinctive social, cultural, and political characteristics. The Wallace group was distinctively southern, Protestant and business-oriented. (See Table 9–2.) Of all candidate groups it also had the lowest median income (see Table 9–3) and the lowest median education. The McGovern group by contrast was distinctively eastern, non-Christian (atheist, agnostic, and Jewish), urban, and geographically mobile and contained an unusually large number of symbol specialists. Median political experience was low in both these groups, and in neither was there much consensus about attitude to party or delegate role. The low levels of consensus concerning party stood in suggestive contrast to their much higher levels of agreement on substantive questions of policy and ideology. (Consensus scores on the solidarity index were McGovern, 28 and Wallace, 42, as compared to scores of 80 to 100 on many substantive issues.) Neither was socially, politically, or geographically homogeneous. The structure of consensus strongly suggests that "ideology" was the glue that held these groups together.

But the presence of these two ideological factions did not mean that by 1972 ideology had become the exclusive basis for political combination. Humphrey and Muskie candidate groups provided a sharp contrast. The long political experience, the high consensus concerning party and organizational support, and the ideological diversity in each of these groups indicate that each was united less by agreement on the controversial issues of the day than by agreement on a candidate. Consensus on issues was relatively low in both groups and lowest of all in the Humphrey group. In that group agreement was greatest on traditional Democratic symbols—government's economic role, civil rights leaders, the poor, and union leaders—and low on the more controversial new issues—busing, welfare, Vietnam, and political demonstrators.[17] The ideological diversity of the Humphrey group is reflected in the relatively low level of agreement on those overarching ideological symbols: liberals and conservatives. (See Table 9–1.) The pattern of consensus in the Muskie group most closely resembled that of the Humphrey support group, but levels of consensus were somewhat higher and the conformity to the traditional New Deal model was less complete. The Muskie group displayed high consensus on inflation and civil rights leaders but less consensus on union leaders and the military. The relatively low ideological cohesion of the Humphrey and Muskie groups extended even to the most controversial convention issues: ousting of the regular Illinois delegation and the "California challenge." On this latter issue McGovern and Wallace consensus scores were 97 and 94 respectively while the Humphrey group, who had a special stake in ousting the solid McGovern delegation chosen

Table 9-2. Section of United States by Party and Candidate Preference and by Party and Ideology (%)

Party and Candidate Preference

	Democrats	Republicans	McGovern	Humphrey	Wallace	Muskie	Nixon
New England–Mid-Atlantic	27	19	35	20	3	27	19
Midwest	31	30	28	44	25	41	30
South and Border	25	33	15	30	69	22	33
Far West	18	18	23	7	3	9	18
N =	1587	825	385	199	68	139	791

Ideology by Section by Party

	Democrats				Republicans			
	NE–MA	MW	S + B	FW	NE–MA	MW	S + B	FW
Ideological Self-Classification								
Radical	13	6	3	9	0	0	0	0
Very liberal	48	41	29	46	1	1	0	0
Somewhat liberal	27	32	31	30	17	9	3	8
Moderate	8	15	19	10	46	41	24	31
Somewhat conservative	3	5	13	3	30	41	52	47
Very conservative	0	2	5	1	8	7	20	14
N =	418	478	381	278	156	242	267	147

NOTE: Data are from the mail questionnaires.

NE–MA = New England–Mid-Atlantic; MW = Midwest; S + B = South and Border; FW = Far West.

Table 9-3. Median Income by Party and Candidate Preference

	Median Income	N
Democrats	4.29	1550
Republicans	6.02	807
McGovern	4.05	872
Humphrey	4.42	195
Wallace	3.79	63
Muskie	5.29	134
Nixon	6.06	774

NOTE: These data are from the mail questionnaires. Delegates were asked to name their "income range" for family income before taxes in 1971. Eight "ranges" were offered as answers; they are listed below with the number code represented in the medians above.

Number code

1	Under $4,999
2	$5,000–$9,999
3	$10,000–$14,999
4	$15,000–$19,999
5	$20,000–$24,999
6	$25,000–$29,999
7	$30,000–$49,999
8	Over $50,000

on the basis of "winner-take-all," had a consensus score of only 43, and the Muskie group of 6.

The relatively low levels of consensus of the Humphrey and Muskie groups demonstrate that both were *aggregative candidate groups* in the sense that each attracted to its cause activists with quite different orientations toward major issues. Confidence in the leadership of their candidate was more important than ideology in holding these groups together. These groups were "moderate" in two senses: one, they tended to take less extreme positions and two, those "for" and "against" tended to cancel out one another, especially on the more controversial issues. Neither the Humphrey nor Muskie groups were ideologically neutral. As compared to Republican groups, both were clearly "liberal" (see Table 9–1). But both contained a broader spectrum of opinion than the McGovern or Wallace groups. A good deal of compromising and aggregating of diverse points of view had apparently taken place *inside* these groups. Because they featured agreement on candidate, attachment to party, and giving priority to electoral victory and disagreement on many of the most controversial issues of 1972, the Humphrey and Muskie groups constituted examples of factions based less on ideology than on interest in contesting and winning.

There were present, then, in the 1972 Democratic Convention not merely different types of individuals, but different types of factions: the one based on agreement on a relatively broad range of issues, the other based on common attachment to candidate, party, and concern with winning. The presence of both "ideological" and "electoral" factions in the Democratic party means that that party did not conform closely to either of the dominant models of parties: it was neither a group of like-minded persons united in pursuit of a conception of the common good *nor* an association principally concerned with "attaining to office, rewarding its followers, adding to its power and continuing its life."[18] Since compromises and coalitions are worked out not merely among individuals but among representatives of groups, the presence of two types of factions within the Democratic party has some interesting implications for the party's potential for success.

The very fact that factions coalesced around different types of values probably enhanced their low regard for one another and exacerbated the difficulty of arriving at understanding, respect, and cooperation. Compromise has no moral standing with an ideological faction. To just the extent that ideological goals are the *raison d'être* of an ideological faction, representatives of such factions will find it difficult if not impossible to compromise their goals—even if they are inclined to do so. Electoral factions should have a larger capacity for compromise on the party program and nominee since, in principle, their goals (party victory) and their values (attachment to party and preserving and enhancing its role) can be served by compromise. There is some reason for believing, furthermore, that compromise has intrinsic value for such groups. However, just as the organizational concerns of the electoral faction enjoy low esteem for an ideological faction, the unwillingness of the ideological faction to make compromises to achieve consensus communicates a disrespect for the basic principles of association of the electoral faction. The result is mutual distrust and disesteem of the sort that blighted Democratic presidential hopes in 1968 and 1972. Should such factions continue to exist within the Democratic party, the success of any faction in securing the nomination may prove a Pyrrhic victory.

The alternative to such factions would appear to be either the disappearance (whether by schism or attenuation) of the ideological factions or the disappearance (whether by schism or attenuation) of factions based on electoral concerns. There remains the possibility that the Democratic party will survive in roughly its existing form. The likelihood that the party will continue as a majority party that includes diverse factions depends not only on the persistence of existing divisions but on the continued presence of some common interests or perspectives. This in turn depends on what the various factions have in common. In the search for common perspectives the *direction* of opinion in each faction is considered and sectional opinion on past and present party leaders is examined.

DIRECTION OF FACTIONAL OPINION ON ISSUES

By the dominant direction of opinion I refer simply to which side of an issue delegates placed themselves on the measure utilized to determine direction of opinion. This measure takes into account neither intensity of feeling nor the number of persons in a group without an opinion; it only establishes whether the preponderance of a group opinion falls on the "liberal" or "conservative" end of the spectrum. When factions are arranged by direction of opinion, it becomes clear that *the McGovern group represented an extreme of the dominant Democratic consensus, while the Wallace group was on the opposite side of most issues from other Democratic candidate groups*. Though the level of group consensus varied markedly, the preponderant opinion in the Humphrey, Muskie, and McGovern groups was the same on such relatively non-controversial issues and symbols as civil rights leaders, inflation, and police, and also on more controversial subjects, such as Vietnam, political demonstrators, welfare recipients, conservatives, liberals, union leaders, abortion, and treating women equally in case of job layoffs. (See Table 9–1.) There were four controversial issues or symbols on which the dominant direction of opinion of the McGovern group differed from that of all other Democratic groups: military, busing, women's liberation, and black militants and two other issues—welfare policy and business interests—on which the dominant direction of opinion in the Humphrey group was opposite to that of the Muskie and McGovern groups. The importance of the differences of opinion between the Humphrey and Muskie groups on the one hand and the McGovern group on the other should not be underestimated. Busing and welfare policy were among the most controversial issues of 1972. The military and black militants are groups closely linked to the authority structure and so to questions of legitimacy. For many, women's liberation symbolizes rejection of important aspects of traditional society. Furthermore, the low Humphrey and Muskie group consensus scores on some other controversial issues indicated that a good many persons in each group disagreed with the dominant party position on these issues. Therefore, although the preponderant opinion in these groups was consistent with the preponderant opinion of the dominant McGovern group, differences among these three candidate support groups were large enough and consistent enough to give each a distinctive ideological flavor. The Humphrey group most closely reflected the traditional Democratic consensus, including support for a foreign policy based on conventional conceptions of the national interest, a large government role in the economy, the Democratic/labor alliance, and support for traditional institutions. Though also relatively moderate and ideologically heterogeneous, the Muskie group displayed somewhat less consensus on these traditional fundamentals. The McGovern group was most committed to the new liberalism, includings its characteristic distrust of authority and authority symbols, its rejection of traditional social institutions, including sex roles, neighborhood schools, and the work ethic. But both the Humphrey and Muskie groups contained substantial numbers who shared the McGovern perspective on all these issues. The ideological distance among these three groups was not so great as to make cooperation impossible; the areas of agreement were sufficiently numerous to provide an ideological basis for alliance.

Was there any common ground on which all Democratic factions—including the Wallace faction—might have stood? The only issues or symbols on which the direction of opinion was the same in *all* Democratic factions were also those on which Republicans and Democrats were agreed: police and politicians toward whom all groups were positive and government activism in dealing with inflation, concerning which all were also favorable. The near complete estrangement of the Wallace faction from other Democratic factions is reflected in group scores on those comprehensive ideological symbols: liberal and conservative. The Wallace group scored liberals a negative 82 and conservatives a positive 71, while all other Democratic groups evaluated liberals positively and conservatives negatively. (See Table 9-1.)

REFERENCE FIGURES

Ratings of past and present leaders were analyzed in an effort to determine whether attitudes toward past or present leaders might have given a sense of community to Democrats who were divided on the major issues. (See Table 9-4.) This inquiry established, first, that the McGovern, Humphrey, and Muskie groups shared a symbolic tradition stretching from

Franklin Roosevelt through Adlai Stevenson, Harry Truman, and John Kennedy to Lyndon Johnson on whom they split sharply (with the Humphrey and Muskie groups characterized by high consensus and a favorable attitude and the McGovern group low consensus and an unfavorable

Table 9-4. Candidate Group Consensus Concerning the Political Traditions

McGovern		Humphrey		Muskie	
		Positive Evaluations			
Roosevelt	+94	Roosevelt	+95	Kennedy	+98
Stevenson	+93	Truman	+94	Truman	+96
Kennedy	+92	Kennedy	+93	Roosevelt	+95
Truman	+79	Stevenson	+82	Stevenson	+84
		Johnson	+78	Johnson	+71
		Dirksen	+2		
		Negative Evaluations			
Goldwater	−90	Goldwater	−77	Goldwater	−80
Dulles	−69	Dulles	−30	Dulles	−46
Dirksen	−44	Taft	−27	Eisenhower	−21
Taft	−31	Eisenhower	−16	Taft	−13
Eisenhower	−21			Dirksen	−4
Johnson	−10				

Nixon		Wallace	
	Positive Evaluations		
Eisenhower	+93	Truman	+42
Dirksen	+78	Goldwater	+35
Taft	+70	Dirksen	+24
Goldwater	+58	Roosevelt	+20
Dulles	+30	Taft	+16
Truman	+3	Kennedy	+2
	Negative Evaluations		
Roosevelt	−55	Dulles	−42
Johnson	−54	Johnson	−24
Kennedy	−48	Stevenson	−22
Stevenson	−43	Eisenhower	−20

NOTE: These are consensus scores. They are calculated by subtracting the percent of a group favorable to a reference figure from the percent of a group negative to a reference figure. Data are from the mail questionnaires.

attitude) and, second, that the Wallace tradition bore little resemblance to that of the other Democratic candidate groups. Wallacites' evaluations of past political leaders symbolized the extent to which that movement transcended conventional party and ideological categories. Reactions to leaders also made it clear that the Wallace movement recognized no clear ancestors nor heros except their own candidate. Other groups were characterized by high levels of consensus and positive affect toward selected past party leaders, but there was no past leader on which the Wallace consensus score reached 50. Leaders toward whom the Wallace faction was on balance positive were found in both parties: Harry Truman and Barry Goldwater inspired greatest admiration; Everett Dirksen and Franklin Roosevelt were also objects of group approbation. Negative evaluations were also bipartisan: John Foster Dulles and Lyndon Johnson; Dwight Eisenhower and Adlai Stevenson. Apart from the McGovern faction's negative score on Lyndon Johnson (which reflected that group's disassociation from an aspect of the Democratic tradition), other candidate group evaluations of past figures followed party lines.

The pattern of group orientations toward contemporary leaders was also suggestive. It established the clear preference of each group for its own candidate and confirmed the relative affinity of the Humphrey and Muskie support groups for each other's leaders; it documented the McGovern group's relatively low regard for Muskie and, especially, for Hubert Humphrey and the negative feeling of the Humphrey faction for McGovern; it reflected the strong tendency for evaluation of leaders to follow party lines; it documented the estrangement of the Wallace group from all other majority party leaders, the unimportance of party affiliation to that group, and the extent to which the Wallace movement rejected most politics and politicians. (See Table 9-5.) Only on George Wallace himself was there high consensus and positive affect and apart from Wallace only Spiro Agnew stimulated more approval than disapproval. The Wallace group's list of negative reference figures read like a bipartisan who's who of the politics of 1972: George McGovern, Nelson Rockefeller, Edward Kennedy, Edmund Muskie, Shirley Chisholm, Hubert Humphrey, and Richard Nixon were all objects of disapproval. The Wallace group's attitudes toward past and present leaders reflected that group's alienation from both parties, and their rejection of the Democratic tradition and of most contemporary political leaders. The evaluations of Wallace by all other candidate groups proved that the disapproval was mutual. *The Wallace delegates' estrangement from the dominant tendencies of the Democratic party and their isolation on the 1972 political scene provide still further evidence that they were separated from the Democratic mainstream by more than race and from the Republicans by more than*

Table 9-5. Candidate Groups and Contemporary Political Leaders

McGovern		Humphrey		Muskie	
Positive Evaluations					
McGovern	+99	Humphrey	+100	Muskie	+96
E. Kennedy	+76	Muskie	+64	E. Kennedy	+60
Chisholm	+59	E. Kennedy	+52	Humphrey	+58
Muskie	+29	McGovern	+3	McGovern	+29
Negative Evaluations					
Nixon	−99	Agnew	−85	Agnew	−91
Agnew	−99	Reagan	−83	Nixon	−91
Reagan	−97	Nixon	−80	Reagan	−85
Wallace	−97	Connally	−74	Connally	−80
Connally	−94	Wallace	−63	Wallace	−77
Rockefeller	−53	Rockefeller	−28	Rockefeller	−30
Humphrey	−13	Chisholm	−17	Chisholm	−2

Nixon		Wallace	
Positive Evaluations			
Nixon	+99	Wallace	+97
Agnew	+65	Agnew	+17
Reagan	+51		
Connally	+34		
Rockefeller	+20		
Negative Evaluations			
McGovern	−96	McGovern	−88
E. Kennedy	−94	Rockefeller	−82
Chisholm	−85	E. Kennedy	−74
Muskie	−82	Muskie	−68
Humphrey	−79	Chisholm	−68
Wallace	−39	Humphrey	−56
		Nixon	−37
		Reagan	−9
		Connally	−2

NOTE: These are consensus scores. They are calculated by subtracting the percent of a group favorable to a reference figure from the percent of a group negative to a reference figure. Data are from the mail questionnaires.

economics. The multi-dimensional estrangement of the Wallace movement within American politics indicates that it will not be readily integrated into either party.

REPUBLICAN CONSENSUS

Republicans shared a common perspective on far more issues than Democrats; however, the scope and the intensity of Republican consensus was less than that of either the McGovern or Wallace factions. Republican consensus was greatest on the defense of the traditional social and political order (see Table 9-6) and least on some change-oriented groups who challenged traditional practices.

Table 9-6. Ideological Consensus in the Republican Party: Rank-Ordered

Nixon Candidate Group	
Police	+92
Cultural conservatism	+89
Sanctions	+86
Military	+80
Black militants	-80
Busing	+76
Politicians	+73
Welfare	-66
Political demonstrators	-58
Liberals	-56
Vietnam	+54
Women's lib	-52
Military policy	+50
Inflation	-49
Business interests	+48
Conservatives	+46
Union leaders	-43
Crime	+35
International idealism	+33
Abortion	+31
Lay off women first	+30
Welfare recipients	-18
Civil rights leaders	0

NOTE: Consensus scores reflect the differences between the percent of a candidate group favorable to a symbol or issue and the percent of a group unfavorable to the symbol or issue.

While not as ideologically homogeneous as Democratic extremes, Republicans were more united than their traditional liberal adversaries—the Humphrey and Muskie groups—and unlike the latter, their consensus extended to the new issues. Republican agreement on busing, welfare, political demonstrators, and cultural conservatism was higher than their agreement on the New Deal issues.

Republican ratings of contemporary political leaders reflected high partisan regularity. (See Table 9–5.) Not only was Nixon himself the object of greatest Republican agreement, McGovern and Kennedy were the objects of near unanimous disapproval, and no Democrat was well-regarded by a majority of Republicans. Republican evaluations of past leaders reflected a similar pattern. They were most united in approval of Eisenhower, least so in their regard for Dulles. Roosevelt remained the Democrat who aroused the most negative feeling, with Johnson not far behind.

There was also a high level of Republican consensus concerning party and organizational maintenance. Altogether, the Republican pattern of consensus suggested a party which, while not monolithic, enjoyed a relatively high degree of agreement on a wide range of people, issues, and groups. The level, scope, and multi-dimensionality of Republican consensus suggests that that party will be far less vulnerable to *ideological* conflict than the Democratic party and it belies the notion that a "realigned" party system featuring one relatively pure conservative party and one relatively pure liberal party would entail deeply splitting both parties. The Republican party is already overwhelmingly conservative. The clear-cut preponderance of negative feeling toward Wallace among this national sample of Republican leaders suggests the extent of the difficulty that would probably confront an effort to integrate the Republican and Wallace groups. The low consensus on Rockefeller suggests his continued divisive potential in this party.

IDEOLOGICAL DISTINCTIVENESS
OF THE PARTIES AND FACTIONS

While each of the parties and each of the principal Democratic factions had a distinctive ideological flavor reflected in the group consensus scores, none was so ideologically distinctive and homogeneous that it lacked any overlap with competing political groups. Ideological self-classification, scores on the Political Culture Index, on foreign policy indexes, and on measures of ideological style all indicated that *even the ideological polarization of the last decade did not result in the coales-*

cence of all like-minded activists into entirely homogeneous ideological groups. The McGovern group was the most ideologically pure; its liberalism score was 95, as compared to the Wallace conservative score of 68, Muskie liberal score of 66, Humphrey liberal score of 52, and Republican conservative score of 47. Scores on the Political Culture Index followed a similar pattern except that the Wallace consensus outstripped the Muskie and Humphrey consensus: 80 to 22 to 17 respectively.

While there was no overlap in the substantive ideological orientations of McGovern and Wallace supporters, each had substantial areas of agreement with other candidate factions. It has already been noted that the preponderant opinion in the Humphrey and Muskie groups put these groups on the same side of most issues as the McGovern group. This tendency is clearly reflected in delegates' ideological self-classification. Ninety-six percent of McGovern delegates, 69 percent of Muskie delegates, 64 percent of Humphrey delegates, 8 percent of Wallace delegates, and 9 percent of Nixon delegates placed themselves on the liberal end of the political spectrum. There were differences in the degree of "liberalism" among these factions. Nearly three-fourths of McGovern delegates said they were radical or very liberal, while about one-half of Humphrey and Muskie delegates described themselves as somewhat liberal. Similarly, while more Wallace than Nixon delegates said they were very conservative, 76 percent of Wallace delegates, 56 percent of Nixon delegates, 11 percent of Humphrey delegates, and 3 percent of Muskie delegates placed themselves on the conservative end of the political spectrum. Ideological common ground among the factions was also reflected in the substantial portions of all groups who classified themselves as "moderates." (Only among McGovern delegates were there no "moderates.") Group distributions on the Political Culture Index overlap in similar patterns: 98 percent of McGovern delegates were "cultural transformers," 100 percent of Wallace delegates "cultural preservers," but the Humphrey and Muskie groups split.

These patterns of overlapping orientations mean that neither the Democratic factions nor either of the two parties had become subcultures with commitments, goals, symbols, and reference figures that differentiated them completely from all other factions or parties. Humphrey and Muskie factions resembled one another most closely and even shared a high regard for one another's candidates. But there were people in each of these candidate preference groups who shared the McGovern orientation, and others who tended to the conservative orientations of Nixon and Wallace. Such overlapping orientations constitute potential links between groups, because they can facilitate communication and enhance the potential for empathy.

The McGovern and Wallace factions symbolized true polarization: their differences were of such scope, intensity, and salience that they could probably neither be compromised nor papered over. Although McGovern strategists hoped that "alienation" from prevailing practices would serve as the basis of a "protest" vote, consensus scores on ideology, issues, groups, and political leaders indicated that substantive differences between the two groups were enormous and that attitudinal links between them were virtually nonexistent. There was nearly complete opposition between the McGovern and Nixon groups, between whom shared expectations, identifications, and demands were few. Different party identifications, organizational orientations, and reference figures reinforced their substantive ideological differences. The McGovern/Nixon pattern of interparty competition was not the familiar one in which marginally differentiated factions compete in support of marginally differentiated candidates. The scope and extent of their disagreement virtually guaranteed that each would project an ideologically distinct image in the campaign. The virtual absence of self-designated "moderates" in McGovern ranks doubtless made it harder for that faction to move to the center in search of votes, and the presence of large numbers of "moderates" in the Republican leadership group probably made it easier for that party to accommodate its strategy and its rhetoric to neighboring points of view. In this sense, the structure of delegate perspectives foreshadowed the Republican capacity to put together a temporary Republican majority.

The structure of opinion among Republican delegates conformed rather closely to the conception of party as a band of like-minded persons united in furtherance of a common view of the national interest; there were no important issues on which Republicans were seriously divided. But the Democratic party lacked any such ideological harmony. Burke argued that persons adhering to a party should find themselves in agreement with it on nine out of ten cases. By this standard, not only the Wallace group, but a substantial minority of the activist supporters of Humphrey, Jackson, and Muskie would have dissolved their ties with the 1972 Democratic presidential party. Only then would the Democratic party have become an ideologically coherent association—united in pursuit of a vision of the public interest. But the liberal and conservative parties that would have resulted from such a realignment would have been a far cry from the familiar Republican/Democratic alignment. Parties include voters as well as activists, and, though more voters consider themselves Democratic than Republican, more held "conservative" opinions on the divisive issues of 1972 than held "liberal" views on these issues. Table 9-7 reflects the disparity between the predominant opinion in the Democratic Convention, on the one hand, and the opinion of Democratic voters on the other. These disparities (discussed further in Chapter 10) reflect the extent and the content of disagreement within the Democratic party.

Table 9–7 confirms that consensus among Republican delegates was substantially higher than among Democratic delegates and that consensus among Republican identifiers was higher than among Democratic identifiers.

Both the Republican elite and rank and file were more divided than the Democratic on questions concerning abortion and on whether in case of a depression women should be laid off before male heads of family. Republican delegates were also more divided than Democrats on their own ideological self-classification, but Democratic identifiers were in substantially less agreement on this matter than were Republican identifiers.

In both parties there was higher consensus among delegates than identifiers about how to rate the ideological labels "liberal" and "conservative." Democratic delegates were much more agreed than their own rank

Table 9-7. Party Consensus on Issues: Delegates and Voters

	Democrats		Republicans	
	Delegates	Voters	Delegates	Voters
Welfare	+29	−47	−66	−65
Busing	−41	+68	+76	+88
Crime	−65	+14	+35	+28
Civil rights leaders	+71	+4	0	−24
Welfare recipients	+47	−17	−18	−36
Political demonstrators	−37	−53	−58	−69
Police	+58	+74	+92	+79
Military	−1	+51	+80	+59
Conservatives	−59	+5	+46	+47
Liberals	+63	+17	−56	−22
Union leaders	+24	+9	−43	−32
Politicians	+55	−2	+73	−9
Inflation	−83	−69	−49	−68
Abortion	+49	−19	+31	−9
Laying off women first	+54	+12	+30	−2
Women's liberation	+30	+5	−52	−17
Business interests	−32	+3	+48	+37
Black militants	−10	−71	−80	−89
Ideological self-classification	−71	−12	+47	+40

NOTE: Consensus scores were calculated by subtracting the percent of a group favorable to a symbol or issue from the percent of a group unfavorable to the symbol or issue.

and file that "liberal" rated approval and "conservative" disapproval, and the Republican elite reciprocated.

The issues on which there was highest consensus *among* the identifiers of each party were also issues on which there was agreement *between* the parties: government's role in the management of inflation, black militants, busing, police, the military, political demonstrators, and welfare. A dramatic indicator of the divisions within the Democratic party was the fact that on a number of these issues on which there was high consensus among Democratic voters, a large portion of Democratic delegates were on the other side—busing, political demonstrators, the military, and welfare were examples.

Table 9–7 also makes clear that on most issues there was much greater distance between the elites of the two parties than between their rank and files, a finding that is, of course, consistent with those of Herbert McClosky and others.[19]

In neither party was there anything approaching perfect consensus on all the social, cultural, and political issues tested. In neither party was the extent of agreement as great as in the McGovern or Wallace factions. The Republican party approached the Burkean model in the sense that a substantial majority of its delegates and rank and file were of a common mind concerning many (though not all) of the most controversial political problems of the period. The Democrats were far too divided on too many issues to qualify as an association of persons united in furtherance of a conception of the common good. The fact that the Republican party is a minority that has distinct and persistent problems in growing may or may not be related to its relative ideological homogeneity. And the massive defeat of the McGovern candidacy may or may not have been a consequence of the still greater ideological homogeneity of that group.

It may be that parties and candidate groups with somewhat diverse supporters find it easier to grow than more homogeneous groups, to reach out in more directions for followers. Leaders of such groups are already practiced in aggregating diverse interests and points of view. Conversely, the party that includes factions whose values and commitments are contradictory is continually threatened by centripetal tendencies.

The social bases of the two parties not only complement but complicate the pattern described. The social diversity of Democrats—among whom Jews, blacks, atheists, Catholics and Protestants, under-educated and highly educated are numerous—provides a sharp contrast to the much more socially homogeneous Republicans. Again, the diversity doubtless constitutes a potential for growth and a continuing invitation to schism while the greater Republican social homogeneity reinforces not only the bonds that hold that group together, but also the potential boundaries hemming in the party.

Each pattern holds the potential for defeat and failure. It was perhaps inevitable that Richard Nixon, architect of the 1972 Republican victory, should have studiously bypassed and transcended his party during the campaign and that the anatomy of the Democratic defeats of 1968 and 1972 reflected the factional schisms of that party.

Two quite different divisions within the Democratic party held the promise of trouble for that party's presidential hopes: the division between ideological factions, symbolized in 1972 by the candidacies of George McGovern and George Wallace, and the division between the liberal activists who dominated the party's decisions and the more conservative Democratic identifiers. Humphrey and Muskie group median positions were not as remote from those of the Democratic rank and file as were the positions of the McGovern group, but these groups were also more "liberal" on both new and old issues than were a large portion of Democratic rank and file. The distance between Democratic elite and mass constitutes a standing invitation to Republican and third party leaders to try to attract Democrats away from the dominant party leadership.

NOTES

1. James Madison, in *The Federalist Papers,* especially his famous treatment in *Federalist,* No. 10; George Washington deals with "the baneful effects of the spirit of party" in the Farewell Address. David Hume, *Political Essays* (New York: Liberal Arts Press, 1953), especially "Of Parties in General," pp. 77-84.
2. Robert MacIver, *The Web of Government* (New York: Macmillan, 1947), p. 212.
3. E. E. Schattschneider, *Party Government* (New York: Farrar and Rinehart, 1942), p. 62.
4. Ibid.
5. Avery Leiserson, *Parties and Politics: An Institutional and Behavioral Approach* (New York: Alfred A. Knopf, 1958), p. 133.
6. Harold D. Lasswell and Abraham Kaplan, *Power and Society: A Framework for Political Inquiry* (New Haven: Yale University Press, 1950), p. 172.
7. Edmund Burke, *The Works of Edmund Burke* (London: 1902), vol. I, pp. 372-378.
8. E. Pendleton Herring, *The Politics of Democracy: American Parties in Action* (New York: W. W. Norton, 1940), p. 111. A similar perspective is that of A. Lawrence Lowell, *The Government of England,* rev. ed. (New York: Macmillan, 1912).
9. Schattschneider, *Party Government* and Herring, *Politics of Democracy.*
10. Erwin K. Scheuch, "Social Context and Individual Behavior," in *Quantitative Ecological Analysis in the Social Sciences,* eds. Mattei Dogan and Stein Rokkan (Cambridge, Mass.: MIT Press, 1969) p. 141.
11. Heinz Eulau, "Some Aspects of Analysis, Measurement and Sampling in the Transformation of Micro- and Macro-Level Unit Properties" (Paper prepared for presentation at the Conference on Design and Measurement Standards for Research in Political Science, Deleran, Wisc., May 13-15, 1974), p. 12.
12. Leiserson, *Parties and Politics,* p. 133.
13. V. O. Key, Jr., *Politics, Parties and Pressure Groups,* 4th ed. (New York: Thomas Y. Crowell Company, 1958), p. 251.
14. Ibid., p. 275.
15. Robert Alford, *Party and Society: The Anglo-American Democracies* (Chicago: Rand McNally & Co., 1963) and *Party Systems and Voter Alignments,* eds. Seymour M. Lipset and Stein Rokkan (New York: The Free Press, 1967). An interesting recent report is John W. Books and JoAnn B. Reynolds, "A Note on Class Voting in Great Britain and the United States." *Comparative Political Studies* 8, no. 3 (1975): 360-376.
16. Donald E. Stokes, "Some Dynamic Elements of Contests for the Presidency," *American Political Science Review* 60 (1966):27.
17. Note that the consensus scores measure level of agreement, not level of support.
18. Herring, *Politics of Democracy,* p. 111.
19. Herbert McClosky, Paul J. Hoffman, and Rosemary O'Hara, "Issue Conflict and Consensus Among Party Leaders and Followers," *American Political Science Review* 54 (1960): 405-427 .

CHAPTER 10

The Presidential Elite
as a Representative Body*

National conventions are part of the institutionalized process of representation through which masses participate in the selection of their rulers. They are also representative bodies in the sense that delegates act in the name of the much larger numbers who comprise the presidential parties. This chapter examines delegates as representatives of the presidential parties. It raises and discusses various questions concerning the theory and practice of representation in the national political conventions of 1972. In what ways was the Democratic Convention of 1972 representative? And of whom? In what ways was the Republican Convention representative? And of whom? How does representation of biological traits relate to representation of opinion? Why is it so difficult to construct a representative national convention? Are the difficulties related to the character of the elite? Does the changing character of activists in presidential politics complicate the problem of securing a representative convention?

Hannah Pitkin has reminded us that "representing and representativeness need not mean exactly the same thing,"[1] and I do not suggest that they are identical. Representation is an emergent characteristic, the outcome of the process that includes the choice of some persons to act as representatives, their interactions and decisions, and their continuing relation to those represented.[2] Representativeness is something else again. It concerns the distribution, as between two groups, one larger, one smaller, of personal characteristics, such as sex, age, color, foot size, or opinions, in some smaller and some larger group. Representation is the desired outcome of the processes of "representative" governments. Representativeness is a desired coincidence of traits. Failure to distinguish

---

*A version of this chapter was presented at the American Political Science Association annual meeting in Chicago, Ill. in 1974 and was reprinted in the *British Journal of Political Science* (1974): 265–373.

between representation and representativeness has theoretical and also political consequences. Both were evident in the discussion and practices of the Democratic party in 1972. In that year the Commission on Party Structure and Delegate Selection announced that after having examined "the level of representation of blacks, women, and young people," it found "that each of these groups was significantly lacking in representation,"[3] and it undertook major reforms to provide them with greater "representation." In so doing, it opened new questions about who can and should represent whom in national political conventions and about how representation can and should take place, and it raised to national significance the "simplistic"[4] approach that identifies representation with representativeness.[5]

The conventions of 1972 provide an especially good opportunity for exploring the problem of making party conventions representative: because the Democratic reforms were explicitly addressed to securing representation of some personal attributes not usually taken account of in the selection of representatives—namely, race, sex, age; because the Republican party's selection process provides an example of an alternative approach to the selection of representatives; and because data are available that permit the comparison of delegates and the various larger collectivities including voters, party identifiers, and persons sharing particular biological and social characteristics.[6]

THE DATA

Three bodies of data will be utilized in comparing personal, social, and ideological characteristics of elite and mass: these are, first, the elite sample on which this book is based; second, a national opinion survey based on a statistically representative sample conducted in December 1971 before the nominating conventions were held.[7] This study comprises face-to-face interviews with 2,014 probable voters chosen on the basis of area probability sampling. Fieldwork was conducted by International Research Associates.[8]

The third set of data is the national study of the electorate designed and conducted by the University of Michigan's Center for Political Studies and carried out in the post-convention period of 1972. This survey was based on face-to-face interviews with people chosen by probability sampling from the entire electorate.

These three data sets contain some identical questions designed to elicit views on issues and groups that figured significantly in the politics of 1972.[9]

THE INTELLECTUAL CONTEXT: A CONSIDERATION
OF POLITICAL REPRESENTATION[10]

The purpose of this section is not to recapitulate the intellectual history of representation, but to remind readers of some essential elements of the theory and practice of representative governments, to provide an intellectual context for the discussion of the events of 1972, and to acknowledge, too, that like all the most important concepts with which political scientists must work, this one has a long history but has no firm, fixed referent by which we may settle disputes and resolve doubts. There have been not one but several views about what constitutes a representative and what is entailed in representation.[11] There will doubtless be others. However, the absence of a fixed definition agreed upon by all does not indicate that this concept has no content, nor that it can be used to mean anything one chooses.

The concept of political representation always suggests that, in relation to some functions, someone stands for or acts for another. Various kinds of people are described as representatives: ambassadors who in diplomatic processes represent their countries vis-à-vis others; politicians elected to represent their constituents in decision-making processes; persons who because they share the personal characteristics of some larger group are said to be representatives. Persons may represent others either "by virtue of their activities, by virtue of the manner of their selection, or by virtue of their personal characteristics."[12] Everyday usage of the term "representation" does not include any specification of the manner of selection of representatives, their activities, or their personal characteristics; a king who inherits power and a dictator who seizes it can, without doing violence to the language, be described as "representatives" of their people in international affairs, and the notion that, *however chosen*, some persons "embody" the will or the spirit of a nation, race, or class and are therefore qualified to "represent" that nation or class is affirmed in virtually all nondemocratic regimes.[13] But the concept of representation has a much more precise meaning within the modern democratic tradition.

In the democratic tradition the concept of representation is firmly associated by theory and practice with the doctrines of consent[14] and accountability and the institutions of popular elections and political parties. It is with that tradition that we are here concerned.[15] The basic tenets of the doctrine of democratic representation are:

First, that laws should be made not merely in the name of the community, but by persons selected in periodic, competitive elections by some large, specified portion of the adult members of the community (e.g., a majority or plurality) to represent them in a specified context (e.g., Congress, a state legislature) for the performance of some specified (and therefore limited) functions.

Second, that political representation requires the representation of the opinions of individual citizens.

Third, that the *responsiveness* of representatives to the will of citizens can be assured by frequent periodic elections which a) limit the tenure of representatives and b) hold them accountable to those who elected them for the quality of their representation.

These principles, largely identical with the "utilitarian" or "radical" theory of representation, are shared by and reflected in the practices of all democratic political systems. Certain aspects of these principles deserve note.[16]

The belief that laws should be made by persons *chosen by* some numerous portion of the adult citizens differentiates the democratic theory and practice of representation from the various doctrines of representation by embodiment, which assert that regardless of how they were chosen some persons "embody" the will or spirit or interests of a nation, race, or class. The belief that individuals are the basic unit of representation distinguishes modern democratic theory and practice from earlier practices which represented estates and guilds and from contemporary doctrines of group representation. Representation of individuals is associated with belief in the reality and value of the individual, with the existence of individual rights and duties, and with the belief that individuals are capable of speaking for themselves. It is also closely associated with representation of *opinion* or of "heads."[17] Note that after once it is decided that individuals shall be represented, there remains the question of what attributes of individuals shall be represented: racial membership, age group, economic status, or what? The answer given by modern democratic theory and practice is that individuals shall be represented as citizens, with opinions about the laws and the rulers under whom they live.[18]

The representation of opinion has been called the "representation of subjective interests," because it is the individual himself who defines his views and priorities. But if individuals are to choose rulers and hold them accountable, they can do so *only* by consulting their own experience and opinion. This is doubtless the reason that all representative governments are in fact based on representation of opinion.

The representation of opinions rests on the beliefs that each citizen is the best judge of his own interests or, at least, that each individual is more likely to be able to judge his own interests than is any other person (especially any ruler), and that government should represent the actual desires, values, and views of individuals as expressed by those individuals.[19] In these assumptions democratic theories differ from embodiment theories[20] of representation. Embodiment theories postulate the existence of "objective" interests, spirit, or will that is the individual's "true" interest or will and is independent of his preferences or desires. They also postulate a doctrine of false consciousness that explains that for some reason—whether because of the perpetual immaturity of the masses or as a consequence of their having been brainwashed by racist imperialists, or a patriarchal society, or a Jewish press—the people are incapable of knowing their own "true" will and therefore cannot make valid decisions about who should rule or to what ends.[21]

Some scholars distinguish between the representation of individual opinions and the representation of individual interests.[22] But theories of democratic representation assume that a person's opinions will reflect the "interests" deriving from his social position as well as his idiosyncratic attributes. Representing individual opinion bypasses questions about the relation of social position to opinion by providing for representation of opinion regardless of its source. Modern electoral systems permit each individual to decide which of his several statuses or values have priority in a given election.[23] A normally Republican Irish Catholic businessman might decide in a particular election that his religious or ethnic identifications take priority over his economic interests. He might also decide to vote none of these identifications, but instead to give his vote to a candidate he regards as most capable in international affairs.[24]

The third basic principle of democratic theories of representation postulates that the responsiveness of elected officials to the opinions of those by whom they are elected can be secured by frequent, periodic elections. Frequent elections both limit the permission granted to serve as representative and condition the relationship between voters and representatives. They give legislators, the *Federalist* authors (and others) argued, "an habitual recollection of their dependence on the people."[25]

Modern democratic electoral systems embody the belief that through frequent free elections assemblies can be secured which will accurately reflect the opinions and interests of the nation—assemblies that will reflect the diverse views of a diverse people. John Adams was not alone in his conviction that a legislature "should be an exact portrait, in miniature, of the people at large, as it should think, feel, reason and act like them."[26] The belief that a legislature should accurately reflect the thoughts and feelings of the nation, that, in James Wilson's words, it should be "an exact transcript of their minds,"[27] and that it *would* do so rested on the conviction that voters could be counted on to elect persons who shared the views and values of the dominant portion of the community and to defeat those who did not.[28]

That persons shaping American electoral institutions held what Pitkin has called the "descriptive" theory of representation can hardly be doubted;[29] *it is also clear that they advocated that version of "descriptive" representation that concerns the opinions of the electorate.* The mirror proposed in classical writings and embodied in democratic practice reflects the *subjective not the objective* traits of the citizens.[30] There is no demand for or expectation of elected officials who have the appearance, the intelligence, the social characteristics, or the leadership capacities of those who elect them. This focus on the representation of opinion is embodied in the electoral systems of all representative democracies. Single member districts, multi-member constituencies, variants of proportional representation—all aim at representing the opinions of individuals about who should rule and to what broad ends.

Doctrines and institutions of democratic representation old and new grew out of the effort to make governments responsive to those who lived under them. But characteristic theories and practices have been applied to many other institutions from voluntary organizations to classrooms and even, of late, to the family. Because of the central role of political parties in representative government, there have been repeated efforts to apply theories of representation to parties.[31] Successive waves of reform have passed through the parties leaving in their wake such institutional monuments to "representation" as primary elections and, most recently, the McGovern-Fraser Commission guidelines.[32] Since parties differ from governments in many important respects, we should not be surprised that efforts to make them representative institutions encounter unexpected obstacles and produce unexpected consequences.

CHANGING CONCEPTIONS OF REPRESENTATION

The meaning and usage of such concepts as freedom, citizenship, and representation change with changing conditions and changing ideas about what is good, what is just, what is appropriate.[33] It frequently happens that very large political changes take place not in the name of the new ideas that stimulate them, but in the name of ancient and honored principles.

Something like this happened in the case of the famous guidelines of the Democratic party's Commission on Party Structure and Delegate Selection,[34] which introduced into American party practice some major changes—and did so in the name of traditional, universally accepted principles. The guidelines had numerous consequences. We are concerned here only with those directly related to the new doctrine of representation and its consequences for the composition of the Democratic Convention.

In the century and a half since the emergence of national conventions, both Republicans and Democrats held conventions that were basically conferences of party leaders and regulars—conferences of people who had devoted and would continue to devote large amounts of time, energy, and (sometimes) money to the party. Obviously, the rise and spread of presidential primaries affected the character of conventions since the selection of delegates by primary provided a vehicle for the representation of voters' views in conventions—and not merely those of state party leaders.[35] But even in states with primaries, slating, endorsements, and apathy have generally resulted in delegations filled by persons who "tended to be representatives of the regular party organizations in their state."[36]

Insofar as conventions were conceived as representative bodies, it was the party organizations—its leaders and regulars from around the country—who were to be represented. This explains the fact noted by McClosky in 1968 that, "Whether a state's delegates are chosen by a primary, state convention, caucus, state central committee, or some variation or combination of these, no special effort is made to represent the state's party membership in proportion to their beliefs or preferences."[37]

The test of a convention was generally believed to be its ability to pick a winner. Its responsiveness to the rank and file was secured—or was believed to be secured—by the party's need to attract and mobilize local party activists, to attract voters, and to win elections.[38]

In 1972 the Republican Convention was organized on the basis of these traditional notions about what a national convention should be.[39] But the ties of the Democratic Convention to the regular organization were fewer and more tenuous.[40] That convention not only reflected new "open" procedures, but also a new conception of who should be represented and how they should be chosen.[41] To that new doctrine of representation we now turn.

THE THEORY OF REPRESENTATION
OF THE McGOVERN COMMISSION

A close reading of the report of the twenty-eight member Commission on Party Structure and Delegate Selection confirms that the Commission was much more concerned with participation than with representation. This emphasis is doubtless in part accounted for by the Commission's mandate to guarantee all Democrats a "full and timely opportunity to participate" in the delegate selection process.[42] It also doubtless resulted from the then widespread belief that many people were being denied the opportunity to participate in the major decision processes of the society. There is no explicit affirmation in the report of the Commission's desire to assure representation of all Democrats or of all voters. The large statements of purpose concern not representation, but participation.

Representing the rank and file is not the same as making sure that everyone who desires to influence the nominating process is able to do so. Perhaps the reason that the McGovern Commission emphasized the latter and never mentioned the former in its statements of purpose is that it was not much concerned with the general question of how to make a convention represent the views and values of the whole body of rank and file Democrats, but rather was concerned with the narrower question of how to make it representative of those with strong presidential preferences and a predisposition to be politically active. Support for this view is found in Austin Ranney's statement, "Most of the guidelines were consciously designed to maximize participation by persons who are enthusiasts for a particular aspirant *in the year of the convention.*"[43]

However, the Commission also asserted that an "issue of special concern" was "the fair representation of supporters of each presidential candidate on the state's delegation."[44] And presumably its decisions to eliminate "winner-take-all" primaries, the unit rule, and untimely selection were prompted by the desire to secure more accurate and timely representation of rank and file presidential preferences[45] or at least of the preferences of active Democrats. Furthermore, we have the assurances of Commission member Ranney that the group was concerned with the representation of Democrats' views as well as their biological and social characteristics.[46] But the most persuasive evidence of the Commission's concern with representation of all Democrats is indirect. Its repeated references to the lack of representation of blacks, women, and youth at least imply that it believed that everyone should be represented in the convention, even if it did not say so. Blacks, women, and youth were said to be "significantly lacking in representation."[47] It was noted that "representation of blacks, women, and youth at the convention was substantially below the proportion of each group in the population."[48] This belief was the basis for requiring all states "to overcome the effects of past discrimination by affirmative steps to encourage representation on the national convention delegation of young people—defined as people of not more than 30 nor less than 18 years of age—and women in reasonable relationship to their presence in the population."[49] These requirements, stated in Guidelines A-1 and A-2, are the centerpiece of the Commission's largely implicit theory of political representation.

In *Mandate for Reform*, Guidelines A-1 and A-2 were presented as part of a continuing effort to eliminate discriminatory procedures from the party's nominating and governing processes.[50] The Commission did not advocate the representation of groups as such. It did not endorse the view that race or sex or age determine political views nor that women, blacks, or youth could or should only be represented by women, blacks, and youths. It did not argue that in an urban mobile society, age, sex, and race had as much importance as geography and that it was as important to secure representation of all groups as it was to secure representation of all areas. It did not argue that a convention's legitimacy depended on its reflecting the racial, sexual, or age composition of the population,[51] nor that social justice required increasing the numbers of women, blacks, and youth in the party's governing councils. It did not argue that having more women, blacks, or youth in governing bodies was more important than letting party members choose for themselves who should make decisions for the party. It only asserted that it was important to eliminate discrimination against these groups—a principle certain to win assent in the Democratic party.[52]

It then made the extraordinary assumption that *if there were no institutional barriers to their participation in party governance*, blacks, women, and youth would be elected to the party's governing councils in rough proportion to their presence in the population.[53] In fact, the guidelines speak not of eliminating discrimination but of "overcoming the effects of past discrimination."[54] The report reads as though a majority of the Commission believed that unequal participation in power could only be a result of discrimination and not of such other attributes as ambition, interest, or skill and that therefore, by definition, as long as there was not equal participation in power, the "effects" of past discrimination had not been eliminated.

The Commission's decisions on representation of blacks, women, and youth 1) committed the party to new practices that emphasized the representation of physical or social characteristics as well as opinion, 2) committed its members and the party to the utilization of procedures that guaranteed outcomes as well as open processes (quotas were, of course, the institutional device for achievement of this goal), and 3) thereby opened the general question about the "representativeness" of the delegates to the convention of the Democratic rank and file.

In separating the delegate selection process from state party organizations and opening the process to amateurs and enthusiasts the McGovern Commission abandoned the conception of the convention as a conference of regulars. In embracing the doctrine of demographic representation the McGovern Commission departed drastically from "radical" theory and practice and adopted a new approach to representation.

Demographic theories of representation differ from radical doctrine and practice in *goals, methods,* and *assumptions*. The goal of demographic theories is an assembly in which some specific physical and/or social characteristics are present in roughly the same proportions as their occurrence in the total electorate. The goal of the radical theories is an assembly that reflects the opinions and orientations of the electorate in its decisions on matters of public policy. The methods of the two differ because proponents of demographic representation propose to achieve the desired outcome through institutional devices, notably quotas, that assure the desired outcomes. Radical representation relies on the dynamics of personal ambition, intraparty and interparty competition, and the preferences of the represent*ed* to determine the composition of the representative assembly. The assumptions of these two doctrines of representation differ first in their view about which personal characteristics are relevant to politics, and second in their view about who should make this determination. The radical doctrine of representation does not deny that sex or race may be importantly related to social position and political views. But it does not *assume* that these characteristics have special, unique, or definitive relevance to political perspectives, roles, or outcomes. It leaves the decision concerning the relevance of different statuses to those to be represented. Blacks (or whites) may choose blacks to represent them. Women (or men) may choose women to represent them. They also may not. *The demographic approach to representation requires that someone other than voters determine which of the many statuses of a person are in fact most important*: the McGovern Commission decided in favor of sex, race, and age.

Since there is no state in the United States, no country in the world, and no major political party in any country in which women and youth are as numerous in the governing bodies as in the population, it seems unlikely that a majority of the twenty-five men and three women on the McGovern Commission actually believed that low participation of women, blacks, and youth in the party's decision processes was a result simply of the party's past discrimination against these groups. These were men and women of large experience. Presumably they had noticed that women, youth, and blacks were scarce in their law firms, their universities, their state governments, and in other power processes in which they participated. Probably they believed that this low participation in power processes resulted from generalized discrimination throughout the society, and probably they desired that their party not reflect the power distributions of the society. Probably they desired, also, to affirm their belief in the equality and "worthiness" of blacks, women, and youth as compared to middle-aged white males and believed "proportional demographic representation" an appropriate means of doing so. Perhaps they believed that race, sex, and age had a special impact on social experience and therefore on political perspectives or that in a real democracy people would be represented by people "like" themselves. Such beliefs were common in the years just preceding the Commission's work—and especially common in "progressive" circles.

It would require a cultural history of the period to account for the fact that the attention of reformers was progressively focused on these three of the many groups who have not shared fully in power (instead of, for example, the poor, the uneducated, or the immigrants).[55] Suffice it to say that blacks, whose predicament had been dramatized as well as ameliorated by the civil rights movement, were a blatant example of a group which because of race had been heavily restricted in the pursuit of values; that the Vietnam war, the obligations of military service, campus disorders, and the peace movement had focused attention on youth; and that the rise of the women's movement dramatized the very low participation of women in politics. By 1972 the attention of the cultural elite had shifted away from economic problems and groups[56] to preoccupation with the political advantages of white middle-aged males. Women, youth, and blacks were described as "new constituencies," and constituencies normally have representatives.

The notion that sex, race, and age are relevant to politics did not originate with the Democratic party's Commission on Party Structure and Delegate Selection. The view that biological characteristics qualify or disqualify persons for participation in political processes has reappeared in history in various forms—the most common of which historically is the belief that adult males are qualified for political participation while others—that is, females and those who have not reached the age defined as adult—are not. And through most of American history being black was a disqualification for full participation in politics in most parts of the nation.[57] Both parties have long made special efforts to "represent" these groups through youth divisions and special organizations of Young Republicans and Democrats, women's divisions and various formal requirements for the "representation" of women at all levels of the party—in such posts as state committeewoman or vice chairman. But until recently no one seems to have found it disturbing that in neither party were women or youth very numerous in national conventions or among top decision makers.[58] By 1972 the position of blacks in both parties was stronger than that of either women or youth. But this stronger position was, at least in part, a consequence of concerted efforts—especially by the national Democratic party—to end the exclusion of blacks.[59] And they still had not gained power proportionate to their numbers, but this was a fact that disturbed only those who believed in the proportional group representation.

Still, the belief that a *really* representative body would mirror biological characteristics was "in the air" in the late 1960s, and it seems likely that it was adopted by the McGovern Commission without much scrutiny either of its foundations, implications, relationship to the doctrine of democratic representation, or its probable consequences. Four years later it is still in the air. The Republicans, who frequently adopt Democratic innovations when they are no longer new, have moved toward this notion of representation at the same time that Democrats are moving away from it. For this reason, an examination of just how "representative" a convention the guidelines produced is of more than historical and more than academic interest.

Which of the two 1972 conventions was more representative of its own rank and file? The Republican Convention which relied on traditional methods of delegate selection and produced a traditional convention of organization Republicans or the reformed Democratic Convention which relied on the new rules to wrest control from the leadership and "open" the party?

In considering these questions we take account of two possible standards for measuring "representativeness": total population and party identification. Both were invoked by the McGovern Commission which, though it called for representation of blacks, women, and youth in proportion to their numbers in the total population, usually wrote as though it were Democrats (not voters) whose participation was sought.[60] The Commission's mandate also spoke of giving all *Democratic* voters an opportunity to participate.

REPRESENTATION OF ASCRIPTIVE CHARACTERISTICS

Certain facts about the "representativeness" of the two conventions were obvious to the naked eye. It was clear, for example, that the Democratic party included more women than the Republican, but that in neither convention did women comprise the same share of delegates as of the total population of which they constitute 51 percent or of party identifiers (roughly 52 percent of the Democrats and 53 percent of Republicans).[61] They comprised approximately 40 percent of the Democratic Convention—up from 13 percent at the previous convention and 30 percent of the Republican delegates as compared with 17 percent in the previous convention.[62]

Blacks comprised some 16 percent of the Democratic Convention (as compared with 5 percent in 1968) and some 5 percent of the 1972 Republican Convention. As compared with their numbers in the total population blacks were overrepresented in the Democratic Convention and underrepresented in the Republican Convention. As compared with the percentage they constituted of party identifiers they were precisely represented in the Republican party since they comprised approximately 4 percent of the total of Republican identifiers; and accurately represented in the Democratic since blacks constituted about 17 percent of the total of party identifiers.[63].

The age structure of the two conventions was quite different. Reflecting the impact of age quotas, delegates from 18 to 29 were three times as numerous in the Democratic as the Republican Convention, comprising 23 percent of Democrats (up from 3 percent in 1968) as compared to 28 percent of the total population over 18, and approximately 25 percent of Democratic party identifiers. This age group constituted only 8 percent of the Republican Convention and about 16 percent of Republican identifiers. Persons from 30 to 50 were overrepresented in the Democratic Convention; people from 40 to 65, in the Republican. Those over 65 were substantially *under*represented at both. At the Democratic Convention delegates over 65 comprised only 4 percent of the total as compared to 15 percent of the population while at the Republican they comprised 9 percent.[64]

The McGovern Commission did not consider the ethnic composition of the convention (except for blacks) but it stimulated a good deal of comment all the same. Blacks, Jews, and the "new" Spanish immigrants were numerous in the Democratic Convention,[65] especially in the McGovern ranks. These are, of course, groups that vote heavily Democratic. WASPs, who vote heavily Republican, were most numerous at the Republican Convention. But the ethnic composition of the two conventions cannot be explained only by party identification and voting habits. Even when these are taken into account, WASPs were overrepresented at the Republican Convention, Jews in the Democratic Convention, and the "white ethnics" were underrepresented in both.[66] Religion is, of course, closely related to nationality, and similar patterns of "imbalance" persist. Republican delegates were overwhelmingly Protestant (79 percent), as compared to about 69 percent of their party identifiers; Catholics comprised 17 percent of their delegates as compared to 23 percent of identifiers; and Jews comprised 2 percent of Republican delegates as compared to 1 percent of identifiers. Among Democrats, Protestants were approximately as numerous among delegates as among party identifiers (52 percent to 55 percent); Catholics were underrepresented comprising 25 percent of delegates and 34 percent of identifiers; Jews were over-represented constituting 11 percent of delegates as compared to 3 percent of identifiers; and persons without religion were most overrepresented of all—they constituted some 11 percent of Democratic delegates and 2 percent of Democratic identifiers. In religious composition McGovern supporters were especially unrepresentative of Democratic identifiers. In this group Protestants comprised only 41 percent, Catholics 24 percent, Jews 18 percent, and atheists and/or agnostics 16 percent.

Obviously, the Democratic reform rules must be counted successful in having increased the number of blacks, women, and youth. The Democratic Convention more accurately mirrored the numbers of these groups in the total population than did the Republican. Obviously, however, neither of the two achieved balanced representation of age, religion, or ethnic groups.[67]

REPRESENTING SOCIAL CLASSES

Little attention was paid in 1972 to the representation of social classes. The McGovern Commission "urged" (but did not require) state parties to "remove all costs and fees involved in the delegation selection process" and to "explore ways of easing the financial burdens on delegates and alternates and candidates for delegate and alternate."[68] But the question of representation for the various socioeconomic classes was not really explored by that group, which was, for reasons known best to its own members, preoccupied with representation of women, blacks, and youth.

The social homogeneity of the two conventions provides an interesting contrast to their biological heterogeneity. Delegates to both conventions and delegates supporting all candidates shared the crucial characteristics that identify political elites everywhere: as compared to most other people they had gone to school longer, made more money, and had better jobs.[69] The social characteristics of women, blacks, and youth were not exactly like those of middle-aged white males, but the differences were marginal. With few exceptions the blacks at the two conventions were middle-class blacks with relatively high education and occupational status and income, not as high as white members of the elite but definitely middle class. The women tended to be professionals themselves or married to professionals. Like the men, they, too, tended to be at least college educated and economically comfortable. Youth delegates were drawn from the same social categories. Neither convention was representative of the economic, educational, and status groups that comprise the two parties' rank and file.

Although in 1970 50 percent of all American families had incomes of under $10,000[70] and 5 percent had incomes of over $25,000, only about 5 percent of Republican delegates and 13 percent of Democrats earned under $10,000 and a portion of these were still students, while 58 percent of Republican and 35 percent of Democrats made $25,000 or over.

The contrasts in education were, if anything, still sharper. While 42 percent of rank and file Democrats and 35 percent of Republicans had not completed high school, this "uneducated" class had virtually disappeared from the ranks of delegates. Only 4 percent of Democratic delegates and 2 percent of Republicans had less than a high school education.[71] Among party identifiers, three-fourths of Democrats and two-thirds of Republicans had no more than a high school education as compared to 18 percent of Democratic delegates and 13 percent of Republican. Approximately 60 percent of both Republican and Democratic delegates had graduated from college. Nearly two-fifths of each had postgraduate or professional training. All candidate support groups were highly educated as compared to the rank and file voters. About 65 percent of McGovern delegates, 56 percent to 58 percent of Muskie and Nixon delegates, 40 percent of Humphrey delegates, and 33 percent of Wallace delegates held college degrees.

Delegates' occupations matched their high educations. Professionals were the most numerous in all candidate support groups of both parties. Approximately one-half of all McGovern and two-fifths of Republican delegates were lawyers, teachers, and other professionals. Professionals comprised 40 percent of all other candidate support groups except Wallace delegates, of whom slightly under one-third were in this category. Lawyers were the most numerous type of professional, but among McGovern delegates they were apparently outnumbered by teachers.[72] The dominance of both conventions by professionals was further accentuated by the large number of women delegates who, though themselves housewives, were married to professionals and by the high percentage of college students headed for professions.

Businessmen and workers were notable for their absence. Self-employed businessmen constituted only 8 percent of the Democratic delegates (down from 29 percent in 1968).[73] Even in the Republican Convention self-employed businessmen comprised only 18 percent of delegates. Workers were still rarer. Obviously, the reforms, upheavals, and rhetoric of 1972 did not alter fundamentally the relationship between socioeconomic status and political participation. The delegates to both conventions were an overwhelmingly middle to upper middle-class group, and they knew it.

REPRESENTATIVE OPINIONS

If the representation of opinion about who should rule and, broadly, to what ends is the heart of the representative process, then the question of whether the two conventions represented the political views and values of their rank and file lies at the heart of an inquiry in the representativeness of these bodies. Such an inquiry was undertaken in the pioneering work of Herbert McClosky nearly two decades ago.[74]

It seems desirable to reaffirm that representation and representativeness, are not identical, that having representative opinions does not assure that a body will actually make decisions reflecting those opinions anymore than having unrepresentative opinions necessarily means the views and values of constituents will be ignored. But in social science as in life we deal in probabilities not certainties, and probably the relationship between representativeness and representation of opinion is closer than insistence on the distinction might suggest. It is more probable that an assembly, a majority of whose members share the general views and values of the community, will represent those views and values in their decisions than will an assembly wherein the majority of whose members do not share them. If conventions are supposed to represent the rank and file of their parties, then the correspondence or non-correspondence of the opinions of representatives and represented matters, and matters a good deal.

Such correspondence or non-correspondence of elite and mass opinion will not tell us whether the political system is democratic, since an autocrat may share the opinions of masses, reflect them in his policies, and still remain an autocrat; or whether the elite's policy decisions will or will not in any specific instance reflect shared opinions, since decision makers who share mass opinions may decide that some overriding concern makes it undesirable to translate those opinions into policy, just as an elite not sharing mass opinion may decide to enact policies reflecting mass opinion either from hope of reelection or out of a sense of obligation; or whether decisions based on shared opinions will be wise, just, or liberal because masses may acquiesce in foolish, oppressive, and discriminatory policies. But the extent of correspondence between mass and elite opinion does tell us whether the system of representation is working in such a way that it offers citizens the opportunity of supporting leaders who share their views and values and opposing those who do not.

The correspondence—or rather the non-correspondence—of Democratic elite and mass opinion concerning candidate preference is readily established. While the McGovern Commission affirmed a "special concern" with the fair representation of all Democratic presidential preferences, Ranney has pointed out that "Nearly two-thirds of the convention's delegates were chosen or bound by presidential primaries but 57 percent of its first-ballot votes and the nomination went to a candidate who won only 27 percent of the popular vote cast in the primaries and who had only 30 percent of the first choice preferences in Gallup's last preconvention poll of Democrats."[75]

Presidential preference is only one aspect of opinion—albeit a very important one. A political party concerned with representation presumably desires that its convention will be representative of and responsive to the views and values of its rank and file on other matters.[76]

VOTERS AND PRESIDENTIAL ELITES: OPINIONS COMPARED IN FIVE POLICY AREAS

A comparison of the political attitudes of voters and presidential elites documents the estrangement of the Democratic presidential elite —and especially the dominant McGovern movement—from the views and values of a majority of Americans. It documents, too, that in 1972 rules and politics combined to produce a Democratic Convention which, though it may (or may not) have resembled the "face of America," did not think, feel, reason, and act"[77] like the American electorate.

Everyday observation and previous research would not have led us to expect leaders—even elected leaders—to reflect exactly the political opinions of the electorate. McClosky, Stauffer, and others have documented the tendency of political leaders to be more involved, informed, and effective, and if liberal, to be more liberal, if conservative, to be more conservative.[78] But the discontinuities in mass and elite opinion are not usually very large in democratic systems, because the voters tend to choose leaders who share their basic views and commitments and to reject those who do not and because understanding this fact normally keeps the parties responsible to the views and values of the electorate.

In 1972, the difference between Democratic mass and elite so far exceeded the norms that on a range of issues central to the politics of that year, the Democratic elite and rank and file were found on opposite sides and the Republican elite held views which were more representative of the views and values of rank and file Democrats than were the views of Democratic delegates.

Because the representativeness of the 1972 Democratic Convention is controversial as well as important, it seems desirable to provide full data on the opinions of both delegates and rank and file as well as comparisons based on difference scores that summarize the extent of correspondence and non-correspondence between rank and file and elite opinions.[79] And because aggregation of interests and opinions may or may not take place in political conventions and is least likely to occur when, as in 1972, ideological differences among factions are large and one faction has all the votes it needs to win, it seems desirable to provide data on the relations of various portions of the Democratic elite to the Democratic rank and file. Aggregate statistics on Democratic delegates not only conceal intra-elite differences, they also obscure the extent of the difference between 1972's dominant party rank and file and the dominant Democratic elite party's rank and file, because they average the views of McGovern delegates who were ideologically homogeneous and in control of the convention, Wallace delegates who were also ideologically homogeneous and utterly without influence on Democratic decisions, and other delegate groups, who though they were less homogeneous were also without influence. The Democratic averages describe an aggregate that did not exist in the political world. In considering the relations between Democratic mass and presidential elite, we therefore look at the opinions of the various candidate support groups as well as of the convention as a whole.

Welfare Policy

A majority of the Democratic and Republican rank and file and Republican elite gave priority to the obligation to work; a majority of the Democratic presidential elite gave priority to abolishing poverty. Analysis of the structure of elite opinion on this issue 1) reveals that the views of all Democratic candidate support groups except Wallace were substantially different from those of Democratic party identifiers (and of their own candidates' rank and file supporters),[80] 2) confirms the existence of an especially large gap between the opinions of the McGovern elite and the party rank and file, and 3) reveals that the views of the Republican elite were closer to those of Democratic rank and file than were those of any Democratic candidate support group. (See Table 10-1.) Difference scores (which range from 0 to 200) summarize these distances: the difference between Democratic delegates and rank and file on this issue is 76 and that between Republican delegates and Democratic rank and file only 19. (That between Republican elite and party identifiers is 1. See Table 10-9.) The difference between McGovern delegates and Democratic identifiers was substantially larger than that between rank and file identifiers and all Democratic delegates. Among Democratic delegates only the Wallace group contained a majority (95 percent) who emphasized the obligation to work. While Wallace delegates were more nearly unanimous than rank and file Democrats in their emphasis on the obligation to work, they were on the same side of the issue as voters.

Table 10-1. Welfare Policy: Rank and File Identifiers and Elite Compared (%)

	Democrats						Republicans	
	Identifiers	All Delegates	McGovern Delegates	Humphrey Delegates	Muskie Delegates	Wallace Delegates	Identifiers	All Delegates
Abolish poverty								
1	12 ⎫	28 ⎫	38 ⎫	15 ⎫	19 ⎫	0 ⎫	8 ⎫	3 ⎫
2	6 ⎬ 22	17 ⎬ 57	24 ⎬ 75	6 ⎬ 33	17 ⎬ 46	2 ⎬ 2	2 ⎬ 13	2 ⎬ 10
3	4 ⎭	12 ⎭	13 ⎭	12 ⎭	10 ⎭	0 ⎭	3 ⎭	5 ⎭
4	9	15	12	21	21	3	8	15
5	7 ⎫	6 ⎫	4 ⎫	11 ⎫	10 ⎫	9 ⎫	6 ⎫	13 ⎫
6	12 ⎬ 69	7 ⎬ 28	3 ⎬ 12	12 ⎬ 45	12 ⎬ 33	8 ⎬ 95	13 ⎬ 79	22 ⎬ 75
7	50 ⎭	15 ⎭	5 ⎭	22 ⎭	11 ⎭	78 ⎭	60 ⎭	40 ⎭
Obligation to work								
Weighted N =	1040	2532	1281	411	277	145	604	1070

Question: "Some people believe that all able-bodied welfare recipients should be compelled to work. Others believe that the most important consideration is that no American family should live in poverty whether they work or not. Suppose the people who stress the obligation to work are at one end of this scale, at point number 7, and the people who stress that no one should live in poverty are at the other end, at point number 1, where would you place yourself?"

NOTE: Data on rank and file identifiers (voters) were taken from the pre-convention study. Data on elites are from the interviews. Percentages do not necessarily add to 100 due to rounding.

Busing

Comparison of opinions concerning court ordered busing of rank and file party identifiers with the party's elite once again reveals very large differences between Democratic delegates and party identifiers. (See Table 10-2.) On busing as on welfare policy all Democratic candidate support groups except Wallace were more liberal than the Democratic rank and file and more liberal than their own supporters within the Democratic party. Again the largest gap is between the Democratic rank and file and delegates supporting George McGovern. While 71 percent of Democratic voters took the strongest possible anti-busing position, only 3 percent of McGovern delegates took this position. Once again the Republican presidential elite closely reflected the opinions of both the Republican' and the Democratic rank and file. Once again, too, Wallace delegates were more unanimous in their support of the anti-busing position than were voters of either party or Republican delegates but were on the same side of the issue as both Republican and Democratic voters, while a majority of McGovern delegates were on the other side.

Difference scores sum up these comparative gaps. The distance between Democratic elite and rank and file was 108 as compared to 9 between Democratic voters and Republican elite. The difference separating McGovern supporters from Democratic voters was still larger, at 147, as compared to 26 for Wallace. Again, the distance between the views of Republican voters and elite was negligible.

Crime

The law and order issue had its origins in the rising crime rates, urban violence, civil disobedience, and popular anxieties of the late 1960s, but by 1972 broad attitudes toward obedience to the law, toward the coercive power of government, the legitimacy of the social order, race, poverty, social causation, and the morality of lawbreakers had become entangled in this issue.

As in the case of welfare policy and busing a question developed by the Center for Political Studies at the University of Michigan was used to probe attitudes toward "getting tough" versus protecting the rights of the accused. (See Table 10-3.) Responses to this question revealed another large disagreement between Democratic voters and elite. About one-half of the Democratic voters gave priority to stopping crime, but 78 percent of the Democratic delegates (and one-third of the voters) gave priority to protecting the rights of the accused. Here, too, the distance between Democratic rank and file and elite views was large (79) and that between rank and file and McGovern delegates larger still (107). Once again the

Table 10-2. Busing Policy: Rank and File Identifiers and Elite Compared (%)

	Democrats						Republicans	
	Identifiers	All Delegates	McGovern Delegates	Humphrey Delegates	Muskie Delegates	Wallace Delegates	Identifiers	All Delegates
Bus to integrate								
1	8 ⎫	34 ⎫	45 ⎫	14 ⎫	17 ⎫	3 ⎫	2 ⎫	2 ⎫
2	4 ⎬ 15	20 ⎬ 66	29 ⎬ 87	11 ⎬ 38	12 ⎬ 41	0 ⎬ 3	1 ⎬ 5	2 ⎬ 8
3	3 ⎭	12 ⎭	13 ⎭	13 ⎭	12 ⎭	0 ⎭	2 ⎭	4 ⎭
4	6	9	7	12	19	2	4	8
5	4 ⎫	4 ⎫	2 ⎫	10 ⎫	8 ⎫	2 ⎫	4 ⎫	7 ⎫
6	7 ⎬ 82	4 ⎬ 25	2 ⎬ 7	8 ⎬ 51	9 ⎬ 41	2 ⎬ 96	8 ⎬ 93	13 ⎬ 84
Keep children in neighborhood schools 7	71 ⎭	17 ⎭	3 ⎭	33 ⎭	24 ⎭	92 ⎭	81 ⎭	64 ⎭
N =	1275	1492	846	184	131	62	867	796

Question: "There is much discussion about the best way to deal with racial problems. Some people think achieving racial integration of schools is so important that it justifies busing children to schools out of their own neighborhoods. Others think letting children go to their neighborhood schools is so important that they oppose busing. Where would you place yourself on the following scale ranging from agreement with busing to achieve integration (point 1) to agreement with keeping children in neighborhood schools (point 7)?"

NOTE: Data on rank and file identifiers (voters) were taken from the 1972 pre-election (post-convention) study. Data on the elite are from the mail questionnaires. Percentages do not necessarily add to 100 due to rounding.

Table 10-3. Get Tough vs. Protect the Accused: Rank and File Identifiers and Elite Compared (%)

	Democrats						Republicans	
	Identifiers	All Delegates	McGovern Delegates	Humphrey Delegates	Muskie Delegates	Wallace Delegates	Identifiers	All Delegates
Protect the accused								
1	19 ⎱ 36	53 ⎱ 78	67 ⎱ 95	32 ⎱ 58	33 ⎱ 59	11 ⎱ 11	15 ⎱ 28	9 ⎱ 21
2	10 ⎰	18 ⎰	22 ⎰	13 ⎰	20 ⎰	0 ⎰	8 ⎰	5 ⎰
3	7	7	6	13	6	0	5	7
4	14	9	4	17	23	10	17	23
5	10 ⎱ 50	5 ⎱ 13	1 ⎱ 2	12 ⎱ 27	9 ⎱ 19	16 ⎱ 79	13 ⎱ 56	20 ⎱ 56
6	11 ⎰	3 ⎰	0 ⎰	5 ⎰	6 ⎰	13 ⎰	15 ⎰	19 ⎰
Stop crime regardless of rights of accused 7	29	5	1	10	4	50	28	17
N =	1013	1493	850	183	128	62	590	769

Question: "Some people are primarily concerned with doing everything possible to protect the legal rights of those accused of committing crimes. Others feel that it is more important to stop criminal activity even at the risk of reducing the rights of the accused. Suppose that those who stress protecting the rights of the accused are at one end of this scale—at point number 1, and those who stress stopping crime even at the risk of reducing the rights of the accused are at the other end—at point number 7, where would you place yourself?"

(This question was included in the CPS post-election study. The Democratic electorate split as follows: 1 = 23 percent; 2 = 10 percent; 3 = 9 percent; 4 = 19 percent; 5 = 12 percent; 6 = 10 percent; 7 = 19 percent. The Republican electorate split as follows: 1 = 14 percent; 2 = 7 percent; 3 = 7 percent; 4 = 19 percent; 5 = 17 percent; 6 = 15 percent; 7 = 21 percent.)

NOTE: Data on rank and file identifiers (voters) were taken from the pre-convention study. Data on the elite are from the mail questionnaires. Percentages do not necessarily add to 100 percent due to rounding.

views of the Republican delegates were more representative of both Republican and Democratic rank and file.

Foreign Policy: Support
for Southeast Asia

Disagreement about United States policy in Southeast Asia continued to divide the rank and file and elite of both parties and to divide Democratic rank and file from the elite. The questions used to measure attitudes to this policy area concerned the amount and kind of aid that should be provided to Southeast Asia. Only McGovern delegates were relatively united on this question: 57 percent were opposed to any aid whatsoever to the area as compared to 23 percent of voters. On balance approximately 40 percent of Democratic voters were more negative than positive to aid for the area, as compared to 75 percent of Democratic delegates. Sixty percent of voters were on balance favorable to some aid for the area as compared to 16 percent of the Democratic elite. On this question too the views of the Republican elite are similar to both those of the Democratic and Republican rank and file.

Inflation

At last, on this New Deal–Fair Deal–Great Society issue that involves the use of government power to solve economic problems, we find substantial agreement between Democratic voters and Democratic delegates. It was, of course, just such issues that united the Roosevelt coalition, welding together white southerners and northern industrial workers. Even in 1972 Wallace and McGovern delegates and their rank and file supporters were found on the same side of this issue. But the Republicans were also on this side. (See Table 10-4.) This is the only issue tested on which a majority of all candidate support groups were in rough agreement. The broad consensus on the desirability of using government to solve the problem of inflation reflects the decline of laissez-faire economics and perhaps also to the fading importance of this issue in distinguishing between the parties.[81] Republican delegates were less overwhelmingly in favor of government activities to halt inflation than were Democrats or rank and file Republicans. But 63 percent were on the same side of this issue as three-fourths of Democratic voters and elite and Republican rank and file. Here opinions of Democratic elite were more representative of Democratic rank and file than those of the Republican elite and furthermore were closer to the views of the Republican voters than were those of Republican delegates.[82]

Table 10-4. Inflation Policy: Rank and File Identifiers and Elite Compared (%)

	Democrats						Republicans	
	Identifiers	All Delegates	McGovern Delegates	Humphrey Delegates	Muskie Delegates	Wallace Delegates	Identifiers	All Delegates
Government action against inflation 1	52 ⎫	43 ⎫	46 ⎫	37 ⎫	37 ⎫	46 ⎫	39 ⎫	23 ⎫
2	13 ⎬ 78	28 ⎬ 87	34 ⎬ 93	22 ⎬ 81	21 ⎬ 82	7 ⎬ 60	16 ⎬ 74	18 ⎬ 63
3	13 ⎭	16 ⎭	13 ⎭	22 ⎭	24 ⎭	7 ⎭	19 ⎭	22 ⎭
4	14	9	6	12	15	20	21	24
5	3 ⎫	2 ⎫	2 ⎫	2 ⎫	2 ⎫	0 ⎫	3 ⎫	7 ⎫
6	2 ⎬ 9	1 ⎬ 4	1 ⎬ 3	2 ⎬ 7	1 ⎬ 4	6 ⎬ 21	1 ⎬ 6	5 ⎬ 14
No government action against inflation 7	4 ⎭	1 ⎭	0 ⎭	3 ⎭	1 ⎭	15 ⎭	2 ⎭	2 ⎭
N =	608	1449	824	183	126	55	394	759

Question: "There is a great deal of talk these days about rising prices and the cost of living in general. Some feel that the problem of inflation is temporary and that no government action is necessary. Others say the government must do everything possible to combat the problem of inflation immediately or it will get worse. Where would you place yourself on this scale, ranging from agreement with total government action against inflation to agreement with no government action against inflation?"

NOTE: Data on rank and file identifiers (voters) were taken from the 1972 CPS pre-election study. Data on the elite are from the mail questionnaires. Percentages do not necessarily add to 100 due to rounding.

GROUPS

Politics is conducted by and in the name of collectivities. Activities are undertaken and demands are made in the name of groups which become the "we" and the "they" in the competition for power and other values.[83] From the most sophisticated to the most rudimentary, ideologies emphasize groups (the proletariat, the imperialists, the Ibo, the Communists, liberals, conservatives, hawks, doves, the Europeans, the enemies of Allah), and groups serve for many as the principal guideposts by which they locate themselves and others in the political arena. There is no more effective way of locating respondents in the political universe than by reference to their orientations to groups.

"Feeling thermometers" were utilized to elicit voters' and delegates' attitudes toward groups that played a role—as contenders and symbols—in the politics of 1972. The results are consistent with the patterns revealed in the preceding analysis of issue positions. With regard to the most controversial groups the sympathies of Democratic voters differed substantially from those of the Democratic elite, and the Republican leaders shared more orientations of Democratic voters than did Democratic delegates. Political demonstrators, civil rights leaders, black militants, welfare recipients, and the military fall in this category. (See Tables 10-5, 10-6, 10-7, and 10-8.) The feelings of McGovern delegates toward these groups were most remote from the feelings of Democratic voters.

Democratic delegates' orientations were closer to their own rank and file on two symbols of New Deal politics, trade unions and business interests, and also on "liberals," a general ideological category of which Democrats have a more favorable opinion than Republicans. Democrats were also closer to one another in their feelings about "politicians" (though the most important fact about attitudes toward politicans is that voters of both parties had a much more negative feeling about politicians than the elites of both).

DEMOCRATIC SCHISMS EXPLORED

It was generally understood that the new issues—war, race, law and order—divided the electorate in new ways different from the old divisions that grew out of the New Deal and the development of the welfare state.[84] But the extent to which the new issues separated normal Democratic voters from the Democratic elite has been less frequently and less systematically discussed.[85] The fact that Democratic rank and file and elite

Table 10-5. Attitudes Toward Political Demonstrators: Rank and File Identifiers and Elite Compared (%)

| | Democrats | | | | | | Republicans | |
	Identifiers	All Delegates	McGovern Delegates	Humphrey Delegates	Muskie Delegates	Wallace Delegates	Identifiers	All Delegates
Unfavorable 0	35	7	1	9	6	40	40	24
10	12	3	1	7	5	11	11	12
20	8 } 67	3 } 22	1 } 8	4 } 38	3 } 27	9 } 69	10 } 76	16 } 72
30	6	4	2	7	8	6	9	10
40	6	5	3	11	5	3	6	10
Neutral 50	18	19	16	16	31	20	16	14
60	4	12	14	12	9	0	3	5
70	4	13	18	13	9	0	2	4
80	3 } 14	14 } 59	18 } 78	11 } 46	14 } 42	5 } 11	1 } 8	3 } 14
90	1	10	15	4	5	0	1	2
Favorable 100	2	10	13	6	5	6	1	0
Weighted N =	1058	2582	1311	428	283	148	619	1036

Question: "This is called a 'feeling thermometer' and we would like to use it to measure your feelings toward various groups. If you don't feel particularly warm or cold toward a group, then you would score yourself at the 50° mark. If you have a warm feeling toward a group, you would give it a score somewhere between 50° and 100°. On the other hand, if you don't feel very favorably toward a group, then you would place it somewhere between 0° and 50°. How would you rate your overall impressions of political demonstrators?"

NOTE: Data on rank and file identifiers (voters) were taken from the pre-convention study. Data on the elite are from the interviews. Percentages do not necessarily add to 100 due to rounding.

Table 10-6. Attitudes Toward Welfare Recipients: Rank and File Identifiers and Elite Compared (%)

	Democrats						Republicans	
	Identifiers	All Delegates	McGovern Delegates	Humphrey Delegates	Muskie Delegates	Wallace Delegates	Identifiers	All Delegates
Unfavorable								
0	10 ⎱	2 ⎱	0 ⎱	2 ⎱	0 ⎱	26 ⎱	11 ⎱	4 ⎱
10	5	1	0	1	0	12	7	5
20	8 ⎰ 43	1 ⎰ 11	1 ⎰ 5	1 ⎰ 11	2 ⎰ 20	13 ⎰ 63	11 ⎰ 53	5 ⎰ 43
30	10	3	1	3	9	7	12	11
40	10	4	3	4	9	5	12	18
Neutral								
50	30	31	32	27	27	24	29	32
Favorable								
60	8 ⎱	10 ⎱	11 ⎱	13 ⎱	13 ⎱	0 ⎱	6 ⎱	7 ⎱
70	7	14	15	16	11	2	4	8
80	4 ⎰ 26	15 ⎰ 58	16 ⎰ 64	16 ⎰ 63	15 ⎰ 53	5 ⎰ 14	2 ⎰ 17	7 ⎰ 25
90	3	10	11	11	10	2	2	1
100	4	9	11	7	4	5	3	1
Weighted N =	1058	2533	1297	420	279	129	619	1003

Question: "This is called a 'feeling thermometer' and we would like to use it to measure your feelings toward various groups. If you don't feel particularly warm or cold toward a group, then you would score yourself at the 50° mark. If you have a warm feeling toward a group, you would give it a score somewhere between 50° and 100°. On the other hand, if you don't feel very favorably toward a group, then you would place it somewhere between 0° and 50°. How would you rate your overall impressions of welfare recipients?"

NOTE: Data on rank and file identifiers (voters) were taken from the pre-convention study. Data on the elite are from the interviews. Percentages do not necessarily add to 100 percent due to rounding.

Table 10-7. Attitudes Toward the Military: Rank and File Identifiers and Elite Compared (%)

	Democrats						Republicans	
	Identifiers	All Delegates	McGovern Delegates	Humphrey Delegates	Muskie Delegates	Wallace Delegates	Identifiers	All Delegates
Unfavorable								
0	4	4	7	1	4	0	1	0
10	2	8	14	1	4	2	2	0
20	1	7	12	1	3	0	2	1
30	5	11	16	4	4	2	3	1
40	4	13	17	8	17	0	4	2
(total)	*16*	*43*	*66*	*15*	*32*	*4*	*12*	*4*
Neutral								
50	16	14	16	14	15	11	18	12
60	8	7	6	5	14	3	7	10
70	12	10	7	16	6	10	15	18
80	13	9	2	21	9	21	16	24
90	13	7	3	14	9	17	12	17
Favorable 100	21	9	2	15	15	34	21	15
(60–100 total)	*67*	*42*	*20*	*71*	*53*	*85*	*71*	*84*
Weighted N =	1058	2619	1330	427	283	148	619	1068

Question: "This is called a 'feeling thermometer' and we would like to use it to measure your feelings toward various groups. If you don't feel particularly warm or cold toward a group, then you would score yourself at the 50° mark. If you have a warm feeling toward a group, you would give it a score somewhere between 50° and 100°. On the other hand, if you don't feel very favorably toward a group, then you would place it somewhere between 0° and 50°. How would you rate your overall impressions of the military?"

NOTE: The data on rank and file identifiers (voters) were taken from the pre-convention study. Data on the elite are from the interviews. Percentages do not necessarily add to 100 due to rounding.

Table 10-8. Attitudes Toward the Police: Rank and File Identifiers and Elite Compared (%)

	Democrats						Republicans	
	Identifiers	All Delegates	McGovern Delegates	Humphrey Delegates	Muskie Delegates	Wallace Delegates	Identifiers	All Delegates
Unfavorable 0	1	1	1	1	0	0	0	0
10	1	1	1	1	0	0	0	0
20	1 (7)	2 (13)	3 (18)	0 (6)	1 (5)	0 (2)	1 (5)	0 (2)
30	2	3	5	0	1	0	2	1
40	2	6	8	4	3	2	2	1
Neutral 50	11	17	24	9	10	12	9	5
60	9	11	14	6	12	0	7	7
70	13	13	16	12	9	4	12	11
80	16 (81)	19 (71)	17 (59)	27 (87)	17 (86)	12 (87)	19 (84)	16 (94)
90	16	15	8	25	27	16	19	32
Favorable 100	27	13	4	17	21	55	27	28
Weighted N =	1058	2616	1327	432	283	148	619	1070

Question: "This is called a 'feeling thermometer' and we would like to use it to measure your feelings toward various groups. If you don't feel particularly warm or cold toward a group, then you would score yourself at the 50° mark. If you have a warm feeling toward a group, you would give it a score somewhere between 50° and 100°. On the other hand, if you don't feel very favorably toward a group, then you would place it somewhere between 0° and 50°. How would you rate your overall impressions of the police?"

NOTE: The data on rank and file identifiers (voters) were taken from the pre-convention study. Data on the elite are from the interviews. Percentages do not necessarily add to 100 due to rounding.

remained essentially united on inflation, union leaders, and business interests reflects the persistence of the New Deal consensus on these questions, but the sharp divisions among Democratic elite and rank and file on the new cultural and social issues provides evidence of how the new issues cut across the older alignments.

The fact that a general consensus on economic policy survived among Democrats in this year of the party's landslide defeat indicates either that the consensus is no longer perceived as having much relevance to interparty conflict, because Republicans have joined Democrats on these issues that formerly divided them[86] or that economic issues were perceived by the electorate as less important in 1972 than the new issues or that economic issues had such low salience for the dominant Democratic elite[87] in 1972 that voters never fully grasped the persistence of differences in orientation between the parties. Probably all three were involved.

The power of welfare state issues to move masses was reflected in Democratic victories from 1932 to 1968. But the massive defeat of George McGovern and the attitudes of defecting Democrats testified to the importance for voters of new cross-cutting issues. Not everyone has views about whether it is or is not desirable to have public or private ownership of communications or whether it is or is not desirable to make new concessions in the SALT talks, but almost everyone has internalized cultural prescriptions concerning obedience to law and punishment for disobedience, the relations of work and rewards, the nation's armed forces, and parents' roles in bringing up their children.[88] While questions about how government should be conducted are not necessarily or frequently perceived as involving the self, cultural prescriptions concerning work, authority, "just desserts," and race become part of the definition of the self. This intimate relation of culture to the self-system gives to cultural politics its capacity to interest and involve masses. It explains why student riots, remote from the experience of most, capture the attention of millions who remain unconcerned by large but impersonal questions of government policy. It also explains why political conflict concerning cultural matters is so often so intense—as in religious, linguistic, national, and tribal wars.[89]

Issues become important in politics because of their perceived relation to political contests and because of their relations to a person's core values and commitments.[90] Identifying these core commitments is problematic. However, by all the indicators available: presence of an opinion,[91] intensity of opinion,[92] direct inquiry about which issue is important in determining vote,[93] salience,[94] factor analysis, and inter-item correlations,[95] the issues on which Democratic elite and rank and file disagreed were important to the politics of 1972.

All the political issues that most sharply distinguished Democratic mass and elite involved the clash of new and old political cultures.[96] Welfare policy had become involved with conflicting views about the achievement ethic, about whether work was an obligation, and about whether deprivation of income was an appropriate response to those who were idle by preference.[97] Law enforcement policy had obvious relevance to questions concerning the legitimacy of the social order and the moral status of coercion used to defend that order. Foreign policy became enmeshed in culture conflict not only because of the affinity of the counter culture and the antiwar movement, but also because the two sides held conflicting conceptions of citizenship and national purpose. Racial policy was entangled in the clash of cultures: because traditional America took white supremacy for granted, because equality is a basic value of the society, because political protest, civil disobedience, and urban riots were associated with the movement for racial equality, and because busing mixes cultures, deprives parents of traditional prerogatives, and challenges some accepted notions about the appropriate functions of government. Attitudes on each of these issues suggest an entire syndrome. Lack of consensus between Democratic elite and mass about these questions of public policy signaled the likelihood of broad differences in perspective and commitments.[98] (See Table 10-12.)

Because George McGovern was the standard-bearer for the new politics as well as the Democratic party, his association with the new issues was especially strong, and the difference between the beliefs, sympathies, and preferences of McGovern delegates and rank and file Democratic identifiers was especially large. On all the issues on which rank and file Democrats were closer to the Republican than the Democratic delegates, a still wider gap separated them from McGovern delegates. On busing, for example, the margin of difference between all Democratic identifiers and all delegates was 108, but the difference between Democratic identifiers and McGovern delegates was 147. The difference between rank and file and McGovern delegates' rating of political demonstrators soared to 123 as compared to a 90 margin of difference for all delegates. On welfare policy and work, the difference between voters and all Democratic delegates was 76, but between Democratic identifiers and McGovern delegates it was 110. On crime, the margin of difference of voters to McGovern delegates was 107 as compared to 79 for all Democratic delegates; on the military, the margin of difference rose from 52 for all Democratic delegates to 97 for McGovern delegates. The pattern is clear and consistent. McGovern delegates were especially unrepresentative of the views and values of the Democratic rank and file.

It is readily observed from Table 10-9 that on all but two groups (union leaders and politicians) McGovern delegates were less representative of

Table 10-9. Differences Between Democratic Rank and File Identifiers and Selected Groups of Convention Delegates

	McGovern Delegates	Humphrey Delegates	Wallace Delegates	Muskie Delegates	Republican Delegates	Democratic Delegates
Welfare	110	35	46	60	19	76
Busing[a]	147	54	26	67	9	108
Crime	107	45	54	54	21	79
Civil rights leaders	94	59	74	69	4	67
Welfare recipients	76	69	32	50	1	64
Political demonstrators	123	61	5	68	5	90
Police	33	7	11	7	18	16
Military	97	5	30	30	29	52
Blacks	34	45	6	37	26	34
Conservatives	89	42	66	48	41	64
Liberals	75	24	99	37	73	46
Union leaders	10	43	52	21	52	15

Politicians	55	76	16	66	75	57
Inflation[a]	21	5	30	9	20	14
Abortion[a]	89	43	2	67	50	68
Laying off women first[a]	54	32	4	38	18	42
Women's liberation[b]	61	32	55	21	57	25
Business interests[b]	57	2	2	15	45	35
Black militants[b]	93	26	15	32	9	61
Vietnam	109	29	14	62	34	79
Ideological self-classification[b]	83	40	80	54	59	59
Mean Differences	77.0	36.9	34.2	43.5	31.6	54.9

[a]These data on rank and file identifiers—used to compute differences—were taken from the 1972 CPS pre-election (post-convention) study.
[b]These data on rank and file identifiers—used to compute differences—were taken from the 1972 CPS post-election study.

The remaining data on rank and file identifiers were taken from the pre-convention study.

NOTE: The difference scores were computed from preponderance scores carried to the first decimal place.

the views of the Democratic rank and file than were delegates to the Republican Convention and that they had fewer views in common with rank and file Democrats than did the delegates supporting all other candidates—including George Wallace. On only three issues or groups—union leaders, liberals, and inflation—were the views of McGovern delegates closer to those of the Democratic rank and file than were the orientations of Wallace delegates. (See Table 10-10.) Delegates supporting the two candidates popularly tagged "moderate" included more persons with views like the Democratic rank and file.[99] But as we have already noted, on questions of welfare policy, busing, crime, political demonstrators, civil rights leaders, etc., no candidate support group at the Democratic Convention as closely represented the views and values of rank and file as did the Republican elite: McGovern, Humphrey, and Muskie delegate groups had views that were too "liberal" on most issues; Wallace delegates were, as a group, too "conservative." Among Democrats, the Humphrey group most closely approximated views of Democratic voters on welfare policy, crime, civil rights leaders, the military, conservatives and liberals, inflation, and ideological self-classification; the Muskie group was closest to Democratic rank and file on women's liberation. Humphrey and Muskie delegates tied as closest on police. Wallace delegates most closely approximated Democratic rank and file views on busing, welfare recipients, political demonstrators, blacks, politicians, abortion, black militants, Vietnam, and job policy for women. Humphrey and Wallace were equally close in attitudes to business interests. McGovern delegates' orientations were closest to those of the Democratic rank and file on a single group: union leaders.

Although there was close correspondence between views of Republican mass and elite, there were a few issues and groups about which the Republican delegates were closer to Democratic than Republican party identifiers: busing, civil rights leaders, blacks, welfare recipients, political demonstrators, job policy for women, and politicians. On each of these, Republican delegates took a view more sympathetic to the group in question than did the Republican rank and file. Democratic identifiers' views were somewhat less unfriendly than the ordinary Republican to these groups, but far less sympathetic than the Democratic elite. Their views therefore meshed nicely with those of the Republican delegates. On a number of subjects, including "liberals," Vietnam, the military, women's liberation, and politicians, the position of the Republican elite was substantially more "conservative" than that of the Republican rank and file and slightly so on inflation, police, business interests, crime, union leaders, and ideological self-classification. The two Republican groups were in virtually complete agreement on welfare policy. Differences between Republican elite and rank and file were not large and were generally consistent with previous findings. Republican elite distances from Democrats as well as Republicans were small enough to permit competition for Democratic votes.

The relative proximity of Democratic rank and file and Republican elite does not indicate that there were no differences between the two mass parties.[100] To the contrary, attitudinal differences between the voters of the two parties were consistent enough to confirm once more that there exist some reliable if not large differences in orientation and emphasis between the mass parties. (See Table 10-11.) Democratic identifiers were more likely to take the position considered "liberal" in 1972 on welfare policy, busing, and crime. They felt somewhat more sympathetic than Republican identifiers toward civil rights leaders, welfare recipients, political demonstrators, liberals, union leaders, and blacks and slightly less warm toward police and the military and definitely less friendly to "conservatives." The mean difference between Democratic and Republican identifiers on busing, welfare, and crime is 17, or slightly more than that which separates Republican voters and delegates. More significant for our purposes here is the fact that *the same issues and symbols that separated the Democratic from Republican rank and file still further separated Democratic voters from their own party elite.* (See Table 10-12.)

In 1956 McClosky concluded that ". . . there is a substantial consensus on national issues between Democratic leaders and Democratic and Republican followers, while the Republican leaders are separated not only from the Democrats but from their own rank and file members as well."[101] By 1972 the position of Republican and Democratic elites had been reversed and the Democratic presidential elite was "odd man out." The Republican presidential elite more faithfully mirrored the views and values of their own party identifiers and of voters generally than did the Democratic elite which did not reflect the views either of ordinary Democrats or of voters generally. Perhaps, though, the Democrats reflected the views of the new constituencies—the women, blacks, and youth who were numerous in the Democratic Convention and important in the electorate. To this possibility we now turn.

SEX, AGE, RACE, AND OPINIONS IN THE TWO CONVENTIONS

Women

Did the Democratic Convention, in which women were especially numerous, represent the views of Democratic women more adequately than the Republican? Is there any necessary relation between the numbers of women present in a convention and the reflection of rank and file

Table 10-10. Least Difference of Democratic Rank and File Identifiers from Various Delegate Groups on Selected Issues

	McGovern Delegates	Humphrey Delegates	Muskie Delegates	Wallace Delegates	Republican Delegates	Democratic Delegates
Welfare					X	
Busing[a]					X	
Crime					X	
Civil rights leaders					X	
Welfare recipients					X	
Political demonstrators				X		
Police		X	X			
Military		X				
Blacks				X		
Conservatives					X	
Liberals		X				
Union leaders	X					

	Col 1	Col 2	Col 3	Col 4
Politicians				
Inflation[a]		X		X
Abortion[a]		X		
Laying off women first[a]		X		
Business interests[b]		X		X
Black militants[b]	X			
Women's liberation[b]			X	
Vietnam		X		
Ideological self-classification[b]				X

[a] Data on rank and file identifiers used to compute least differences on these issues were taken from the 1972 CPS pre-election (post-convention) study.

[b] Data on rank and file identifiers used to compute least differences on these issues were taken from the 1972 CPS post-election study.

The remainder of the data on rank and file identifiers were taken from the pre-convention study.

NOTE: This table is based on difference scores computed from preponderance scores carried to the first decimal place.

women's views? The answer to both questions is "no." Women's political opinions were no better represented than men's in the Democratic Convention.

It is quite clear that on the major issues of 1972 women's views split about like those of men. As Table 10-16 shows, there is no correlation

Table 10-11. Differences on Selected Issues: Democratic and Republican Rank and File Identifiers and Party Elites Compared

	Republican/Democratic Voters	Republican/Democratic Elite
Welfare	18	95
Busing[a]	21	117
Crime	14	100
Civil rights leaders	28	71
Welfare recipients	19	65
Political demonstrators	16	95
Police	5	34
Military	8	81
Blacks	17	8
Conservatives	42	105
Liberals	39	119
Politicians	7	18
Union leaders	41	67
Inflation[a]	1	34
Abortion[a]	10	18
Laying off women first[a]	14	24
Women's liberation[b]	22	82
Business interests[b]	34	80
Black militants[b]	18	70
Vietnam	1	113
Ideological self-classification[b]	52	118
Mean Differences	20	72

[a]The data on rank and file identifiers for these issue-questions were taken from the 1972 CPS pre-election (post-convention) study.

[b]The data on rank and file identifiers for these issue-questions were taken from the 1972 CPS post-election study.

All other data on rank and file identifiers were taken from the pre-convention study.

NOTE: The difference scores were computed from preponderance scores carried to the first decimal place.

Table 10-12. Rank Order of Difference Scores on Selected Issues

Difference Scores: Democratic Identifiers vs. All Democratic Delegates		*Difference Scores: Democratic Identifiers vs. All McGovern Delegates*		*Difference Scores: Republican Identifiers vs. All Republican Delegates*	
Busing	108	Busing	147	Politicians	82
Political demonstrators	90	Political demonstrators	123	Blacks	43
Vietnam	79	Welfare	110	Abortion	40
Crime	79	Vietnam	109	Women's liberation	35
Welfare	76	Crime	107	Vietnam	35
Abortion	68	Military	97	Liberals	34
Civil rights leaders	67	Civil rights leaders	94	Laying off women first	32
Welfare recipients	64	Black militants	93	Civil rights leaders	24
Conservatives	64	Abortion	89	Military	21
Black militants	61	Conservatives	89	Inflation	19
Ideological self-classification	59	Ideological self-classification	83	Welfare recipients	18
Politicians	57	Welfare recipients	76	Police	13
Military	52	Liberals	75	Busing	12
Liberals	46	Women's liberation	61	Political demonstrators	11
Laying off women first	42	Business interests	57	Business interests	11
Business interests	35	Politicians	55	Union leaders	11
Blacks	34	Laying off women first	54	Black militants	9
Women's liberation	25	Blacks	34	Crime	7
Police	16	Police	33	Ideological self-classification	7
Union leaders	15	Inflation	21	Welfare	1
Inflation	14	Union leaders	10	Conservatives	1

between sex and political opinion at the mass level. And Table 10-13 shows that on 16 of 21 measures the opinions of women delegates to the Democratic Convention were even less representative of Democratic rank and file women than the opinions of male delegates were representative of male party identifiers.

On most issues *inter*party differences among women exceeded intraparty sex differences—a fact that demonstrates the strong tendency of opinion to follow partisan rather than sexual identifications. There was no "woman's position" on any issue in either party. Within the Democratic Convention women's opinions followed ideology and candidate preference, not sex. McGovern supporters behaved like McGovern supporters; Wallace supporters like Wallace supporters.

Even on questions with a special "women's" angle, sex had no significant relation to opinion so the views of women delegates were not especially representative of those women rank and file. Democratic delegates—male and female—had much more liberal views on abortion, personnel policy, and the women's liberation movement than did rank and file Democratic women. Sixty percent of Democratic women voters and 25 percent of Democratic women delegates took a rather conservative position on the availability of abortion; 46 percent of Democratic women voters and 20 percent of Democratic women delegates believed that in times of economic depression women should be laid off before male heads of families. Attitudes toward women's liberation reflected the same type of mass–elite discrepancies. Forty percent of Democratic women voters felt "warm" toward women's liberation as compared to 67 percent of Democratic women delegates. Differences between Republican and Democratic women delegates on this last issue was marked. Sixty percent of Republican women delegates were unsympathetic to women's liberation, while 67 percent of Democratic women were sympathetic. Though they were more conservative on this symbolic issue than the rank and file of either party, the Republican female elite was nonetheless somewhat closer than the Democratic female elite to the women in the rank and file of both parties.

Race

Did the blacks in the Democratic and Republican conventions share the views and values of black party identifiers? Did black Democratic delegates share the views and values of the black rank and file to a greater extent than white delegates shared those of the white rank and file? What of the Republicans who were so very unsuccessful in attracting black support in 1972? Were black Republican delegates representative of such few black Republican identifiers as existed?

Table 10-14 shows that on most of the major issues of 1972 black Democratic delegates were more in step with black Democratic voters than were their white counterparts. On four of the five major policy areas tested—busing, crime, welfare, inflation—the distance between black delegates and voters is less than that between whites. The same relationship holds for groups which in 1972 had become entangled with race: civil rights leaders, welfare recipients, black militants, and political demonstrators. Black Democratic elite and mass opinions were more similar than those of white delegates and voters. However, the difference in black elite and mass opinion remained very large on a number of issues, and the direction of these differences is the same as that which characterized the relation between Democratic whites: delegates were more liberal than rank and file (except, of course, for Wallace delegates who were more conservative); they were less supportive of authority, more supportive of challenges to authority and challengers, more concerned about integration than about maintaining neighborhood schools, and so forth. On busing, welfare policy, welfare recipients, political demonstrators, and black militants the difference scores range from 43 to 85, and on each item the black delegates were more liberal than the black rank and file. (See Table 10–14.) Black Democratic identifiers were much more divided than white about busing, preferring neighborhood schools by a small margin (7 percent). But black Democratic delegates were overwhelmingly in favor of busing (by a margin of 67 percent). Black identifiers were also less united than white about emphasizing the obligation of the able-bodied to work (the margin of blacks is 22 percent as compared to 51 percent for whites), but by a 37 percent margin black delegates emphasized the abolition of poverty even if it meant using public funds to support some able-bodied but lazy persons.

Unlike sex, race is related to political perspectives on several issues, and the differences between black and white views are large enough to put the majority of black delegates and the majority of Democratic delegates on the same side of several questions as black voters. On responses to major policy areas and groups, such as inflation, busing, crime, welfare recipients, civil rights leaders, and black militants, white Democratic voters were closer to the Republican than the Democratic elite in views. But only on the question that juxtaposes getting tough on crime versus protecting the rights of the accused were black voters closer to the Republican than the Democratic elite.

Obviously, since McGovern delegates were more pro-busing, pro-welfare, pro-rights of the accused, pro-demonstrator, pro-black militant, and pro-welfare recipient than the average of Democratic delegates, the distance of McGovern delegates from black voters was greater than from all Democratic delegates. Although these differences were large, larger

Table 10-13. Difference Scores for Women Only: Rank and File Identifiers and Delegates Compared

	Democratic Women Identifiers/ All Democratic Women Delegates	Democratic Women Identifiers/ McGovern Women Delegates	Democratic Women Identifiers/ All Republican Women Delegates
Welfare	105	131	4
Busing[a]	117	145	17
Crime	86	108	8
Civil rights leaders	73	93	30
Welfare recipients	65	73	20
Political demonstrators	101	129	3
Police	21	38	12
Military	71	110	16
Blacks	30	28	44
Conservatives	73	94	8
Liberals	53	77	42

Union leaders	13	9	17
Politicians	56	52	85
Inflation[a]	15	19	23
Abortion[a]	86	102	62
Laying off women first[a]	52	60	38
Women's liberation[b]	46	69	21
Business interests[b]	36	49	4
Black militants[b]	64	88	9
Vietnam	94	114	23
Ideological self-classification[b]	65	83	4
Mean Differences	63.0	79.6	23.3

[a] These data on rank and file identifiers (voters) were taken from the 1972 CPS pre-election (post-convention) study.
[b] These data on rank and file identifiers (voters) were taken from the 1972 CPS post-election study.

The remainder of the data were taken from the pre-convention study.

NOTE: The difference scores were computed from preponderance scores carried to the first decimal place.

Table 10-14. Difference Scores: Rank and File Identifiers and Delegates Compared by Race

	Identifiers/ Delegates Democratic Whites	Identifiers/ Delegates Democratic Blacks	Identifiers/ Delegates Republican Whites	Identifiers/ Delegates Republican Blacks
Welfare	76	61	2	2
Busing[a]	118	74	9	57
Crime	82	68	5	30
Civil rights leaders	80	14	23	1
Welfare recipients	64	43	19	6
Political demonstrators	94	85	10	27
Police	14	15	15	17
Military	56	26	19	34
Blacks	41	10	45	7
Conservatives	64	67	4	38
Liberals	50	34	36	6

Union leaders	19	10	10	17
Politicians	63	45	83	64
Inflation[a]	15	10	19	38
Abortion[a]	69	69	40	60
Laying off women first[a]	44	22	35	19
Women's liberation[b]	27	8	36	55
Business interests[b]	36	15	10	14
Black militants[b]	62	48	8	24
Vietnam	73	116	33	63
Ideological self-classification[b]	66	24	8	36
Mean Differences	57.8	41.1	22.3	29.3

[a]These data on rank and file identifiers (voters) were taken from the 1972 CPS pre-election (post-convention) study.
[b]These data on rank and file identifiers (voters) were taken from the 1972 CPS post-election study.

The remainder of the data on rank and file identifiers (voters) were taken from the pre-convention study.

NOTE: These difference scores were computed from preponderance scores carried to the first decimal place.

than expected mass–elite differences, the views of McGovern delegates were nonetheless more similar or less dissimilar to those of black than white Democrats.

The situation was reversed among Republicans. White delegates more closely mirrored the views of white party identifiers. As Table 10–14 illustrates, the distance between black identifiers and delegates was greater than that separating white Republicans on several issues and groups. Still, the mean difference on busing, crime and welfare between black Republican voters and delegates was 30, while the mean difference between black Democratic voters and delegates was 68. Thus among blacks as well as among whites the distance between Democratic mass and elite was much larger than that between Republican mass and elite.

Youth

The twenty-five million first-time voters were the resource, "the real sleeper," on which McGovern strategists counted for victory. Fred Dutton forecast that McGovern would get thirteen million of the new youth to five million for Nixon and that this margin would sweep him to victory.[102] But the relationship between young delegates and party identifiers was largely the same as for other groups. Like race, age is positively, though rather weakly, related to opinions on several issues. Among delegates, those under 30 were most numerous in the McGovern ranks, and the opinions of that group were remote from those of rank and file Democratic identifiers of any age. The mean differences between youthful Democratic voters (18 to 30) and their counterparts within the convention was 47. The mean difference for all the comparable Republican groups was 28. On many issues and groups—notably busing, inflation, crime, the military, black militants, and conservatives—under-30 voters who identified with the Democrats had views closer to the young Republican than the young Democratic elite. (See Table 10-15.)

There were differences among age groups on some of the major questions of 1972, and these differences were especially marked on the new issues: crime, abortion, welfare, and busing, and especially policy questions affecting women. On these questions voters under 30 and over 65 had somewhat distinctive views on numerous questions. As between the two groups, Democratic delegates were somewhat closer to the views of youth than older voters, but they remained far more liberal than youth in general, or Democratic youth in particular. (See Table 10–15.)

The differences between young Republican rank and file and delegates are greater than for the middle-aged; however, they are small as compared to those separating the Democrats.

Table 10-15. Difference Scores for Youth (18-30): Rank and File Identifiers and Delegates Compared[a]

	Democratic Identifiers 18–30/ Democratic Delegates 18–30	Republican Identifiers 18–30/ Republican Delegates 18–30
Busing[b]	112	23
Crime[c]	61	18
Civil rights leaders[c]	53	89
Police[c]	26	6
Military[c]	68	20
Blacks[c]	14	36
Conservatives[c]	92	28
Liberals[c]	28	21
Inflation[b]	16	32
Abortion[b]	50	62
Laying off women first[b]	12	22
Women's liberation[c]	41	18
Business interests[c]	36	28
Black militants[c]	58	6
Ideological self-classification[c]	43	6
Mean Differences	47.3	27.7

[a]Unfortunately, the pre-convention study's "age" variable could not be coded to achieve an 18–30 category. Consequently, the data used here are entirely from the CPS surveys.

[b]These data on rank and file identifiers (voters) were taken from the 1972 CPS pre-election (post-convention) study.

[c]These data on rank and file identifiers (voters) were taken from the 1972 CPS post-election study.

NOTE: The difference scores were computed from preponderance scores carried to the first decimal place.

SOME CONCLUSIONS AND COMMENTS

The McGovern-Fraser Commission made a self-conscious effort to achieve desired goals through party reform. Certain of its goals—notably increased numbers of women, blacks, and youth in the national convention and the opening of the party to new faces and ideas—were achieved. But it is clear that the new rules did not result in a convention that was representative of the views and values of ordinary Democratic voters.

The experience demonstrates that it is much easier to change the processes through which delegates are selected than it is to secure a more "representative" convention. The new rules, like the old, produced a convention whose members had much higher incomes, higher education, higher social status, and less religious commitment than regular Democratic voters, a convention in which some age and ethnic groups were clearly unrepresented. It also produced a convention whose majority did not reflect and was not responsive to the values, views, and policy preferences of most Democrats or most voters. The Democrats' landslide defeat was consistent with the large differences between the views of the Democratic voters and elite.

I do not mean to suggest that the political unrepresentativeness of the Democratic Convention was a result only or perhaps even mainly of the new rules.[103] In retrospect, it seems likely that many contemporaneous accounts exaggerated the impact of the reform rules on the composition of the Democratic Convention. But they made it more likely that verbal specialists, youth, and others with relatively weak attachments to party would be chosen as delegates and this probably had the unanticipated, unintended effect of reducing the convention's concern for winning the election, unifying the party, and attracting the support of the rank and file.

PARTICIPATION AND REPRESENTATION

Since the prestige of participatory processes is currently very large, political parties are under heavy internal and external pressure to opt in favor of "open" processes that at least appear to provide for mass participation of the rank and file in the party's major decisions. But it is extremely difficult to devise procedures that will *in fact* represent rank and file voters. Very few voters ever participate in caucuses and conventions—*however "open"*—and those who do are, for various reasons, likely to be very unrepresentative political types. Primaries provide for wider participation but their electorates are also often not "representative" of all the party's voters.[104] They, too, frequently feature low turnout, multiple candidates, and no run-off; delegates in primary states are usually elected by a plurality of those who vote who in turn constitute only a minority of the voters whose support the party will need to win the election. Winning by a plurality in several states multiplies the problem but does not solve it. Eliminating winner-take-all primaries does not affect problems arising from turnout.

One factor with important consequences for all efforts to make national conventions representative of large numbers is that habits of participation are related to social class. Existing data on representation suggest that the processes that take place well in advance of general elections, that emphasize issue conflict, and that require attending meetings are almost certain to result in the choice of delegates by ideologically motivated upper middle income skill groups whose views are not typical either of rank and file voters or their own parties.

Although the data linking habits of participation (joining, volunteering, attending) to education, income, and occupation are convincing, they are rarely considered when political reforms are considered. Participatory politics may not be an upper middle-class sport (as one friend suggested),[105] but indubitably it requires social, economic, and psychological resources that are not evenly distributed in society. (The impact of this distribution on organizational behavior has most recently been examined by James Q. Wilson.)[106]

Not only are some classes and groups less likely to turn out for the neighborhood meetings through which participatory procedures typically operate,[107] but the middle-class persons *most* likely to participate in processes remote from major salient decisions have some other special characteristics that have been studied in the United States and elsewhere with similar results. Activists are more likely than rank and file to have strong ideological convictions, and their ideologies are likely to be more extreme than those of average voters. They are more likely to be what Bagehot termed "immoderate persons."[108] It is not that party elites and activist identifiers are *extremist* in their views, only that, as compared to party rank and file, their views are less moderate. Studies of amateur or "middle-class" politics[109] confirm the special importance of ideological incentives to the middle-class activists most attracted to participatory politics. There is the tendency already discussed for a self-perpetuating style to develop: persons with high ideological interests and commitments are most likely to become active in politics, the presence of persons with strong ideological interests strengthens the ideological component of politics; the more ideological or issue-oriented politics becomes, the more attractive it is to middle-class activists who have strong ideological commitments, and so forth.

The result is not only that parties will continue to be governed by an elite comprising persons of relatively high income, education, and occupational status. These are characteristics of elites everywhere. Participatory politics poses a special pitfall for political parties: the danger of mistaking those who turn out to participate in party governance for "the people," for the voters to whom the party is answerable on election day. The Democratic experience of 1972 not only demonstrates the persistence of class characteristics of political elites, it illustrates the errors of concluding that "open" processes and thousands of meetings will produce a convention in which "the people" are represented. Herein lies the reason that conventions based on "open" participatory politics may turn out (as in 1972) to be less representative of party rank and file (and other voters) than conventions peopled by labor leaders, political "bosses," and public officials. The middle income symbol specialist elected by those who turned out for a party conference or ward meeting is likely to feel his job is to represent those who chose him—that is, to represent other politically active middle-class symbol specialists. But the "boss" and the labor leader, even if also middle income professionals, know that they represent different and broader constituencies. A characteristic of the "new breed" may be its remoteness from the party rank and file, and a major consequence of the new rules may have been to open the way for selection of delegates unrepresentative of and unaccountable to either the party rank and file or any ongoing organization whose welfare depends on responsiveness to that rank and file.

The noncoincidence of the total population that should be represented and the minority that turns out for party meetings is a major problem that confronts any effort to mix the forms of intraparty democracy with the realities of mass political behavior. Delegates are elected by an activist minority and "responsible to" the whole body of Democratic identifiers—or the whole electorate. If the job of a delegate is defined as representing the opinions and interests of those who choose him, then it is very unlikely that the views and values of average voters will be represented in political conventions.

Quotas do not solve this problem. The structure of opinion and the experience of 1972 demonstrate that the quotas did not substantially enhance the representation of the political views of women, blacks, or youth. Indeed, it seems likely that, with the exception of the seating of the Illinois delegation, *the quotas probably had little impact on the political composition of the convention.*[110] The opinions of women, youth, and blacks supporting McGovern in the convention were essentially like those of the white middle-aged males supporting McGovern.[111] The views of women, youth, and even the black or two supporting Wallace were in basic respects like those of middle-aged white male Wallacites, and so forth. The quotas had a small impact on the political composition of the convention because there are no large or reliable relationships between age, sex, race, and political perspectives (Table 10-16), and because all candidate groups obviously adapted to the requirements—filling their "women" slots with women who shared their political opinions, and so forth. The quotas therefore can be blamed neither for the failure of the Democratic Convention to represent more accurately or more adequately the political views of rank and file Democrats, nor for the party's landslide defeat. But neither does the experience of 1972 support the view that the *quality of political representation* is enhanced by providing quotas for specified groups.[112] 1972 Democratic delegates were less representative of the views and values of voters than were delegates to the "unreformed" Republican Convention, and the "new" political type concentrated in the McGovern ranks were least representative of all.[113]

Table 10-16. The Relationships Between Social Position and Political Views: All Voters

	Sex[a]	Race[a]	Religion[a]	Education[b]	Income[b]	Age[b]
Busing[c]	0.00	0.13	0.01	0.03	0.09	0.01
Crime	0.00	0.01	0.00	-0.12	-0.03	0.17
Welfare	0.00	0.02	0.00	-0.05	0.01	0.11
Inflation[c]	0.01	0.01	0.01	0.11	0.05	-0.05
Civil rights leaders	0.00	0.17	0.00	0.04	-0.03	-0.14
Police	0.00	0.01	0.01	-0.05	0.00	0.14
Conservatives	0.00	0.01	0.01	-0.05	0.00	0.14
Military	0.00	0.00	0.02	0.27	0.10	0.14
Politicians	0.00	0.01	0.00	-0.13	-0.03	-0.02
Blacks	0.01	0.16	0.00	0.07	0.01	0.14
Union leaders	0.00	0.04	0.00	-0.21	-0.09	-0.03
Liberals	0.00	0.04	0.01	0.00	0.03	0.15
Welfare recipients	0.00	0.06	0.01	-0.11	-0.16	-0.02
Political demonstrators	0.00	0.06	0.02	0.11	0.03	-0.26
Black militants[d]	0.00	0.13	0.00	0.06	-0.03	0.23

Women's liberation[d]	0.00	0.02	0.00	0.03	-0.01	0.07
Abortion[c]	0.00	0.01	0.03	0.30	0.19	0.19
Laying off women first[c]	0.01	0.01	0.01	0.02[a]	0.00[a]	0.04[a]
Business interests[d]	0.00	0.00	0.01	-0.09	-0.03	0.21
Vietnam	0.00	0.00	0.01	-0.09	-0.02	0.09
Ideological self-classification[d]	0.00	0.04	0.02	-0.06	0.06	0.18

[a]These measures of association are "eta" statistics, measuring the relationship between nominal and interval variables.

[b]These measures of association are Pearson's R correlation coefficients.

[c]The data for these variables were taken from the 1972 CPS pre-election (post-convention) study.

[d]The data for these variables were taken from the 1972 CPS post-election study. The remainder of the data were taken from the pre-convention study.

NOTE: *Coding*: The following variables were coded with these positions receiving the *highest* values: 1. Busing: "children in neighborhood schools"; 2. Crime: "stop crime regardless of rights of accused"; 3. Welfare: "obligation to work"; 4. Inflation: "government action against inflation"; 5. Abortion: "abortion okay if woman wants it"; 6. Vietnam: "aid to Southeast Asia"; 7. Ideological self-classification: "very conservative." "Laying off women first" was a nominal variable and was so treated throughout this analysis. The remainder of the variables were feeling thermometers with the highest value in each case representing a favorable impression of the group listed.

NOTES

1. Hannah F. Pitkin, *The Concept of Representation* (Berkeley: University of California Press, 1967), p. 77.
2. A good discussion of representation as an emergent characteristic is Heinz Eulau and Kenneth Prewitt, *Labyrinths of Democracy: Adaptation, Linkages, Representation and Policies in Urban Politics* (Indianapolis: Bobbs-Merrill, 1973), pp. 37–53.
3. The Commission on Party Structure and Delegate Selection, *Mandate for Reform* (Washington, D.C.: Democratic National Committee, 1970), p. 26.
4. Pitkin so termed this approach. *Concept,* p. 76.
5. These efforts have been discussed in various places that will be cited in the course of this chapter. Notable among them are Austin Ranney's "The Line of Peas: The Impact of the McGovern-Fraser Commission's Reforms and Their Probable Impact in 1972 and Beyond" (Paper delivered at the annual meeting of the Southern Political Science Association, Gatlinburg, Tenn., November 11-13, 1971); and Ranney, *Curing the Mischiefs of Faction: Party Reform in America* (Berkeley: University of California Press, 1975).
6. Whether representation is treated as an attribute of an interpersonal relationship or a system characteristic depends of course on one's observational standpoint. The importance of observational standpoint has always been emphasized by Harold D. Lasswell. The most complete explication is perhaps that found in "Person, Personality, Group, Culture," *Psychiatry 2* (1939): 533–561. This article is available in the Bobbs-Merrill reprint series on the Social Sciences, P.S. 163, and in Harold D. Lasswell, *The Analysis of Political Behavior* (New York: Oxford University Press, 1948).
7. The preconvention questionnaire was designed by Evron Kirkpatrick and myself with some participation of Warren Miller for use in the presidential campaign of Hubert Humphrey.
8. A New York-based polling organization founded by the late Elmo Wilson which conducted opinion studies in many countries.
9. There are also a good many measures that are included in one but not both of the voter studies. Where a measure was included in both voter studies, I have cited the CPS data because of the high regard in which these data are held. In fact, the two mass studies' findings are highly consistent.
10. I am convinced that in considering representation in a particular year or institutional context, such as political conventions, it is important to relate the discussion to the theory and practice of political representation more generally. I have provided a brief overview of this theory and practice with references to some relevant literature. The reader who is knowledgeable about this subject may wish to skip this discussion and go directly to page 286 where the discussion of representation in the political conventions of 1972 begins.
11. Hannah Pitkin examines and analyzes conceptions of representation in her book which has been previously cited. Charles E. Gilbert identifies five intellectual traditions concerned with representation in "Operative Doctrines of Representation," *American Political Science Review* 57 (1963): 604–618. John A. Fairlie catalogues approaches to representation in "The Nature of Political Representation I," *American Political Science Review* 34 (1940): 236–248, and "II," *American Political Science Review* 34 (1940): 456–466. The Nomos volume discussed the most important aspects of representation: J. Roland Pennock and John W. Chapman, *Representation*, Nomos X (New York: Atherton Press, 1968). Also, Dale A. Neuman, "Operative Conceptions of Political Representation in the United States: Some Preliminary Findings," *Journal of Politics* 33 (1971): 831–839. A. H. Birch, *Representative and Responsible*

Government (Toronto: The University of Toronto Press, 1964) is a useful source on the Anglo-Saxon tradition.

12. Birch, *Representative*, p. 16.

13. What I call the "embodiment" theory of representation is one variant of what Pitkin terms the "conception of representation by authorization." See her discussion of this view in Pitkin, *Concept*, pp. 38–59.

14. Harvey Mansfield, Jr., notes that "Medieval representation used 'representative machinery' to secure consent. But 'representative government' is government that uses representative machinery because it is authorized solely and entirely by consent." "Modern and Medieval Representation" in Pennock and Chapman, *Representation*, p. 78.

15. Of course, these concepts were not always associated with the theory or practice of representation. Representative institutions were initially established by strong governments who sought the help—usually financial—of notable citizens. In Charles Beard's words, "It began its career as an instrument of power and convenience in the hands of the state. . . . " Charles A. Beard, "The Teutonic Origins of Representative Government," *American Political Science Review* 26 (1932): 44. Also, Birch, *Representative*, p. 1. Also Charles A. Beard and John D. Lewis, "Representative Government in Evolution," *American Political Science Review* 26 (1932): 223–240.

16. *The Federalist* No. 52, emphasized the *modern* character of the "scheme of representation, which was "at most but very imperfectly known to ancient policy." Alexander Hamilton, John Jay and James Madison, *The Federalist* (Washington, D.C.: National Home Library Foundation), p. 343. The notion that a representative body was a substitute for a meeting of all citizens and can speak for them was expressed in the sixteenth century by Sir Thomas Smith, who wrote that the Parliament of England "representeth and hath the power of the whole realme both the head and the bodie. For everie Englishman is entended to be there present, either by person or by procuration and attornies, of whatever preheminence, state, dignitie or qualities soever he be, from the Prince (be he King or Queen) to the lowest person of England, and the consent of Parliament is taken to be everie man's consent." *De Republica Anglorum*, 1583 ed. L. Alston (Cambridge University Press, 1906), p. 49. Quoted in Beard and Lewis, "Representative Government," p. 225.

17. Beard and Lewis, "Representative Government," p. 235, assert that in modern representation, "speaking politically, all adult heads are equal and alike, each having an equal share of governing power." They also refer, p. 236, to the proposed change from a time when economic classes were represented to one which substituted "the representation of free and equal heads."

18. Some democratic governments, notably the Fifth French Republic and the German Federal Republic, have undertaken to represent individuals as incumbents of economic and social roles. However, the bodies based on these representative principles have lesser policy-making roles and most power is vested in legislative bodies which represent citizen opinion. For a good discussion of functional representation, see Herman Finer, *Theory and Practice of Modern Government*, vol. 2 (New York: The Dial Press, 1932); Carl J. Friedrich, *Constitutional Government and Democracy* (Boston: Ginn and Company, 1946); and Carl J. Friedrich, *Man and His Government* (New York: McGraw-Hill, 1963), also Pitkin, *Concept*. The representation of groups takes place in various ways in modern governments. These are discussed in a British context in Samuel Beer, *British Politics in the Collectivist Age* (New York: Alfred A. Knopf, 1965) and, briefly, in A. H. Birch, "The Theory and Practice of Representation: Some Preliminary Notes" (Paper prepared for the International Political Science Association Round Table in Warsaw, 1966).

19. Rousseau was, of course, the author of the most famous theory distinguishing between the existential opinions and the "real" will of the people. Idealist conceptions of the state typically postulate this distinction. See, e.g., Hegel, Frichte, Bosanquet. Most modern nondemocratic theories also make this distinction. For a discussion of this distinction, see R. M. MacIver, *The Web of Government* (New York: The Free Press, 1965).

20. In democratic theory and practice the legitimacy of rulers depends on their selection as representatives in lawful competitive processes. In embodiment theories of representation the ruler's claim to legitimacy rests on his prior claim to "embody" this true will or these true interests.

21. Monarchism, communism, nazism, and dictatorship in the "new" nations have all been justified by some version of the doctrine of false consciousness. For versions of this doctrine, see, e.g., J. Bodin, *Six Books of the Commonwealth* (Oxford: Blackwell, 1955), vol. I; V. I. Lenin, *Imperialism: The Last Stage of Capitalism*; A. Hitler, *Mein Kampf*; Franz Fanon, *The Wretched of the Earth* (New York: Grove Press, 1956). For an unexpected defense of this doctrine as applied to colonial peoples, see J. S. Mill, *Considerations On Representative Government*. Doctrines that postulate the existence of abstract or objective individual interests deny the individual freedom to choose or to change his identifications. They are incompatible with the premises and practice of democratic government and constitute the epistemological and moral basis of despotism. The figure of the philosopher-king who knows better than those he governs their true, objective interests is familiar to students of political philosophy: Plato's formulation in *The Republic* remains the classic statement of this doctrine. An interesting variation is John of Salisbury, *Policraticus*, trans. Dickinson (New York: Alfred A. Knopf, 1927). Most recently this doctrine has reappeared in the writings of certain theorists associated with the New Left politics, for example, Herbert Marcuse, *One Dimensional Man* (Boston: Beacon Press, 1964).

22. This distinction is grounded in the historical association of the representation of groups and interests, and of opinions with individual representation.

23. This characteristic distinguishes contemporary systems of individual representation from functional representation, which is based on a single status determined not by the individual but by the system.

24. Research on voting has demonstrated that for many, the aspects of social position most salient for elections vary through time and space.

25. *The Federalist*, No. 57, p. 372. The importance of frequent elections for securing responsiveness and accountability is emphasized repeatedly by the authors of the *Federalist Papers*. Publius makes clear that frequent elections are not only useful for the person seeking reelection must "account" for his stewardship, but also because they *limit* the power of the lawmaker. This latter aspect is sometimes overlooked in discussions of representative institutions. Note that the *limits* are the same whether or not the lawmaker seeks reelection. Earlier, in *The Federalist*, No. 52, Publius asserted: "As it is essential to liberty that the government in general should have a common interest with the people, so it is particularly essential that the branch of it under consideration should have an immediate dependence on, and an immediate sympathy with, the people. Frequent elections are unquestionably the only policy by which this dependence and sympathy can be effectively secured" (p. 343). Note that the authors of the *Federalist Papers* also expected representatives to be restrained by the fact that "they can make no law which will not have its full operation on themselves and their friends, as well as on the great mass of the society" (p. 373). These and many similar statements demonstrate that at least in American practice frequent elections have been

regarded as the principal institutional guarantee of responsiveness. The duty of those elected officials and the strategy of accountability was defined by Thomas Paine who said of representatives that they "are supposed to have the same concerns at stake which those have who appointed them, and who will act in the same manner as the whole body would act if they were present. . . ." Further, "that the *elected* might never form to themselves an interest separate from the electors, prudence will point out the propriety of having elections often." *The Writings of Thomas Paine*, ed. M. D. Conway (New York: 1894–95), vol 1, pp. 70–71; quoted in Birch, *Representative*, p. 42.

26. John Adams, "Letters to John Penn," *The Works of John Adams, Second President of the United States with A Life of the Author* (Boston: Little. Brown, 1951), vol. IV, p. 205.

27. Quoted in Fairlie, "The Nature I," p. 243.

28. In *The Federalist*, No. 35, Hamilton notes that "all that can be reasonably meant by a knowledge of the interests and feelings of the people" is that the representative "should be acquainted with the general genius, habits and modes of thinking of the people at large and with the resources of the country" (p. 216).

29. For a discussion of this theory of representation, see Pitkin, *Concept*, ch. 4. Her discussion notes that "In politics, too, representation as 'standing for' by resemblance, as being a copy of the original, is always a question of which characteristics are politically relevant for reproduction" (p. 87).

30. Hannah Pitkin's book passes almost imperceptibly from discussion of an assembly which "mirrors" opinions to one which looks like—is a visual representation of—the whole people. See Pitkin, *Concept*, ch. 4. In *The Federalist*, No. 3, Hamilton explicitly examines the idea "that all classes of citizens should have some of their own number in the representative body, in order that their feelings and interests may be the better understood and attended to" (p. 124). This argument, he says, is "very specious and seducing" but also "impracticable," "unnecessary," and "altogether visionary" (pp. 212–213). Furthermore, he asserts, "This will never happen under any arrangement that leaves the votes of the people free" (p. 21). Other major democratic theorists—Burke, Locke, Rousseau, Adams—were also concerned with representing opinions and interests, not with representing physical or social characteristics.

31. Giovanni Sartori says, ". . . parties become for some the type of political organism that most closely resembles, or should resemble, the prototype of every authentic democratic form." *Democratic Theory* (Detroit: Wayne State University Press, 1962), pp. 120–121.

32. In his book on party reform, Austin Ranney suggests that within American parties there has been a longstanding "three-cornered dispute among purists-for-representativeness, purists-for-direct-democracy, and professionals-for-competitiveness." *Curing the Mischiefs*, p. 142. And he asserts that in this dispute the purists-for-representation have most frequently carried the day. The "responsible party" debate has received most attention from academics. Important proponents have been E. E. Schattschneider, *Party Government* (New York: Farrar & Reinhart, 1942); Stephen K. Bailey, *The Condition of our National Parties* (New York: Fund for the Republic, 1959); James MacGregor Burns, *The Deadlock of Democracy* (Englewood Cliffs: Prentice-Hall, 1963); David S. Broder, *The Party's Over: The Failure of Politics in America* (New York: Harper and Row, 1972). A comprehensive review of this debate is Evron M. Kirkpatrick's " 'Toward a More Responsible Two-Party System': Political Science, Policy Science or Pseudo-Science?" *American Political Science Review* 65 (1971): 965–990, and Austin Ranney, *The Doctrine of Responsible Party Government* (Urbana, Ill.: University of Illinois Press, 1954).

33. Robert G. Dixon, Jr., emphasizes the revolution in conceptions of representation which led to the "one man, one vote" decision. See *Democratic Representation: Reapportionment in Law and Politics* (New York: Oxford University Press, 1968), pp. 3–98.
34. The guidelines are published in *Mandate for Reform*.
35. William H. Lucy, "Polls, Primaries and Presidential Nominations," *Journal of Politics* 35 (1973): 830–848, provides an account of the relations of these three.
36. David W. Abbott and Edward T. Rogowsky, "The Linkage Process: An Essay on Parties and Opinions," in *Political Parties: Leadership, Organization, Linkage*, eds. Abbott and Rogowsky (Chicago: Rand McNally, 1971), p. 518. Until 1972 the characterization of David, Goldman, and Bain remained essentially accurate: "The party conventions bring together a cross section of officialdom from the executive and legislative branches of all levels of government and from all parts of the party hierarchy." Paul T. David, Ralph M. Goldman, and Richard C. Bain, *The Politics of National Party Conventions* (Washington, D.C.: Brookings Institution, 1960), p. 343.
37. Herbert McClosky, "Are Political Conventions Undemocratic?" *New York Times Magazine*, August 4, 1968, pp. 10–11, 62–68. McClosky added, "Primaries, in fact, sometimes turn out to be the least representative since they assign the entire states' delegation to the presidential candidate who gets a plurality."
38. A good description of the traditional convention is Nelson W. Polsby, "Decision-Making at the National Convention," *Western Political Quarterly* 13 (1960): 609–619. A good description of the entire presidential nominating process is Nelson W. Polsby and Aaron B. Wildavsky, *Presidential Elections: Strategies of American Electoral Politics*, 3rd ed. (New York: Charles Scribner's Sons, 1971). Also, Aaron B. Wildavsky, "On the Superiority of National Conventions," *Review of Politics* 24 (1962): 307–319.
39. Though note that the Republican party adopted new rules that aimed at providing "timely" selection and wider representation of rank and file.
40. The absence of a contest in the Republican party doubtless enhanced the identification of the party organization and the convention.
41. The following is typical of the many popular accounts that emphasize this change:

> "Actually, there are two Democratic parties now. One was in the convention hall, relishing its ascension to power. The other, beaten and bitter, was on the sidelines. It was not just Richard Daley, but included scores of Democratic Governors, Senators, Congressmen, state party chairmen, local officeholders— all the regulars unhorsed by the McGovern reforms and outorganized by what is now the McGovern machine. Only 19 of the nation's 30 Democratic Governors came to Miami Beach, and none played a significant role." *Time*, July 24, 1972.

Theodore White noted, perceptively, "There were quite clearly two Democratic parties on the floor, and a third, far beyond Miami, watching." Theodore H. White, *The Making of the President 1972* (New York: Atheneum, 1973). p. 179.
42. The mandate is contained in the "Minority Report of the Rules Committee," adopted by the convention on August 27, 1968, *Mandate for Reform*, p. 53.
43. Ranney, *Curing the Mischiefs*, p. 153.
44. *Mandate for Reform*, p. 32.
45. In an informal endorsement of "representativeness," the Commission described *itself* as representing "all ideological and geographical elements of the Party." Ibid., p. 15.
46. Ranney, *Curing the Mischiefs*, pp. 108–109.

47. *Mandate for Reform*, p. 26.
48. Ibid., p. 10.
49. Ibid.
50. Eli Segal, chief counsel to the McGovern Commission also describes this as the purpose of the treatment of women, blacks, and youth in "Delegate Selection Standards: The Democratic Party's Experience," *George Washington Law Review* 38 (1970): 880–881.
51. No argument is made that "if a group's numerical strength at a convention is increased, then the members of that group in society at large will be inclined to accord more legitimacy to the convention's decisions," which is described as a chief justification of quotas by Dennis G. Sullivan, Jeffrey L. Pressman, Benjamin I. Page, and John J. Lyons, *The Politics of Representation: The Democratic Convention 1972* (New York: St. Martin's Press, 1974), p. 35. This book is very friendly to group quotas.
52. Note that the rationale endorsed by the commission does not provide a basis for permanent group quotas, but only for as long as may be needed to overcome the vestiges of past discrimination. The other arguments, not included in the commission report, would have provided a rationale for permanent quotas for these groups.
53. A similar assumption is, of course, made by the various "affirmative action" programs which use the absence of "appropriate" proportions of various categories of people—especially women and blacks—as prima facie evidence of discrimination. Only such an assumption can serve as the basis for regarding racial, sexual, or age "imbalance" as prima facie evidence of discrimination. There is no discussion in the report of this assumption.
54. *Mandate for Reform*, Guidelines A-1 and A-2, p. 40, and the "Summary," p. 34.
55. In *Curing the Mischiefs*, p. 114, Ranney provides some information on this point: "Many people have asked since, why only *those* groups? Why not also guarantee representation for, say, people over 65, or labor union members, or poor people? The answer is simple, if not edifying: the commissioners who believed in descriptive representation spoke only for the special interests of women, youth, and minority ethnic groups; and those of us who sought a different kind of representation did not counter by pressing for the special interests of other groups. Such political realities constitute an adequate explanation for decisions, but are obviously irrelevant to moral justification."
56. This shift of attention is consistent with the lower salience of economic questions for the elite, especially the elite (liberal Democratic) most concerned with representing the new constituencies.
57. Note that although age is a biological characteristic with a relationship to power, it has some distinctive characteristics. It is not a permanent characteristic in the way that sex and color are permanent; everyone who lives long enough is every age. Furthermore, age has a special relationship to biological and social maturation. In most political systems (except monarchy) long periods of apprenticeship typically precede access to power.
58. The scarcity of women in top political positions is a characteristic of virtually all modern governments—democratic and nondemocratic. In the contemporary world, only in India, Ceylon, and Israel have women achieved top posts, and these governments are also heavily dominated by males.
59. The "Mississippi Compromise" of 1964 provided that in subsequent years racial discrimination in party processes would be the grounds for exclusion of state delegations. The Special Equal Rights Committee asserted that "failure to comply [with the non-discrimination call] can and in our opinion will mean forfeiture of the right to be seated

at the 1968 Democratic National Convention.'' See *Report of the Special Equal Rights Committee*, April 20, 1966, on file with the Democratic National Committee. The 1968 Credentials Committee rejected quotas and the shifting of evidentiary burdens but ''In fact, the Committee's judgment was certainly affected by an evident 'under-representation' of Negroes.'' For a discussion of this, see John R. Schmidt and Wayne W. Whalen, ''Credentials Contests at the 1968 and 1972 Democratic National Convention,'' *Harvard Law Review* 82 (1969): 1445–1454.

60. This principle is most clearly reflected in the practice of giving ''bonuses'' in the form of additional votes to states carried by the party in previous elections. The courts specifically upheld this as a legitimate practice in *Bode* vs. *The National Democratic Party* (452 #F2d #1302, D.C. Cir. 1971, cert. denied 92 S.Ct. 684, 1972). The practice of American and other political parties is to take account of political affiliations as well as total numbers, awarding a larger voice within the party to groups which support the party. This practice is compatible with the view that a party should be governed by its ''members''—loosely, by persons sympathetic to it.

61. The estimates of the percent that various population categories constitute of the total party identifiers were derived from the preconvention study. The figures on women are from the CBS study. All others on delegates are derived from the delegate study. These latter differ slightly from those of other surveys (notably the CBS survey and the *Washington Post* survey) which also disagree slightly with each other. All these differences are small and without substantive importance.

62. In 1968 women comprised 13 percent of Democratic and 17 percent of Republican delegates. For a survey (though not up-to-date) of women's presence in national political conventions, see Marguerite J. Fisher and Betty Whitehead, ''Women and National Party Organization,'' *American Political Science Review* 38 (1944): 895–903. Additional comparative data on delegates are found in David, et al., *Politics*, pp. 325–354.

63. And they constituted about 19 percent of the total Democratic presidential vote in 1968, and 5 percent of the Republican. My source for this figure is Paul R. Abramson, ''Why the Democrats are No Longer the Majority Party'' (Paper prepared for delivery at the annual meeting of the American Political Science Association, New Orleans, La., September 4–8, 1973). In 1972 they cast 26 percent of the total McGovern vote according to Arthur H. Miller, Warren E. Miller, Alden S. Raine, and Thad A. Brown, ''A Majority Party in Disarray: Party Polarization in the 1972 Election'' (Paper prepared for delivery at the annual meeting of the American Political Science Association, New Orleans, La., September 4–8, 1973), p. 76.

64. The ''imbalance'' of the age composition of the two conventions is relevant to the clientele of the two groups. Gallup estimates that in 1968 persons under 30 gave Humphrey 47 percent of their votes as compared to 38 percent for Nixon and 15 percent for Wallace, and that the votes of persons over 50 split 41 percent for Humphrey, 47 percent for Nixon and 12 percent for Wallace. In 1964 71 percent of persons under 30 supported Lyndon Johnson, as compared to 63 percent over 50. In fact, voters under 30 have given 50 percent of their votes to Democratic candidates in all but two presidential elections since 1952. In 1956 they voted 57 percent to 42 percent for Eisenhower, and in 1972 they voted 52 percent to 48 percent for Nixon. If a party convention should represent its regular clientele, then one would expect to find relatively more persons over 30 at a Democratic Convention and more over 50 at a Republican Convention.

65. Lloyd A. Free and Hadley Cantril, *The Political Beliefs of Americans* (New Brunswick, N.J.: Rutgers University Press, 1967). Note that one-third of their sample did not have a grandparent born in the United States and that of these 52 percent

consider themselves Democrats as compared to 42 percent of respondents at least some of whose grandparents were born in the United States, (p. 151).

66. Charges were heard repeatedly during the period of the Democratic Convention that the "reforms" had resulted in the gross underrepresentation of those Democratic stalwarts—so-called "white ethnics." One widely broadcast charge was that of *Chicago Daily News* columnist, Mike Royko, whose column was widely reprinted. In it, he compared the "balance" of the "Singer" delegation, which was finally seated with that of the ousted Daley group. In this column addressed to Singer, Royko noted that "About half of your delegates are women. About a third of your delegates are black. Many of them are young people. You even have a few Latin Americans" but "There's only one Italian name there. . . . Are you saying that only one out of every 59 Democratic votes cast in a Chicago election is cast by an Italian? And only three of your 59 have Polish names. . . . Does that mean that only 5 percent of Chicago's voting Democrats are of Polish ancestry? . . . Your reforms have disenfranchised Chicago's white ethnic Democrats, which is a strange reform." Reprinted as a full-page advertisement in the *Miami Herald* during the convention.

67. The composition of the McGovern delegate group and of the Democratic Convention bore less resemblance to those who had voted for the party in 1968 than to those who would cast their votes for George McGovern in 1972.

68. *Mandate for Reform*, p. 41.

69. All qualify for membership in what David Apter has termed the "national elite." *Ideology and Discontent* (Glencoe, Ill.: The Free Press, 1964), pp. 38–39. Recently the social correlates of political participation have received new emphasis. Wilson, Eulau, Prewitt, Thompson, Verba and Nie, for example, have explored the links between social status and organizational participation. James Q. Wilson, *Political Organizations* (New York: Basic Books, 1973), esp. pp. 56–77. Heinz Eulau and Kenneth Prewitt, "Social Bias in Leadership Selection, Political Recruitment, and Electoral Context," *Journal of Politics* 33 (1971): 293–315; Dennis F. Thompson, *The Democratic Citizen* (Cambridge, Eng.: Cambridge University Press, 1970), pp. 53–85; Sidney Verba and Norman Nie, *Participation in America: Political Democracy and Social Equality* (New York: Harper and Row, 1972), pp. 123–223.

70. This and other figures on national population income and education are from the 1970 United States Census.

71. A growing body of evidence suggests that views on the "new issues" may be more influenced by the kind than by the amount of education and more influenced by the character of occupation than by the associated income. Gallup reported that juniors and seniors were more likely than freshmen and sophomores to support McGovern, and that students in the humanities and social sciences supported McGovern 58 percent to 37 percent as compared to students in the physical sciences, math, and engineering who supported Nixon 51 percent to 42 percent. Miller, et al., "Majority Party," report that education was related to opinion in 1972. See also Alfred O. Hero, Jr., "Liberalism-Conservatism Revisited: Foreign vs. Domestic Federal Policies, 1937–1967," *Public Opinion Quarterly* 33 (1969): 407. Also Reo M. Christenson and Patrick J. Capretta, "The Impact of College on Political Attitudes: A Research Note," *Social Science Quarterly* 49 (1968): 315–320.

72. The percent of teachers was described as a "healthy" 22 percent of the total delegates in Miami by Sullivan, et al., *Politics*, p. 24.

73. In 1952, businessmen constituted 57 percent of Republican delegates as compared to 18 percent in 1972. See David, et al., *Politics*, p. 340. The 1968 Democratic figure is from the CBS survey.

74. McClosky's classic article is Herbert McClosky, et al., "Issue Conflict and Consensus Among Party Leaders and Followers," *American Political Science Review* 54 (1960): 406–427. An aspect of mass/elite opinion which has had more attention from political scientists concerns attitudes toward the "rules" of democratic competition. See Herbert McClosky, "Consensus and Ideology in American Politics," *American Political Science Review* 58 (1964): 361–382; J. W. Prothro and C. M. Grigg, "Fundamental Principles of Democracy: Bases of Agreement and Disagreement," *Journal of Politics* 22 (1960): 276–294; S. A. Stouffer, *Communism, Conformity and Civil Liberties* (Garden City, N.Y.: Doubleday, 1955); Robert A. Dahl, *Who Governs? Democracy and Power in an American City* (New Haven: Yale University Press, 1961); Charles F. Cnudde, "Elite-Mass Relationships and Democratic Rules of the Game," *American Behavioral Scientist* 13 (1969): 189–200.
75. Ranney, *Curing the Mischiefs*, p. 196.
76. The correlations among candidate preference and various issue positions in 1972 confirmed that these two dimensions were related in 1972.
77. Adams, "Letters to John Penn."
78. The tendency of the political elite to be either more liberal or more conservative than the rank and file has been noted and documented in McClosky, et al., "Issue Conflict"; McClosky, "Consensus"; Stouffer, *Communism;* Edmond Costantini and Kenneth H. Craik, "Competing Elites Within a Political Party: A Study of Republican Leadership," *Western Political Quarterly* 22 (1969): 879–904. V. O. Key discusses political stratification and opinion on issues in *Public Opinion and American Democracy* (New York: Alfred A. Knopf, 1961), pp. 184–195. A book devoted to examining relations between mass/elite opinion in Britain is Ian Budge, *Agreement and the Stability of Democracy* (Chicago: Markham, 1970).
79. Difference scores reflect the direction of opinion, not the intensity. They were calculated simply by finding the difference between those who supported and opposed a position or group. This difference, termed a "preponderance score," reflects the consensus on an issue. If the preponderance score of a group of delegates on busing is +14 and the Democratic rank and file preponderance score is +60, then the difference score is 46. Had the delegate preponderance score been −14, then obviously the difference score would have been 74. Difference scores range from 0 to 200.
80. Data are available to check the correspondence of opinion of supporters of candidates and their preconvention mass supporters. Analysis, which will not be presented here, demonstrates that Democratic delegate groups other than Wallace's were more liberal than their rank and file, and that the Wallace group of delegates was more conservative than its mass support.
81. McClosky, et al., found large interparty elite differences on welfare state economic questions. "Issue Conflict," p. 411.
82. McClosky, et al., found that on such questions the views of the Republican rank and file were closer to the Democratic elite than their own party's elite. Ibid., p. 422.
83. Converse places respondents who evaluate parties and candidates in terms of their expected treatment of groups in the third level of ideological sophistication. I tend to think that this classification underestimates the universality with which politics is conceived in terms of groups. Philip E. Converse, "The Nature of Belief Systems of Mass Publics," in *Ideology and Discontent*, ed. David Apter (Glencoe, Ill.: The Free Press, 1967), pp. 216–217.
84. See, e.g., Philip E. Converse, W. E. Miller, J. G. Rusk and A. C. Wolfe, "Continuity and Change in American Politics: Parties and Issues in the 1968 Election," *American Political Science Review* 63 (1969): 1083–1105.

85. Miller, et al., describe the ideological gaps between Democrats who did and did not support McGovern. "Majority Party," pp. 10–13.
86. Wilson emphasizes the rise of general consensus about the enlarged powers of government in *Political Organizations*, pp. 330–332.
87. Perhaps the lower salience of economic questions for the presidential elite reflected their relatively high socioeconomic status. Perhaps it was a consequence of the diminishing role of business and labor in American politics. In any case, it is significant that among McGovern voters four times as many mentioned foreign policy as *the* principal problem as mentioned an economic problem.
88. See note 91 for specific data on the widespread presence of opinion on these issues.
89. Lasswell's conception of political perspectives emphasizes the relation to self. See especially Harold D. Lasswell, *World Politics and Personal Insecurity* (New York: McGraw-Hill, 1935), *Power and Personality* (New York: Viking, 1948), pp. 7–107. Also Lasswell and Abraham Kaplan, *Power and Society: A Framework for Political Inquiry* (New Haven: Yale University Press, 1950), esp. pp. 3–28. Robert E. Lane also emphasized the centrality of identifications in political perspectives: see especially in *Political Ideology: Why the Common Man Believes What He Does* (New York: The Free Press, 1962). Also, Lane's *Political Thinking and Consciousness* (Chicago: Markham, 1969), and "Patterns of Political Belief" in *Handbook of Political Psychology*, ed. Jeanne Knutson (Washington: Jossey-Bass, 1973). This perspective may be contrasted with those approaches that focus on cognitive aspects of belief systems as found, e.g., in Converse, "Continuity," pp. 206–261. Cantril also distinguishes between opinion which does and does not concern ego values: Hadley Cantril, *The Psychology of Social Movements* (New York: John Wiley & Sons, 1941), pp. 74–75. For a discussion of some of the issues involved, see Giovanni Sartori, "Politics, Ideology and Belief Systems," *American Political Science Review* 63 (1969): 398–411, and Roger W. Cobb, "The Belief-Systems Perspective: An Assessment of a Framework," *Journal of Politics* 35 (1973): 121–153.
90. No students of politics believe that all elements of a belief system are equally important. Converse asserts that ". . . idea elements within a belief system vary in a property we shall call *centrality*, according to the role they play in the belief system as a whole." "Continuity," p. 203. His discussion includes a useful comment on "felt" interrelations among belief, but he is principally concerned with logical constraints. (Ibid.) A suggestive critique of this emphasis on intellectual constraints is Lane, "Patterns of Political Belief," pp. 98–105. My own view is that depth interviews probably provide the most reliable basis for determining centrality, but since it is impossible to be certain that the few persons interviewed in depth are in fact representative of large collectivities, depth interviews do not solve the problem of how to determine centrality. Robert E. Lane has pushed further than anyone else the effort to determine the structure of political beliefs from long interviews with a few persons. Good examples of this approach are Lane, *Political Ideology* and *Political Thinking*. The same approach is, of course, exemplified in Robert Cole's excellent work on white southerners.
91. Over 50 percent of voters of both parties have an opinion for or against all issues and symbols discussed here. The highest percent of "neutral" responses are to the ideological labels "liberal" and "conservative," to the abstract category "black" and the "politicians." At least 70 percent have positive or negative views about other groups, and over 85 percent have positive or negative views about the specific policy areas tested—crime, welfare, busing, inflation, Southeast Asia. Note however that, as V. O. Key pointed out, there may be wide agreement on issues about which no one feels

strongly. He called this "permissive consensus" (*Public Opinion*, pp. 32–35) but might have easily called it "prohibitory consensus" since negative consensus can prohibit as well as positive consensus can permit.

92. Feeling was intense on a number of the policy areas tested. Seventy-one percent of Democratic voters and 81 percent of Republicans took the strongest possible anti-busing position. Eight percent of Democrats and 2 percent of Republicans took the strongest possible pro-busing position. Fifty percent of Democratic voters and 60 percent of Republican voters gave the strongest endorsements possible to the proposition that the able-bodied had an obligation to work; another 12 percent of Democrats and 8 percent of Republicans took the extreme opposite view—that abolishing poverty had priority over the obligation to work. Twenty-eight percent of Republicans took the extreme "anti-crime" position, while 19 percent of Democrats and 15 percent of Republicans were equally strongly committed to protecting the rights of the accused. (The extreme position on these measures is considered either one or seven on a seven-point scale.) On feeling thermometers an eleven-point scale is offered, which reduces the likelihood of respondents choosing the "extreme" position, but nonetheless, 35 percent of Democratic voters and 40 percent of Republicans took the strongest possible "anti" demonstrator position; approximately 27 percent of each group offered the strongest possible support for the police, and 21 percent of both for the military.

93. Forty-four percent of Democratic and 36 percent of Republican party identifiers described busing as very important to them in deciding how to vote; 75 percent of Democrats and 68 percent of Republicans said it was at least somewhat important. Fifty-five percent of Democratic and 56 percent of Republican voters reported that the question of welfare vs. work was very important, while 88 percent of Democrats and 90 percent of Republicans said it would be at least somewhat important in deciding their vote for president. Sixty percent of Democrats and 53 percent of Republicans described government initiative in solving inflation as very important, while 89 percent and 87 percent respectively said it was at least somewhat important in determining their vote.

94. Responses to questions about "the most important problem facing this country" confirm the existence of large discontinuities between the Democratic elite and rank and file but offer only limited confirmation to the importance of the issues separating Democratic elite and rank and file. Voters—87 percent of Democrats and 82 percent of Republicans—mentioned an economic issue in answer to this question: the high cost of living, high taxes, unemployment, and related "pocketbook issues." Law and order ranked second, with 62 percent of Democrats and 65 percent of Republicans; Vietnam ranked a close third with 62 percent of Democrats and 59 percent of Republicans; 31 percent of Democratic voters and 21 percent of Republicans mentioned race relations as a major problem.

95. A factor analysis provides still further confirmation of the centrality of many of these issues and groups to voters in 1972. Busing, civil rights leaders, liberals, black militants, welfare recipients, and political demonstrators are all importantly related to the most inclusive issue dimension. Police, the military, politicians, and courts comprise a second factor. Busing, crime, police, conservatives, and the military are linked in a factor. At the elite level interconnections are still stronger and broader—busing, crime, conservatives, liberals, black militants, welfare policy, civil rights leaders, the military, welfare recipients, political demonstrators, and women's liberation occur in the same most inclusive factor. An example of the use of factor analysis to explore centrality is Norman R. Luttbeg, "The Structure of Beliefs among Leaders and the Public," *Public Opinion Quarterly* 32 (1968): 398–409. (The criterion for inclusion in each of these factors was .4 or above.)

96. I am using the term "culture" in the sense that it is normally used in the social sciences, namely, to refer to patterns of meaning, to the web of values, valuations, cognitions, goals, and symbols characteristic of a group. Some important components of political culture are conceptions of citizenship, authority, legitimacy, and obligation, of the appropriate application of deprivations and indulgence, of the appropriate spheres of government activity, and of the appropriate modes of political behavior of government and in politics. Political culture is not the only aspect of culture which may be involved in the political arena. Other aspects of culture, such as work and child-rearing, may become political issues. Culture may be analytically differentiated from society as the system of identifications, beliefs, and goals associated with patterned behavior. This conception of culture is broader than that found in some recent discussions that use cultural issues to refer to more limited phenomena, such as drugs, abortion, women's liberation, and rock festivals. See, e.g., Teresa Levitan and Warren E. Miller, "The New Politics and Partisan Realignment." (Paper delivered at the annual meeting of the American Political Science Association, Washington, D.C., September 5–9, 1972). A somewhat broader conception of culture, but one still narrower than that employed here is found in Miller, et al., "Majority Party." As I am using the term, culture includes clashing conceptions of authority, of indulgences and deprivations, and of socialization; that is, it includes a large part of what has been termed the "social issue" by Richard M. Scammon and Ben J. Wattenberg, *The Real Majority* (New York: Coward-McCann, 1970). I have dealt with the salience of culture in the 1972 elections in Jeane Kirkpatrick, "The Revolt of the Masses," *Commentary*, 2 (1973): 58–62. Related explanations of the politics of 1972 are Seymour Martin Lipset and Earl Raab, "The Election and the National Mood," *Commentary*, 1 (1973): 43–50. Also, Michael Novak, *The Rise of the Unmeltable Ethnics: Politics and Culture in the Seventies* (New York: Macmillan, 1971).

97. This relationship is illustrated in a letter disseminated by supporters of Alabama Governor George Wallace which stated the governor's concern with five issues. One read, "I am concerned that most politicans in Washington want to take a lot of your money and give a guaranteed income to people even if they are healthy and refuse to work," quoted in the column of William J. Buckley, Jr., published in the *International Herald Tribune*, July 4, 1974.

98. V. O. Key noted the prevalence of consensus among the electorate on many such "concrete but broad questions of public policy." *Public Opinion*, p. 50.

99. Both the candidate support groups included persons with diverse views, suggesting that a good deal of issue aggregation had gone on *within* these groups.

100. Wilson emphasizes the rise of general consensus about the enlarged powers of government in *Political Organizations*, pp. 330–332.

101. McClosky, et al., "Issue Conflict," p. 423.

102. *Time*, July 17, 1972. More conservative estimates in the McGovern camp gave their candidate a net plurality of 3.6 million votes among young voters (*The National Journal*, September 23, 1972, p. 1504). Note that at the same time that McGovern strategists predicted a youth landslide for their candidate, psephologist Richard Scammon predicted that the youth vote would divide about like that of their parents—with perhaps 5 percent to 10 percent more liberal (Ibid.). Scammon's prediction proved correct, as the votes of persons 18 to 30 split almost evenly between McGovern and Nixon. Note also that Fred Dutton, author of the most optimistic estimate, was an active and influential member of the McGovern Commission.

103. In its vulnerability to an ideologically unified, well-coordinated nationwide campaign the "reformed" Democratic party was not unique. The Goldwater phenomena of 1964 had demonstrated that an unreformed convention could be taken by a movement that did not enjoy the support of a majority of the party. Note though that Leon D. Epstein points out that in Wisconsin the McGovern and Goldwater candidacies had a very different impact on their respective parties' voters, "Who Voted for McGovern: The Wisconsin Case," *American Politics Quarterly* 1 (1973): 465–477.

104. On this question, see especially Austin Ranney and Leon D. Epstein, "The Two Electorates: Voters and Non-Voters in a Wisconsin Primary," *Journal of Politics* 28 (1966): 598–616; Ranney, "Turnout and Representation in Presidential Primary Elections," *American Political Science Review* 66 (1972): 21–37; and Ranney, "The Representativeness of Primary Electorates," *Midwest Journal of Political Science* 12 (1968): 224–238.

105. The friend in question is Richard Schifter, a paragon of effective citizen participation.

106. Wilson, *Political Organizations*.

107. Voters who do not turn out also cannot "screen out" persons whose views and values are not acceptable to the constituency, a function the late V. O. Key, Jr. described as one of the important sanctions available to force compliance with constituency opinion. *Public Opinion*.

108. Walter Bagehot, quoted in Birch, *Representative*, p. 124. See his discussion of this point as applied to Britain on pp. 124–125. Also David Butler, "The Paradox of Party Difference," *The American Behavioral Scientist* 4, no. 3 (1960): 3–5.

109. Especially James Q. Wilson, *The Amateur Democrat: Club Politics in Three Cities* (Chicago: University of Chicago Press, 1962); Leon D. Epstein, *Political Parties in Western Democracies* (New York: Frederick A. Praeger, 1967); Dennis S. Ippolito, "Motivational Reorientation and Change Among Party Activists," *Journal of Politics* 31 (1969) 1098–1101; Francis Carney, *The Rise of Democratic Clubs in California* (New York: Holt, Rinehart, and Winston, 1958); Stephen A. Mitchell, *Elm Street Politics* (New York: Oceana Publications, 1959); Robert H. Salisbury, "The Urban Party Organization Member," *Public Opinion Quarterly* 29 (1965–66): 550–564.

110. The Illinois case is, of course, different. The ousting of the delegation elected in the primary and headed by Richard Daley and its replacement by the pro-McGovern "Singer" group affected the political composition of the convention. But it would doubtless have been possible for the Daley delegation to have had the prescribed racial, sexual, and age "balance" without having altered its political composition.

111. The priority of political over sexual identifications was most dramatically demonstrated when scores of female McGovern delegates voted—for political reasons—against the Women's Caucus challenge to the seating of South Carolina and against a more liberal abortion plank in the Democratic platform.

112. The view that people can only be *truly* represented by someone like themselves is enormously influential in our times. As developed by some critics of democracy, the observation that elected representatives are drawn from relatively privileged strata of society *proves* that "representative" government is fundamentally a sham perpetrated by a ruling class on a gullible mass who only thinks it "chooses" its leaders. Others conclude only that the system of representation should be overhauled. The most impressive version of this view is Roberto Michels, *Political Parties: A Sociological Study of the Oligarchical Tendencies of Modern Democracy* (Glencoe, Ill.: The Free Press, 1949). Also, C. Wright Mills, *The Power Elite* (New York: Oxford University Press, 1956), and Floyd Hunter, *Community Power Structure* (Chapel Hill: University of North Carolina Press, 1953), and *Top Leadership, U.S.A.* (Chapel Hill: University of North Carolina Press, 1959).

113. A politics dominated by symbol specialists is likely to differ in both style and substance from a politics in which businessmen and workers are more numerous. The business

and trade union ethos alike stress material concerns and self-interest. Professionals tend to be more interested in rectitude and power than in the pursuit of material rewards. Harold D. Lasswell notes some special characteristics of such politics in *Power and Personality*, pp. 47–50. Also Lasswell and Daniel P. Lerner, eds., *World Revolutionary Elites: Studies in Coercive Ideological Movements* (Cambridge: MIT Press, 1965); Talcott Parsons, *Essays in Sociological Theory: Pure and Applied* (Glencoe, Ill.: The Free Press, 1949), p. 186; F. A. Hayek, "The Intellectuals and Socialism," *University of Chicago Law Review* (1949): 417; and Wilson, *Amateur Democrat*, p. 62. A politics dominated by symbol specialists will have a higher ideological content and a lower concern for goods and services; the political process will be conceived rather more as an arena for debating and resolving moral questions and less as an arena for maximizing and compromising material interests.

I discuss the problems of making national conventions representative in more detail in Kirkpatrick, "Representation," *British Journal of Political Science* 5 (1975): 313–322.

CHAPTER 11

A New Politics?

Almost all observers of American politics have been impressed by accumulating symptoms of change. This book, which is also concerned with change, views presidential politics from the perspective of the delegates to the two conventions in 1972. Those delegates were not only in the position to influence convention decisions, they comprised a cross section of activists in both parties. They were not strictly representative of all activists engaged in presidential politics in 1972, nor did they reflect exactly the persons who are active in presidential politics today. Issues change, people change, the relative influence of the various factions changes. However, the delegates to the 1972 conventions reflected all the major political tendencies in contemporary American politics, and while the politics of 1976 is not identical with that of 1972, there is substantial continuity. The war has ended but many of the antiwar activists have remained active in politics. Indeed, as James Sundquist noted, "In many places, the anti-Vietnam firebrands are now leaders of the party."[1] There is no contemporary equivalent of the McGovern movement, but the Democratic forums demonstrate the continued presence of many of the people and concerns who coalesced around that movement. Although American parties are characterized by high turnover and responsiveness to rapidly changing social and political concerns, there is nonetheless substantial continuity within the political elite from one presidential election to the next. The 1972 Democratic Convention was a legitimate successor to the 1968 convention, whose majority abolished the unit rule and authorized creation of a commission on party reform whose explicit purpose was to "open" the party. The McGovern majority in the 1972 convention was a more numerous version of the "peace" delegates of 1968 who precipitated a searing debate on Vietnam policy. Neither the McCarthy, the Mc-Govern, the Goldwater, nor the Wallace movements burst upon the national stage between conventions. Persons sharing the perspectives associated with each were present in their party's conventions before and after the conventions at which each movement made its greatest impact on presidential politics. Observation and experience alike argue that the perspectives that shaped the presidential politics of 1972 will not rapidly disappear from the national political scene, particularly since rules changes reinforce and stabilize some of the trends of the past decade. The previous chapters have described the diverse characteristics of delegates to the two conventions that I believe to be significant for understanding contemporary presidential politics. This chapter recapitulates an interpretation of contemporary politics to which the data and arguments are relevant. The following chapters analyze and describe the role of women in the presidential elite.

The entire analysis rests on the assumption that an institution, such as a political party, lasts just as long as participants in that institution share expectations about what it should do and what they should do. When the understandings and goals of participants change, the institution changes. Elites are participants with a strategic impact on the stability of institutions.

Three principal hypotheses guided the inquiry: that there were among the delegates to the two conventions new political types whose personal and political goals, resources, and ideological styles differed in identifiable ways from those of the people who have dominated American politics since at least World War II; that the goals, expectations, and styles of some new political types are incompatible with the established patterns of institutional behavior and with conventional descriptions of American parties; and that the changing characteristics of the parties' elites may have adverse consequences for the capacity of the parties to aggregate and integrate diverse interests and perspectives and to represent the party rank and file.

The absence of strictly comparable data on past convention delegates is an obvious handicap, but is not ultimately disabling. Enough data exist on certain social and political characteristics of delegates to earlier conventions to establish the fact and direction of the changing composition of the elite with regard to certain important characteristics including occupation, education, religion, and past experience in party and public office. More important are the numerous descriptions of American party leadership provided by observers. Some of these, such as Samuel Eldersveld's careful and suggestive study of Detroit, focus on local activists and party leaders; some are based on what we have come to call "empirical" research (interviews with or a quantified description of a specified population), some are not. Some, such as the enormously useful Nelson Polsby and Aaron Wildavsky volumes,[2] collect, integrate, analyze, and interpret available information on the nominating process. And there are other accounts, among which Theodore White's chronicles[3] are notable, that reflect the opinions, observations, and interpretations of persons who have more or less closely and more or less insightfully observed the political scene. It is not true that there exists no base line for measuring "change" in the elite of the presidential parties. It did not require a survey of delegates to the 1960 and 1964 Republican conventions to establish that some significant changes had occurred, nor a survey of delegates to the 1964, 1968, and 1972 Democratic conventions to confirm that significant change was in progress. Knowledge of these events has about the same status as most of our knowledge of the world.

This book could not and did not attempt to measure a sample of 1972 delegate population against a comparable sample of previous delegates; it has attempted to identify some ways in which the 1972 delegates differed from the available description of previous party elites and to describe some characteristics of 1972 delegates that may have special importance for the future of American presidential politics. A special effort was made to identify incipient trends. Although there is more discussion today about the possible disappearance or disintegration of the Republican party, most of the dramatic evidences of change were discernible in the heterogeneous Democratic party. The most important of these evidences of change concerned the following:

1) changing incentives to political participation among effective activists in presidential politics, notably the presence of significant numbers of delegates for whom support for party was not a significant incentive to political activity;
2) changing attitudes toward organizational maintenance, notably the presence of significant numbers of Democrats with negative attitudes toward those practices generally regarded as necessary to preserving an organization;
3) changing ideological styles, notably the rise of holistic, internally consistent ideologies at both ends of the political spectrum;
4) changing patterns of the "group basis" of presidential parties, notably the rise of "constituencies" based on race, sex, age, and candidate preference and a concomitant decline in the concern of some political activists for those geographical constituencies that are the traditional units of American politics and the basis of the federal system; and
5) changing social composition of the political elite, notably a continued decline in the political role of labor and business and the continuing rise in the political influence of symbol specialists.

Two aspects of these changes deserve special note: they are related to age, experience, and social structure in ways that indicate trends, not merely temporary fluctuations in personnel, and they are so interrelated as to complement and reinforce one another. Younger and less experienced delegates had weaker attachment to party, less interest in organizational maintenance, and more comprehensive, intense, consistent ideologies. Similarly, persons for whom attachment to party was not an important motivation to political activity were also those most likely to have negative attitudes to organizational maintenance, to have holistic, comprehensive, consistent, intensely held ideologies and most likely to prefer demographic and candidate groups as units of political action and to be engaged in occupations that feature symbol manipulation.

Continuation of these trends will almost surely create increasing difficulties for the preservation of aggregative, pragmatic, stable two-party politics. The remainder of this chapter discusses some of the implications and consequences of these trends.

First, changing patterns of incentives. The presence in decision-making roles of substantial numbers of persons whose motivation to political participation is independent of party should have a major impact on the stability of parties, their aggregative potential, and their electoral strategies.

Strong attachment to a party is a source of diffuse (as compared to specific) support.[4] Attachment to a party constitutes a focus of identification that links together all those who share it. In the American system (and other enduring two-party systems), it has generally been a more inclusive symbol of identification than a particular issue or candidate. Therefore, loyalty to party modifies the impact of disagreement on specific issues. It provides a context of shared identification and common interest (in the welfare of the party) within which conflicting interests and perspectives can be reconciled or compromised. If a party's decision makers do not feel an attachment to party that transcends a particular election or issue, an important incentive to compromise is removed.

Attachment to party provides a reason for tolerating frustration of particular policies, goals, and ambitions and preferring "voice" or acquiescence over "exit,"[5] because when there is genuine identification with party, personal collective goals (that is, satisfactions derived from the successes of the party) are real and the promise of sharing in a collective reward—victory of one's party—remains even if one's preferred candidate or platform is defeated.

Weakening attachment to party among decision makers not only increases the likelihood that decisions will be made without regard to organizational well-being, it affects electoral strategies and may diminish concern with winning. Note that concern with winning constitutes another incentive to compromise. When a decision maker's focus of loyalty and identification is a subgroup of the party (based on an issue, candidate, or some other more restricted symbol of identification), then "winning" may be conceived in terms of the subgroup rather than the party. Victory for a faction is not identical with victory for a party. Where factional identifications are stronger than party identification, intraparty goals frequently take precedence over interparty victory. In fact, a good many Democratic delegates who were motivated more by attachment to policy than party did not give high priority to winning the election.

We know from the study of other political systems (and minor parties in the American system) that political parties may pursue goals other than electoral victory. A party's leadership may value self-expression more than winning and may see an electoral campaign more as an opportunity for the education and moral edification of voters than as a chance to win control of government. It may seek long-range goals to which victory in a particular election campaign is seen as irrelevant. Its leaders may be more interested in consolidating their own power within the organization than in winning an election.

The assumption that winning elections is the prime goal of political leaders and parties is the foundation of the theory and practice of two-party politics as we have known it. American (and British) parties have featured widespread, relatively stable identification of voters with one of two major parties who are locked in a continuing competition to win elections (and control of government). The assumption that political leaders desire above all to win elections is the foundation of most models of party competition (for example, Anthony Downs, and Richard Scammon and Ben Wattenberg).[6] The desire of parties to win leads them to endorse platforms and choose candidates believed to be acceptable to a majority of voters and to seek to accommodate diverse interests and perspectives. *The assumption that parties will continue to make winning elections their principal goal is the basis of an expectation that American parties will continue to be inclusive, aggregative, pragmatic, responsive, and representative. Any deemphasis on winning elections would profoundly alter the fundamental character of the American parties by removing the "discipline of the market."* But, in fact, a substantial number of persons who did not give top priority to winning were present among the delegates to the two conventions. Most Democrats for whom party solidarity was not a motive to activity also had negative attitudes to organizational maintenance. They opposed practices normally regarded as important to recruiting and retaining members and training leaders; they declined to take account of the impact of decisions on organization. In short, some Democrats did not conceive of themselves as having responsibility for the well-being and future of the organization; they did not accept organizational constraints as binding on their decisions.

The most direct effect of decision makers with a negative attitude toward organizational maintenance will almost surely be the weakening of the organization itself. An organization almost exclusively based on intangible and/or collective benefits is difficult to maintain at best. One held together only by a shared cause has a still more tenuous existence. James Q. Wilson has argued with particular clarity that the dramatic decline in the importance and prestige of material benefits has already left American parties heavily dependent on solidary and ideological incentives.[7] Organizations dependent on solidary incentives require careful nurturing of identification, of the feeling of "belonging" and solidarity; these are the rewards for loyalty. Such organizations must be carefully guarded against divisiveness and interpersonal unpleasantness. But the rising importance of issues in American politics and the increasing prestige of ideology as an incentive to political action give "issues" growing importance in political organizations, and "issues" are very divisive. They have already appeared in several "movements" (McCarthy, McGovern, and Wallace) based on principle and personality that valued spontaneity and resisted institutionalization. It is most striking that a good many McGovern and Wallace supporters who disagreed intensely on almost all substantive issues resembled one another in their organizational and ideological styles. Both these movements were ad hoc organizations bound together by shared commitment to specified policies and an explicit disdain for bureaucratic political structures, relationships, and preoccupations. It is fascinating that many followers of both had a propinquity for direct action (marches, massive resistance, demonstrations), that is, for a type of political action characteristic of systems with weak institutionalization.

Weak parties would appear to be the principal result of decisions made by persons who accept no responsibility for organizational maintenance, and weak parties cannot contain or channel the demands of a mobilized population. American political parties are not bureaucratic structures which can act through an established chain of command. They depend on the dedication, intelligence, and skill of the volunteers who act in their name to do what needs to be done within the broad framework of some broad basic understandings. Their institutional strength is heavily dependent on the policies of those who at any given time "are" the party. Low organizational concern on the part of persons occupying influential roles will result in further weakening already weak institutions.

Though the reform of the Democratic party was accompanied by repeated references to the desirability of more responsible parties, in retrospect it is clear that those reforms significantly weakened that party. While responsible party advocates have desired "centralized, disciplined, and cohesive national bodies dedicated to formulating, expounding, and implementing policy programs,"[8] the principal demands of the post-1968 Democratic reformers concerned access and participation. While the responsible party tradition requires strengthening party organization as well as clarifying and implementing programs, the McGovern-Fraser reforms stood in what Noble Cunningham, Richard Hofstadter, Allan Sindler, and Austin Ranney have termed the anti-party tradition[9] that views party organization as an obstacle to popular government and seeks through such mechanisms as the direct primary and the "open" party to bypass an "entrenched" party leadership.

That the declining cohesion of the majority party should have occurred alongside the rise of "direct" action (marches, massive resistance, demonstrations, violence) is important; that both should have occurred during a period of rising challenges to the legitimacy of government, declining confidence in the society's basic institutions, decreasing voter attachment to the parties (as reflected in split ticket voting and the success of "independents"), and declining levels of party identification clarifies the significance of the process. That this entire process occurs alongside the rising salience of issues in American politics is, of course, enormously suggestive.

The fact that issues achieved new importance during a period when bread and butter issues were *not* salient violates some firmly held expectations about what moves and does not move voters. The nature of the issues and the scope and the intensity of responses indicated that basic values had become involved in the presidential politics of 1964, 1968, and 1972. Disagreements between and within the parties (especially the Democratic party) proved unusually difficult to compromise because their scope was wide and the associated feeling intense. Compromise was also made more difficult by the fact that many persons most concerned about the issues were also least concerned about party and winning and had least confidence in the system.

An interesting correlative to these trends is the rise to political prominence of a new social type whom, following Harold Lasswell, I have termed "symbol specialists." The declining role of businessmen in presidential politics and the rising importance of professionals, especially symbol specialists has been predicted and noted by various commentators on industrial and post-industrial society. This process is related to, but not identical with, the rise of the managerial class. Symbol specialists share with managers a position based on skills deriving from higher education rather than one based on wealth, ownership, or heredity. But the nature of their skills is substantially different, as is their social and economic position. Managers are specialists in the organization, production, and transmission of goods and services. Their skills are highly compensated, and their economic interest and social status are closely allied to those of the owners of the enterprises which they manage. Symbol specialists are experts in the production, manipulation, and communication of the symbols with which we interpret events, define goals, and attribute meanings. These are the teachers, advertisers, journalists, clergy, and other wordsmiths, including publishers and commentators. But symbol specialists not only communicate values and myths, they are also guardians, destroyers, and creators of the collective myths that bind together and rip apart communities and societies. A society that does not reward its symbol specialists neglects its foundations, for, as many political philosophers have understood, a society that loses its sense of rectitude does not long endure. It is symbol specialists who manipulate and ultimately control common understandings of the meaning and morality of events.[10] The evolution of the welfare state in capitalist nations demonstrates that capitalists are not compulsively driven to maximize profits—as Marx believed. But there is a good deal of evidence that they are obsessively concerned with "practical" material outcomes and have always underestimated the importance of symbols and symbol smiths. Symbol specialists, who have achieved power in most of the twentieth century's revolutionary regimes (communist, fascist, nationalist) receive relatively low financial, power, and status rewards in democratic, capitalist regimes—a fact that may or may not be related to the generally low opinion writers, teachers, clergy, and moralists have held of bourgeois societies.

Symbol specialists' enhanced role in American politics reflects the increased importance of symbol manipulation under conditions of mass communications and the elevated prestige of symbol skills in a society that features a huge educated class. Governments and politicians always stand in need of symbol skills, but the rise of electronic media—especially television—has greatly increased the political importance of symbols. The number of symbol specialists has multiplied alongside their ever-growing potential audience of relatively highly educated persons who value the persuasive skills.

I do not argue here that American politics has fallen under the sway of a communications-based knowledge elite, but that presidential politics is heavily dominated by professionals and others (e.g., housewives) of similar education and that the training and skills of such persons predispose them to value persuasive skills above, for example, negotiating skills, physical strength, courage, business, or legislative accomplishments.[11]

It is not inevitable that American politics should be dominated by symbol specialists or highly educated professionals, but *the importance of public relations image and style assures that communications specialists will play a significant role. And the adoption of presidential nomination and delegate selection processes that make success dependent on self-presentation gives communication skills a special value, so does the salience of ideology and style in politics.* The relatively high prestige of symbol specialists also constitutes a political asset of large importance.

The political role of symbol specialists is important to just the extent that they have distinctive perspectives on American politics. And as this analysis demonstrates beyond reasonable doubt, while these delegates did not hold a single point of view, they, more than any other occupational group, were carriers of new ideological and organizational styles.

Because many symbol specialists stand in an adversary posture vis-à-vis the dominant culture, the process of demoralization of traditional myths, understandings, and beliefs can be expected to continue, and because persuasive moral criticism requires a standard against which to measure existing institutions, the creation and/or introduction of alternative conceptions of legitimacy—the remoralization of politics—can be expected to proceed apace. Both processes—of demoralization and remoralization—are far advanced. The politics of demoralization proceeds by calling into question the justice or fairness or morality of outcomes, the legitimacy of procedures, and the authority of agents of government. This process has become a familiar aspect of contemporary politics. The process of remoralization provides new criteria for resolving debates, distributing scarce resources, and establishing legitimacy and authority in the light of which past and present policies may be judged. Both processes involve rejecting old values and standards of value in favor of new values and standards of value. Both processes proceed by linking small questions to large ones and treating policy problems as moral issues. Of course, all this expands the scope of conflict, heightens its intensity, and complicates its resolution.

The fact that so many symbol specialists are critics and opponents of the traditional culture and that they have an important influence on the focus of attention and the formulation of issues has an impact on the capacity of the parties to represent voters, most of whom are attached to traditional views and values.

As Table 11-1 demonstrates, the views of Democratic symbol specialists and students (many of whom are doubtless on their way to becoming symbol specialists) were least representative of the views of rank and file Democrats; and material specialists' views were closest to those of Democratic identifiers. (The mean difference between Democratic students and rank and file was 75.5; of symbol specialists and rank and file, 72.2; of lawyers and rank and file, 48.9; housewives and rank and file, 63.5; and material specialists and rank and file, 33.6.) These differences are large enough and consistent enough to be taken seriously. Still, the differences between symbol specialists and rank and file were not as great as those between McGovern delegates and the rank and file. (See Table 10-9.) The facts that some symbol specialists were found supporting each of the candidates and that in the Republican party symbol specialists were *not* so remote from their party's rank and file (Table 11–2) make clear (in case anyone ever doubted it) that perspectives do not necessarily follow occupation. But various middle-class occupational groups present at the Democratic Convention did have distinctive orientations to both ideology and organization. A recent study of the political views of university professors by Lipset and Ladd confirms that the distinctive character-

Table 11-1. Difference Scores: Democrats

	Democratic Categories of Delegates from Democratic Rank and File				
	Symbol Special-ists	Lawyers	Material Special-ists	Housewives	Students
Welfare	97	71	41	96	105
Busing	137	105	61	130	139
Crime	101	96	34	97	108
Civil rights leaders	92	72	40	70	91
Welfare recipients	74	54	47	71	70
Political demonstrators	118	71	65	101	119
Police	26	5	3	17	61
Military	71	35	4	74	121
Blacks	39	24	35	33	29
Conservatives	79	61	40	71	81
Liberals	70	39	14	54	51
Union leaders	17	15	12	14	0
Politicians	64	64	65	52	42
Inflation	14	0	8	19	6
Abortion	74	65	44	84	103
Laying off women first	58	32	36	44	62
Women's liberation	51	5	14	35	73
Business interests	55	24	14	41	53
Black militants	99	52	46	64	82
Vietnam	98	74	70	98	114
Ideological self-classification	82	63	13	68	76
Mean difference	72.2	48.9	33.6	63.5	75.5

NOTE: The difference scores were computed from preponderance scores carried to the first decimal point.

istics of symbol specialists at the Democratic Convention were not an accidental by-product of the McGovern candidacy.[12] The characteristics of Democratic symbol specialists have much greater importance than those of Republicans since persons in these professions are overwhelmingly Democratic.

Talcott Parsons long ago pointed out that the rise of the professional

Table 11-2. Difference Scores: Republicans

	Republican Categories of Delegates from Republican Rank and File				
	Symbol Specialists	Lawyers	Material Specialists	Housewives	Students
Welfare	1	3	16	16	22
Busing	8	23	0	7	12
Crime	20	12	7	13	128
Civil rights leaders	33	9	5	23	124
Welfare recipients	36	6	15	18	4
Political demonstrators	6	3	26	1	49
Police	12	5	20	18	21
Military	10	6	35	27	59
Blacks	47	35	44	47	71
Conservatives	17	26	28	4	13
Liberals	18	33	39	38	42
Union leaders	12	10	9	24	28
Politicians	65	81	89	95	31
Inflation	3	36	5	27	1
Abortion	31	37	25	58	109
Laying off women first	38	62	8	22	74
Women's liberation	35	39	35	24	57
Business interests	25	5	25	2	3
Black militants	17	5	20	3	11
Vietnam	68	10	52	33	15
Ideological self-classification	0	0	17	9	0
Mean difference	23.9	21.2	24.8	24.2	41.6

NOTE: The difference scores were computed from preponderance scores carried to the first decimal point.

classes enhanced the importance of the processes and institutions through which they were recruited and trained, notably the universities.[13] It also enhances interest in the distribution of the resources of that class. From the rising influence of the verbalist professionals it should also have been possible to predict the development of culture classes and a culture class struggle. The growing power of the professional verbalist elite greatly enhances the importance of the distribution of related educational resources in the society, accentuates their unequal distribution in the population, and illuminates the existence of a deprived class. Each value can and does serve as the basis of a class structure; class struggles occur when events dramatize the importance of a value distribution to the lives of the relatively deprived. The American culture class struggle emerged after the development and consolidation of power by a cultural elite— comprising persons of relatively high education and specialized skills who shared values and perspectives different from those of the majority. That class struggle became the basis of the Wallace revolt, the Nixon victory, and several interesting hypotheses concerning the future of the American party system.[14]

Another aspect of the elite politics of 1972 that has especially interesting implications for the future concerns the relations between secularism and politics. Unlike sex, age, color, state, or candidate preference, no special effort was made to make sure that various religious persuasions were represented in the convention. But differences in religious preference turn out to have been strongly associated with candidate preference and ideological and organizational style. There was little difference in the political orientations of Catholics and Protestants. Both tended toward traditional political styles: toward moderate, eclectic, ideological views and toward party solidarity as well as policy interests. Atheist and agnostic delegates, in contrast, were most likely to be "purists" in politics motivated by issue commitments, unconcerned about party, very liberal to radical in ideology, very liberal in cultural orientation, and very likely to have comprehensive, internally consistent ideological orientations. Jewish delegates more closely resembled the atheist–agnostic delegates in political style. (See Tables 11–3, 11–4, and 11–5.) (Once again, Wallace delegates were an exception to the dominant pattern: they combined intense comprehensive ideological perspectives with strong Protestant religious identifications.) This is not the appropriate place to speculate on why persons who have abandoned religion are especially susceptible to more comprehensive, extreme, change-oriented political ideologies, but the marked association between the two is suggestive. The relations between religion and political style indicate a trend from a politics dominated by Protestant and Catholic leaders to a politics based on secular assumptions[15] and dominated by a non-Christian elite. The relations between

Table 11-3. Ideological Substance and Style by Religious Preference (%)

		Protestant	Catholic	Jewish	Atheist - Agnostic
Ideological Self-Classification					
Radical		2	4	6	16
Very liberal		15	25	54	56
Somewhat liberal		21	29	30	16
Moderate		25	25	7	7
Somewhat conservative		28	13	3	5
Very conservative		8	4	0	1
N =		1301	492	162	358
Political Culture					
Very liberal	1	18	27	37	67
	2	27	32	52	28
	3	36	27	10	6
Very conservative	4	19	13	1	0
Holism					
Very eclectic		10	9	5	5
Eclectic		56	51	50	29
Programmatic		25	34	36	42
Holist		8	6	10	25
Domestic Policy – Intensity					
Low	1	12	11	3	5
	2	45	47	29	22
High	3	43	42	67	73
Foreign Policy – Intensity					
Low	1	2	0	0	0
	2	43	43	25	12
High	3	55	57	75	88
Weighted *N* (interview) =		2161	810	308	291
Weighted *N* (intersect) =		1217	404	181	184

NOTE: Ideological self-classification is from the mail questionaires; foreign policy intensity from the interviews; the remainder of the above measures are from the intersect sample. For a complete explanation of these indexes, see Appendix C.

religion and political style underscore the cultural dimensions of the politics of 1972 and *suggest that ideological politics may be a by-product of growing secularism—as if the abandonment of other worldly religions enhanced the attractions of ideological politics.*

McGovern delegates stood at one end of the 1972 ideological spectrum; Wallace delegates, at the other. Both were characterized by relatively intense, highly ideological world views that linked diverse issues into more comprehensive political perspectives. These perspectives had much in common: they emphasized ideological commitment over organizational identifications; they featured relatively comprehensive internally consistent ideologies rather than eclectic orientations. They saw foreign policy, governmental legitimacy, domestic policy, and party disputes as aspects of a larger struggle. Both had distinctive social composition: symbol

Table 11-4. Organizational Style by Religious Preference (%)

		Protestant	Catholic	Jewish	Atheist–Agnostic
Specialists					
Solidary specialists		14	11	6	3
Rectitude specialists		19	24	48	55
Synthesizers		65	61	42	39
Neither important		2	4	4	4
Solidarity					
Low	1	6	11	29	32
	2	13	18	25	31
	3	35	33	29	21
High	4	47	37	16	16
Policy Orientation					
Low	1	4	3	1	4
	2	30	30	17	12
	3	47	44	48	38
High	4	20	23	35	47
N =		974	361	116	260

NOTE: These data are from the mail questionnaires. For a complete explanation of these indexes, see Appendix C. *N*'s are from the solidarity table; other *N*'s are comparable in size.

specialists were most numerous in McGovern ranks; self-employed persons, in the Wallace group. Both had distinctive religious orientations: Jews, atheists, and agnostics were most numerous in McGovern ranks; Protestants, in the Wallace group. Wallace delegates were most unequivocally committed to a defense of traditional political culture; McGovern delegates were most unequivocally engaged in challenging that culture.

What are the implications of these patterns for the present and future? The issues of 1976 are different from those of 1971; so are the candidates. Once again the Republicans have an incumbent, but this time it is the heir of Watergate, a man who was never chosen by his party to run for national office, never elected by the voters to serve in national office. Unlike Richard Nixon, Gerald Ford faces a major challenge from within his party and the prospect of a bruising series of primary battles.

The Democrats have a plethora of candidates, but no overriding issues with which to outrage and mobilize activists, and from the bitterness of defeat some *anciens combattants* of the antiwar movement have apparently acquired a taste for winning and a feel for aggregative politics.

What then does the future hold? Will 1976 feature Republican factionalism and Democratic compromise?

Table 11-5. Views on Women by Religious Preference (%)

		Protestant	Catholic	Jewish	Atheist – Agnostic
New Woman					
Old breed	1	12	9	5	2
	2	44	36	19	14
	3	33	40	46	43
New breed	4	11	16	31	41
Intensity – Women					
Low	1	18	18	9	10
	2	42	37	25	22
High	3	41	45	66	68
N =		1232	458	156	325

NOTE: These data are from the mail questionnaires. For a complete explanation of these indexes, see Appendix C. *N*'s are from "Newwoman" table; other *N*'s are comparable in size.

THREE HYPOTHETICAL FUTURES

Discussions of the future of American presidential parties usually canvass at least three alternative futures: the restoration of traditional alignments and patterns, the prospect for realignment, and the possibility of decomposition. Most discussion of these possibilities focuses on voter behavior and takes less account of activists. But the influence of activists on parties' decisions and structures is more immediate and more constraining than that of masses.

Organizations are not merely individuals writ large, and their purposes are not the sum of purposes of their members. The fallacies involved in attributing to a collectivity the characteristics of its members are too well-known to require elaboration here.[16] Political parties feature an unequal division of power, a degree of structure, and some regularized procedures, all of which affect the influence of attitudes on organization. And, in addition, the process of aggregation itself affects the organizational reflection of individual purposes. Nonetheless, there is an intrinsic relation between individual purposes and styles and organizational behavior, and that relation is especially important in such permeable, porous voluntary organizations as political parties. The following consideration of the parties' futures therefore takes account of the elite perspectives explored in this study.

The No Change Model

The no change model is one of three alternative futures that have been predicted by students of American parties. The no change model postulates a continuation of the party system as we have known it, with two aggregative pragmatic parties competing to determine who shall rule and, broadly, to what ends. It assumes that most people will continue to think of themselves as Republicans and Democrats and that, after the intense politics of the late 1960s, party competition will settle back into familiar grooves. The principal arguments for this model are first, that there are no extremely divisive salient issues on the horizon that threaten to divide the parties and, second, that the extant party system is grounded in the identifications and habits of millions of voters and that these attitudes are not easily changed. The problem with the no change model is that it requires a reversal of existing trends, specifically, the reversal of the decline in party identification; the reversal of the trend to weakened party attachment in activities as well as voters; the reversal of the trend toward domination of American politics by symbol specialists; the reversal of the declining confidence in government; the reversal of disenchantment with traditional political culture; and the reversal of the trend toward issue-based politics. Although existing trends have not yet transformed the political habits of enough Americans to fundamentally alter institutional practices, their continuation would presumably have sweeping institutional consequences. As the murmurings of John Connally, Charles Mathias, George Wallace, and Eugene McCarthy made clear, the weakness of the parties constitutes an invitation to ambitious, discontented politicians to try to circumvent and further weaken them. But the apparent failure of any of these third or fourth party threats to materialize also illustrates the continuing power of two-party practices. Nonetheless, the likelihood that all of these trends toward change will be reversed is diminished by the various electoral reforms that make it difficult to conduct politics as in the past. The post-1972 reformed Democratic reform rules prompted further proliferation of primaries, left diminished the role that state party organizations and elected officials can play in the nominating process, left the party open to nonparty groups and candidates with a special interest in presidential politics, and enhanced the competitive position of the candidates who can mobilize activists; and the "proportional representation" rule makes it less likely that the preconvention process will produce a winner. The increased numbers of primaries and the campaign financing reforms will also affect the Republican party. With the rules of the game and the disposition of the players so changed, it is difficult to see how the party system can revert to the familiar patterns of the already receding past.

The Realignment Hypothesis

Some observers see split ticket voting, declining party identification and intraparty schisms as symptoms of a major realignment of voters, such as those which occurred in 1800, 1828, 1860, 1896, and 1932. In the past, major realignments have occurred when large numbers of voters abandoned their traditional party loyalties. James Sundquist, whose *Dynamics of the Party System* is the most comprehensive analysis of past party realignments, has identified as a minimal precondition of a massive shift in voters' loyalties the rise of a new issue or issues that cut across existing alignments and polarize millions of voters for a sustained period of time.[17] Such new cross-cutting issues must be more powerful than the issues associated with traditional party alignments and more powerful than the previous institutional identifications. Realignment does not necessarily entail the appearance of new parties, but may involve the redistribution of voters between existing parties. It is distinguished from such transient phenomena as split ticket voting by its greater durability and the large numbers who alter their institutional identifications.

A currently popular scenario concerning the future of the American parties predicts their realignment into a "conservative" and a "liberal" party, each of which will be more ideologically homogeneous than the existing parties. There are two main versions of the realignment scenario. One is that of William Rusher who proposes that American conservatives "form a new party that will replace the Republican party *in toto* as one of America's major parties."[18] Rusher's new conservative majority party is to be based on a coalition of social conservatives, many of whom are Democratic neopopulists, and economic conservatives, most of whom are now found in the Republican party. The new conservative coalition will reflect a new social and economic reality that "pits the hard hats, blue collar workers, and farmers . . . against a new and powerful class of non-producers comprised of a liberal verbalist elite . . . and a semi-permanent welfare constituency all coexisting happily in a state of mutually sustaining symbiosis."[19] The resulting party structure will, Rusher argues, provide an institutional expression of the conservative majority that is currently divided between the parties.

James Sundquist denies that any such realignment is in prospect. There seems to him no cross-cutting issue of sufficient power to restructure the electorate. However, Sundquist does believe there is in progress a process of "convergence" that "has made each of the major parties far more homogeneous nationally, and hence has sharpened the difference between them."[20] Like Rusher's realignment, Sundquist's convergence will result in two ideologically distinctive parties: one liberal and one conservative. But Sundquist's parties are structured on the old New Deal principles, while Rusher's are structured on the newer social and cultural issues. Since most opinion studies indicate that a majority of voters are liberal on economic and welfare state issues and conservative on cultural issues, the type of issue that "structures" the electorate will importantly influence which is the majority and which is the minority party.

The convention study provides no basis on which to reject definitively either of these hypotheses, but it does illuminate certain aspects of the argument. First, it is clear that in 1972 cultural issues were more central than economic issues to the structure of conflict at the elite level. Second, it is also true that the structure of conflict linked many items of social, cultural, and domestic and foreign policy that Rusher describes as dividing his "new" conservative party from its liberal opponents. Third, many of the views that are attributed to Rusher's new conservatives were views on which a good many Democratic delegates *agreed* with Republican delegates and *disagreed* with the dominant McGovernites. On the important question of whether military superiority should have priority as a goal of foreign policy, a majority of Humphrey and Jackson delegates and just under one-half of Muskie delegates agreed with large majorities of Wallace and Nixon delegates and disagreed with over three-fourths of McGovern delegates. In attitudes toward the military, the lineup was similar: a majority of Humphrey, Muskie, and Jackson supporters agreed with a still larger majority of Wallace and Nixon delegates and disagreed with McGovern supporters; and on a range of other issues that involved basic values large minorities of the supporters of traditional "liberal" candidates agreed with the "conservative" cultural position.

The data make quite clear that many of the issues of 1972 cut across traditional party lines, dividing Democrats from one another and creating new areas of agreement between social conservatives in both parties. And, confirming Rusher, religion or, more specifically, secularism was linked to the new issue alignments.

The patterns of division of convention delegates demonstrate that Rusher's hypothesis was grounded in the politics of 1972, but they do not prove that the future holds the predicted realignment. Several actual and potential obstacles stand in the way of such a development. It is frequently pointed out that, while the politics of the late 1960s and early 1970s featured cultural conflict, the divisive issues of those years have receded at the same time that traditional economic issues have reasserted themselves. Certainly, it is true that economic issues have greater salience in 1976 than in 1972. Sundquist argues that the resurgence of welfare state issues will reverse trends away from the New Deal party alignments. "Ever since the 1930's," he asserts, "whenever a political issue has revolved around the question of expanding the governmental role in our society, or has reflected class division, the two major parties have tended naturally to gravitate to opposite sides."[21] To document the case that 1976 will lead to further "convergence," he points to the list of Gerald Ford's vetoes: "control of strip mining, an education appropriations bill, an emergency bill to create public jobs for the unemployed, a bill to stimulate housing, a bill to control oil prices, and so on. . . ."[22] Sundquist's list, however, is not exactly a roster of New Deal programs. Like many other "environmental" and "growth" issues, the strip mining bill pitted Democrat against Democrat in much the same way as busing or welfare. Education is not a bread and butter issue, and price controls raise issues marginally relevant to traditional alignments. It is not certain that the "economic" issues of 1976 will be presented in the familiar ways and will stimulate familiar responses, because there are few proponents of laissez-faire among the elite of either party, because inflation affects more people and raises different questions from unemployment, because the strong anti-business sentiments in the McGovern wing of the Democratic party suggest that the structure of the economy may be called into question, and because the notion of expanded government functions now stimulates the fear of greater bureaucratization as well as the promise of delivery from existing ills. It is, therefore, not certain that the economic issues of 1976 will reinforce rather than cross cut traditional party alliances. And it is not certain that the salience of inflation and unemployment will prevent Rusher's predicted realignment. Sundquist rests his argument against this type of realignment on the belief that no cross-cutting, polarizing issue exists: neither Vietnam, race, nor the "social issue" has the needed salience, durability, and power to polarize. But Sundquist does not consider the *cumulative* impact of divisive issues on traditional alignments. The possibility that the traditional culture has itself become a political issue of which specific questions such as busing or abortion are indicators, is not discussed by him. But this possibility is central to the Rusher thesis and to elite politics in 1972. Certainly, there is less anti-system rhetoric today than in 1972 and fewer and less strident challenges to the legitimacy of the system. The muting of cultural conflict may diminish the power of these issues to move voters from traditional loyalties. But it is also clear that those traditional loyalties are weaker than they once were—and, for this reason, more susceptible to change.

From the perspective of the 1972 delegates, the most powerful argument against the realignment hypothesis is that it does not take account of the existence of substantial numbers of political influentials who were and may remain without a significant attachment to any organization. As conventionally stated, *the realignment hypothesis assumes that voters and parties will divide on a single dimension* (e.g., economic issues or cultural issues) *and that parties will form around "core" positions on either side of the center*. It assumes that a two-party system and widespread, relatively stable voter identification are the "normal state" that will reemerge after a period of electoral instability. In consequence, such alternatives as the persistence of multi-dimensional conflict are not considered. A combination of economic conservatives and social conservatives, such as envisioned by Rusher, might prove possible, but it should be noted that most democratic parties in most democratic systems offer the opposite combination; namely, social conservatism and welfare state economics. And it should be noted too that the groups that Rusher hopes to unite may find it impossible to subordinate their disagreements on economics to shared cultural values. Many political systems feature multi-dimensional conflict and institutions of varying stability and effectiveness.

Another interesting, rarely noted, aspect of the realignment hypothesis is that it is less concerned with representation than with choice. It emphasizes the importance of providing voters with a choice between distinct approaches and programs. Less attention has been paid to the importance of providing an opportunity to vote for persons and programs who reflect the views and values of the majority of the voters.[23] Political parties are not merely or even principally vehicles for enabling or forcing voters to choose among alternative policies. They are agencies of *representation*. The dynamics of competition and the operation of self-interest tend to guarantee parties' responsiveness to voter opinion. The whole edifice of representative, responsible institutions is designed to insure that those who make decisions for the society will remain responsive to the values and preferences of majorities. It is possible, even likely, that the ideologically distinct parties foreseen by the realignment hypothesis may leave unrepresented and dissatisfied millions of voters who will be available for mobilization by some other leaders or groups. The notion that voters are more attracted by relatively "extreme" parties belies the undoubted fact that party identification is most widespread in systems featuring "aggregative" parties, that moderate parties attract more support than extreme parties, and that party identification has declined during a period (1964–1972) that has featured sharper differences between the parties, and that it was more widespread and more stable during the 1950s and early 1960s when "consensus" politics was strongest. A choice between, for example, George Wallace and George McGovern would almost surely leave millions of voters longing for an echo of the moderate politics of the past.

Finally, the prospect that there will be a realignment resulting in two ideologically distinct parties is further clouded by the fact that some of the evidence necessary to the realignment hypothesis is also consistent with other interpretations.

The Decomposition Hypothesis

A third hypothesis has recently appeared in most discussions of the future of the American parties that emphasizes the possibility that parties will neither continue in their familiar form nor undergo some realignment during which voters will redistribute themselves into two new parties. Loosening of traditional party loyalties, weakening of traditional organization, breaking of traditional patterns of political behavior, and proliferation of electoral alternatives precede classical realignments. But weak loyalties, weak organizations, and volatile political behavior are also stable characteristics of some types of party systems.

It is striking that among Democrats the increasing importance of issues has accompanied decreasing organizational attachment. At the mass level, the increased importance of issues has been associated with a rise in split ticket voting and an increase of "independents" who identify with no party.[24] Among 1972 delegates, motives emphasizing party solidarity and roles emphasizing policy concerns were negatively related to solidary incentives and roles stressing institutional preservation.[25] This could be a prelude to realignment. European Communist and Socialist parties demonstrate that there is no necessary incompatibility between strong ideological commitment and strong organization.[26] However, the negative relations between issue concerns and organizational attachment may prove a more permanent feature of the political scene. Where ideological identification (as with right or left) is more widespread and more intense than organizational attachment, institutions are typically fragile. France, Italy, Argentina, and other "Latin" political systems provide examples of politics in which many mobilized people identify with a tendency (e.g., "left," "Peronista," "radical") rather than an institution.[27] In these traditions, attachment to a party often lasts just as long as the party is perceived as an effective institutional means to desired policy ends. Such systems stand in sharp contrast to those in which organizations are the foci of identification and loyalty.[28] These latter, of which Britain and the United States are examples, are characterized by institutional stability. *The projection of a negative relation between solidary and rectitude incentives, between ideological and organizational commitments, would indicate that the rising importance of issues in American politics does not necessarily herald the rise of strong programmatic parties on the British model* (because British parties are powerful symbols of identification that persist through changing problems and programs), *but may portend the development of factional politics featuring strong policy commitments and weak parties of a multi-party or a "no party" system.*

It is important, as always, not to exaggerate. Approximately one-half of the 1972 Democratic presidential elite and nearly three-fourths of the Republican were motivated by concern with both policy and party.[29] Almost all Republicans and many Democrats also accepted organizational constraints on their decisions. The delegate study provides small reason to suppose that the Republicans will suffer from withdrawal of diffuse support of its leadership. And it may be that Democratic delegates' lack of attachment to party only reflected their alienation from a party with those policies they had disagreed. However, the presence of a good many McGovern and Wallace delegates with long political experience and weak attachment to party suggests a more fundamental and permanent attitude toward organizations.

In fact, there are several problems with the common explanation of low attachment to party as a function of disagreement with party policy. The notion that a very conservative Republican will remain attached to his party *as long as* he perceives the party as serving conservative values and a very liberal Democrat will be attached to his party *provided* that the party devotes itself to very liberal causes assumes that attachment to party is instrumental and that attachment to policy fundamental. But this conception of the relation between party and policy conflicts with our understanding of party identification and social identifications more generally. If party identification is largely hereditary, acquired at a fairly young age, if it later functions to screen communications helping determine the focus of attention and the direction of affect, if it is a powerful identification that links the self into the political system, if it grows stronger with activity, with attachment to specific persons, and with organizational responsibilities, then it is not simply a function of the relation perceived to exist at any given time between personal policy preferences and the party platform. A purely instrumental relation to an organization does not involve *identification* of the self with the institution. Perhaps persons for whom party solidarity was not a motive for political activity and for whom organizational concerns were not constraining would *not* develop stronger identifications, simply because their faction took control of the party machine any more than a temporary or limited policy disagreement destroys the attachment to party of persons who identify with the fate of the institution (that is, who feel themselves part of the institution and who feel the institution to be part of themselves).

Attitudes toward organization are a neglected aspect of political orientations.[30] The experience of other nations indicates that the presence or absence of ideology is not in itself an adequate explanation of why some political parties become the foci of identification while others are the foci only of instrumental attachment. American parties are examples of loosely structured, pragmatic organizations that have been highly successful in attracting *identification*. The British Labour party and some European parties of the left demonstrate that ideological politics are not necessarily antagonistic to organizational solidarity, and the experience of countries whose politics feature high ideological content and low institutional coherence suggests that attitudes toward party may be associated with virtually any point on the political spectrum.

Fragile, fissiparous institutions are frequently associated with political traditions described as "individualistic." The political cultures of such polities typically deemphasize associational activities and emphasize the priority of the individual conscience.[31] The "privatization of politics" that Polsby and Wildavsky detected prior to 1972[32] may be relevant to the presence in influential roles of activists not moved by party solidarity. This process, which they believed they saw at work in the Goldwater and McCarthy movements, makes the individual conscience the center of the political world. Obviously, it is hostile to group solidarity. A habit of self-reference and a preoccupation with individual purity is profoundly antagonistic to the development of strong identification with a collectivity, because the pursuit of group interests involves a concern with collective gains and losses, solidarity and growth, which have *no immediate intrinsic relevance to individual moral objectives.* Building a strong party may be prerequisite to the accomplishment of desired policy goals, but organizational development will require activities remote from these goals. To just the extent that a person's political participation is motivated by pure issue concern, that person may be offended by the regulars' preoccupation with organizational maintenance. To the extent that the ideologically committed remain unconcerned with organizational interests and preservation they remain outsiders.

Weak institutional loyalties produce weak parties. The dilution of party loyalty and the rise of new issues may foreshadow the emergence of a multiparty or a no party system which reflects multi-dimensional political conflict. The dynamics of personal ambition reinforce the prospects of a proliferation of parties. As long as two parties monopolize access to high office, the activities of the ambitious will be channeled through these parties, but when there are plausible possibilities outside the two parties, ambition can be expected to reinforce ideological conflict—and heighten the likelihood that new parties will emerge to nominate more candidates. Weak porous parties are vulnerable to personal ambition in yet another sense. Where nominations can be settled by a surge of popularity and party leaders have no control over who competes in primaries, parties can be "captured" and transformed in a single presidential year.

Some polities feature a variety of organizational styles as well as a range of groups who differ on ideological substance. France is such a polity: disciplined, cohesive parties of the left coexist with leftist parties subject to schism and with a range of center and right parties. Maoist, communist, socialist, liberal, center, conservative, far right groups exist in a variety of embodiments: some disciplined and cohesive, some loose, fissiparous coalitions; some enduring, some transient "surge" parties or personalist movements.

One future of American politics consistent with existing trends toward a political class in which increasing numbers are *not* moved by party nor constrained by its organizational needs is *the proliferation of parties and of organizational styles. Why should we not expect that as the ideological variety of American politics increases, the range of organizations and of organizational and anti-organizational styles would increase also?*

The rise of personalist politics is also a likely concomitant of the decline of traditional parties. Personalist movements—organized around men on or off horseback—are a common feature of polities with low levels of party identification and weak organization.

There has been less discussion in this chapter of the Republican party than the Democratic because the 1972 Republican Convention provided little evidence of tension or likelihood of change. Judged from the perspectives of 1972, that party's problems appear to derive not from internal discord but from its dwindling popular appeal. Those problems are especially relevant to the decomposition hypothesis, because Republican decline contributes to a growing number of "no party" voters whose lack of institutional attachment is an important source of electoral volatility.

In the years following 1972 the Republican party has suffered numerous disasters—notably the resignation of Agnew, the fall, indictment, and conviction of so many in the Nixon White House, and the electoral defeat of 1974. The fact that the Republican party's continuing decline has been accompanied by a resurgence of internal dissension illustrates that *a relatively high level of ideological homogeneity in a party does not guarantee unity or cohesion*. The ambition and skills of leaders are also major determinants of party unity.

Other scenarios point to other futures. The progressive domination of politics by a single class, for example, verbalist professionals, could easily result in a politics increasingly remote from voters' values. An early symptom of elite estrangement may have been the curious reluctance of both parties to give the voters what public opinions of the last decade clearly indicate that voters wanted—welfare state economic policies that ensure minimum levels of comfort and security *and* defense of traditional values and institutions. The potential for elite estrangement from voters is enhanced by a culture that reserves special esteem for issue and style activists and by rules that permit parties to be captured by mobilized minorities.

The dynamics of participatory politics under conditions of mass communication and democratic politics intensify and diversify demands at the same time that they dilute broad identifications and weaken the institutions through which those demands might be met. The end of this process is not yet in sight and, as always, it is more difficult to discern the shape of the future than to observe the disintegration of the present.

NOTES

1. "The American Party System: Its Past and Its Future," (Paper prepared for the Symposium on the Two-Party System, California State College, Long Beach, Fall 1975).
2. Nelson W. Polsby and Aaron B. Wildavsky, *Presidential Elections: Strategies of American Electoral Politics*, 3rd. ed. (New York: Charles Scribner's Sons, 1971).
3. Theodore White, *The Making of the President 1960, 1964, 1968, 1972* (New York: Atheneum, 1961, 1965, 1969, 1973).
4. A suggestive discussion of institutional support is David Easton, "A Re-Assessment of the Concept of Political Support," *British Journal of Political Science* 5, pt. 4 (1975): 435–457.
5. Albert O. Hirschman, *Exit, Voice and Loyalty: Responses to Decline in Firms, Organizations and States* (Cambridge, Mass.: Harvard University Press, 1970).
6. Anthony Downs, *An Economic Theory of Democracy* (New York: Harper and Row, 1957); Richard M. Scammon and Ben J. Wattenberg, *The Real Majority* (New York: Coward-McCann, 1970).
7. James Q. Wilson, *Political Organizations* (New York: Basic Books, 1974).
8. Austin Ranney's *Curing the Mischiefs of Faction: Party Reform in America* (Berkeley: University of California Press, 1975), p. 42.
9. Noble E. Cunningham, Jr., ed. *The Making of the American Party System, 1789–1809* (Englewood Cliffs, N.J.: Prentice-Hall, 1965), pp. 65–74; Richard Hofstadter, *The Idea of a Party System: The Rise of Legitimate Opposition in the United States 1780–1840* (Berkeley: University of California Press, 1969), p. ix; Ranney, *Curing the Mischiefs*, pp. 25–57; Allan P. Sindler, *Political Parties in the United States* (New York: St. Martin's Press, 1966), p. 5. Also John H. Bunzel, *Anti-Politics in America: Reflections on the Anti-Political Temper and Its Distortions of the Democratic Process* (New York: Alfred A. Knopf, 1967). As I have noted elsewhere, the O'Hara Commission recommendations were inspired by the responsible party tradition.
10. Lasswell noted, "If traditional elites are indifferent or hostile (as in China), the intellectuals may become alienated and radicalized to a degree that largely determines the course of politics." Harold D. Lasswell in Harold D. Lasswell and Daniel Lerner, eds. *World Revolutionary Elites: Studies in Coercive Ideological Movements* (Cambridge, Mass: MIT Press, 1965) p. 20.
11. A recent indicator of the esteem in which one class of symbol specialists is held is the Gallup report of a survey of college students that rates the honesty and ethical standards of college teachers higher than all other occupational categories tested (70 percent rate college teachers high or very high as compared to 66 percent, medical doctors; 58 percent, engineers; 50 percent, psychiatrists; 49 percent, journalists; 40 percent, lawyers; 21 percent, building contractors; 20 percent, business executives; 19 percent, labor union leaders; 9 percent, political officeholders; 6 percent, advertising practitioners). *The Gallup Opinion Index*, September 1975, Report No. 123, p. 13.
12. Everett Carll Ladd, Jr. and Seymour Martin Lipset, "Faculty Democrats Disagree with Party's Rank and File," *The Chronicle of Higher Education,* December 15, 1975, p. 11. Lasswell notes that symbol specialists are especially prone to a politics of conflict and crisis because "In a symbol-rich and action poor environment human beings become the scene of internal conflict whose details are both symbolic and physiological." Lasswell and Lerner, *World*, p. 90.
13. Talcott Parsons, "Distribution of Power in American Society," in *C. Wright Mills and The Power Elite*, eds. G. William Domhoff and Hoyt B. Ballard (Boston: Beacon Press, 1968), pp. 60–87. This is a version of a review originally printed in *World Politics*, 1957.

14. Richard Whalen has suggested that John Kennedy was a transitional figure in this process. Kennedy, he suggests, was felt by the new cultural elite to be one of their own, while he also embodied the habits and perspectives of the traditional professional politician. There are good grounds however for believing that Adlai Stevenson may have been the catalytic figure in the rising political identity of this group. Richard J. Whalen, *Taking Sides* (New York: Houghton Mifflin, 1974). I discuss the culture class struggle in Jeane Kirkpatrick, "The Revolt of the Masses," *Commentary* 55, no. 2 (1973): 58–62.

15. Perhaps the most important secular assumption is that if it is to be attained at all, the good life must be realized in this world.

16. The literature on the pitfalls of the ecological fallacy, renamed by Heinz Eulau as the "fallacy of division" and the "fallacy of composition" is quite large. Eulau's discussions are especially useful for political science. See especially his *Micro-Macro Political Analysis: Accents on Inquiry* (Chicago: Aldine Publishing Co., 1969). Also, Eulau and Kenneth Prewitt, *Labyrinths of Democracy: Adaptation, Linkages, Representation and Policies in Urban Politics* (Indianapolis: Bobbs-Merrill, 1973), ch. 2; also Eulau's still unpublished paper, "Some Aspects of Analysis, Measurement and Sampling in the Transformation of Micro and Macro-Level Unit Properties" (Paper presented at the Conference on Design and Measurement Standards for Research in Political Science, Lake Lawn Lodge, Develan, Wisc., May 13–15, 1974). I wish to thank Professor Eulau for providing me with a copy of this paper and for permitting its citation. Eulau's approach is consistent with and, in part, derived from Harold D. Lasswell. See especially Lasswell's "Person, Personality, Group, Culture," *Psychiatry* 2 (1939), reprinted in the Bobbs-Merrill Reprint Series in the Social Sciences, No. 1.5.163.

17. James L. Sundquist, *Dynamics of the Party System: Alignment and Realignment of Political Parties in the United States* (Washington, D.C.: Brookings Institution, 1973).

18. William A. Rusher, *The Making of the New Majority Party* (New York: Sheed and Ward, Inc., 1975), p. xviii.

19. Ibid., p. xxi.

20. James L. Sundquist, "The American Party System: Its Past and Its Future" (Paper delivered at the Symposium on the Two-Party Political System, California State College, Long Beach, September 25–26, 1975).

21. Ibid. p. 28.

22. Ibid.

23. The tendency to value choice over representation is clearly reflected in Albert O. Hirschman's proposal that to satisfy the activists (whose views are more extreme as well as more forcefully articulated) the two parties should position themselves nearer the ends of the political spectrum. The competitive position of neither party will suffer providing that each eschews moving to the center in search of votes. Even more serious than the practical shortcomings of this proposal is Hirschman's assumption that *it is more important for the electoral* process to represent the views and values of activist minorities than of the majority of voters. His view that the ideological commitments of activists take precedence over the views and values of voters is an unusually clear-cut example of political elitism whose purpose is to give greater weight to the preferences of the ideological classes. Hirschman, *Exit*.

24. See, inter alia, Walter De Vries and Lance Terrance, Jr., *The Ticket Splitters: A New Force in American Politics* (Grand Rapids, Mich.: Eerdmens, 1972). Also Walter Dean Burnham, *Critical Elections and the Mainsprings of American Politics* (New York: W. W. Norton, 1970); David Broder, *The Party's Over: The Failure of Politics in America* (New York: Harper and Row, 1972); Sundquist, *Dynamics*, pp. 340–354.

25. A composite measure of role expectation emphasizing policy is negatively associated with a composite measure comprising orientations to organization, $r = .23$.

26. Note, however, that these parties of the left are formed not on the basis of specific *policy* goals but on the basis of broad ideological goals. The latter are presumably more enduring than the former.

27. James Payne finds that conflict in the politics of Colombia is a consequence of the structure of incentives. James L. Payne, *Patterns of Conflict in Colombia* (New Haven: Yale University Press, 1968). An excellent discussion of the impact of status incentives on French politics is Nathan Leites, *The Game of Politics in France* (Stanford, Calif.: Stanford University Press, 1959). Status concerns and institutional fragility in Argentina are discussed in Jeane Kirkpatrick, *Leader and Vanguard in Mass Society: A Study of Peronist Argentina* (Cambridge, Mass.: MIT Press, 1971), pp. 232–233.

28. David E. Butler and Donald Stokes, *Political Change in Britain: Forces Shaping Electoral Choice* (New York: St. Martin's Press, 1969); Samuel H. Beer, *The British Political System* (New York: Random House, 1974), pp. 201–221; Philip E. Converse and Georges Dupeux, "Politicization of the Electorate in France and the United States," *Public Opinion Quarterly* 26, no. 1 (1962): 1–23.

29. Previous research indicates that ideological or policy concerns long have been widespread among the presidential elite. McClosky's article comparing the orientations of convention delegates and voters established that delegates to the two conventions had coherent, distinctive views that not only differentiated them from the rank and file, but also from each other. Herbert McClosky, et al., "Issue Conflict and Consensus Among Leaders and Followers," *American Political Science Review* 54 (1960): 406–427. See also McClosky, "Consensus and Ideology in American Politics," *American Political Science Review* 58 (1964): 361–382. Neither the Goldwater nor the McGovern movements burst into the political system from outside it; both represented ideological tendencies present in the parties before and after the nomination of those candidates.

30. Brian Barry recently noted that, "In the rigorous, unified social science which is waiting to be born the relative strength of instrumental and non-instrumental orientations toward different kinds of groups will itself have to be explained." Brian Barry, "Review Article: 'Exit, Voice, and Loyalty'," *British Journal of Political Science* 4 (1974): 94.

31. Often the fortress family that protects the individual from the rest of society is the most inclusive social unit in societies that feature individualistic politics.

32. Polsby and Wildavsky, *Presidential Elections*, pp. 35–59. This insight of Polsby and Wildavsky is confirmed for the delegates. Delegates who are strongly identified with party and are committed to serving organizational interests are less given to introspection and self-reference than persons who define the delegates' role chiefly in terms of policy issues and ideology. The Pearson's r's summarizing the relation between a Solidarity Index and a Subjectivity Index is $r -.29$ for the whole presidential elite, $r -.25$ for the Democrats, and $r -.30$ for Republicans.

PART II

Women in the Presidential Elite

CHAPTER 12

Personal Characteristics of Women Delegates

In the history of humankind, group efforts to seize territory, possessions, or governments by force have been the province of men. So have efforts to resist the incursions of others. Societies are rare indeed that have placed women in the front ranks of their armies. Forceful person-to-person power struggles . . . whether for blood or "sport," have also been almost exclusively male endeavors. Why should this be so?[1]

Few aspects of social life are more completely or universally male dominated than politics. Here and there, from time to time a Golda Meir, or Indira Gandhi, or Elizabeth I, or Catherine the Great breaks the male monopoly on power positions, but these exceptions to the contrary notwithstanding, eastern, western, Arab, Christian, Buddhist, communist, capitalist, socialist, developed, traditional democracies, and autocracies have in common the fact that their political structures especially at the highest levels are heavily dominated, often exclusively populated, by males. The advent of democracy and of women's suffrage has given women a voice in important political decisions in some countries, but in the United States and elsewhere, universal suffrage has had a limited impact on male dominance of power processes.

Why, almost everywhere almost all the time, men have governed and women have not is a fascinating question that cannot be pursued here. Note, however, that its thoughtful exploration would require confronting certain basic facts: that women are *not* a minority, that women have acquiesced in male dominance of politics, and that acquiescence in governance by others is not a sex specific trait—untouchables have acquiesced in a caste system that deprives them of the most basic attributes of human dignity, slaves have acquiesced in slavery, peasants in serfdom, and subjects in tyranny, providing that by acquiescence we mean generalized conformity to the expectations and demands characteristic of the system.

Obviously human beings have a large capacity for submission to and acquiescence in systems that do not seem hospitable to their interests.

The Nineteenth Amendment gave women access to the political system. After a slow start, characteristic of newly enfranchised groups (as the low turnout of 18 to 21-year-olds has recently reminded us), women began to vote in proportions roughly equal to men;[2] and at the lower levels of volunteer politics, where the coffee is poured, the dollars collected, and the teas organized, women have been as numerous as men. But as we move up to levels where decisions are made that influence communities, states, and nations, the proportions of women dwindle to insignificance. Except in monarchies, very few women have won political roles to which large power attaches. No woman has ever been nominated as president or vice-president by a major party, or even by a party sufficiently important to count as a "third" party, and only one has been elected to the Senate or chosen as governor in her own right. But some women have made it to presidential nominating conventions as delegates—to wield whatever power attaches to that role. Existing prejudices against women in influential roles constituted an informal inhibition even to the selection of women as delegates. Before 1972 the number of women in national conventions was somewhat greater in the Republican than the Democratic party, but never constituted as much as one-fifth of either convention.[3]

One of the most interesting political phenomena of recent history has been the emergence of women as a symbol in whose name political grievances are stated and demands made. Since women comprise somewhat more than one-half the adult population, the symbol "women" constitutes an identification of great potential importance. Its practical influence depends on whether or not substantial numbers of women come to see their sex as relevant to politics in the way they see party, region, or economic interest as relevant and/or whether or not large numbers of politically influential persons come to *believe* that sex has become a determinant of women's political behavior. In 1972 "women" emerged as a symbol sufficiently powerful that Theodore White termed women "a third new historic power force."[4] Perhaps he exaggerated. What was true, however, was that some women, speaking in the name of other women, persuaded the men who made up the Democrats' Commission on Party Structure and Delegate Selection of the validity of women's grievances and the reality of their potential power. Most observers saw the rise of the women's movement as a part of the political turmoil of the 1960s, and the fact that it occurred alongside the rising demands of two other groups—youth and blacks—is probably significant. Popular rhetoric termed 1972 the "year of the woman," and women's role in the new politics was emphasized in many contemporaneous accounts. It was duly noted that women outnumbered men by more than five million and that they were voting in ever larger numbers. The new sense of the potential importance of "woman power" had multiple impacts on the politics of 1972.

Before 1968 women were chosen delegates on approximately the same formal basis as men. But in 1972 the McGovern-Fraser guidelines declared that as victims of past discrimination, women should henceforth be represented in the national convention in proportion to their numbers in the population.[5] This provision did not result in a convention which was 51 percent female; however, it did lead to a marked increase in the proportion of Democratic delegates who were women. Presumably, the Democratic action on behalf of women constituted informal pressure on Republican managers to include more women in that convention. The result was a Democratic convention in which nearly 40 percent of delegates were women and a Republican convention at which almost 30 percent were women. Because of "quotas" established by the reform guidelines, the Democratic women who became delegates in 1972 were chosen on a somewhat different basis than previously.[6] There were other evidences of the increasing political salience of women.

The National Women's Political Caucus made its appearance on the political scene to speak for newly mobilized women. Describing itself as a "coalition of women from various backgrounds, economic levels, and political affiliations who have joined together for political action . . . in the interest of *all* women,"[7] the NWPC argued for increased representation of women in both conventions and described one of its functions as "evaluating political candidates' races and targeting in on those who are weak on women's causes."[8] Certainly, there was more discussion in 1972 than in previous presidential years about where candidates stood on women and women's issues. Frederick Dutton, a top McGovern strategist, said that the feminist factor "affects our campaign organization, the symbols that we signal, the issues we choose and the personality and style of our candidate. . . ."[9] This was not the first time that reform politics had been linked to participation of women. Leon Epstein had long since noted the distinctive role of women in "middle-class politics:"

> A special feature of these (new) clubs is the prominence of women in their activities. Again the contrast to the patronage machines is sharp— . . . women in the American clubs do much of the canvassing and mailing—not to mention home-based coffee hours. All this is a long way from the male political world of a party's saloon headquarters.[10]

Dutton and certain other McGovern strategists believed that the "Nylon Revolution," as one termed it in an off-guard moment,[11] constituted an important new resource for a candidate like McGovern. This belief rested on the assumption, widely held among some spokespersons and fellow travellers of the women's movement, that new women entering politics in unprecedented numbers were more humanistic, liberal, and generous[12] than the men who had hitherto dominated politics.

Since slightly over one-half the population is female, a significant change in women's political identifications, expectations, and demands could have a major impact on the political system.

Gaining access to power is not the same as gaining power. Various events at the two conventions raised questions about whether the women present in Miami were new women more determined to claim a fresh share of power, whether their views were, after all, very different from those of men, and whether the larger numbers of women in fact signalled greater power for women.

The three chapters in this section discuss the ways in which women who achieved delegate status in 1972 resembled or did not resemble male delegates and one another. Special attention is paid to whether or not there were present significant numbers of new women whose future political behavior is likely to be substantially different from that of women in the past. Because so much less is known about women's political characteristics and behavior, these subjects will be discussed in somewhat more detail than would be required in comparable discussions of men.

INCOME, EDUCATION, OCCUPATION

The personal and social characteristics of women delegates were in most respects very similar to those of the men. Both sexes showed the same basic characteristics of elites everywhere: as compared to most people, they had gone to school longer and had higher incomes, and had relatively high status jobs. But on each of these conventional indicators of socio-economic status women's position was somewhat less high than men's. Table 12–1 shows that at the Democratic Convention 29 percent of men and 21 percent of women had family incomes of over $30,000. Among Republicans the contrast was greater with 54 percent of men and 32 percent of women having family incomes over $30,000.[13] And in each candidate group except Muskie's there were relatively fewer affluent women than men and more men than women with incomes over $20,000. The picture is the same in regard to education.[14] Among Democrats 38 percent of men and 17 percent of women held some advanced degree. This contrast is heightened by the fact that most women with advanced degrees had master's degrees; while a majority of the men had law degrees or doctorates. Conversely 50 percent of women and 38 percent of Democratic men had

Table 12-1. Delegate Income by Sex, Party by Sex, Candidate Preference by Sex (%)

Income/year	All Men	All Women	Democrats Men	Democrats Women	Republicans Men	Republicans Women	McGovern Men	McGovern Women	Humphrey Men	Humphrey Women	Wallace Men	Wallace Women	Muskie Men	Muskie Women
Less than $10,000	9	14	10	17	5	7	14	18	11	24	17	11	0	8
$10,000–20,000	28	34	34	37	14	25	36	38	31	33	21	61	44	26
$20,000–30,000	27	29	27	26	28	36	27	25	32	29	35	11	17	34
$30,000–50,000	19	13	16	11	25	21	15	9	14	10	10	6	23	23
Over $50,000	18	10	13	10	29	11	8	10	12	5	17	11	17	9
Weighted *N* =	2210	1431	1516	1063	694	368	662	655	301	119	87	36	179	107

Question: "Please look at this card and tell me the letter of the income group that includes the income of all members of your family in 1971 before taxes. This figure should include dividends, interest, salaries, wages, pensions, and other income."

NOTE: These data are from the interviews.

not finished college. Among Republicans an even greater contrast is evident: four times as many men as women held a post-graduate degree (43 percent as compared to 10 percent). (See Table 12–2.) The same pattern of more highly educated men and relatively less educated women holds in each candidate group. Among McGovern delegates 43 percent of men and 22 percent of women held a post-graduate degree; 28 percent of men and 43 percent of women had less than a college education. Among Humphrey delegates 22 percent of men and 14 percent of women held a graduate degree; 56 percent of men and 72 percent of women did not complete college, and so forth. *The point is not that women were poor or uneducated. As compared to women generally they were neither, but as compared to the males with whom they were associated in Miami, they were less advantaged.* Since both women and men were at least middle class in socioeconomic status, would it have mattered that women had less income and education? It seems unlikely that income would have been relevant to the political interactions that take place prior to and during a convention. But, since education may breed verbal skills, it seems likely that persons with less education may have felt themselves, and in fact, may have been at a relative disadvantage. Edmond Costantini and Kenneth Craik comment concerning their California activists applies as well to the convention delegates: ". . . the present data suggest that women party leaders—probably already handicapped by being engaged in an activity considered properly the domain of men—operate in politics with whatever disadvantages accompany relatively lower class achievement."[15] The discrepancy in education was probably enhanced by the greater professional experience of male delegates.[16]

There is good reason to believe that working in a reasonably high status, relatively responsible job enhances self-confidence. The ability to perform in a public role reinforces a sense of personal competence, and the responses of co-workers provide consensual validation that one is in fact performing an important role in a satisfactory manner. Many middle-class jobs also provide practice in the persuasive skills—in dealing with others, presenting facts or arguments in a convincing manner. However satisfying, the traditional wife/mother role provides practice in other skills. However appreciative the husband, his praise may not be as reassuring about one's *competence* as that of adult colleagues to whom one is related in a less personal, more functional manner.[17]

Approximately 60 percent of Democratic women and 46 percent of Republican women were employed outside the home at the time of the convention, and only 30 percent of Democrats and 49 percent of Republicans described themselves as housewives. (See Table 12–3.) There was no Democratic candidate group in which housewives comprised more than 35

Table 12-2. Delegate Education by Sex, Party by Sex, Candidate Preference by Sex (%)

Education	All Men	All Women	Democrats Men	Democrats Women	Republicans Men	Republicans Women	McGovern Men	McGovern Women	Humphrey Men	Humphrey Women	Wallace Men	Wallace Women	Muskie Men	Muskie Women
Less than high school	4	3	4	4	2	2	2	2	10	5	15	22	2	6
High school grad	11	14	12	13	7	18	6	9	25	24	12	48	12	9
Some college	22	35	22	33	23	38	20	32	21	43	29	22	27	28
College graduate	24	32	24	31	25	32	29	36	23	15	27	4	15	45
M.A.	10	12	11	14	8	7	16	17	6	11	0	0	10	4
Ph.D. or equivalent	5	1	6	1	5	1	11	2	1	0	0	0	3	2
LL.B.	21	3	19	3	26	2	15	3	13	3	18	0	28	7
M.D.	2	0	2	0	4	0	1	0	2	0	0	4	3	0
Weighted *N* =	2270	1475	1546	1095	724	380	671	663	304	131	102	46	179	109

Question: "What was the highest grade of school or year of college you completed?"

NOTE: Data are from the interviews.

Table 12-3. Employment Status by Sex, Party by Sex, Candidate Preference by Sex (%)

Employment Status	All Men	All Women	Democrats Men	Democrats Women	Republicans Men	Republicans Women	McGovern Men	McGovern Women	Humphrey Men	Humphrey Women	Wallace Men	Wallace Women	Muskie Men	Muskie Women
Presently working	94	56	92	59	97	46	90	55	94	71	92	52	97	54
Housewife	0	35	0	30	0	49	0	32	0	23	0	35	0	35
Student	3	5	4	6	1	2	7	8	2	2	0	4	3	2
Unemployed, laid off temporarily, looking for work	1	3	1	4	1	2	3	6	1	0	3	4	0	2
Retired	2	2	2	2	1	2	1	0	3	5	6	4	0	7
Weighted *N* =	2287	1495	1555	1111	732	384	674	675	304	131	108	46	179	111

Question: "Are you presently employed, or are you unemployed, retired, a housewife, a student, or what?"

NOTE: Data are from the interviews.

percent; they were least numerous among Humphrey's women delegates of whom only 23 percent were housewives. Among employed women, professionals were most numerous. Among McGovern delegates, for example, 40 percent of women and 49 percent of men were professionals or highly qualified technical experts; among Humphrey delegates 31 percent of women and 42 percent of men fell in this category; among Muskie delegates it was 28 percent of women and 46 percent of men; for Nixon it was 24 percent of women and 38 percent of men. Self-employed women were even scarcer than self-employed men,[18] but there were somewhat more women than men in clerical jobs. On balance, the women at the conventions closely resembled the men in the socioeconomic characteristics except that approximately one-half of Republican women and one-third of Democratic women were housewives. (Table 12–4 compares occupations of delegates and spouses.)

The data suggest that though many of the women worked outside the home, few worked as long as males at these jobs. Nearly one-half of all men in the presidential elite reported working more than fifty-one hours a week;

Table 12-4. Occupation and Spouse's Occupation by Sex (%)

	Own Occupation		Spouse's Occupation	
	Men	Women	Wives	Husbands
Professional — Technical	42	22	17	50
Managers — Salaried	29	13	3	16
Managers — Self-employed	12	4	2	12
Clerical workers	3	13	9	3
Sales workers	3	3	2	3
Craftsmen	2	0	1	5
Operatives	2	1	1	3
Service workers	1	1	2	2
Farmers and Farm Managers	1	0	0	2
Laborers	1	0	0	1
Housewives	0	35	64	0
Students	3	5	1	1
Unemployed	1	3	0	0
Weighted N =	2263	1468	1853	1034

Questions: "What is your main occupation? What sort of work do you do?" "What is your spouse's main occupation? What sort of work does he/she do?"

NOTE: These data are from the interviews.

only about one-third as many employed women said that they worked such long hours—a fact that is probably accounted for by the greater household duties of the employed married women.

Although M. Kent Jennings and Norman Thomas reported that working women were no more likely than housewives to be politically ambitious,[19] the high numbers of employed women among the presidential elite suggests that employment outside the home may be more compatible with political activism—despite the fact that unemployed women often have more flexible, less overcrowded schedules. We know that occupation is generally related to political activity—that lawyers, teachers, journalists, and insurance and real estate agents, for example, all of whom have high levels of verbal skills, are more likely to be active in politics than farmers, chemists, engineers, or industrial workers. Perhaps housewife should be added to the category of occupations that are not conducive to political activity. It will not be possible to determine this until substantial numbers of women are employed in the professions from which more political participants are drawn. If employment in the "persuasive" professions is more conducive than housewifery to women's political participation, then women's activity should be expected to increase alongside their greater participation in these occupations.

Upward social mobility was a characteristic widely shared by both women as well as men.[20] Most women delegates were substantially more well-educated than their mothers, and many of the employed had higher status jobs than their mothers. For women intergenerational occupational mobility also included a trend toward moving out of the home into remunerative jobs. In both parties and in every candidate group, except Wallace supporters, there was a sharp decline in the proportion of housewives from one generation to the next. Among McGovern's women supporters 54 percent of delegates' mothers were housewives as compared to 26 percent of delegates; among Humphrey women it was 55 percent of mothers to 39 percent of delegates; among Nixon supporters 73 percent of women delegates' mothers were housewives as compared with 42 percent of delegates. Among women as well as men the low status jobs and low levels of education virtually disappeared from the parent to the delegate generation. Substantial portions of the maternal generation had only an eighth grade education; a majority had not gone beyond high school. Mothers of delegates employed outside the home were more likely than their daughters to have been employed in clerical jobs and service trades, less likely to have achieved professional status. The status mobility of women delegates means that they shared this essential characteristic of American political elites, so that whatever the psychological and political effects of social mobility, they were present among women as well as men. It also means that women delegates shared the same basic class interests as the men: they too constituted a socially mobile group whose status and incomes derived from family membership in a middle income skill group requiring relatively high levels of education.

Since the social status of a wife typically follows that of a husband, the class character of the women delegates is also reflected in the husband's occupation. Women delegates' husbands were even more likely than the male delegates to be professionals: for example, while 49 percent of male McGovern delegates were professionals, 63 percent of the spouses of his women delegates fell in this category;[21] whether they were wage earners or were supported by husbands, most women delegates owed both their status and incomes to family membership in a middle income skill group.

While this survey of sexes establishes the basic similarity of the socioeconomic characteristics of the two sexes, it also confirms that women dispose of fewer of the base values associated with access to power. The women in this study, like the men, had relatively high educations, incomes, and professions—much higher than the national average. However, their positions were not as strong as those of the male delegates, and for a good many, their status was more a function of the achievement of their husbands than of personal achievement.[22]

WOMEN IN A SOCIAL CONTEXT: FAMILY

The most basic and important social unit is, of course, the family, and the aspect of the woman's roles generally believed to be most important to her political behavior is her family status. It is the presumed conflict between the roles of wife and mother and any other role that causes many women to devote themselves entirely to family-centered concerns at least during the years that they have young children at home. It is generally true that: "While children are a real achievement, a source of joy and fulfillment, they are also time-consuming and energy-depleting, a major source of responsibility and anxiety. In today's child-centered milieu, with the decline of the extended family and the dearth of adequate child care facilities, the responsibility for child-rearing falls directly on the mother alone."[23] Freedom from the exclusive or near exclusive responsibility for young children has figured importantly in the demands of some women for new sex role distributions. One characteristic of the new woman as she is described by both detractors and defenders is that she has declared herself free to participate in public and professional affairs even during the years that her children are young. Presumably then the new women in Miami, if such there were, would not have been deterred from attending the convention because of the responsibility for young children at home. She would, instead, have had a supportive spouse who accompanied her to the convention where he looked after the children *or* one who assumed the care of the children at home. How many women were there in Miami who had small children? Were there differences among the liberals and the conservatives? How many men were there in Miami who had young children?

First, marital status: most delegates, like most adults, were married. The largest percent of single delegates was found among McGovern supporters, of whom almost 30 percent were unmarried—the same candidate support group that had the largest number of delegates under 30. The unmarried were distributed approximately equally between the sexes. Just as McGovern delegates were younger and more likely to be unmarried, more were also childless. However, almost 70 percent of the women in the McGovern group and over 75 percent of those in other candidate support groups had at least one child. Small families were common for both male and female delegates. A majority of delegates of both sexes had two or three children; large families (four or more children) were not uncommon, but neither were they numerous.[24] Apparently, the number of children had little effect on whether a woman was active and effective enough to become a delegate.[25]

Table 12-5 shows that while there were no significant sex differences in the number of children, there were differences in the ages of delegates' children. As expected, more men than women had very young children; three times as many Republican men as women had children under 6; so did nearly as many Democratic men. More significant for women's political role is the fact that in all candidate support groups there were female delegates with children under 5, and even more with children under 10. For one-third to one-half of these women of varying values and beliefs, there was no insurmountable role conflict between mothering small children, being active in presidential politics, and leaving home to spend a week in Miami as a delegate. Until recently this type of mobility has been conceived as a male monopoly. That large numbers of married women with small children found it possible to play an active political role that involved temporary transfer of location demonstrates that small children were not an insurmountable handicap to the participation in such roles as delegate and effective local volunteer and suggests also that males may no longer have as important a political advantage as in the past.

Whether mothers and wives *can* combine political activity and their traditional roles is one question; the impact of these activities on the family is another matter. It is very interesting and highly suggestive that substantially more women than men reported that their spouses were very

Table 12-5. Delegates' Number of Children and Age of Youngest Child by Sex, Party by Sex, and Candidate Preference by Sex (%)

	All Men	All Women	Democrats Men	Democrats Women	Republicans Men	Republicans Women	McGovern Men	McGovern Women	Humphrey Men	Humphrey Women	Wallace Men	Wallace Women	Muskie Men	Muskie Women	Nixon Men	Nixon Women
Number of children																
None	22	23	26	26	14	17	36	29	16	19	19	13	15	24	14	17
1	9	11	8	10	10	13	8	8	8	11	14	17	9	7	11	13
2	23	26	22	26	25	26	22	27	24	26	21	13	18	16	24	27
3	21	21	19	20	25	23	15	19	18	21	33	26	24	33	25	23
4	14	10	13	9	15	13	11	9	20	7	7	17	18	9	15	12
5	5	5	4	4	6	6	3	4	6	5	5	9	4	4	6	6
6 or more	6	4	7	5	5	3	5	4	8	11	2	4	14	7	5	3
N =	1406	973	883	673	523	300	429	438	142	57	43	23	80	55	503	287
Age of Youngest Child																
1–5	25	16	29	21	19	6	38	25	16	9	33	15	21	17	18	6
6–12	27	29	27	31	28	25	24	31	31	35	12	40	25	33	28	24
13–18	21	23	20	22	24	25	19	23	24	22	9	15	21	14	24	26
Over 18	27	32	25	27	30	44	19	21	30	35	46	30	33	36	30	44
N =	1068	729	633	493	435	236	265	307	115	46	33	20	67	42	420	226

Questions: "How many children do you have?" "What is the age of your youngest child?"

NOTE: These data are from the mail questionnaires.

much in favor of their political activity (58 percent to 71 percent among Democrats; 45 percent to 81 percent among Republicans) and that substantially fewer women said that their political activity interfered much with their family life. The contrast among Republicans is especially sharp: 43 percent of Republican women and only 18 percent of men reported politics did not interfere at all with the family. What do these patterns mean? Are husbands more willing than wives to see their spouses spend time and energy on political activities? Or are women less likely than men to participate in the face of their spouse's disapproval? Do women whose spouses offer less than wholehearted approval of their political activity forego the activity? Regardless of their reported enthusiasm for their wives' political activities, fewer husbands accompanied their delegate-wives to Miami than women accompanied their delegate-husbands. But more women than men delegates were accompanied by other members of their families. Despite popular impressions to the contrary, meeting the expenses of the convention constituted no more a problem for women than for men.

WOMEN IN A SOCIAL CONTEXT: COMMUNITY

We know from previous research that small towns have contributed through time substantially more than their demographic share of political participants;[26] we know too that political participants are likely to have lived for many years in their communities[27] and to be "joiners"[28]—active not only in politics but in other community affairs as well. There is little reason to suppose that the demographic patterns associated with political participation generally are not descriptive of women as well as men, and, in fact, the social characteristics of the two sexes are in all essential respects identical. That is not to say that all delegates are alike in these respects, but that differences are a function not of sex but of other factors. Both male and female delegates from very large cities, for example, are most numerous in the McGovern ranks; both male and female McGovern delegates were less likely than supporters of other candidates to have lived in their communities for more than twenty years. (See Table 12-6.) Patterns of geographic mobility differ by candidate group and age group, but not by sex.

What of participation in other organizations?

Various stereotypes concerning women are relevant to their participation in voluntary associations. They are said to be more likely to focus all concerns on the immediate family, to be more concerned with personal than with public matters, to find socializing in the absence of intimacy

Table 12-6. Years in Local Community by Sex and Candidate Preference by Sex (%)

Years in Local Community	All Men	All Women	Democrats Men	Democrats Women	Republicans Men	Republicans Women	McGovern Men	McGovern Women	Humphrey Men	Humphrey Women	Wallace Men	Wallace Women	Muskie Men	Muskie Women
One year or less	2	3	3	4	2	1	5	5	1	0	0	0	1	0
2–5	12	15	14	19	8	5	21	23	7	10	7	30	6	3
6–10	12	17	14	19	10	14	16	21	8	14	5	17	11	15
10–20	25	30	25	28	25	34	29	28	20	28	21	35	14	27
Over 20	49	36	45	31	55	46	30	23	64	48	68	17	68	54
N =	1415	973	899	676	516	297	440	437	142	58	44	23	80	59

Years in local community question: "How many years have you lived in your present community?"

NOTE: Data on number of years in local community are from the mail questionnaires.

especially difficult. In his cross-cultural study of women and politics, Maurice Duverger largely explains women's low participation by this tendency to turn inward on the family rather than outward to the community.[29] In America, however, there is another stereotype—that of the clubwoman—that pictures middle-aged housewives engaging in an endless round of public and social activities: running from the school board, the PTA, and the Red Cross to the bridge club and back again while dinner burns on the stove at home. Previous studies of women active in American politics suggest that they resemble politically active men in their tendency to join and lead voluntary associations.[30] The data on convention delegates provided an unprecedented opportunity to compare the participation patterns of large numbers of politically active males and females. To determine whether there were distinctive patterns of participation of women and men and to identify them if they existed it was necessary to consider both the quantity and the quality of group memberships. Table 12-7 shows that among both Democrats and Republicans both women and men are joiners. Over four-fifths of males and females of both parties belonged to at least one voluntary organization, and differences in the number of memberships of men and women were insignificant. Although women supporting Humphrey, Muskie, and Nixon belonged to somewhat more voluntary organizations than the men in their candidate support group, the differences are slight and statistically insignificant. Women supporting Wallace were least likely to be members of voluntary groups; however 70 percent were active in at least one organization. Differences between Wallace men and women delegates were slight. The conclusion is clear. *Among this political elite there were no significant differences in the readiness of men and women to join groups outside the family. Both sexes tended to be participants and to show a capacity for collective endeavor and a habit of group activity.* This is true in spite of the fact that in a national survey of college-educated women inquiring about what the women would most admire and would like most for themselves, "Fewer than 5 percent showed any interest in success as a prominent leader of a voluntary organization or as a national figure holding an elective or appointive political office."[31]

Turning from quantity of affiliations to type, more significant sex differences might be expected. Traditional women's roles give women a special responsibility for the home and the care and education of children. Traditionally, too, women, serving as keepers of the community conscience, have been more active than men in church affairs. Therefore more women than men might have been expected to belong to church and social groups and fewer to service and occupational organizations. Since women were widely believed to have more leisure time than men, or at least more

Table 12-7. Civic Participation by Sex, Party by Sex, Candidate Preference by Sex (%) (Number and Type of Memberships in Voluntary Associations)

	All		Democrats		Republicans		McGovern		Humphrey		Wallace		Muskie		Nixon	
	Men	Women	Men	Women	Men	Women	Men	Women	Men	Women	Men	Women	Men	Women	Men	Women
Total Number of Memberships																
None	20	15	20	16	20	14	21	17	13	3	27	30	21	12	20	14
1–2	32	36	37	38	25	29	44	44	34	36	29	26	24	20	24	28
3–4	34	34	32	32	37	40	28	30	37	40	38	35	41	42	37	41
5 or more	14	15	11	14	19	18	8	9	17	21	7	9	15	25	19	18
N =	1452	996	913	687	539	309	445	445	144	58	45	23	81	59	518	296
Professional, Service, Social Club Memberships																
None	42	56	48	63	33	41	58	74	35	35	44	57	31	32	32	41
Some activity	46	41	43	34	50	55	40	25	52	59	44	39	47	59	50	55
A great deal of activity	12	4	9	3	18	4	3	2	13	7	11	4	22	9	18	4
N =	1452	996	913	687	539	309	445	445	144	58	45	23	81	59	518	296

Female-Civic Group Memberships (Feminist Groups, League of Women Voters, Civic Groups)																
None	71	45	68	39	77	56	63	36	70	45	78	61	77	44	77	56
Some activity	29	50	32	54	23	43	37	56	30	55	22	39	24	46	23	43
A great deal of activity	0	5	0	7	0	1	0	9	0	0	0	0	0	10	0	1
N =	1452	996	913	687	539	309	445	445	144	58	45	23	81	59	518	296

Church-School Group Memberships																
Neither	52	48	56	53	46	38	61	59	47	28	49	48	46	37	45	37
One	29	28	29	27	31	29	25	27	25	33	33	26	28	34	32	30
Both	19	24	16	20	24	33	5	14	28	40	18	26	26	29	24	33
N =	1452	996	913	687	539	309	445	445	144	58	45	23	81	59	518	296

NOTE: These data are from the mail questionnaires. For the method of index construction and the specific constituent variables comprising each of these indexes, see Appendix C.

control over their time, they might have been expected to join more purely social clubs.

Such expectations turned out to be only partly correct. Among Humphrey, Wallace, Muskie, and Nixon delegates, more women than men were involved in church and/or school related organizations, but this pattern did not hold for McGovern delegates, among whom men and women were equally likely to belong to church or school groups. McGovern, Wallace, and Nixon women delegates were less likely than men to belong to service, occupational, or social clubs, but Humphrey and Muskie women delegates were approximately as active as men in these two candidate support groups. Women were, of course, much more likely than men to belong to feminist groups.

PERSONALITY FACTORS: MALE AND FEMALE

The most common explanation of the differences between male and female political behavior derives from their presumably different personalities. Males are often said to be more dominant, more aggressive than females; females to be naturally submissive, naturally focused on the intimacies characteristic of family relations, and more concerned with subjective than objective factors. Whether such personality differences are seen as innate or conditioned matters less for our purposes than the fact that such differences are more often postulated than demonstrated.

The question is not whether there are psychological differences between the sexes, but *whether there are such differences that are relevant to political behavior*. There is general agreement among students of personality and politics about some of the traits which have an important influence on who participates in politics. Ego strength, self-esteem, and sociability have been found by many researchers to be highly correlated with political participation, so have achievement and dominance. It is more than coincidence that each of these traits which are widely believed to be essential for political participation has been described by some reputable scholar to be a trait which women are distinctly lacking. Women have been said to be submissive, to have low feelings of personal competence, low self-esteem, low achievement needs, less sociability—all as compared to men. The authors of the *American Voter* and the *Civic Culture* have reported that women are lower than men in efficacy;[32] James David Barber reported that women were numerous among his Spectator Group—his most inefficacious, generally inept legislator;[33] Duverger attributed to women a special tendency to turn inward toward the family rather than outward toward the world;[34] Lane described women as less achievement oriented than men;[35] and a long line of authorities including

Aristotle, St. Paul, Charles Darwin, and Sigmund Freud have described women as submissive by nature.[36] The fact that all these investigations were conducted and reported by men does not necessarily prove that they are wrong. But we now know that some of their generalizations are mistaken. Fortunately, Eleanor Maccoby and Nancy Jacklin have recently collected the scattered studies relevant to some of these questions and reported them in *The Psychology of Sex Differences*,[37] a book that is indispensable for anyone interested in this subject. A body of research is beginning to accumulate on sex specific behavior, which provides a better source of hypotheses concerning psychological differences relevant to politics. Data on convention delegates cast some new light on these hypotheses.

SOCIABILITY

"Sociable personalities are more likely to enter politics than nonsociable personalities," Milbrath reported, summarizing a widely held belief that because it involves continuous social interactions democratic politics attracts sociable people.[38] If sociability facilitates political participation, then it matters whether women share this trait. Popular lore is of two minds: on the one hand, women are said to be less interested than men in socializing outside a circle of intimacy;[39] on the other hand, women are said to be more oriented to persons than tasks and to have greater affiliative needs than men.[40] These two positions may be somewhat less contradictory than they at first appear to be because the "sociability" needed to enjoy politics is often rather impersonal and may not be satisfying to persons with strong affiliative needs. Alice Rossi, a distinguished student of women's social behavior, commented on the existence of a "tendency of women to define themselves in terms of their intimate affiliation with other people rather than in terms of their own unique abilities."[41] But we are concerned here not with what has been said about all women's affiliative needs or capacity for purposive socializing, but with what the data indicate about the predispositions of women in the presidential elite. Presumably, a process of self-selection would operate to attract to politics gregarious women who enjoy non-intimate, purposive socializing. But we did not know. Did women in this political elite have greater affiliative needs than men? Did they enjoy the social aspects of politics as much as, less than, or more than men? What of their other activities? Do they reflect a tendency toward a withdrawal or a participant style of citizenship?

To tap global affiliative, achievement, and power needs, several questions were asked which invited respondents to choose among alternative responses to particular interpersonal situations. Each question provided the respondent an opportunity to emphasize affiliative, achievement, or power alternatives. The respondent's choice presumably indicated personal predisposition. Responses were combined in simple, additive indexes that permitted scoring each respondent on affilation, achievement, and power.[42] Judging by scores on the Affiliation Index (Table 12–8), relatively few of the presidential elite—male or female—had high affiliation needs; and among those who did, women were no more numerous than men. Republican women scored somewhat higher than Republican men on affiliation, but the difference was small and not statistically significant.

A second set of measures was designed to tap enjoyment of the socializing that takes place in a political context. Those measures inquired about incentives to political participation and listed various alternatives that might play a role in stimulating political activity. Responses indicate that there was no consistent "female" tendency to be either attracted or repelled by the social aspects of politics: women supporting Humphrey, Muskie, and Wallace were more likely than men to stress social incentives to participation.

In all candidate groups women were somewhat more likely than men to mention social ties and the participation of friends and family as having played an important role in their original political involvement. Apparently social ties may have played a more important role for women in their initial recruitment to political activity, but there were no differences in the two sexes' enjoyment of socializing once they had embarked on political participation. Neither the women nor the men displayed an overriding need to seek affection and approval through political activities; both enjoyed the purposive socializing that is characteristic of volunteer politics.[43]

We have already seen, too, that women in both parties were "joiners," that they not only displayed the well-known tendency of political types to seek and enjoy organizational affiliations, but that both the quantity and quality of their participation in other community organizations was very similar to that of comparable men. This finding is also consistent with mass behavior where there are no sex differences in participation in voluntary organizations, and it provides further confirmation of the Maccoby and Jacklin conclusion that ". . . the two sexes are equally interested in social (as compared to nonsocial) stimuli."[44]

EGO STRENGTH AND SELF-ESTEEM

Both ego strength and self-esteem involve feelings of personal competence, efficacy, self-confidence, self-control, and autonomy, all of which have been repeatedly found to be correlated with political activity.[45]

Table 12-8. Personality Traits by Party and Candidate Preference, by Sex (%)

	Democrats M	Democrats W	Republicans M	Republicans W	McGovern M	McGovern W	Humphrey M	Humphrey W	Wallace M	Wallace W	Muskie M	Muskie W	Nixon M	Nixon W
Affiliation Index														
Low 1	20	22	20	15	23	24	26	13	12	17	16	22	20	15
2	34	36	35	38	31	40	38	35	44	35	35	23	35	37
3	31	28	28	23	32	24	24	39	35	39	20	36	28	23
4	11	9	14	19	10	8	10	8	6	4	24	11	14	20
High 5	4	5	4	5	4	4	2	5	3	4	5	8	4	5
Weighted N =	1504	1040	688	352	656	631	289	121	102	46	179	105	672	348
Achievement Index														
Low 1	1	1	2	0	1	1	0	0	3	0	2	6	2	0
2	11	8	6	4	13	7	9	7	3	13	8	10	7	4
3	25	27	17	16	30	25	16	25	29	35	15	31	17	16
4	35	34	36	36	31	36	43	30	29	30	54	23	37	36
High 5	28	30	38	44	26	30	32	39	35	22	21	31	38	44
Weighted N =	1504	1040	688	352	656	631	289	121	102	46	179	105	672	348
Power Index														
Low 1	14	14	26	31	11	10	16	26	12	9	22	21	26	32
2	28	28	26	32	27	30	26	30	32	22	29	15	25	33
3	30	31	26	24	30	32	28	26	38	39	33	39	26	24
4	22	20	15	11	26	20	25	13	15	26	12	17	15	24
High 5	6	8	7	1	7	8	5	5	3	4	5	8	7	1
Weighted N =	1504	1040	688	352	656	631	289	121	102	46	179	105	672	348

NOTE: Data are from interviews. For method of index construction and the specific constituent variables that comprise these indexes, see Appendix C.

There are many grounds for supposing that women are less convinced than men of their competence, worth, and autonomy. Like every other world religion, the Judeo-Christian tradition unequivocally subordinates females to males in both social and religious matters; the Freudian tradition conceives the woman as a male manqué doomed to suffer permanent feelings of inferiority because of a missing member;[46] the failure to enfranchise women until this century makes perfectly clear that when they spoke of "men," the Founding Fathers and other national leaders meant *men* and did not include women in the class of people for whom self-government was a basic right.[47] And there are no more grounds for believing that granting women the vote eradicated the memory of a previous condition of servitude than for believing that emancipation of slaves eliminated the psychological and social consequences of slavery. This is especially true because both men and women have a lesser opinion of the work normally done by women than that performed by men.[48]

> In spite of an egalitarian ideal in which the roles and contributions of the sexes are declared to be equal and complementary, both men and women esteem masculine qualities and achievements. . . . When male criteria are the norms against which female performance, qualities, or goals are measured, then women are not equal. It is not only that the culture values masculine productivity more than feminine productivity. The essence of derogation lies in the evolution of the masculine as the yardstick against which everything is measured. Since the sexes are different, women are defined as not men and that means not good, inferior. It is important to understand that women in this culture, as members of the culture, have internalized these self-destructive values.[49]

It is therefore hardly surprising that women have sometimes been found to have a lower sense of political efficacy and self-esteem than men.[50] It is more surprising that females ever achieve levels of self-esteem comparable to males.[51]

Available evidence suggests that adolescent girls consider themselves more competent socially than men,[52] but, with adolescence, many girls who have till then been task-oriented turn their attention to interpersonal relations, and maintaining close affiliative relations becomes the highest priority task.[53] Beginning with the college years, women have less confidence than men about their ability to do well on assigned tasks and have less sense of being able to control their environments.[54] But not all girls lose interest in public affairs, nor lack the self-confidence needed to function effectively in arenas that feature impersonal, task-oriented interactions.

The women state legislators studied by Kirkpatrick had a very good opinion of themselves and high confidence in their ability to achieve desired goals.[55] Costantini and Craik found that "the ways in which female party leaders differ from most other women is remarkably similar to the ways in which male party leaders differ from most other men,"[56] and Emmy Werner and Louise Bachtold concluded that the women state legislators studied by them "shared certain key personality characteristics"[57] with male politicians. As Robert Lane noted more than two decades ago, ". . . if a sense of effectiveness tends to increase political participation, might it not be true also that political participation tends to increase a sense of political effectiveness?"[58]

Various measures aimed at exploring these dimensions of self-concept were included in this study. One set of questions inquired about expectations of influence in various areas and about the influence a respondent believed he had in his state delegation on platform issues and on credentials; other questions inquired about which aspects of politics delegates found most and least satisfying; still others asked which of their personal qualities were best and least suited to politics, and about how difficult the respondent found various situations. Finally, individuals were asked which of various opposite traits best described them (confident/insecure, dependent/independent, and so forth). Some of these questions were open-ended; some forced choices. These multiple measures checked and reinforced one another, and in combination, these questions provide substantial insight into respondents' self-conception.

The findings reveal a striking similarity in the self-concept of politically active women and men. Both sexes are very efficacious, but not absurdly so. Roughly equal proportions of men and women felt they had some influence in their state delegations; influence in their candidate groups, and on credentials and platform decisions; and approximately equal numbers of both sexes thought they were without much influence. A majority of both sexes felt that their actual influence was about as expected. Almost all had a very good opinion of themselves, many describing themselves as self-confident, independent, rational, and decisive. It is significant, however, that men were still more likely than women to rate themselves as high as possible on all these items, while women, though giving themselves high marks, were less likely to claim the highest possible degree of these qualities. Perhaps this reflects the male tendency toward defensiveness noted by Maccoby and Jacklin;[59] perhaps it reflects a slightly less optimistic self-conception in female respondents. In any case both sexes' feelings of personal competence and efficacy are high, and similarities far outweigh the differences.

In addition to sociability and a conviction of personal competence, the recipe for success in democratic politics is believed to include flexibility and a sense of comfortable self-control. The unending round of non-intimate purposive socializing characteristic of democratic politics requires the capacity for empathy and compromise with persons of diverse temperaments and values. Inflexibility and/or anxiety not only handicap interpersonal relations, they also render them unpleasant and so are less compatible with prolonged or extensive involvement in politics. Of course, self-ratings are not entirely reliable instruments for assessing these characteristics widely regarded as undesirable, although they were the basis on which Costantini and Craik attributed to women a "fretful uncertainty about themselves and their situation," and a degree of "anxiety and readiness for psychological change" not characteristic of male political leaders,[60] and the grounds on which Werner and Bachtold found "little evidence of ego-defensiveness or anxiety."[61] And it is the type of measure included in the delegate study.

Both sexes rated themselves as calm rather than anxious, flexible rather than inflexible, and as neither very emotional nor unemotional. Sex differences in self-ratings emerged on two characteristics: women saw themselves as more sympathetic and less competitive than men. These differences are consistent with stereotypes according to which women have larger capacities than men for both empathy and sympathy, while men react more positively to competition.

There were also small but theoretically suggestive differences in male and female ratings of how difficult they find certain tasks: men were somewhat more likely than women to report that they have no difficulty in losing, competing, being with others, or compromising their convictions. Although women are often believed to have greater needs for privacy, there were no differences between the sexes in their response to this question.

When individual traits were factor analyzed, five dimensions emerged and indexes were constructed to tap orientations to these dimensions: order, subjectivity, defensiveness, self-confidence, and competitiveness. Since these composite measures discriminated more sharply than single questions, population distributions on these measures further illuminate sex differences. (See Table 12–9.) Both sexes scored relatively high on the competitiveness index; however, more men than women scored very high. This finding is consistent with other investigations of the two sexes' reactions to competition in nonpolitical situations.[62] Competition is conflict and like all conflict, it involves other traits that are believed to be preeminently male, notably dominance and aggressiveness. While the physiological basis of competitive behavior remains obscure, the cultural component is easily discernible. Boys are socialized not only

Table 12-9. Personality Traits by Party by Sex and Candidate Preference by Sex (%)

	Democrats M	Democrats W	Republicans M	Republicans W	McGovern M	McGovern W	Humphrey M	Humphrey W	Wallace M	Wallace W	Muskie M	Muskie W	Nixon M	Nixon W
Competitiveness/Aggression														
Low	2	9	2	9	4	12	0	5	0	0	0	5	2	9
	27	39	27	43	31	44	28	32	29	36	19	32	27	42
High	71	53	72	49	65	45	72	63	71	64	81	63	72	50
Weighted N =	1516	1083	706	376	662	667	298	125	102	44	170	111	690	368
Subjectivity														
Low	9	8	17	16	4	6	17	10	12	14	12	11	17	16
	73	70	67	72	72	67	71	78	59	86	80	74	67	72
High	18	22	16	12	24	27	12	12	29	0	8	15	16	13
Weighted N =	1520	1087	706	374	662	669	301	125	102	42	179	107	690	366
Defensiveness														
Low	42	30	41	26	39	26	53	32	37	23	40	32	40	27
	53	59	52	62	54	62	46	54	57	77	51	53	53	61
High	6	11	7	12	7	12	1	14	6	0	8	14	7	13
Weighted N =	1532	1096	708	370	668	664	301	131	105	44	179	111	692	362
Rationality/Confidence/Decisiveness														
Low	3	7	2	5	4	6	2	10	6	14	0	5	2	5
High	97	93	98	95	96	94	98	90	94	86	100	95	98	95
Weighted N =	1519	1077	700	376	662	661	301	125	102	44	167	111	682	368

NOTE: Data are from interviews. For method of index construction and the specific constituent variables that comprise these indexes, see Appendix C.

to engage in competition but to enjoy it. Competitive sports provide practice in reacting positively to competition. Women, to the contrary, are not expected to relish competition. Cultural norms operate to restrict the satisfactions that girls and women derive from conflict, especially conflict with males. And there is some evidence that women are more likely than men to deemphasize or find unappealing the conflictual aspects of politics.[63] Political competition, to be sure, is limited, stylized, institutionalized. But it is nonetheless conflict. For these reasons it is not surprising to find fewer women than men saying that they are very competitive, but differences are not large. More surprising is the fact that women delegates scored higher than men on the "defensiveness" index. Previous studies have found boys quicker to adopt ego defensive behavior than girls, and girls more willing to disclose their weaknesses.[64] Costantini and Craik found women more "counseling ready"—which surely means less defensive.[65] But in each candidate group women delegates scored higher than men on defensiveness, and though the differences are not large, they are consistent and statistically significant. They establish that at least in this specialized adult population, women are no less ego defensive than men, and probably more so. Defensiveness signals vulnerability. Since women are widely believed to be more vulnerable than men to criticism[66] and to losing, women who engage in relatively conflictual arenas may have special needs to defend themselves against their own doubts. One wonders whether these women are more vulnerable to disapproval generally, or whether they are only more vulnerable in specific arenas to disapproval from specific persons. It may be important that this is a study of adults, not adolescents. The tendency to greater defensiveness is not, in any case, sufficiently strong to indicate weak egos, only egos slightly weaker than those of the men in the sample. People who are very much involved in protecting themselves from internal and external assaults lack the energy and inclination for socializing that characterizes most women and men in the delegates. Both the men and women in the presidential elite are unusually well-integrated, confident of their effectiveness, confident of their self-control, their social skills, and their knowledge of the political arena.

There are virtually no sex differences in regard to subjectivity and self-confidence. Both sexes scored relatively low on subjectivity, confirming that the political activist shares with the politician a disinclination to turn inward and a preference for acting upon the world. Both sexes scored high on the self-confidence index, confirming the solid confidence in their own stability that is commonly found among the politically active of both sexes. This study offers no support for the view of women as more oriented to the self or more involved in internal than external events.

The character of political activity probably screens out introverted women and men alike. We do not know how many women there are in the society interested in acting in the world, confident enough to attempt it, and skillful enough to have enjoyed a modicum of success in gaining influence. Neither do we know the size of the pool of men whose psychological and social characteristics make them eligible for effective participation in politics.

In sum, there was little difference between male and female delegates in regard to self-esteem, self-confidence, and ego strength. Both sexes have high confidence in their personal competence and political efficacy; both sexes display autonomy and are comfortable in their sense of internal control. There is slight but consistent female tendency to be less competitive and more defensive, and while these are consistent with popular sex stereotypes, the differences do not extend to most women delegates of the two parties.

DOMINANCE, ACHIEVEMENT, AND AMBITION

Everyone understands that politics is intimately and ultimately concerned with power. It has both a historic and an existential relationship to force and authority, both of which are associated with leadership and dominance. Dominance may be achieved and exercised by peaceful or violent means, physical or psychological means or all of these. It is widely believed to be a peculiarly male trait. For many students of social behavior, the "natural" tendency to male dominance of social life is explanation enough of the fact that almost all power processes almost everywhere have been dominated by men and that relatively few women have either sought or exercised power. Charles Darwin found the origins of society in a dominant male. Sigmund Freud also saw society as rooted in force and authority and conceived both of these as male properties. More recently, Lionel Tiger has asserted that "there is a very rigid nature in the relationship between force and maleness which can be observed cross-culturally."[67] This relationship, he believes, excludes women from participation in high politics and guarantees continued male dominance of society. Even Maccoby and Jacklin are impressed by the greater aggressiveness of the male and with the relations between aggressiveness and dominance. However, they also note that although "Dominance among groups of primates or young boys is largely achieved by fighting or threats. . . . In human groups, particularly as humans move from childhood into adulthood, they begin to outgrow their reliance upon aggression as the chief means for achieving dominance."[68] But they also comment that even among boys the ability to maintain coalitions is a factor in establishing and maintaining dominance. Dominance, Maccoby and Jacklin argue, is not *necessarily* founded on aggressiveness, and therefore, male dominance of society and politics is not *necessarily* decreed by human nature.

This investigation provides no direct information on sex differences of delegates in regard to dominance per se. However, there are data on the structure of influence in state delegations, and this is a useful indicator of dominance in a specific political arena. All respondents were asked to name the three members in their state delegations whom they believed to be most influential. Since influence is the distinguishing property of dominance, answers to the question on influence will tell us who between the two sexes was *believed* to be most influential, that is, most dominant. Of course, influence in a delegation may derive from superior experience and knowledge of the arena, or from position in another influence structure, and may therefore be a function of factors unrelated to sex. Still, influence requires leadership skills and dominance and however elusive these are, they must be taken into account by any serious effort to understand the psychology of politics and political participants.

Answers to the question on influential persons in each delegation also provide a basis for judging the extent to which influence in a delegation was susceptible to manipulation through rules regulating the composition of the delegation. If power necessarily follows numbers, then 40 percent of the "most influential" Democrats should be women, and so forth.

Such did not occur. *Analysis by sex of respondents' views concerning who in their delegations were most influential establishes the continued male dominance of state delegations.*[69] Approximately 62 percent of all respondents mentioned *no* woman as among the three most influential persons in the delegation; 26 percent mentioned one or two women; the remainder declined to answer. The pattern of male dominance held in both parties. Among Democrats 71 percent of those who answered the question mentioned no women; 27 percent mentioned one woman; and 2 percent mentioned two women. Among Republicans, 69 percent named no women; 29 percent, one; and 2 percent, two women.[70] McGovern delegates were most likely to name a woman as influential; Wallace delegates least likely; but the differences were not large. Among those responding, the percent mentioning no woman was 56 percent McGovern; 64 percent Humphrey; 63 percent Muskie and Nixon; and 73 percent Wallace.

Women were somewhat more likely than men to perceive other women as influential. While 66 percent of Democratic and 71 percent of Republican males perceived no women as among the three most influential persons in their delegations, only 53 percent of Democratic and 51 percent of

Republican women perceived no woman as influential; 20 percent of Democratic males and 34 percent of women perceived one woman as influential, as compared to 22 percent of Republican men and 38 percent of Republican women. Whether this difference in perception reflects men's greater realism or their reluctance to see women in positions of power is not clear. Perhaps women were more sensitive to other women's influence, because they were more interested in the activities of other women. Perhaps women's higher estimates of other women's influence reflect wishful thinking. Perhaps men's lesser perceptions of women's influence reflected an inability to believe it could be true that in a large group of influential people a woman had become one of the three most powerful persons present. In any case sex differences in influence perception were limited, but they were large enough and consistent enough to suggest the operation of selective perception on the part of one or both sexes, though not large enough to leave any doubt about which sex dominated the delegations to the convention.[71]

The fact that persons of both sexes, both parties, and all generations were in substantial agreement about the sex of the influential delegates gives us greater confidence that their opinions reflected with some accuracy the realities of power distributions, and assuming that this is the case, then *it is very clear that increasing the numbers of women in the two conventions did not increase correspondingly the influence of women in their state delegations—nor, presumably, in the convention.* Probably the meager number of female influentials constitutes an increase over past conventions. We cannot know. Certainly, however, the finding of low female influence not only illustrates the difficulty of reforming power distributions in intended ways, it also testifies to the continued dominance of presidential politics by males—even at the level of the state delegation. No research was needed to demonstrate continued male dominance of candidacies, campaign staffs, rulemakers, and convention managers.

Neither the past nor the present power of men in political processes demonstrates that they are biologically destined to dominate politics nor that males are more "dominant" by nature, but the ubiquity of male dominance of power processes increases the likelihood that this is the case.

Political leadership is a complex phenomenon in which are linked the capacities, skills, and ambitions of the leader and the wants, needs, and/or fears of followers. Dominance is one determinant of leadership capabilities, but ambition and skills are also important determinants of influence. Power, it is sometimes said, goes to those who seek it—provided that they have the skills needed to translate the personal predisposition into an interpersonal reality. *It is neither necessary nor desirable to postulate an ambiguous trait, such as dominance, to explain why and how men dominate influence structures unless or until explanations more accessible to investigation have been exhausted.* The fact that women generally have lacked training and expertise in the "persuasive skills" is too well understood to require documentation here. The paucity of women in law and occupations from which political leaders are recruited is but one evidence of women's relative lack of training and experience relevant to political roles. A congruent professional role is not a prerequisite to political leadership, but it almost surely helps; and the role of housewife, or clerk, or secretary provides less practice in political skills than the roles of lawyer, insurance agent, teacher, or real estate agent. The educational and occupational backgrounds of women delegates indicated that they probably had lower level skills than men. The greater political experience of Democratic (though not of Republican) men also probably gave men an advantage in these arenas. Though women in the presidential elite had quite high levels of social and psychological capabilities, it nonetheless seems likely that women, on the average, brought somewhat less highly developed skills and psychic capacities to politics than men.

What of the other major dimensions of political leadership—achievement and ambition? Did these politically active women *desire* to achieve roles to which power attaches? Or did they find such roles less attractive than such nurturant roles as wife, mother, nurse? Were these women less "achievement oriented" than men?

ACHIEVEMENT

Some people explain the fact of women's low participation in power by their low aspirations and drive. Women, it is asserted, do not achieve power, because they do not seek it, do not desire it, and are not willing to work for it. Elizabeth Douvan and Joseph Adelson found that after earning better grades and higher test scores throughout their school years, on reaching puberty girls begin to abandon interest in achievements in the public sphere and become preoccupied with winning approval.[72] The desire for achievement fades, and affiliation needs come to dominate their psychic functioning.

Achieving most goals is a complex task; it involves adopting and working toward a goal, developing skills, and deferring gratifications. Psychologists believe it is meaningful to talk about the need to achieve as such, independently of any particular goal. Some people, they believe, have greater achievement needs than others; such people are task-oriented and seek goals involving many skills, much effort, and deferral of gratification.[73]

As it is normally defined, achievement and the need to achieve is related to *occupations outside the home and does not include achievement in interpersonal relations*. This focus is one of the reasons that women who have traditionally been especially concerned with social relations, especially family relations, have often been regarded as having lower achievement needs than men. When in a nationwide survey conducted by the University of Chicago's National Opinion Research Center (NORC), college-educated women were asked which kinds of success they most admired and which kinds they would most like to have for themselves, a majority said they desired success as a mother and wife.[74] The normal social scientific interpretation of these findings is that women have lower achievement needs than men. Judith Bardwick and Elizabeth Douvan report that girls are socialized to be ambivalent about achievement, noting that though young girls are rewarded for academic achievement with the onset of puberty "definitions of femininity change." . . . "Now behavior and qualities that were rewarded, especially successful competing, may be perceived negatively."[75] Maccoby and Jacklin's analysis confirms the absence of sex differences in achievement need in prepubertal subjects, but they also cite Martin's study demonstrating that "introducing competition into a task has a different effect upon the achievement striving of the two sexes."[76] Competition inhibited girls and had no such effect on boys. How much can be validly inferred about adult political or other real life behavior from children tossing bean bags is uncertain. But convention and practice in many countries support the notion that males are stimulated by competition in ways that females are not. Apparently girls are no less achievement oriented than boys in regard to the principal tasks of childhood, notably school work, but after puberty most girls give top priority to achieving interpersonal rather than other occupational goals.[77] Obviously the culture and social structure play major roles in these choices, so perhaps do natural predispositions.

Bardwick and Douvan argue that socialization encourages girls to measure themselves by their success in sustaining intimate relations and to develop personal qualities needed for satisfactory performance of traditional nurturant roles. They further state that those characteristics are antithetical to those required for career success.

"Whether you are male or female, if you have traditionally masculine personality qualities—objectivity rather than subjectivity, aggression rather than passivity, the motive to achieve rather than a fear of success, courage rather than conformity, and professional commitment, ambition and drive—you are more likely to succeed in masculine roles."[78]

"Achievement need" as conceived by psychologists, is very closely related to ambition, providing that by ambition we mean not merely a wish, but a powerful motive that mobilizes and channels energy. But while achievement need is general, ambition is focused on particular goals.

Bardwick and Douvan share with many others who have written on this subject the conviction that cultural norms simultaneously discourage girls from developing task-oriented achievement goals and the personality traits necessary to successful pursuit of such goals. This view found powerful confirmation in Matina Horner's fascinating finding that "precisely those women who most want to achieve and who are most capable of achieving" fear success.[79] Not only are femininity and competitive achievement defined as incompatible mutually exclusive ends, but girls come to believe that powerful sanctions await persons of their sex who succeed in competition with males.

To just the extent that women are less achievement oriented than men, that they dislike competition and/or fear success they should less often desire or seek to achieve political office. As a result, ". . . until now very few women have succeeded in traditionally masculine roles, not only because of disparagement and prejudice, but largely because women have not been fundamentally equipped and determined to succeed."[80]

Political ambition involves seeing oneself as having substantial influence over public outcomes. It is another name for the desire for power. However pure or unconscious the motive, in politics the person of high ambition is a power seeker. The effort to identify power needs (or desires) in this study has already been described in Chapter 4. Two types of measure were utilized: one that tapped a generalized orientation to power in interpersonal relationships, another that inquired specifically about ambition for party and public office. Of the three measures (general orientation to power, desire for public office, desire for party office) ambition for public office has most direct relevance to political power. To estimate the seriousness of the ambition, a second question inquired how hard the respondent was prepared to work to achieve the desired office; a third inquired whether or not the respondent expected to achieve the office.

Repeated studies have confirmed that elected officials even at quite low levels are characterized by very high achievement orientations.[81] Despite these findings, the problems of role conflict, and the fact that "making it" in politics is often harder for a woman than a man, there were good grounds for expecting that women who gained entrance to the presidential elite might be at least as achievement oriented *and as ambitious* as men. But they were not.

Although there were no significant sex differences in orientation to power, in interpersonal relations, or in the desire for party office, *in both parties, in all candidate groups, and in all age cohorts women had significantly lower levels of ambition for public office than men, were prepared to make less effort, and had lower expectations of political achievement.* There were no sex differences in desire for party office, but ambition for public office is a more reliable indicator of power motivation than is desire for party office. *Public* officials participate directly in the major power processes of the society. Party officials have influence in party affairs, but they do not often make decisions that have the force of law.[82]

Tables 12–10 and 12–11 demonstrate that sex differences in ambition for public office were quite large. Only the Chisholm candidate support group was an exception to this pattern. In that group women's levels of ambition and effort equalled or exceeded those of men, and so did their expectation of success. More than twice as many women as men had no ambition; more than twice as many men as women expressed a desire to achieve high public offices (here defined as governor, congressman, senator, president or vice-president). When ambition and effort categories were combined in a single measure, men with high ambition prepared to work harder to achieve it than anything else outnumbered women by more than two to one. And when expectations of success (Table 12–12) were combined with effort, into a single "effort/expectation" measure, about three times as many men as women were prepared to work extremely hard to achieve high public office and expected to be successful in the effort. (See Table 12–13.) The possibility that women would be willing to work very hard to achieve middle or local level public offices was also investigated and rejected. It seems clear that, for whatever reason, few women in the presidential elite were prepared to give top priority to achieving any level of public office. Relatively more women than men said they would like to achieve a state level office and were prepared to work somewhat harder than before in order to achieve it. These ambitions and efforts reflect substantial but modest goals.

In his study of ambition and politics, Schlesinger noted, "To slight the role of ambition in politics . . . or to treat it as a human failing to be suppressed, is to miss the central function of ambition in political systems."[83] To slight the role of ambition is also to miss its important function in personal lives. Previous studies of political recruitment and of personality and politics reveal that while ambition is not a *sine qua non* of achieving public office—Barber, Kirkpatrick, Patterson, Bowman, Boynton and others have provided examples of reluctant officeholders— people with little or no ambition are unlikely to gain or retain a significant voice in significant decisions.[84] Presumably, women's lesser achievement drives in politics are *part* of the explanation of their low participation in power processes.

Although students of "ambition theory" have argued that the presence of ambition for higher office affects many aspects of political behavior,[85] it has proved easier to establish the socioeconomic and psychological correlates of ambition than to demonstrate its behavioral consequences. Still it is almost certainly an error to discount the importance for politics of the

Table 12-10. 1972 Convention Delegates: Ambitions for Public Office by Sex and Party by Sex (%)

Public Office Ambition	All Men Delegates	All Women Delegates	Democrats Men	Democrats Women	Republicans Men	Republicans Women
President– vice-president	10	2	12	3	7	0
U.S. senator	28	14	28	17	27	6
U.S. representative	11	6	11	7	11	3
Appointed national office[a]	12	11	12	11	13	10
Governor	7	1	5	1	9	1
Other state office[b]	11	19	10	16	12	24
Mayor	1	1	1	1	1	2
Other local office[c]	3	7	3	7	2	5
No ambition for public office	18	39	17	35	19	49
$N =$	1452	996	913	687	539	309

Question: "Thinking of all the possible offices and positions in politics, from local to national . . . which of the following would you most like to be if you could have your personal choice? Consider public office." (The question was accompanied by a specific list of offices that included those mentioned, as well as a "no interest" category.)

[a]"Appointed national office" includes cabinet member, ambassador, federal judge, federal prosecutor, or "other" national office.

[b]"Other state office" includes lieutenant governor, state judge, state administrative posts, state senator, state representative, or "other" state office.

[c]"Other local office" includes council member or "other" local office.

NOTE: These data are taken from the mail questionnaires. Percentages do not necessarily add to 100 due to rounding.

desire for power when precisely this predisposition has often been seen as *the* distinguishing characteristic of "political man."[86]

This inquiry indicates that differences in ambition are not necessarily accompanied by different perceptions of the political process, nor by different political goals, nor by distinctive self-concept.

The implications of these findings on aspiration levels seem important. To be sure, sex differences were not very large, and neither sex was monolithic in regard to them. Not all men had high political ambitions, nor did all women lack them. Nonetheless, the findings confirm that *even among women who are interested and active in politics*, fewer women than men desire high office, and fewer can be expected to seek it. Since the route to high elective office is long, fraught with many obstacles and booby traps, it is very unlikely that anyone who does not have an intense desire for high office will travel it to the end. Furthermore, women's lower level aspirations are accompanied by a lesser drive to achieve them. It is not the level of ambition but the contrast with men that is significant here. The findings prove nothing about innate characteristics of the two sexes, but they offer important clues to contemporary male domination of power processes. Why these differences exist and whether they will be, indeed can be, influenced by changing conceptions and role distributions are questions that will be pursued in a later chapter.

AMBITIOUS AND UNAMBITIOUS WOMEN: TWO PROFILES

Because ambition affects how hard a person will work at winning influence, and, often, how successful she will be at attaining it, women's lower levels of political aspirations and achievement goals merit close attention. Profiles were constructed of two "pure" co-relation types: those who desired high public office and were prepared to work harder than for anything else and those without ambition for public office. The former comprise 15 percent of the total sample of women ($n = 141$); the latter 42 percent ($n = 391$).[87] Women with particularly high and low political achievement drives are found in all age groups, all sizes of families, and all ideological groups. The assertions in the following profiles that they are more likely to be young and/or unmarried, and/or very liberal means that as compared to other groups, persons in that category were more likely to have high political ambitions. Many of the characteristics of women with high political ambitions are shared by ambitious men. Presumably, however, there are some sex specific determinants of political ambition, or else as many politically active women as men would aspire to high public office and would expect to work hard to achieve their goal.

Table 12-11. Ambition for Public Office by Candiate Preference and by Sex (%)

	McGovern Men	McGovern Women	Humphrey Men	Humphrey Women	Wallace Men	Wallace Women	Muskie Men	Muskie Women	Nixon Men	Nixon Women	Chisholm Men	Chisholm Women
No ambition	15	36	18	43	29	35	10	37	19	49	11	5
Low ambition	2	6	5	9	0	17	1	5	2	5	11	5
Moderate ambition	8	15	13	26	18	22	17	20	13	26	11	25
High ambition	75	43	65	22	53	26	72	37	66	21	67	65
$N =$	445	445	144	58	45	23	81	59	518	296	9	20
Effort for Public Office by Candidate Preference and by Sex (%)												
Some effort	9	13	7	24	3	8	17	16	13	20	29	6
More than before	44	49	49	38	47	62	31	45	39	45	43	56
More than for anything else	47	38	44	38	50	31	52	39	47	35	29	39
$N =$	352	263	106	29	30	13	64	31	369	131	7	18

Public Office Ambition and Effort by Candidate Preference and by Sex (%)

High ambition/high effort	37	18	31	11	28	10	42	15	34	10	25	32
High ambition/ moderate effort	33	19	30	7	21	19	18	17	25	8	38	32
Moderate ambition/ moderate effort	4	8	7	7	12	14	10	8	6	12	0	21
N =	418	423	132	54	43	21	72	53	469	275	8	19

Ambition question: "Thinking of all the possible offices and positions in politics, from local to national—which of the following would you most like to be if you could have your personal choice? Consider public office."

"High ambition" was measured by a choice of president, vice-president, U.S. senator, congressperson, cabinet member, ambassador, federal judge, federal prosecutor, "other" national office, or state governor.

"Moderate ambition" was measured by a choice of lieutenant governor, state senator, state representative, state judge, state administrative post, "other" state office, or mayor.

"Low ambition" was measured by a choice of council member or "other" local office.

"No ambition," of course, included all those without any public office aspiration.

Effort question: "If there were a real chance to hold the position you think is most desirable, how much effort would you be willing to make to get that position?" Possible answers: 1) would work harder and make more sacrifices than for any other goal in life; 2) would work harder than before in politics; and 3) would make some additional effort.

NOTE: These data are from the mail questionnaires.

**Table 12-12. Expectation of Success in Achieving Public Office
by Party and Sex (%)**

| | Democrats | | Republicans | |
	Men	Women	Men	Women
No expectation	27	52	33	67
Low expectation	9	14	5	10
Moderate expectation	28	22	24	17
High expectation	37	12	37	7
$N =$	851	640	515	285

Question: "Now, all things considered, which of all these positions do you think you are *most likely to hold* at the top of your career in politics?"

"High expectation" includes any national offices—appointed or elected—and state governorships.

"Moderate expectation" includes state offices other than governor, and includes mayor.

"Low expectation" includes local offices other than mayoralties.

NOTE: These data are from the mail questionnaires.

**Table 12-13. Expectation of Success in Achieving Public Office
by Effort, Party, and Sex (%)**

| | Democrats | | Republicans | |
	Men	Women	Men	Women
High exp/high effort	15	5	13	3
High exp/mod effort	18	6	15	3
High exp/low effort	4	1	7	2
Mod exp/high effort	4	4	4	2
Mod exp/mod effort	16	12	11	8
Mod exp/low effort	6	5	6	5
Low exp/high effort	1	2	0	0
Low exp/mod effort	3	6	1	5
Low exp/low effort	3	4	3	3
No interest	31	56	40	71
$N =$	747	596	431	269

This table is based on the "expectation" question cited in Table 12-12 and the following "effort" question:

"How much effort will you have to make to reach this position?" Possible answers: 1) will work harder and make more sacrifices than for any other goal in life (high effort); 2) will work harder than before in politics (moderate effort); and 3) will make some additional effort (low effort).

NOTE: These data are from the mail questionnaires.

As compared to women without ambition, those who aspire to high pub-lic office are more apt to see themselves as competitive, aggressive, ambitious, and somewhat surprisingly, they also consider themselves to be more subjectively oriented. Those self-evaluations, which were also characteristic of very ambitious men, suggest a person of high self-confidence who is comfortable with the idea of self-assertion and competi-tion. Presumably women with such self-conceptions would be compara-tively uninhibited in their pursuit of goals even when this involved direct competition.

The woman with high hopes and intense drive for public office is most likely to be under 30 (Table 12–14); however, she might be virtually any age under 65. Like all delegates, she is probably married; however, much higher percents of unmarried than married women have high ambition; conversely, married women are more likely than unmarried to have no political ambition whatsoever. Similarly, while having children is not in-compatible with strong achievement drives, women without children are most likely to have high political ambition.[88] However, women with very young children are no less likely than women with older children to lack political ambition (perhaps because the effects of the women's age coun-terbalance the effects of young children). Most women with high political ambitions report that their political activity interferes little or not at all with family life—probably because their spouse approves it, but women who are separated or divorced from their husbands constitute nearly twice as large a portion of the very ambitious as the unambitious, suggest-ing that combining high ambition for achievement in male domains with a stable marriage may still pose special problems. Still, only 12 per-cent of the women with high ambition were estranged from their husbands.

Ambitious women were more likely to be currently employed outside the home, and to work at relatively high status jobs, or to be students with high aspirations. Housewives were twice as numerous among those with-out ambition as among those with high ambition. A majority of the ambitious women saw some combination of wife/mother and professional roles as ideal. A quarter would like to ease role problems with respon-sible household help; one-fifth regarded intermittent employment as an ideal work pattern; only 12 percent of the most ambitious (and 30 percent of those without ambition) preferred not to be employed outside the home.

Though Protestants were most numerous among both the ambitious and the unambitious, they were somewhat more likely to fall in the former than the latter category; Catholics and women with no religion were most numerous among the very ambitious. As expected, ambition was related to education; however, many highly educated women had no political ambition. Income, place of birth, and ethnic background had a slight relation to ambition levels. Women with very low income, blacks, and Irish were slightly more likely to have high ambition; those with very high incomes, rural origin, or Anglo-Saxon descent were a little less likely to have high political ambition, but the differences were marginal. Like the political participants generally, ambitious women were generally long-time residents of their communities and "joiners."

Table 12-14. Public Office Ambition/Effort by Age and Sex (%)

	No Ambition	High Ambition/ High Effort	High Ambition/ Mod Effort	Mod Ambition/ High Effort	Mod Ambition/ Mod Effort	N
Under 30						
Men	8	55	27	3	4	234
Women	25	29	21	4	11	171
Age 30–39						
Men	10	45	27	3	4	271
Women	36	13	23	7	10	197
Age 40–49						
Men	20	29	30	3	7	384
Women	46	14	12	6	8	292
Age 50–65						
Men	30	22	23	2	7	330
Women	52	12	9	6	8	217
Over 65						
Men	46	17	18	4	4	72
Women	68	3	3	3	13	31

Cramer's V:

For under 30 = .38
30–39   = .47
40–49   = .38
50–65   = .32
Over 65   = .41

NOTE: These data are from the mail questionnaires. For the questions on which this table is based, see footnote to Table 12-11.

The political characteristics of women who desired high public office were also mixed. Women of high political ambition were found in all candidate groups but were especially numerous among McGovern supporters and scarcer among Republicans. Few (16 percent) had experience in public office and fewer than one-third of these would-be high achievers had not held party office. Over one-third had held a party office at the national or state level. Just as young delegates were "overrepresented" among the very ambitious, so were persons of brief political experience. Those recruited to politics during or after 1968 comprised 37 percent of the most ambitious. The ambitious were neither more nor less strongly attached to party than the unambitious, though they were somewhat more likely to give very high priority to policy.

Like other delegates whose policy interests were the main incentives to political activity highly ambitious women were likely to have intense, relatively extreme policy commitments, but they were no more likely than the unambitious to have comprehensive, internally consistent ideologies. Radicals and the very liberal were definitely "overrepresented" among the ambitious; conservatives comprised twice as large a portion of the unambitious as the ambitious.

The most important characteristic differentiating the ambitious from the unambitious was not their beliefs about war and peace, welfare and inflation, but their beliefs about women. Ambitious women were substantially more likely than those without ambition to deny that there are innate sex differences that disqualify women from exercising power, less likely to believe that there are profound or unmanageable conflicts between family and political roles, and more likely to believe that men discriminate against women in the political sphere. Since views about women constitute part of a woman's self-conception, it is hardly surprising that they should play an important role in facilitating and inhibiting power seeking behavior. A later chapter, which is devoted to analyzing delegates' conceptions of femininity, will further illuminate relations among these and other aspects of political life.

NOTES

1. Eleanor Emmons Maccoby and Carol Nagy Jacklin, *The Psychology of Sex Differences* (Stanford, Calif.: Stanford University, 1974), p. 227.

2. Sex differences in political participation have been widely noted, especially in, Gabriel A. Almond and Sidney Verba, *The Civic Culture: Political Attitudes and Democracy in Five Nations* (Princeton: Princeton University Press, 1963). However, economic and social modernization erodes these differences: Lester Milbrath, *Political Participation: How and Why Do People Get Involved in Politics* (Chicago: Rand McNally & Co., 1965), p. 136; also Stein Rokkan and Angus Campbell, "Norway and the United States of America," *International Social Service Journal* 12, no. 1 (1960): 66–99. Women's rights are described as an indicator of modernity in Alex Inkeles and David H. Smith, *Becoming Modern: Individual Change in Six Developing Countries* (Cambridge, Mass.: Harvard University Press, 1974), p. 26.

3. In 1968 women comprised 13 percent of Democratic and 17 percent of Republican delegations. For a survey (unfortunately not up-to-date) of women's presence in national political conventions, see Marguerite J. Fisher and Betty Whitehead, "Women and National Party Organization," *American Political Science Review* 38 (1944): 895–903. Additional information on delegates' characteristics is available in Paul T. David, Ralph M. Goldman, Richard C. Bain, *The Politics of National Party Conventions* (Washington, D.C.: Brookings Institution, 1960), p. 343.

4. Theodore White, *The Making of the President 1972* (New York: Atheneum, 1973), p. 36.

5. The guidelines did not make clear whether women (or blacks or youth) should be represented in proportion to their numbers in the total population of a state, the nation, or among a party's identifiers or voters. The guidelines are discussed in Chapter 2.

6. The "quotas" were not born in a vacuum. They resulted at least in part from new demands made by and on behalf of women and in part from established practice. Note that both parties had long included both a man and a woman from each state on the national committees, and various states have had special rules aimed at securing equal representation of the two sexes at decision-making levels—for example, a requirement that the county chairman and vice chairman should be of different sexes.

7. Quoted from a mimeographed statement of the National Women's Political Caucus which was distributed at the Democratic Convention. Despite its efforts at bipartisanship, the NWPC was in fact heavily McGovernite in perspective, perhaps because several of its most prominent leaders—among whom were Gloria Steinem and Bella Abzug—were publicly associated with McGovern's campaign. Although Shirley Chisholm was active in the NWPC, she did not succeed in winning much support from its leadership for her presidential bid.

8. Ibid.

9. *The National Journal*, September 23, 1972, p. 1512.

10. Leon D. Epstein, *Political Parties in Western Democracies* (New York: Frederick A. Praeger, 1967), p. 126.

11. White, *Making of the President*, p. 38.

12. Susan Tolchin and Martin Tolchin, *Clout: Women Power and Politics* (New York: Coward, McCann and Geoghegan, 1974), believe that women will bring to politics a more "humanistic perspective," p. 247.

13. This finding is consistent with findings of Edmond Costantini and Kenneth H. Craik, "Women as Politicians: The Social Background, Personality and Political Careers of Female Party Leaders," *Journal of Social Issues* 28, no. 2 (1972): 217–235, esp. p. 220. Also Jeane Kirkpatrick, *Political Woman* (New York: Basic Books, 1974), p. 38.

14. Costantini and Craik also found California male activists better educated than women. "Women as Politicians," p. 220.
15. Ibid.
16. Studies of political participation have repeatedly found that "professional persons are the most likely to get involved in politics," Milbrath, *Political Participation*, p. 126.
17. Bardwick and Douvan emphasize the negative effects of "absence of independent and objective achievement." Judith M. Bardwick and Elizabeth Douvan, "Ambivalence: The Socialization of Women," *Women in Sexist Society: Studies in Power and Powerlessness*, eds. Vivian Gornick and Barbara K. Moran (New York: Basic Books, 1971), pp. 225–239.
18. It seems clear that the entry of more women into politics may result in further diminution of economic perspectives and a "broker's" view of politics. Kirkpatrick, *Political Woman*, pp. 154–159.
19. M. Kent Jennings and Norman Thomas, "Men and Women in Party Elites: Social Roles and Political Resources," *Midwest Journal of Political Science* 12 (1968): 469–492, esp. p. 488.
20. Costantini and Craik, "Women as Politicians," p. 221, found women less upwardly mobile than men. The active women studied by them were more likely than men to have high status parents.
21. Note that women were much more likely than men to have spouses with high education and high status jobs.
22. In this society and most others family status is a function of the husband's occupation and income and is only marginally affected by the wife's occupation.
23. Bardwick and Douvan, "Ambivalence," p. 236.
24. Kirkpatrick found that women legislators had fewer children than male legislators, *Political Woman*, p. 55.
25. Bardwick and Douvan, "Ambivalence," p. 237. Also Kirkpatrick, *Political Woman*, pp. 229–240.
26. Donald Matthews, *U.S. Senators and Their World* (Chapel Hill: University of North Carolina Press, 1960), p. 17. Kirkpatrick, *Political Woman*, p. 31; Page Smith, *As a City Upon a Hill: The Town in American History* (New York: Alfred A. Knopf, 1966). But note that Milbrath argues that "the larger the community the higher the rate of participation." Milbrath, *Political Participation*, p. 130, but he is discussing mass participation.
27. Robert E. Agger, Daniel Goldrich, and Bert E. Swanson, *The Rulers and the Ruled: Political Power and Impotence in American Communities* (New York: John Wiley & Sons, 1964), pp. 333–334; Robert E. Lane, *Political Life: Why People Get Involved in Politics* (Glencoe, Ill.: The Free Press, 1959); Milbrath, *Political Participation*, p. 133.
28. Milbrath, *Political Participation*, p. 131; Kirkpatrick, *Political Woman*, pp. 43–45; note that Costantini and Craik, "Women as Politicians," found women to be members of fewer organizations than men, p. 232. Murray Hausknecht, *The Joiners: A Sociological Description of Voluntary Association Membership in the United States* (New York: Bedminster, 1962). Also Almond and Verba, *Civic Culture*, note that membership in voluntary associations is related to participation. Milbrath, *Political Participation*, p. 17, notes "it is probably easier for a person who enjoys social activity to enter politics than it is for a person who shuns social and community participation." Lester W. Milbrath and Walter Klein, "Personality Correlates of Political Participation," *Acta Sociologica* 6, fasc. 1–2 (1962): 53–66.
29. Maurice Duverger, *The Political Role of Women* (Paris: UNESCO, 1955), p. 128.
30. Kirkpatrick, *Political Woman*, pp. 42–45; on the tendency of state legislators to be "joiners," see Thomas R. Dye, "State Legislative Politics" in *Politics in the American*

States: A Comparative Analysis, eds. Herbert Jacob and Kenneth N. Vines (Boston: Little, Brown, 1965), pp. 168–169. Also Frank J. Sorauf, *Party and Representation: Legislative Politics in Pennsylvania* (New York: Atherton, 1963), p. 79. Patricia Gorence Bach reports the same pattern of multiple memberships in "Women in Public Life in Wisconsin," unpublished manuscript, Alverne Research Center on Women, p. 13.

31. Alice Rossi, "Barriers to the Career Choice of Engineering, Medicine or Science Among American Women," *Readings on the Psychology of Women,* ed. Judith M. Bardwick (New York: Harper and Row, 1972), p. 81.

32. Angus Campbell, Philip E. Converse, Warren E. Miller and Donald E. Stokes, *The American Voter* (New York: John Wiley & Sons, 1960), pp. 474–493. Almond and Verba, *Civil Culture,* pp. 209–212; Lane, *Political Life,* p. 149.

33. James David Barber, *The Lawmakers: Recruitment and Adaptation to Legislative Life* (New Haven: Yale University Press, 1965), pp. 23–66.

34. Duverger, *Political Role,* p. 128.

35. Lane, *Political Life,* pp. 212–213.

36. Kirkpatrick discusses the views concerning the "natural" basis of male dominance in *Political Woman*, pp. 9–13. Virginia Woolf, *A Room of One's Own* (New York: Harcourt, Brace, 1929) is always interesting on this subject.

37. Maccoby and Jacklin, *Psychology.*

38. Milbrath, *Political Participation.* He also provides citations on the large literature on sociability and politics, see p. 75.

39. Maurice Duverger explained the low levels of political activity of European women by their tendency to withdraw from contact with the larger world. *Political Role,* p. 128.

40. J. E. Gorai and A. Scheinfeld, "Sex Differences in Mental and Behavioral Traits," *Genetic Psychology Monographs* 77 (1968): 169–299.

41. Rossi, "Barriers to the Career Choice," p. 81. Douvan and Adelson emphasize special concern of the adolescent girl with opinions and feelings of those in her immediate circle. Elizabeth Douvan and Joseph Adelson, *The Adolescent Experience* (New York: John Wiley & Sons, 1966). Maccoby and Jacklin discuss differences and similarities in the socializing of boys and girls. *Psychology,* pp. 200–214.

42. These indexes are also discussed in Chapter 4. For a description of their composition, see Appendix C.

43. For further discussion of the type of socializing characteristic of politics, see Kirkpatrick, *Political Woman,* pp. 97–99 and 115–118.

44. Maccoby and Jacklin, *Psychology,* p. 349.

45. Important among these are Barber's study of the Connecticut legislature, *Lawmakers;* Campbell et al., *American Voter*; Almond and Verba, *Civic Culture*; Robert Dahl, *Who Governs? Democracy and Power in an American City* (New Haven: Yale University Press, 1961): Lane, *Political Life,* pp. 147–155. On self-esteem, see especially Paul M. Sniderman's *Personality and Democratic Politics: Correlates of Self-Esteem* (Berkeley: University of California Press, 1975); Stanley A. Renshon, *Psychological Needs and Political Behavior: A Theory of Personality and Political Efficacy* (New York: The Free Press, 1974) focuses on the need for personal control as a motive of political participation.

46. Freud's negative conception of women is made clear in many of his works. A good discussion of his misogyny is Philip Rieff, *Freud: The Mind of the Moralist* (New York: Viking, 1959), pp. 173–185. For a more recent psychoanalytic view, see Erik H. Erikson, "Inner and Outer Space: Reflections on Womanhood," *Daedalus* 93 (1964): 582–606.

47. Because this is sometimes treated as a unique or distinctive American failing, I wish to emphasize that the United States was among the first nations to enfranchise women. A

recent useful and interesting essay is Victoria Schuck, "Sexism and Scholarship: A Brief Overview of Women, Academia, and the Disciplines," *Social Science Quarterly* 55, no. 3 (1974): 563–585. Also Barbara Tovey and George Tovey, "Women's Philosophical Friends and Enemies," *Social Science Quarterly* 55, no. 3 (1974): 586–604.

48. H. N. Mischel, "Professional Sex Bias and Sex-role Stereotypes in the U.S. and Israel," reported in Maccoby and Jacklin, *Psychology*, p. 543. Note also "The hero in America has been white, Protestant and male," Dixon Weeter, *The Hero in America* (Ann Arbor, Mich.: University of Michigan Press, 1963), cited by Patricia S. Kruppa, "The American Woman and the Male Historian," *Social Science Quarterly* 55, no. 3 (1974): 605.

49. Bardwick and Douvan, "Ambivalence," pp. 233–234.

50. In addition to the previously cited studies reporting women's lower levels of political efficacy, note that Bardwick found that "women have lower levels of self-esteem than men," Judith M. Bardwick, *The Psychology of Women: A Study of Bio-Cultural Conflicts* (New York: Harper and Row, 1971), p. 155.

51. "We found that on most measures of self-esteem girls and women show at least as much satisfaction with themselves as do boys and men. During the college years some sex differentiation does occur. At this time, women have less confidence than men in their ability to perform well on a variety of tasks assigned to them; they have less sense of being able to control the events that affect them, and they tend to define themselves more in social terms." Maccoby and Jacklin, *Psychology*, p. 162.

52. R. Carlson, "Stability and Change in the Adolescent's Self-Image," *Child Psychology* 36 (1955):659–666. No differences were found at the preadolescent level. Girls are also less defensive; R. L. Williams and H. Byars, "Negro Self-Esteem in a Transitional Society," *Personnel and Guidance Journal* 47 (1968): 120–125; also N. Bogo, C. Winget and G. C. Gleser, "Ego Defenses and Perceptual Styles," *Perceptual and Motor Skills* 30 (1970): 599. Both of these studies are included in Maccoby and Jacklin's annotated bibliography, *Psychology*.

53. Douvan and Adelson, *Adolescent Experience*. Also, J. S. Coleman, *The Adolescent Society* (New York: The Free Press, 1961).

54. Relevant studies of particular interest are J. W. Julian, C. R. Regula, and E. P. Hollander, "Effects of Prior Agreement by Others on Task Confidence and Conformity," *Journal of Personality and Social Psychology* 9 (1968): 171–178; N. T. Feather, "Change in Confidence Following Success or Failure as a Product of Subsequent Performance," *Journal of Personality and Social Psychology* 9 (1968): 38–46. Note that although women in this study had lower expectations of success, their performance was equal to that of men. Also, N. T. Feather, "Attribution of Responsibility and Valence of Success and Failure in Relation to Initial Confidence and Task Performance," *Journal of Personality and Social Psychology* 13 (1969): 129–144. For further citations of studies on this question, see Maccoby and Jacklin, *Psychology*, p. 155.

55. Kirkpatrick, *Political Woman*, pp. 52–53.

56. Costantini and Craik, "Women as Politicians," p. 225.

57. Emmy E. Werner and Louise M. Bachtold, "Personality Characteristics of Women in American Politics," in *Women in Politics,* ed. Jane S. Jaquette (New York: John Wiley & Sons, 1974), p. 83. Also, E. R. Kruschke, "Level of Optimism as Related to Female Political Behavior," *Social Science* 41 (1966): 67–75.

58. Lane, *Political Life*, p. 153.

59. Maccoby and Jacklin, *Psychology*, pp. 157–160.

60. Costantini and Craik, "Women as Politicians," p. 226.

61. Werner and Bachtold, "Personality Characteristics," p. 83.
62. J. C. Martin, "Competitive and Non-competitive Behavior of Children in Bean Bag Toss Game," University of California, 1973, cited in Maccoby and Jacklin, *Psychology*, p. 534.
63. Fred I. Greenstein, "Sex Related Political Differences in Childhood," *Journal of Politics* 23 (1961): 353–371. Kirkpatrick, *Political Woman*, p. 143, found that women legislators deemphasized conflict as a dimension of politics.
64. Maccoby and Jacklin, *Psychology*, p. 157.
65. Costantini and Craik, "Women as Politicians," pp. 223–225.
66. Bogo, Winget, and Glesen, "Ego Defenses."
67. Lionel Tiger, *Men in Groups* (New York: Random House, 1969), p. 81.
68. Ibid.
69. The classification by sex was based on names. There are obvious pitfalls in this process; however, there seemed no alternative short of asking the respondents to indicate the sex of the persons they listed and thus making them self-conscious in their responses.
70. This question was included in the mail questionnaires: 2,272 delegates responded; 315 gave no answer.
71. There was virtually *no* generational difference in the perception of male and female influence in state delegations.
72. Douvan and Adelson, *Adolescent Experience*, pp. 72–77.
73. David C. McClelland, *The Achievement Motive* (New York: Appleton-Century-Crofts, 1953); McClelland found that women's N/ach scores were higher than men's under neutral conditions, but that women's scores did not improve as a result of instructions designed to arouse achievement drives while men's scores improved appreciably under these conditions.
74. Rossi, "Barriers to the Career Choice," p. 81.
75. Bardwick and Douvan, "Ambivalence," p. 229.
76. Maccoby and Jacklin, *Psychology*, p. 141.
77. The difficulty of finding language to juxtapose wife/mother roles and other "occupations" is fascinating and suggestive. In fact traditional wife/mother roles are occupations and involve many of the same interpersonal skills as managerial and political roles. But we do not *think of them* as occupations. Occupations are only what one is paid for.
78. Bardwick and Douvan, "Ambivalence," p. 233.
79. Matina Horner, "The Motive to Avoid Success and Changing Aspirations of College Women," reprinted in Bardwick, *Readings*, p. 62.
80. Bardwick and Douvan, "Ambivalence," p. 233.
81. Jennings and Thomas, "Men and Women" and Costantini and Craik, "Women as Politicians," pp. 227–231, report women's lower levels of political ambition.
82. Court decisions that give party rules the force of law have, of course, enhanced their authoritative character and perhaps transformed party officials into authoritative rule makers for the society.
83. Joseph A. Schlesinger, *Ambition and Politics: Political Careers in the United States* (Chicago: Rand McNally & Co., 1966), p. 2.
84. Jennings and Thomas, "Men and Women"; Costantini and Craik, "Women in Politics," pp. 227–235; Barber, *Lawmakers*, pp. 23–66; Kirkpatrick's "personalizer" is an example of a type of woman legislator without political ambition, *Political Woman*, pp. 197–207. On the importance of being asked for (rather than seeking) office, see Lewis Bowman and George R. Boynton, "Recruitment Patterns Among Local Party Officials: A Model and Some Preliminary Findings in Selected Locales," *American Political Science Review* 60 (1966): 667–676; also Ingunn Nordeval Means, "Women in Politics: The Norwegian

Experience," *Canadian Journal of Political Science* 5 (1972): 381–382. Also with reference to state legislators who do and do not wish to return, see John Wahlke, Heinz Eulau, William Buchanan, and Leroy Ferguson, *The Legislative System: Explorations in Legislative Behavior* (New York: John Wiley & Sons, 1962); Charles S. Hyneman, "Who Makes Our Laws," in *Legislative Behavior: A Reader in Theory and Research,* eds. John C. Wahlke and Heinz Eulau (Glencoe, Ill.: Free Press, 1959).

85. John W. Soule, "Future Political Ambitions and the Behavior of Incumbent State Legislators," *Midwest Journal of Political Science* 13 (1969): 439–454; Kenneth Prewitt and William Nowlin, "Political Ambitions and the Behavior of Incumbent Politicians," *Western Political Quarterly* 22 (1969): 298–308.

86. Lasswell's conception of political man as power maximizer is explicated in many of his works. Good sources are Harold D. Lasswell, *Power and Personality* (New York: Viking Press, Compass Books, 1962), pp. 39–58, and *Psychopathology and Politics* (Glencoe, Ill.: Free Press, 1951), pp. 47–53. George E. Catlin proposes that we conceive "political man" as a power maximizer in *The Science and Method of Politics* (New York: Alfred A. Knopf, 1927).

87. The high aspiration/high effort index was utilized on the assumption that *effective* ambition includes both aspiration and achievement drive (effort). The percents of men in the high aspiration/high achievement category and the no ambition category were 35 percent ($n = 459$) and 19 percent ($n = 256$) respectively.

88. Men with high aspiration and achievement drive are also more likely to be young, single, or, if married, childless, and are more likely than women to say that their political ambitions conflict with their family lives.

CHAPTER 13

Political Characteristics of Women Delegates

This chapter explores the political characteristics of women in the presidential elite. It inquires into the processes by which women became delegates and their reasons for desiring to serve as delegates and for political participation more generally. It discusses how they conceived the role of delegate and how they in fact spent their time at the conventions. Finally, it examines both the substance and the style of women's political beliefs. The central questions throughout are comparative: how did women's political styles and behavior compare with men's? Did women have different reasons from men for participating in politics? Did they have distinctive personal and political goals? Was women's focus of attention different from men's? Were their perspectives on the major problems of the day different from men's perspectives? Did women react to foreign policy like wives and mothers whose most precious relationships are threatened by war or did they react as partisans of particular ideologies?

Exploration of these questions will not only tell us what some women seek through politics, but will identify the probable social and political consequences of their increased political participation. Determining whether women have distinctive political attitudes on issues is not difficult; it is only necessary to ask them about their attitudes and compare their responses with men's. This procedure does not go to the more basic questions about whether, if women had a larger role in the whole society, the political system would be different from what it is or the culture would be different from what it is; nor whether, if women had their "consciousness raised," they would think differently from what they now do. It only asks why women in today's world become politically active, how they behave, and what they think about some major political issues. That men dominate the culture and politics and therefore have a decisive effect in determining patterns of political interaction and salience of issues does not prove that women would create different patterns of political interaction or would focus attention on different issues, though we cannot be sure that they would not do so. We simply do not and cannot know what a political world in which women had equal influence would be like. It might be just like the political world in which we now live. It might be quite different.[1] The question dealt with here is whether, our life and times being what they are, women who have managed to reach positions of political influence behave differently from men and have different perspectives on salient political questions of the day.

RECRUITMENT

Did the quotas and other pressures on candidates to include women in state delegations result in different methods of recruitment for women and men? Contemporary talk frequently stated or implied that to fill women's "quotas" women were being recruited in different ways from men: that men were taking initiatives and winning delegates' positions while women were being placed in delegations—presumably by some male activist desirous of achieving a "balanced" slate. This investigation indicates the contrary: *there were no significant differences in the recruitment of male and female delegates*. (See Table 13–1.) In motives, methods of pursuing the nomination, contests, and campaigns, the patterns of recruitment for women and men were indistinguishable.

Although Costantini and Craik reported "unmistakable sex differences" among the California party leaders studied by them in regard to motivation,[2] the motives of the two sexes in seeking to become delegates were very similar; both were stimulated chiefly by the desire to see their preferred candidate elected, by a general interest in politics and a habit of political participation. Women were no more oriented to candidates than men and no more or less likely to be motivated by moral concerns.[3] Having decided they desired to become delegates, women and men followed the same courses of action. Approximately equal proportions of each sex took the initiative in contacting others and/or campaigning. The women at the convention were neither more passive nor less active than men in winning delegates' seats. Some of each sex won seats without competition; some of each sex had tight races; some ran as part of a slate; some did not. *There were no sex specific incentives to become a delegate and no sex specific routes to delegate status*.

Although there were no significant differences in the recruitment of male and female delegates, there was one important difference in the political backgrounds of Democratic women and men.[4] The men had more political experience than the women. In both parties and all candidate support groups fewer women than men had attended previous conventions, and fewer had held public office. Democratic women also had been active less long than their male counterparts and had less experience in party offices. This was not true of Republican women whose longevity and experience in party office equalled that of Republican men.

Scores on the index constructed to measure delegates' total political experience confirm that Democratic women had less cumulative experience in party politics than Democratic men. Table 13–2 shows that 36 percent of Democratic women scored low on the Party Experience Index as compared to 22 percent of their male counterparts. This relationship between sex and experience held for all candidate groups. (See Table 13.3.) In the McGovern, Humphrey, and Muskie candidate support groups, substantially more women than men scored low on political experience; fewer scored high. Nearly as many Democratic women as men had held party office, but the offices they held were frequently at lower levels; very few had held public office. For example, 65 percent of McGovern women and 73 percent of McGovern men reported having held party office, but nearly twice as many men as women had held public office. One unintended side effect of the Democrats' requirements for increased numbers of women was to lower the percentage of delegates with experience in public office.

The Republican pattern is quite different. Although women comprised a somewhat smaller portion of the Republican than the Democratic Convention, the women present at the Republican Convention were as experienced as the men. Approximately 5 percent of both Republican men and women scored low on the Political Experience Index; approximately 45 percent of each scored high. Republican women had been active as long as men and even more had held party office. Their apprenticeship in party affairs also equalled that of men. Only in experience in public office did the record of Republican women not equal or exceed that of men. Nearly one-half of Republican men had held some elective public office as compared to only 28 percent of Republican women.

Women with previous experience in party and public office were distributed fairly evenly among the various Democratic candidate support groups. No Democratic candidate support group was characterized by unusually large numbers of women with prior experience in public office. Each candidate group contained some women who held party and public office, but in each, the proportion of such was less than the percent of men.

It seems likely that Democratic women's lesser experience in party and public office constituted a disadvantage leaving them with lesser reputations for leadership and less advantageous locations in communications networks. It is tempting to believe that these disadvantages contributed to women's lesser influence.

The differences in political experiences of women and men may have

Table 13-1. Method of Delegate Selection by Party and Candidate Preference by Sex (%)

	Democrats		Republicans		McGovern		Humphrey		Wallace		Muskie		Nixon	
	M	W	M	W	M	W	M	W	M	W	M	W	M	W
Method of Selection														
Primary	45	36	34	22	52	45	48	35	36	14	44	24	34	22
State convention	29	30	46	53	21	21	36	39	33	57	48	49	46	52
State-local committee	7	9	11	14	6	8	6	9	16	14	3	7	11	15
Mixed system	19	24	9	11	21	26	9	18	16	14	5	20	9	11
N =	902	668	531	299	442	433	140	57	45	21	79	59	510	286
Was There a Contest for Your Delegate Post?														
Very close contest	31	31	13	16	33	31	30	40	22	17	28	23	13	16
Somewhat close	25	25	16	17	25	27	27	26	22	26	26	29	16	16
Not too close	34·	33	31	27	34	33	33	28	33	39	38	32	31	27
No contest at all	10	11	41	41	9	10	11	5	22	17	9	16	41	41
N =	905	672	535	297	443	435	142	57	45	23	80	56	514	285

Who, If Anyone, Approached You and Encouraged You to Seek a Position as a Delegate to the National Convention This Year?[a]

Decided on my own	24	33	15	23	27	38	20	22	18	17	16	19	15	22
Close friends and associates	12	16	17	31	9	15	13	21	9	9	8	16	17	29
Party members, unofficially	29	37	3	6	40	45	22	22	36	39	19	14	3	6
Candidate supporters	4	6	1	2	5	8	3	7	2	0	0	0	1	2
Civic groups or their members	7	10	25	43	4	7	13	17	4	9	6	14	25	43
Party official	3	8	0	2	4	11	2	2	2	0	1	2	2	2
Issue supporters	3	6	4	5	3	4	5	7	2	9	1	12	4	5
Others	56	42	61	40	52	38	48	50	51	52	69	55	60	40
N =	908	678	532	302	443	438	144	58	45	23	80	58	511	289

What Did Your Campaign Involve?[a]

No campaign	23	25	46	45	22	25	20	26	18	26	35	25	46	45
Speeches to party and civic groups	38	29	20	15	42	32	35	24	27	13	37	37	21	15
Television-radio appearances	6	5	2	2	8	7	6	3	2	0	4	0	2	2
Newspaper ads	17	12	5	3	19	14	23	14	20	4	15	9	5	3
Television-radio ads	5	3	1	0	6	4	6	2	13	4	4	2	1	0
Door-to-door	24	25	5	3	32	32	17	14	33	35	15	9	4	3
Mail circulars	28	30	18	20	31	34	24	19	20	9	24	34	18	20
Telephone campaigns	33	35	18	18	36	36	32	31	33	30	20	41	18	17
Donate services to party or candidate	20	25	13	15	21	26	25	28	29	26	12	25	13	16
N =	913	687	539	309	445	445	144	58	45	23	81	59	518	296

[a]Eight possible responses recorded, therefore, percentages can add to more than 100.

NOTE: Data are from mail questionnaires.

been compounded, too, by the fact that women were less numerous than men at both conventions. Since state delegations make relatively few advance preparations and conventions are of short duration, the position of a delegate within the delegation's influence structure is chiefly a function of his position in other arenas. Resources brought into the arena are even more important than in arenas that feature more sustained interaction. However, Republican women constituted a kind of control group concerning the relations of sex, experience, and influence. And, as we have seen, though their experience was equal to that of Republican men, few were named as one of the three most influential persons in their state delegations.

INCENTIVES AND ROLE PERCEPTIONS

Women sought to become delegates for much the same reasons as men. Did they also seek and find the same satisfactions in political participation? Previous studies have frequently found women's political motives and

Table 13-2. Political Experience by Party by Sex (%)

	Democrat Men	Democrat Women	Republican Men	Republican Women
Low experience	22	36	4	5
	52	47	50	51
High experience	27	17	46	44
N =	890	674	519	300

NOTE: These data are from the mail questionnaires. For a complete explanation of the Political Experience Index, see Appendix C.

Table 13-3. Political Experience by Candidate Preference by Sex (%)

	McGovern		Humphrey		Wallace		Muskie		Nixon	
	M	W	M	W	M	W	M	W	M	W
Low	32	41	11	32	36	32	5	20	4	5
Middle	54	49	44	46	41	64	48	36	50	51
High	14	10	46	23	23	5	47	44	46	44
N =	434	441	142	57	44	22	79	59	499	288

NOTE: These data are from the mail questionnaires. For a complete explanation of the Political Experience Index, see Appendix C.

Table 13-4. Important Incentives to Political Participation by Candidate Preference by Sex (%)

Incentives	McGovern Men	McGovern Women	Humphrey Men	Humphrey Women	Wallace Men	Wallace Women	Muskie Men	Muskie Women	Nixon Men	Nixon Women
Support particular candidate	99	98	96	95	96	96	96	95	94	97
Influence party on policy	95	91	88	70	93	100	88	84	83	75
Sense of civic responsibility	68	69	89	84	71	74	82	79	86	94
Politics is my way of life	70	65	84	79	46	57	85	78	76	87
Support the party	41	46	86	95	43	50	84	81	89	94
Friendships and social contacts	47	49	70	79	50	65	65	65	64	77
Fun and excitement	47	47	65	72	50	61	61	64	59	72
Near people doing important work	37	34	57	59	56	55	47	49	47	53
Want career in politics	40	27	46	30	26	22	41	31	41	21
Visibility and recognition	27	18	47	34	41	36	41	37	38	35
Family-friends active in party	16	26	40	47	29	29	25	44	32	42
Business-professional contacts	8	7	23	7	14	17	18	7	14	8
N =	440	441	139	56	44	23	80	58	507	287

Question: "We are interested in peoples' reasons for being involved in politics. How important are each of the following reasons to your own participation in politics?" Possible answers for each incentive listed above: extremely important, quite important, not very important, not at all important.

This table describes those for whom each incentive was extremely important or quite important.

NOTE: These data are from the mail questionnaires. N's are from "Support Particular Candidate" table; other N's are comparable in size.

satisfactions to be quite different from men's. Robert Lane attributed to American women a more "moralistic orientation,"[5] and Costantini and Craik reported that men's motives were more "self-serving" in nature than those of women, while "women leaders grant significantly greater importance than the male leaders to strong party loyalty." They found sex differences "particularly magnified on those items which most clearly tap a power orientation, . . . principally on 'interest in running for public office' and 'search for power and influence'."[6]

Table 13–4 shows that women who participated in the two conventions in 1972 were attracted to politics for the same reasons as men—with one minor and one major exception. Women were neither more nor less single-minded, neither more nor less strongly attached to their parties, neither more nor less morally concerned or interested in influencing policy, nor concerned with civic duty, nor attracted by the fun and excitement of politics. Like men, women were most interested in seeing particular candidates elected and preferred policies adopted. And, like men, some were motivated by party solidarity and some were not—and whether they were depended on factors other than sex. Few women or men were motivated by the desire to become rich or famous through politics. Somewhat larger percents of women than men reported that participation of friends and family were important to their participation, but the differences were not large enough to establish that women were more likely than men to seek affection or approval in politics. Many delegates of both sexes enjoyed the social aspects of politics, and affiliation needs were no stronger in women than men. The fun and excitement of politics were no more important to women than to men. But in both parties fewer women than men were attracted to politics by the hope of building a political career. There were no "women's reasons" for participating in politics, but there was one predominant "men's reason"—political ambition and career enhancement. If political ambition is an indicator of the desire for power (as I have argued), then the important sex difference in motives for political participation is that significantly fewer women were motivated to participate by the hope of maximizing power. Whether women's lesser political ambition is a function of existing role distributions (which leave fewer women than men interested in all traditionally male occupations) or of innate disinterest in power, or of a disinclination to seek positions that entail competition with men—the result is the same. Women's lesser interest in political careers was also identified by Jennings and Thomas as the most striking difference between Michigan's women and men delegates.[7] Costantini and Craik described ambition for public office as the key variable in what they termed the "public office oriented" and the "intraparty oriented" styles of political participation. The public office style was most characteristic of male activists; the intraparty style was most attractive to female activists.[8] Most students of sex and politics agree that women's non-careerist orientation is related to the whole pattern of sex role distributions and that it affects other aspects of women's orientation to politics. Sometimes it is argued that this makes women more disinterested and more moral.[9]

The conviction that cultural revolution is producing a new woman stimulated some observers to attribute to young women at the 1972 conventions motives and styles different from their older colleagues. However, the relation of incentives, roles, and age does not indicate that experienced female activists reflected traditional predispositions while the younger, more liberated women purveyed different motives and styles. Such generational differences as exist (for example, concerning party solidarity) were characteristic of both sexes.

This investigation provides no evidence that political participation of women is more likely than that of men to be motivated by moral concerns. Many members of both sexes gave high priority to rectitude concerns. The attraction of rectitude incentives, solidary incentives, and status incentives varied by candidate preference, age, ideology, and political experience but not by sex. Since a distinctive tendency to "moralism" has long been attributed to women, the finding that this national sample of women were no more likely than men to display "a kind of bloodless love of the good"[10] requires comment. A plausible explanation of the absence of sex differences lies, I believe, in the declining importance of material incentives in politics and the large number of men who in 1972 were motivated by "idealism" rather than material or career incentives.

Similarities between the sexes also existed with regard to role perceptions. (See Tables 13–5 and 13–6.) Women were no more nor less likely than men to be institutional preservers or institutional transformers, nor to see the delegate's role as that of policy maker. They were neither more nor less likely than men to have local concerns nor to emphasize personality as a factor in decision making. Since women were relatively more numerous in McGovern ranks than elsewhere, relatively more Democratic women displayed the distinctive characteristics of that candidate group. But Republican women had political characteristics similar to Republican males, and the distaff supporters of Humphrey, Muskie, and Wallace displayed the characteristics of males in those groups. Although Epstein and Wilson noted unusually large numbers of women in the reform clubs and the middle-class suburban political organizations, and Robert Lane spoke of the "image of the female vote as a 'reform' vote,"[11] in this study women displayed no distinctive propensity for being amateurs, purists, or professionals. Again, the explanation may lie in the evolution of party organizations—from heavily male urban machines and courthouse groups to the

Table 13-5. Organization Support by Candidate Preference by Sex (%)

	McGovern		Humphrey		Wallace		Muskie		Nixon	
	Men	Women	Men	Women	Men	Women	Men	Women	Men	Women
Very low	33	29	1	2	28	22	3	0	1	0
Low	32	33	14	5	24	22	17	15	9	3
High	27	26	32	27	28	33	32	43	38	25
Very high	9	11	53	66	21	22	48	43	53	72
N =	321	296	118	41	29	9	65	40	427	221

NOTE: These data are from the mail questionnaire. For a description of the construction of this measure, see Appendix C.

Table 13-6. Policy Orientations by Candidate Preference by Sex (%)

	McGovern		Humphrey		Wallace		Muskie		Nixon	
	Men	Women	Men	Women	Men	Women	Men	Women	Men	Women
Very low	0	1	6	2	0	0	6	5	4	6
Low	11	9	39	49	16	18	39	49	39	38
High	45	43	49	46	38	27	47	38	47	47
Very high	44	47	6	2	46	55	8	8	11	9
N =	389	366	109	41	37	11	64	37	381	192

NOTE: Data are from the mail questionnaires. For a description of the construction of this measure, see Appendix C.

"volunteer" style of participatory politics typical of the last two decades. The latter are obviously more hospitable to women's participation than the former.

The similarity of the sexes with regard to incentives and roles strongly implies that in 1972 both sexes perceived similar opportunities for value maximization in the political arena, that they formed similar attachments to groups and to ideas, and that they shared the same political culture. These findings coincide with those of Jennings and Thomas who reported that "members of the Michigan elites do not differ substantially by sex in their perceptions of the political process, the nature of their political party, and the party's role in the political process."[12]

ORIENTATIONS OF WOMEN TO PUBLIC ISSUES

If women bring any distinctive perspectives into politics, then these should be manifested in foci of attention and distinctive attitudes on public issues. The belief that women have special interests has been widespread among scholars and public alike. Robert Lane's view that "Women have special reasons to be interested in problems of price control, housing, zoning, education, playgrounds, prevention of war. . ."[13] reflected the once nearly ubiquitous belief that women have distinctively "feminine perspectives" on events. Lane summed it up thus: "A moralized political orientation characteristic of women arising from maternal responsibilities, exclusion from more socially achieved areas of activity, and narrower orbits tends to focus female political attention upon persons and peripheral 'reform' issues."[14] The fact that women voted very much like men did not stimulate revision of expectations concerning the political relevance of sex differences but prompted such explanations as that of Duverger, who suggested that the tendency of women to vote much like men reflected the fact that "They (women) still have the mentality of minors in many fields and particularly in politics, they usually accept paternalism on the part of men."[15] Such interesting interpretations of the *similarities* of the sexes' political perceptions and attitudes reflect the tenacity of the belief in politically relevant sex differences.[16]

This notion—that there are innate sex differences relevant to politics— has been familiar in America since frontier days. There are theoretically sound reasons for expecting that the sexes' distinctive socialization, roles, and life experiences would lead to different interests, assumptions, and approaches.[17] The belief that women were keepers of the community conscience, that they had special purity and special sensitivity, has been the stock in trade of male chauvinists who justified keeping women out of the political arena on grounds that they should be protected from the gross, vulgar reality and of women's partisans who claimed that women's greater purity constituted a reason for their participation. Both notions—that the greater purity of women is advantageous and disadvantageous in politics—share the premise that the political behavior of the two sexes will differ significantly because of the psychological and moral differences between them. The historical association of women's suffrage with temperance and anti-slavery movements reinforced the expectation that women would bring more intense moral concerns to politics. Popular stereotypes also suggested that women might be more pacific than men, less aggressive and warlike. The argument that women would end war and corruption received a setback when women, once enfranchised, voted much like men voted, except in somewhat smaller numbers.[18] But with the advent of the women's movement and new demands for a larger voice in the society's decision process, this argument was dusted off and updated.

Three questions are examined in the following paragraphs: first, did the focus of attention of women delegates differ from that of men's? Second, did women's opinions on substantive policy questions differ from those of men, including their opinions on questions believed to be of special concern to women? Third, were there identifiable differences in ideological style between sexes, such as a tendency to judge events and persons more or less harshly or a tendency to have more or less extreme opinions?

In examining the structure of political opinions by sex, it is, as always, important to control for candidate preference. Most Democratic delegates were chosen as supporters of particular candidates. The women chosen as McGovern delegates were selected, not from among all women or all Democratic women but from among women who supported McGovern. Those chosen may or may not have had views like the majority of women of their party or of the nation—that is a question that will be examined later. *But if women as women feel and think differently from men about issues, then the opinions of women of all partisan affiliations should differ at least marginally from men's.*[19] Focus, direction, intensity, and scope of opinions on issues were examined in the effort to identify sex-based differences.

Focus of attention is reflected in delegates' responses to open-ended questions about the most important problems facing government and the most important problems facing people like themselves. Although the question concerning the most important problems facing the nation invites responses that deal with national rather than local affairs, national concerns may be either concrete or abstract, personal or remote, rectitude or power oriented. And, possible responses to the question concerning problems facing "persons like you" provide even larger scope for the expression of different objects of attention.

The most important fact concerning women's focus of attention is that virtually none of them in either party identified women's status and role as salient public or personal issues. Neither did they mention women in describing their reasons for desiring to become a delegate. These priorities cast light on the fate of the so-called "women's issues" at the Democratic Convention.

Previous research provided good grounds for supposing that women delegates would be more likely than men to mention problems related to nurturant, welfare functions (health, education, and child care), more likely to focus on local, state, or national problems than international, and more likely to focus on concrete than abstract issues. But there were no significant differences between the sexes. As with incentives and organizational style, the salience of issues was associated with candidate preference, but not with sex.[20] Not only were differences among candidates much larger than differences between sexes, but there were no consistent differences between the sexes. Women supporting McGovern and Wallace were more likely than men in these candidate groups to mention economic problems, but women supporting other candidates were not.

Analysis of issue orientations and policy preferences by sex establishes that *on most major issues of public policy, including those concerning education and the poor, the views of women delegates were virtually identical with those of men.* On welfare policy women were no more generous than men; on law and order they were neither more nor less "tough-minded" than men; on busing, too, they shared the views characteristic of men with their general ideological position. And symbolizing these similarities is the fact that women placed themselves on the ideological spectrum in the same ways as men. They were no more liberal—as some studies have found[21] and some contemporary spokespersons claim—nor more conservative, as they have often been believed to be. Both men and women supporting George McGovern tended to take positions unsupportive of authority and the status quo on a range of issues; both women and men supporting Nixon or Wallace were consistently likely to support existing institutions. Women were not more generally idealistic about foreign affairs than men; they were no more likely to advocate greater support for the United Nations, nor foreign aid, nor normalization of relations with Cuba.

The single exception to this general pattern of similarity in issue orientations of the sexes concerns opinions on military policy. Women were somewhat less likely than men to support the resolution of problems by force. Consistent though not large sex differences existed on whether the United States should withdraw all troops from Asia, on whether American military intervention would be justified only by an attack on the United States itself, and on whether it is ever justifiable to use nuclear weapons.

Despite these small but consistent differences, there was no "women's position" on issues involving the use of military force. On these questions, too, women, like men, tended to split on ideological rather than sexual lines with a large majority of McGovern's women supporters advocating total withdrawal from Southeast Asia and a large majority of Nixon's distaff supporters opposing withdrawal.

The feminine disinclination to use force in foreign policy did not extend to domestic policy. McGovern women were slightly more "tender-minded" than men in their candidate support group; Humphrey and Muskie women were much more "tender-minded" than their male counterparts; but both Wallace and Nixon women were somewhat more "tough-minded" than the men in their candidate support groups. Could it be that whatever the dominant ideological direction of the group, women of that group tend, as a group, to be somewhat "more so"? V. O. Key's observation about the attitudes of the upward mobile comes to mind: "Perhaps the common denominator is the tendency of persons who gain a valued status or position to adopt in special degree the perceived norms of their new status or group connection."[22]

Sex distributions on the Political Culture Index appear to provide limited confirmation for this hypothesis. More McGovern women delegates held the extremely "new politics" position and favored cultural transformation; more Wallace and Nixon women delegates scored on the extreme end of the "cultural conservative" position. And in Humphrey and Muskie ranks, more women than men held moderate views. But examination of attitudes on a range of subjects establishes that women did not hold whatever opinion they have in a distinctively extreme degree.

Unusual intolerance has also been attributed to women.[23] But women did not judge those of whom they disapproved more harshly than men. Women supporting McGovern and Wallace were somewhat more likely than men in those groups to make the most negative possible evaluation of those of whom they disapproved, but women in the Nixon, Muskie, and Humphrey camps did not.

In sum, it can be said that there were no consistent differences in the views of women and men delegates concerning which public or private problems were most pressing and important, nor was there a "women's" position on any of the salient issues of 1972. Although there was a discernible tendency for greater numbers of women to oppose war, even on foreign policy issues examined in this study women reacted like Republicans and Democrats and liberals and conservatives rather than as women. There was also no discernible difference between the sexes in ideological intensity and no general tendency for women to be either more or less tolerant or extreme in their evaluations of people or events. The fact that the same issues cohered when factor analyzed suggests that the same ideological connections and patterns of inference operated on both sexes. Women were as likely as men to have comprehensive ideological positions and to be eclectic in their views. Roughly equal portions of both sexes were holistic, pragmatic, and eclectic in their views. One of the most definitive indicators of the ideological diversity of politically active women in 1972 was the simple fact that they supported different presidential candidates.

These findings argue that the socialization of the sexes with reference to general questions of public affairs is probably more similar than different. Public affairs and political culture are areas to which formal education is enormously relevant. Girls and boys take the same civics, political science, and history courses; they read the same newspapers and listen to the same television programs. Gross differences in the cognitive capacities or styles of the sexes would probably be required to overcome the years of common schooling, reading, and viewing habits. Obviously such gross differences do not exist.

The finding of ideological similarity of the sexes does not settle larger, subtler questions about sex-based differences in perception, cognition, and feeling. But it has important implications for the emergence of women as a distinctive political bloc. But what of the questions often thought to have special appeal to women? Even if women divided like men on the most salient questions, perhaps they had more distinctive perspectives on subjects specifically oriented to their traditional concerns or more specifically involving their welfare.

Jane Jaquette has suggested that women may bring to politics distinctive perspectives on "issues which were formerly relegated to the private sphere, issues involving sexual relations, new forms of marriage, changes in the family structure, and areas of corporate decision-making such as hiring and promotion. . . ."[24] But do they? Was there a women's position in 1972 on issues widely believed to be of special interest to women?[25]

Several questions were included in the delegate study on issues that have a special relevance to women's past and present status. Specifically, opinions were elicited on day care programs, abortion laws, personnel policy, women's liberation, and the National Women's Political Caucus.

There was no issue on which the women delegates of either party were unanimous, but there was more support for abortion on demand, day care centers, egalitarian personnel policies, and women's liberation among women than among men. A majority of women in each convention believed the sexes should be treated equally in case economic depression forced layoffs; a majority believed in easy abortion (though not necessarily abortion on demand); and a majority supported a national day care program. Views on these "women's" issues were closely related to orientations toward other social and political policies. For example, while 56 percent of McGovern's women supporters took the view that abortion should be available to any woman who desired it, only 39 percent of Muskie's women delegates, 23 percent of Humphrey's, 18 percent of Nixon's, and 9 percent of Wallace's agreed. A national day care program drew the strong endorsement of 82 percent of McGovern women and 66 percent of the women supporting Muskie, but under one-half of Humphrey's distaff supporters, one-fourth of Nixon's women supporters, and only 13 percent of Wallace women were equally convinced. Republican women who were generally united on issues and organizational orientations were split on whether in case of a depression, women should be laid off before male heads of family and on the women's liberation movement. Male opinions on these issues also followed general ideology and provided further confirmation that each of these issues involved not just women, but other values and views concerning society and politics. (The relation of opinions on busing and a national day care program, for example, was gamma .88.) These relations between social, political, and sexual ideology partially explain women's attitudes toward women's liberation. A large majority of Republican women and supporters of George Wallace were negatively disposed to women's lib as were some moderate Democrats (a fact that partly explains the difficulties of state and national equal rights amendments). Most delegates of both sexes saw women's issues as part of broader disagreements between those who desired to preserve the society and those who sought to transform it, but a few women who were quite conservative on most political issues supported easy abortion, national day care, and women's liberation. (See Tables 13–7 and 13–8.) The possibility that women will become an effective political pressure group is dependent on the extent to which women's issues and identifications develop the power to align women in new ways.

WOMEN'S LIBERATION AND THE NATIONAL WOMEN'S POLITICAL CAUCUS

The National Women's Political Caucus constituted the first major effort of an organization of women to function within the conventions as a pressure group articulating women's interests. The NWPC presented itself as a bipartisan organization, had officers drawn from both parties, and was active in both conventions. It aroused widespread interest among women of all political persuasions. Nearly four-fifths of women in all candidate preference groups said they were interested in its activities. Nearly two-thirds of Democratic women delegates participated in some women's activity, and many of these were sponsored by the NWPC whose influence

Table 13-7. Views on Abortion, Day Care, and Employment Policy by Party by Sex, Candidate Preference by Sex, Political Generation by Sex (%)

| | Democrats | | Republicans | | McGovern | |
	Men	Women	Men	Women	Men	Women
Views on Abortion						
Abortion, never	4	4	5	2	2	2
If life and health of woman in danger	26	15	35	24	19	8
If woman and doctor agree	41	35	44	57	42	33
If the woman wants it	29	47	17	18	37	56
Weighted *N* =	1501	1073	674	362	653	661
Views on Day Care						
Very much in favor	56	70	17	25	75	82
Somewhat in favor	27	19	36	28	22	14
Undecided	4	2	9	6	0	2
Somewhat opposed	5	5	23	22	1	2
Very much opposed	8	4	15	18	1	1
Weighted *N* =	1543	1099	704	378	668	671
Views on Employment Policy						
Lay off women first	25	20	34	38	19	16
Treat sexes equally	75	80	66	62	81	84
Weighted *N* =	1475	1075	684	362	641	655

(Table continued)

Questions: "There has been some discussion about abortion in recent years. Which one of these opinions best agrees with your own view? 1) Abortion should never be permitted; 2) abortion should be permitted only if the life and health of the woman are in danger; 3) if a woman and her doctor agree, she should be able to have a legal abortion; 4) any woman who wants to have an abortion should be able to have one."

"How do you feel about the proposal to establish a national day care or child care program for working mothers? Are you very much in favor, somewhat in favor, somewhat opposed, very much opposed, or what?"

"Sometimes a company has to lay off part of its labor force. Some people think that the first workers to be laid off should be women whose husbands have jobs. Others think that male and female employees should be treated the same. Which of these opinions do you agree with?"

Table 13-7. **Views on Abortion, Day Care, and Employment Policy by Party by Sex, Candidate Preference by Sex, Political Generation by Sex (%)—Continued**

	Humphrey		Wallace		Muskie		Nixon	
	Men	Women	Men	Women	Men	Women	Men	Women
Views on Abortion								
Abortion, never	2	5	9	9	2	8	5	2
If life and health of woman in danger	35	35	44	61	24	19	34	24
If woman and doctor agree	41	38	31	22	49	34	45	57
If the woman wants it	22	23	16	9	26	39	16	18
Weighted N =	298	127	96	46	176	97	658	354
Views on Day Care								
Very much in favor	51	44	11	13	45	66	16	25
Somewhat in favor	31	34	11	13	30	22	37	28
Undecided	4	5	14	0	10	6	9	6
Somewhat opposed	7	12	3	13	10	6	23	23
Very much opposed	7	5	61	61	5	0	15	18
Weighted N =	301	131	108	46	179	107	686	370
Views on Employment Policy								
Lay off women first	23	38	50	38	26	23	34	37
Treat sexes equally	77	62	50	62	74	77	66	63
Weighted N =	298	131	96	42	173	103	668	354

Table 13-7. Views on Abortion, Day Care, and Employment Policy by Party by Sex, Candidate Preference by Sex, Political Generation by Sex (%)—Continued

Pre–1945		1946–1959		1960–1967		1968–1972	
Men	Women	Men	Women	Men	Women	Men	Women
0	3	3	3	4	3	2	2
30	35	28	18	24	15	25	7
45	37	45	41	46	49	40	36
25	25	24	38	26	33	33	55
139	75	467	322	412	322	245	269
37	42	40	54	39	59	60	64
25	31	33	22	35	23	22	24
11	0	5	6	5	2	6	2
10	17	14	10	13	10	4	7
18	10	8	9	9	7	9	3
142	83	471	328	437	328	262	269
31	34	33	30	24	23	29	21
69	66	67	70	76	77	71	79
138	83	465	324	412	318	255	267

NOTE: These data are from the interviews.

was much broader than its formal membership. Substantially fewer women later said that they approved its conduct, though only among Wallace supporters did it stimulate outright disapproval. Many women described their reactions to the NWPC as mixed. It won kudos mainly for its effort to stimulate women's participation in politics and to eliminate discrimination against women. It was criticized chiefly on grounds that its own activities created a negative impression. Only about one-half of McGovern women and one-quarter to one-third of women in other candidate support groups reported that most women in their delegations had a favorable opinion of the NWPC. Curiously, more men than women believed the women in their delegations thought well of the NWPC,[26] and there was a widespread impression that men in both conventions thought less well of the NWPC than women. No more than one-quarter of the Democrats (and 10 percent of the Republicans) believed the NWPC had had a great deal of influence, but a majority of delegates believed it had had an impact on the course of their conventions. (See Table 13-9.)

It is not surprising that the NWPC encountered less than unanimous approval from women. Disagreements among women delegates were extensive; common ground on public issues was scarce. Women in the Democratic and Republican conventions disagreed with each other on busing and day care, on foreign policy and welfare. They did not even agree

Table 13-8. Attitudes Toward Women's Liberation (%)

	Democratic Men	Democratic Women	Republican Men	Republican Women
0	8 ⎫	6 ⎫	27 ⎫	28 ⎫
1	5 ⎪	2 ⎪	12 ⎪	8 ⎪
2	8 ⎬ 33	4 ⎬ 19	14 ⎬ 72	9 ⎬ 60
3	5 ⎪	4 ⎪	11 ⎪	10 ⎪
4	7 ⎭	3 ⎭	8 ⎭	5 ⎭
5	18	15	18	17
6	9 ⎫	10 ⎫	5 ⎫	9 ⎫
7	11 ⎪	10 ⎪	2 ⎪	7 ⎪
8	11 ⎬ 49	14 ⎬ 67	2 ⎬ 10	4 ⎬ 24
9	10 ⎪	12 ⎪	1 ⎪	2 ⎪
10	8 ⎭	21 ⎭	0 ⎭	2 ⎭
N =	875	663	509	292

NOTE: Data are from the mail questionnaires. This table reflects responses to a thermometer rating of women's liberation.

Table 13-9. Reaction to National Women's Political Caucus (%)

	McGovern	Humphrey	Wallace	Muskie	Nixon
Favorable	55	29	2	36	38
Mixed	38	58	40	51	50
Unfavorable	7	13	59	13	12
Weighted N =	1281	365	111	265	838

	McGovern		Humphrey		Wallace		Muskie		Nixon	
	Men	Women	Men	Women	Men	Women	Men	Women	Men	Women
Favorable	61	48	27	35	0	7	44	23	42	31
Mixed	32	44	60	54	44	27	43	63	47	56
Unfavorable	7	7	13	11	56	67	13	14	12	13
Weighted N =	626	655	250	115	81	30	164	101	510	328

Question: "What was your reaction to the National Women's Political Caucus? Was it favorable, unfavorable, mixed, or what?"

NOTE: The data are from the interviews.

on women's liberation. The women who participated in such activities had some distinctive characteristics that identified them as more feminist than nonparticipants and more feminist than women generally. Participants were much more likely than nonparticipants to support a national day care program strongly, to advocate equal treatment of women in employment, to favor abortion on demand, and to have a positive view of the women's liberation movement and the NWPC.

WOMEN'S ISSUES AND POLITICAL PRIORITIES

Conflict on women's issues within the Democratic party cut across candidate preference lines creating an especially intense conflict in McGovern ranks. The issues involved therefore provided a particularly good opportunity to observe the relative priority which *women* gave to women's issues (the abortion plank and the South Carolina challenge) and to candidate selection. Since the majority of the most vocal supporters of abortion on demand and a larger voice for women were found in McGovern's ranks, the McGovern leaders' decision not to support the South Carolina challenge and the abortion on demand plank was potentially explosive.

Abortion is an issue that touches the most profound convictions concerning life and death. For some delegates (and voters) abortion was quite simply murder—the murder of unborn and helpless children. For other delegates the availability of abortion involved the most basic of women's rights: the right to control her own body. For most political strategists (virtually all of whom were men) convention action concerning abortion involved another issue as well: whether the platform would saddle the candidate with a plank that would cost him votes in the general election. In consequence, an effort was made to finesse the issue. Doing so meant giving the electoral function of the party priority over the educative function of the platform. Disagreement over these priorities produced some deep divisions among Democratic delegates supporting various candidates.

The Tolchins described the floor fight on abortion as "one of the most passionate battles of the convention . . . 'It was a fight that divided sister against sister,' reported Myra MacPherson in the *Washington Post* with Bella Abzug taking off on Shirley MacLaine, who spoke against the minority plank. It was a fight that had Gloria Steinem's usually controlled monotone quivering as she wept in rage, verbally attacked Gary Hart and called McGovern strategists 'bastards'."[27] When interviewed later, a bare majority of McGovern's women supporters said they supported the decision to abandon the abortion plank, and a substantial minority (41 percent) disagreed. Women in other candidate support groups were also split. The South Carolina credentials challenge produced a similar division within McGovern ranks. While 43 percent of McGovern's women supporters agreed with the decision to give convention strategy priority over support for a challenge supported by the National Women's Political Caucus, 36 percent disagreed.

INFLUENCE

Disagreement on issues and preoccuption with the presidential nomination and race doubtless weakened the potential influence of women in both conventions. We have already seen that few respondents named a woman as one of the three most influential members of their delegation. However, when respondents of both sexes were asked about whether women had participated in state delegations as fully as men, 90 percent to 95 percent of each sex agreed that this had been the case, and approximately four-fifths of both Democrats and Republicans said in response to a general question that women had been as influential as men in their delegation's proceedings.

It is possible that women as a group could have been as influential as men in a delegation and still have none or few of their number rank among the three most influential delegation leaders—but it is not likely. It seems more likely that the general description of women being as influential as men reflects an impression that women did indeed take part in convention deliberations, did not suffer obvious discrimination, and had some impact on decisions. But when delegates were confronted with a specific question about the power structure in their delegation, it was men's names that leaped to mind.

NOTES

1. To the best of my knowledge no feminist utopias exist. Shulamith Firestone's *The Dialectic of Sex: The Case for Feminist Revolution* (New York: William Morrow, 1970), take steps in this direction. Wilhelm Reich's picture of sensual non-authoritarian matriarchal society is one man's vision of a feminist utopia—*The Mass Psychology of Facism* (New York: Farrar, Straus and Giroux, 1970), esp. ch. II.

2. Edmond Costantini and Kenneth Craik, "Women as Politicans: The Social Background, Personality, and Political Careers of Female Party Leaders," *Journal of Social Issues* 28, no. 2 (1972): 233–235.

3. Previous studies of mass behavior which have found women more oriented to candidates include Angus Campbell, Philip E. Converse, Warren E. Miller, and Donald E. Stokes, *The American Voter* (New York: John Wiley & Sons, 1960), pp. 483–493; Maurice Duverger, *The Political Role of Women* (Paris: UNESCO, 1955), p. 143; Robert E. Lane, *Political Life: Why People Get Involved in Politics* (Glencoe, Ill.: The Free Press, 1959), p. 213.

4. This finding is consistent with the study of Michigan activists by M. Kent Jennings and Norman Thomas, "Men and Women in Party Elites: Social Roles and Political Resources," *Midwest Journal of Political Science* 12 (1968): 469–492, especially p. 490.

5. Lane, *Political Life,* p. 212.

6. Costantini and Craik, "Women as Politicians," p. 234.

7. Jennings and Thomas, "Men and Women," pp. 490–491.

8. Costantini and Craik, "Women as Politicians," pp. 227–232.

9. Joseph A. Schlesinger, *Ambition and Politics: Political Careers in the United States* (Chicago: Rand McNally & Co., 1966).

10. This is Lane's phrase. *Political Life,* p. 212.

11. Leon D. Epstein, *Political Parties in Western Democracies* (New York: Frederick A. Praeger, 1967), p. 126; James Q. Wilson, *The Amateur Democrat: Club Politics in Three Cities* (Chicago: University of Chicago Press, 1962); Lane, *Political Life,* p. 212.

12. Jennings and Thomas, "Men and Women," p. 484.

13. Lane, *Political Life,* p. 209.

14. Ibid., p. 216.

15. Duverger, *Political Role,* p. 129.

16. Unless I am mistaken, Jane S. Jaquette continues this tradition when she asserts "that women have always been sensitive to the gap between the norms and reality of democratic politics in the United States seems clear; however, such sensitivity has until very recently been very unfashionable." Jane S. Jaquette, "Introduction: Women in American Politics," *Women in Politics,* ed. Jaquette (New York: John Wiley & Sons, 1974), pp. xiii–xxxvii, xxiv.

17. See especially, Herbert H. Hyman, *Political Socialization: A Study in the Psychology of Political Behavior* (New York: The Free Press, 1959); Fred I. Greenstein, *Children and Politics* (New Haven: Yale University Press, 1969); David Easton and Jack Dennis, *Children in the Political System: Origins of Political Legitimacy* (New York: McGraw-Hill, 1969); Robert D. Hess and Judith V. Torney, *The Development of Political Attitudes in Children* (Garden City, N.Y.: Doubleday, Anchor, 1968); D. B. Lynn, "Sex Role and Parental Identification," *Child Development* 33 (1962): 555–564.

18. See, e.g., Gabriel Almond and Sidney Verba, *The Civic Culture: Political Attitudes and Democracy in Five Nations* (Princeton: Princeton University Press, 1963), p. 325; also

Duverger, *Political Role;* Campbell, et al., *American Voter;* Carl N. Diegler, "Revolution Without Ideology: The Changing Place of Women in America," in *The Women in America*, ed. Robert Jay Lifton (Boston: Houghton, Mifflin, 1965); Morris Levitts' useful study on women's voting behavior, *Political Attitudes of American Women: A Study of the Effects of Work and Education on their Political Role* (Ann Arbor, Mich: University Microfilm, 1960); also Martin Gruberg, *Women in American Politics: An Assessment and Sourcebook* (Oshkosh, Wis.: Academia Press, 1968).

19. Among previous studies which revealed different foci of attention were James G. March, "Husband-Wife Interaction Over Political Issues," *Public Opinion Quarterly* 17 (1953–1954):461–470; Jaquette, *Women*, pp. xxiii–xxiv; and Jeane Kirkpatrick, *Political Woman* (New York: Basic Books, 1974), pp. 153–159.

20. The studies which have found women activists to be more liberal than comparable males include Gruberg, *Women*, p. 95. Costantini and Craik report no differences among Republicans but greater liberalism in Democratic women, "Women as Politicians," p. 234.

21. Duverger, *Political Role*, whose data were drawn heavily from Europe asserts that women have voted somewhat more conservatively than men. French polling data in the last presidential election confirmed Duverger's view—for France.

22. V. O. Key, *Public Opinion and American Democray* (New York: Alfred A. Knopf, 1961), p. 147.

23. Samuel A. Stouffer noted that women were less tolerant of deviant views and behavior than men, *Communism, Conformity and Civil Liberties: A Cross Section of the Nation Speaks Its Mind* (Garden City, N.Y.: Doubleday, 1955), ch. 6

24. Jaquette, *Women*, p. xxxiii. Jaquette also asserted: "As the definition of politics expands to include issues which were formerly relegated to the private sphere, issues involving sexual relations, new forms of marriage, changes in the family structure, and areas of corporate decision-making such as hiring and promotion, the examination of the role of women in politics and a conscious awareness of male bias may revitalize our thinking on some of the fundamental questions of equity, obligation, and representation on which the study of politics has traditionally been based."

25. A good discussion of the organizational evolution of the women's movement and its factional problems is Jo Freeman, *The Politics of Women's Liberation* (New York: David McKay, 1975).

26. For example: 63 percent of McGovern men, 56 percent of McGovern women; 51 percent of Humphrey men, 32 percent of Humphrey women; 16 percent of Wallace men, 13 percent of Wallace women; 41 percent of Muskie men, 32 percent of Muskie women; 37 percent of Nixon men, 25 percent of Nixon women reported that the women in their delegations had favorable impressions of the NWPC.

27. Susan Tolchin and Martin Tolchin, *Clout: Womanpower and Politics* (New York: Coward, McCann and Geoghegan, 1974), p. 45.

CHAPTER 14

Femininity, Masculinity, and Power

Because women comprise slightly over one-half the electorate, because their nonpower seeking political behavior is distinctive and relatively un-examined, because it is widely claimed and believed that women will figure much more importantly in the new politics than in the old, because if women are to play a larger role in power processes they will be recruited from among women interested and active in politics, such as the women in the 1972 presidential elite, this chapter will examine women delegates' understanding of their sex's capacities and possibilities. The exploration of women's views about themselves and men's views of women will tell us a great deal not only about women in the political elite, but about women in the American political system. This chapter discusses reports of what actually happens to women when they become active, how they are treated by the men who control the gateways to power, and women's and men's views about why women do not have a larger voice in decision processes, and it assays women's prospects for the future. The purpose is to discern the impact of women's enlarged role in presidential politics and the likelihood that in the foreseeable future women will alter traditional ways of conducting politics.[1] It asks: what is the situation of women in politics in the United States today? Do women have an equal opportunity in politics? What are women's principal handicaps? What is the attitude of (male) party leaders toward women? Are women emotionally suited for the political world? What of their families? Is the price too high? Do the children suffer? What of the future? Will there be more women seeking and wielding political power? Or will things stay about as they are?

Four principal arguments are made in this chapter: 1) that women who participate in power processes are more likely than men or than other women to describe women as victims of male discrimination; 2) that women who participate in power processes are less likely than women in general to have conceptions of femininity that define femininity as incompatible with political success; 3) that women who participate in power processes are less likely than others to see conflict between family and political roles as inevitable or necessarily negative in its results; and 4) that conceptions of femininity are related to political ambition with the result that women with more restrictive conceptions of femininity have less political ambition and vice versa.

The result of this discussion should be a fairly comprehensive picture of elite expectations concerning what women can, should, and might do in politics, the price women must pay for political success, the extent to which they are victims of discrimination by men, and the extent to which women comprise a major new force in politics.

Women delegates constitute a sample of the pool of politically active women from which women candidates will be recruited; men in the presidential elite constitute a national sample of males who stand at the gateways to power through which women must pass if they are to achieve more important roles in power processes. Voters have the last word in determining whether women may or may not win greater influence in government, but the prior decisions of elites—of women deciding to run or not run, of men and women deciding to support or not to support women candidates—largely determine choices confronting electorates. Until now voters have rarely been asked to choose between male and female candidates; women have opted out or been selected out of the nomination prior to the stage at which voters are involved. This chapter explores some reasons why this has occurred and some reasons why it may continue.

MALE DISCRIMINATION

It is not possible to establish definitely the actual behavior of male party leaders from the data provided by this survey. A different kind of study would have been required to establish the facts about male discrimination against women seeking public office. But the perception of party leaders' attitudes is itself a fact with important consequences for women's behavior. The belief that her candidacy would be welcomed by party leaders might encourage a woman to pursue it; and the perception of party leaders as inhospitable might easily have the opposite effect. The preception of the situation becomes one of the facts defining the situation.

When delegates were asked an open-ended question about why women rarely run for public office, four major categories of response were offered: about one-third of all delegates answered with general references to society, smaller numbers alluded to family responsibilities and lack of motivation as the principal inhibitions, and a few identified male discrimination against women as the chief cause of women not running for office.

Table 14–1 indicates that in neither party did politically active women have at the top of their minds a belief that male prejudice and discrimination prevents women from nomination and election to public office. When women's answers were coded to reflect the principal group by reference to which the respondent explained low participation, a similar pattern emerged: respondents of both sexes rarely mentioned men as playing a principal role in women's failure to run for public office; both sexes were more likely to explain it with a reference to society, or to identify women themselves as the source of their sex's nonpower seeking behavior. However, when specific questions were posed concerning male attitudes and treatment of women, much higher percentages of women asserted that yes, in fact, women were not treated equally in their parties.

For example, a majority of delegates of both parties agreed that "men prevent women from seeking political careers," and a majority of Democrats, though not of Republicans, agreed that "most men in the party organization try to keep women out of leadership roles." Nearly one-half of all delegates disagreed with the assertion that "women have just as much opportunity as men to become political leaders." But on the other hand Table 14–2 shows that many delegates said that in their own city or county party leaders generally encouraged women to run for office. Furthermore a majority of women denied ever having been personally discriminated against. In fact, as many women report having received preferential treatment as having been victims of prejudice: 36 percent of Democratic women and 27 percent of Republican women said they never personally

Table 14-1. Why Women Rarely Run for Public Office, by Party and Sex (%)

| | Democrats | | Republicans | |
	Women	Men	Women	Men
Society in general	32	38	17	27
Lack of motivation	12	15	26	16
Family responsibilities	13	14	15	26
Male discrimination	6	6	1	3
Weighted N =	1099	1504	380	714

Question: "In general, there have been fewer women candidates for political office than men. Why do you think this has been the case?"
NOTE: These data are from the interviews.

Table 14-2. Party Leaders' Attitudes Toward Women Seeking Higher Office by Candidate Preference and by Sex (%)

	McGovern		Humphrey		Wallace		Muskie		Nixon	
	Men	Women	Men	Women	Men	Women	Men	Women	Men	Women
Encourage them	40	36	46	48	42	44	56	57	69	74
Neither encourage nor discourage	20	17	20	39	39	22	9	23	17	11
Discourage	33	39	24	3	3	28	30	28	9	11
Other	7	8	10	16	16	6	5	12	5	4
Weighted N =	635	621	299	93	36	86	170	103	670	374

Why Party Leaders Have These Attitudes

Women as referent	11	3	0	0	100	0	13	0	15	16
Men's beliefs	19	30	18	9	0	25	27	21	22	26
Male chauvinism	15	18	9	17	0	25	0	21	7	16
Men fear competition	17	16	9	22	0	0	13	10	7	11
Other male reference	11	9	18	17	0	0	13	7	0	5
Society in general	18	9	25	9	0	50	33	28	15	21
Family responsibility	0	3	0	17	0	0	0	0	22	0
Women cannot win	9	4	18	0	0	0	0	7	7	0
Weighted N =	199	235	68	23	3	8	45	29	54	38

Questions: "What is the attitude of party leaders in your city or county toward women becoming candidates for public office? Would you say they encourage women to run for office, discourage them, or what?" "Why do party leaders feel that way?" (Asked only of those who said party leaders have a negative attitude.)

NOTE: These data are from the interviews.

experienced discrimination because of sex; slightly larger numbers (37 percent of Democrats and 35 percent of Republicans) said they had been given preferential treatment. What are we to make of these contradictory reports: do male party leaders (that is, virtually all party leaders) attempt to keep women at the lowest levels of the party where the coffee is poured and bar them from political careers? Why did so many more women affirm the existence of anti-female prejudice when they were specifically asked than when they were simply asked about why women rarely run for public office? Why did so many women who said they themselves had never experienced anti-woman discrimination believe that it exists in their party? Perceptions of sex and power within the parties are mixed and contradictory. That some delegates should have perceived discrimination where others saw encouragement for women could be easily explained by the fact that delegates' responses reflected their different experiences. Since politics in the United States varies by locality and state, it is likely that persons in different places have different experiences growing out of local habits and norms. However, this does not account for why delegates who did not themselves mention sex discrimination affirmed that it did occur when asked directly, and neither did it account for the fact that women were more likely than men, and liberals more likely than conservatives, to perceive women as victims of discrimination. The latter tendencies could be clearly perceived in responses to the important question of whether city and county party leaders encourage or discourage women: 36 percent of McGovern delegates asserted that party leaders discourage women from seeking higher office as compared to 29 percent of Muskie delegates, 19 percent of Humphrey delegates, 20 percent of Wallace delegates, and 10 percent of Nixon delegates. The facts concerning the treatment of women in politics and the perception of that treatment by women and men obviously warrant close examination.

To secure a more accurate measure of views, a unidimensional index was constructed on the basis of a factor analysis comprising several questions on women's access to public office. The composite measures constitute a better indicator of perception of discrimination than single items that concern only single aspects of the relation of active women to male gatekeepers. When delegates were arrayed on this measure, relationships become still clearer. (See Table 14–3.) McGovern delegates were more likely than other candidate groups to perceive women as victims of discrimination, and in each preference group women were more likely than men to perceive male party leaders as discriminating against women. There are also statistically significant relations between perception of discrimination against women and political culture (r .42), foreign and domestic policy orientations, political experience (r .25), and a weak relationship to education (r .14).

Persons who considered themselves liberal or radical were much more likely than moderates and conservatives to see women as victims of discrimination in politics. (See Table 14–4.) The relationships were strong enough to indicate a systematic difference in interpretation of experience. It is hardly likely that conservative women in all geographical areas had the good luck to encounter male party leaders who were fair-minded, while liberal women had the misfortune of being confronted with male chauvinist pigs. It is more likely that liberal women interpreted as discriminatory behavior what conservative women found normal, natural, and appropriate.

Most contemporary liberal and radical ideologies are egalitarian.[2] Egalitarian expectations create new ideas about what is fair and unfair and so determine whether a given action will be considered fair and acceptable or unfair and discriminatory.[3] Expectations also affect the demands one makes; the higher the expectations, the greater the demands, and the greater the likelihood that they will be rebuffed or frustrated. The lower perception of discrimination by conservatives and moderates probably reflects part of a larger satisfaction with things as they are. Not all radicals and liberals perceive women as discriminated against and some conservatives do, but the association is strong enough to confirm that in 1972 perceptions of women's actual situation as well as of their political potential was part of a much larger view about the society and culture.

Personal ambition might be expected to have the same effects as ideology on the perception of discrimination, because persons without ambition are probably more satisfied with their situation and because the expression of political ambition by a woman may stimulate latent resistance to sharing power with women. But women with political ambition were no more likely than those without ambition to perceive their sex as victims of sexual discrimination.

Professional women were much more likely than housewives to see males as discriminatory, perhaps because filling traditionally male roles had sensitized the former to men's resistance to role-busting activity. But the fact that female students also perceive discrimination probably indicates the presence of ideology rather than experience. Women delegates apparently did not find women's situation as disadvantageous as the popular impression indicates that it is. Most comments on the attitudes of party leaders toward women in politics describe them as frankly discriminatory. For example, Peggy Lamson, commenting on the scarcity of women candidates, asserted, "If blame is to be attached to any group of men it must not be to those who pull the voting machine lever inside the polling booth but to those who pull the strings inside the political parties." Statements by party leaders who should know also attest to the continuing frustration suffered by women

Table 14-3. Perception of Discrimination Against Women by Sex and Candidate Preference by Sex (%)

	All Delegates	All Men	All Women	McGovern Men	McGovern Women	Humphrey Men	Humphrey Women	Wallace Men	Wallace Women	Muskie Men	Muskie Women	Nixon Men	Nixon Women
Low 1	15	19	9	6	2	15	9	11	9	21	9	30	19
2	30	34	24	20	17	44	25	53	27	42	24	41	34
3	35	35	35	48	36	32	40	29	59	34	28	25	32
High 4	20	12	32	27	45	9	26	7	5	3	40	4	14
N =	2376	1406	970	434	437	138	57	45	22	76	58	505	288

NOTE: These data are from the mail questionnaires. For a complete explanation of the Perception of Discrimination Index, see Appendix C. Percentages do not necessarily add to 100 due to rounding.

Table 14-4. Perception of Discriminaton Against Women by Ideological Self-Classification: All Delegates (%)

	Radical	Very Liberal	Somewhat Liberal	Moderate	Somewhat Conservative	Very Conservative
Low perception of discrimination	15	23	39	61	67	62
High perception of discrimination	85	77	62	39	33	38
N =	118	629	530	477	447	131
		(gamma = −.49)				

NOTES: These data are from the mail questionnaires. For a complete explanation of the Perception of Discrimination Index, see Appendix C.

seeking party endorsement. India Edwards, for many years the vice chairman of the Democratic National Committee, noted, "If the party backs a woman you can be pretty sure they do it because they think it's a lost cause but they know they have to have *some* candidate." And John Bailey, national chairman of the Democratic party and for years the leading power broker in the state of Connecticut, asserted, "The only time to run a woman is when things look so bad that your only chance is to do something dramatic."[4] Women state legislators also reported encountering resistance from party leaders when they sought their party's nomination, when they entered their legislatures, and when they attempted to move into the inner citadels of power,[5] and Frieda Gehlen reported the refusal of congressmen to admit women into the informal political networks which are an important source of strength in Congress.[6] The Tolchins provide a plethora of examples of casual discrimination by male political leaders against women in politics.[7]

Given the paucity of women in decision-making roles and the widespread impression that men who control the gateways to power are not enthusiastic about permitting women to pass through, it is surprising that more women did not perceive themselves and their sex as victims of discrimination; surprising, too, that more did not see male attitudes as a significant cause of women's failure to seek public office. Three explanations suggest themselves. It might be that men active in politics are actually less prejudiced against women power seekers than is commonly believed. It might be that politically active women exclude themselves from power—by low political ambition and effort. It might be that politically active women disregard evidences of male exclusiveness, because they like the men with whom they associate and desire to preserve cordial relations with them. We have already seen that enjoyment of the social aspects of politics is important to many men and women in the presidential elite; we know too that resentment and hostility are incompatible with either enjoyment or ease. It is psychologically plausible that the desire to preserve valued relationships would leave women insensitive to evidences of rejection by leaders of their "team." By blaming themselves or society men and women alike can preserve the sense of comradeship and team spirit that is so important to a volunteer activity held together by solidary incentives. The fact that women strongly committed to party are least likely to perceive party leaders as attempting to exclude women from public office (gamma–.41) constitutes indirect evidence that perceptions of discrimination may be inhibited by the desire to protect and preserve valued identifications. Since parties are people as well as principles, it is reasonable that women's attachment to party should be related to their views about whether the men in charge are or are not fair to people like themselves. The perception of leaders as antagonistic to sharing power with women might result in decreased support for the Constitution but the reverse may also be true: strong identification with the party may inhibit negative perceptions of leaders.

The general picture is, in any case, clear: a substantial minority of Democratic women and a smaller percent of Republican women perceived their party's leaders as antagonistic to sharing power with women, and perception of discrimination was related to ideology, candidate preference, and attitude toward party, but not to ambition.

An additional clue to who does and does not perceive women as victims of discrimination and why is found in respondents' views about how much power women actually exercise and whether they were satisfied to have their sex be the "power behind the throne." (See Table 14–5.) The "power behind the throne" role is a traditional women's role according to which women can be most effective not by aggressively seeking power, but by using feminine wiles to influence male policy makers. Exercising power behind the scenes is one strategy by which traditional feminine role requirements and power-seeking behavior can be harmonized. A woman who is content with this role would not perceive it as discriminatory. But power is one of the deference values, and most persons interested in power also desire the associated symbols of deference. Women who desire equality and deference rejected the "power behind the throne" role along with other traditional sex role distributions. Conservatives were more likely than liberals to believe women have more power than they appeared to. And delegates who believed women had more power than they seemed to were less likely than others to believe women victims of discrimination.

NATURE, SEX, AND POLITICS

Expectations concerning women's capacities and roles are, of course, part of a culture that also defines men's capacities and political roles.[8] Beliefs about the "nature" of the sexes are part of a society's basic values and beliefs that serve as the often inarticulate premises of specific opinions about who should rule, how, and to what broad ends. Beliefs about legitimacy, force, authority, human nature, causes and effects, and purposes of government are important parts of the political culture that have received a good deal of attention in recent years. But the aspect of political culture with which we are concerned has received less attention—perhaps because it involves a still deeper level of assumptions: this is the question of *who might govern*; who comprises the pool of eligibles from among whom rulers are chosen.

Table 14-5. Perceptions of Women as "Powers Behind the Throne" by Sex and Candidate Preference by Sex (%)

	All Delegates	All Men	All Women	McGovern Men	McGovern Women	Humphrey Men	Humphrey Women	Wallace Men	Wallace Women	Muskie Men	Muskie Women	Nixon Men	Nixon Women
Low 1	6	4	8	9	14	1	2	2	0	3	7	2	1
2	24	24	25	35	36	18	24	11	18	18	25	17	12
3	48	53	42	46	38	55	44	53	32	60	46	58	51
High 4	21	19	24	9	12	26	31	33	50	20	22	24	35
N =	2380	1417	962	433	428	139	55	45	22	80	59	507	288

NOTE: These data are from the mail questionnaires. For a complete explanation of the "Power Behind the Throne" Index, see Appendix C. Percentages do not necessarily add to 100 due to rounding.

Certain aspects of this question have attracted scholars' attention: Marxism, for example, calls attention to the economic class basis of the political elite, and argues that it should and will be altered, and such political theorists as Aristotle, Montesquieu, and Mosca have also emphasized the relations between social structure and access to political power. *At any given time views about who should govern closely resemble the characteristics of the regnant elite, and alternative doctrines state the special qualifications and claims of the counterelite.*

The belief that men of certain kinds comprise the pool of eligibles and that women are not included in that pool constitutes an aspect of the political culture of the United States and most other nations. The notion that rulers should be drawn from one sex rather than the other is so deep-rooted as to have so far escaped notice almost entirely, a fact that goes far toward explaining why generations of male radicals bent on uprooting and transforming societies wholesale have taken so little notice of the relations between sex and power. The reason so few questions have been raised about women's participation—and especially their nonparticipation—in power is that men and women alike have found it natural for men to govern public affairs.

Today many are no longer sure that biology has destined men to govern and women to be governed. Questions concerning the relevance of innate sex differences to politics have received new attention, and beliefs concerning the psycho-physical characteristics of the sexes have become involved in the politics of the age.

Beliefs about the "nature" of women and of men are not only important parts of our beliefs about the world; they become part of the self-concept of the two sexes. Views about the nature of things underlie demands: because they define what is possible as well as what is, they occupy a strategic position in the process of social change. Demands are taken seriously only to the extent that their objects do not violate existing conceptions of the "nature" of things, people, and possibilities.

Culture provides essentialist definitions of the sexes. Because its definitions of the nature of men and women serve as goals in the socialization process, emergent feminine and masculine natures confirm the aptness of the definitions. As acorns develop into oaks, girls and boys of a specific culture develop into men and women who illustrate and confirm existing conceptions of the sexes. In stable societies, culture, socialization, personality, role distribution, and the organization of indulgences and deprivations insure the operation of an endless process of social teleology.

Through the socialization process little girls learn what it is to be a girl, what girls do and do not do, what girls want and do not want, what girls *are* and what boys *are*. And in a parallel process boys acquire expectations about girls and boys, men and women. Internalized, these cultural requirements are felt as demands of the self on the self and others. The credibility of culture derives in part from its relation to basic needs and the life cycle of each human, in part from its daily reinforcement by social reality. Culture provides operational definitions of femininity which point females (and males) toward some activities and away from others and provide a sense of "fitness" that underpins, justifies, and preserves sex role distributions. Where socialization is successful, appropriate behavior is felt not as a demand on the self but as self-fulfillment; even where unsuccessful, socialization produces anxiety to accompany nonconformity. Horner's studies demonstrate how "inappropriate" behavior creates discomfort, fear, and flight.[9] Traditionally, little girls not only learn that politics is "man's work," they see that the political world *is* a male world—that presidents, senators, congressmen, mayors, judges, ambassadors are men. Practices create expectations, expectations create practices. The character-culture manifold shapes and reflects, reflects and shapes the pattern of interpersonal relations that characterizes the society,[10] and this pattern of relations reinforces itself through a continuing demonstration that experience is indeed as described in the culture.

It is not suggested that culture is entirely arbitrary, only that it shapes self-conceptions, interpersonal relations, role system, and that even though each is rooted in biology, definitions of femininity and masculinity as of childhood, maturity, and old age vary among cultures. Culture provides identity, motives, and meaning; it constitutes a statement of the society's expectations. Beliefs concerning femininity have obvious relevance to women's participation in public power: they condition the expectations of men and women alike concerning who can (and cannot) *appropriately* exercise power in the society. In stable societies the roles available to women illustrate and elaborate cultural definitions of femininity. The core of the feminist critique of male dominated societies (and all societies are to a greater or lesser extent male dominated) is that cultural norms arbitrarily restrict women's personal development, limit the choices available to them, and prevent their participation in power and other values. But as the very existence of the feminist movement demonstrates, conceptions of femininity are changing. This means that alternative conceptions of femininity are already available and that some women have internalized deviant (that is, nontraditional) conceptions of femininity that deny that innate sexual characteristics bar women from political roles to which power is attached. Studies of women in political roles indicate that most of the women who occupy such roles do not share the expectations concerning femininity that are believed to be most disabling for women.[11] But studies of the whole population establish that cultural norms inhospitable to women's participation in power are still widely shared among the adult population. A useful Virginia Slims poll, for example, revealed that as of 1972, 63 percent of the adult women agreed that "most men are better suited emotionally for politics than are most women."[12]

We hypothesized that quite different conceptions of femininity would be found among the presidential elite, that younger women would be more likely than older women to define femininity as compatible with successful political participation. But we also expected that views concerning the "nature" of women would be related to general political ideology, candidate preference, level of political experience, political ambition, and employment. Women who had held public office or relatively high levels of party office and/or who had high levels of political ambition, and/or who were regularly employed, and/or whose general political views were more liberal than conservative were expected to reject the view that women are innately unfit for politics; and women of generally conservative political views, and/or no experience in public or upper level party office, and/or little or no political ambition, and/or not employed outside the home were expected to express opposite views.

Because the delegates were drawn from fifty states, diverse ideological persuasions, and different professional and political experience, they provided an especially good opportunity to discover whether nontraditional conceptions of femininity are a precondition to political activity and whether politically active men as well as women were affected by changing sex conceptions.

Table 14–6 shows that while there was not unanimity among women concerning women's innate "fitness" for politics, there was an unexpectedly broad consensus. A large majority of women delegates denied that women were "naturally" unsuited for politics or that men were better suited emotionally for politics than most women. Even larger majorities affirmed that women in public office can be as logical and rational as men and denied that "women who succeed in politics have to sacrifice their femininity to get there." On all these questions women in the political elite were significantly less divided than women voters and much less convinced that their sex is innately incapacitated in the political sphere. Over nine-tenths of Democratic and four-fifths of Republican women rejected the view that biologically based sex differences bar women from political roles.

SEX, POWER, AND IDEOLOGY

There was limited confirmation for the hypothesis that women's views concerning the innate sex characteristics were related to ideology and candidate preference.

Table 14-6. Perceptions of Innate Sex Differences by Sex and Candidate Preference by Sex (%)

	All Delegates	All Men	All Women	McGovern		Humphrey		Wallace		Muskie		Nixon	
				Men	Women	Men	Women	Men	Women	Men	Women	Men	Women
Low 1	48	33	69	64	87	22	68	7	39	26	58	16	51
2	26	30	19	25	11	33	16	20	22	35	22	36	29
3	22	30	10	10	2	33	13	47	26	35	19	40	18
High 4	5	7	2	1	0	13	4	27	13	4	2	8	2
N =	2391	1412	978	432	438	138	56	45	23	80	59	508	292

NOTE: These data are from the mail questionnaires. For a complete explanation of the Innate Sex Differences Index, see Appendix C. Percentages do not necessarily add to 100 due to rounding.

Republicans were substantially more conservative than Democrats, and they were also more likely than Democrats to see existing political sex role distributions as rooted in the "natures" of men and women. Twenty-one percent of Republican and 8 percent of Democratic women thought that innate differences restrict women's participation in power; 49 percent of Republican and 30 percent of Democratic males saw political sex roles as rooted in biology. Within parties as well as between them the more liberal the political ideology, the more egalitarian the sex conceptions. (See Table 14–7.) But there was no necessary relationship between political and sexual views (a fact made clear by the histories of most radical movements and by male dominance of all contemporary "revolutionary" governments). Women are as rare in the leadership circles of Communist parties as they are rare in the top levels of most conservative parties.[13] The Maoist, Soviet, and Castro governments share with Vorster's South Africa, Amin's Uganda, and Anglo-Saxon and European democracies the condition of male dominance. Most "liberal" Democratic males denied the existence of innate sex differences relevant to politics, but roughly one-third did not. Most conservative Democratic males believed the contrary, but about one-third of the delegates doubted that innate sex differences doomed women to exclusion from power, and among Democratic women four-fifths of the moderates and conservatives denied that political sex roles reflected biological realities. Among the more ideologically

Table 14-7. Ideological Self-Classification by Conceptions
of Femininity: Women Only (%)

	Traditional Woman	Medium	New-Woman
Radical	1	4	10
Very liberal	10	28	58
Somewhat liberal	15	29	21
Moderate	31	18	7
Somewhat conservative	29	19	4
Very conservative	13	2	0
Reactionary	0	5	0
N =	230 (gamma –.60)	417	272

NOTE: For method of index construction and the constituent variables of each of the indexes, see Appendix C. These data are from the mail questionnaires.

homogeneous Republicans, relations between the liberal/conservative political spectrum and beliefs concerning the nature of women were still weaker.

Innate Sex Characteristics and Experience, Income, and Education

The hypothesis that women's views concerning innate sexual characteristics and politics were related to their level of political experience and civic participation and to political ambition and achievement needs was also confirmed. There was a positive, but not very strong, relationship (r .28) between the quantity and quality of political experience and views concerning innate sex differences. And while there was a very weak association between sex conceptions and membership in voluntary organizations generally, women who belonged to the League of Women Voters and to feminist groups were less likely to believe that femininity was politically disabling. This relationship, however, is not as strong (r .23) as might have been expected.

The 1973 Virginia Slims report that 71 percent of women with an eighth grade education, 66 percent of those with a high school education, and 52 percent of women who had gone to college agreed that men were emotionally better suited for politics than women[14] suggested that among delegates, too, education might be related to sex conceptions of power positions. But the relation turned out to be unimportant among Democrats and Republicans of both sexes.[15]

The possibility, also suggested by the Virginia Slims poll, that younger women and men in the elite would be less likely than older ones to have internalized and/or retained restrictive conceptions of femininity was confirmed.

Men's Conceptions and Women's Conceptions

If sex role conceptions are a function of ideology, as some radical feminists and the sociology of knowledge suggest, men should cling more tenaciously than women to traditional sex role conceptions. Men have a "vested interest" in women's unfitness for power, entirely comparable to the "vested interest" of an industrialist in tax law, a trade unionist in collective bargaining, or an urban civil servant in the city's budget. Compared to women, men enjoy advantages in the pursuit of various values, including political power. The relative advantage of males and disadvantage of females in relation to power roles might be expected to sensitize women to the "ideology" that supports existing role distributions. (Of course, it is equally true that women interested in gaining political power have a "vested interest" in denying sex differences relevant to politics.)

These expectations were confirmed. In each party, each candidate group, and each regional, age, and education group, men were less likely than women to doubt conventional stereotypes concerning sex and power. More male than female delegates agreed that women are less suited to politics than men; more men than women agreed that women must sacrifice their femininity to succeed in politics; more men than women doubted that women in public office can be just as logical and rational as men. These differences between the sexes were substantial and consistent. Thirty percent of Democratic males and 8 percent of Democratic females affirmed the importance for political roles of innate sex characteristics. Among Republicans, 49 percent of males and 21 percent of females agreed that innate sex characteristics leave women at a disadvantage in power processes. This contrast between male and female opinions held across the political spectrum.

Disagreement between the sexes at the elite level stands in suggestive contrast to agreement between male and female voters. The Virginia Slims polls, which constitute an invaluable source of information on popular conceptions of masculinity and femininity, reveal broad agreement between men and women concerning the relations between femininity, masculinity and power. Among voters roughly equal portions of each sex (65 percent) believed women emotionally ill-suited for politics; approximately equal portions (75 percent) agreed that "women in public office can be just as logical and rational as men."[16] Male delegates were in general agreement with voters of both sexes. *It is politically active women who had deviant conceptions.* But the fact that women's and men's ideologies diverged on questions of women's political abilities and ambitions does not necessarily indicate biologically based differences in perceiving and cognizing social issues any more than finding that the views of coal miners differed from those of the mine's management would necessarily imply that labor and capital had different cognitive capacities.

ROLE CONSTRAINTS: HOW DISABLING ARE THEY?

The incongruity of women's wife/mother roles with political roles is also a popular explanation for women's low participation in major decision processes of the society. The cultural explanation of women's nonparticipation in high power identifies the personality of women (and men) as the principal cause of the scarcity of women in politics; the explanation by role constraint deemphasizes personality and emphasizes social system. Culture explains, justifies, and protects role distributions. Roles, of course, occur not in isolation, but in systems: some roles are congruent; some incongruent. In this and most other cultures women's primary roles have been nurturant roles—wife, mother, daughter roles—and these have been thought incompatible with most other roles, especially those involving autonomy and the exercise of power. The roles of son, husband, and father, on the other hand, have been conceived as congruent with professional and political roles. The roles of husband, father, and provider encourage males to prepare themselves by education and experience for autonomous activity in the political and other spheres; until recently the roles of wife, mother, and daughter have been thought incongruent with all political roles except those of volunteer. As recently as 1972, nearly one-half of all women in the electorate agreed that "it is almost impossible to be a good wife and mother and hold public office, too."[17] And over one-half agreed that "to be really active in politics women have to neglect their husbands and children." The presumed incompatibility of wife/mother roles and roles involving the exercise of political power has discouraged women from acquiring the education and skills needed for decision making in the public arena and from attempting to enter arenas believed to be unsuited to their skills and temperaments. The traditional role system made it difficult for a woman to prepare herself for a political career; difficult to begin a political career before middle age; difficult to change her place of residence; difficult to develop the skills and acquire the resources needed for a political career; difficult to find a husband who would tolerate a wife that engaged in such activities; difficult to persuade voters to support such efforts—difficult, but not impossible, and not equally difficult for all women. But today, when equality is the dominant passion of the age, when power is won with social skills rather than physical force, when there are no legal barriers to women's seeking, gaining, and exercising power, and when some women make political demands in the name of all women, roles as well as beliefs are in a state of flux.

It seems clear that belief in the incompatibility of "women's" roles and professional roles has itself been a source of role incompatibility. The belief that wife/mother roles are incompatible with political roles discourages girls and women from desiring political office, from acquiring the needed skills, and from making the needed efforts. Available evidence suggests that women who actually run for public office are much less likely than women generally to believe in the inevitability of role conflict and much more likely to believe that it is possible to harmonize the roles of wife/mother and political participant.[18]

It was expected that experience with combining wife/mother roles with other activities would create a greater sense of confidence in the possibility of harmonizing traditional and nontraditional roles. Therefore, women who were employed outside the home and who had longer political experience would, we thought, be more optimistic about dealing with role conflict than women who had not attempted such role juggling. It was also expected that heavy demands of mothering young children might leave women with children under, say, 12 less optimistic than others about the prospects of harmonizing nurturant and political roles. Many of these expectations were not confirmed by the data.

The level of agreement and the optimism of women delegates in both parties were high. Three-fourths of both Republican and Democratic women delegates denied that "It is almost impossible to be a good wife and mother and hold public office, too." But at the same time, over 85 percent of each group agreed that "Family responsibilities have kept women from participating in politics." In other words, there was wide agreement that role conflict has inhibited women's political participation and equally wide agreement that it need not do so. (See Table 14–8.)

Over four-fifths of the women of both parties scored low on a composite Role-Conflict Index. Republican women were somewhat more likely than Democratic women to see a serious role conflict between nurturant and political roles, and McGovern's women delegates less likely than women supporting other candidates to see role conflict as intractable.[19] Many women who disagreed intensely on issues of public policy and partisan loyalty were in general agreement on this issue.

Single women were less likely than married ones to give importance to role conflict, but the differences were not large. More interesting is the fact that young children did not seem to increase the respondents' sense of the difficulties of combining wife/mother roles with a political career. Women with children under 6 were *less* likely than those with children over 18 to score high on the Role Conflict Index. (See Table 14–9.)

The number of children also had less effect on how these women perceived role conflict than might have been expected. Women with two or more children were no more likely than the childless to be high scorers. Employment turned out to be a more important factor in the perception of role conflict. Women employed as professionals and technical experts were much *less* likely than housewives to see role conflict as intractable, doubtless because many of them were already juggling traditionally incongruent roles. Most women delegates—married and unmarried, childless and with young children—agreed that the problem could be handled. (See Table 14–10.)

It was also expected that perception of role conflict might be related to

Table 14-8. Perceptions of Female Role-Conflict by Sex and Candidate Preference by Sex (%)

	All Delegates	All Men	All Women	McGovern Men	McGovern Women	Humphrey Men	Humphrey Women	Wallace Men	Wallace Women	Muskie Men	Muskie Women	Nixon Men	Nixon Women
Low 1	40	26	59	43	70	18	54	11	17	24	48	18	52
2	31	34	27	35	22	31	25	24	44	35	31	36	31
3	21	29	11	16	7	35	18	33	22	29	14	35	13
High 4	8	11	3	6	1	16	4	31	17	11	9	12	5
$N =$	2356	1386	969	422	432	137	56	45	23	79	59	496	291

NOTE: These data are from the mail questionnaires. For a complete explanation of the Role-Conflict Index, see Appendix C. Percentages do not necessarily add to 100 due to rounding.

Table 14-9. Perceptions of Female Role-Conflict by Age of
Youngest Child: Women Only (%)

Age of Youngest Child	Perceptions of Role-Conflict				All Women with Children (%)
	Lowest	Low	High	Highest	
1–5	17	17	17	0	17
6–12	33	22	31	20	30
13–18	21	25	18	25	22
Over 18	29	35	35	55	32
$N =$	413	198	78	20	709

NOTE: The data are from the mail questionnaires. For a complete explanation of the Role-Conflict Index, see Appendix C.

the extent of political and other community activity, because the experience of being active in several organizations would demonstrate the possibility of being a good wife and mother and carrying on regular activities outside the home. But among neither Democratic nor Republican women was perception of role conflict positively associated with political or other organizational experience.

It also seemed likely that differences in income might affect the perception of role conflict, because money can buy household help which in turn can resolve problems of child and home care. In fact, however, there was no relation at all between income and perception of role conflict. The relation of role conception to education was somewhat stronger, but still weak.

As compared with women generally, women delegates were more sanguine about the possibility of harmonizing wife/mother roles and political activity. Differences were not large but they were predictable and consistent. Apparently, politically active women have a more optimistic, expansive conception of women's innate political capacities and of their ability to harmonize traditional nurturant roles with political participation —including running for office.

Their views about women in political roles are part of a more general rejection of traditional sex role conceptions. Large majorities denied that women are unsuited for the professions,[20] and over one-half denied that the children of working mothers necessarily suffer. Views on these more general questions were similar to those concerning political sex roles: women delegates were less likely than women generally to hold traditional

Table 14-10. Perceptions of Female Role-Conflict by Employment Status, by Party, and by Candidate Preference: Women Only (%)

Role-Conflict	Democrats		Republicans		McGovern		Humphrey	
	Employed	Housewife	Employed	Housewife	Employed	Housewife	Employed	Housewife
Low 1	66	56	52	50	69	67	46	68
2	26	28	30	32	23	24	32	21
3	7	15	15	12	7	9	18	11
High 4	12	2	3	7	0	0	4	0
N =	365	181	145	123	242	106	28	19

Role-Conflict	Wallace		Muskie		Nixon	
	Employed	Housewife	Employed	Housewife	Employed	Housewife
Low 1	13	30	58	38	51	51
2	63	20	26	33	31	30
3	13	30	7	25	14	12
High 4	13	20	10	4	4	7
N =	8	10	31	24	142	116

NOTE: These data are from the mail questionnaires. For a complete explanation of the Role-Conflict Index, see Appendix C. Percentages do not necessarily add to 100 due to rounding.

views and more likely to believe things could be worked out. Views on the broader subject of working mothers were also related to general ideological position, with McGovern delegates least frequently and Wallace delegates most frequently expressing views that a working woman's family pays a heavy price.

WOMEN AND MEN VIEW WOMEN'S ROLES

Politically active women not only had a more optimistic view than women generally about the abilities of their sex and their ability to combine traditionally incompatible roles, they were also more optimistic than their male counterparts at the convention about women's abilities generally. Since the men and women in this elite agreed about almost everything, it comes as something of a surprise that there are substantial sex differences in attitudes concerning women's nature and women's place. Yet in each candidate support group men were more likely to believe 1) that women already have an equal opportunity in politics, 2) that women are "naturally" unsuited for politics, 3) that families suffer when mothers are active in politics, and 4) that women must sacrifice their femininity in order to succeed in politics. In all candidate support groups men were more likely to doubt 1) that men try to exclude women from leadership roles in politics, 2) that women are as logical and rational as men, 3) that mothering and politics mix, 4) that women's roles will be very different ten years from today.

Women in each candidate support group were more likely to take the position that women are well-suited for politics by nature, that men try to exclude women, that women do not have an equal opportunity in politics at the present time, that women are as rational as men, that families need not suffer when women develop political (or other) careers, that women will gain greater influence in politics in the next decade, and so forth.

Because McGovern delegates were very homogeneous ideologically and because they had the most explicit and articulate commitment to a new deal for women, they provided a particularly interesting example of the differences between male and female perceptions of the political world.

On questions concerning discrimination against women, the difference between McGovern men and women was 10 to 15 percent. On the question that most directly concerned male chauvinism among political leaders 17 percent of men and 29 percent of women strongly agreed that men in party organizations try to exclude women from leadership roles. Even male

McGovern supporters who, more than other men, saw women as suffering discrimination were not as sensitive to women's disadvantages as their female counterparts.

On key questions concerning the "nature" of women, the differences between male and female McGovern supporters were still greater. Forty-six percent of men and 75 percent of women disagreed strongly with the assertion that "most men are better suited emotionally for politics than are most women." Only 73 percent of male McGovernites strongly agreed that "women in public office can be just as logical and rational as men," as compared to 92 percent of McGovernite women. In a less direct but no less definitive confirmation of the unsuitability of politics for women, only 45 percent of male and 75 percent of female McGovern supporters strongly disagreed with the statement that "women who succeed in politics usually have to sacrifice their femininity to get there." Again, McGovern men were more likely than men supporting other candidates to regard women as naturally and emotionally "fit" to perform major political roles, but were not as convinced of this as were McGovern's women supporters.

Differences in how men and women perceive role conflicts are in some ways most interesting of all, because, in principle, women should feel these conflicts most keenly, but men turn out to estimate role conflicts as more insurmountable than women. Fifty-two percent of McGovern's women supporters but only 30 percent of the men were sure that it is *not* true that it is nearly impossible to be a good mother and hold public office too.

The point is not that McGovern's male delegates were sexist. As compared to men in other candidate support groups they were enormously supportive of women's liberation (to which 89 percent pronounced themselves favorable), and sympathetic to feminist complaints about the status quo. McGovern men, for example, tended to be more pro-women's liberation than most of the women delegates supporting the other Democratic candidates. The point is that even *in the movement where support for women's liberation was the strongest, substantial portions of the men did not have beliefs associated with equal political roles for women.*

In other candidate support groups greater numbers of men had attitudes toward women in politics that, at a minimum, were not likely to facilitate women's efforts to gain and exercise increased influence. For example, only 10 percent of male Humphrey supporters, 15 percent of male Muskie supporters, 8 percent of male Nixon supporters, and 2 percent of male Wallacites strongly disagreed with the view that men are emotionally better suited for politics. In each case at least four times as many women strongly disagreed. Or, on the question of whether women in public office could be as logical and rational as men, only 38 percent of male Humphrey delegates, 44 percent of male Muskie delegates, 32 percent of male Nixon delegates, and 16 percent of male Wallacites were strongly convinced that it was true. The substantial gaps demonstrate that even among men and women with similar social, economic, and educational backgrounds, similar personalities, similar conceptions and styles of citizenship, similar views about social, economic, and foreign policy, *even, in brief, among men and women who have everything but gender in common, there was disagreement about the nature, situation, role, and future of women.*

FEMININITY AND AMBITION

If culture, personality, socialization, and role system are interrelated in the manner generally believed, beliefs about masculinity and femininity exist not as ideas but are internalized as standards guiding males and females to appropriate desires and behaviors, discouraging inappropriate aspirations, and suggesting and rewarding with psychic comfort and approval, conventional masculine and feminine role behavior which is then further rewarded and reinforced by society. If culture shapes aspirations, then beliefs about women should shape the ambitions that women develop. The most powerful and disabling inhibitions are anchored in the self-system. A restrictive conception of femininity, which, for example, conceives men as the natural governors of society and women as the natural subjects, should discourage women from developing political ambitions or ambitions for achievement in any other traditional male role. Matina Horner's studies revealed "fear of success" in talented, achievement oriented young women at an elite college and suggested the psychological dynamics by which success in "inappropriate" jobs produces anxiety and flight. The fantasies in which successful women "got their comeuppance" demonstrate the workings of one success-inhibiting mechanism. Conceptions of femininity that discourage women from desiring "male" roles and call into question the femininity of the nonconformer should be very inhibiting. *All that is required to control sex role distributions is that each sex not desire roles assigned to the opposite sex.*

There are many reasons for which people might not desire to run for public office. Running for office entails competition and risk; it requires a large investment of time; winning entitles one to work long hours for low pay and constant criticism. Few men desire to run for public office, and no one has proposed to explain this as a consequence of crippling sex stereotypes. But the belief that power seeking is incompatible with femininity poses special problems for women.

To test the hypothesis that restrictive beliefs about women are associated with low political ambition, several different analyses were undertaken. *All measures confirmed that beliefs about women are in fact quite strongly related to political ambitions.* Women who believed there are innate sex differences that are relevant to politics were most likely not to desire public office or, if they did, to desire only low level office. Women who believed wife/mother roles are incompatible with political participation were less likely than others to aspire to hold public office. These relationships are reflected graphically in Figures 14–1, 14–2, 14–3, 14–4, and 14–5. Views concerning innate sex characteristics are most strongly related to ambition (as they were also most closely related to political ideology), and this relationship illustrates the practical consequences of beliefs about the nature of the sexes.

To tap respondents' general conception of femininity scales dealing with innate sex differences, role conflict, discrimination, and "power behind the throne" were combined in a single composite measure which I call the "Newwoman Index."

High scorers on the Newwoman Index rejected traditional beliefs that women are innately less suited than men to exercise political power, that conflicts between wife/mother role and holding political office are intractable, that women get a fair deal in politics, and that women can and do wield more power behind the scenes through traditional feminine wiles than they are generally believed to.

Low scoring women have traditional views about the political characteristics of women and men and accept traditional definitions of women's roles and men's roles. They are therefore not disposed to regard male domination of politics and government as implying or involving discrimination against women. To identify the distinguishing characteristics of women with nontraditional and traditional beliefs about women in politics, high scorers and low scorers on the Newwoman Index were isolated. A preliminary analysis established the characteristics that seemed most relevant to these two conceptions of women in politics, and discriminant analysis was undertaken to determine which of these characteristics distinguished most sharply between newwomen and traditional women. The ambition/achievement index was revealed to discriminate most powerfully between these groups. Occupational experience, political ideology, political experience, education, and subjectivity were also distinguishing traits of traditional and nontraditional women, but

ambition and achievement were most important. Conceptions of femininity
and political ambition/achievement were more highly related to each other
than to such "objective" characteristics as age, education, and occupational experience.

The relations between political ambition/achievement need and conceptions of femininity do not definitively establish that traditional conceptions
of femininity cause women to lack political ambition, but they provide
further confirmation that the two are significantly related.

"Newwoman" had some other distinctive characteristics. She was most
likely to be urban and middle class in origin, to come from the Northeast
or the Midwest, and to have had both a mother and a father with a good
education. Like most delegates she was probably married and was only
slightly more likely than traditional women to be separated or divorced.
Over one-fourth of all newwomen were childless, more than one-third had
three or more children. Newwomen were most likely to be under 40 and
more likely than traditional women to have young children. Both newwomen and traditional women probably had some experience working

**Figure 14-1. Perceptions of Innate Sex Differences by Ambition Levels
for Public Office: Women Only (Z-scores)**

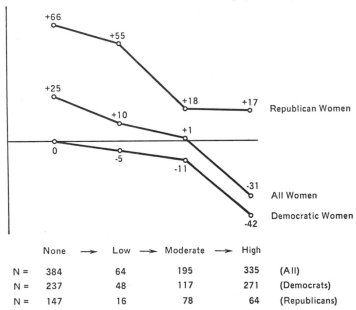

NOTE: These data are from the mail questionnaires. Z-scores were multiplied by 100
before graphing. For a complete explanation of the Innate Sex Differences Index, see
Appendix C. For an explanation of each ambition level, see Chapter 12, Table 11.

Figure 14-2. Perceptions of Discrimination Against Women by Ambition
Levels for Public Office: Women Only (Z-scores)

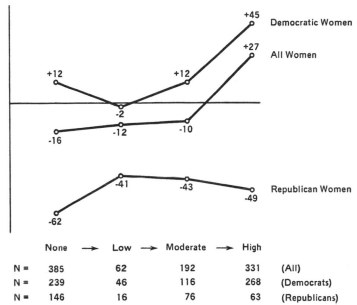

N =	385	62	192	331	(All)
N =	239	46	116	268	(Democrats)
N =	146	16	76	63	(Republicans)

NOTE: These data are from the mail questionnaires. Z-scores were multiplied by 100 before graphing. For a complete explanation of the Perception of Discrimination Index, see Appendix C. For an explanation of each ambition level, see Chapter 12, Table 11.

Figure 14-3. Perceptions of Female Role-Conflict by Ambition
Levels for Public Office: Women Only (Z-scores)

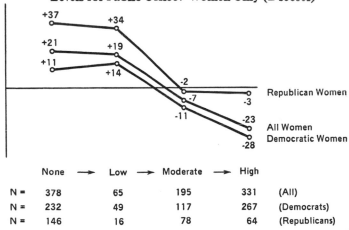

N =	378	65	195	331	(All)
N =	232	49	117	267	(Democrats)
N =	146	16	78	64	(Republicans)

NOTE: These data are from the mail questionnaires. Z-scores were multiplied by 100 before graphing. For a complete explanation of the Role-Conflict Index, see Appendix C. For an explanation of each ambition level, see Chapter 12, Table 11.

outside the home, but newwomen were more likely than their more traditional counterparts to have had a career punctuated by interruptions for childbirth and rearing.

Newwomen were much more likely than traditional women to be employed regardless of the age of their children. (See Tables 14–12 and 14–13.) Among newwomen whose youngest child was under 5, 56 percent were employed and 44 percent unemployed; among newwomen whose youngest child was between 6 and 12, 61 percent were employed and 39 percent unemployed; among newwomen whose youngest child was between 13 and 18, 65 percent were employed and 35 percent unemployed; among newwomen with no child under 18, 78 percent were employed and 22 percent unemployed.

For many newwomen the ideal work pattern would be to be employed and have good household help; relatively few of either newwomen or traditional women would prefer no employment outside the home (9 percent of newwomen and 18 percent of traditional women), but newwomen were most unanimously convinced of the desirability of mixing family and occupational roles. One of the reasons is that newwoman probably had a relatively high status occupation for which she spent some years preparing: 52 percent of newwomen were professional or managerial types, as compared to 38 percent of traditional women. (See Table 14–14.)

Figure 14-4. Perceptions of Women as "Powers Behind the Throne" by Ambition Levels for Public Office: Women Only (Z-scores)

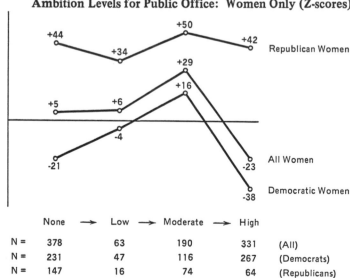

NOTE: These data are from the mail questionnaires. Z-scores were multiplied by 100 before graphing. For a complete explanation of the Power Behind the Throne Index, see Appendix C. For an explanation of each ambition level, see Chapter 12, Table 11.

**Figure 14-5. Overall Conceptions of Femininity by Ambition Levels
for Public Office: Women Only (Z-scores)**

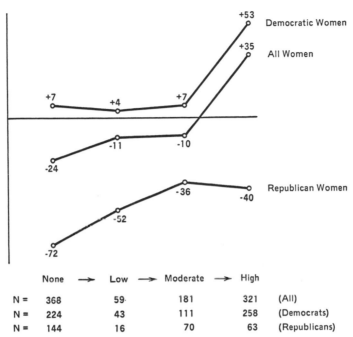

	None →	Low →	Moderate →	High	
N =	368	59	181	321	(All)
N =	224	43	111	258	(Democrats)
N =	144	16	70	63	(Republicans)

NOTE: These data are from the mail questionnaires. Z-scores were multiplied by 100 before graphing. For a complete explanation of the Newwoman (or "Conceptions of Femininity") Index, see Appendix C. For an explanation of each ambition level, see Chapter 12, Table 11.

**Table 14-11. Relationships Between Conceptions of Femininity and Reactions
to the Women's Liberation Movement: Women Only (gammas)**

"Femininity" Indexes		N
Innate sex differences	−.58	942
Perception of discrimination	.46	935
Role-conflict	−.40	932
Power behind the throne	−.48	926
Newwoman	.66	896

The question on the women's liberation movement was a "feeling thermometer" on which delegates were asked to indicate their "warm" or "cold" feelings toward the movement.

NOTE: These data are from the mail questionnaires. For a complete explanation of these indexes, see Appendix C.

Politically, newwoman saw herself as very liberal or radical, and her views on specific issue areas confirm the accuracy of this self-classification. She was more likely than traditional woman to have a comprehensive internally consistent ideology—to be idealistic in international affairs, to oppose the use of force in both domestic and foreign affairs, to be "tender-minded" on domestic issues, and to have especially intense feelings about women's role in politics. It is most likely that she supported George McGovern in 1972 though women who shared her perspectives were also numerous among the supporters of Shirley Chisholm. Her views on what in 1972 were tagged "women's issues" were characteristic of the National Women's Political Caucus and included abortion on demand, a national day care program, sexual equality in employment practices, and support for the women's liberation movement.

Newwoman had many of the characteristics associated with Wilson's "amateur" politican: an urban background, relatively brief experience in her local community, Jewish or no religion, college education, and middle-class status. Despite her relatively shallow community roots she was probably a joiner, but belonged to fewer organizations than traditional woman. Her political experience was probably brief; about one-third had held no party office. Like the amateur, she was motivated by intense interest in policy and tended to define the delegate's role as that of

Table 14-12. Conceptions of Femininity by Employment and
Age of Youngest Child: Women Only (%)

| | Age of Youngest Child | | | |
	1–5	6–12	13–18	18+
Newwoman				
Employed	56	61	65	78
Housewife	44	64	35	22
N =	43	64	37	37
Traditional Woman				
Employed	39	30	58	62
Housewife	61	70	42	39
N =	18	43	38	65

NOTE: These data are from the mail questionnaires. For a complete explanation of the Newwoman (or Conceptions of Femininity) Index, see Appendix C.

policy maker. Her concern with party reform and expanded participation outweighed her attachment to party and interest in its preservation. Securing party unity and picking a winning team were less important to her than to traditional woman and less important than issue articulation or party reform. Solidary incentives, status, the fun of the game, and local concerns were also all less important to her than to traditional woman.

Newwoman and traditional woman differed in many ways relevant to politics: in political experience, in attitude toward party, and in attitude

Table 14-13. Present Work Pattern by Conceptions of
Femininity: Women Only (%)

	Traditional Woman	Medium	Newwoman
Employment/no family	4	7	7
Employment/maid	5	4	4
Employment/housewife	37	22	23
Employment/with interruptions for children	5	6	18
Intermittent employment	12	25	17
Employment before marriage	12	11	13
No significant employment	24	22	16
Part-time employment with no help	0	1	0
Part-time employment with help	3	3	2
Weighted N =	222	437	271

Present-work-pattern question: "Women have many ways of combining work and family. Which of these patterns best describes your own work pattern?"

1. Continuous employment outside the home with no family responsibilities.
2. Continuous employment outside the home with homemaking responsibilities assumed by someone else.
3. Continuous outside employment, combining both work and homemaking throughout adult life.
4. Outside employment with interruptions for child raising.
5. Outside employment on and off in no regular pattern—working as often as needed or desired.
6. Outside employment only before marriage and/or children.
7. No employment for any significant period.
8. Part-time employment with no help in home.
9. Part-time employment with help in home.

NOTE: These data are from the intersect sample. For a complete explanation of the Newwoman (or Conceptions of Feminity) Index, see Appendix C.

toward foreign, domestic, and "feminist" issues. (See Table 14–15.) Traditional woman was more likely to have long political experience and to have served in several party offices, to be motivated by solidary as well as ideological incentives, and to be relatively conservative, especially on cultural and social questions. Traditional woman displayed a predilection for defining the delegates' role in terms of electoral and aggregative functions. Her ideology was more eclectic than holistic, more eclectic than that of newwoman. There was no agreement among traditional women on abortion or day care; there was a higher degree of consensus on the women's liberation movement: two-thirds were against it. Traditional woman had many characteristics in common with Wilson's "professional": rural or small town origins, longer political experience, a commitment to preservation of the party and concern for organizational preservation, and less concern with internal procedures than with winning and maintaining the organization interest.

Traditional woman was more likely than newwoman to have strong attachments to family, party, and state and an abiding concern with local and state issues.[21]

These patterns of political, social, and cultural traits confirm the extent to which political issues were enmeshed and intertwined in 1972.

CONCLUSIONS AND COMMENT

The pattern of beliefs about women described in the previous pages has important implications for both the present and future of women in politics.

Table 14-14. Type of Employment by Conceptions of
Femininity: Women Only (%)

	Traditional Woman	Medium	Newwoman
Professional/technical	25	31	43
Managerial/salaried	6	7	7
Manager, etc./self-employed	7	7	2
Clerical, etc.	11	7	5
Housewife	41	35	26
Student	6	9	12
N =	213	394	266

NOTE: These data are from the mail questionnaires. No more than 2 percent of women fell in any employment category other than those listed. For a complete explanation of the Newwoman (or Conceptions of Femininity) Index, see Appendix C.

Table 14-15. Opinions on Three "Women's Issues" by Conceptions of Femininity: Women Only (%)

	Traditional Woman	Medium	Newwoman
Abortion			
Abortion never	2	4	0
Life/health of woman	30	14	7
If woman/doctor agree	48	46	34
If woman wants it	20	37	59
Weighted N =	218	435	269
(gamma .44)			
National Day Care Program			
Very much favor	35	54	78
Somewhat favor	29	27	14
Undecided	2	3	4
Somewhat opposed	20	10	3
Very much opposed	15	6	1
Weighted N =	228	439	277
(gamma –.47)			
Employment Policy			
Lay off women first	41	25	13
Treat sexes same	59	75	87
Weighted N =	224	433	269
(gamma .44)			

Questions: "There has been some discussion about abortion in recent years. Which one of the options on this card best agrees with your own view? 1) Abortion should never be permitted; 2) abortion should be permitted only if the life and health of the woman is in danger; 3) if a woman and her doctor agree, she should be able to have a legal abortion; 4) any woman who wants to have an abortion should be able to have one."

"How do you feel about the proposal to establish a national day care or child care program for working mothers? Are you very much in favor, somewhat in favor, somewhat opposed, very much opposed, or what?"

"Sometimes a company has to lay off part of its labor force. Some people think that the first workers to be laid off should be women whose husbands have jobs. Others think that male and female employees should be treated the same. Which of these opinions do you agree with?"

NOTE: These data are from the intersect sample. For a complete explanation of the Newwoman (Conceptions of Femininity) Index, see Appendix C.

First, it makes it clear that women—at least at the elite level—are no longer their own worst enemies. The belief that women hold women back, that women are unwilling to support the political aspirations of other women, is widespread, but it is not true that politically active women have a poorer opinion of women than do their male counterparts. To the contrary, the relative reluctance of men in both parties to believe that women *are* suited for political roles and *can* manage to combine them with marriage and children indicates that at this time, *it is men rather than women who are most likely to oppose individual women's efforts to move into more important roles in power processes.*[22]

Doubts of men in the party elite about women's political capacities are consistent with the widespread impression that male party leaders attempt to bar women from political careers: a majority of men in both parties agreed that this was the case. It seems quite clear that women's low participation in power today derives from relatively low political ambition *and* from male prejudice. The opinions of men and women at both the mass and elite level indicate that widespread male discrimination is not only an open secret, it is no secret at all. It is not universal, and the evidence suggests that it may readily give way under challenge[23] but it is nonetheless real.

There is less agreement between the sexes about women's nature and women's place at the elite than at the mass level. Among voters as many women as men believed that men are better suited for politics. Politically active males had more conventional views about sex roles, but politically active women were much more sanguine about women's capabilities than conventional wisdom counsels.

Part of the difference in women's views of women was due to differences in education. The Virginia Slims poll indicated that 52 percent of women who had gone to college believed men were especially fit for politics as compared to 66 percent of those with a high school education and 71 percent of women who had not gone beyond eighth grade.[24] But education alone did not explain the entire difference, because women delegates were much more optimistic about women's political capacities than the most educated category of women voters.

It is not clear how or why politically active women were less likely than others to have acquired or retained less restrictive views of femininity and role possibilities. Perhaps it is because American society is pluralistic and socialization practices vary greatly. Perhaps these active, self-confident women never learned that girls were less effective or less concerned with public affairs than boys. Perhaps their adult experiences were reinforcing, confidence building experiences.

One consequence of optimism about the political efficacy of their sex was that more often than men women delegates foresaw much larger political roles for women in the future than the past. Almost all women and men in both parties agreed that there would be a major change in women's political roles in the next ten years, but more women than men were certain that this would be the case.

Still these data raise serious questions about how soon women will seek or achieve de facto political equality. Lower aspirations, lesser achievement drives, male doubts and resistance, anticipated voter resistance, and women's hypersensitivity to potential voter resistance,[25] all foreshadow obstacles to women's seeking and winning political power. None of these obstacles need be insurmountable. We have already seen that changing beliefs about femininity, masculinity, and political power are related to political aspirations, because desires are rooted in the perception of the fitting and the possible. We have seen too that conceptions of femininity are related to employment and that women in professional roles are especially likely to have high political aspirations *and* a conception of femininity and wife/mother roles that is compatible with the pursuit of political ambitions.

But even though women employed as professionals and in managerial roles were definitely more likely than housewives to aspire to high office, women employed in occupations from which political candidates are normally recruited were much less likely than men in comparable occupations to desire high office or to be willing to work to achieve it. Only among female college students were there more women with high ambition/high achievement drives than without ambition, and even among students, the familiar sex differences are present. As compared to persons already engaged in other occupations, students of both sexes were most likely to harbor ambition for high office; but when the two sexes were compared, it was clear that substantially more males than females had aspirations and strong achievement drives. A determined effort to identify personal, social, and political factors that contribute to women's ambitions yielded suggestive if rather unsatisfying results. (See Table 14–16.)

Conception of femininity was more strongly related to ambition than were education, age, occupation (Table 14–17), political experience, or political ideology. (Although young men and women were more likely than older ones to have high political ambitions, the highly educated were more ambitious than the less educated, and professionals were more ambitious than other occupational groups.) Only sex itself was a more powerful predictor of ambition than were sex conceptions. Still, all these factors explain only about one-quarter of the variance between delegates with high ambition, moderate ambition, and low ambition.

Why? The problem is perhaps less puzzling than it first appears.

Women's lower level of ambition is a complex psycho-social phenomenon, one to which all aspects of women's lives are potentially relevant. And, as Robert MacIver noted,

> ... the discovery of the causes of social phenomena is progressive and always approximate, always incomplete. We seek to trace the routes of specific transitions within the larger flux. What we designate causes are the various conjunctures of things in the process of creating some difference that arrests our attention; effects are then particular properties—or differences—manifested by things in their various conjunctures.[26]

The conjuncture of events that shapes a woman's subjective response to political opportunity includes many factors not even touched upon in this study. Residues of early socialization, fears, anxieties, and the self-denying ordinances through which each of us attempts to ward these off, values that determine priorities in ways too subtle to be available through standardized interviews, situational constraints too complex to be readily explained—all these and the interactions among them are doubtless relevant to women's lower political ambitions and to our problem in explaining them.

The data indicate that there is a new breed of woman, and while she is not necessarily new to politics, she differs from traditional woman in her more expansive self-conception,[27] her greater demands for power, and her higher power orientation. Because views about women are a basic aspect of culture, they are of course involved in broad processes of cultural

Table 14-16. Femininity, Age, Occupation, Education, and Ambition: Women Only

Ambition by occupation[a]	.19
Ambition by age[a]	−.17
Ambition by education[a]	.16
Ambition by conception of femininity[a]	.28
Ambition by conception of femininity[b]	
Controlling for occupation	.26
Controlling for age	.26
Controlling for education	.25
Controlling for occupation and education	.24
Controlling for age and education	.22
Controlling for age, education, occupation	.21
N =	736

[a]Zero order correlations.
[b]Partial correlations.
NOTE: Data are from the mail questionnaires.

Table 14-17. Ambition for Public Office by Occupation (%)

	Symbol Specialists	Lawyers	Material Specialists	Housewives	Students	Clerical & Sales	Public Employees	Salaried Managers	Health Personnel	Other Professionals	Other
None	26	13	30	56	7	30	9	22	44	19	30
Low	1	3	4	6	2	9	7	1	0	5	5
Moderate	11	12	12	18	4	22	21	20	17	13	12
High	63	72	54	21	87	39	64	57	40	63	53
Weighted *N* =	305	273	280	395	90	288	185	177	48	164	200

NOTE: These data are from the intersect data set. For an explanation of the measures, see Appendix C.

change. Attitudes toward femininity and masculinity are enmeshed with attitudes toward such diverse phenomena as busing, welfare policy, the United Nations, and rock festivals. It appears that for now, women with nontraditional views about themselves and their sex are also likely to have nontraditional views about other aspects of society and culture. New breed women will not necessarily be liberal Democrats but they are more likely to be, and since high ambition is associated with new conceptions of femininity, women running for high office are more likely to be Democratic than Republican, liberal than conservative. The fact that male liberals are also more likely than conservatives to believe that women can manage political roles means that liberal political milieus will be more hospitable to women's political ambitions. But since there is no necessary or perfect association between conceptions of femininity and political liberalism, more conservative women candidates for high office are also a possibility. There were present in the Republican party more women of long experience and high ambition and some men who believed in women's political potential. In sum, increased numbers of women candidates for high office are likely to appear in both parties. Both their numbers and their success will depend largely on the progressive elimination of disabling conceptions of femininity and restrictive role distributions.

In their now famous study, the Brovermans and their associates confirmed the existence of "a double standard of health . . . wherein ideal concepts of health for a mature adult, sex unspecified, are meant primarily for men, less so for women."[28]

The Brovermans argued that the conception of femininity conventional among clinical psychologists "conceals a powerful, negative assessment of women." Clinicians, they note, were "more likely to suggest that healthy women differ from healthy men by being more submissive, less independent, less adventurous, more easily influenced, less aggressive, less competitive, more excitable in minor crises, having their feelings more easily hurt, being more emotional, more conceited about their appearance, less objective, and disliking math and science. This constellation," they added, "seems a most unusual way of describing any mature, healthy individual."[29] The "feminine" traits described by the Brovermans hardly equip women for important political roles.

A suggestive parallel to the Brovermans' discovery is available in the conception of modern man. In their recent book, *Becoming Modern*, Inkeles and Smith argue that women's status in society is integrally related to modernity. They note that most traditional societies are "vigorously male dominated." They predicted "that the liberating influence of the forces making for modernization would act on men's attitudes and incline them to accord to women status and rights more nearly equal to those enjoyed by men."[30]

Women's changing position is seen by Inkeles and Smith as part of a more general trend away from distributing roles on the basis of ascriptive characteristics, such as sex, and toward greater egalitarianism in human affairs. The association of women's rights and modernity seems reasonable enough since women have made strides in the contemporary period and in the most modern nations toward gaining a larger share of political power with the result that women enjoy legal equality in most industrial nations. But there are two bothersome aspects of this argument. The first is that modern as well as traditional countries are "vigorously male dominated." Some Western nations were ruled by women monarchs in the pre-modern period; in the contemporary period women have achieved leadership mainly in new nations—India, Ceylon, Israel. But that is not all. There is also a striking resemblance between characteristics usually ascribed to modern men and those ascribed to *men* in modern societies.

Inkeles and Smith summed modern man's character as consisting of four general traits:

> He is an informed, participant citizen; he has a marked sense of personal efficacy; he is highly independent and autonomous in his relations to traditional sources of influence, especially when making basic decisions about how to conduct his personal affairs; and he is ready for new experiences and ideas; that is, he is relatively open-minded and cognitively flexible.[31]

But if these traits are associated with modernity rather than maleness and it is also true that the characteristics of modern man comprise a syndrome of interrelated characteristics that are affected by education, employment, and similar experiences, then we might conclude 1) that women in the presidential elite were more "modern" than most women, since they are participant, efficacious, and open, and 2) that newwomen, defined as those who have discarded traditional conceptions of femininity derived from example and conventional wisdom in favor of other conceptions derived from formal education and egalitarian ideologies, are most modern of all. If this is true, then there are grounds for expecting that increasing education, mobility, and employment outside the home will lead to increasing numbers of newwomen in whom new beliefs about what it is to be a woman will have led to new self-conceptions and new patterns of behavior.

The presence of a new breed of women in 1972 does not foreshadow the emergence of a new feminist voting bloc, but it probably does portend persistent demands for increased power by increasing numbers of women to whom it is not self-evident that men are the natural governors of society.

NOTES

1. I discuss four hypothetical constraints to women's participation in power in Jeane Kirkpatrick, *Political Woman* (New York: Basic Books, 1974), pp. 8–20.

2. Note that some contemporary radical ideologies, e.g., the Black Muslims, reject sexual and racial equality and emphasize traditional distinctions between the sexes.

3. For this reason, demands should be studied in conjunction with expectations. Not only do demands derive from expectations (only that which is conceived as possible is demanded), but they also specify their content and designate the appropriate strategy for pursuing them. On the interrelation of demands, expectations, and identifications, see Harold D. Lasswell and Abraham Kaplan, *Power and Society: A Framework for Political Inquiry* (New Haven: Yale University Press, 1950), pp. 16–28.

4. Peggy Lamson, *Few Are Chosen: American Women in Political Life Today* (Boston: Houghton Mifflin, 1968), p. xxiii.

5. Kirkpatrick, *Political Woman*, p. 127.

6. Frieda L. Gehlen, "Women in Congress: Their Power and Influence in a Man's World," *Transaction*, October 1969, pp. 36–40.

7. Susan Tolchin and Martin Tolchin, *Clout: Womanpower and Politics* (New York: Coward, McCann and Geoghegan, 1974).

8. A good statement of the argument that culture arbitrarily defines femininity and socializes women to accept exclusion from many aspects of life is Margaret Mead, *Sex and Temperament in Three Primitive Societies* (New York: New American Library, Mentor Books, 1950), also Mead, *Male and Female: A Study of the Sexes in a Changing World* (New York: New American Library, Mentor Books, 1955). Also, Judith M. Bardwick and Elizabeth Douvan, "Ambivalence: The Socialization of Women," in *Woman in Sexist Society*, eds. Vivian Gornick and Barbara K. Moran (New York: Basic Books, 1971); S. L. Bern and D. J. Bern, "Case Study of a Non-Conscious Ideology: Training the Woman to Know Her Place," *Beliefs, Attitudes and Human Affairs*, ed. D. J. Bern (Belmont, Calif.: Brooks/Cole, 1970). A fascinating article on beliefs concerning the "normal" woman is Inge K. Broverman, Donald M. Broverman, Frank Clarkson, Paul S. Rosenkrantz, and Susan R. Vogel, "Sex-Role Stereotypes and Clinical Judgments of Mental Health," *Journal of Consulting and Clinical Psychology* 34, no. 1 (1970): 1–7; on socialization into sex roles, see Lenore J. Weitzman, Deborah Eifler, Elizabeth Hokada, and Catherine Rosse, "Sex-Role Socialization in Picture Books for Pre-School Children," *American Journal of Sociology* 77 (1972): 1125–1150. One of the most interesting studies of the effect of culture on professional aspirations is Matina S. Horner's "Femininity and Successful Achievement: A Basic Inconsistency," in *Feminine Personality and Conflict*, ed. Judith Bardwick (Belmont, Calif.: Brooks/Cole, 1970); also Nancy Chodorow, "Being and Doing," in *Woman in Sexist Society*.

9. Matina Horner, "The Motive to Avoid Success and Changing Aspirations of College Women," in *Readings on the Psychology of Women*, ed. Judith Bardwick (New York: Harper and Row, 1972). On sex stereotyping and politics, see also Lynne B. Iglitzin, "The Making of the Apolitical Woman: Femininity and Sex Stereotyping in Girls," in *Women in Politics*. ed. Jane S. Jaquette (New York: John Wiley & Sons, 1974). Her findings are inconclusive as regards the relation between sex stereotyping and politicization, p. 30.

10. The concept of the character-culture manifold is Harold Lasswell's. A good description is found in Harold D. Lasswell, "The Democratic Character," in *The Political Writings*

of Harold D. Lasswell (Glencoe, Ill.: The Free Press, 1951), pp. 487–489. A useful version of this concept is Heinz Eulau, "The Maddening Methods of Harold D. Lasswell," in *Micro-Macro Political Analysis: Accents of Inquiry* (Chicago: Aldine, 1969), pp. 119–137. This conception is related to that of George Herbert Mead; for a succinct account, see, e.g., Anselm L. Strauss, *The Social Psychology of George Herbert Mead* (Chicago: University of Chicago Press, Phoenix Books, 1956), pp. 212–260.

11. Kirkpatrick, *Political Woman*. Also, Kirkpatrick, "Women in Power Processes: A Preliminary Examination of Four Hypothetical Constraints Affecting Women's Political Participation" (Paper delivered at the annual meeting of the Southern Political Science Association, New Orleans, La., November 1974).

12. The 1972 Virginia Slims American Women's Opinion Poll (A study conducted by Louis Harris), p. 15.

13. It is, of course, interesting that it was in the Conservative party that a woman, Margaret Thatcher, first won the leader's position in an Anglo-Saxon democracy.

14. Virginia Slims Poll, p. 15.

15. This finding is consistent with a number of other studies demonstrating that relations between socioeconomic characteristics and perspectives tend to disappear within the elite.

16. Virginia Slims Poll, p. 29.

17. Ibid., p. 30.

18. Kirkpatrick, "Women in Power Processes."

19. Persons who describe themselves as radicals and very liberal see role conflict as less inevitable than those who are "somewhat liberal" who, in turn, see it as less important than moderates and conservatives. Among Democratic women the relationship of ideological self-classification to role conflict is .23; among the more homogeneous Republican women, it is .16.

20. Among Wallace women the majority is not so large; only 55 percent are convinced that their sex is fully suited to the professions.

21. The relations for the relationship among newwoman, traditional woman, and the various characteristics mentioned are expressed in the following statistics: age: gamma .26; religion: Cramer's V .25; education: gamma .31; income: V .06; occupation: V .12; church attendance: gamma .25; place of origin: V .12; region residing: V .18; ethnicity: V .18; self-perceived social class: gamma $-.03$; candidate preference: V .33; political generations: gamma .26; sanctions: gamma $-.53$; international idealism: gamma .48; military policy: gamma $-.40$; cultural conservation: gamma .61; tough and tender: gamma .56; intensity of women's questions: gamma .72; abortion: gamma .44; day care: $-.47$; layoffs, women first in depression: gamma .44; women's liberation movement: gamma .69; voluntary organization membership: gamma $-.04$; years in community: gamma $-.28$; insider: gamma .41; lots of fun: gamma $-.31$; status index: gamma $-.31$; reformer index: gamma .41; policy-maker index: gamma .31; party leader index: gamma $-.24$; local leaders index: gamma $-.25$.

22. The tenacity and enthusiasm with which many women assert that it is women who block women seems to be curious and suggestive. I suspect that it is related to the tendency to repress and understate male discrimination. This tendency of politically active men was also noted in Kirkpatrick, *Political Woman*, and "Women in Power Processes."

23. Kirkpatrick, *Political Woman*; Gehlen, "Women in Congress."

24. Virginia Slims Poll, p. 15.

25. The following statistics reflecting the percentages of delegates who strongly agree that many voters will not vote for women reflect women's greater perception of voter resistance to women: McGovern men—13 percent, women—26 percent; Humphrey

men—19 percent, women—29 percent; Wallace men—9 percent, women—25 percent; Muskie men—0 percent, women 24 percent; Nixon men—6 percent, women—19 percent.

26. Robert MacIver, *Social Causation* (New York: Harper and Row, Torchbooks, 1964), p. 382.

27. One study of the attitudes of women toward women found that local party committeewomen had a higher evaluation of women's political capacities than did women registered voters. See Audrey Siess Wells and Eleanor Cutri Smeal, "Women's Attitudes Toward Women in Politics: A Survey of Urban Registered Voters and Party Committeewomen," in *Women in Politics*, pp. 54–72.

28. Broverman, et al., "Sex-Role Stereotypes," p. 2.

29. Ibid., pp. 4–5.

30. Alex Inkeles and David H. Smith, *Becoming Modern: Individual Change in Six Developing Countries* (Cambridge, Mass.: Harvard University Press, 1974), p. 290. David Riesman noted a relation between modernization and sex roles in his introduction to Daniel Lerner's *The Passing of Traditional Society: Modernizing the Middle East* (Glencoe, Ill.: The Free Press, 1958), pp. 7–8. ". . . The ingenuity needed to escape the all-too-evident impasses in the Middle East can neither be imported nor be locally engendered without a lessening of the dominant male values, what the Spaniards term 'machismo.' A greater equality between the sexes would seem to be requisite before many of the approaches toward modernization can make sense. . . ."

31. Inkeles and Smith, *Becoming Modern*, p. 290.

APPENDIX A

Mail Questionnaire and Interview Schedule

MAIL QUESTIONNAIRE

DIRECTIONS: Your responses will be read by an optical mark reader. Your careful observance of these few simple rules will be most appreciated.

Use only black lead pencil (No. 2½ or less).
Make heavy black marks that fill the circle.
Erase cleanly any answer you wish to change.
Make no stray markings of any kind.

EXAMPLE: Yes   No
Will marks made with ball pen or
fountain pen be properly read? . . . . ◯ . . ●

1. Have you ever attended a National Convention as a delegate or alternate before? If yes, mark each year in which you attended. (Mark all that apply)

Never attended as a del-   1956 . . . . . . ◯
  egate or alternate . . . ◯   1952 . . . . . . ◯
1968 . . . . ◯   1948 . . . . . . ◯
1964 . . . . ◯   1944 . . . . . . ◯
1960 . . . . ◯   1940 . . . . . . ◯

2. Who, if anyone, approached you and encouraged you to seek a position as a delegate to the National Convention this year? (Mark all that apply)

Some close personal friends and associates. . . . . ◯
Some party members, although they did not speak
  officially for the party . . . . ◯
Supporters for a particular candidate . . . . ◯
Some civic groups and organizations or their members . ◯
The county chairman, precinct chairman, or some
  other party official . . . . ◯
Supporters of a particular issue. . . . . ◯
Other. . . . . ◯
I decided to run on my own. . . . . ◯

3. Were you selected as a delegate to this year's National Convention: (Mark one)

Through a party primary . . . . ◯
Through a state convention . . . . ◯
Through a state or local committee . . . . ◯
Through some type of mixed system . . . ◯

4. What were the circumstances of your election as a delegate to the National Convention? Was there: (Mark one)

Very close contest for the position . . . . . . ◯
Somewhat close contest for the position. . . ◯
Not too close contest for the position . . . . ◯
No contest at all. . . . . ◯

5. Did you run for delegate as a member of slate?
      Yes. . . . ◯   No. . . . ◯

6. Did you have to campaign personally to become a delegate or did the slate assume the burden of campaigning? (Mark one)

Campaigned personally . . ◯   Both . . . . ◯
Slate assumed burden . . . ◯   No campaign. . ◯

7. (If campaigned personally) what did this involve? (Mark all that apply)

Speeches to party and civic groups . . . . ◯
Appearances on television and radio programs . . . ◯
Ads in the newspaper . . . . ◯
Ads on radio and television . . . . ◯
Door-to-door canvassing . . . . ◯
Mail circulars to prospective voters . . . . ◯
Telephone campaigns . . . . ◯
Donate services to party or candidate . . . . ◯

8. About how much of your own money did you have to invest in the contest? (Mark one)

$ 0 – $ 49 ....○ $300 – $399 ....○
$ 50 – $ 99 ....○ $400 – $499 ....○
$100 – $199 ....○ $500 & More ...○
$200 – $299 ....○

9. What is your opinion of the process by which you were selected as a delegate this year as compared to that of previous years? For each of the following indicate whether it was more, about the same, or less than in previous years.

(Mark one in each row)

	More than in Previous Years	About the Same	Less than in Previous Years	Don't Know No Opinion
Open to any interested party member	○	○	○	○
Representativeness of slate	○	○	○	○
Fairness of selection process	○	○	○	○
Likelihood of producing winner in the election	○	○	○	○

10. How many members of the state delegation were you personally acquainted with before you ran for delegate? (Mark one)

All ..... ○   A few ... ○
Most .... ○   None .... ○
Some .... ○

11. How important would you say each of the following qualities is for a delegate to have?

(Mark one in each row)

	Very Important	Somewhat Important	Not Too Important	Not a Consideration
Works hard for party	○	○	○	○
Dependable	○	○	○	○
Will represent best interests of state	○	○	○	○
Contributes financially to the party	○	○	○	○
Ran for or held public office	○	○	○	○
Strong policy views	○	○	○	○
Held party office	○	○	○	○
Likeable personality, easy to get along with	○	○	○	○
Well known in local community	○	○	○	○
Will represent best interests of party	○	○	○	○

12. Now, some comparisons of women and men. First, in politics, would you say:

(Mark one in each row)

	Strongly Agree	Moderately Agree	Slightly Agree	Slightly Disagree	Moderately Disagree	Strongly Disagree
Women have just as much opportunity as men to become political leaders	○	○	○	○	○	○
Most men in the party organization try to keep women out of leadership roles	○	○	○	○	○	○
Many will not vote for women candidates	○	○	○	○	○	○
We can expect to see really big changes in the role and power of women in the political parties within the next ten years	○	○	○	○	○	○

13. Next, in politics and public office:
(Mark one in each row)

	Strongly Agree	Moderately Agree	Slightly Agree	Slightly Disagree	Moderately Disagree	Strongly Disagree
While women hold few public offices, they work behind the scenes and really have more influence in politics than they're given credit for	○	○	○	○	○	○
Most men are better suited emotionally for politics than are most women	○	○	○	○	○	○
To be really active in politics, men have to neglect their wives and children	○	○	○	○	○	○
Women have more time to be involved in politics than men	○	○	○	○	○	○
Women in public office can be just as logical and rational as men	○	○	○	○	○	○
Feminine charm and diplomacy can be a woman's greatest asset in getting ahead in politics	○	○	○	○	○	○
It is almost impossible to be a good wife and mother and hold public office, too	○	○	○	○	○	○
Women who succeed in politics usually have to sacrifice their femininity to get there	○	○	○	○	○	○

14. Now, thinking more generally about women in our society:

(Mark one in each row)

	Strongly Agree	Moderately Agree	Slightly Agree	Slightly Disagree	Moderately Disagree	Strongly Disagree
Although not always recognized, women have more real power than men	○	○	○	○	○	○
Successful career women are usually competitive and agressive	○	○	○	○	○	○
Children of working mothers tend to be less well-adjusted than children of women who stay at home	○	○	○	○	○	○
Women are emotionally less well suited than men for business and professional careers	○	○	○	○	○	○

15. (Mark one in each row):   DEMOCRATS   REPUBLICANS

When you entered the contest to become a delegate were you publically identified with any candidate? .... No ○ ...... Yes, Muskie ○ .. Yes, Humphrey ○ .. Yes, McGovern ○ .. Yes, Wallace ○ .. Yes, Mills ○ .. Yes, Chisholm ○ .. Yes, Jackson ○ .. Yes, Kennedy ○ .. Yes, Other ○ ...... Yes, Nixon ○ .. Yes, Ashbrook ○ .. Yes, McCloskey ○

When you go to the Convention will you be bound by state law or party convention to vote for a candidate? .... ○ ...... ○ .. ○ .. ○ .. ○ .. ○ .. ○ .. ○ .. ○ .. ○ ...... ○ .. ○ .. ○

16. (Mark one in each row):   DEMOCRATS   REPUBLICANS

Whether committed or not, whom do you most prefer as your party's nominee for President? .... McGovern ○ .. Chisholm ○ .. Humphrey ○ .. Kennedy ○ .. Mills ○ .. Wallace ○ .. Jackson ○ .. Muskie ○ .. Other ○ ...... Ashbrook ○ .. Nixon ○ .. McCloskey ○ .. Other ○

Whom do you consider the least acceptable as your party's nominee for President? ...... ○ .. ○ .. ○ .. ○ .. ○ .. ○ .. ○ .. ○ .. ○ ...... ○ .. ○ .. ○ .. ○

Who do you think will win your party's nomination for President? .... ○ .. ○ .. ○ .. ○ .. ○ .. ○ .. ○ .. ○ .. ○ ...... ○ .. ○ .. ○ .. ○

Who do you think will win the election? .... ○ .. ○ .. ○ .. ○ .. ○ .. ○ .. ○ .. ○ .. ○ ...... ○ .. ○ .. ○ .. ○

17. In thinking about the decisions that will be made at the Convention, which of the following factors will you favor and which will you oppose?

(Mark one in each row)

Strongly Favor / Favor / Oppose / Strongly Oppose / No Position

Counting service to the party heavily in nominating candidates .... ○○○○○

Working to minimize disagreement within the party .... ○○○○○

Standing firm for position even if it means resigning from party.... ○○○○○

Minimizing the role of the party organization in nominating candidates for office .... ○○○○○

Playing down some issues if it will improve the chances of winning. .... ○○○○○

Encouraging widespread participation in making most party decisions. .... ○○○○○

Selecting a nominee who is strongly committed on the issue .... ○○○○○

18. To what extent do you think the actions of the Convention will be fair in dealing with the wishes of each of the following groups? For each group indicate whether the Convention will probably Always be very fair, Generally quite fair, Probably quite unfair, or will Largely ignore the group.

(Mark one in each row)

Always Very Fair / Generally Quite Fair / Probably Quite Unfair / Convention Will Largely Ignore

Delegates favoring your candidate for nomination .... ○ .. ○ .. ○ .. ○

Delegates in favor of reform... ○ .. ○ .. ○ .. ○

Rank and file delegates ...... ○ .. ○ .. ○ .. ○

Women. .... ○ .. ○ .. ○ .. ○

Labor union delegates .... ○ .. ○ .. ○ .. ○

Conservative delegates ...... ○ .. ○ .. ○ .. ○

Delegates supporting the leading contender for nomination . ○ .. ○ .. ○ .. ○

Radical delegates .... ○ .. ○ .. ○ .. ○

Young delegates. .... ○ .. ○ .. ○ .. ○

Middle Americans .... ○ .. ○ .. ○ .. ○

Liberal delegates .... ○ .. ○ .. ○ .. ○

Black delegates .... ○ .. ○ .. ○ .. ○

Members of your state delegation .... ○ .. ○ .. ○ .. ○

Convention leadership. ...... ○ .. ○ .. ○ .. ○

Other delegates like you ..... ○ .. ○ .. ○ .. ○

Farm delegates. .... ○ .. ○ .. ○ .. ○

Business interests delegates ... ○ .. ○ .. ○ .. ○

19. Think ahead to the Convention and to the problem of keeping track of what is going on. Do you think you will have access to as much information as you want about:

(Mark one in each row)

As well informed as I want to be / Some difficulty in becoming well informed / Not as well informed as I want

What is going on <u>within your state</u>
  <u>delegation</u> .... O .. O .. O
Knowing what <u>your candidate</u> and
  his staff are doing .... O .. O .. O
Following what is going on in the
  <u>platform committee</u> .... O .. O .. O
Following what is going on in other
  state delegations .... O .. O .. O
What will be going on in the <u>Cre-
  dentials Committee</u> .... O .. O .. O
<u>Other groups</u> you are particularly
  interested in, such as Women's
  Caucus, Labor, Blacks, etc. .... O .. O .. O

20. Once you get to the Convention, how much opportunity do you think you will have to participate in:

(Mark one in each row)

Much Opportunity / Some Opportunity / Not Much Opportunity

The activities of <u>your delegation</u> ... O .. O .. O
Meetings and caucuses on behalf
  of one of the <u>candidates</u> .... O .. O .. O
Decisions on <u>platform</u> or <u>creden-
  tials</u> issues .... O .. O .. O
<u>Party reform</u> activities .... O .. O .. O
<u>Other groups</u> you are interested
  in, such as Women's Caucus,
  Labor, Blacks, etc. .... O .. O .. O

21. Once your National Convention is under way, how much influence do you think you will have on:

(Mark one in each row)

Great Deal of Influence / Some Influence / Little Influence / No Influence at All

Decisions made by your <u>state's</u>
  <u>delegation</u> .... O .. O .. O .. O
Decisions in meetings or cau-
  cuses on behalf of one of the
  <u>candidates</u> for nomination ... O .. O .. O .. O
Decisions in meetings or cau-
  cuses concerning <u>platform</u> or
  <u>credentials</u> issues .... O .. O .. O .. O
Decisions involving <u>party</u>
  <u>reform</u> .... O .. O .. O .. O
Decisions made by <u>other groups</u>
  you are particularly interested
  in, such as Women's Caucus,
  Labor, Blacks, etc. .... O .. O .. O .. O

22. At your National Convention, what do you expect to be of greatest interest to you?

(Mark one in each row)

Great Interest / Quite a Bit of Interest / Not Very Interested / Not at all Interested

The nomination of the candidate
  for President .... O .. O .. O .. O
The activities of the Women's
  Caucus .... O .. O .. O .. O
Decisions on the party's platform . O .. O .. O .. O
Experiencing the excitement of
  the Convention .... O .. O .. O .. O
Disagreements within your state
  delegation .... O .. O .. O .. O
Taking part in an important
  event .... O .. O .. O .. O
Decisions on the seating of state
  delegations .... O .. O .. O .. O
The activities of the Black dele-
  gates .... O .. O .. O .. O
Discussions or debates over party
  reform .... O .. O .. O .. O
Getting acquainted with other
  delegates................. O .. O .. O .. O
Being able to see and meet nation-
  al political leaders........... O .. O .. O .. O
Making contact with important
  people .... O .. O .. O .. O
Learning more about politics .... O .. O .. O .. O

23. What do you think are the most important things the Convention can do? Below are listed five different functions that the Convention performs. Please rank them from FIRST through FIFTH most important.

(Mark one in each column)

FIRST most important / SECOND most important / THIRD most important / FOURTH most important / FIFTH most important

Unifying the party .... O O O O O
Putting together a team that will
  win the election .... O O O O O
Adopting correct positions on im-
  portant national issues......... O O O O O
Reforming the party .... O O O O O
Nominating the most deserving
  candidates................. O O O O O

24. What year did you first become active in politics?
(Write the year in the boxes)

|1|9| | | ⓪①②③④⑤⑥⑦⑧⑨
             ⓪①②③④⑤⑥⑦⑧⑨

25. Have you been <u>continuously</u> active ever since?
    Yes ... O   No ... O

26. Have you ever been a supporter of a different political party?
    Yes ... O   No ... O

27. When you vote in a general election, do you vote a straight party ticket? (Mark one)

All of the time. . . .○   Almost never. . .○
Most of the time . .○   Never. . . . . . .○
Some of the time . .○

28. For the following party positions, mark those which you have held and those which you presently hold.

(Mark all that apply)	Positions I have held	Positions I now hold
National Party Staff	○	○
Presidential Campaign Staff	○	○
National Committeeman/ Committeewoman	○	○
Other National Role	○	○
State Party Chairman	○	○
State Central Committee	○	○
State Campaign Director	○	○
Other State Position	○	○
District Chairman	○	○
District Campaign Manager	○	○
County Chairman/Chairwoman	○	○
County Board	○	○
County Campaign Director	○	○
Other County Position	○	○
City Chairman	○	○
Other Local Organization Position	○	○

29. For the following public positions, mark those which you have held and those which you presently hold.

(Mark all that apply)	Positions I have held	Positions I now hold
Vice President	○	○
U.S. Senator	○	○
Congressman	○	○
Cabinet Member	○	○
Federal Judge	○	○
Federal Prosecutor	○	○
Ambassador	○	○
Other National Office	○	○
Governor	○	○
Lt. Governor	○	○
State Senator	○	○
State Representative	○	○
State Judge	○	○
State Administrative Post	○	○
Other State Office	○	○
Mayor	○	○
Council Member	○	○
Other Local Office	○	○

30. Do you plan to be active during the general election campaign?

Yes . . . ○   No. . .○

31. Were (are) one or both of your parents active in politics? If active, in which party? (Mark one)

Father active Republican . . . .○
Mother active Republican . . . .○
Both active Republicans . . . .○
Father active Democrat . . . .○
Mother active Democrat . . . .○
Both active Democrats . . . .○
Father active Republican, Mother active Democrat .○
Father active Democrat, Mother active Republican .○
One or both active in party other than Republican or Democratic. . . . .○
Neither parent active . . . .○

32. If active in politics, did (do) either of your parents hold any elective or party office(s)?

Yes . . .○   No . . .○

33. (If married) how about your present family? Does your spouse share your political interests?

Yes . . . ○   No . . .○

34. (If married) does your spouse approve of your political party? (Mark one)

Strongly approves. .○   Somewhat disapproves.○
Somewhat approves ○   Strongly disapproves. .○
Indifferent . . . . . .○

35. We are interested in peoples' reasons for being involved in politics. How important are each of the following reasons to your own participation in politics?

(Mark one in each row)

	Extremely Important	Quite Important	Not Very Important	Not at all Important
Personal friends or members of my family are active in the party (as workers, candidates or office holders)	○	○	○	○
I want to see particular candidates elected	○	○	○	○
Party work helps me make business or professional contacts	○	○	○	○
Politics is a part of my way of life	○	○	○	○
I am strongly attached to the party and want to give it my support	○	○	○	○
I enjoy the friendships and social contacts I have with other people in politics	○	○	○	○
I like the fun and excitement of conventions and campaigns	○	○	○	○
I want to have a personal career in politics	○	○	○	○
Party work gives me a sense of fulfilling civic responsibility	○	○	○	○
I want to get the party and its candidates to support the policies I believe in	○	○	○	○
I like the feeling of being close to people who are doing important work	○	○	○	○
Party work gives one visibility and recognition	○	○	○	○

36a. Thinking of all the possible offices and positions in politics, from local to national and from public office to positions in the party organization, which of the following would you most like to be if you could have your personal choice? First consider public office. (Mark only one)

President . . . . O	State Senator . . . . . O
Vice President . . . . . O	State Representative. . O
U. S. Senator. . . . . . O	State Judge. . . . . . . O
Congressman . . . . . . O	State Administrative
Cabinet Member. . . . O	Post. . . . . O
Ambassador . . . . . . O	Other State Office . . . O
Federal Judge . . . . . O	Mayor . . . . O
Federal Prosecutor . . . O	Council Member. . . . . O
Other National Office . O	Other Local Office . . . O
Governor . . . . O	No Interest in Public
Lt. Governor . . . . . . O	Office . . . . O

b. If there were a real chance to hold the position you think is most desirable, how much effort would you be willing to make to get that position? (Mark one)

Would work harder and make more sacrifices than
for any other goal in life . . . . O
Would work harder than before in politics . . . . O
Would make some additional effort . . . . O
Will probably hold that position if I do no more than
I have done in the past . . . . O

37a. Next, consider party positions. Which of the following would you most like to be if you could have your personal choice? (Mark only one)

National Party Chairman . O	County Chairman/
Presidential Campaign	Chairwoman . . . . . . O
Manager . . . . O	County Board . . . . . . O
National Committeeman/	County Campaign
Committeewoman . . . . O	Director . . . . O
Other National Role . . . . O	Other County Position O
State Party Chairman . . . O	City Chairman. . . . . . O
State Central Committee . O	Other Local
State Campaign Director . O	Organization Position O
Other State Position . . . . O	No Interest in Party
District Chairman. . . . . . O	Offices . . . . O
District Campaign	
Manager . . . . O	

b. If there were a real chance to hold the position you think is most desirable, how much effort would you be willing to make to get that position? (Mark one)

Would work harder and make more sacrifices than
for any other goal in life . . . . O
Would work harder than before in politics . . . . O
Would make some additional effort . . . . O
Will probably hold that position if I do no more than
I have done in the past . . . . O

38a. Now, all things considered, which of all of these positions do you think you are most likely to hold at the top of your career in politics? (Mark only one, either public or party office, not both)

No interest in public or party office . . O

Public Office

President . . . . O
Vice President . . . . O
U. S. Senator. . . . . O
Congressman. . . . . O
Cabinet Member . . . . O
Ambassador . . . . O
Federal Judge . . . . O
Federal Prosecutor . . . . O
Other National Office . . . . O
Governor . . . . O
Lt. Governor. . . . . O
State Senator . . . . O
State Representative. . . . . O
State Judge. . . . . O
State Administrative Post . . . . O
Other State Office . . . . O
Mayor . . . . O
Council Member . . . . O
Other Local Office . . . . O

Party Office

National Party Chairman . . . . O
Presidential Campaign Manager. . . . . O
National Committeeman/
Committeewoman . . . . O
Other National Role. . . . . O
State Party Chairman . . . . O
State Central Committee . . . . O
State Campaign Director . . . . O
Other State Position. . . . . O
District Chairman. . . . . O
District Campaign Manager . . . . O
County Chairman/Chairwoman. . . . . O
County Board . . . . O
County Campaign Director . . . . O
Other County Position . . . . O
City Chairman . . . . O
Other Local Organization Position. . . O

b. How much effort will you have to make to reach this position?

Will work harder and make more sacrifices than for
any other goal in life . . . . O
Will work harder than before in politics . . . . O
Will make some additional effort. . . . . O
Will probably hold that position if I do no more
than I have done in the past . . . . O

39. There is a great deal of talk these days about rising prices and the cost of living in general. Some feel that the problem of inflation is temporary and that no Government action is necessary. Others say the Government must do everything possible to combat the problem of inflation immediately or it will get worse. Where would you place yourself on the following scale, ranging from agreement with total government action against inflation to agreement with no government action against inflation? Now where would you place each of the following declared candidates and other possible candidates for President?

(Mark one in each row)	TOTAL Government Action Against Inflation						NO Government Action Against Inflation
	1	2	3	4	5	6	7
Yourself	O	O	O	O	O	O	O
Shirley Chisholm	O	O	O	O	O	O	O
Edmund Muskie	O	O	O	O	O	O	O
Richard Nixon	O	O	O	O	O	O	O
George McGovern	O	O	O	O	O	O	O
Nelson Rockefeller	O	O	O	O	O	O	O
Hubert Humphrey	O	O	O	O	O	O	O
Spiro Agnew	O	O	O	O	O	O	O
George Wallace	O	O	O	O	O	O	O
Ronald Reagan	O	O	O	O	O	O	O
Edward Kennedy	O	O	O	O	O	O	O
John Connally	O	O	O	O	O	O	O

40. There is much discussion about the best way to deal with racial problems. Some people think achieving racial integration of schools is so important that it justifies busing children to schools out of their own neighborhoods. Others think letting children go to their neighborhood schools is so important that they oppose busing. Where would you place yourself on the following scale ranging from agreement with busing to achieve integration to agreement with keeping children in neighborhood schools? Now where would you place each of the following declared candidates and other possible candidates for President?

(Mark one in each row)	Busing to Achieve Integration						Keeping Children in Neighborhood Schools
	1	2	3	4	5	6	7
Yourself	O	O	O	O	O	O	O
Spiro Agnew	O	O	O	O	O	O	O
Shirley Chisholm	O	O	O	O	O	O	O
John Connally	O	O	O	O	O	O	O
Hubert Humphrey	O	O	O	O	O	O	O
Edward Kennedy	O	O	O	O	O	O	O
George McGovern	O	O	O	O	O	O	O
Edmund Muskie	O	O	O	O	O	O	O
Richard Nixon	O	O	O	O	O	O	O
Ronald Reagan	O	O	O	O	O	O	O
Nelson Rockefeller	O	O	O	O	O	O	O
George Wallace	O	O	O	O	O	O	O

41. Even though most of the American troops have been withdrawn from South Vietnam, there is still a lot of discussion about the United States' action in Indo-China. Some people think we should end all American military assistance and economic aid to South East Asia. Others say we should give military assistance and economic aid to the governments of South Vietnam, Cambodia, Laos. Where would you place yourself on the following scale, ranging from agreement with no U.S. military assistance or economic aid to agreement with U.S. military assistance and economic aid? Now where would you place each of the following declared candidates and other possible candidates for President?

(Mark one in each row)	No U.S. Military Assistance or Economic Aid						U.S. Military Assistance and Economic Aid
	1	2	3	4	5	6	7
Yourself	O	O	O	O	O	O	O
George Wallace	O	O	O	O	O	O	O
Nelson Rockefeller	O	O	O	O	O	O	O
Ronald Reagan	O	O	O	O	O	O	O
Richard Nixon	O	O	O	O	O	O	O
Edmund Muskie	O	O	O	O	O	O	O
George McGovern	O	O	O	O	O	O	O
Edward Kennedy	O	O	O	O	O	O	O
Hubert Humphrey	O	O	O	O	O	O	O
John Connally	O	O	O	O	O	O	O
Shirley Chisholm	O	O	O	O	O	O	O
Spiro Agnew	O	O	O	O	O	O	O

42. Some people are primarily concerned with doing everything possible to protect the legal rights of those committing crimes. Others feel that it is more important to stop criminal activity even at the risk of reducing the rights of the accused. Where would you place yourself on the following scale, ranging from agreement with protecting the rights of the accused to agreement with stopping crime regardless of rights of accused. Now where would you place each of the following declared candidates and other possible candidates for President?

(Mark one in each row)	Protect Rights of Accused						Stop Crime Regardless of Rights of Accused
	1	2	3	4	5	6	7
Yourself	O	O	O	O	O	O	O
George McGovern	O	O	O	O	O	O	O
Edmund Muskie	O	O	O	O	O	O	O
Edward Kennedy	O	O	O	O	O	O	O
Richard Nixon	O	O	O	O	O	O	O
Hubert Humphrey	O	O	O	O	O	O	O
Ronald Reagan	O	O	O	O	O	O	O
John Connally	O	O	O	O	O	O	O
Nelson Rockefeller	O	O	O	O	O	O	O
Shirley Chisholm	O	O	O	O	O	O	O
George Wallace	O	O	O	O	O	O	O
Spiro Agnew	O	O	O	O	O	O	O

43. As you know, there will be many groups at the Convention that will be trying to get the party to see things their way. For each of the following groups indicate your feeling toward them on what we call a "feeling thermometer."

Here's how it works: If you don't feel either particularly warm or cold toward a group, then you should place them in the middle of the thermometer, at the 50° mark.

If you have a warm feeling toward a group, or feel favorably toward them, you would give them a score somewhere between 50° and 100°, depending on how warm your feeling is toward that group.

On the other hand, if you don't feel very favorably toward a group--that is, if you don't care much for them--then you would place them somewhere between 0° and 50°. Remember 50° means you feel neutral toward the group.

(Mark one in each row)	Unfavorable · · · · · Neutral · · · · · Favorable
	0° 10° 20° 30° 40° 50° 60° 70° 80° 90° 100°
National Women's Caucus	O O O O O O O O O O O
Conservatives	O O O O O O O O O O O
Convention Leaders . . .	O O O O O O O O O O O
Leaders in Party Reform Activity	O O O O O O O O O O O
Middle Americans	O O O O O O O O O O O
Women's Liberation Movement	O O O O O O O O O O O
Negroes/Blacks	O O O O O O O O O O O
Liberals	O O O O O O O O O O O
Union Leaders	O O O O O O O O O O O
Business Interests	O O O O O O O O O O O

44. Now, using the thermometer again, where would you place Democrats taken together as a group? Where would you place Republicans?

(Mark one in each row)	Unfavorable · · · · · Neutral · · · · · Favorable
	0° 10° 20° 30° 40° 50° 60° 70° 80° 90° 100°
Democrats	O O O O O O O O O O O
Republicans	O O O O O O O O O O O

45. We would like to get your feelings toward some of the declared candidates as well as other possible candidates for President. Please use the thermometer again--this time indicate your feelings toward these persons.

(Mark one in each row)	Unfavorable · · · · · Neutral · · · · · Favorable
	0° 10° 20° 30° 40° 50° 60° 70° 80° 90° 100°
Richard Nixon	O O O O O O O O O O O
George McGovern	O O O O O O O O O O O
Hubert Humphrey	O O O O O O O O O O O
Shirley Chisholm	O O O O O O O O O O O
Nelson Rockefeller	O O O O O O O O O O O
George Wallace	O O O O O O O O O O O
John Connally	O O O O O O O O O O O
Spiro Agnew	O O O O O O O O O O O
Edmund Muskie	O O O O O O O O O O O
Ronald Reagan	O O O O O O O O O O O
Edward Kennedy	O O O O O O O O O O O

46. Using the thermometer again, where would you place your feelings about the following past and present political leaders?

(Mark one in each row)	Unfavorable · · · · · Neutral · · · · · Favorable
	0° 10° 20° 30° 40° 50° 60° 70° 80° 90° 100°
Franklin D. Roosevelt . .	O O O O O O O O O O O
Harry Truman	O O O O O O O O O O O
Robert Taft	O O O O O O O O O O O
Dwight Eisenhower	O O O O O O O O O O O
Adlai Stevenson	O O O O O O O O O O O
John Foster Dulles	O O O O O O O O O O O
John F. Kennedy	O O O O O O O O O O O
Everett Dirksen	O O O O O O O O O O O
Lyndon Johnson	O O O O O O O O O O O
Barry Goldwater	O O O O O O O O O O O

47. People have different ideas about the government in Washington. These ideas don't refer to Democrats or Republicans in particular, but just to the government in general. We want to see how you feel about these ideas — for example:

a. Do you think that people in the government waste a lot of the money we pay in taxes, waste some of it, or don't waste very much of it? (Mark one)

   Not much . . . O   Some . O   A lot . O

b. How much of the time do you think you can trust the government in Washington to do what is right — just about always, most of the time, or only some of the time? (Mark one)

   Always . . . . O
   Most of the time . . . . . . O
   Some of the time . . . . . . O

c. Would you say the government is pretty much run by a few big interests looking out for themselves or that it is run for the benefit of all the people? (Mark one)

   For benefit of all . . O   Few big interests . . . . . . O

d. Do you feel that almost all of the people running the government are smart people who usually know what they are doing, or do you think that quite a few of them don't seem to know what they are doing? (Mark one)

   Know what they're doing . . . . O
   Don't know what they're doing . . . . O

e. Do you think that quite a few of the people running the government are a little crooked, not very many are, or do you think hardly any of them are crooked at all? (Mark one)

   Hardly any . O   Not many . O   Quite a lot . . O

48. Now, how about the media:

(Mark one in each row)

Usually Fair and Accurate · *Sometimes Fair and Accurate* · *Rarely Fair and Accurate*

How fair and accurate do you find television news reporting? Would you say TV news coverage is: . . . . O . . O . . O

How about the newspapers? Would you say newspaper coverage of events is: . . . . O . . O . . O

49. What is your sex?   Male . . . . . O
Female . . . . O

50. In what year were you born?

(Write the year in the box)

⟶ [ ] ⓪①②③④⑤⑥⑦⑧⑨
⓪①②③④⑤⑥⑦⑧⑨

51. What is your marital status?

Single . . . . O
Married . . . . O
Separated or divorced . . . . . O
Widowed . . . . O
Other. . . . . O

52. How many children do you have?

None . . . . . . O   Four . . . . . . O
One. . . . . . . O   Five . . . . . . O
Two. . . . . . . O   Six or more . O
Three. . . . . . O

53. (If you have children) what is the age of your youngest child? (Write in the age as of June 1)

⟶ [ ] ⓪①②③④⑤⑥⑦⑧⑨
⓪①②③④⑤⑥⑦⑧⑨

54. To which ethnic or racial groups do you belong?

(Mark all that apply)

Black/Negro/Afro-
 American . . . . . . O   Polish. . . . . O
Jewish . . . . O   Slavic. . . . . O
English/Scottish/   Other Eastern
 Welsh. . . . . O   European . . . . . . O
Irish . . . . O   Arabic . . . . O
Germanic . . . . O   Chicano . . . . O
Italian . . . . O   Cuban . . . . O
Greek. . . . . O   Puerto Rican . . . . O
French . . . . O   American Indian . . O
Scandinavian . . . . . O   Japanese. . . . . . . O
Other Western   Chinese . . . . O
 European . . . . O   Other Asian . . . . . . O
                                 No Identification . . O

55. In which social class would you place yourself? (Mark one)

Lower class . . . . O
Working class . . . . O
Middle class . . . . O
Upper middle class . . . . O
Upper class . . . . O

56. How many years of education did:

you complete?
your spouse complete? (if married)
your mother complete?
your father complete?

Ⓨ Ⓢ Ⓜ Ⓕ

(Mark only four responses, one in each column)

Grade school or less / 0 - 8 years . . Ⓨ Ⓢ Ⓜ Ⓕ
High school / 9 - 12 years . . . . . . Ⓨ Ⓢ Ⓜ Ⓕ
Some college / 13 - 15 years. . . . . Ⓨ Ⓢ Ⓜ Ⓕ
College graduate. . . . . Ⓨ Ⓢ Ⓜ Ⓕ
Some graduate school . . . . Ⓨ Ⓢ Ⓜ Ⓕ
Master's degree . . . . Ⓨ Ⓢ Ⓜ Ⓕ
M.D., Ph.D., LL.B., etc. . . . . Ⓨ Ⓢ Ⓜ Ⓕ

57. Are you retired?   Yes . O   No . O

58. What is (was):

your occupation?
your spouse's occupation? (if married)
your mother's occupation?
your father's occupation?

Ⓨ Ⓢ Ⓜ Ⓕ

(Mark only four responses, one in each column)

Professional, technical. . . . . Ⓨ Ⓢ Ⓜ Ⓕ
Managers, officials and proprietors – salaried. . Ⓨ Ⓢ Ⓜ Ⓕ
Managers, officials and proprietors – self
 employed . . . . Ⓨ Ⓢ Ⓜ Ⓕ
Clerical and kindred workers . . . . Ⓨ Ⓢ Ⓜ Ⓕ
Sales workers. . . . . Ⓨ Ⓢ Ⓜ Ⓕ
Craftsmen, foremen and kindred workers. . . . Ⓨ Ⓢ Ⓜ Ⓕ
Operatives and kindred workers . . . . Ⓨ Ⓢ Ⓜ Ⓕ
Private household workers. . . . . Ⓨ Ⓢ Ⓜ Ⓕ
Service workers, except private household . . . Ⓨ Ⓢ Ⓜ Ⓕ
Laborers, except farm. . . . . Ⓨ Ⓢ Ⓜ Ⓕ
Farmers and farm managers. . . . . Ⓨ Ⓢ Ⓜ Ⓕ
Farm laborers and foremen . . . . Ⓨ Ⓢ Ⓜ Ⓕ
Member of armed forces. . . . . Ⓨ Ⓢ Ⓜ Ⓕ
Student . . . . Ⓨ Ⓢ Ⓜ Ⓕ
Housewife . . . . Ⓨ Ⓢ Ⓜ Ⓕ
Unemployed . . . . Ⓨ Ⓢ Ⓜ Ⓕ
Permanently disabled . . . . Ⓨ Ⓢ Ⓜ Ⓕ
Occupation not known . . . . Ⓨ Ⓢ Ⓜ Ⓕ

59. What is your religious preference? (Mark one)

None . . . . ○	Church of Christ . . . . ○
Presbyterian , ... ○	Latter Day Saints,
Lutheran. . . . . ○	Mormon . . . . ○
Congregational. . . . . . . ○	Other Protestant . . . . ○
Episcopalian . . . . ○	Catholic . . . . ○
Methodist . . . . ○	Eastern Orthodox. . . . ○
Baptist . . . . ○	Jewish . . . . ○
United Church of Christ . ○	Non-Christian, other
Church of God. . . . . . . ○	than Jewish . . . . ○
Pentecostal or Assembly	Agnostic, Atheist . . . . ○
of God . . . . ○	Other religions. . . . . . ○

60. (If some religious preference) how often would you say you attend religious services?

Almost every week . . . ○	A few times a year . . . ○
Once or twice a month ○	Almost never. . . . . . . ○

61. Where were you born? (Mark one)

New England (Conn., Mass., N.H., R.I., Vt., Me.) . . . . . ○
Middle Atlantic (N.Y., N.J., Del., Penn.). . . . . ○
North Central (Ill., Ind., Mich., Ohio, Ia., Kan., Mo.,
Wisc., Minn., Neb., N.D., S.D.) . . . . ○
South (Ala., Ark., Fla., Ga., La., N.C., S.C., Va.,
Miss.). . . . . ○
Border States (Ky., Md., Tenn., W.Va., D.C.) .· . . . . . ○
Southwest (Tex., Okla., N.M., Ariz.) . . . . ○
Mountain States (Colo., Id., Nev., Mont., Ut., Wyo.) . . ○
Pacific Coast States (Cal., Oreg., Wash.) . . . . ○
External States and Territories . . . . ○
Foreign Country . . . . ○

62. Where did you grow up? (Mark one)

Rural Area . . . . ○
Town (500 — 24,999) . . . . ○
Small city (25,000 — 300,000) . . . ○
Large city . . . . ○
Suburb. . . . . ○

63. How many years have you lived in your present community? (Write the number of years in the box)

⓪①②③④⑤⑥⑦⑧⑨
⓪①②③④⑤⑥⑦⑧⑨

64. What was the approximate annual income of your present family last year ---before taxes? (Mark one)

Under $ 4,999 . . ○	$20,000 — $24,999 . . ○
$ 5,000 — $ 9,999 . . ○	$25,000 — $29,999 . . ○
$10,000 — $14,999 . . ○	$30,000 — $49,999 . . ○
$15,000 — $19,999 . . ○	$50,000 and over . . . . ○

65. Are you a member of any of the following organizations? If a member, indicate whether active or not active. (Mark all that apply)

	Active Member	Not Active Member
Church, synagogue or other religious groups	○	○
Service clubs (Rotary, Lions, Veterans) .	○	○
Non partisan civic groups (Environmental Groups, Better Government Organizations)	○	○
School and school-related groups (PTA, Safety Committees, Fund-raising projects, etc.)	○	○
Professional or occupationally-related groups	○	○
Labor Unions	○	○
Partisan political groups	○	○
Feminist groups, new women's groups (NOW, WEAL, Women's Liberation groups).	○	○
The League of Women Voters.	○	○
Social Clubs	○	○

66. How would you compare your political activity with your involvement in other groups? Would you say your political party work is: (Mark one)

More important . . . . . ○
About as important . . ○
Less important. . . . . . ○

67. How would you describe your political views? (Mark one)

Radical . . . . ○
Very liberal. . . . . ○
Somewhat liberal . . . . . . ○
Moderate . . . . ○
Somewhat conservative . . ○
Very conservative. . . . . . ○
Reactionary. . . . . ○

68. Who would you say are the three most influential persons on your state delegation?

_____

_____

_____

THANK YOU FOR YOUR COOPERATION

Please return your completed questionnaire in the envelope provided to:

Convention Delegate Study
c/o Intran Processing Center
4555 W. 77th Street
Minneapolis, Minnesota 55435

INTERVIEW SCHEDULE

1. I'm mainly interested in talking to you about your experience as a delegate to your party's National Convention. I'd like to begin by asking you about the process by which you were selected as a delegate. Had you ever attended a National Convention as a delegate or as an alternate before 1972?

                                               (GO TO Q. 2)

  1a. Which years did you attend?

        19____ (YEAR)   19____ (YEAR)   19____ (YEAR)

2. What were the main reasons why you decided to seek a delegate position this year?

    _____

    _____

    _____

    _____

    _____

  2a. Anything else? _____

    _____

    _____

    _____

    _____

3. After deciding to run what course of action did you follow in order to ensure your selection as a delegate?

_____

_____

_____

_____

_____

4. (CARD 1-YELLOW) How were you <u>finally</u> chosen as a delegate to this year's National Convention. Were you chosen in a party primary, at a state convention; by a state or local committee, or by some combination of these systems or what?

       1️⃣ IN A PARTY PRIMARY

       2️⃣ AT A STATE CONVENTION

       3️⃣ BY A STATE OR LOCAL COMMITTEE

       4️⃣ BY COMBINATION OF SYSTEMS (SPECIFY) _____

         _____

         _____

5. When you went to the Convention were you bound by state law or instructed by party convention to vote for a particular presidential candidate or were you chosen as an uncommitted delegate?

| 1. BOUND OR INSTRUCTED | | 3. UNCOMMITTED | 8. DK |

(TURN TO P.4, Q.6)

5a. To which candidate were you bound?

_____

6. Which of your party's candidates for President did you personally prefer?

_____

7. How often did you meet with the entire state delegation: all of the time, most of the time, some of the time, seldom or never?

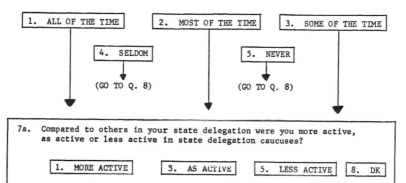

| 1. ALL OF THE TIME | 2. MOST OF THE TIME | 3. SOME OF THE TIME |

| 4. SELDOM | 5. NEVER |

(GO TO Q. 8)   (GO TO Q. 8)

7a. Compared to others in your state delegation were you more active, as active or less active in state delegation caucuses?

| 1. MORE ACTIVE | 3. AS ACTIVE | 5. LESS ACTIVE | 8. DK |

8. Was there a serious contest for the office of state delegation chairman?

| 1. YES | 5. NO | 8. DK |

(TURN TO P.5, Q.9)

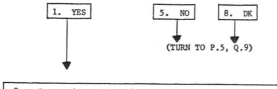

8a. Compared to others in your state delegation were you more active, as active or less active in this contest?

| 1. MORE ACTIVE | 3. AS ACTIVE | 5. LESS ACTIVE | 8. DK |

9. Do you feel the reform movement in your party had a good effect, bad effect or no effect on your party?

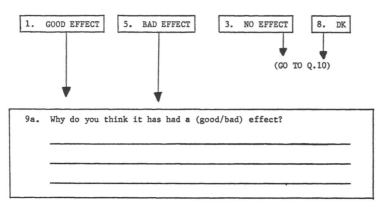

| 1. GOOD EFFECT | 5. BAD EFFECT | 3. NO EFFECT | 8. DK |

(GO TO Q.10)

9a. Why do you think it has had a (good/bad) effect?

_____

_____

_____

10. Once the Convention was underway, what were the main things that you did in addition to voting?

_____

_____

_____

11. Did you have any specific responsibilities or tasks assigned to you?

| 1. YES | 5. NO | → (TURN TO P.6, Q. 12)

11a. What were they? _____

_____

_____

12. Did the women in your delegation participate in the decisions of the delegation as fully as the men did?

1. YES   5. NO   8. DK

13. In general, how influential were the women compared to the men in your state delegation? Were they more influential, as influential or less influential?

1. MORE INFLUENTIAL 3. AS INFLUENTIAL 5. LESS INFLUENTIAL 8. DK

14. Were there groups in your state delegation who met separately?

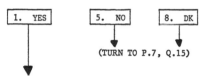

1. YES   5. NO   8. DK

(TURN TO P.7, Q.15)

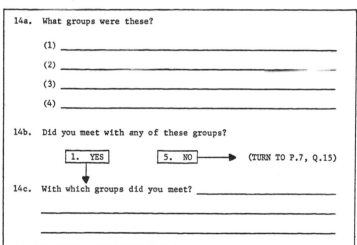

14a. What groups were these?

(1) _____

(2) _____

(3) _____

(4) _____

14b. Did you meet with any of these groups?

1. YES   5. NO ⟶ (TURN TO P.7, Q.15)

14c. With which groups did you meet? _____

_____

_____

15. (CARD 2-GREEN) Thinking back to the Convention and the problem of getting information about what was going on, did you have as much information as you wanted about what went on within your state delegation?

    ☐1 I WAS AS WELL INFORMED AS I WANTED TO BE.

    ☐3 I HAD SOME INFORMATION, BUT NOT AS MUCH AS I WANTED.

    ☐5 I WAS NOT AT ALL WELL INFORMED.

    ☐6 I WAS NOT INTERESTED.

16. (CARD 2-GREEN) How about information about what your candidate and his staff were doing?

    ☐1 I WAS AS WELL INFORMED AS I WANTED TO BE.

    ☐3 I HAD SOME INFORMATION, BUT NOT AS MUCH AS I WANTED.

    ☐5 I WAS NOT AT ALL WELL INFORMED.

    ☐6 I WAS NOT INTERESTED.

17. (CARD 2-GREEN) How about information about what went on in other state delegations?

    ☐1 I WAS AS WELL INFORMED AS I WANTED TO BE.

    ☐3 I HAD SOME INFORMATION, BUT NOT AS MUCH AS I WANTED.

    ☐5 I WAS NOT AT ALL WELL INFORMED.

    ☐6 I WAS NOT INTERESTED.

18. (CARD 2-GREEN) How about information about what went on in the Platform Committee?

    ☐1 I WAS AS WELL INFORMED AS I WANTED TO BE.

    ☐3 I HAD SOME INFORMATION, BUT NOT AS MUCH AS I WANTED.

    ☐5 I WAS NOT AT ALL WELL INFORMED.

    ☐6 I WAS NOT INTERESTED.

19. (CARD 2-GREEN) How about information about what went on in the Credentials Committee?

    ☐1 I WAS AS WELL INFORMED AS I WANTED TO BE.

    ☐3 I HAD SOME INFORMATION, BUT NOT AS MUCH AS I WANTED.

    ☐5 I WAS NOT AT ALL WELL INFORMED.

    ☐6 I WAS NOT INTERESTED.

20. (CARD 2-GREEN) How about information about activities of other groups in which you were particularly interested, such as Women's Caucus, labor, Blacks, youth, etc?

    (INDICATE TO WHICH GROUP(S) R IS REFERRING _____)

    ☐1 I WAS AS WELL INFORMED AS I WANTED TO BE.
    ☐3 I HAD SOME INFORMATION, BUT NOT AS MUCH AS I WANTED.
    ☐5 I WAS NOT AT ALL WELL INFORMED.
    ☐6 I WAS NOT INTERESTED.

21. Once you got to the Convention, how much did you participate in the activities of your delegation? Aside from voting, did you participate a great deal, somewhat or not very much?

    | 1. A GREAT DEAL | 3. SOMEWHAT | 5. NOT VERY MUCH |

22. How much did you participate in meetings on behalf of the candidates?

    | 1. A GREAT DEAL | 3. SOMEWHAT | 5. NOT VERY MUCH |

23. How much did you participate in decisions on platform issues?

    | 1. A GREAT DEAL | 3. SOMEWHAT | 5. NOT VERY MUCH |

24. How much did you participate in decisions on credentials issues?

    | 1. A GREAT DEAL | 3. SOMEWHAT | 5. NOT VERY MUCH |

25. How much did you participate in decisions on rules issues?

    | 1. A GREAT DEAL | 3. SOMEWHAT | 5. NOT VERY MUCH |

26. How much did you participate in activities of other groups or were you not interested?

1. A GREAT DEAL	3. SOMEWHAT	5. NOT VERY MUCH

6. NOT INTERESTED IN OTHER GROUPS

27. (CARD 3-ORANGE) During the Convention, how much influence did you feel you had on the following decisions? First, in decisions made by your state's delegation, would you say you had a great deal of influence, some influence, little influence or no influence at all?

1. GREAT DEAL OF INFLUENCE	2. SOME INFLUENCE	4. LITTLE INFLUENCE	5. NO INFLUENCE AT ALL

28. (CARD 3-ORANGE) How about decisions in meetings on behalf of the candidates for nomination?

1. GREAT DEAL OF INFLUENCE	2. SOME INFLUENCE	4. LITTLE INFLUENCE	5. NO INFLUENCE AT ALL

29. (CARD 3-ORANGE) How about decisions in meetings concerning platform issues?

1. GREAT DEAL OF INFLUENCE	2. SOME INFLUENCE	4. LITTLE INFLUENCE	5. NO INFLUENCE AT ALL

30. (CARD 3-ORANGE) How about decisions in meetings concerning credentials issues?

1. GREAT DEAL OF INFLUENCE	2. SOME INFLUENCE	4. LITTLE INFLUENCE	5. NO INFLUENCE AT ALL

31. (CARD 3-ORANGE) How about decisions involving the rules?

1. GREAT DEAL OF INFLUENCE	2. SOME INFLUENCE	4. LITTLE INFLUENCE	5. NO INFLUENCE AT ALL

32. (CARD 3-ORANGE) How about decisions made by other groups.

1. GREAT DEAL OF INFLUENCE	2. SOME INFLUENCE	4. LITTLE INFLUENCE	5. NO INFLUENCE AT ALL

33. (CARD 4-BROWN) Compared to your expectations, did you have as much influence at the Convention as you thought you would have?

    1⃞ MUCH MORE THAN EXPECTED

    2⃞ SOMEWHAT MORE THAN EXPECTED

    3⃞ ABOUT AS MUCH AS EXPECTED

    4⃞ A BIT LESS THAN EXPECTED

    5⃞ MUCH LESS THAN EXPECTED

    8⃞ DK

    0⃞ HAD NO EXPECTATION

[ASK WOMEN DELEGATES ONLY]

34. Did you go to any of the meetings or activities for women outside of your delegation?

    | 1. YES | 5. NO | 8. DK |

35. What was your reaction to the National Women's Political Caucus? Was it favorable, unfavorable, mixed or what?

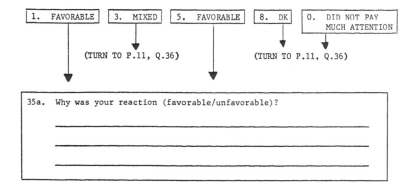

| 1. FAVORABLE | 3. MIXED | 5. FAVORABLE | 8. DK | 0. DID NOT PAY MUCH ATTENTION |

(TURN TO P.11, Q.36)   (TURN TO P.11, Q.36)

35a. Why was your reaction (favorable/unfavorable)?

_____

_____

_____

36. How do you think most of the <u>women</u> delegates of your party felt about the
National Women's Political Caucus? Was their reaction favorable, unfavorable,
mixed or what?

| 1. FAVORABLE | 3. MIXED | 5. UNFAVORABLE | 8. DK | 0. DID NOT PAY MUCH ATTENTION |

37. How do you think most of the <u>men</u> delegates of your party felt about the
National Women's Political Caucus? Was their reaction favorable, unfavorable,
mixed or what?

| 1. FAVORABLE | 3. MIXED | 5. UNFAVORABLE | 8. DK | 0. DID NOT PAY MUCH ATTENTION |

38. How much impact do you think the National Women's Political Caucus had on
events at the convention; a great deal, some, not much or none at all?

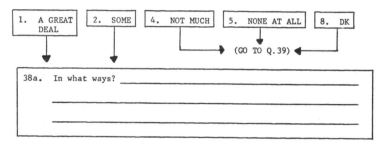

39. What was your reaction to the Black Caucus? Was it favorable, unfavorable,
mixed or what?

| 1. FAVORABLE | 3. MIXED | 5. UNFAVORABLE | 8. DK | 0. DID NOT PAY MUCH ATTENTION |

40. How much impact do you think the Black Caucus had on events at the Convention, a great deal, some, not much or none at all?

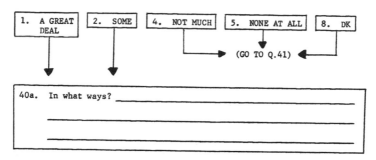

40a. In what ways? _____

_____

_____

41. What was your reaction to the role of labor at the Convention? Was it favorable, unfavorable, mixed or what?

| 1. FAVORABLE | 3. MIXED | 5. UNFAVORABLE | 8. DK | 0. DID NOT PAY MUCH ATTENTION |

42. How much impact do you think labor had on events at the Convention, a great deal, some, not much or none at all?

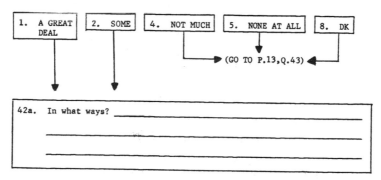

42a. In what ways? _____

_____

_____

INTERVIEWER CHECK BOX A

☐ R IS REPUBLICAN ──────➤ TURN TO P. 15, Q.51

☐ R IS DEMOCRAT

[ASK DEMOCRATIC DELEGATES ONLY]

43. (CARD 5-BLUE) Thinking of the fights over credentials and the seating of delegates, how did you feel about the final outcome concerning the challenge of the South Carolina delegation? Did you strongly agree, somewhat agree, somewhat disagree or strongly disagree with the decision?

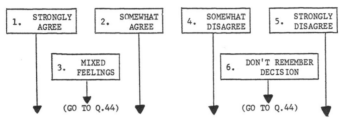

| 1. STRONGLY AGREE | 2. SOMEWHAT AGREE | 4. SOMEWHAT DISAGREE | 5. STRONGLY DISAGREE |

| 3. MIXED FEELINGS | 6. DON'T REMEMBER DECISION |

(GO TO Q.44)   (GO TO Q.44)

43a. Why did you (agree/disagree)? _____

_____

_____

_____

_____

44. (CARD 5-BLUE) How did you feel about the final decision concerning the seating of the California delegation? Did you strongly agree, somewhat agree, somewhat disagree, or strongly disagree with the decision?

| 1. STRONGLY AGREE | 2. SOMEWHAT AGREE | 4. SOMEWHAT DISAGREE | 5. STRONGLY DISAGREE |

| 3. MIXED FEELINGS | 6. DON'T REMEMBER DECISION |

45. (CARD 5-BLUE) Finally, how did you feel about the final decision on the challenge of Mayor Daley's delegation from Illinois?

| 1. STRONGLY AGREE | 2. SOMEWHAT AGREE | 4. SOMEWHAT DISAGREE | 5. STRONGLY DISAGREE |

| 3. MIXED FEELINGS | 6. DON'T REMEMBER DECISION |

46. Regardless of how you feel about the outcomes of these decisions, what did you think of the <u>procedures</u> that were used to handle the fights over credentials and the seating of delegates? Were they very fair, somewhat fair, not too fair or not at all fair?

| 1. VERY FAIR | 2. SOMEWHAT FAIR | 4. NOT TOO FAIR | 5. NOT AT ALL FAIR | 8. DK |

(COMMENTS) _____

_____

47. (CARD 5-BLUE) Turning now to the fights over the platform, did you strongly agree, somewhat agree, somewhat disagree or strongly disagree with the Convention's final decision on the busing plank?

| 1. STRONGLY AGREE | 2. SOMEWHAT AGREE | 4. SOMEWHAT DISAGREE | 5. STRONGLY DISAGREE |

| 3. MIXED FEELINGS | 6. DON'T REMEMBER DECISION |

48. What about the abortion issue: did you strongly agree, somewhat agree, somewhat disagree or strongly disagree with the convention's final decision?

| 1. STRONGLY AGREE | 2. SOMEWHAT AGREE | 4. SOMEWHAT DISAGREE | 5. STRONGLY DISAGREE |

| 3. MIXED FEELINGS | 6. DON'T REMEMBER DECISION |

49. What about the plank concerning Israel: did you strongly agree, somewhat agree, somewhat disagree or strongly disagree with the Convention's final decision?

1. STRONGLY AGREE	2. SOMEWHAT AGREE	4. SOMEWHAT DISAGREE	5. STRONGLY DISAGREE

3. MIXED FEELINGS	6. DON'T REMEMBER DECISION

50. Regardless of the results of the platform fights, what did you think of the procedures that were followed in handling them? Did you think they were very fair, somewhat fair, not too fair or not at all fair?

1. VERY FAIR	2. SOMEWHAT FAIR	4. NOT TOO FAIR	5. NOT AT ALL FAIR	8. DK

(COMMENTS) _____

_____

(TURN TO P.16, Q. 54)

[ASK REPUBLICAN DELEGATES ONLY]

51. (CARD 5-BLUE) How did you feel about the manner in which Rule 30, the apportionment of delegates to the 1976 Convention, was handled? Did you strongly agree, somewhat agree, somewhat disagree or strongly disagree with the final decision?

1. STRONGLY AGREE	2. SOMEWHAT AGREE	4. SOMEWHAT DISAGREE	5. STRONGLY DISAGREE

3. MIXED FEELINGS	6. DON'T REMEMBER DECISION

TURN TO P.16,Q.52   TURN TO P.16,Q.52

51a. Why did you (agree/disagree)? _____

_____

_____

_____

[ASK REPUBLICAN WOMEN DELEGATES ONLY]

52. (CARD 5-BLUE) How did you feel about the Convention's handling of the issues of day care and abortion? Did you strongly agree, somewhat agree, somewhat disagree or strongly disagree with the final outcome?

| 1. STRONGLY AGREE | 2. SOMEWHAT AGREE | 4. SOMEWHAT DISAGREE | 5. STRONGLY DISAGREE |

| 3. MIXED FEELINGS | 6. DON'T REMEMBER DECISION |

53. (CARD 5-BLUE) Finally how did you feel about the Convention's handling of representation of women in the 1976 Convention?

| 1. STRONGLY AGREE | 2. SOMEWHAT AGREE | 4. SOMEWHAT DISAGREE | 5. STRONGLY DISAGREE |

| 3. MIXED FEELINGS | 6. DON'T REMEMBER DECISION |

[ASK MARRIED DELEGATES ONLY]

54. Did your spouse accompany you to the Convention?

1. YES   5. NO

55. Did any (other) members of your family accompany you to the convention?

1. YES   5. NO

56. I would like to ask you about a different aspect of the Convention. About how much did the Convention cost you personally (apart from the costs of other members of your family who may have accompanied you)?

(COST INCLUDES FOOD, LODGING, TRANSPORTATION, ETC.)

$ _____ (FOR DELEGATE ONLY)

57. Convention expenses pose difficulties for some delegates. Did the cost of the Convention pose a problem for you?

| 1. YES | 5. NO | 8. DK |

58. I would now like to ask you some questions about yourself and your reaction to and participation in politics.

Do you hold any party position now?

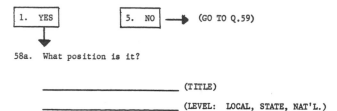

| 1. YES | 5. NO | → (GO TO Q.59)

58a. What position is it?

_____ (TITLE)

_____ (LEVEL: LOCAL, STATE, NAT'L.)

59. Have you ever held public office?

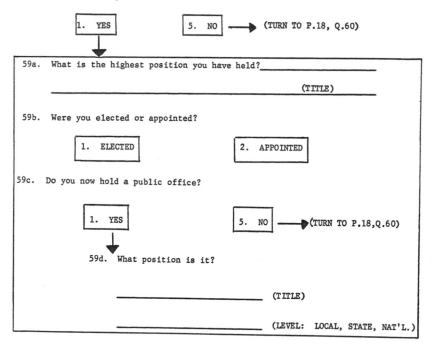

| 1. YES | 5. NO | → (TURN TO P.18, Q.60)

59a. What is the highest position you have held? _____

_____ (TITLE)

59b. Were you elected or appointed?

| 1. ELECTED | 2. APPOINTED |

59c. Do you now hold a public office?

| 1. YES | 5. NO | → (TURN TO P.18, Q.60)

59d. What position is it?

_____ (TITLE)

_____ (LEVEL: LOCAL, STATE, NAT'L.)

INTERVIEWER CHECK BOX B

☐ R IS NOT MARRIED ⟶ TURN TO P. 19, Q.63
☐ R IS MARRIED

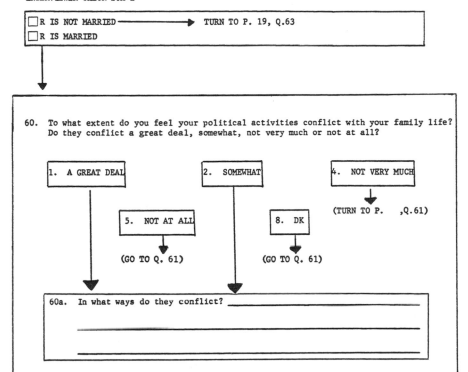

60. To what extent do you feel your political activities conflict with your family life? Do they conflict a great deal, somewhat, not very much or not at all?

1. A GREAT DEAL   2. SOMEWHAT   4. NOT VERY MUCH

(TURN TO P.   ,Q.61)

5. NOT AT ALL   8. DK

(GO TO Q. 61)   (GO TO Q. 61)

60a. In what ways do they conflict? _____
_____
_____

61. Is your husband/wife active in politics?

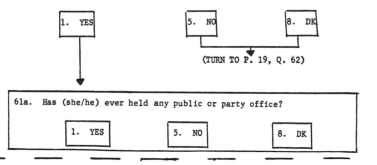

1. YES   5. NO   8. DK

(TURN TO P. 19, Q. 62)

61a. Has (she/he) ever held any public or party office?

1. YES   5. NO   8. DK

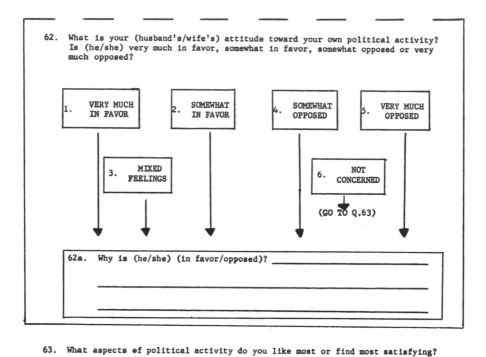

62. What is your (husband's/wife's) attitude toward your own political activity? Is (he/she) very much in favor, somewhat in favor, somewhat opposed or very much opposed?

1. VERY MUCH IN FAVOR

2. SOMEWHAT IN FAVOR

4. SOMEWHAT OPPOSED

5. VERY MUCH OPPOSED

3. MIXED FEELINGS

6. NOT CONCERNED

(GO TO Q.63)

62a. Why is (he/she) (in favor/opposed)? _____

_____

_____

63. What aspects of political activity do you like most or find most satisfying?

_____

_____

_____

_____

64. What aspects of political activity do you dislike most or find least satisfying?

_____

_____

_____

_____

65. Which of your own personal qualities make you particularly well suited to politics?

_____

_____

_____

66. Which, if any, of your own personal qualities do you see as liabilities in politics?

_____

_____

_____

67. (CARD 6-WHITE) How difficult would you find each of the following situations that can arise in political activity?

		Very Difficult	Somewhat Difficult	Uncertain	Not Very Difficult	Not At All Difficult
a.	Dividing your time and attention to meet many different demands	[1]	[2]	[3]	[4]	[5]
b.	The loss of privacy	[1]	[2]	[3]	[4]	[5]
c.	Opening yourself to attack and criticism	[1]	[2]	[3]	[4]	[5]
d.	Having to argue with people about issues	[1]	[2]	[3]	[4]	[5]
e.	Having to compromise your convictions	[1]	[2]	[3]	[4]	[5]
f.	Having to work with incompetent people	[1]	[2]	[3]	[4]	[5]
g.	Having to compete with others	[1]	[2]	[3]	[4]	[5]
h.	The possibility of losing	[1]	[2]	[3]	[4]	[5]

I will now read several hypothetical situations that could happen. Please imagine that each of these has happened to you.

68. You are a candidate for public office. Your opponent has been conducting a personally insulting, nearly slanderous campaign against you. What would your reaction be?

_____

_____

_____

69. The media find you a particularly personable and appealing candidate. Every-where you go, reporters and cameras follow you, asking for details of both your personal and political life. What would your reaction be?

_____

_____

_____

_____

70. You want to be elected to public office. The success of your campaign would depend heavily on the support of many people. It appears that their initial enthusiasm for your campaign has weakened considerably. What would your reaction be?

_____

_____

_____

_____

71. (CARD 7-YELLOW) Here is a card on which several scales describing individual qualities of people are represented. Where would you place yourself in general on each of these scales? The first scale ranges from confident to insecure. Where would you place yourself on this scale?

    a. confident: insecure   _____

    b. dependent: independent   _____

    c. ambitious: not ambitious   _____

    d. calm: anxious   _____

    e. rational: irrational   _____

    f. non-competitive: competitive _____

    g. unsympathetic: sympathetic   _____

    h. emotional: unemotional   _____

    i. subtle: direct   _____

    j. flexible: inflexible   _____

    k. decisive: indecisive   _____

72. (CARD 8-GREEN) In general, which of the following events would upset you most?

    ☐ a. FINDING THAT A FRIEND IS ANGRY WITH ME

    ☐ b. FINDING THAT MY VIEWS ARE IGNORED

    ☐ c. FAILING IN SOMETHING THAT I'VE TRIED TO DO

72a. (CARD 8-GREEN) Which would upset you least?

    ☐ a. FINDING THAT A FRIEND IS ANGRY WITH ME

    ☐ b. FINDING THAT MY VIEWS ARE IGNORED

    ☐ c. FAILING IN SOMETHING THAT I'VE TRIED TO DO

73. (CARD 9-ORANGE) Which of the following is most important to you?

    ☐ a. HAVING IDEAS THAT CAN BE USED TO SOLVE POLITICAL PROBLEMS

    ☐ b. MAKING FRIENDS WITH INTERESTING PEOPLE ACTIVE IN POLITICS

    ☐ c. HAVING INFLUENCE AND POWER OVER WHAT POLITICAL LEADERS DO

73a. (CARD 9-ORANGE) Which is least important to you?

    ☐ a. HAVING IDEAS THAT CAN BE USED TO SOLVE POLITICAL PROBLEMS

    ☐ b. MAKING FRIENDS WITH INTERESTING PEOPLE ACTIVE IN POLITICS

    ☐ c. HAVING INFLUENCE AND POWER OVER WHAT POLITICAL LEADERS DO

74. (CARD 10-BROWN) Regardless of whether or not you have children or regardless of what your children are actually like, what would you want for them? Imagine that you have a daughter, which one of the following three things would you most like her to do?

      ☐ a. EXCEL IN SPORTS

      ☐ b. HAVE MANY FRIENDS, BE POPULAR

      ☐ c. BE A LEADER

74a. (CARD 10-BROWN) Which would you second most like for her to do?

      ☐ a. EXCEL IN SPORTS

      ☐ b. HAVE MANY FRIENDS, BE POPULAR

      ☐ c. BE A LEADER

75. (CARD 11-BLUE) Which of these other three things would you most like your daughter to do?

      ☐ a. SHOW KINDNESS TOWARDS PLAYMATES

      ☐ b. FIGHT, NOT RUN, IF ATTACKED BY ANOTHER CHILD

      ☐ c. BE EXCELLENT IN SCHOOL WORK

75a. (CARD 11-BLUE) Which would you second most like for her to do?

      ☐ a. SHOW KINDNESS TOWARDS PLAYMATES

      ☐ b. FIGHT, NOT RUN, IF ATTACKED BY ANOTHER CHILD

      ☐ c. BE EXCELLENT IN SCHOOL WORK

76. (CARD 10-BROWN) Now imagine that you have a son. Which one of the following things would you most like him to do?

    ☐ a. EXCEL IN SPORTS

    ☐ b. HAVE MANY FRIENDS, BE POPULAR

    ☐ c. BE A LEADER

76a. (CARD 10-BROWN) Which would you second most like for him to do?

    ☐ a. EXCEL IN SPORTS

    ☐ b. HAVE MANY FRIENDS, BE POPULAR

    ☐ c. BE A LEADER

77. (CARD 11-BLUE) Which of these other three things would you most like your son to do?

    ☐ a. SHOW KINDNESS TOWARDS PLAYMATES

    ☐ b. FIGHT, NOT RUN, IF ATTACKED BY ANOTHER CHILD

    ☐ c. BE EXCELLENT IN SCHOOL WORK

77a. (CARD 11-BLUE) Which would you second most like him to do?

    ☐ a. SHOW KINDNESS TOWARDS PLAYMATES

    ☐ b. FIGHT, NOT RUN, IF ATTACKED BY ANOTHER CHILD

    ☐ c. BE EXCELLENT IN SCHOOL WORK

78a. Here are a number of statements about other people. First, generally speaking, would you say you can trust most people or that you can't be too careful in dealing with most people?

    ☐ YOU CAN TRUST MOST PEOPLE

    ☐ YOU CAN'T BE TOO CAREFUL IN DEALING WITH MOST PEOPLE

78b. Would you say that most of the time people try to be helpful or that they mostly look out for themselves?

    ☐ PEOPLE TRY TO BE HELPFUL

    ☐ PEOPLE LOOK OUT FOR THEMSELVES

78c. Do you think most people, if they are given a chance, try to take advantage of you or do you think most people try to treat you fairly?

    ☐ MOST PEOPLE TRY TO TAKE ADVANTAGE OF YOU

    ☐ MOST PEOPLE TRY TO TREAT YOU FAIRLY

79. (CARD 12-WHITE) I will read a number of statements about how people see themselves. Although you may find some statements difficult to apply to yourself, please tell me as best as you can how much each statement is true of you.

	Very true	Somewhat True	Not Very True	Not At All True
a) I enjoy work that requires attention to details	1	2	4	5
b) Other people know me better than I know myself	1	2	4	5
c) I am a very competitive person	1	2	4	5
d) There are lots of things about myself I'd change if I could	1	2	4	5
e) I enjoy situations and problems which seem to have no obvious solutions	1	2	4	5
f) I'm not embarrassed when people praise me for things I've done well	1	2	4	5
g) I enjoy careful planning and scheduling of my activities	1	2	4	5
h) I like to argue both sides of an issue	1	2	4	5
i) I get so involved in other people that I lose track of my own needs and feelings	1	2	4	5
j) I prefer doing one thing at a time to being involved in several things at once	1	2	4	5
k) I don't think about my own motives for doing things	1	2	4	5

As you well know, there are many serious problems in this country and in other parts of the world, I would now like to ask your opinion about some of them.

80. What do you personally feel are the most important problems facing our government?

_____

_____

_____

_____

_____

81. What do you personally feel are the most important problems facing people like you these days?

_____

_____

_____

_____

_____

82. (CARD 5-BLUE) I will now read you several statements on American foreign policy. For each please tell me whether you strongly agree, somewhat agree, somewhat disagree, or strongly disagree.

	Strongly Agree	Somewhat Agree	Uncertain	Somewhat Disagree	Strongly Disagree
a. American military superiority should have priority in American foreign policy	1	2	3	4	5
b. The U.S. should be generous with economic aid to needy nations	1	2	3	4	5
c. All U.S. troops should be withdrawn from Asia	1	2	3	4	5
d. The U.S. should resume normal diplomatic relations with Cuba	1	2	3	4	5
e. American troops should be withdrawn from Europe	1	2	3	4	5
f. The only justification for this country's becoming involved in another war would be an attack on the United States itself	1	2	3	4	5
g. The use of nuclear weapons by the United States would never be justified	1	2	3	4	5
h. The U.S. should give more support to the United Nations	1	2	3	4	5

83. Sometimes a company has to lay off part of its labor force. Some people think that the first workers to be laid off should be women whose husbands have jobs. Others think that male and female employees should be treated the same. Which of these opinions do you agree with?

> 1. LAY OFF WOMEN FIRST

> 2. TREAT MALE AND FEMALE EMPLOYEES THE SAME

> 8. DK

84. (CARD 13-YELLOW) There has been some discussion about abortion during recent years. Which one of the opinions on this card best agrees with your own view?

> 1. ABORTION SHOULD NEVER BE PERMITTED

> 2. ABORTION SHOULD BE PERMITTED ONLY IF THE LIFE AND HEALTH OF THE WOMAN IS IN DANGER

> 3. IF A WOMAN AND HER DOCTOR AGREE, SHE SHOULD BE ABLE TO HAVE A LEGAL ABORTION

> 4. ANY WOMAN WHO WANTS TO HAVE AN ABORTION SHOULD BE ABLE TO HAVE ONE

> 7. OTHER (SPECIFY) _____

> 8. DK

85. How do you feel about the proposal to establish a national day care or child care program for working mothers? Are you very much in favor, somewhat in favor, somewhat opposed, very much opposed or what?

| 1. VERY MUCH IN FAVOR | 2. SOMEWHAT IN FAVOR | 3. UNDECIDED | 4. SOMEWHAT OPPOSED | 5. VERY MUCH OPPOSED |

86. (CARD 14-GREEN) Some people believe that no American family should live in poverty whether they work or not. Others believe that no able bodied individual who does not work should receive welfare. Also, there are those with opinions in between. Where would you place yourself on this scale?

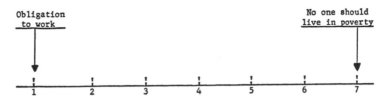

Obligation to work

No one should live in poverty

1   2   3   4   5   6   7

87. (CARD 15-ORANGE) This next card is called a "feeling thermometer," and we would like to use it to measure your feelings toward various groups. If you don't feel particularly warm or cold toward a group, then you should place it at the 50° mark. If you have a warm feeling toward a group, you would give it a score somewhere between 50° and 100°. On the other hand, if you don't feel very favorably toward a group, then you would place it somewhere between 0° and 50°.

The first group is civil rights leaders. Where would you put them on the thermometer?

    a. Civil rights leaders _____

    b. Policemen _____

    c. Judges _____

    d. People who go to rock festivals _____

    e. Politicians _____

    f. The Military _____

    g. Whites _____

    h. Blacks _____

    i. Welfare recipients _____

    j. Political demonstrators _____

    k. Black militants _____

88. Turning now to questions about people in politics, what do you think are the most important characteristics or qualities a person needs to be a success in politics?

_____

_____

_____

89. In general, there have been fewer women candidates for political office than men. Why do you think this has been the case?

_____

_____

_____

90. (CARD 5-BLUE) Here are some statements about women in politics. Please tell me how much you agree or disagree with each statement.

	STRONGLY AGREE	SOMEWHAT AGREE	UNCERTAIN	SOMEWHAT DISAGREE	STRONGLY DISAGREE	DK
a) Family responsibilities have kept women from participating in politics.	1	2	3	4	5	8
b) Women don't support other women who run for political office.	1	2	3	4	5	8
c) Women are taught not to want political careers.	1	2	3	4	5	8
d) Men prevent women from seeking political careers.	1	2	3	4	5	8
e) Women by nature are unsuited to politics.	1	2	3	4	5	8
f) There will be many more women running for public office within the next few years.	1	2	3	4	5	8
g) Women are sometimes given an advantage in politics just because they are women.	1	2	3	4	5	8

91. What is the attitude of party leaders in your city or county toward women becoming candidates for public office? Would you say they encourage women to run for office, discourage them or what?

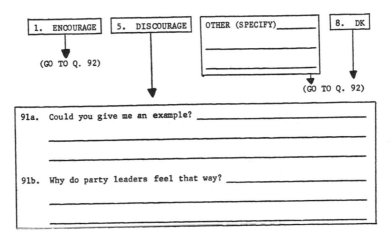

```
┌──────────────┐  ┌──────────────┐  ┌─────────────────────┐  ┌──────────┐
│ 1. ENCOURAGE │  │ 5. DISCOURAGE│  │ OTHER (SPECIFY)_____ │  │ 8.  DK   │
└──────────────┘  └──────────────┘  │ _____ │  └──────────┘
                                     │ _____ │
   (GO TO Q. 92)                     └─────────────────────┘
                                              (GO TO Q. 92)
```

> 91a. Could you give me an example? _____
>
> _____
>
> _____
>
> 91b. Why do party leaders feel that way? _____
>
> _____
>
> _____

[ASK WOMEN DELEGATES ONLY]

92. Have you personally, ever experienced discrimination in politics because you are a woman?

   | 1. YES | | 5. NO | | 8. DK |

93. Have you ever been given preferential treatment in politics because you are a woman?

   | 1. YES | | 5. NO | | 8. DK |

94. In general, what is your attitude toward the Women's Liberation Movement?
Would you say you are strongly in favor, somewhat in favor, somewhat opposed,
strongly opposed to it or what?

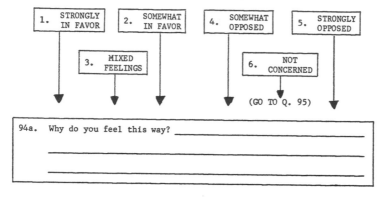

(GO TO Q. 95)

94a. Why do you feel this way? _____
_____
_____

Now I would like to find out a little about the politics of your state and home
community.

95. (CARD 16-BROWN) Generally, how would you describe party competition in
statewide elections within your state?

　　　　1 VERY COMPETITIVE - BALANCE BETWEEN PARTIES

　　　　2 SOMEWHAT COMPETITIVE - FAVORING REPUBLICAN PARTY

　　　　3 SOMEWHAT COMPETITIVE - FAVORING DEMOCRATIC PARTY

　　　　4 NON-COMPETITIVE - REPUBLICAN PARTY DOMINANT

　　　　5 NON-COMPETITIVE - DEMOCRATIC PARTY DOMINANT

96. (CARD 16-BROWN) Next, how would you describe party competition between
parties within your congressional district?

　　　　1 VERY COMPETITIVE - BALANCE BETWEEN PARTIES

　　　　2 SOMEWHAT COMPETITIVE - FAVORING REPUBLICAN PARTY

　　　　3 SOMEWHAT COMPETITIVE - FAVORING DEMOCRATIC PARTY

　　　　4 NON-COMPETITIVE - REPUBLICAN PARTY DOMINANT

　　　　5 NON-COMPETITIVE - DEMOCRATIC PARTY DOMINANT

97. (CARD 16-BROWN) Finally, how would you describe party competition between parties within your own precinct or ward (or whatever is the smallest district in your community)?

    1 VERY COMPETITIVE - BALANCE BETWEEN PARTIES

    2 SOMEWHAT COMPETITIVE - FAVORING REPUBLICAN PARTY

    3 SOMEWHAT COMPETITIVE - FAVORING DEMOCRATIC PARTY

    4 NON-COMPETITIVE - REPUBLICAN PARTY DOMINANT

    5 NON-COMPETITIVE - DEMOCRATIC PARTY DOMINANT

98. Is the party organization in your local community (city, town) very strong, fairly strong, not very strong or not strong at all?

| 1. VERY STRONG | 2. FAIRLY STRONG | 4. NOT VERY STRONG |

| 5. NOT STRONG AT ALL | 8. DK |

99. Do women tend to participate in your local party organization (city, town) in the same ways as men or do they engage only in certain types of party work?

| 1. SAME AS MEN | 5. CERTAIN WORK ONLY |

[ASK WOMEN DELEGATES ONLY]

100. Are you active in any women's political organizations in your area, outside the organizations in the party (i.e., League of Women Voter's)?

| 1. YES | 5. NO ——▷ (TURN TO P.35, Q.101) |

    100a. Which organizations are these?

        (1) _____

        (2) _____

        (3) _____

        (4) _____

101. In the past have you ever worked in a campaign on behalf of a candidate or a political issue?

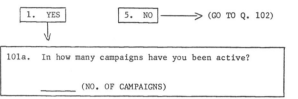

| 1. YES | | 5. NO | ——> (GO TO Q. 102) |

101a. In how many campaigns have you been active?

_____ (NO. OF CAMPAIGNS)

102. How did you originally get involved in politics?

_____

_____

_____

103. For whom do you plan to vote in November?

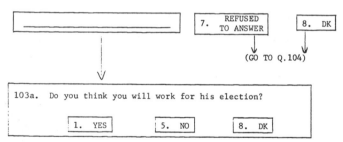

| _____ | 7. REFUSED TO ANSWER | 8. DK |

(GO TO Q.104)

103a. Do you think you will work for his election?

| 1. YES | 5. NO | 8. DK |

104. Will you work for the election of any state or local candidates?

| 1. YES | 5. NO | 8. DK |

105. Will you contribute money to the campaign of a presidential candidate?

| 1. YES | 5. NO | 8. DK |

<u>DEMOGRAPHIC DATA</u>

We would like a little background information on you and your family.

106. What is your date of birth _____   _____
                                        (month)   (year)

107. In addition to being an American, what do you consider to be your <u>main</u> ethnic or nationality group?

_____

_____

108. What was the highest grade of school or year of college you completed?

GRADE SCHOOL	COLLEGE
00 01 02 03 04 05 06 07 08 09 10 11 12	13 14 15 16 17+

(TURN TO P. 38, Q. 109)

108a. Did you get a high school graduation diploma or pass a high school equivalency test?

1. YES   2. NO

108b. Do you have a college degree?

4. YES   3. NO

(TURN TO P. 38, Q.109)

108c. What degree is that?

_____

TWO - PAGE RESPONDENT

109. Are you presently employed, or are you

| 1. WORKING NOW | 2. TEMPORARILY LAID OFF |

| 3. LOOKING FOR WORK | 4. UNEMPLOYED |

110. What is your main occupation? (What sort of work do you do?) IF NOT CLEAR: Tell me a little more about what you do.

_____

_____

_____

110a. What kind of (business/industry) is that in?

_____

110b. Do you work for someone else, yourself, or what?

| 1. SOMEONE ELSE | 2. BOTH SOMEONE ELSE AND SELF |

| 3. SELF ONLY |

110c. About how many hours do you work on your job in the average week?

_____HOURS A WEEK

110d. Were you out of work at any time during the last twelve months?

| 1. YES | 5. NO |

TURN TO P. 40, CHECK BOX C

111. Have you ever done any work for pay?

| 1. YES | 5. NO | ———> TURN TO P.40 CHECK BOX C

111a. What sort of work did you do on your last regular job? (What was your occupation?)

_____

_____

111b. What kind of (business/industry) was that in?

_____

111c. Did you work for someone else, yourself, or what?

| 1. SOMEONE ELSE | 2. BOTH SOMEONE ELSE AND SELF |

| 3. SELF ONLY |

111d. Have you had a job in the past twelve months?

| 1. YES | 5. NO | ———> TURN TO P.40 CHECK BOX C

111e. About how many hours did you work on your last job in the average week?

_____HOURS A WEEK

TURN TO P. 40, CHECK BOX C

EMPLOYMENT SECTION

unemployed, retired, (a housewife), (a student), or what?

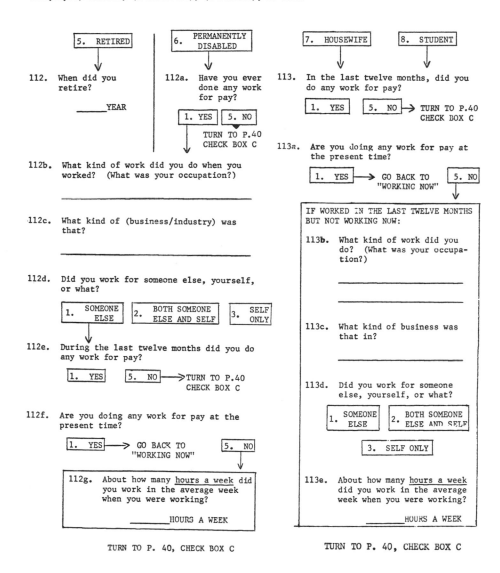

112. When did you retire?

_____YEAR

112a. Have you ever done any work for pay?

1. YES   5. NO

TURN TO P.40
CHECK BOX C

112b. What kind of work did you do when you worked? (What was your occupation?)

112c. What kind of (business/industry) was that?

112d. Did you work for someone else, yourself, or what?

1. SOMEONE ELSE   2. BOTH SOMEONE ELSE AND SELF   3. SELF ONLY

112e. During the last twelve months did you do any work for pay?

1. YES   5. NO → TURN TO P.40
CHECK BOX C

112f. Are you doing any work for pay at the present time?

1. YES → GO BACK TO "WORKING NOW"   5. NO

112g. About how many <u>hours a week</u> did you work in the average week when you were working?

_____HOURS A WEEK

TURN TO P. 40, CHECK BOX C

---

7. HOUSEWIFE   8. STUDENT

113. In the last twelve months, did you do any work for pay?

1. YES   5. NO → TURN TO P.40
CHECK BOX C

113a. Are you doing any work for pay at the present time?

1. YES → GO BACK TO "WORKING NOW"   5. NO

IF WORKED IN THE LAST TWELVE MONTHS BUT NOT WORKING NOW:

113b. What kind of work did you do? (What was your occupation?)

113c. What kind of business was that in?

113d. Did you work for someone else, yourself, or what?

1. SOMEONE ELSE   2. BOTH SOMEONE ELSE AND SELF

3. SELF ONLY

113e. About how many <u>hours a week</u> did you work in the average week when you were working?

_____HOURS A WEEK

TURN TO P. 40, CHECK BOX C

TWO - PAGE SPOUSE

INTERVIEWER CHECK BOX C

| 1. | R IS NOT MARRIED $\longrightarrow$ |
| 2. | R IS MARRIED -- ASK ABOUT SPOUSE. |

114. We would also like to know about your (husband/wife)................................

| 1. WORKING NOW | 2. TEMPORARILY LAID OFF | | 3. LOOKING FOR WORK | 4. UNEMPLOYED |

115. What is his/her main occupation? (What sort of work does he/she do? (IF NOT CLEAR: Tell me a little more about what he/she does.)

_____

_____

_____

115a. What kind of (business/industry) is that in?

_____

115b. Does he/she work for someone else, him-self/herself, or what?

| 1. SOMEONE ELSE | 2. BOTH SOMEONE ELSE AND SELF |

| 3. SELF ONLY |

115c. About how many hours does he/she work on his/her job in the average week?

_____ HOURS A WEEK

115d. Was he/she out of work at any time during the last twelve months?

| 1. YES | 5. NO |

TURN TO P. 42, Q. 119

116. Has he/she ever done any work for pay?

| 1. YES | 5. NO | $\rightarrow$ TURN TO P. 42, Q. 119

116a. What sort of work did he/she do on his/her last regular job? (What was his/her occupation?

_____

_____

116b. What kind of (business/industry) was that in?

_____

116c. Did he/she work for someone else, himself/herself, or what?

| 1. SOMEONE ELSE | 2. BOTH SOME-ONE ELSE AND SELF | 3. SELF ONLY |

116d. Has he/she had a job in the past twelve months?

| 1. YES | 5. NO | $\rightarrow$ TURN TO P. 42, Q. 119

| 116e. About how many hours did he/she work on his/her last job in the average week?

_____ HOURS A WEEK |

TURN TO P. 42, Q. 119

EMPLOYMENT SECTION

TURN TO P. 42, Q. 119

Is (he/she) working now, looking for work, retired, (a housewife), (a student), or what?

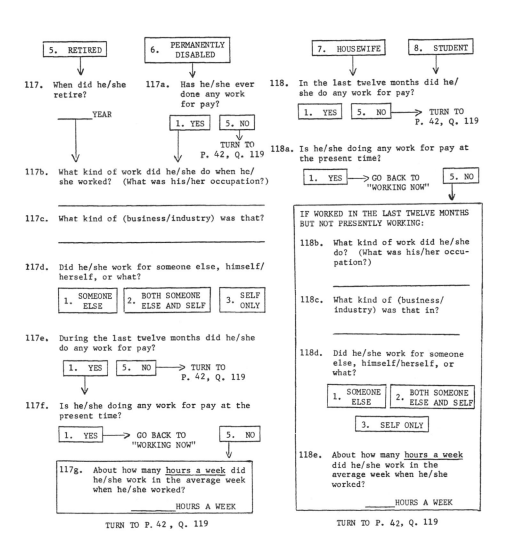

| 5. RETIRED |

117. When did he/she retire?

_____ YEAR

117b. What kind of work did he/she do when he/she worked? (What was his/her occupation?)

_____

117c. What kind of (business/industry) was that?

_____

117d. Did he/she work for someone else, himself/herself, or what?

| 1. SOMEONE ELSE | 2. BOTH SOMEONE ELSE AND SELF | 3. SELF ONLY |

117e. During the last twelve months did he/she do any work for pay?

| 1. YES | 5. NO | → TURN TO P. 42, Q. 119

117f. Is he/she doing any work for pay at the present time?

| 1. YES | → GO BACK TO "WORKING NOW" | 5. NO |

117g. About how many hours a week did he/she work in the average week when he/she worked?

_____ HOURS A WEEK

TURN TO P. 42, Q. 119

| 6. PERMANENTLY DISABLED |

117a. Has he/she ever done any work for pay?

| 1. YES | 5. NO |

TURN TO P. 42, Q. 119

| 7. HOUSEWIFE | | 8. STUDENT |

118. In the last twelve months did he/she do any work for pay?

| 1. YES | 5. NO | → TURN TO P. 42, Q. 119

118a. Is he/she doing any work for pay at the present time?

| 1. YES | → GO BACK TO "WORKING NOW" | 5. NO |

IF WORKED IN THE LAST TWELVE MONTHS BUT NOT PRESENTLY WORKING:

118b. What kind of work did he/she do? (What was his/her occupation?)

_____

118c. What kind of (business/industry) was that in?

_____

118d. Did he/she work for someone else, himself/herself, or what?

| 1. SOMEONE ELSE | 2. BOTH SOMEONE ELSE AND SELF |

| 3. SELF ONLY |

118e. About how many hours a week did he/she work in the average week when he/she worked?

_____ HOURS A WEEK

TURN TO P. 42, Q. 119

119. (CARD 17-BLUE) Women have many ways of combining work and family. Which of these patterns best describes your own work pattern?

☐ a. CONTINUOUS EMPLOYMENT OUTSIDE THE HOME WITH NO FAMILY RESPONSIBILITIES

☐ b. CONTINUOUS EMPLOYMENT OUTSIDE THE HOME WITH HOMEMAKING RESPONSIBILITIES ASSUMED BY SOMEONE ELSE

☐ c. CONTINUOUS OUTSIDE EMPLOYMENT, COMBINING BOTH WORK AND HOMEMAKING THROUGHOUT ADULT LIFE

☐ d. OUTSIDE EMPLOYMENT WITH INTERRUPTIONS FOR CHILD RAISING

☐ e. OUTSIDE EMPLOYMENT ON AND OFF IN NO REGULAR PATTERN - WORKING AS OFTEN AS NEEDED OR DESIRED

☐ f. OUTSIDE EMPLOYMENT ONLY BEFORE MARRIAGE AND/OR CHILDREN

☐ g. NO EMPLOYMENT OUTSIDE THE HOME FOR ANY SIGNIFICANT PERIOD

☐ h. OTHER (SPECIFY) _____

☐ DK

120. (CARD 17-BLUE) What would be your ideal work pattern, the one you would most like to follow if you could?

☐ a. CONTINUOUS EMPLOYMENT OUTSIDE THE HOME WITH NO FAMILY RESPONSIBILITIES

☐ b. CONTINUOUS EMPLOYMENT OUTSIDE THE HOME WITH HOMEMAKING RESPONSIBILITIES ASSUMED BY SOMEONE ELSE

☐ c. CONTINUOUS OUTSIDE EMPLOYMENT, COMBINING BOTH WORK AND HOMEMAKING THROUGHOUT ADULT LIFE

☐ d. OUTSIDE EMPLOYMENT WITH INTERRUPTIONS FOR CHILD RAISING

☐ e. OUTSIDE EMPLOYMENT ON AND OFF IN NO REGULAR PATTERN - WORKING AS OFTEN AS NEEDED OR DESIRED

☐ f. OUTSIDE EMPLOYMENT ONLY BEFORE MARRIAGE AND/OR CHILDREN

☐ g. NO EMPLOYMENT OUTSIDE THE HOME FOR ANY SIGNIFICANT PERIOD

☐ h. OTHER (SPECIFY) _____

☐ DK

121. Is your religious preference Protestant, Catholic, Jewish or something else?

| PROTESTANT | ROMAN CATHOLIC | JEWISH | OTHER; (SPECIFY) |

(GO TO Q. 122)

121a. What church or denomination is that? _____

122. Where were you born? (IF UNITED STATES) Which state? _____

_____

123. Were you brought up mostly in the country, in a town, in a small city, or in a large city?

| 1. COUNTRY | 2. TOWN | 3. SMALL CITY | 4. LARGE CITY | 7. OTHER (SPECIFY) |

124. (CARD 18-WHITE) Please look at this card and tell me the letter of the income group that includes the income of all members of your family in 1971 before taxes. This figure should include dividends, interest, salaries, wages, pensions and all other income. (IF UNCERTAIN: What would be your best guess?)

☐ a. UNDER $4,999

☐ b. $5,000 - $9,999

☐ c. $10,000 - $14,999

☐ d. $15,000 - $19,999

☐ e. $20,000 - $24,999

☐ f. $25,000 - $29,999

☐ g. $30,000 - $49,999

☐ h. $50,000 AND OVER

That's all the questions I have. Thank you very much for your time and participation.

INTERVIEWER'S SUPPLEMENT

S1. Respondent's sex is: | 1. Male | | 2. Female |

S2. Respondent's race is: | 1. White | | 2. Negro | | OTHER: _____ |

S3. Relationship of R to head: | 1. Is head | | 2. Is wife | | OTHER: _____ |

S4. Other persons present at interview were: (CHECK MORE THAN ONE BOX IF NECESSARY)

| None | | Children under 6 | | Older children | | Spouse |

| Other relatives | | Other adults |

S5. Respondent's cooperation was:

| 1. Very good | | 2. Good | | 3. Fair | | 4. Poor | | 5. Very poor |

S6. Respondent's general level of information about politics and public affairs seemed:

| 1. Very high | | 2. Fairly high | | 3. Average | | 4. Fairly low | | 5. Very low |

S7. Rate R's apparent intelligence?

| 1. Very high | | 2. Above average | | 3. Average | | 4. Below average | | 5. Very low |

S8. How suspicious did R seem to be about the study, <u>before</u> the interview?

| 1. Not at all | | 3. Somewhat | | 5. Very suspicious |

S9. Overall, how great was R's interest in the interview?

| 1. Very high | | 2. Above average | | 3. Average | | 4. Below average | | 5. Very low |

S10. How sincere did R seem to be in his answers?

1. COMPLETELY SINCERE	2. USUALLY SINCERE	3. OFTEN SEEMED TO BE INSINCERE

S11. Were there any particular parts of the interview for which you doubted R's sincerity? If so, name them by section or question numbers:

_____

_____

_____

THUMBNAIL SKETCH

APPENDIX B

The Sample

The study was based on analysis of data derived from a mail questionnaire sent to all delegates (or hand delivered in Miami to Democratic delegates chosen at the last minute) and from face-to-face interviews with a carefully selected probability sample of delegates. The following description of the sample was provided by Warren Miller under whose direction the sample was drawn and the interviewing conducted.

The overall response rate was slightly over 86 percent on the interviews which exceeded expectations and resulted in completion of 1,336 interviews of approximately one hour and ten minutes each.

The response rate on the mail questionnaire was predictably much below that for the personal interviews with approximately 55 percent of all of the delegates returning fully completed and usable questionnaire forms to us. (Summary information about response rates for both data collections are presented in Table 1.) Initially, we were somewhat disappointed with the response rate because the staff had made exceptional efforts to obtain the cooperation of all of the delegates. However, as Table 2 demonstrates, the efforts were obviously not in vain. We were successful in avoiding the bias that is often associated with a low response rate. The response rate from the interview sample gives us great confidence that it is a faithful reproduction of the population of the convention delegates; the virtually identical distributions on items of information collected both in the questionnaire and in the interview authenticates the mail questionnaire response as being equally representative of the total population of delegates. Indeed, given the fact that the interviews were taken with a sample, albeit a sample that was an unusually large fraction of the total population, we would normally expect sampling variability alone to provide larger discrepancies than those that can be found in the comparisons of the distributions in Table 2.

The original design would have been ideally executed if all mail questionnaires had been completed prior to the conventions and all interviews completed in the interval between the conventions and the election. For a

Table 1. Response Rates and Weighted Numbers of Cases for Interviews and Questionnaires

Interview Data Set

Total response rate	86.4%	N 1336
		Wt. N 3747
Response rate of Democrats	87.6%	N 985
		Wt. N 2672
Response rate of Republicans	85.6%	N 351
		Wt. N 1120

Mail Questionnaires

Total response rate	55.0%	N 2449
Response rate of Democrats	51.3%	N 1601
Response rate of Republicans	62.9%	N 848
Percent of interviews with matching mail questionnaires	63.5%	Wt. N 2426
Percent of Democratic interviews with matching mail questionnaires	59.9%	Wt. N 1618
Pre-convention questionnaires– Pre-election interviews	48.0%	Wt. N 784
Post-convention questionnaires– Pre-election interviews	21.0%	Wt. N 342
Post-convention questionnaires– Post-election interviews	30.0%	Wt. N 488
Percent of Republican interviews with matching mail questionnaires	72.1%	Wt. N 807
Pre-convention questionnaires– Pre-election interviews	88.0%	N 711
Post-convention questionnaires– Pre-election interviews	4.0%	N 36
Post-convention questionnaires– Post-election interviews	7.0%	N 60

NOTE: This and all other tables in this appendix were prepared at the Center for Political Studies and provided by Warren Miller.

variety of reasons, including our inability even to identify some Democratic delegates until they were ultimately seated by action of the convention itself, it was clearly impossible to complete all of the mail questionnaire portion of the study before the conventions. In analogous fashion, given the heavy involvement of many delegates in the ensuing campaigns, it was also impossible to complete all of the interview portion of the study prior to the election. In each instance we were most apprehensive about the likely distortions in the data that would be associated with the points in time at which the data were collected.

There was, in fact, virtually no systematic difference between those delegates who completed the mail questionnaire before the convention and those who filled out the questionnaire after the convention. There are, of course, some expected distortions. The surprise is that the impact was as limited as it was. The general conclusion that follows from a detailed inspection of these and other comparative distributions is that the total set of mail questionnaires can be treated as a single body of data with relatively minor, continuing attention to distortions associated with the time period in which the questionnaires were completed.

A similar conclusion follows from the comparison of interview data obtained prior to and following the election. Again, there are some discrepancies of a predictable sort. However, on such important symbolic convention issues as the seating of the Illinois delegation, there is very little evidence of distortion resulting from post-election reinterpretations of the convention decision. The two parts of the interview sample, even more than the two parts of the mail questionnaire, are so similar as to permit their combination into the single sample that was intended.

At the level of overall comparison of these two data collections and the two major parts within each collection, the uniformity and stability of the data are very impressive. The most telling question comes, however, as one examines the intersection of the two data collections. The total set of objectives being sought in the study called for a more extensive collection of information than could be gathered in either of the two data collections taken alone. Consequently, the total task of information collection was divided between the interview and the questionnaire. The ability to reassemble the parts to form one integrated set of data is contingent on having the respondents who participated in both data collections be representative of the total universe of delegates. In other words, even though Table 2 demonstrates that data from the complete sample are closely matched by data from the complete set of mail questionnaire respondents, it does not necessarily follow that we can treat the delegates who provided both sets of information as though they also represent the delegates who failed to participate in one or the other of the two data collections.

Table 2. Selected Comparisons of Delegate Attributes from National Interviews of Samples and Responses from Mail Questionnaire

| | Republicans | | Democrats | |
	Sample	Mail Questionnaire	Sample	Mail Questionnaire
Age				
18–30	8%	9%	24%	24%
31–49	50	49	48	47
50+	40	39	27	26
No answer	2	3	1	3
	100%	100%	100%	100%
Sex				
Male	66%	64%	58%	57%
Female	34	36	42	43
	100%	100%	100%	100%
Ethnic Identification				
White	94%	94%	79%	79%
Negro	5	3	16	12
Puerto Rican	–	–	–	–
Chicano	–	1	2	3
Oriental	–	–	–	–
American Indian	1	1	1	4
Other	–	1	–	1
No answer	–	–	2	1
	100%	100%	100%	100%
Education				
Up to 8th grade	1%	–%	1%	1%
9–12 grades	12	11	15	11
Some college	28	24	26	23
B.A.	27	20	27	15
Some graduate school	–	8	–	12
M.A.	8	6	12	13
Ph.D. etc.	23	18	17	18
No answer	1	13	2	7
	100%	100%	100%	100%

Table 2. Selected Comparisons of Delegate Attributes from National Interviews of Samples and Responses from Mail Questionnaire—(Continued)

| | Republicans | | Democrats | |
	Sample	Mail Questionnaire	Sample	Mail Questionnaire
Income				
Under $4,999	2%	1%	5%	4%
$5,000–9,999	3	4	8	10
$10,000–14,999	7	11	16	20
$15,000–19,999	10	11	18	18
$20,000–24,999	15	15	15	13
$25,000–29,999	14	10	10	8
$30,000–49,999	22	21	13	13
$50,000 and over	22	22	11	10
No answer, Don't know	5	5	4	4
	100%	100%	100%	100%
Marital Status				
Single	11%	10%	20%	18%
Married	80	79	75	75
Separated or Divorced	4	5	2	4
Widowed	5	5	1	2
Other	—	1	2	1
	100%	100%	100%	100%
Attended Convention Before				
Yes	34%	30%	17%	17%
No	66	66	83	79
No answer	—	4	—	4
	100%	100%	100%	100%
Number of Conventions Attended				
One	66%	64%	83%	77%
Two	23	20	10	10
Three	5	5	4	3
Four	2	2	2	1
Five or more	3	3	1	3
No answer	1	6	—	6
	100%	100%	100%	100%

Table 2. Selected Comparisons of Delegate Attributes from National Interviews of Samples and Responses from Mail Questionnaire—(Continued)

	Republicans		Democrats	
	Sample	Mail Questionnaire	Sample	Mail Questionnaire
Method of Selection as Delegate				
Party primary	29%	29%	36%	40%
State convention	41	47	30	29
State-local committee	13	12	15	8
Combination	2	10	4	21
Other elective	10	—	9	—
Other selective	3	—	3	—
Don't know	—	—	—	—
No answer	2	2	3	2
	100%	100%	100%	100%
Candidate Preference at Convention				
Ashbrook	–%	1%		
McCloskey	—	—		
Nixon	98	96		
Other Republican	1	1		
No answer	1	2		
	100%	100%		
McGovern			50%	56%
Chisholm			3	2
Humphrey			16	13
Kennedy			2	7
Mills			1	—
Wallace			6	4
Jackson			5	5
Muskie			11	9
Other Democrat			3	2
Don't know			—	—
No answer			3	2
			100%	100%

Table 3 presents a partial answer to the question of whether those respondents who provided both interview and questionnaire information differed in some way from those individuals who provided only interview information while failing to respond to the mail questionnaire. The evidence does not quite match the rather phenomenal comparability of the two complete data collections taken separately. For example, it is evident that women who were included in the interview sample were more likely to return mail questionnaires than were the men in the sample. This means, of course, that among delegates who were not in the sample to be interviewed, it was the men rather than the women who responded in larger proportions to the request for answers on the mail questionnaire. These two biases cancel each other out when one makes the overall comparisons as detailed in Table 2. In like manner it is apparent that the population participating in both data collections underrepresents non-whites when contrasted with the population that provided only interview data and overrepresents non-whites when compared to the population that provided only mail questionnaire information.

These two discrepancies are the most notable among those contained in Table 3. More generally, information like that contained in Table 3 has led us to the conclusion that we can treat the subset providing information from both sources as closely representative of the total population of delegates. We have pursued this question on a number of additional levels. For example, analogous questions may be addressed to the question of interrelationships or correlations among variables. At a simple level one can ask whether the correlation between age and education is different among those who participated in both data collections than among those who provided information only in one or the other of the data collections. Such inquiries have uniformly supported the conclusion that the various subsets of our delegates exhibit relational as well as distributional uniformity.

A still more rigorous set of tests takes us back to our concern with the specific time of data collection with each of the two instruments. For example, among the Democrats, approximately 48 percent of those participating in *both interview and questionnaire* collection fitted the ideal design by returning their questionnaires before the convention and giving their interviews between the convention and the election. (See Table 1.) Another 21 percent did not return their questionnaires until after the convention although they did give their personal interviews before the election. The final 31 percent of the Democrats completed their questionnaires some time after the convention and gave their interviews only after the election. This group would presumably be least likely to provide reliable information to be used in reconstructing pre-convention expectations or pre-election assessment of the conventions. Analysis suggests

Table 3. Selected Comparisons of Delegate Attributes of Those Who Responded and Failed to Respond to a Mail Questionnaire, within a National Sample of Delegates

	Republicans		Democrats	
	Questionnaire Returned	Questionnaire Not Returned	Questionnaire Returned	Questionnaire Not Returned
Age				
Under 35	9%	6%	25%	23%
35–50	50	50	49	47
Over 50	40	40	25	29
No answer	1	4	1	1
	100%	100%	100%	100%
Sex				
Male	61%	78%	55%	63%
Female	39	22	45	37
	100%	100%	100%	100%
Ethnic Identification				
White	97%	87%	84%	72%
Negro	3	8	11	23
Puerto Rican	—	—	—	1
Chicano	—	1	2	2
Oriental	—	—	—	—
American Indian	—	3	1	1
Other	—	—	—	—
No answer	—	1	2	1
	100%	100%	100%	100%
Education				
Up to 8th grade	1%	1%	1%	2%
9–12 grades	14	6	14	17
Some college	29	24	26	27
B.A.	27	26	28	26
Some graduate school	7	10	15	8
Graduate degree	21	30	16	18
No answer	1	3	—	2
	100%	100%	100%	100%

Table 3. Selected Comparisons of Delegate Attributes of Those Who Responded
and Failed to Respond to a Mail Questionnaire, within a National Sample
of Delegates–(Continued)

| | Republicans | | Democrats | |
	Questionnaire Returned	Questionnaire Not Returned	Questionnaire Returned	Questionnaire Not Returned
Income				
Under $4,999	2%	2%	4%	5%
$5,000–9,999	3	3	8	8
$10,000–14,999	6	8	18	14
$15,000–19,999	12	4	18	17
$20,000–24,999	16	13	17	13
$25,000–29,999	14	14	10	10
$30,000–49,999	22	22	13	13
$50,000 and over	21	23	9	14
No answer	4	11	3	6
	100%	100%	100%	100%
Marital Status				
Single	10%	8%	18%	24%
Married	80	87	76	75
Separated	1	1	1	–
Divorced	4	3	4	1
Widowed	5	1	1	–
	100%	100%	100%	100%
Number of Conventions Attended				
One	66%	67%	86%	78%
·Two	24	18	9	10
Three	6	6	3	6
Four	2	3	1	3
Five or more	2	5	1	2
No answer	–	1	–	1
	100%	100%	100%	100%

Table 3. **Selected Comparisons of Delegate Attributes of Those Who Responded and Failed to Respond to a Mail Questionnaire, within a National Sample of Delegates—(Continued)**

	Republicans		Democrats	
	Questionnaire Returned	Questionnaire Not Returned	Questionnaire Returned	Questionnaire Not Returned
Method of Selection as Delegate				
Inap. (Alternates)	—%	6%	—%	4%
Party primary	30	26	37	35
State convention	43	35	31	29
State-local committee	13	14	13	18
Combination	1	5	5	4
Other elective	10	8	10	8
Other selective	2	3	3	2
Don't know	—	1	—	—
No answer	1	2	1	—
	100%	100%	100%	100%
Candidate Preference at Convention				
Nixon	95%	98%		
McCloskey	—	—		
Other Republican	2	—		
No answer	3	2		
McGovern			56%	42%
Chisholm			2	5
Humphrey			15	19
Kennedy			2	3
Mills			—	1
Wallace			3	9
Jackson			6	5
Muskie			11	11
Other Democrat			3	2
Don't know			1	—
No answer			1	3
	100%	100%	100%	100%

that the 31 percent reflecting the least adequate execution of our basic design are not, in fact, substantially different from the 48 percent who match perfectly the design requirements.

This rather remarkable finding is explicable, of course, if one concludes that most of the delegates participating in either data collection were providing information about matters of considerable importance to themselves. For the deeply involved, heavily engaged individual, it is not at all unreasonable to expect that ability to recall, recollect, and reconstruct one's own attitudes and actions from earlier points in time will be relatively free of influence from intervening events. We would, of course, predict and expect with a high degree of certainty that large proportions of the general electorate would behave in a very different fashion. Pre-election preferences of non-voters, for example, are notoriously subject to errors of memory after the election when one aspect of the bandwagon effect causes the uninvolved to "remember" preferring the candidate who actually won the election. Delegates to a convention are more deeply and continuously involved in politics than are most members of the national electorate, and the focus of our information collecting efforts on precisely those aspects of politics most salient and central to the delegates simply enhanced their ability to respond with great reliability, whatever the point in time at which they provided the information.

In sum, our most critical scrutiny of the quality of the data has produced a virtually unbroken array of reassuring evidence. The stability and congruity of marginal distributions have been closely matched by the comparability of internal correlations. This is not to argue that the entire data collection is totally free of error. There are minor problems that must be related to sampling error, and there are slightly larger problems that undoubtedly stem from the biasing influence of convention and election events. In general, however, we are well satisfied that all aspects of the analysis proceeded very much as though the most ideal features of the research design had been executed.*

---

*The size of the mail questionnaire sample utilized in this study differs somewhat from the size of the sample distributed through the Inter-University Consortium (ICPR) because the latter includes some responses which became available only after this analysis was well underway.

APPENDIX C

Index Construction

Indexes used in this book, with few exceptions,[1] are constructed on the basis of factor analyses performed with varimax rotation. All indexes are additive with equal weight assigned to each constituent variable.

Factor scores were not used for at least two reasons: 1) very different scores resulted from identical problems performed on different subgroups, e.g., Republicans, Democrats, McGovern supporters, etc., and 2) Democrats in the sample were twice as numerous as Republicans and factor solutions (and scores) for the whole elite were always biased toward the structure of Democratic opinion.

An effort was made to include in each index items that comprised a single component when Democrats and Republicans were considered separately and when the resulting factor was theoretically relevant to the inquiry.

What follows is a description of each index used in the book, its constituent variables, its minimum and maximum values in "long form," and the way(s) it was recoded for crossruns with other variables. Where variables with varying numbers of value points form an index (e.g., a 10-point thermometer and a 7-point proximity measure), they have been recoded to the same number of value points (e.g., perhaps the 7 and 10-point measures were first aggregated to 5-point scales) before adding—to insure equal weight for each variable.

Where measures were constructed in any way different from this general method, this appendix takes note of it.

---

[1]These include ambition, power, achievement, affiliation, "joiners," holism, and others. Differences are noted in this appendix.

INDEXES MEASURING SUBSTANTIVE IDEOLOGY

1. *Sanctions (Intersect Sample)*

   CONSTITUENT VARIABLES:
   a. Proximity measure on crime: closer to "stop crime" or "protect the accused"?
   b. "American military superiority should have priority in American foreign policy": strongly agree to strongly disagree
   c. Feeling thermometer: the police
   d. Feeling thermometer: the military

   All the above were converted to 5-point variables with a "pro-sanctions" attitude receiving the high score.

   Maximum value: 20
   Minimum value: 04

   Recodings: 4-way: 1) 4-7 2) 8-12 3) 13-16 4) 17-20
               3-way: 1) 4-8 2) 9-15 3) 16-20

2. *International Idealism (Interview Sample)*

   CONSTITUENT VARIABLES:
   a. "American military superiority should have priority in American foreign policy."
   b. "The United States should be generous with economic aid to needy nations."
   c. "The United States should resume normal diplomatic relations with Cuba."
   d. "The United States should give more support to the United Nations."

   All of the above are 5-point measures with answers ranging from "strongly agree" to "strongly disagree." The "international realist" or more "conservative" position was given the high score.

   Maximum value: 20
   Minimum value: 04

   Recodings: 4-way: 1) 4-7 2) 8-12 3) 13-16 4) 17-20
               3-way: 1) 4-8 2) 9-15 3) 16-20

3. *Military Policy (Interview Sample)*

   CONSTITUENT VARIABLES:
   a. "All United States troops should be withdrawn from Asia."

b. "American troops should be withdrawn from Europe."
c. "The only justification for this country's becoming involved in another war would be an attack on the United States itself."
d. "The use of nuclear weapons by the United States would never be justified."

All of the above are 5-point measures with answers ranging from "strongly agree" to "strongly disagree." The "pro-military" position was given the highest score.

Maximum value: 20
Minimum value: 04

Recodings: 4-way: 1) 4-7   2) 8-12   3) 13-16   4) 17-20
             3-way: 1) 4-8   2) 9-15   3) 16-20

4. *Cultural Conservatism (Intersect Sample)*

CONSTITUENT VARIABLES:
a. Proximity measure on welfare: closer to "obligation to work" or "no one should live in poverty"?
b. Feeling thermometer: black militants
c. Feeling thermometer: women's liberation
d. Feeling thermometer: the military

All of the above were recoded to 5-point variables before adding with the "culturally conservative" position receiving the highest score.

Maximum value: 20
Minimum value: 04
Recodings: 4-way: 1) 4-7   2) 8-12   3) 13-16   4) 17-20
             3-way: 1) 4-8   2) 9-15   3) 16-20

5. *Political Culture Index (Intersect Sample)*

CONSTITUENT VARIABLES:
a. "American military superiority should have priority in American foreign policy": strongly agree to strongly disagree.
b. "The United States should be generous with economic aid to needy nations": strongly agree to strongly disagree.
c. "The United States should resume normal diplomatic relations with Cuba": strongly agree to strongly disagree.
d. "The use of nuclear weapons by the United States would never be justified": strongly agree to strongly disagree.
e. "The United States should give more support to the United Nations": strongly agree to strongly disagree.

f. Proximity measure on busing: closer to "children in neighbor-hood schools" or "bus to integrate"?
g. Proximity measure on crime: closer to "stop crime" or "protect the accused"?
h. Proximity measure on welfare: closer to "obligation to work" or "no one should live in poverty"?
i. Feeling thermometer: the military
j. Feeling thermometer: liberals
k. Feeling thermometer: civil rights leaders
l. Feeling thermometer: rock festival people
m. Feeling thermometer: welfare recipients
n. Feeling thermometer: political demonstrators
o. Feeling thermometer: black militants

Each variable above was coded so that a 5-point scale resulted with the "conservative" viewpoints receiving highest scores.

Maximum value: 75
Minimum value: 15

Recodings: 4-way: 1) 15-28   2) 29-43   3) 44-58   4) 59-75
2-way: 1) 15-43   2) 44-75

INDEXES MEASURING ATTITUDES TOWARD WOMEN

1. *Innate Sex Differences Index*
   (Mail Questionnaire)

   CONSTITUENT VARIABLES:
   a. "Most men are better suited emotionally for politics than are most women."
   b. "Women in public office can be just as logical and rational as men."
   c. "Women are emotionally less well-suited than men for business and professional careers."

   All the above had six possible responses ranging from "strongly agree" to "strongly disagree." Variables were coded so that belief in "innate sex differences" received the highest scores.

   Maximum value: 18
   Minimum value: 03

   Recodings: 4-way: 1) 3-6   2) 7-10   3) 11-14   4) 15-18
   2-way: 1) 3-10   2) 11-18

2 ·*Perception of Discrimination Index*
(Mail Questionnaire)

CONSTITUENT VARIABLES:
a. "Women have just as much opportunity as men to become political leaders."
b. "Most men in the party organization try to keep women out of
leadership roles."
c. "Many will not vote for women candidates."

All the above had six possible responses ranging from "strongly
agree" to "strongly disagree." Variables were coded so that belief in
the reality of discrimination received the highest scores.

Maximum value: 18
Minimum value: 03

Recodings: 4-way: 1) 3-6 2) 7-10 3) 11-14 4) 15-18
            2-way: 1) 3-10 2) 11-18

3. *Role-Conflict Index (Mail Questionnaire)*

CONSTITUENT VARIABLES:
a. "It is almost impossible to be a good wife and mother and hold
public office too."
b. "Women who succeed in politics usually have to sacrifice their
femininity to get there."
c. "Children of working mothers tend to be less well-adjusted than
children of women who stay at home."

All of the above had six possible responses ranging from "strongly
agree" to "strongly disagree." Variables were coded so that belief in
the role-conflict received the highest score.

Maximum value: 18
Minimum value: 03

Recodings: 4-way: 1) 3-6 2) 7-10 3) 11-14 4) 15-18
            2-way: 1) 3-10 2) 11-18

4. *Power Behind the Throne (Mail Questionnaire)*

CONSTITUENT VARIABLES:
a. "While women hold few public offices, they work behind the
scenes and really have more influence in politics than they're
given credit for."
b. "Feminine charm and diplomacy can be a woman's greatest assets
in getting ahead in politics."

c. "Although not always recognized, women have more real power than men."

All of the above had six possible responses ranging from "strongly agree" to "strongly disagree." Variables were coded so that belief in female "power-behind-the-throne" received the highest score.

Maximum value: 18
Minimum value: 03

Recodings: 4-way: 1) 3-6   2) 7-10   3) 11-14   4) 15-18
2-way: 1) 3-10   2) 11-18

5. *Conceptions of Femininity or Newwoman Index
(Mail Questionnaire)*

Constituent Variables:
1. Innate Sex Differences Index
2. Perception of Discrimination Index
3. Role-Conflict Index
4. Power-Behind-the-Throne Index

The four-way recoding was used to construct this new index from the four previous ones. Rejection of innate sex differences, perception of discrimination, rejection of role conflict, and rejection of female power-behind-the-throne received the highest scores.
This was intended to be an overall measure of attitudes toward women in politics and society.

Maximum value: 16
Minimum value: 04

Recoding: 4-way: 1) 4-7   2) 8-10   3) 11-13   4) 14-16

INDEXES MEASURING POLITICAL STYLE AND ORGANIZATIONAL SUPPORT

I. Incentives

1. *"Lots of Fun" Index (Mail Questionnaire)*

Constituent Variables:
a. Degree of interest in: experiencing the excitement of the convention
b. Degree of interest in: taking part in an important event

c. Degree of interest in: getting acquainted with other delegates
d. Degree of interest in: being able to see and meet national political leaders
e. Degree of interest in: making contact with important people
f. Degree of interest in: learning more about politics

Possible answers for each of the above were: "great interest," "quite a bit of interest," "not very interested," and "not at all interested." All were coded so that "great interest" in all of the above received the highest score.

Maximum value: 30
Minimum value: 06

Recodings: 3-way: 1) 6-13   2) 14-22   3) 23-30
                 2-way: 1) 6-18   2) 19-30

2. *Status Index (Mail Questionnaire)*

CONSTITUENT VARIABLES:
a. Why active: "I enjoy the friendships and social contacts I have with other people in politics."
b. Why active: "I like the feeling of being close to people who are doing important work."
c. Why active: "Party work gives one visibility and recognition."

Possible answers: "extremely important," "quite important," "not very important," "not at all important." All were coded so that "very important" in all of the above received the highest score.

Maximum value:15
Minimum value: 03

Recodings: 3-way: 1) 3-7   2) 8-11   3) 12-15
                 2-way: 1) 3-9   2) 10-15

3. *Party Reform Index (Mail Questionnaire)*

CONSTITUENT VARIABLES:
a. Degree of interest in: activities of the women's caucus
b. Degree of interest in: activities of the black delegates
c. Degree of interest in: discussions or debates over party reform

Possible responses: "great interest," "quite a bit of interest," "not very interested," "not at all interested." All of the above were coded so that "great interest" received the highest score.

Maximum value: 15
Minimum value: 03

Recodings: 3-way: 1) 3-7   2) 8-12   3) 13-15
2-way: 1) 3-9   2) 10-15

4. *Organizational Support Index (Mail Questionnaire)*

CONSTITUENT VARIABLES:
a.   Delegate quality desirable: works hard for the party
b.   Delegate quality desirable: will represent best interests of the party
c.   Favor or oppose: counting service to the party heavily in nominating candidates
d.   Favor or oppose: working to minimize disagreement within the party
e.   Favor or oppose: minimizing role of the party organization in nominating candidates for office
f.   Why active: "I am strongly attached to my party and I want to support it."

Each of the above variables was coded so that the pro-party response received the highest value.

Maximum value: 24
Minimum value: 06

Recodings: 4-way: 1) 6-14   2) 15-17   3) 18-20   4) 21-24
3-way: 1) 6-15   2) 16-19   3) 20-24

5. *Incentive Specialties: Rectitude, Solidarity,
Synthesizers (Mail Questionnaire)*

N.B. This index was not constructed from factor analysis as such, but from theoretical considerations confirmed by various factor analyses and other examinations of the data.

CONSTITUENT VARIABLES:
a.   Why active: "I am strongly attached to my party and I want to support it."
b.   Why active: "I want to get the party and its candidates to support the policies I believe in."

Possible answers: "extremely important," "quite important," "not very important," "not at all important."

Those who found party support "extremely" or "quite important" but who found policy advocacy "not very" or "not at all important" were classed as "Solidary Specialists."

Those who found policy advocacy "extremely" or "quite important" but who found party support "not very" or "not at all important" were classed as "Rectitude Specialists."

Those who found both items "extremely" or "quite important" were classed as "Synthesizers."

Those who found neither item "extremely" or "quite important" constituted a small, unnamed residual category.

II. Roles

1. *Policy Orientation Index (Mail Questionnaire)*

   CONSTITUENT VARIABLES:
   a. Delegate quality desirable: strong policy views
   b. Favor or oppose: standing firm for position even if it means resigning from the party
   c. Favor or oppose: encouraging widespread participation in making most party decisions
   d. Favor or oppose: selecting a nominee who is strongly committed on the issues
   e. Why active: "I want to get the party and its candidates to support the policies I believe in."

All of the above were coded so that strong policy views, standing firm, widespread participation, commitment to issues, or policy advocacy received the highest score.

   Maximum value: 20
   Minimum value: 05

   Recodings: 4-way: 1) 6-11   2) 12-14   3) 15-17   4) 18-20
                   3-way: 1) 6-12   2) 13-16   3) 17-20

2. *Job of the Convention Measures*
   (Mail Questionnaire)

   N.B. These measures are simply recodings of existing variables in the mail questionnaire sample.

   In question 23 of the questionnaire delegates were asked to rank-order convention functions:

1. unifying the party
2. putting together a team that will win the election
3. adopting correct positions on important national issues
4. reforming the party
5. nominating the most deserving candidates

These were transformed into five variables, with the values being the "rank" assigned to the convention function by each delegate.

3. *Amateur Orientations Index (Mail Questionnaire)*

CONSTITUENT VARIABLES:

a. Delegate quality desirable: strong policy views
b. Favor or oppose: counting service to party heavily in nominating candidates
c. Favor or oppose: standing firm for position even if it means resigning from the party
d. Favor or oppose: minimizing role of party organization in nominating candidates for office
e. Favor or oppose: playing down some issues if it will improve chances of winning
f. Favor or oppose: encouraging widespread participation in making party decisions
g. Favor or oppose: selecting a nominee who is strongly committed on the issues
h. Why active: "I want to get the party and its candidates to support the policies I believe in."

All of the above were coded so that strong policy views, discounting party service, standing firm, minimizing party organization, keeping all issues in view, participation, committed nominee, and policy advocacy received the highest score.

Maximum value: 32
Minimum value: 08

Recoding: 3-way: 1) 8-20 2) 21-24 3) 25-32

INDEXES·MEASURING IDEOLOGICAL STYLE

1. *Holism Measure (Intersect Sample)*

N.B. This measure is not based on factor analysis. Rather, it is an attempt to measure "consistency" of "liberal" or "conservative" positions across a number of issue-areas. The following "issue-clusters" were selected in the construction of this measure.

a. RACE:
   a. Feeling thermometer: civil rights leaders
   b. Feeling thermometer: black militants
   c. Proximity on busing: closer to "children in neighborhood schools" or "bus to integrate"?
b. AUTHORITY ORIENTATIONS:
   a. Feeling thermometer: the military
   b. Feeling thermometer: political demonstrators
   c. Proximity on crime: closer to "stop crime" or "protect the accused"?
c. WOMEN:
   a. Feeling thermometer: women's liberation
   b. Strongly agree to strongly disagree: national day care program
   c. Favorable or unfavorable opinion of National Women's Political Caucus
d. FOREIGN POLICY:
   a. Strongly agree to strongly disagree: "American military superiority should have priority in American foreign policy."
   b. Strongly agree to strongly disagree: "The United States should resume normal diplomatic relations with Cuba."
   c. Strongly agree to strongly disagree: "The United States should give more support to the United Nations."
e. ECONOMIC POLICY:
   a. Proximity on inflation: closer to "no government action to stop inflation" or "total government action"
   b. Feeling thermometer: union leaders.
f. COUNTER CULTURE:
   a. Feeling thermometer: rock festival people
   b. Feeling thermometer: political demonstrators
   c. Proximity on welfare: closer to "obligation to work" or "no one should live in poverty"?

To be considered "consistent" within any one of the above issue-areas, a delegate had to respond as a "liberal" or "conservative" to all three (or in the case of economic policy: two) component variables of a cluster.

The "holism" measure then defined delegates according to their consistency *within and across* issue clusters:

1. Holists: consistent within and across five or six issue clusters
2. Programmatics: consistent within and across three or four issue clusters
3. Eclectics: consistent within and across one or two issue clusters
4. Very Eclectic: consistent within or across no issue areas

2. *Intensity: Women in Politics (Mail Questionnaire)*

N.B. This index was not based on factor analysis, but rather on a theoretical desire to measure intensity of views about women in politics.

CONSTITUENT VARIABLES:
a. "Most men are better suited emotionally for politics than are most women."
b. "Women in public office can be just as logical and rational as men."
c. "It is almost impossible to be a good wife and mother and hold public office too."
d. "Women who succeed in politics usually have to sacrifice their femininity to get there."

Since the object of this index was a measure of style-related intensity rather than substantive views, "strongly agree" and "strongly disagree" were coded with highest scores; "moderately agree" and "moderately disagree" with the next highest; and "slightly agree" and "slightly disagree" with the lowest scores.

Maximum value: 12
Minimum value: 03

Recodings: 3-way: 1) 4-6 2) 7-9 3) 10-12
            2-way: 1) 4-8 2) 9-12

3. *Intensity: Domestic Policy (Intersect Sample)*

N.B. This index was not based on factor analysis, but rather on a theoretical desire to measure the intensity of delegate views on vital domestic issues in 1972.

CONSTITUENT VARIABLES:
a. Proximity on inflation: closer to "no government action against inflation" or "total government action"?
b. Proximity on busing: closer to "children in neighborhood schools" or "bus to integrate"?
c. Proximity on crime: closer to "stop crime" or "protect the accused"?
d. Proximity on welfare: closer to "obligation to work" or "no one should live in poverty"?

Since the object was to measure intensity rather than substantive views, the most extreme responses (at either end) were given the highest scores, the next most extreme the second highest score, and so forth.

Maximum value: 12
Minimum value: 00

Recodings: 3-way: 1) 0-4 2) 5-8 3) 9-12
            2-way: 1) 0-6 2) 7-12

4. *Intensity: Foreign Policy (Interview Sample)*

N.B. This index was not based on factor analysis, but rather on a theoretical desire to measure intensity of views on important foreign policy issues of 1972.

CONSTITUENT VARIABLES:
a. "American military superiority should have priority in American foreign policy."
b. "All United States troops should be withdrawn from Asia."
c. "The use of nuclear weapons by the United States would never be justified."
d. "The United States should give more support to the United Nations."

The component variables of this measure were recoded the same way as those for domestic policy intensity, i.e., most extreme positions receiving highest scores, etc.

Maximum value: 08
Minimum value: 00

Recodings: 3-way: 1) 0-2 2) 3-5 3) 6-8
            2-way: 1) 0-4 2) 5-8

PERSONALITY INDEXES

1. *Ambitious-Competitive Index (Interview Sample)*

CONSTITUENT VARIABLES:
a. Proximity measure: closer to "ambitious" or "not ambitious"?
b. Proximity measure: closer to "competitive" or "not competitive"?
c. "I am a very competitive person": very true, somewhat true, not very true, or not at all true.

The above variables were recoded to a 5-point scale before adding. The ambitious and competitive self-conceptions received the highest scores.

Maximum value: 15
Minimum value: 03

Recodings: 3-way: 1) 3-6   2) 7-11   3) 12-15
2-way: 1) 3-9   2) 10-15

2. *Rational-Decisive Index (Interview Sample)*

CONSTITUENT VARIABLES:
a.   Proximity measure: closer to "confident" or "insecure"?
b.   Proximity measure: closer to "rational" or "irrational"?
c.   Proximity measure: closer to "decisive" or "indecisive"?

Confident, rational, and decisive ends of the scales received the highest scores.

Maximum value: 21
Minimum value: 03

Recoding: 2-way: 1) 4-12   2) 13-21*

*Because of the extremely low number of cases registering low on this index, a two-way split was the only reasonable possibility.

3. *The Defensiveness Index (Interview Sample)*

CONSTITUENT VARIABLES:
a.   How difficult for you: opening yourself to attack and criticism?
b.   How difficult for you: having to argue with people about issues?
c.   How difficult for you: the possibility of losing?

Highest scores were assigned where criticism, arguing, and losing were judged most difficult.

Maximum value: 15
Minimum value: 03

Recoding: 3-way: 1) 3-6   2) 7-11   3) 12-15

4. *The Orderly Index (Interview Sample)*

CONSTITUENT VARIABLES:
a.   "I enjoy work that requires attention to details": very true, somewhat true, not very true, not at all true?

b. "I enjoy careful planning and scheduling of my activities": very true, somewhat true, not very true, not at all true?

For both variables above, a very true response was given the highest score.

Maximum value: 08
Minimum value: 02

Recodings: 3-way: 1) 2-3 2) 4-6 3) 7-8
2-way: 1) 2-5 2) 6-8

5. *The Subjectivity Index (Interview Sample)*

CONSTITUENT VARIABLES:
a. "Other people know me better than I know myself": very true, somewhat true, not very true, not at all true?
b. "I get so involved in other people that I lose track of my own needs and feelings": very true, somewhat true, not very true, not at all true?
c. "I don't think about my own motives for doing things": very true, somewhat true, not very true, not at all true?

Variables above were coded so that knowing oneself, *not* losing track of feelings, and thinking about one's motives received the highest scores.

Maximum value: 12
Minimum value: 03

Recodings: 3-way: 1) 3-5 2) 6-9 3) 10-12

6. *Power, Affiliation, and Achievement*
Indexes (Interview Sample)

N. B. These three indexes were not created from factor analyses, but from theoretical considerations arising from a series of interdependent questions.

The constituent variables for all three indexes were the questions with interpretation of responses marked in the three columns on the following page.

	Affiliation Response	Achievement Response	Power Response
A. In general, which of the following events would upset you most?			
1) finding that a friend is angry with me	X		
2) finding that my views are ignored			X
3) failing in something that I've tried to do		X	
B. Which would upset you least?			
1) finding that a friend is angry with me		X	X
2) finding that my views are ignored	X	X	
3) failing in something that I've tried to do	X		X
C. Which of the following is most important to you?			
1) having ideas that can be used to solve political problems		X	
2) making friends with interesting people active in politics	X		
3) having influence and power over what political leaders do			X
D. Which is least important to you?			
1) having ideas that can be used to solve political problems	X		X
2) making friends with interesting people in politics		X	X
3) having influence and power over what political leaders do	X	X	

Since only one response was possible for questions B and D, either response in a given column to each of those questions counted as "1" in the index construction. Consequently, each of the three resulting indexes had possible values from 0 to 4. No recoding was necessary.

POLITICAL GENERATIONS AND POLITICAL EXPERIENCE MEASURES

1. *Political Generations (Mail Questionnaire)*

   N.B. This measure is simply a single variable recoded for crossruns with several other variables in this study.

   Question: "What year did you first become active in politics?"

   Recoding: 1) Before 1945
   2) 1946–59
   3) 1960–67
   4) 1968–72 (newcomers)

2. *Political Experience Index (Mail Questionnaire)*

   N.B. This measure was not based on factor analysis, but was simply the theoretical and actual combination of two other variables: political generations and officeholding experience.

   Constituent Variables:
   1. What year did you first become active in politics?
      Coding for this index: 0=1968–72
      1=1960–67
      2=1946–59
      3=pre–1945
   2. Officeholding experience (party or public office):
      Coding: 0=no offices ever held
      1=one office held
      2=two offices held
      3=three or more offices held

   Maximum value: 06
   Minimum value: 00

   Recoding: 3-way: 1) 0-1   2) 2-4   3) 5-6

CONVENTION PARTICIPATION INDEXES

1. *Levels of Elite Activism (Ordinal Measure)*
   (Interview Sample)

   N.B. This measure was not based on factor analysis, but was constructed from theoretical considerations about levels of activism. The operational definition is on the following page.

	Measure of Quality and Scope of Participation	Measure of Intensity and Scope of Participation
Levels of Activism as Defined by Party	Ques.: What were the main things you did in addition to voting? (two responses recorded)	Ques.: How much did you participate in: state delegation* candidate meetings credentials decisions rules decisions* platform decisions other groups that met* (possible responses to each: a great deal, somewhat, not very much, not at all)

High or Combative Activism		
Democrats (22%)	Cited two significant acts related directly to convention business[1]	Cited a great deal or some participation in at least four of the above six categories
Republicans (23%)	Same as Democrats[1]	Cited a great deal or some participation in at least two of the three starred (*) activities above[2]
Low or Supportive Activism		
Democrats (14%)	Cited two acts that were either passive or not related directly to convention business (or cited one such act and gave no second response)[3]	Cited a great deal or some participation in fewer than three activities above
Republicans (16%)	Same as Democrats[3]	Cited a great deal or some participation in only one of the starred (*) activities above
Moderate Activism Democrats—64% Republicans—61%	Anyone who did not fit either of the above definitions for his or her party was placed in this category.	

[1] This included both official and unofficial tasks: membership on any convention committee, any state delegation position, speech-making from the podium, participation in any special interest caucus, work for any candidate or work with any specific convention challenge or policy issue. Percents cited above are percents *within* each party in each category.

[2] Candidate meetings, credentials, and platform decisions were of little importance at the Republican Convention and so were not included in the measure of Republican activism.

[3] This included: social activity, keeping informed, listening to speeches, and consulting with others.

2. *Styles of Elite Activism: Democrats*
   (Interview Sample)

N.B. Once again, this measure was not constructed from factor analysis, but from theoretical considerations about modes of convention participation.

The following is the operational definition of styles of elite activism among Democrats:

	State Delegation Participation[1]	Interest Group Activity[2]	Dispute Orientation[3]	Percentage of Delegates
General activists	+	+	+	26.0%
Interest group specialists	0	+	0	7.1%
Dispute specialists	0	0	+	6.3%
State delegation specialists	+	0	0	12.1%
Interest-oriented disputants	0	+	I	7.4%
Interest-oriented state participators	+	+	0	11.9%
State-oriented disputants	+	0	+	19.4%
Observers	0	0	0	9.9%

Weighted $N =$ 2378

[1] State Delegation Participation was measured by an index combining the following questions.

  a. Once you got to the convention, how much did you participate in the activities of your state delegation?

  Possible answers: a great deal, somewhat, not very much, none.

  b. Compared to others in your state delegation, were you more active, as active, or less active in state delegation caucuses?

  Possible answers: more active, as active, less active.

Since almost all delegates reported high state delegation participation, this index was used to ascertain the *most active* participants. On an index with possible scores ranging from 1 to 6, those who scored 5 or 6 were given a "+" in this column and considered significantly active state participants.

[2] A "+" in this column simply means that a delegate reported participating in *some* interest group activity at the convention, including caucuses of women, blacks, Chicanos, youth, senior citizens, labor, gay liberation, the New Democratic Coalition, or other minority or interest groups. It also included any mention of substate delegation caucuses.

[3] Dispute orientation was measured by an index of participation in platform, rules, and

3. *Styles of Elite Activism: Republicans* *(Interview Sample)*

N.B. This measure was not constructed from factor analysis, but from theoretical considerations about modes of convention participation for Republicans in 1972.

The operational definitions of styles of participation among Republicans are as follows:

	State Delegation Participation[1]	Interest Group Activity[2]	Percentage of Delegates
General Activists	+	+	27.4%
Interest group specialists	0	+	6.9%
State delegation specialists	+	0	48.8%
Observers	0	0	16.9%
		Weighted N =	1014

[1] State delegation participation for Republicans was measured in the same way as for Democrats. See footnote 1 in preceding table.

[2] A "+" in this column simply means that a delegate reported participating in *some* interest group at the Republican Convention. Caucuses of women, blacks, and youth were the principal interest groups active at this convention, although small groups of labor representatives, Chicanos, and a caucus interested in the distribution of 1976 delegates also reported meeting.

4. *Number of Subgroups (Interview Sample)*

N.B. This measure was not constructed through factor analysis, but was simply the aggregation of subgroup affiliations claimed by each delegate. These affiliations included the following:

credentials decisions—the "great disputes" at the Democratic Convention. The basic question(s) on which the index was based were:

How much did you participate in: credentials decision?
decisions on platform issues?
decisions on rules issues?

Possible responses to each question included: a great deal, somewhat, not very much, none.

Those who scored on the upper half of this index were given a "+" in this column. (A preliminary factor analysis indicated that these three dispute-related arenas of participation comprised a single dimension of participation.)

1. Women's groups
2. Black groups
3. Youth groups
4. Labor groups
5. Chicano groups

An individual's affiliations were coded in this way:
0 = participated in no subgroup meetings at convention
1 = one group
2 = two groups
3 = three or more groups

CIVIL PARTICIPATION INDEXES

1. *Joiners (Mail Questionnaire)*

N.B. This measure was not constructed from factor analysis but is simply a tally of the number of civic group memberships claimed by each delegate. Only active memberships were counted.

The groups included:
1. Church, synagogue or other religious groups
2. Service clubs (Rotary, Lions, etc.)
3. Nonpartisan civic groups (environmental groups, better government organizations, etc.)
4. School and school-related groups (PTA, safety committees, fund-raising projects, etc.)
5. Professional or occupationally related groups
6. Labor unions
7. Partisan political groups
8. Feminist groups, new women's groups (NOW, WEAL, women's liberation groups)
9. League of Women Voters
10. Social clubs

Maximum value: 10
Minimum value: 00

Recoding: 4-way: 1) 0 memberships 2) 1-2 3) 3-4 4) 5 or more

2. *Service-Occupational-Social Memberships (Mail Questionnaire)*

CONSTITUENT VARIABLES:
a. Professional or occupationally related groups

    b.   Service clubs
    c.   Social clubs

This variable assigned high scores to active membership, second highest to inactive membership, lowest to non-membership.

Maximum value: 06
Minimum value: 00

Recoding: 3-way: 1) 0-1   2) 2-4   3) 5-6

3. *Civic Women's Group Memberships*
   (Mail Questionnaire)

CONSTITUENT VARIABLES:
a.   Nonpartisan civic groups
b.   Feminist groups
c.   League of Women Voters

The coding for constituent variables was the same as No. 2 above.

Maximum value: 06
Minimum value: 00

Recoding: 3-way: 1) 0-1   2) 2-4   3) 5-6

4. *Church-School Memberships (Mail Questionnaire)*

CONSTITUENT VARIABLES:
a.   Church, synagogue, or other religious groups
b.   School or school-related groups

The coding of these two constituent variables was the same as No. 2 above.

Maximum value: 04
Minimum value: 00

Recoding: 3-way: 1) 0-1   2) 2   3) 3-4

AMBITION AND AMBITION-EFFORT INDEXES

1. *Public Office Ambition (Mail Questionnaire)*

   N.B. This measure is simply a recoding of the following variables:

    "Thinking of all the possible offices and positions in politics, from local to national and from public office to positions in the party organization, which of the following would you most like to be if you could have your personal choice? First consider public office."

Coding of this variable:

0 = no interest in public office

1 = low level of interest: council member, other local office

2 = moderate level of interest: lieutenant governor, state senator, state representative, state judge, state administrative post, other state office, mayor

3 = high level of interest: president, vice-president, United States senator, United States representative, cabinet member, ambassador, federal judge, federal prosecutor, other national office, governor.

2. *Party Office Ambition (Mail Questionnaire)*

N.B. This measure is simply a recoding of the following variable:

"Next, consider party positions. Which of the following would you most like to be if you could have your personal choice?"

Coding of this variable:

0 = no interest in party office

1 = low interest level: district chairman, district campaign manager, county chairman/chairwoman, county board, county campaign manager, other county position, city chairman, other local organization position

2 = moderate level of interest: state party chairman, state central committee, state campaign director, other state position

3 = high level of interest: national party chairman, presidential campaign manager, national committeeman/committeewoman, other national role

3. *Public Office Ambition-Effort*
   (Mail Questionnaire)

This variable was simply a combination of the public office ambition recoding above (No. 1) with the following "effort" question:

"If there were a real chance to hold the position you think is most desirable, how much effort would you be willing to make to get that position?"

1. High effort: would work harder and make more sacrifices than for any other goal in life
2. Moderate effort: would work harder than before in politics
3. Low effort: would make some additional effort

These categories were mixed with the four public office ambition categories into a new measure with discrete categories: high ambition-high effort, high ambition-moderate effort, etc. Where analysis demanded that this measure be ordinal, those categories not clearly higher or lower than others in overall effort and ambition were dropped from the ordinal measure.

4. *Party Office Ambition-Effort*
   (Mail Questionnaire)

This variable was simply a combination of the party office ambition recoding above (No. 2) with the following effort question:

> "If there were a real chance to hold the position you think is most desirable, how much effort would you be willing to make to get that position?"

1) High effort: would work harder and make more sacrifices than for any other goal in life
2) Moderate effort: would work harder than before in politics
3) Low effort: would make some additional effort

These categories were mixed with the four party office ambition categories into a new measure with discrete categories: e.g., high ambition-high effort, high ambition-moderate effort, etc. Where analysis demanded that this measure be ordinal, those categories not clearly higher or lower than others in overall effort *and* ambition were dropped from the ordinal measure.

5. *Expectation Indexes (Mail Questionnaire)*

With the same set of offices (public and party) as possible responses, delegates were also asked about their expectations:

> "Now, all things considered, which of all these positions do you think you are *most likely to hold* at the top of your career in politics?"

Responses for public office were coded in exactly the same way as those for public office ambition (No. 1 above). List of offices was the same as No. 1.

Responses for party office were coded in exactly the same way as those for party office ambition (No. 2 above). List of offices was the same as No. 2.

Where expectations were combined with effort, the effort question ("How much effort will you have to make to reach this position?") had the same set of possible responses as Nos. 3 and 4 above.

Expectation-effort measures were constructed from expectation and effort questions—exactly parallel to the ambition-effort measures described above.

STATE DELEGATION INFLUENTIALS MEASURE

1. *Influentials (Interview Sample)*

   This variable is simply a coding of delegate responses to a question that asked them to name the three most influential people in their state delegation. The coding of the question was as follows; the emphasis was on the sex of the person named:

   1. Three mentions, all three women
   2. Two mentions, both mentions women
   3. One mention, one woman mentioned
   4. Three mentions, two of them women
   5. Two mentions, one woman mentioned
   6. Three mentions, one woman mentioned
   7. One mention, no woman mentioned
   8. Two mentions, no women mentioned
   9. Three mentions, no women mentioned

   If the respondent said "governor," "senator," or "congressman," without giving a specific name, it was assumed that the person was male.

OCCUPATIONS *(Interview Sample)*

This measure is simply a recoding of the occupation variable into the following categories:

1. *Symbol Specialists*

   authors
   clergy
   public relations people, publicity writers
   college presidents, professors, instructors
   editors and reporters
   religious workers
   social scientists
   teachers

2. *Lawyers*

lawyers and judges

3. *Material Specialists*

farm owners
self-employed: construction managers
                    manufacturing managers
                    transportation managers
                    wholesale trade people
                    retail trade: food stores, general merchandise,
                      apparel and accessories stores, home furnishings,
                      motor vehicles, eating and drinking places,
                      hardware and farm equipment, other retail trade
                    banking, credit, securities, brokerage, investment
                    insurance and real estate
                    advertising and miscellaneous business services
                    auto repair and garage
                    other types of self-employment
boilermakers
brickmasons, stonemasons, tile setters
cabinetmakers
carpenters
electricians
metal industry craftsmen
textile industry craftsmen
telephone/telegraph linemen-servicemen
machinists
auto mechanics
plumbers and pipe fitters
metal filers, grinders, polishers
street/subway/el motormen
sewers and stitchers
taxi drivers and chauffeurs
truck and tractor drivers
welders and flame-cutters
hairdressers and cosmetologists
mineral/stone workers
metal industry workers
motor vehicle workers
miscellaneous manufacturing workers

hospital attendants
barbers
firemen
guards, watchmen, doorkeepers
housekeepers and stewards
laborers: meat industry, construction, wholesale-retail trade
manufacturing checkers, examiners, inspectors

4. *Housewives*

5. *Students*

6. *Clerical and Sales*

file clerks
clerical agents
library attendants and assistants
bank tellers
bookkeepers
cashiers
dispatchers and vehicle starters
messengers and office boys
office machine operators
stenographers, receptionists, typists, secretaries
telephone operators
clerical and kindred workers
hucksters and peddlers
insurance agents, brokers, underwriters
real estate agents and brokers
sales: manufacturing, wholesale trade, retail trade, other industries
stock clerks and storekeepers

7. *Public Employees*

state public administration—inspectors
public officials and administrators
federal public administration and postal service
state public administration
local public administration
government police/detectives
sheriffs and bailiffs

8. *Salaried Managers*

construction managers
manufacturing managers
transportation managers
communications, utilities, sanitary services managers
wholesale trade managers
retail trade: general merchandise, eating and drinking places, other
   retail trade
banking, credit agencies, securities, brokerage, investment
insurance and real estate
advertising and miscellaneous business services
personal services
other salaried officials

9. *Health Personnel*

dentists
professional nurses
osteopaths
pharmacists
physicians and surgeons
medical and dental technicians
veterinarians

10. *Other Professionals*

accountants and auditors
actors and actresses
airplane pilots and navigators
architects
artists and art teachers
chemists
designers
draftsmen
electrical engineers
industrial engineers
mechanical engineers
other engineers
funeral directors and embalmers
librarians
musicians and music teachers
natural scientists

personnel and labor relations workers
photographers
recreation and group workers
social and welfare workers
sports instructors and officials
electrical-electronic technicians
other professionals

11. *Others*

buyers and store department heads
credit men
building managers and superintendents
ship officers, pilots, pursers, engineers
officials: lodge, society, union, etc.
purchasing agents and buyers
members of armed forces, including officers
campaign workers

Index